CW00432899

Managerial Level

Paper P4

Organisational Management and Information Systems

CIMA Study Text

PUBLISHING

British Library Cataloguing-in-Publication Data

A catalogue record for this book is available from the British Library.

Kaplan Publishing UK

Unit 2 The Business Centre

Molly Millars Lane

Wokingham

RG41 2QZ

ISBN 978-1-84710-679-7

© Kaplan Financial Limited, April 2007

Printed and bound in Great Britain by Ashford Colour Press Ltd, Gosport, Hants.

Acknowledgements

We are grateful to the Chartered Institute of Management Accountants, the Association of Chartered Certified Accountants and the Institute of Chartered Accountants in England and Wales for permission to reproduce past examination questions. The answers have been prepared by Kaplan Publishing.

INTRODUCTION

This is a new edition of CIMA Paper P4 Study Text. It has been fully updated and revised in order to produce an even better, more syllabus-tailored, exam-focused and student-friendly publication. To achieve this we have worked closely with numerous CIMA tutors and experts, and we are confident that this Study Text forms the best resource for your exam preparation.

It covers all syllabus topics to the required depth, and contains a wealth of exam-style and practice questions. Throughout the text you will find plenty of relevant examples, activities, diagrams and charts. These will put the subject matter in context and help you absorb the material easily.

The following points explain some of the concepts we had in mind when developing the layout of this book.

DEFINITION

- **Definitions**. The text defines key words and concepts, placing them in the margin with a clear heading, as on the left. The purpose of including these definitions is to focus your attention on the point being covered.

KEY POINT

- **Key points**. Also in the margin, you will see key points at regular intervals. The purpose of these is to summarise concisely the key material being covered.

- **Activities**. The text involves you in the learning process with a series of activities designed to catch your attention and make you concentrate and respond. The feedback to activities is at the end of each chapter.

- **Self-test questions**. At the end of each chapter there is a series of self-test questions. The purpose of these is to help you revise some of the key elements of the chapter. All the answers to these questions can be found in the text.

- **End of chapter questions**. At the end of each chapter we include examination-type questions. These will give you a very good idea of the sort of thing the examiner will ask and will test your understanding of what has been covered.

Good luck with your studies!

CONTENTS

SYLLABUS AND LEARNING OUTCOMES

Syllabus outline

The syllabus comprises:

Topic and study weighting

A	Information Systems	20%
B	Change Management	10%
C	Operations Management	20%
D	Marketing	20%
E	Managing Human Capital	30%

Learning aims

Students should be able to:

*   describe the various functional areas of an organisation and how they relate to one another,

*   apply theories, tools and techniques appropriate to a functional area in support of the organisation's strategy,

*   prepare reports and plans for functional areas,

*   evaluate the performance of functional areas.

Below we reproduce the learning outcomes and syllabus content. The numbers in brackets denote the chapters in which each topic is covered.

Learning outcomes and syllabus content

A – Information Systems – 20%

Learning outcomes

On completion of their studies students should be able to:

(i) explain the features and operations of commonly used information technology hardware and software; (1)

(ii) explain how commonly used technologies are used in the work place; (1)

(iii) identify opportunities for the use of information technology (IT) in organisations, particularly in the implementation and running of the information system (IS); (2)

(iv) evaluate, from a managerial perspective, new hardware and software and assess how new systems could benefit the organisation; (3)

(v) recommend strategies to minimise the disruption caused by introducing IS technologies; (4)

(vi) explain how to supervise major IS projects and ensure their smooth implementation; (4)

(vii) evaluate how IS fits into broader management operations. (2)

Syllabus content

*   Introduction to hardware and software in common use in organisations. (1)

*   Hardware and applications architectures (i.e. centralised, distributed, client server) and the IT required to run them (PCs, servers, networks and peripherals). (1)

*   General Systems Theory and its application to IT (i.e. system definition, system components, system behaviour, system classification, entropy, requisite variety, coupling and decoupling). (2)

*   Recording and documenting tools used during the analysis and design of systems (i.e. entity-relationship model, logical data structure, entity life history, dataflow diagram, and decision table). (3)

*   Databases and database management systems. (Note: Knowledge of database structures will not be required.) (3)

*   The problems associated with the management of in-house and vendor solutions and how they can be avoided or solved. (4)

*   IT-enabled transformation (i.e. the use of information systems to assist in change management). (4)

*   System changeover methods (i.e. direct, parallel, pilot and phased). (4)

*   IS implementation (i.e. methods of implementation, avoiding problems of non-usage and resistance). (4)

*   The benefits of IT systems. (2)

*   IS evaluation, including the relationship of sub-systems to each other and testing. (4)

*   IS outsourcing. (4)

*   Maintenance of systems (i.e. corrective, adaptive, preventative). (4)

B – Change Management – 10%

Learning outcomes

On completion of their studies students should be able to:

(i) explain the process of organisational development; (5)

(ii) discuss how and why resistance to change develops within organisations; (5)

(iii) evaluate various means of introducing change; (6)

(iv) evaluate change processes within the organisation. (6)

Syllabus content

- External and internal change triggers (e.g. environmental factors, mergers and acquisitions, re-organisation and rationalisation). (5)

- The stages in the change process. (5)

- Approaches to change management (e.g. Beer and Nohria, Kanter, Lewin and Peters, Senge et al.). (6)

- The importance of managing critical periods of change through the life cycle of the firm. (5)

C – Operations Management – 20%

Learning outcomes

On completion of their studies students should be able to:

(i) evaluate the management of operations; (7, 8)

(ii) analyse problems associated with quality in organisations; (10)

(iii) evaluate contemporary thinking in quality management; (10)

(iv) explain the linkages between functional areas as an important aspect of quality management; (10)

(v) apply tools and concepts of quality management appropriately in an organisation; (10)

(vi) construct a plan for the implementation of a quality programme; (10)

(vii) recommend ways to negotiate and manage relationships with suppliers; (9)

(viii) evaluate a supply network; (9)

(ix) explain the concept of quality and how the quality of products and services can be assessed, measured and improved. (10)

Syllabus content

- An overview of operations strategy and its importance to the firm. (7)

- Design of products/services and processes and how this relates to operations and supply. (7)

- Methods for managing inventory, including continuous inventory systems (e.g. Economic Order Quantity, EOQ), periodic inventory systems and the ABC system (Note: ABC is not an acronym. A refers to high value, B to medium and C to low value inventory). (8)

- Strategies for balancing capacity and demand including level capacity, chase and demand management strategies. (8)

- Methods of performance measurement and improvement, particularly the contrast between benchmarking and Business Process Re-engineering (BPR). (10)

- Practices of continuous improvement (e.g. Quality circles, Kaizen, 5S, 6 Sigma). (10)

- The use of benchmarking in quality measurement and improvement. (10)

- Different methods of quality measurement (i.e. operational, financial and customer measures). (10)

- The characteristics of lean production: flexible workforce practices, high commitment human resource policies and commitment to continuous improvement. Criticisms and limitations of lean production. (10)

- Systems used in operations management: Manufacturing Resource Planning (MRP), Optimised Production Technologies (OPT), Just-in-Time (JIT) and Enterprise Resource Planning (ERP). (8)

- Approaches to quality management, including Total Quality Management (TQM), various British Standard (BS) and European Union (EU) systems as well as statistical methods of quality control. (10)

- External quality standards (e.g. the various ISO standards appropriate to products and organisations). (10)

- Use of the Intranet in information management (e.g. meeting customer support needs). (10)

- Contemporary developments in quality management. (10)

- The role of the supply chain and supply networks in gaining competitive advantage, including the use of sourcing strategies (e.g. single, multiple, delegated and parallel). (9)

- Supply chain management as a strategic process (e.g. Reck and Long's strategic positioning tool, Cousins' strategic supply wheel). (9)

- Developing and maintaining relationships with suppliers. (9)

D – Marketing – 20%

Learning outcomes

On completion of their studies students should be able to:

(i) explain the marketing concept; (11)

(ii) evaluate the marketing processes of an organisation; (11, 12, 13)

(iii) apply tools within each area of the marketing mix; (12)

(iv) describe the business contexts within which marketing principles can be applied (consumer marketing, business-to-business marketing, services marketing, direct marketing, interactive marketing); (13)

(v) evaluate the role of technology in modern marketing; (13)

(vi) produce a strategic marketing plan for the organisation. (12)

Syllabus content

- Introduction to the marketing concept as a business philosophy. (11)

- An overview of the marketing environment, including societal, economic, technological, physical and legal factors affecting marketing. (11)

- Understanding consumer behaviour, such as factors affecting buying decisions, types of buying behaviour and stages in the buying process. (13)

- Market research, including data gathering techniques and methods of analysis. (11)

- Marketing Decision Support Systems (MDSS) and their relationship to market research. (13)

- How business to business (B2B) marketing differs from business to consumer (B2C) marketing. (13)

- Segmentation and targeting of markets, and positioning of products within markets. (11)

- The differences and similarities in the marketing of products and services. (13)

- Devising and implementing a pricing strategy. (12)

- Marketing communications (i.e. mass, direct, interactive). (12)

- Distribution channels and methods for marketing campaigns. (12)

- The role of marketing in the strategic plan of the organisation. (11)

- Use of the Internet (e.g. in terms of data collection, marketing activity and providing enhanced value to customers and suppliers) and potential drawbacks (e.g. security issues). (13)

- Market forecasting methods for estimating current (e.g. Total Market Potential, Area Market Potential and Industry Sales and Market Shares) and future (e.g. Survey of Buyers' Intentions, Composite of Sales Force Opinions, Expert Opinion, Past-Sales Analysis and Market-Test Method) demand for products and services. (11)

- Internal marketing as the process of training and motivating employees so as to support the firm's external marketing activities. (13)

- Social responsibility in a marketing context. (12)

E – Managing Human Capital – 30%

Learning outcomes

On completion of their studies students should be able to:

(i) explain the role of the human resource management function and its relationship to other parts of the organisation; (15)

(ii) produce and explain a human resource plan and supporting practices; (15)

(iii) evaluate the recruitment, selection, induction, appraisal, training and career planning activities of an organisation; (16, 17, 18)

(iv) evaluate the role of incentives in staff development as well as individual and organisational performance; (14, 16, 17, 18)

(v) identify features of a human resource plan that vary depending on organisation type and employment model; (15)

(vi) explain the importance of ethical behaviour in business generally and for the Chartered Management Accountant in particular. (14)

Syllabus content

- The relationship of the employee to other elements of the business plan. (15)

- Determinants and content of a human resource (HR) plan (e.g. organisational growth rate, skills, training, development, strategy, technologies and natural wastage). (15)

- Problems in implementing a HR plan and ways to manage this. (15)

- The process of recruitment and selection of staff using different recruitment channels (i.e. interviews, assessment centres, intelligence tests, aptitude tests, psychometric tests). (16)

- Issues relating to fair and legal employment practices (e.g. recruitment, dismissal, redundancy, and ways of managing these). (16)

- Issues in the design of reward systems (e.g. the role of incentives, the utility of performance-related pay, arrangements for knowledge workers, flexible work arrangements). (14)

- The importance of negotiation during the offer and acceptance of a job. (16)

- The process of induction and its importance. (16)

- Theories of Human Resource Management (e.g. Taylor, Schein, McGregor, Maslow, Herzberg, Handy, Lawrence and Lorsch). (14)

- High performance work arrangements. (14)

- The distinction between development and training and the tools available to develop and train staff. (17)

- The importance of appraisals, their conduct and their relationship to the reward system. (18)

- HR in different organisational forms (e.g. project-based firms, virtual or networked firms). (14)

- Personal business ethics and the CIMA Ethical Guidelines. (14)

HELPING YOU WITH YOUR STUDIES

Take control

Create favourable conditions and a positive attitude

- Plan to study at specific times each week. Devise a schedule and set goals.

- Choose a location where you can concentrate.

- Ask questions to be an active learner and to generate interest.

- Continually challenge yourself.

Study

Develop good learning techniques

- Use the **SQR3** method – it works with reading accountancy and management subjects. **Survey** (get an overall picture before studying in detail), **Question** (important things to learn are usually answers to questions), **Read** actively (to answer your questions), **Recite** (recall what you have read and connect topics) and **Review** (what you have covered and accomplished).

- Use the **MURDER** method – **Mood** (set the right mood), **Understand** (issues covered and make note of any uncertain bits), **Recall** (stop and put what you have learned into your own words), **Digest** (go back and reconsider the information), **Expand** (read relevant articles and newspapers), **Review** (go over the material you covered to consolidate the knowledge).

- Create **associations** and analogies to relate new ideas to what you already know and to improve understanding.

Practise

Practise under exam conditions

- **Practise** as much as possible – go through exam style and standard questions under exam conditions.

Prepare for the exam

Develop exam technique

- Be familiar with the structure of your exam and know how to approach and answer the questions.

THE EXAMINATION

Format of the examination:

There will be a written examination paper of three hours, plus 20 minutes' reading time, with the following sections:

	Marks
Section A: a variety of compulsory objective test questions, each worth between 2 and 4 marks. Mini-scenarios may be given, to which a group of questions relate.	40
Section B: six compulsory short answer questions, each worth 5 marks. A short scenario may be given, to which some or all questions relate.	30
Section C: one question, from a choice of two, worth 30 marks. Short scenarios may be given, to which questions relate.	<u>30</u>
TOTAL	<u>100</u>

Note: The first 20 minutes of your exam is reading time. During reading time you can read, annotate and highlight the question paper, but you are not allowed to open the answer book, write in the answer book, add any loose sheets/supplements to your answer book or use a calculator.

Before sitting the exam make sure that you are familiar with CIMA's *Exam Rules & Regulations*. You can find this document on the CIMA website (www.cimaglobal.com).

Examination tips

- Spend the first 20 minutes of the examination **reading the paper** and where you have a **choice of questions**, decide which ones you will do.

- **Divide the time** you spend on questions in proportion to the marks on offer. One suggestion is to allocate 1½ minutes to each mark available, so a 10-mark question should be completed in 15 minutes.

- Unless you know exactly how to answer the question, spend some time **planning** your answer. Stick to the question and **tailor your answer** to what you are asked.

- **Fully explain** all your points but be **concise**. Set out all workings **clearly and neatly**, and state briefly what you are doing. Don't write out the question.

- If you do not understand what a question is asking, **state your assumptions**.

- If you **get completely stuck** with a question, leave space in your answer book and **return to it later.**

- Towards the end of the examination spend the last **five minutes** reading through your answers and **making any additions or corrections**.

KAPLAN PUBLISHING

Answering the questions

- **Multiple-choice questions**: Read the questions carefully and work through any calculations required. If you don't know the answer, eliminate those options you know are incorrect and see if the answer becomes more obvious. Remember that only one answer to a multiple-choice question can be right!

- **Objective test questions**: These might ask for numerical answers, but could also involve paragraphs of text which require you to fill in a number of missing blanks, or for you to write a definition of a word or phrase, or to enter a formula. Others may give a definition followed by a list of possible key words relating to that description.

- **Essay questions**: Make a quick plan in your answer book and under each main point list all the relevant facts you can think of. Then write out your answer developing each point fully. Your essay should have a clear structure; it should contain a brief introduction, a main section and a conclusion. Be concise. It is better to write a little about a lot of different points than a great deal about one or two points.

- **Computations**: It is essential to include all your workings in your answers. Many computational questions require the use of a standard format: company profit and loss account, balance sheet and cash flow statement for example. Be sure you know these formats thoroughly before the examination and use the layouts that you see in the answers given in this book. If you are asked to comment or make recommendations on a computation, you must do so. There are important marks to be gained here. Even if your computation contains mistakes, you may still gain marks if your reasoning is correct.

- **Reports, memos and other documents**: Some questions ask you to present your answer in the form of a report or a memo or other document. Use the correct format – there could be easy marks to gain here.

Chapter 1

COMPONENTS AND STRUCTURE OF A COMPUTER SYSTEM

Syllabus content

- Introduction to hardware and software in common use in organisations.

- Hardware and applications architectures (i.e. centralised, distributed, client server) and the IT required to run them (PCs, servers, networks and peripherals).

Contents

1   IT systems and hardware

2   Software

3   Computer communications

4   Applications architectures

5   Network-enabled technologies

6   Designing systems to suit the user's requirements

1 IT systems and hardware

Organisations use information technology (IT) to:

- process data

- store data and information

- produce output for operational use or for management reports

- communicate information.

IT systems are computer systems, which consist of:

- hardware

- software, and

- in many cases, communications links, including links to the Internet.

1.1 Hardware

All information systems require computer hardware and software to make them operate effectively. This section introduces (or revises, if you are already familiar with this detail) the common hardware and software that are found in most information systems.

The term 'hardware' is used to describe the equipment in a computer system, including the computer itself. Peripherals is a collective term for input, output and storage devices i.e. any device other than the CPU.

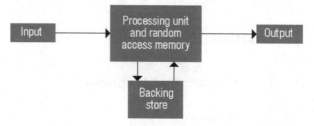

The diagram shown above can represent all computers. Data is entered through input devices, data may be used from the backing store, and output is produced. Records on the backing store may also be updated.

Of course, the sizes of computer can differ greatly from supercomputers down to laptops, and there will be choices as to the types of input, output and backing store devices used.

Peripherals are hardware devices other than processors or networks. The term 'peripherals' commonly refers to input, output and communication hardware. Some of these devices are covered below.

DEFINITION

The term 'hardware' is used to describe the equipment in a computer system, including the computer itself.

KEY POINT

Peripherals is a collective term for input, output and storage devices, i.e. any device other than the CPU.

1.2 Input devices

Examples of input hardware devices are:

- keyboard and mouse
- bar code reader
- touch screen
- optical mark reading
- optical character recognition
- magnetic ink character recognition
- scanner
- plastic swipe card.

You should be thoroughly familiar with many of these devices, but it is important to recognise how (and why) they might be used in the computer systems of organisations.

Keyboard and mouse

A keyboard and mouse are commonly used input devices in office systems, in conjunction with visual display screens (VDUs). Many office workers, including managers, have a personal computer (PC) or other terminal on their desk top, with keyboard and mouse (or tracker ball) and the VDU for input and output.

Using a mouse is usually quicker than a keyboard, and input errors are fewer, when the computer system provides a **graphical user interface** (GUI). This is a way of presenting data and information to users, and offering processing choices to users, in the form of an easy-to-understand graphical presentation on screen. Although it is now usual for computer systems to have a GUI, the term originated because interaction between a computer user and the computer at one time was by text-and-keyboard instructions. GUI, in contrast, uses graphical displays and pull-down menus, which the computer user can control with a mouse.

For example, computer users have grown accustomed to WIMP computer system design. WIMP stands for either **Windows, Icons, Mouse and Pointer**, or **Windows, Icons, Mouse and Pull-down menus**.

- Windows allows users to view two or more different programs or parts of the computer system at the same time on their screen, each in a different window or box.

- Icons are used to represent data files or processing options. The computer user can choose a file or processing option by moving the screen pointer or cursor to the icon, and clicking the mouse to select the icon.

- The pointer or cursor is an arrow head or similar image on the screen that can be moved around by the mouse and used for selecting options.

- Pull-down menus are lists of files or processing options. Pull-down menus might be shown along the top of the VDU screen, which can be selected with the pointer and mouse. A list of choices in the menu then drops down on to the screen, from which the computer user makes a selection, also with pointer and mouse.

However, both keyboard input and input with a mouse are slow methods of input, since they are dependent on the speed of the human operator. They are inappropriate input devices for high volume, high-speed automated processing systems and, where possible, faster input methods should be preferred.

Bar code reader

A bar code is a pattern of black and white stripes representing a code, often an inventory item code.

The code is read by a scanner or light pen, which converts the bar code image into an electronic form acceptable to the computer. Bar codes are used widely at checkout points in supermarkets and shops (electronic **point of sale systems** or E**POS systems**). They allow the point of sale system to recognise the item being purchased and to add its price to the customer's total bill. They speed up the checkout process and reduce the risk of input error by the checkout clerk.

EFTPOS

Another input method associated with EPOS is EFTPOS – electronic funds transfer at point of sale. This system allows a customer to pay for their purchases using a magnetic stripe or chip & pin card (see below) by their card being read by a card reader at the supermarket checkout. Funds are then transferred from the customer's debit or credit card account to the supermarket electronically; no cash changes hands.

Touch screen

A touch screen is another form of point of sale device, which might be used in a cafeteria or restaurant. The screen displays a range of items that are available for sale, and the salesperson inputs the customer's order by touching the appropriate icon with a finger. The screen recognises the instruction and converts it into an electronic command for the computer.

Optical mark reading (OMR)

Optical mark reading (OMR) involves making marks, usually with a pencil or pen, on a standard document. The document is then read by an optical mark reader, and the positioning of the mark or marks on the document can be interpreted as data for processing by the computer. The individual completing the OMR document for input is guided as to where the marks should go, and is instructed to draw a circle round or put a cross through chosen numbers or letters on the document.

Examples of OMR include:

- answer sheets for multiple-choice examination questions, where candidates are required mark their chosen answer, e.g. A, B, C or D, to each question

- national lottery tickets, where the lottery numbers are selected by marking the chosen numbers on the ticket.

Optical character recognition (OCR)

With optical character recognition (OCR), a reader can recognise hand-written characters from their shape, and convert them into electronic data format. OCR applications have included meter reading forms for electricity and gas meters. The person reading the meter records the meter reading in boxes on a standard form, and the form is then input into the processing system through an OCR reader.

Magnetic ink character recognition (MICR)

With MICR, a special reader can detect characters on a standard form in 'magnetic ink' characters. The use of MICR is uncommon, although its most well-known use is the automatic reading of characters on bank cheques.

Scanner

A scanner is a device that can read any form of image and convert it into an electronic form for acceptance by a computer system. Scanners can therefore be used to input diagrams and pictures, signatures and other visual images, as well as images of text. Scanners are widely used in the publishing industry, for the processing of diagrams and other pictures in books, magazines and newspapers. They can also be used in other industries where diagrams and drawn plans are important, such as the construction and civil engineering industries. However, they have wider applications as general document readers.

Plastic cards (magnetic stripe and chip & pin)

Plastic swipe cards hold data in electronic form on a magnetic strip on the card. Plastic cards or other items might hold data in electronic form in an electronic chip. These can be read by a special reading device (either reading the magnetic stripe on the card or the chip in case of a chip & pin card) and fed into the computer system. The uses of plastic cards should be very familiar to you: they are used in banking systems, credit cards, security passes and so on.

Smart cards

The next generation of plastic cards will have funds actually on the card itself (rather than simply providing online authorisation to transfer funds). The card will be read in the same way as chip & pin cards, but funds then transferred direct from the card to the supermarket's (or other seller's) bank account. The smart card will be 'recharged' with more money at specialist ATMs. Experiments with smart cards have already been carried out in some cities, while Traveller's Cheque smart cards are already available.

Voice recognition

Voice recognition systems receive input as the spoken word. They are currently used in a limited number of situations such as routing calls within call centres ("please choose from the following six options") and as an alternative to keyboard input on computers.

Activity 1

The banks make use of MICR in their processing, with cheques being pre-encoded with certain data. What MICR data can you identify on your cheques?

Feedback to this activity is at the end of the chapter.

1.3 Output devices

Output from a computer system is often stored, in which case the output is transferred to a storage device. The other most common forms of output are:

- printer, and

- VDU screen.

Printers

Different types of printer are available. The most commonly used are now either:

- ink-jet printers for smaller computers and low-volume output, and

- laser printers, which are capable of faster output and so can handle much higher print volumes, with high print quality.

Printers can be used for the output of diagrams and pictures as well as text, and have widespread applications in business. In some computer systems, output can be printed on the standard pre-printed stationery, to produce documents such as sales invoices and statements.

VDU screen

Output to a VDU screen is temporary, whereas printed output is more permanent. However, many computer systems rely on output to VDU, where the computer user can simply read the information provided. There are many examples of VDU output, but examples are:

- e-mail messages, which can be printed out but are more usually read on screen

- customer service centres, where customer sales orders and queries by telephone can be handled by a customer service representative with access to central computer records through keyboard, mouse and VDU screen.

Other output devices

The other most commonly used output devices are for storing data in electronic form, and include floppy disks, compact disks or DVDs. Data can also be output onto microfilm (for which a computer output on microfilm or COM device is needed). Storage devices are discussed below.

1.4 Storage devices

Storage devices are devices for holding data or information (and programs) in electronic form. They are used for both input of data into a computer system and for output of data and information for storage. A distinction is made between:

- internal storage within the central processing unit, and

- external storage, which refers to all other electronic storage.

Internal storage

Data and programs can be stored in the internal RAM of the computer, or in a hard disk

RAM (read access memory) is volatile memory (the contents are lost when the computer is turned off) but it is accessible directly by the computer.

Hard disks provide the permanent storage in a computer. The contents of memory remain intact without the need for power supply, but there is a small time delay involved in accessing data and files stored on the disks. CDs can also provide disk storage, although CD/RW drives are needed to read and write to this storage medium.

External storage

The function of external storage is to maintain files of data and programs in a form intelligible to the computer. The principal requirements of external storage are:

- that sufficient storage capacity exists for the system to function adequately
- that the stored data can be quickly input to the computer when required
- that the stored data can be quickly and accurately amended when necessary and the updated files are easily created.

Magnetic tape

Magnetic tape is still occasionally used as a back-up storage device, where its low cost is a significant advantage, or where it is maintained because other, more recent, systems have not been implemented. Tape can be used to take a fast back up of the contents of the hard disk on a microcomputer. The device used to do this is a tape streamer. It would be normal to keep several editions or 'generations' of back ups.

Floppy disks, zip disks, CDs and DVDs

These are the main types of disks, which come in different forms and with different storage capacities. Storage capacity is measured in bytes. A byte is a unit of eight binary digits or bits, and can be used to represent one character (one number, one letter or one punctuation mark, etc).

- A kilobyte (Kb) is about 1,000 bytes (it is actually 1,024 bytes).
- A megabyte (Mb) is about 1,000,000 bytes (it is actually 1,024 × 1,024 bytes).
- A gigabyte is about 1,000 million bytes.

The storage capacity of a standard floppy disk is 1.44 Mb. Zip disks hold data in a compressed form. With **data compression**, the data held on the file is reduced in size, so that it does not require one byte to represent one character. Zip disk drives compress the data for storage purposes and de-compress it when it is needed for processing. They have a capacity of 150 Mb, 250 Mb or 750 Mb. (Zipped files are also used for transmitting large files more quickly via the Internet.)

The storage capacity of a CD-ROM is 650 Mb, and data can be retrieved by the computer from a CD more quickly than from a floppy disk. CDs are therefore faster devices as well as having larger storage capacity. DVDs hold between 4 Gb and 15 Gb, and are faster devices than CDs.

Storage capacity within computers can vary significantly, but the storage capacity of the hard drive of a PC might be 300 Gb or more.

DVDs are now the most popular form of disk storage.

Pen drives (compact storage devices that attach to the USB port on a computer) are also becoming more common. They enable limited amounts of data (up to about 2 megabytes) to be transferred easily between computers. The limited storage capacity means that, at present, they are not used for permanent system backup.

1.5 The central processing unit (CPU)

The central processing unit (CPU) is the computer itself. It consists of several component elements:

- a control unit, which supervises and co-ordinates all the computer's processing, in accordance with its programmed instructions

- an arithmetic and logic unit, which carries out mathematical computations and logic tests on data

- internal storage or memory.

The central computer must have a small amount of ROM and some RAM. It will also have some instantly accessible permanent storage, commonly referred to as the **hard drive**.

The CPU controls all the input, output and storage devices of the computer, holds the program that is currently being worked on and executes the program instructions.

1.6 Types of computer

Computers are categorised by their size and power. In addition to their storage capacity, computers are also compared by their processing speed, which is measured in MegaHertz (MHz) or GigaHertz (1GHz = 1,000 MHz). A PC, for example, might have a processing speed of 3.8 GHz or more.

Servers

The term 'server' is now used for any shared IT processing or storage device. Although servers vary widely in their technical design, the most important issue for a user such as a management accountant is to recognise the need for a server and specify its performance features. The technical specification of hardware and software is an issue for IT specialists – members of the organisation's IT department or supplier organisations.

The following sections look briefly at the different types of storage and processing hardware available to organisations. Later, we will look at the different ways in which servers can be used in IT architecture.

Mainframe computers

Much of the computer processing in large and medium-sized organisations is carried out on large mainframe computers. This type of computer is well suited to basic operational systems – payroll, stock control, invoicing, etc. – that are crucial to an organisation. Mainframe servers tend to be run by specialist staff, usually employed within the IT department, and tend to run only specially written or bespoke application software. Data may be input by operators within the IT department, or it may be input through VDUs operated by staff within user departments.

Minicomputers

The minicomputer came to be recognised as such when only mainframe computers existed. Now less powerful mainframe computers equate with the upper end of the minicomputer range and microcomputers cover the bottom end of the range.

Minicomputers may act as the main computing resource in small or medium-sized organisations, or may be used as departmental servers within large organisations. Off-the-shelf software packages are available for minicomputers.

Personal computers

In recent years, personal computers (PCs) have become the most widespread and commonly used computer resource. Their versatility and cheapness, combined with the wide variety of software that is available, allow their use in almost every business.

PCs may be used on a stand-alone basis, or they may be linked together via a local area network (LAN), or they may be linked with minicomputers or mainframes via a wide area network (WAN).

There are four or five common designs of computer chips that have been built into many hundreds of differently labelled PCs. Those chips have made possible the vast expansion of computer production in recent years.

The PC is cheap enough for an individual to have one all to him or herself either in business or at home. Typically, they cost between £400 and £3,000.

Adding extra memory, additional processing power or more peripheral devices can enhance the PC.

Portable or laptop PCs

In recent years, computers have been developed that are truly portable. Many of them use screens that are less power hungry than those on standard PCs, which enables them to be powered by rechargeable batteries. These batteries give several hours of continuous operation before needing to be recharged. This enables portable PCs to be used by business people while travelling.

Portable PCs are compatible with desktop PCs, which enable work carried out on the portable PC to be downloaded onto office computers (either via diskette or via a communications link). Many laptops have a docking station into which they can be placed to link them into a local area network.

Portable PCs may also be used for specialist applications, such as carrying out market research surveys.

Hand-held computers are used in some business applications. These are much smaller than laptops, and as the name indicates, are hand-held (and powered by re-chargeable battery). Uses of hand-held computers include parcel delivery company systems (where the recipient of the parcel signs for the receipt on the screen of the computer), electricity meter reading systems and warehouse systems (for example, for recording inventory counting).

2 Software

Computer software is the term used to describe collections of instructions to the computer hardware. You need to be aware of the different types of computer software available.

2.1 Types of software

There are five different types of software available for computers:

• utilities

• programming tools

• operating systems

• bespoke applications

• off-the-shelf applications.

Utilities packages are software tools designed to improve the way in which the operating system works. These might automate routine operations such as file management or back up (as with 'Norton Utilities'), or might make the whole operating system easier to use (as with 'Windows®' when used with a conventional operating system such as DOS).

Programming tools include the programming language itself, the tools to allow programmes to be written (such as compilers or assemblers) or more advanced tools such as computer-aided software engineering (CASE) packages.

Operating systems software

The operating system is the most important piece of software in any computer system, as without it the system will not work at all. It consists of a number of tools to allow the following functions:

• communication between the operator and the computer

• control of the processor and storage hardware

• the management of files

• the use of peripherals such as printers and modems.

When the computer is multi-tasking, and running several application programs simultaneously, the operating system allocates internal storage space to each application, chooses which programs should be run in which order of priority and decides how much CPU time to give to each application

There are two different types of operating systems in common use in business:

• command-driven operating systems, such as DOS, which are sometimes used with a graphical user interface (GUI) utility

• WIMP (Windows®, icons, mouse and pointer) operating systems such as Windows® XP, which have their own GUI.

The GUI allows a reduction in the amount of training required to use the system, and prevents the selection of invalid or unreasonable options or instructions.

Bespoke applications

Bespoke (tailor-made or purpose-written) applications have been constructed to meet the specific needs of the particular organisation in which they are found. The process of programming these is extremely time-consuming and expensive, but is often the only alternative if the application is very specialised.

Advantages of bespoke systems include the following:

- they precisely fit the organisation's information needs
- the organisation has complete discretion over data structures
- the system can be integrated with other applications within the organisation
- the system can be modified to fit changing needs.

If the programs are of interest to other organisations, they can be sold (or licensed). The information services group can thus become a profit centre.

Disadvantages of bespoke systems include:

- development takes a long time, which delays the implementation of the system
- bespoke systems are costly to develop and test
- there is a greater probability of bugs in a bespoke system – most of the errors in packages will have been found by other users
- support of a bespoke system will be expensive.

Off-the-shelf applications

These are pieces of software, often called application packages, which have been created by a software manufacturer, tested and documented, then copied many times. They are sold in a form that is ready to install and use straight away.

Examples of off-the-shelf applications include spreadsheets, word processing, databases, accounting and communications packages.

These applications tend to be generalist in nature, that is, used by many different organisations for basic word processing and spreadsheet work. Specialist packages are also available for specific areas such as production scheduling, order processing or maintenance of employee details. These packages tend to be more expensive, but again they can be used in many different types of organisation.

The advantages and disadvantages of off-the shelf packages are outlined below:

Advantages	Disadvantages
• Cheaper to buy than bespoke packages are to develop • Short lead-times are available, as the software is simply bought and installed • Likely to come with good training programmes and documentation • New, updated versions are likely to be available on a regular basis • They have been tried and tested and have less risk of errors and bugs	• They do not fit precisely the needs of the organisation – the users may need to compromise what they want with what is available • Dependency on an outside supplier for maintenance; many software suppliers are difficult to influence • May not have all of the required functions • Different packages used by the organisation may have incompatible data structures

2.2 Computer applications

Many computer users have the same applications. For example, any business has to have systems for word processing, payroll, sales ledger, bought ledger and stock control. Very often the requirements for these applications are similar for a wide range of companies. An application package is a standard program, or suite of programs, designed to perform a specific task. It saves users from having to develop application programs that are essentially the same as those already developed.

All applications ultimately depend on the processing of data, but they can be sub-divided into three main groups:

- **Commercial**, in which the computer performs administrative data-processing tasks including the maintenance of accounting records. Typically this involves large volumes of data and large file sizes. The main input peripheral is a keyboard, possibly combined with some form of data capture equipment. Large-scale storage devices with rapid access are needed for file handling, and disk-based systems are now the most common.

- **Scientific**, carrying out complex statistical analysis or mathematical manipulation. Relatively small volumes of data may be involved, but they will be subjected to complex processing involving many millions of computer instructions. Especially large processors may be needed for this work to allow more accurate floating-point arithmetic and greater speed of computation.

- **Process control**, in which the computer runs a machine or even a whole factory on the basis of data supplied from the process itself via special sensors and data transmission systems. Examples already implemented range from individual robots to entire steelworks, including automated decision-making processes to optimise the use of raw materials or other resources.

The dividing line between these applications is not always clear, and a computer in use in a particular installation may be involved in more than one type, although there is a certain amount of necessary specialisation to fit them for their particular tasks.

Packages with common interfaces

Some programs, or packages of programs, can perform more than one task, e.g. office administration packages that comprise word processing, creating and using a database, spreadsheets and business graphics. These are called 'integrated packages' because they bring these varied tasks together, an example being Microsoft Office. However, each application within these packages still retains its own data files.

Integrated packages

Many organisations will use an integrated applications package as an alternative to buying in a number of dedicated application packages. An integrated packages provides one set of data files for use by all programmes within that package. Key features of integrated packages include:

- systems communicate with each other inside the computer instead of outside it

- input of a transaction results in *all* relevant files being updated

- output is produced only for communication to the user. It is not produced to communicate with another system

- all files can be accessed by programs as needed; a program is not limited to access to a single file.

An example of an integrated package is Sage Accounting Plus (SAP) (see below).

Fully integrated accounting packages

At their simplest level accounts packages can be considered as electronic ledgers, with the routine transactions recorded on a computer system, rather than on paper, and the general principles of double entry bookkeeping being incorporated in the software.

There are many advantages in computerising an accounts system, e.g. the software package *Sage Accountant Plus* includes sales invoicing, stock control and report generation, as well as the basic sales, purchase and nominal ledgers. The format of invoices can be set by the user as pre-printed forms and other features that can be expected from even the simplest packages would include some form of security and auditing controls. More advanced (and more expensive) packages would be expected to provide such options as payroll, multiple currency accounts, and cheque production facilities with integrated word processors and spreadsheets so that information can be used anywhere in the system and incorporated into financial modelling routines and reports or letters as required.

Desk Top Publishing (DTP)

DTP packages, such as PageMaker and Microsoft Publisher are popular as they let a user combine text and art to present reports in a much more professional looking way. Applications for a DTP package include:

- output of financial reports, incorporating the use of high quality graphics

- preparation of in-house journals and magazines

- reports used in consultancy work, which may incorporate graphs, charts, etc.

DTP has had a major impact upon both the computing world and the business world. There are a wide range of DTP applications on offer to businesses. DTP is attractive to businesses in that it allows for the production of a high quality publication without the need to use a specialist printing firm.

3 Computer communications

Where an organisation has several locations, it may be more effective to process data locally rather than at one central installation. By doing this, individual managers will be able to schedule their own processing and will have more control over the contents of their database systems. Any system that requires computers to communicate with each other will need specialised hardware and software such as:

- modems, broadband or network connection

- communication programs

- network circuits and software.

3.1 Modems

The modem (MOdulator/DEModulator) is the interface between the electronic pulses used to transfer data within the computer system and the signals needed for transmission through the telephone system. It is controlled by communications software running on the computer and provides an input and output link with the telephone system. With appropriate software, intelligent modems (those with built-in control circuitry) can handle communications with minimum manual intervention, allowing redialling of engaged numbers and call answering to be performed automatically. Many models are also capable of adjusting their information reception rate to match the transmission rate of the calling modem.

Modem transmission speeds are quoted in baud rates, which correspond to bits per second.

3.2 Broadband connections

A broadband connection allows the transfer of digital signals along a telephone line. This means that a modem is not required because computer signals do not have to be converted to analogue. Transferring of computer signals directly along a telephone line allows much faster baud rates to be achieved. Rates of up to 2 megabytes are now common with some advanced systems quoting 8 megabytes.

3.3 Communications software

Specialist software is needed to handle the communications process itself, and the software used by the transmitter and the receiver must be compatible. To achieve this, certain standard protocols (that is, an agreed format for the communication being used between the different communication devices) have been developed so that systems can signal to each other the start and finish of transmission and reception and any problems experienced with data, and so priorities of use of the communication channel can be properly maintained.

3.4 Local area networks (LANs)

A local area network (or LAN) consists of a network which connects the computers to each other and contains the hardware needed for efficient communication (often in the form of expansion cards which plug directly into the computers' circuitry), and software to run the network. The software provides for appropriate priority control over data transmission and reception and allows the system to cope with multiple users having access to the same files. This involves extra protocols to cover simultaneous access by different users, security over data, and so on. The network may be setup using cables to join the computers and other devices, although wireless networking (using local radio signals to link computers) is becoming common. Wireless networks, as the name suggests, have the benefit that they do not require cables, thus making installation of a network easier.

LANs can be made up of several identical computers, often to allow shared access to an expensive piece of equipment, such as a laser printer, to maximise its cost-effectiveness. In some cases, several microcomputers provide input to one or more servers, so that they can be used independently within their own locations and as intelligent terminals to the shared machine(s).

Local area network - star configuration

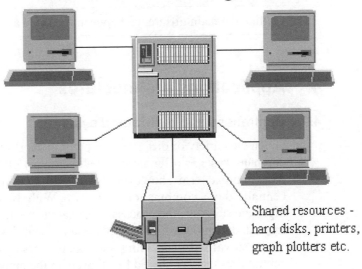

Shared resources - hard disks, printers, graph plotters etc.

Advantages of local area networks

- Data can be shared amongst all users.

- The network can be gradually extended as the organisation grows. Each new machine brings with it additional processing power.

- Users can share expensive resources such as high quality printers.

- If one machine breaks down, the others can continue working.

- They are cost effective for large numbers of users.

- Members of the network can send electronic mail to one another, reducing the amount of paperwork.

The distance over which an LAN can be set up is limited by the efficiency of the cables connecting the machines or the power of the radio signals in a wireless network. They are typically used within relatively small areas because of the expense of long-distance connections. Within these limits, they provide an efficient and secure means of communication and can significantly extend the computing power of an organisation at low cost. It is also possible to set up connections between networks over longer distances specialised cabling and software, so that the range of options available for computer communications within an organisation and between organisations is potentially limitless.

An extended network of this sort is often referred to as the wide area network or WAN.

3.5 Wide area networks (WANs)

Wide area networks permit multiple users to have access to a remote computer via the telecommunications network. Network users are required to 'log-on' to the system. A network user would also have a personal password to reduce the risk of unauthorised access.

A modem or broadband connection is often used to gain access to a WAN, though some other devices may be used if the WAN is permanently available. Any device that gives access to a WAN is known as a **gateway**. Although accessing remote computers, the response time over a WAN may be only a fraction of a second.

Response time is defined as the interval between data entry by the terminal user and receipt of the result of any processing activity that has taken place.

Activity 2

Outline the main difference between the LAN and the WAN.

Feedback to this activity is at the end of the chapter.

4 Applications architectures

4.1 Centralised and distributed systems

Given the variety of different computer networks that can be constructed, computer systems offer a computer user many different ways of processing data. In broad terms, however, the processing of data is either distributed, centralised or a combination of the two. With **distributed data processing**, as the name suggests, the processing of data is not done by a central computer. Instead, data processing takes place at a 'local' level, remote from the centre. With **centralised processing**, the data processing occurs centrally, by updating central files that are shared by all users in the network.

The justification for a decision to centralise information technology may be as follows:

Only one set of files is needed. Everyone in the organisation uses the same data, which is readily accessible in a standard format.

Economies of scale. It may be advantageous to acquire one large computer, with greater processing capabilities, rather than several small computers. Centralisation of personnel may also remove unnecessary duplication of activity and allow for regulation and control of analysis and programming functions. It is necessary, however, to balance the cost element against the benefits derived by users (the latter may be greater with decentralisation).

Staff shortages/turnover. Centralisation mitigates the effect of both, so that individuals are less indispensable, and they can be provided with greater scope in their working experience. Fewer employees may be needed, so higher quality staff and specialists may be affordable.

Ease of control. Senior management is better placed to control operating functions, particularly when a standard reporting system is being utilised.

The arguments in favour of decentralised or distributed systems are as follows:

Local knowledge. Computer personnel are advantageously positioned when they are close to the problem. They are more likely to arrive at an appropriate solution than if they were remotely located. They will also focus on the business problem rather than technical computer considerations.

Speed of response. Operational decisions can be made more quickly. Line managers can respond more rapidly to change, as they are better placed to appreciate the local conditions and to be aware of other relevant factors.

Greater appreciation of financial targets. Costs may be decentralised together with decentralisation of equipment and staff. Senior managers and users will be more attentive to the costs associated with computing activities as this will have a direct effect on the budgets and profitability of their department.

Greater ownership of the information and hence greater pride in getting it right.

KEY POINT

Reasons for centralising include: only one set of files is needed; economies of scale; mitigate staff shortages/turnover and ease of control.

KEY POINT

Reasons for decentralising are local knowledge, speed of response, greater appreciation of financial targets, ownership and greater flexibility.

Flexibility. While centralisation promotes increased efficiency and control, decentralisation permits greater flexibility. Inherently, attempting to attain these two objectives creates a conflict. In practice, new and improved technologies have diluted the merits of either structure; it may be most effective to have some aspects of the information system centralised, and others decentralised.

Some information technology activities can be more satisfactorily accomplished centrally. These include:

- devising an IT strategy for the group

- initiating IT standards

- procuring hardware and software

- monitoring standards

- supply of communication needs

- human resource management

- technical support

- support for computer auditing.

The conflict between centralised and distributed systems caused problems for organisations for many years. In many organisations, parallel systems developed with both centralised mainframe or minicomputer services existing alongside PCs and LANs. It is common to find this type of situation in examination questions, where the theme of the question is 'Can we do better?'

Activity 3

Explain the difference between distributed processing and centralised, multi-user processing.

Feedback to this activity is at the end of the chapter.

4.2 Client-server architecture

The term **architecture** is used in IT, as in its normal usage, to describe the physical appearance of the system and the way in which its component parts relate to one another. In client server architecture, a 'client' is a computer requesting a service and a 'server' is another computer providing that service. For example, one computer can request access to a specific printer and the printer server will provide that access.

The hardware elements in a client-server system include:

Client workstations	These are normally PCs used by individual users.
Local or departmental servers	These are shared by a few users with the same computing needs.
A central or corporate server	This is shared by all users throughout the organisation.

These are illustrated in the following figure:

The applications carried out by the organisation's users are split between the available hardware, according to how many users need access to them and how much processing power is required.

Client applications are software tools that are used for processing on client hardware. Although a number of client applications may have many users (e.g. spreadsheet, word processing), they work as individuals rather than together. Some client applications (e.g. decision support systems) may be unique to one user. Sometimes these tools are called personal applications.

Local applications are software tools that are used for processing on a local or departmental server. Local applications are common to users within a section or department and the application is shared by a number of users (e.g. shared databases within an application such as Notes).

Corporate applications – the processing using corporate applications takes place on the corporate server. Such applications are shared by users from many departments (e.g. the organisation's MIS). This allows the very high processing power of the corporate server to be used to its best effect.

4.3 Batch processing and real time processing

Data processing of transactions within a system might be by batch processing or online one transaction at a time.

- With **batch processing**, a quantity of similar transactions is processed at the same time, in a single 'batch'. All the transactions in the batch might be given a batch number, to identify when they were processed: this can improve data control procedures. When input is via a terminal with keyboard, screen and mouse, the computer operator keys in all the transactions. Having input the entire batch of transactions, a command is then given for the computer to process the entire batch. Batch processing might be used in an accounting system. For example, an accounts clerk might process a batch of purchase invoices as a batch, rather than processing each invoice individually when it is received. Similarly, it is usual to process the monthly payroll in a batch processing procedure.

- As an alternative to batch processing, transactions might be processed individually as they occur. This is necessary in systems where the data files have to be kept fully up-to-date, such as booking systems for travel or hotel accommodation reservations. When the central files are updated immediately, so that each user is continually working with fully up-to-date files, the system is said to operate in **real time**. An example of real time update is an ATM machine. After you withdraw cash from the ATM, the balance will have decreased by the amount of cash withdrawn.

5 Network-enabled technologies

Computer systems are able to make use of various technologies through WANs.

5.1 Internet

Users in a computer network are often able to access the Internet through the network server. The Internet gives computer users access to huge amounts of external information on the websites of other organisations. (The term 'world wide web' or 'www' refers to the Internet software tool for network navigation.)

Access to the Internet is invaluable for many businesses.

- Information can be obtained from other organisations quickly. Without the Internet, this information would take much longer to obtain and, in many cases, would be unobtainable. Examples of external information include published financial information by companies (and other investor information), government guidelines and statistics and information about the products and services of other suppliers and competitors.

- An organisation can provide information about itself on its own website, including information about its products or services. Customers might be able to place orders via the Internet and even pay for the order. **E-commerce**, a term for buying and selling via the Internet, continues to grow rapidly.

5.2 Intranets

An intranet is a 'private' computer network operated by an organisation. It uses the same technology as the Internet, but the web pages are only available to computers within a specific company. Information normally placed on an Intranet can include in-house manuals, reference material, job vacancies, telephone lists, etc.

5.3 E-mail

Electronic mail (e-mail) allows messages and data files to be transmitted between users instantly, without the need for paper or disks as transmission media. The network might be a LAN or a WAN. When users are allowed to send and receive e-mail messages to computers outside the network, the system uses the Internet.

The obvious advantages of e-mail are:

- more communication of information

- faster communications and faster responses than communication of paper documents

- convenience: an e-mail can always be sent to a recipient, whereas a telephone call does not always get through immediately.

Although e-mail systems are essential for many organisations, the also create some risk of inefficiency. The disadvantages of e-mail are:

- large volume of e-mail messages are 'junk mail' or of little information value

- computer users can take a long time reading through e-mail messages and waste much of this time unnecessarily

- users often fail to organise their e-mail messages by filing the useful messages in an organised way (and deleting the rest)

- attachments to e-mail messages received from external sources might contain a virus.

5.4 Teleconferencing

Telephone conferencing is a method of communication that enables several participants in different geographical locations to hold a conversation. Video conferencing is similar, except that visual images of the conference participants are provided through computer screens. The benefit of teleconferencing and video conferencing is that it can reduce the time and money spent by business executives on travelling to meetings in other countries.

5.5 Electronic data interchange (EDI)

In theory, the computer systems of one organisation should be able to communicate with the computer systems of other organisations. The Internet makes some communication possible. For example, a person in one company can send an e-mail message to someone in a different company, and attach files to the message. Organisations can also communicate with each other by providing information through their websites.

With current technology, however, there is a problem if a large bespoke computer system of one organisation wishes to send data to the bespoke computer system of another system. Much of the problem lies in the fact that computer records are structured differently in each organisation's computer system.

Direct communications between computer systems of different companies might be desirable, however, in the case of companies and their major suppliers. A purchase system would operate more efficiently and quickly, and with much less paperwork, if a company could:

- send a purchase order automatically from its own inventory control and purchasing system, direct to the computer system of a major supplier, and

- the supplier's computer system could automatically confirm availability, delivery date and price.

Electronic data interchange or EDI is a system for enabling the computer systems of different organisations to communicate without the need for paperwork. Typically, it is used to link the purchasing and invoicing systems of suppliers and their customers. EDI is used predominantly by large business organisations with bespoke computer systems. It works by converting messages, such as purchase orders and invoices, into a standard format that the computer systems of both participants can interpret and respond to.

The advantages of EDI are:

- **speed**: transactions are transmitted between the computer systems quickly, without delays in printing and posting at the sender's end and entering the data at the recipient's end

- **reliability**: there is less chance of messages being lost in transmission, compared with the postal delivery system for paper documents

- **accuracy**: the risk of error is virtually eliminated, because transactions and messages are generated automatically, without human intervention

- **labour cost savings** owing to savings in time and improved efficiency.

5.6 Teleworking

Computer and communications technology make it possible for individuals to work away from the office. They can be linked to the computer systems of the organisation through remote terminals linked to the organisation's intranet, allowing them to download programs and data files, and also to input data to the organisation's systems for processing. They can communicate with colleagues via e-mail, telephone and fax.

Teleworking allows employees to work from home. The benefits include:

- giving an employer the option to recruit employees who do not live close to its premises

- giving an employer the option to recruit employees who want to work from home

- lower accommodation costs and related expenses for the employer, if significant numbers of employees work from home

- greater flexibility in working hours: in theory, homeworkers can access the computer system at any time during the day and so can often adjust their working times to suit their convenience

- for employees, a change in the quality of life, because time spent travelling to and from work each day is eliminated.

6 Designing systems to suit the user's requirements

The range of computer software, hardware and communications technology means that organisations have considerable flexibility in their choice of computer system (subject to the constraints of cost). For your examination, you should be prepared to deal with a question that asks you to recommend the most appropriate type of system structure (or 'architecture') for a particular processing application.

Summary

- IT systems consist of hardware and software and, in many cases, telecommunications links.

- 'Hardware' describes the physical make-up of a system. It consists of central processing units and peripheral equipment, and (in systems using the telecommunications network) modems. Peripheral equipment is used for input and output and for external data storage.

- Many systems are designed to provide a graphical user interface (GUI), so that the computer user can use a screen with icons, pointer and mouse.

- Memory for storage of data may be RAM, ROM or permanent storage. Permanent storage is provided by the computer's hard drive and external data storage items such as floppy disk, CD and DVD.

- 'Software' describes the programs for a computer system. Categories of software are the operating system for a computer, applications software, utility software and programming tools, such as program language translation software.

- Application software might be bespoke programs or off-the-shelf software. Off-the-shelf software has made computer systems accessible to small businesses.

- Many computer systems are structured as networks of inter-linked computers and peripheral equipment. Networks might have a hub computer, distributed servers, file servers (for holding shared data and program files), network servers (for linking the network to the telecommunications network/Internet) and dumb terminals or intelligent terminals for the system users.

- LANs are networks where the hardware items within one local linked by standard cabling or 'wireless' networks. WANs are networks that link LANs over large distances, e.g. between cities. Networks can be designed and structured to provide distributed data processing, centralised processing or client/server architecture.

- Networks and communications links have enabled businesses to make use of the Internet, intranets, e-mail, electronic data interchange, teleconferencing and teleworking.

Having completed your study of this chapter, you should have achieved the following learning outcomes:

- explain the features and operations of commonly used information technology hardware and software

- explain how commonly used technologies are used in the work place.

Self-test questions

1   Name two hardware devices that can be used for both input and output. (1.1)

2   List seven types of input device. (1.2)

3   What is GUI? What is WIMP? (1.2)

4   What is a CD-ROM and a DVD? (1.4)

5   What are the three basic elements in a central processing unit of a computer? (1.5)

6 What are the advantages and disadvantages for a business of using bespoke application software? (2.1)

7 List four types of general purpose package. (2.1)

8 What is the difference between a LAN and a WAN? (3.4, 3.5)

9 What is meant by client/server architecture? (4.2)

10 What is an intranet? (5.2)

11 What are the advantages and disadvantages for a business of using e-mail? (5.3)

12 What is EDI? (5.5)

13 What are the potential benefits for an employer of teleworking? (5.6)

Practice questions

Question 1

Which of the following is an item of software?

A Firewall

B Icon

C Modem

D Disk drive

Question 2

Which of the following types of disk typically has a storage capacity of 650 megabytes?

A Zip disk

B CD

C DVD

D Computer hard drive

Question 3

When a computer system provides for the immediate updating of its data files by input from users so that any subsequent user has access to the updated file, the system is said to operate in _____ .

Question 4

Explain in less than 30 words the meaning of data compression.

Question 5

A compiler is an example of:

A   an operating system

B   application software

C   utility software

D   a programming tool.

Question 6

National Counties Hotels plc (National) runs a chain of 40 major hotels. Most of the hotels are in major cities, but some are located in areas of natural beauty and away from towns. Each hotel has a general manager and separate managers for its restaurant, conferences and group bookings. The housekeeper, chef, and senior barman also have some management responsibility.

The company's head office is in London. Each week head office receives a report from every hotel in the chain; this is used for planning and evaluation purposes. Head office also has a reservations section that can take bookings for all the hotels; alternatively, guests can ring up specific hotels. Touring guests staying at a National can make a booking from one to another of the group's hotels for onward travel.

The company is reviewing its information systems, as there have been some problems of late in several of the company's hotels or at head office. These have included:

- Arrangements made by a group bookings manager had not been properly recorded and individual bookings were subsequently accepted when no rooms were available.

- Conference booking information was not picked up by the kitchens and lunches that had been arranged could not be provided.

- A general manager wanted to review room occupancy by week and profitability. The analysis had to be performed by hand.

- At year-end, head office prepared accounts and it was discovered that an advert, which had been placed in a travel magazine, had been inadvertently allowed to appear every month. Invoices had been received and paid each month and the cost overrun was in the order of £9,000.

- There has been some revenue lost because room numbers have not been correctly recorded when services to guests have been provided. For example, in the restaurant or bar, guests can charge purchases to their rooms. So far guests have merely had to quote their room numbers without having to show any proof of identity.

You have been asked to advise the company on certain matters and have had a preliminary meeting with a head office official. In response to these problems, the official has said: 'What the company needs is a proper operating system. If we had that we would be assured that we would be supplied with the proper information that would allow the company to operate more efficiently.'

You are required to:

Produce a memorandum to the Head Office official that covers the following:

(a)   Describe the major components of National in terms of its activities and explain the linkages that may exist between these various activities.

(9 marks)

(b)   Explain the purposes and functions of an operating system.   **(8 marks)**

(c)   Suggest a data capture method that would improve the accuracy of charging for services. Justify your choice in terms of fulfilling the requirements of National and in terms of guest convenience.   **(3 marks)**

(Total: 20 marks)

For the answers to these questions, see the 'Answers' section at the end of the book.

Feedback to activities

Activity 1

The data that is pre-encoded on the cheques used in the UK banking system includes:

*   the cheque number

*   the bank's branch sort code, and

*   the customer's account number.

Activity 2

A local area network (LAN) is a network of one or more computers and their peripheral equipment where there is no transmission of data over the telecommunications network. The items of hardware in the system are therefore linked by cable or wireless network.

A wide area network (WAN) is a computer network that links LANs over large distances.

Activity 3

Distributed processing is where the system includes more than one processing unit which are connected, allowing the processing to be 'distributed' around the system.

Key features of distributed processing

*   Computers can be distributed or spread over a wide geographical area.

*   Processing is either carried out centrally or at dispersed locations.

*   Each computer can access the information files of other computers in the system.

*   Each computer within the system can process data 'jointly' or 'interactively'.

Centralised processing means having the data/information processing carried out in a central place, such as a computer centre at the head office. At head office there would be the following items:

*   a central computer; probably a mainframe computer

*   central files, containing all the files needed for the system.

Many users could be connected to the same computer and could carry out processing work simultaneously. The terminals need not all be in the same building as the central computer. With a multi-user system, the terminals are 'dumb' terminals, which means that they do not include a Central Processing Unit (CPU) and so cannot perform independent data processing. Instead, they rely on the central computer for data processing power.

Chapter 2

INFORMATION SYSTEMS

Syllabus content

- General Systems Theory and its application to IT (i.e. system definition, system components, system behaviour, system classification, entropy, requisite variety, coupling and decoupling).

- The benefits of IT systems.

Contents

1   Systems theory

2   Control systems

3   Relevance of General Systems Theory to IT/IS

4   Information systems and decision making

5   Different information systems

6   Benefits of IT

1 Systems theory

1.1 General Systems Theory (GST)

General Systems Theory (GST) was first developed during the 1930s, when scientists in a variety of different disciplines (biology, psychology, sociology) realised that there were certain broad principles that applied to the systems they studied and worked with.

GST attempts to describe the common properties of systems, to categorise types of system and to describe how systems react to environmental influences.

1.2 Information technology and information systems

DEFINITION

Information technology (IT) is a term used to describe hardware, software and communications links, which are combined to create IT systems.

Information technology (IT) is a term used to describe hardware, software and communications links, which are combined to create IT systems. Information technology has many uses within organisations.

- Within manufacturing systems, IT technology (robotics) is used in production machinery and equipment.

- It is used within many products that are sold to consumers, such as motor cars, kitchen equipment and home entertainment systems.

- It can be used in security systems.

IT systems are also used extensively to create information systems (IS).

In order to design an IS, it can be very useful to have an understanding of what a system is, and to be able to relate the concepts of General Systems Theory to IT systems and IS. The same concepts of General Systems Theory can also be applied to organisations, such as companies, and so the theory also has relevance for management in general.

1.3 Description of a system

There is no easy, universally accepted definition of the word 'system'. However, it is a term that most people understand, because it is used so frequently; for example, solar system, digestive system, ecosystem, political system, trading system, judicial system, central heating system and purchasing system. A suitable definition for examination purposes is:

DEFINITION

A system is a group of related elements or activities that are organised for a specific purpose or to achieve a common objective.

KEY POINT

Every system has a boundary, which is the limit of the system.

- A **system** is a group of related elements or activities that are organised for a specific purpose or to achieve a common objective.

- System properties include a boundary, inputs/outputs, transformation, purpose or goal, requisite variety, adaptive content and measures of performance.

System boundary and environment

Every system has a **boundary**, which is the limit of the system. Outside the boundary is the system environment: inside the boundary is the system. A company is a system whose boundary might be defined by the people who work for it or the other assets that it controls. Outside the organisation boundary, and so part of the environment of the company, are its customers, suppliers, the tax authorities, and the regulatory authorities. Shareholders are within the company, but lenders and potential investors are outside.

If the system under examination is the 'finance system' then sales, production and purchasing become part of the environment, and within the system boundary will be found smaller subsystems such as product costing, financial accounting and treasury.

Activity 1

List as many items as you can that constitute the external environment of an accounting system.

Feedback to this activity is at the end of the chapter.

Systems are systematic – they do something in a specific order.

Inputs, outputs and the transformation process

The purpose of systems is to change inputs into outputs. This change is called the transformation process, as is shown in the diagram below.

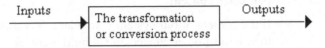

- **Inputs** – for an organisation the inputs may include people, capital, and managerial skills, as well as technical knowledge and skills.

- **The transformation process** – in a manufacturing organisation this would be the production department; in an insurance company it would be the underwriting department.

- **Outputs** – these will vary with the enterprise but include the following: products, services, profits and satisfaction. Outputs can also include waste/undesirable conditions

Requisite variety

Requisite variety is the ability of the system to respond to a variety of inputs from the environment. If there is a change in the environment, resulting in a change of input to the system, and the system is unable to cope then it lacks requisite variety and requires amendment. However, if the change in input is handled by the system, then it has appropriate requisite variety. If this new input occurs regularly, then we can make amendments to this system to allow for this input.

For example, every university offers more places than they have available. Say they have 75 places and offer 150. If the 150 accept and the university can handle this within its existing system, it has **requisite variety.** If this happens every year, this must be recognised as a consistent change to the input and the system must be changed to offer 150 places.

We now have a system. All the concepts identified so far are General Systems' concepts, in that they all relate to any or all systems views.

However, our concern is with a very particular class of systems, i.e. organisations. These display the additional systems properties of 'purposeful' behaviour, as well as the ability to change or modify this behaviour.

System purpose, goal or objective

A system must have a purpose, objective or goal. This is the reason for the existence of the system. With organisations, the senior management specify the objective of the organisation and the way in which it is specified can be crucial to what the organisation does and how it develops in response to changes in its environment. For example, a company whose objective was to manufacture horse-drawn carriages in the early days of the motor car would have seen the car as a threat to its future. In contrast, an organisation whose objective was to provide transport to the people would be more likely to see the motor car as a major new opportunity, and not a threat.

Information systems should also have a clear objective in their design and development. The objective of an IS is to provide information, but for what particular purpose or purposes? Unless there is an objective, a system cannot function properly, and much of its operation will be inefficient and wasteful.

Adaptive content

If the content of our system is to adapt to consistent changes in the environment, then it must be organised and should include:

- operating processes
- communication processes
- control processes
- decision-making processes
- information provision processes
- resources for all of the above.

Management information systems

Management information systems help to monitor, evaluate and take action to make the system adaptive to the environment.

Open and closed systems

Open system

An **open system** interacts with its environment. It exchanges material, information and energy with its environment, and continually changes and evolves in response to changes in the environment.

Organisations can be viewed as systems that take inputs from the environment and through a series of activities convert or transform these inputs into outputs to achieve some objective. This means that the organisation is open to and in continual communication with the external environment of which it is a part. It must respond to the opportunities and challenges and the risks and limitations presented to it. Changes in the environment, e.g. advances in IT or pressure group campaigners, will affect inputs and changes in inputs will affect the transformation or conversion process and hence the outputs.

The model below shows how the organisation, as an open system, receives inputs, transforms them and exports the outputs to the environment.

Feedback – some of the outputs may become inputs again e.g. the satisfaction of employees becomes an important human input. Similarly; profits, the surplus of income over costs, are reinvested in cash and capital goods, such as machinery; equipment, buildings and stock.

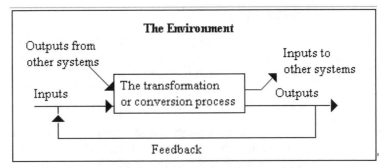

Nearly all organisations are open systems; they have to be in order to survive. It is therefore vital that information systems gather data from outside the organisation as well as from the inside. Examples of such external information include analyses of customer satisfaction, observation of competitors' behaviour, including pricing policy and responses by the local community to environmental policy.

The systems approach expresses a manager's role as being a co-ordinator of the elements of a system, of which people are only one part. A manager is encouraged to spend greater time and effort in improving, planning, controlling and operating systems than motivating staff, since this will lead to greater efficiency.

Closed system

A **closed system** is self-contained and does not interact with its environment in any way.

KEY POINT

A **closed system** is self-contained and does not interact with its environment in any way.

Completely closed systems are not found in business. Monasteries or ghettos come close to being closed systems and the term 'closed economy' is used for a country or region, which does not import or export significantly. An organisation, department or individual being a closed system is likely to be a disadvantage because closed systems will clearly find it difficult to adapt to changing circumstances.

Semi-closed systems

Semi-closed systems react to the environment in a limited and predictable way. For example, a thermostat system is designed to regulate the temperature of its environment. It reacts to the temperature in a controlled and predictable way by switching the heating on or off accordingly. Systems of this type are described later in this chapter under the heading 'control systems'. In some organisations the budgetary control system, whereby actual results are compared with budgets, is treated as a semi-closed system. The results from the environment are measured, but the resulting action taken is pre-defined. Junior management and computer controlled operations may be used for managing semi-closed systems.

Entropy in systems

DEFINITION

Entropy means the tendency for a system to become more and more disorganised over a period of time.

Entropy means the tendency for a system to become more and more disorganised over a period of time. This happens with closed systems, since by their very nature they fail to take into account relevant information from the environment. An open business system overcomes this condition by receiving inputs from the outside environment to take into account new information and conditions. In this way the system can become even more organised, displaying 'negative entropy'. An example of entropy in an information system is the decay that will happen in the system if it is not updated with new information from its environment. For example, a sales invoicing system will suffer entropy if it is not updated with information about changes in the rate of sales tax and data about new customers.

1.4 Subsystems

A system is a group of related elements or activities. Some of these elements may in fact themselves be systems within the system. They are known as subsystems, which may be broken down into further systems, differentiated from each other by such things as function, location, people, time, automation or formality. The area of contact between subsystems is known as the **interface.**

When looking at the organisation as a system, the most obvious way to break it down into subsystems is by organisation structure. The example given earlier in this chapter was of an organisation consisting of production, sales, purchasing and finance functions, where the finance function had several departments including product costing, financial accounting and treasury.

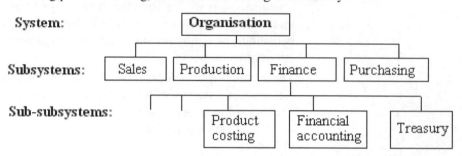

Another obvious way in which to break down an organisational system into subsystems is by **geography** (e.g. the country is divided into regions, which are divided into individual operating units).

Goal congruence and sub-optimisation

Subsystems, like systems, have their own objectives or goals. Systems work most efficiently when the goals of subsystems work in the same direction as the goal of the overall system. If this happens successfully, it is said that there is **goal congruence** (or agreement). Sometimes, however, subsystems pursue their own goals at the expense of the system as a whole. There is then said to be **sub-optimisation,** or **sub-optimality**.

Many examples occur when the organisation is divided into different sections:

- The manager of division B wishes to maximise B's profits. He decides to buy cheaper engines from another source rather than division A. This increases his or her profits, but moves division A into a loss-making situation. Overall the profits of the firm suffer.

- A purchasing manager achieves his or her objective of buying at the minimum unit price by ordering large quantities of raw materials in order to receive a high quantity discount. The results of his or her department look good, but overall the firm may suffer because of unnecessary stockholding cost.

Sub-optimisation can usually be reduced by careful systems design. The design of information systems plays a vital part in this because often the problem arises not out of malice or self-interest but because people simply do not know the consequences of their actions. The key is to encourage goal congruence through education, team building, awareness and reward structures.

1.5 Subsystem connections and decoupling

The relationship between subsystems may be described in terms of the closeness of connection between them.

Coupling describes the way in which subsystems are linked to each other, and the extent to which they depend on each other. For example, although the personnel department may operate relatively independently of the finance function, there needs to be very close connections between the employee details held by the personnel and finance records systems. Or, to take another example, in a manufacturing firm, the system for ordering raw materials and the production system should be well coordinated.

The problem with coupled subsystems is that such co-ordination can be technically difficult and time consuming. Further, a breakdown in one subsystem will affect all the other subsystems that are connected to it.

For example, consider the following simplified description of the manufacturing activities of a firm. Raw materials are purchased and are processed in two stages before being sold as finished goods. The output from one system is used immediately by the next.

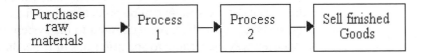

The efficient working of the firm means that there must be very closely controlled co-ordination between all these activities. Even when this co-ordination is achieved, unusual events can upset the system. For example, highly fluctuating demand for finished goods must be very quickly reflected in the orders placed for raw materials. However, any breakdown in Process 1 or 2 will cause the whole line to stop.

The whole system would be easier to control if the subsystems could be **decoupled.** Decoupling means reducing the linkage or interdependence between two subsystems, so that the systems are able to work independently, and a problem in one subsystem will not affect the other subsystem. This is, of course, possible by introducing **stock** between each of the subsystems. In systems theory, stock is classified as a **decoupling device**.

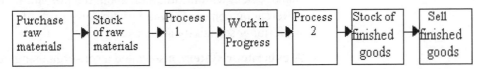

Stock acts as a cushion between each of the subsystems and allows them to operate with more independence. Overall, the system becomes more flexible to changing circumstances. An example of decoupling in information systems might be having separate computer systems for the main ledger and the payroll system so that, if the main ledger system has a fault, the payroll system can still operate.

Activity 2

Examine your own organisation, or one that you know, to find other examples of decoupling devices.

Feedback to this activity is at the end of the chapter.

DEFINITION

Coupling describes the way in which subsystems are linked to each other, and the extent to which they depend on each other.

DEFINITION

Decoupling means reducing the linkage or interdependence between two subsystems, so that the systems are able to work independently.

The Japanese exposed the weaknesses of stock holding and other decoupling devices when they developed the 'just in time' (JIT) system for materials and production. By obtaining good information about future demand for products, by meticulous production planning and reliable machinery and employees, and by careful planning with suppliers, organisations using JIT are able to reduce stock-holdings to the bare minimum and hence abolish costs that were previously regarded as unavoidable. Note how this is a good example of the openness of a system. An organisation cannot operate JIT unless it deliberately interacts with the environment (in this case customers and suppliers) to such an extent that the organisation could be considered as a subsystem of a large system, which also contains all the other relevant organisations.

1.6 Deterministic, probabilistic and cybernetic systems

The systems operating in business organisations, including information systems, can be explained as one of three different types of system:

- deterministic systems (mechanistic systems)
- probabilistic systems (stochastic systems), and
- cybernetic systems.

A **deterministic system**, also called a mechanistic system, is a system in which the outputs of the system can be predetermined from its inputs, provided that the system is error-free. A given input to the system will be processed in a specified way, according to specific rules or procedures, in order to produce a predetermined output. A transaction processing system might be designed in a deterministic way, so that every transaction is processed according to specific rules and procedures.

A **probabilistic system**, also called a stochastic system, is one in which the output cannot be predicted with certainty for a given set of inputs. However, the outputs can be forecast in terms of probabilities of various different outputs happening. For example, in a manufacturing system, it might be predicted that for a given quantity of input to a process, there will be an expected loss rate of 5%. However, the actual loss might be higher or lower than 5%, and the probabilities that the loss will be 1%, 2%, 3%, 4%, 5%, 6% and so on can be measured.

Management information systems might be probabilistic systems, providing management with information about the probability distribution of possible different outcomes. They are particularly useful for forecasting and for performing sensitivity analysis.

A **cybernetic system**, also called a self-organising or adaptive system, is a system that learns from its experiences and mistakes and adapts itself accordingly. The output from a cybernetic system cannot be predicted, not even as a probability distribution of different possible outcomes.

2 Control systems

2.1 Control systems: system feedback

Most systems include control systems, and the control systems are therefore subsystems of the overall system. The purpose of a control system is to keep the system functioning in a desirable way. The basic concepts of a control system are that:

- each system or subsystem is controlled by its control system

- the system has a goal that the control system will help it to achieve.

Whatever the nature of control, there are five elements to a control system, as shown in the diagram

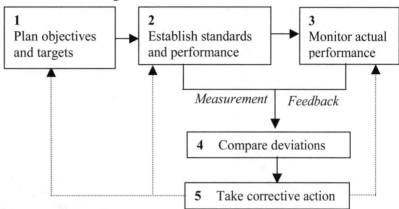

1   Control system planning involves clarification of the goals to be achieved. People need to know exactly what should happen and what is required of them. Objectives and targets should be specified clearly. Planning is the framework for control.

2   Establishing standards of performance against which the level of success can be measured requires realistic measurements, preferably in quantitative terms. Planning and measurement are prerequisites of control.

3   Monitoring actual performance requires feedback and a system of reporting information that is accurate, relevant and timely and in a form that enables management to highlight deviations from the planned standard of performance. Feedback also provides the basis for decisions to adjust the control system, e.g. to revise the original plan. Feedback should relate to the desired end result and also the means designed to achieve them.

4   Comparing actual performance against planned targets requires a means of interpreting and evaluating information to give details of progress, reveal deviations and identify possible problems.

5   Taking corrective action requires consideration of what can be done to improve performance. It requires authority to take appropriate action to correct the situation, to review the operation of the control system and to make any adjustments to objectives, targets or standards of performance.

2.2 Application to an accounting system – budgetary control

In a budgetary control system the financial performance of a department is compared with the budget. Action is then taken to improve the department's performance if possible. The elements of the control system are:

- **standard:** the budget (e.g. standard costs)

- **sensor:** the costing system, which records actual costs

- **feedback:** the actual results for the period, collected by the costing system

- **comparator:** the 'performance report' for the department, comparing actual with budget (e.g. variance analysis)

- **effector:** the manager of the department, in consultation with others, takes action to minimise future adverse variances and to exploit opportunities resulting from favourable variances.

Budgetary control system

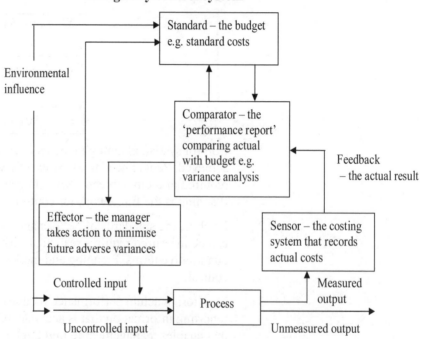

The opportunity may also be taken to adjust the standard (i.e. the budget) if it is seen to be too easy or too difficult to achieve.

A number of complications have been included in the budgetary control system illustrated above:

- the impact of the environment on the system, e.g. prices of raw materials may rise uncontrollably or interest rates may increase

- differences between actual and budgeted results may not be controllable directly by the departmental manager, e.g. rises in certain input costs may be caused by another department

- the accounting system cannot measure all the output of the department, hence feedback may be incomplete, e.g. an investment for longer term profits may have been made at the expense of short-term cost control.

Control is maintained through a network of information flow, which is the means of control. When such information is not fed back it is of no value to the system. This process of routing back into parts of the system is known as 'feedback'. It is a fundamental aspect of any control system.

2.3 Double loop feedback

Double loop feedback, or higher level feedback, is when information is transmitted to a higher level in the system. It indicates differences between actual and planned results allowing for control adjustments to be made to the plan itself. Double loop feedback gathers information from both the system output and the environment.

The diagram below shows the production system of an organisation seen as a double loop feedback control system:

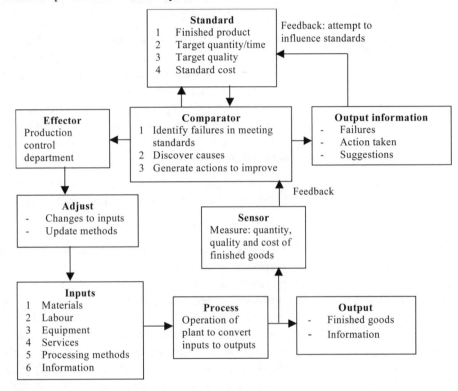

2.4 Feedback and feedforward control

Feedback control is the measurement of differences between planned outputs and outputs achieved, and the modification of subsequent action and/or plans to achieve future required results. The control system responds to the information received from the comparator and initiates corrective action. In order to take any action, the comparator e.g. a manager, must consider:

- the accuracy of the information fed back (the feedback)

- the significance of the variation from standard or norm

- what inputs are required to restore the system to an acceptable standard or a reasonable degree of stability.

Control systems might be mechanical and operate automatically. A system for controlling temperature, for example, might use a thermostat that triggers action to increase or lower the temperature of a room when the temperature falls or rises to a set level.

In business organisations, many control systems are operated by human intervention and are based on reports. Information systems are often designed as a control system for management. Examples of feedback in business include:

- error reports
- performance reports
- cost variance reports.

Feedforward control

Feedback control is concerned with past events being compared with targets or standards. However, systems can be made more adaptive if an attempt is made to anticipate future events in the light of the latest information. This is known as feedforward control.

In other words, feedforward control provides a comparison between current forecast and the target.

Feedforward should be used extensively in budgetary control systems. For example, if in January there is a shortfall of sales against target, this feedback is used to take whatever corrective action is possible. However, it may be that what is being indicated by the January results is a longer-term effect, which will impact on the results for the whole year. These effects should be predicted and used to revise the sales forecast for the whole year, because many decisions (production, distribution, etc) will depend on the forecasts being realistic.

Similar feedforward techniques can be used for all the cost elements of the budget and also for the cash budget, where it is especially important.

Positive and negative feedback

Positive feedback results in deviations from the plan being continued or increased, which can cause the system to repeat or further intensify the particular condition being considered. You may have heard the term 'virtuous circles' where a chain of effects circulates in an ever-increasing manner; this is a form of positive feedback. It may well be that a favourable deviation has occurred and the organisation may want to increase this. For example, where sales orders are higher than expected, the firm takes action to maintain, or preferably increase, these by boosting advertising. In some respects it could be said that the whole idea of growth is a form of positive feedback where, arising from an initial small start, things just get bigger and bigger. They also tend to be unstable and things get out of control more quickly.

Negative feedback is information, which shows that the system is deviating from its planned course in a way that is detrimental to its operation. Action is needed to return the system to its original course. This is the most common kind of feedback, which arises when action is taken in the opposite direction to offset the variance. In other words, the control activity reverses the direction of the tendency to bring the system back to its intended course.

A typical example is where a thermostat controls a central heating system. Defined limits are set on the required room temperatures and if it becomes too warm, then the thermostat records this and, in effect, adjusts the heating system, usually by switching it off temporarily. We sometimes use the term 'self-regulating' to describe such systems. Negative feedback systems are on the whole more stable and likely to conform to accepted standards and norms.

KEY POINT

Feedforward control provides a comparison between current forecast and the target

---

KEY POINT

Positive feedback results in deviations from the plan being continued or increased, which can cause the system to repeat or further intensify the particular condition being considered.

KEY POINT

Negative feedback is information, which shows that the system is deviating from its planned course in a way that is detrimental to its operation. Action is needed to return the system to its original course.

2.5 Requisite variety and control

One of the concepts of system control theory is the law of requisite variety to maintain control. A practical definition would be that there must be at least as many different states of control available to be applied as there are ways for the system to get out of control. The law of requisite variety in GST states that, if a system is to survive, the variety of response available within the system must be at least as great as the variety of changes that arise from the environment. The variety within the system must be at least as great as the variety in the environment within which it is trying to regulate itself.

Control systems are intended to provide control and regulation to a system. However, they will not do this effectively if the variety of different things that might happen in the system is greater than the variety of controls that the control system provides.

Example

A company might have an inventory control system. In a very simple system where there is just one item of inventory and one supplier, the only control necessary is provided by a reorder level and a reorder quantity:

Has inventory fallen below the re-order level?	
No	Yes
No action	Order the reorder quantity

If the variables in the system are changed, so that there is only one item of inventory, but two suppliers each charging a different price, the control system must be more varied itself. It has to be capable of responding in three ways:

- no action
- order the reorder quantity from Supplier 1
- order the reorder quantity from Supplier 2.

As more suppliers are entered in the inventory system, and as more items of inventory are added, there must be more controls to meet all the possible situations that could arise for which a different control measure is required.

In human or organisational terms, a manager who wishes to control a stock system which has 8,000 different stock items needs to have access to detailed data on each stock item and to generate a control response for each possible variation in the state of each stock item. This is clearly impossible for one individual to do in terms of the capacity to receive and transmit data and in terms of processing capacity to generate the necessary variety of control responses. Organisations deal with this by assigning standard control procedures that can be applied to all stock items and providing decision rules to stock-keeping staff for generating the variety of responses required to control the stock system.

The law of requisite variety is particularly important in information system design, where control information will be produced. The system designers need to consider all the possible variations that might arise for which a different control measure or response might be appropriate. If the controls provided by the control system are less than the variety of situations that might occur, the control system might be ineffective and so unsuccessful.

3 Relevance of General Systems Theory to IT/IS

GST can be applied to the design of information technology/information systems (IT/IS). Many systems are large and complex, and are designed as linking subsystems. A systems approach to design should help the designer to:

- recognise the purpose of the system as a whole

- design the subsystems of the system, specify the purpose of each subsystem within the whole system and specify how the subsystems should inter-connect with each other

- consider the extent to which the system can or should be de-coupled (or coupled)

- consider the possible variations that the system must be able to deal with, and design as much variety into the system as necessary.

In particular, it is easier to design a large system as subsystems than to try designing the system as a whole.

Information can arise from sources both within and outside the organisation. For example, in making 'selling price decisions', information about production possibilities and costs will arise from within the organisation, whereas information about potential demand for the products will be found by market research, which is an external source. Information concerning competitors' pricing policies and other aspects of 'market intelligence' is also external.

There are usually several information systems collecting internal data. These include formal systems for producing accounts, production statistics, sales analysis and personnel records. In most organisations the accounting system is one of the most powerful internal information systems because it is the only one that expresses the firm's inputs and outputs in the same unit of measurement – monetary value. These formal information systems require clear procedures for the collection of data, its conversion to information and the filing and communication of this information.

Note also, however, that managers may receive information from informal systems, which include formal and informal meetings, face-to-face exchanges, telephone conversations, ad hoc memoranda and 'grape-vine' rumours. Since many managers prefer to receive information verbally, informal information systems are of great importance and do not receive sufficient attention in many organisations.

- External sources of information can also be formal and informal. Examples of formal systems include accounting systems and production systems. An informal system is the office 'grape vine'.

- Identifying subsystems gives logical structure to the overall system, and each subsystem or sub-subsystem can be designed separately before they are integrated. Since each subsystem or sub-subsystem is less complex than the system as a whole (since it is only a part of the whole), it should be easier to design and develop.

- However, by developing total systems as a number of inter-related and integrated subsystems, there are risks of sub-optimisation and risks that the output from one subsystem cannot be understood by another subsystem, or is available at the wrong time or in the wrong amount of detail.

A GST approach should help the system designers to understand how the subsystems need to inter-relate in order to achieve goal congruence – in other words, in order to achieve the objectives of the total system.

Activity 3

If you have access to the Internet, visit a website of an organisation such as a company or a government department. The website is a type of IS, providing information to visitors to the site. Try to establish how the IS is designed as a collection of related subsystems, by listing the subsystems.

Feedback to this activity is at the end of the chapter.

4 Information systems and decision making

4.1 Data and information

An information processing system is one where data is input to the system and information is output.

Information is different from data. Although the two terms are often used interchangeably in everyday language, it is important to make a clear distinction between them.

The word 'data' means facts. Data consists of numbers, letters, symbols, raw facts, events and transactions, which have been recorded but not yet processed into a form that is suitable for making decisions. Data on its own is not generally useful.

Information is data that has been processed in such a way that it has a meaning to the person who receives it, who may then use it to improve the quality of decision-making. For example, in cost accounting the accounting system records a large number of facts (data) about materials, times, expenses and other transactions. These facts are then classified and summarised to produce accounts, which are organised into reports that are designed to help management to plan and control the firm's activities.

4.2 Sources of external information

Systems for external information include:

- Legal and regulatory update information: changes to company law, tax law, employment law, accounting standards, environmental protection, etc.

- Research intelligence: information about technology changes or new discoveries that may have an impact on the organisation.

- Other forms of market intelligence: for example the formal collection of feedback forms from customers, salesmen and others 'in the field', such as maintenance staff.

Information is gathered informally from external sources through employees reading newspapers, watching television and talking to their friends and business contacts. In a healthy organisation, informal information obtained by employees can be channelled to those who can use it to improve the operations of the firm. This requires an open approach to employees and the cultivation of an atmosphere in which useful information will be readily exchanged.

4.3 System outputs

The output of a system is the result of processing the data. Before a system can be designed, the user must decide what outputs are required, e.g.:

- Routine reports or transaction documents are those required to conform to business conventions, such as payslips, invoices sent to customers, purchase orders sent to suppliers and works orders sent to the factory, day book listings or standard letters. Large numbers of these documents are produced, perhaps in electronic form and displayed on screens or perhaps as 'paperwork'. There is not much scope within the business conventions to vary the contents or format of routine reports.

- Management information in the form of reports which are summaries of or extracts from the data which has been processed, e.g. labour cost analyses, sales analyses, stock reports. These reports summarise many hundreds of thousands of individual transactions into a few key figures, so giving management an overall picture of the organisation's performance. Compared to the large number of transaction documents, relatively few reports are produced, but it is these documents that provide the feedback to enable management to take decisions and exercise control.

4.4 Structured and unstructured decisions

The process of problem solving and decision making varies according to the amount of structure involved in defining the problem or making the decision.

We can distinguish between structured and unstructured problems and decisions:

- A structured problem is one in which there is a defined number of elements and it is possible to go about solving the problem in a systematic way.

- An unstructured problem is less easy to analyse, as it appears to lack any obvious logical underlying procedures for solving it.

Structured decisions (sometimes called programmable) tend to be repetitive and well defined (e.g. inventory replenishment decisions):

- a standardised approach is used to make the decision

- a specific methodology is applied routinely

- the type of information needed to make the decision is known precisely.

It is easy to provide information systems' support for these types of decisions. Many structured decisions can be made by the system itself (e.g. rejecting a customer order if the customer's credit with the company is less than the total payment for the order). Yet managers must be able to override these 'system decisions' because they have information that the system does not have (e.g. the customer's order is not rejected because alternative payment arrangements have been made with the customer).

In other cases the system may make only part of the decision required for a particular activity (e.g. it may determine the quantities of each inventory item to be reordered, but the manager may select the most appropriate vendor for the item on the basis of delivery lead time, quality and price).

Unstructured decisions (non-programmable) tend to be unique (e.g. policy formulation for the allocation of resources):

- the information needed for decision making is unpredictable
- no fixed methodology exists
- multiple alternatives are involved
- the decision variables as well as their relationships are too many and/or too complex to fully specify.

The manager's experience and intuition play a large part in making the decision.

Semi-structured decisions – the information requirements and the methodology to be applied are often known, but some aspects of the decision still rely on the manager, e.g. selecting the location to build a new warehouse. Here the information requirements for the decision such as land cost, shipping costs are known, but aspects such as local labour attitudes or natural hazards still have to be judged and evaluated by the manager.

4.5 Levels of decision making

Types of decision within an organisation vary according to the management level at which the decision is made. In overview, senior managers tend to make more unstructured decisions and junior managers more structured decisions. This section provides additional detail on the types of decision made by different management levels.

It is useful to start by considering the information needs of managers at the strategic, tactical and operational levels assumed in the 'Anthony triangle'. These are shown in the diagram below:

Strategic information is mainly used by directors and senior managers to choose between alternative courses of action, to plan the organisation's overall objectives and strategy and to measure whether these are being achieved. It is essentially forward looking, consisting of forecasts and estimates, including:

- profitability of main business segments
- prospects for present and potential markets
- investment appraisal studies
- cash requirements
- availability and prospects for raising long-term funds, etc.

Strategic information is, in short, used for strategic planning and is prepared irregularly, when required. Decision making tends to be unstructured (non-programmable).

Tactical information is used by managers at all levels, but mainly at the middle level for tactical planning and management control activities, such as pricing, purchasing, distribution and stocking.

Examples of information of this type include:

- sales analysis

- stock levels

- productivity measures

- current purchasing requirements

- budgetary control and variance reports

- labour turnover statistics.

Tactical information is prepared regularly (e.g. weekly or monthly). Decision-making is semi-structured, relying quite heavily on the skills of managers.

Operational information is used mainly by managers on the operational level such as foremen and section heads who have to ensure that routine tasks are properly planned and controlled, although, as described earlier, all managers have some operational tasks.

Examples of this information include:

- listings of debtors and creditors

- payroll details

- raw materials requirements and usage

- listings of customer complaints

- machine output statistics

- delivery schedules.

Operational decisions are highly structured and usually repetitive (i.e. 'programmable'). Information is presented very regularly: weekly, daily, hourly or even minute-by-minute.

Activity 4

At what level of management would information on the profitability of main business segments be required?

Feedback to this activity is at the end of the chapter.

5 Different information systems

5.1 Levels of hierarchy

Management information systems (MIS) can be viewed as being constructed to serve various levels and the three levels of management discussed above. The effectiveness of their support to each level is cumulative because informed decision-making at each level depends on the MIS constructed for that level plus those of any lower levels.

The levels represent the three types of decision made in organisations:

- Strategic planning decisions – where the decision-maker develops objectives and allocates resources to achieve these objectives. Decisions in this category are characterised by long time periods and usually involve a substantial investment and effort. Decisions are seen as unstructured or non-programmed.

- Managerial control decisions – deal with the use of resources in the organisation and often involve personnel or financial problems. For example, an accountant may try to determine the reason for a difference between actual and budgeted costs. In this case the accountant is solving a managerial control problem.

- Operational control decisions – deal with the day-to-day problems of the organisation. These decisions are structured or programmed.

These types of decisions and the relationships to those levels are shown below:

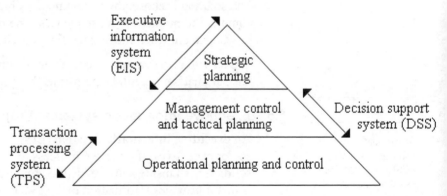

5.2 Transaction processing systems (TPS)

KEY POINT

Transaction processing systems are systems for the processing of routine business transactions, often in large volumes.

Transaction processing systems represent the lowest and most basic use of information within an organisation, and are an integral part of the operation of the organisation. Essentially, these systems record the individual transactions in an organisation, such as each sale and purchase made.

TPSs are vital for the organisation, as they gather all the input necessary for other types of systems. Think about how one could generate a monthly sales report for middle management or critical marketing information to senior managers without TPS. They provide the basic input to the company's database. A failure in the TPS often means disaster for the organisation. Imagine what happens when the reservation system of an airline fails: all operations stop, no transactions can be carried out until the system is up again.

5.3 Management information systems (MIS)

KEY POINT

Management information systems (MIS) are designed to provide information to management, typically at all levels within the organisation.

The purpose of an MIS is to provide information to management to enable them to make timely and effective decisions for planning and controlling the activities for which they are responsible. The value of an MIS should be that it helps management to make better and more effective decisions than they would if they did not have the information.

Today MISs are becoming more flexible by providing access to information whenever needed (rather than pre specified reports on a periodic basis). Users can often generate more customised reports by selecting subsets of data (such as listing the products with 2% increase in sales over the past month), using different sorting options (by sales region, by salesperson, by highest volume of sales) and different display choices (graphical, tabular).

KEY POINT

A decision support system (DSS) is an IS used by managers for helping them with unstructured or semi-structured problems.

5.4 Decision support systems (DSS)

DSS are computer systems that are used by management as an aid in making decisions when presented with semi-structured or unstructured problems. The DSS does not make a decision for managers. It enables them to move through the phases of decision-making:

- intelligence (gathering information and identification of situations requiring decisions)

- design of possible solutions

- choice of a solution.

The solution is chosen by setting up possible scenarios and asking the computer to predict the consequences. The manager must then use his or her judgement when making the final decisions.

A DSS will also summarise data from the underlying TPS. Alternatively, this summarisation will be performed by a separate MIS.

KEY POINT

An executive information system (EIS) is a purpose-built system for senior executives.

5.5 Executive information systems (EIS)

An **executive information system** (EIS) is a purpose-built system for senior executives. It gives them access to information from a variety of sources, both inside and outside the organisation. A key feature of an EIS is that it provides information to the executive in a summarised form, but also gives the executive the option to 'drill down' to a greater level of detail.

Typical features of an EIS include:

- the ability to call up summary data from the organisation's main systems (e.g. a summary profit statement for the month and related balance sheet)

- the ability to 'drill down' to a more detailed level (e.g. to call for a breakdown of the stock figure in the balance sheet)

- the ability to manipulate the summary data (e.g. re-arrange its format make comparisons with similar data, etc)

- built-in graphics, charts and other presentational aids

- the ability to set up templates so that information from different areas is always summarised in the same format

- the provision of analysis tools, similar to those found in spreadsheets, to enable the computation of ratios, identification of trends and 'what-if' analysis.

KEY POINT

An expert system holds specialist (expert) knowledge and allows non-experts to interrogate the system for information, advice and recommended decisions.

5.6 Expert systems

Expert systems hold specialist (expert) knowledge and allow non-experts to interrogate the system for information, advice and recommended decisions. Expert systems now exist in many areas, for example: law (conveyancing); taxation; banking (granting credit); and medicine (diagnosis of symptoms). The subsystems of an expert system are:

- a knowledge base (facts and rules held on the system database)

- an inference engine (the processing software that applies the knowledge base to the user's problem and produces advice or a recommended solution)

- an explanation program, which provides an explanation of the reasoning applied by the system in reaching a particular recommendation

- a knowledge acquisition program, that enables the knowledge base to be updated, corrected or expanded.

Expert systems can be used in all management levels. At the simplest level they can give factual answers to technical questions. At a more complex level they can suggest how a decision should be made, recommending a course of action. In this respect they go further than decision support systems.

6 Benefits of IT

6.1 Developments in information technology

As explained above, an organisation will always try and ensure that the IT strategy is driven by the organisation's objectives and information requirements. However, taking this perspective does not mean that new developments in information technology cannot be monitored or that new ideas cannot be brought to the attention of key decision makers. Knowing what IT solutions are possible in the real world is part of the IS strategy; the trick is to ensure that any new developments in IT are used to meet specific business needs, rather than the business implementing new IT systems because it seems like a good idea.

New developments

The problem with including a section on new developments in IT is that any comment made will almost certainly be out-of-date before the book is published. However, in this section, we look at a few trends in IT and give some indications where those trends may offer new opportunities to organisations.

Trading on the Internet

Trading on the Internet is already commonplace, with most major organisations having a web site and offering on-line purchasing of goods and services. Current jargon includes B2B (business to business) and B2C (business to consumer) trading with some web sites also offering C2C (consumer to consumer) trading in the form of auctions. Perhaps the main trend to watch in the next year or so is the development of large B2B sites, with large market-places being developed to bring many customers and suppliers together. The co-operation between the major motor manufacturers in the USA in setting up a single trading site to purchase parts for their cars is an example of this trend.

Access to organisation databases

Access to organisation databases in the form of extranet and intranet links is another trend that is becoming more commonplace. Rather than provide information on request, organisations allow favoured customers to access their own databases direct through Internet connections. For example, the Dell organisation allows access to its fault and error databases on computers to major clients. Provision of information in this way will have an impact on the IT infrastructure needed to provide access, as well as ensuring that the overall organisation strategy is to allow this provision of information. The issue of payment for information may also arise if free access is provided where information was previously charged for.

Mobile computing

Mobile computing is becoming more and more common with laptop computers having more power and communication capabilities. This should enable better client service to be given, particularly in situations where information would previously have been obtained from databases held at head office. There is now the opportunity to copy those databases onto the laptop or provide on-line access from any telephone connection (or even via satellite and mobile telephone). A technician requiring a particular plan or drawing to mend faulty equipment can now obtain this via communication link rather than arrange for a fax to be sent.

Improved telecommunication structure

Improved telecommunication structure also allows work to take place at a location convenient to the employee rather than the employer. In other words, employees can work from home where particular jobs or tasks do not require formal meetings. The use of broadband technology will continue to improve data transfer rates, making transfer of information and even video-conferencing from home quite feasible.

Look out for other new developments in the computing press and supplements to quality newspapers as you continue studying this topic.

Activity 5

Take 30 minutes to try to find out about new IT products and services that became available in the last month.

Feedback to this activity is at the end of the chapter.

6.2 Competitive advantage

There are various examples where information systems (IS) and information technology have given competitive advantage to an organisation. When they are analysed, they can be classified into those instances where IS:

- links the organisation to customers or suppliers

- creates effective integration of the use of information in a value-adding process

- enables the organisation to develop, produce, market and deliver new products and/or services based on information

- gives senior management information to help develop and implement strategy.

However they are categorised, the revolution caused by information technologies has permanently changed:

- distribution channels, e.g. ATMs have changed the way cash is distributed

- production economies and product life cycles, e.g. CAD/CAM and robotics have altered the physical production industries

- value-added services, e.g. provision of online tracking of parcels in a courier firm for 'free'.

6.3 IT and the five competitive forces

Michael Porter identified five forces that determine the extent of competition in an industry. This section explains how IT can be used to provide competitive advantage with each of these forces.

1 **Threat of entry** – new entrants into a market will bring extra capacity and intensify competition. The strength of the threat from new entrants will depend upon the strength of the barriers to entry and the likely response of existing competition to a new entrant.

   IT can have two possible roles to counteract the threat:

   – **Defensively,** by creating barriers that new entrants to the market find difficult to overcome. IT can increase economies of scale by using computer-controlled production methods, requiring a similar investment in the technology of new entrants.

   – **Offensively,** by breaking down the barriers to entry. An example is the use of telephone banking which reduces the need to establish a branch network. Automated teller machines (ATMs) created new distribution channels enabling 'bank branches' to be set up in airports, by out-of-town supermarkets and other areas where there are many potential customers. These machines provided not only expansion of the total market, but also a low-cost method of overcoming the barriers to entry in the areas where the cost of entry was high and space was at a premium.

2 **Intensity of competitive rivalry** - this is rivalry between firms making similar products, or offering the same services, and selling them in the same market. Cost leadership can be exploited by IT, for example, where IT is used to support just-in-time (JIT) systems and therefore lower the cost of production. Alternatively, IT can be used as a collaborative venture, changing the basis of competition by setting up new communications networks, and forming alliances with complementary organisations for the purpose of information sharing. When Thomson Holidays introduced their on-line reservation system into travel agents' offices, they changed the basis of competition, allowing customers to ask about holiday availability and special deals and book a holiday in one visit to the travel agent.

3 **Threat of substitute products** – this threat is across industries (e.g. rail travel with bus travel and private car) or within an industry (e.g. long life milk as substitute for delivered fresh milk). In many cases information systems themselves are the substitute product. Word processing packages are a substitute for typewriters. Computer-aided design and computer-assisted manufacture (CAD/CAM) have helped competitors to bring innovative products to the market more quickly than in the past.

4 **Bargaining power of buyers** – customers can be affected by using IT to create switching costs and 'lock' the buyer in to your products and services. The switching costs may be in both cash terms and operational inconvenience terms. Companies develop customer information systems to inform them about the customer's behaviour, purchases and characteristics. This information enables them to target customers in terms of direct marketing and other forms of incentive such as loyalty schemes.

5 **Bargaining power of suppliers** – and hence their ability to charge higher prices will be limited by some IT applications. Where an organisation is dependent on components of a certain standard in a certain time, IT can provide a purchases database that enables easy scanning of prices from a number of suppliers. Suppliers' power can be shared so that the supplier and the organisation both benefit from performance improvements. The Ford Motor Company set up CAD links with its suppliers with the intention of reducing the costs of design specification and change. The time taken and the error rate were reduced because specifications did not have to be re-keyed into the suppliers' manufacturing tools.

6.4 Porter's generic strategies

Porter identified three generic strategies for dealing with the competitive forces. The two basic strategies are overall cost leadership and differentiation. The third strategy – a focus strategy – concentrates on a particular segment of a product line or geographical market – a niche. Porter maintains that organisations wishing to gain competitive advantage must make a choice between these three strategies.

If it is known which strategy an organisation is currently using to promote their products and/or services, it should be possible to define a role for IS to enhance that strategy.

Overall cost leadership – is about competing by offering products or services at low cost and value for money. The emphasis is on cost reduction, primarily through simplification and automation. For example, driving down inventory levels, with the assistance of IT for supply chain planning and scheduling, can reduce costs. Application packages are available to generate sales forecasts that can be fed into manufacturing resources planning applications. In turn these can be used in shop floor planning and scheduling applications.

Differentiation is about showing that your product or service is different from those of your competitors through, for example, brand image, customer service or design. A way of differentiating may be to make the ordering process as easy and flexible as possible. This can be done by providing on-line information services e.g. expert systems to identify the most appropriate product or service, followed up by a simple on line ordering process. Where the differentiation is by customisation, CAD can reduce costs effectively. IS can also be used to compare customer purchases of the organisation's goods with those of other suppliers, allowing an organisation to differentiate its products on factors other than price.

Focus – this strategy concentrates on a niche market, e.g. a particular buyer group, market, geographic area, segment or product line. The opportunities for IS/IT include providing access to customer information, trends and competitors so as to maximise competitive thrust and exclude competitors.

6.5 IT as a strategic weapon

Porter also explained that information technology can be used as a strategic weapon in a number of ways.

- It is a potential supplier of competitive advantage to an organisation. We have seen this in travel agents where the choosing and reserving a holiday can be done in much less time and more conveniently when the agent is on-line to the suppliers.

- Information technology and systems can be used as a strategic weapon to improve productivity and performance. CAD and CAM are two examples where this might be the case.

- IT can be used in the development of new business. For example, selling the analysis of a large supermarket's sales to market research companies so that they can identify trends in product purchasing.

- Information systems can be used to change the management and organisational structure of the organisation to achieve competitive advantage. Computers with modems enable people to work from home, reducing the cost of travel and office space. Teleconferencing and video conferencing are available to managers, reducing the necessity for them to travel to meetings and making their time more productive.

Summary

- IT describes the hardware, software and communication systems in a computer system. IT systems are used extensively to create information systems.

- A system is a group of related elements (subsystems) organised for a specific purpose or towards a common goal.

- General systems theory attempts to analyse systems and develop concepts or theories that apply to all types of system, including business organisations and information systems.

- A system (and subsystem) must have a goal or objective.

- A system has a boundary and an environment. An open system interacts with its environment. A closed system does not interact at all with its environment. Some systems and subsystems might be semi-closed, but not entirely closed.

- Entropy is a tendency towards disorder and deterioration. Open systems display entropy unless they receive continual inputs from their environment.

- Systems can be described as deterministic (mechanistic), probabilistic (stochastic) or cybernetic, according to the extent to which the output from the system can be predetermined for a given set of inputs.

- A system consists of subsystems and sub-subsystems, which interact with each other. The objectives of each subsystem should be consistent with each other, and should support the goals or objectives of the organisation as a whole. In other words, there should be goal congruence. However, there is a possibility that subsystems will not show goal congruence, sub-optimisation.

- Subsystems within a system are linked to a greater or lesser extent. Closely linked subsystems are 'coupled' and subsystems that are not closely linked are 'decoupled'. When subsystems are coupled, one subsystem relies on the output from the other system to function properly.

- Every system has a control system. A control system often takes the form of reporting back information about the output from the system to a 'controller', which initiates control action where necessary to keep the system in order. Control information obtained from the system outputs is called feedback, which might be negative or positive in its control effect.

- The law of requisite variety states that, if a system is to survive, the variety of responses of which it is capable must be at least as great as the variety of changes that might occur in its environment. This law is highly relevant to the design of control systems (including information systems).

- Different types of IS are used by organisations: transaction processing systems, decision support systems, executive information systems and expert systems.

- Porter identified five forces that determine the extent of competition in an industry:

    – Threat of entry

    – Intensity of competitive rivalry

    – Threat of substitute products

    – Bargaining power of buyers

    – Bargaining power of suppliers.

- Porter identified three generic strategies for dealing with the competitive forces – overall cost leadership, differentiation and focus.

Having completed your study of this chapter, you should have achieved the following learning outcomes:

- identify opportunities for the use of information technology (IT) in organisations, particularly in the implementation and running of the information system (IS)

- evaluate how IS fits into broader management operations.

Self-test questions

1   Explain the difference between an IT system and an IS. (1.2)

2   Define a system. (1.3)

3   What is goal congruence in a system and what is sub-optimisation? (1.4)

4   What is a deterministic system and what is a stochastic system? (1.6)

5   What is feedforward? (2.4)

6   What is the law of requisite variety? (2.5)

7   How might General Systems Theory be relevant to the design of information systems? (3)

8   What is a management information system and how does it differ from a decision support system? (5.4)

9   What is an expert system? (5.6)

10   What are the five competitive forces? (6.3)

Practice questions

Question 1

Information reported to management about historical performance that indicates the need for control action is called:

A   entropy

B   negative feedback

C   positive feedback

D   feedforward control

Question 2

A system that interacts with its environment is called:

A   an open system

B   a closed system

C   a deterministic system

D   a stochastic system

Question 3

Briefly, describe entropy in systems.

Question 4

HZ Hospital

The HZ Hospital has invested in computer systems to assist its doctors with the diagnosis of patients' ailments and the treatment of patients. Two systems that are now available to the doctors are as follows:

System 1 is a management information system (MIS) that provides information on the medical history of each patient. It includes detailed factual information on past illnesses and any recurring symptoms, as well as the patient's name, address and other personal information.

System 2 is an expert system that is used to assist with the diagnosis of illnesses. The expert system is linked to the MIS to access data about the medical history of any individual patient. From this information, and the symptoms of the current illness, the expert system provides an initial diagnosis. The doctor uses this diagnosis in making a decision about the treatment of the patient. The diagnosis is stated in terms of probabilities of what the illness could be, rather than reaching a definite conclusion.

Required:

(a)   Explain the differences in the characteristics of the information provided by the two systems.   **(5 marks)**

(b)   Explain the hardware and the software requirements for the expert system.

(5 marks)

(Total: 10 marks)

Question 5

Competitive edge

Using examples, illustrate how IT can be used to give an organisation a competitive edge. **(20 marks)**

For the answers to these questions, see the 'Answers' section at the end of the book.

Feedback to activities

Activity 1

Your list could be very long. Ideally, it should be varied. The environment of an accounting system includes:

- the providers of documents that contain accounting transactions for input to the system (suppliers, employees and so on) and the recipients of documents output by the system (customers, management, the tax authorities and so on)

- the business transactions themselves that generate accounting transactions

- regulatory systems, such as the regulatory system for the preparation of financial accounts

- the physical environment in which the accounting system is located, and the people who operate the system

- the economic environment, which affects the volumes of transactions handled by the system

- the technological environment, which might affect how data is captured from the environment (for example, the development of e-commerce via the Internet)

- the organisation's bank or banks.

Activity 2

Examples of decoupling devices include over-staffing, duplication of information systems, and deliberately allowing idle time in production schedules to cope with possible peak loads. What these situations have in common is that they cost money. Decoupling increases flexibility but also increases cost. In the case of stock the cost is the lost interest that could have been earned on the money that is tied up in stock.

Activity 3

Most websites of companies and large organisations try to structure the information that is available, by giving the user choices about the type of information to look at. These choices are made available through menus, buttons, icons or hyperlinks. There might also be a search option, which is itself a subsystem of the IS.

Activity 4

Strategic management would be most interested in information on the profitability of main business segments.

Activity 5

There are various sources of information to assist you in your search. Consider viewing or buying the following:

On the Internet check out news sites such as www.FT.com, especially the IT and Internet sections. You can even have daily updates sent direct to your PC if you subscribe to this site (no cost involved!).

In your bookshop, look out for PC-related magazines such as *PC PRO* and *Computer Weekly*. Both of these products provide reviews of current technology as well as examples of how that technology is being used in practice. Also, buy the *Financial Times* on a Wednesday – the last Wednesday of the month has an Internet magazine with stories from Europe, while the first Wednesday has an FT IT supplement.

Chapter 3

DESIGN OF INFORMATION SYSTEMS

Syllabus content

- Recording and documenting tools used during the analysis and design of systems (i.e. entity relationship model, logical data structure, entity life history, data flow diagram and decision table).

- Databases and database management systems. (Note: Knowledge of database structures will not be required.)

Contents

1 Evaluating a new IS

When an organisation sees a possibility for introducing a new IT-based information system, an evaluation of the new system should be made to decide whether the potential benefits are sufficient to justify the costs.

The costs of a new system will consist of initial costs and running costs.

Initial costs will include:

- costs to design and develop the system, if the software is bespoke

- the purchase price of the software, if the software is off-the-shelf

- the purchase cost of the new hardware required for the system

- the costs of testing and implementing the new system – conversion costs might be quite high if new files have to be created for the new system by keying in the data.

Running costs might include:

- the cost of labour time to run the system

- costs of materials (paper, spare parts)

- the costs of software support (for example, a 'help desk' service for off-the-shelf software).

However, total running costs with the new system might be less than the running costs with the current system, and so one of the possible benefits of a new system could be lower annual running costs. (On the other hand, the new system might be more costly to operate than the current system, and would therefore involve an additional cost.)

1.1 Benefits of a new IS

The potential benefits from a new IS could be much more difficult to quantify in money terms. They might include the following:

- **Enhanced efficiency**. There might be improvements in the efficiency of operations, resulting in savings in labour time and other costs.

- **Better quality of information**. The new system might provide information of a better quality, which should result in better management decisions. 'Better quality' could mean:
  - more reliable information (more accurate information, or information in greater detail)
  - more timely information
  - possibly, information that is more relevant to the users' requirements
  - possibly, a larger quantity of information.

- **Better access to information**. A new system might give better access to data files and program files, and access to external information sources, for example by means of an intranet.

- **Sharing common databases**. A new system might create a single central database for all users, so that users have access to the same files and same information. Updating files is quicker and less expensive because there is only one database to update instead of several different files for a number of different systems.

- **Improved interaction with users**. The new system might be easier to use, and provide a better interface (GUI) with users. The system might also encourage the use of a mouse with icons and menus, rather than input by keyboard: this should reduce the error rate in both the data and the processing.

- **Improved communications**. For example, the introduction of an e-mail system, or an enhanced e-mail system, might improve communications within the organisation and with people in external organisations.

- **Capacity to handle growth in the system**. A new system might be able to handle a larger volume of transactions than the current system. When growth in operations is forecast, a new system might be essential if the current system is reaching its efficient capacity.

Improvements in system efficiency

There are several ways in which a new system might contribute towards higher sales revenues or lower running costs:

Direct benefits	• Lower operating costs
	• Higher sales turnover, as a result of improvements in a sales ordering system
	• Increased output or cheaper unit costs of output, due to the automation of a production facility
	• Improvements in working capital management, due to a more efficient inventory control system or debt collection system
Indirect benefits	• Better decision-making with information of a better quality
	• Improved customer service
	• A potential for achieving competitive advantage, if competitors do not have a similar system themselves

1.2 Potential disadvantages with a new system

When a new IS is assessed, it should also be recognised that there could be disadvantages as well as benefits:

- **Security problems: risks of unauthorised access and fraud**. Protecting the data against unauthorised access and manipulation, and preventing fraud, might be more difficult. If the new system is a network giving access to many users at many different terminals in remote locations, the risks of unauthorised 'hacking' are high.

- **Failure of the system to meet its objectives**. A new system might fail to provide the benefits that were expected of it. There could be unexpected problems with operating the system or with the quality of the information that it provides. If the system is more complex to operate than expected, running costs and labour efficiencies might be worse than with the current system.

- **Redundant data**. The new system might provide a large amount of information that no one finds useful. The data will therefore be unnecessary and 'redundant'.

- **Maintenance problems**. If the new system is more complex than the current system, there might be a requirement for more system maintenance support. If the software is bespoke, a team of programmers might be required to correct errors in the system or make small changes to the programs. If the software is off-the-shelf, it might be necessary to negotiate 'help desk' support from a software company.

1.3 Comparing costs and benefits

Where the expected costs and benefits of a new system are both expressed in money terms, a financial appraisal of the new system can be carried out to decide whether the new system should be introduced. Different methods of financial evaluation are possible, for example, discounted cash flow (DCF) analysis.

2 Systems development life cycle

There is a high risk that, unless the benefits of a new system are properly evaluated, the system will fail to provide the expected benefits. It is therefore important that management should assess very carefully what the expected benefits will be. To do this, they must look at the planned system design, and understand how the system will operate and how it will provide the planned benefits.

2.1 Bespoke software

This analysis should take place at the appropriate stage in the systems development life cycle. When the new system is specially designed for the user, and the software is bespoke, the stages in the system development life cycle are as follows:

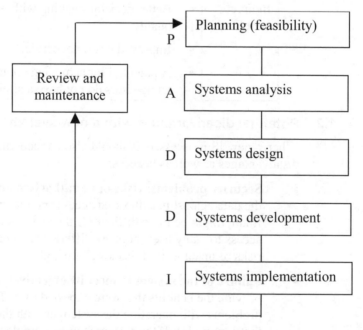

Planning

Planning should begin by establishing the objectives of the new system, and evaluating its expected benefits and costs. Within a formal reporting system, this stage of planning might take the form of a **feasibility study** and a **feasibility report**.

It will be necessary to prepare an outline design of the planned new system at this stage.

The planning stage ends when a decision is made to go ahead to a more detailed analysis of the new system requirements.

System analysis

System analysis is the first stage in the design or selection of the new system. It should begin with a detailed analysis of the current system in order to establish how the system operates, and:

- how the current system meets the users' needs, but

- how the current system fails to meet the users' needs.

The strengths and weaknesses of the current system will give the system designers the information they need for developing a new system design.

System design

In the system design stage, the requirements of the new system are set out in detail. The original outline system design in the feasibility study and report might be changed at this stage. The design must also go into much greater detail, in terms of software requirements, hardware requirements and communication networks.

System development

When the detailed system design has been approved, the next stage in the system development is to:

- write the software, and

- acquire the hardware and network links.

The overall software system will consist of many different programs, and during this implementation stage the programmers will test each program independently to ensure that it appears to perform the tasks required of it.

System implementation

When the system has been developed, it can be implemented. Before implementation, however, there should be testing to make sure that the system operates properly and that there are no design faults or software errors. Systems testing should reveal any errors that exist whereby the output from one program cannot be read or processed by another program. In other words, the system as a whole should be tested, not just the individual programs independently.

The users' files must be converted to the format required for the new system. The user might also wish to carry out additional user tests prior to the system 'going live'. After testing, the new system is implemented and becomes operational.

Review and maintenance

After implementation, the system should be reviewed and maintained.

- A review is required to ensure that the system has achieved the expected benefits.

- Maintenance is required because errors might be discovered in the software after the system has become operational, and the errors should be corrected by writing the amendments and producing a new version of the software. The user's requirements might also change, and new software can be written to meet them.

2.2 Buying off-the-shelf software

When a major new system is introduced using off-the-shelf software, the systems development cycle is similar to the development cycle for bespoke software, but with the following differences:

- There should be a system design, outlining the users' requirements of the new system. At the feasibility study stage, the software that will probably be selected should have been identified, so that a cost and benefit analysis can be carried out.

- During the system analysis stage, the off-the-shelf software should be studied in detail, to establish:
  - whether it will meet the users' requirements, and
  - what changes the user will have to make to its operating procedures in order to use the software.

Since the software has already been written, there is no requirement for system development. When software has been purchased for a large system, it will be sensible to plan user tests for the system before it is introduced operationally. The system changeover to the new system should also be planned carefully to avoid disruption.

2.3 Prototyping

When bespoke software is produced for a new system, there are two approaches to system implementation.

- The **'traditional'** method of system development is to produce a fully completed system, and to test the system thoroughly before handing it over to the user for implementation.

- **Prototyping** – a prototype is a working model of a new system, but not in its final form.

When prototyping is used, the system analysts and programmers produce a working model of the system, which is then handed over to the user. The user introduces this prototype model into operational use and, on the basis of its experience using the model, the user then asks for amendments or corrections. A new prototype is then produced.

This process might be repeated several times until a final version of the system is developed. Each prototype gives the user a chance to test the system ad make sure that it meets the system requirements. If it does not, changes can be specified and designed into the next prototype model.

Two important advantages of prototyping are:

- shortening the time before the new system is available for use. It is quicker to develop a prototype for use than a fully designed and completed system. The user is able to introduce a prototype operationally that fulfils most of the system requirements

- giving the user more time to consider the system requirements. In a traditional systems development life cycle, the user is required to finalise the specifications for the new system before detailed design work begins. With prototyping, the user has an opportunity to alter the system specifications at a later time in the development process and as a result of actual experience with a prototype of the system.

2.4 Alternatives to the SDLC – methodologies

An alternative to the SDLC is the use of structured methodologies. A systems development methodology is a collection of procedures, tools, techniques and documentation aids, which help in the implementation of a new system. Such methodologies have the following advantages.

- They involve users more closely in the design and development process, so avoiding user resentment.

- They analyse the 'needs' of the organisation in a more fundamental way, by looking at the way information is processed at the operational level together with the information needs of managers at the tactical and strategic levels of management.

- They permit flexibility of systems, in that systems can be integrated and can share information.

- They produce easily understood documentation, such as data flow diagrams, entity relationship models, etc.

- They integrate the development process with the disciplines of project management, to ensure that the system arrives at the correct time and to an agreed level of budget.

Examples of software development methodologies are:

- SSADM (Structured Systems Analysis and Design Methodology)

- JSD (Jackson Structured Design)

- Structured Analysis for real-time Systems (Yourdon).

One single development methodology cannot prescribe how to tackle the great variety of tasks and situations encountered by the systems analyst. Methodologies are constantly changing to accommodate new technological advances and ideas in systems development. The main differences are between process driven, data driven and user driven methodologies.

Process driven approach

Process driven methodologies concentrate on the processes that the system performs. For example, the reason for computerising a manual payroll operation may be to reduce staff costs, as well as to improve the quality and efficiency of the payroll process.

In this example, a shortcoming of this process driven approach is that no attempt is made to consider how the information contained within the payroll system can be harnessed for the benefit of managers at the tactical or strategic levels of management.

The main features of the process driven approach are as follows:

- It concentrates on analysing the different activities that form a system.

- Each process is analysed in terms of how it converts inputs into outputs.

- The emphasis of the system is on the 'activities' or 'functions' carried out in the system and on improving the way information is processed.

- An improvement in the way things were done (e.g. by computerising a manual system) will produce a better and more efficient system.

The process diagram shown below is a high level order fulfilment process that begins when a customer places an order for some bicycles and ends when they are delivered.

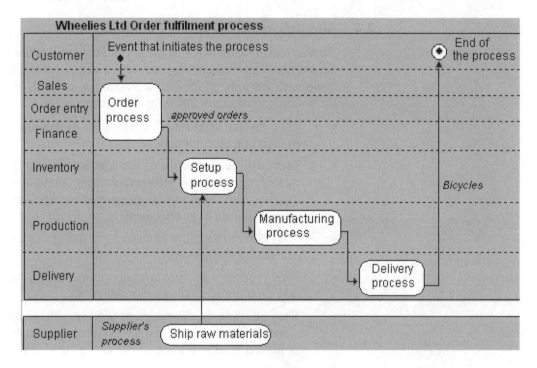

The disadvantages of developing systems based on a process driven approach are as follows.

- It leads to an exact duplication of manual activities.

- It doesn't force the analyst to critically examine how the organisation operates.

- The systems produced are inflexible in the type of information generated, and no attempt is made to link systems (e.g. a payroll system with a personnel system – common data being employee details).

Data driven approach

Data driven methodologies focus on the data items regardless of the processes they are related to. This is because the type of data an organisation needs is less likely to change than either the processes, which operate on it or the output information required of it.

The data driven approach is based on the following considerations.

- Data needs are much more stable and constant irrespective of how the information is processed e.g. we can change the way sales invoices are processed but a sales report that summarises the sales for the period will still be required.

- Systems are designed according to a study of the data in the system, which will lead to more stable and flexible systems.

The data driven approach is often associated with the adoption of a database strategy.

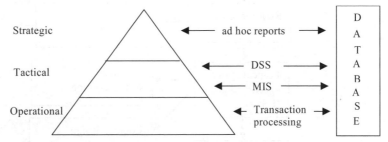

To design a system using this approach the analyst uses tools and techniques that help him or her understand the ways in which data items relate together (e.g. entity life histories, entity relationship model, normalisation).

User driven approach

This approach considers the needs of users, as expressed in the outputs or potential outputs required of the system. The users' requirements should determine the type of data collected or captured by the system.

3 Structured methodologies for system design

A structured systems development methodology has the following characteristics.

- It focuses on the logical design of the system, rather than the physical design. The logical design of the system is concerned with the types of data in the system, the relationships between data items and how data is processed. The logical design is agreed before starting to write the software or choose the hardware.

- The approach to the system design takes a systems approach, starting with the requirements for the system as a whole, and then working down into greater levels of detail for individual applications or programs.

- It uses precise documentation and graphical techniques for documentation such as data flow diagrams and entity relationship models. (These are described later.)

3.1 An example of a structured methodology: SSADM

One of the more popular structured methodologies has been SSADM (Structured Systems Analysis and Design Methodology), and this will be used as an illustration of a structured methodology for design. This uses a five-module approach to system design, but with seven stages of design work and documentation, as follows:

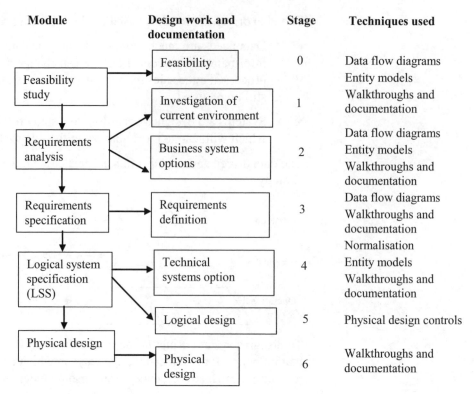

Module	Design work and documentation	Stage	Techniques used
Feasibility study	Feasibility	0	Data flow diagrams Entity models
	Investigation of current environment	1	Walkthroughs and documentation
Requirements analysis	Business system options	2	Data flow diagrams Entity models Walkthroughs and documentation
Requirements specification	Requirements definition	3	Data flow diagrams Walkthroughs and documentation Normalisation
Logical system specification (LSS)	Technical systems option	4	Entity models Walkthroughs and documentation
	Logical design	5	Physical design controls
Physical design	Physical design	6	Walkthroughs and documentation

Stage 0: Feasibility study

This stage is called Stage 0 in SSADM because it is not compulsory in SSADM projects. The feasibility study assesses a new system or project in terms of its technical and operational feasibility, and its financial justification. The feasibility study has four steps:

- carrying out a feasibility study
- preparing a Problem Definition Statement: this is a statement of the problems that a new system should resolve
- selecting a preferred feasibility option from the various system options that are available
- preparing the feasibility report.

Stage 1: Investigation of current system

The current system is investigated and analysed, using techniques such as observation, questionnaires and an investigation of files and records. The current system is then documented.

Stage 2: Business system options

The users' requirements are specified in detail. There will usually be a number of different possible solutions to the users' problems, from which a selection should be made. At this stage of design, several system options are designed in outline, with a brief description and costing, and the user is asked to make a choice.

Stage 3: requirements specification

In this stage, the users' chosen option for a system design is defined in much greater detail, using a variety of documentation techniques such as:

- data flow diagrams (DFDs)
- relational data analysis
- entity life histories.

Stage 4: Technical systems option

The user is now asked to decide on the physical features of the system, in terms of hardware, network structure and some aspects of software. Options might include:

- the hardware configuration

- software options, such as the choice of operating system for the network server.

Stage 5: Logical design

The data and file structures for the entire system are now designed in detail. This stage of development includes:

- the specification and design of outputs from the system and their format (for example, the design and format of transaction documents such as invoices and the content and design of routine management reports)

- the type of dialogue that users will have with the system: typically, a Windows-style graphical user interface is used.

Stage 6: Physical design

The logical system specification and the technical system specification are now used to create a physical database design and a set of program specifications for each of the program modules within the overall system. Physical design involves:

- defining in greater detail the processing required, for example by considering the requirements for audit, security and control

- writing the program specifications, which set out in detail what a particular program is supposed to achieve

- assessing each program for its performance, for example by estimating how long a program will take to run and making sure that this is acceptable, both for the operating needs of the system as a whole and for the requirements of the user

- detailed design of file specifications (and records on each file), including database specifications

- preparing documentation for the user, such as operating manuals and help files.

3.2 Documentation and logical analysis in a structured methodology

A structured methodology to system design is based largely on a logical analysis of the system requirements and documenting the logic of the system. In order to understand the system design, and to contribute meaningfully, users must have some understanding of the recording and documenting 'tools' that might be required. The following tools are described in the next paragraphs:

- data flow diagrams

- entity relationship models entity life histories

- entity life histories

- logical data structures

- decision tables.

4 Data flow diagrams

DEFINITION

A data flow diagram (DFD) shows how data flows through a system in the form of a chart or picture.

A data flow diagram (DFD) shows how data flows through a system in the form of a chart or picture. DFDs are drawn at different levels of detail:

- the top level gives a general description of the data flows
- each further level gives an increasing amount of detail to describe the data flows in the system.

DFDs therefore provide a top-down structured approach to understanding the needs of a system. They are a user-friendly method of documenting the flow of data into the system, within the system and out of it.

Note that you will be not asked to produce a DFD in the examination, but the study guide does state that knowledge of DFDs is examinable.

4.1 Symbols used

Only four symbols are used in data flow diagrams using the SSADM methodology. These are:

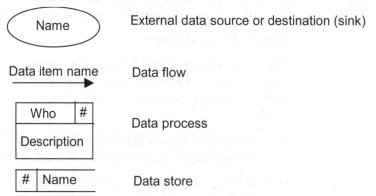

Oval shape with 'Name' inside	This symbol indicates a source of and/or destination for data. The name of this data source or destination is written inside the shape.
Arrowed line with 'name of data item'	A line indicates a flow of data, with an arrow head to show the direction of the data flow. The item of data is identified in words.
Who # / Description	A box represents processing of data. The nature of the processing is written into the bottom part of the box. The person or automatic process doing the processing is identified in the top part of the box. The box is also numbered. The number inside the top right-hand corner of the box indicates the level of detail in the DFD hierarchy.
# Name	A data store is a file or other place where data is held for reference or holding on file. A process might make reference to a data file, by extracting data from the file or updating the data held on file. Each data file is identified with a unique identity number (D1, D2, D3 and so on) and a description or name.

4.2 Context diagrams/level diagrams

When a DFD is used to describe data flows within a system, the diagrams are drawn in a series of levels, starting with level 0, which is the 'context-level' diagram. The context level diagram shows the entire system as one process, and the various sources and destinations of data. The following is an example of a context-level DFD.

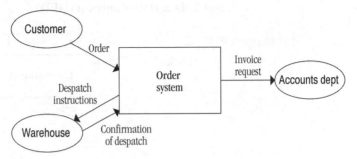

The context level diagram is then 'exploded' into a more detailed Level 1 diagram.

- The Level 1 diagram also shows the system as a whole, with the main processes and data stores.

- Each process in the Level 1 diagram is given a unique number 1, 2, 3, 4 and so on.

The context-level DFD shown above might be 'exploded' into a Level 1 DFD as follows:

Level 1 data flow diagram (DFD)

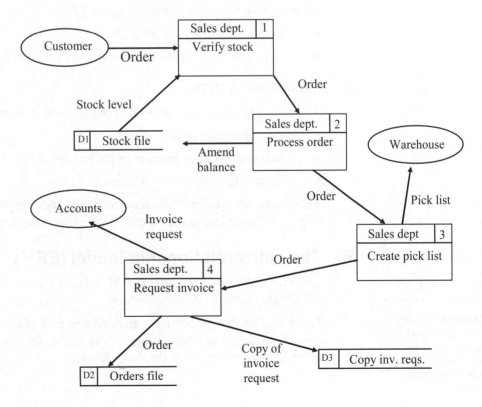

Each process in the Level 1 diagram might then be exploded into a Level 2 diagram, showing data flows and processes in even more detail. In the example above, Process 2 in the Level 1 diagram might be exploded into a Level 2 diagram as below. Note the numbering of the process boxes: each number is unique and provides a hierarchical code system for numbering all processes down through Levels 3 and 4 and so on in the DFD hierarchy.

Level 2 data flow diagram (DFD)

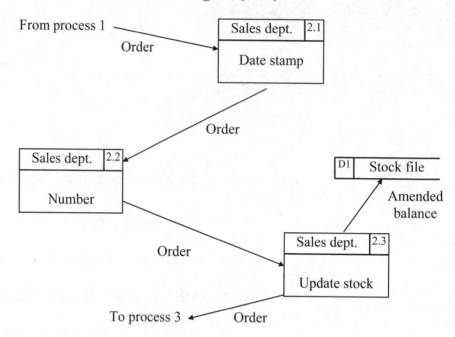

In the examination, you might be required to:

- *interpret an aspect of a DFD*
- *show your understanding of what a DFD is and how it works.*

4.3 Limitations of DFDs

There are limitations to what a DFD shows about a system. It does not show:

- the sequencing of data flows
- how many times a process might be carried out
- the timing of the processing events.

To obtain a description of the sequencing of processing events in a system, it might be appropriate to use an entity life history diagram.

5 The entity relationship model (ERM)

An **entity relationship model (ERM)** reflects a static view of the relationship between different entities.

Entity relationship modelling is an important part of several structured system development methodologies. It is used in the design of databases, to provide an overview of the database design.

The objectives of entity relationship modelling are to:

- identify the relationships between all data items in the system

- provide the user with an opportunity to confirm that the entity relationships shown are in fact correct, so that the database can be designed correctly

- optimise the use of shared data within the system

- avoid data duplication within the system.

An **entity** is something of significance to a system about which data must be held.

An entity might be:

- something physical, such as a customer, an employee or a product sold

- something conceptual such as an order, a job or a training course

- something active, such as a delivery.

Entities, relationship and attributes

The three basic concepts of an ERM are entities, attributes, and relationships. An entity is an individual person or object that is important to an organisation; an attribute is an individual piece of information to help describe that entity; and a relationship is a logical link between two entities.

An ERM is a diagram showing the different entities in the system, and the relationships between them.

- Each entity is described using a set of attributes. For example, if the entity is a customer, the entity attributes will include customer identity number, customer name, address, telephone number, e-mail address and so on.

- One (or more) of these attributes is a key attribute for the entity, by which the entity is uniquely identified. In the case of a customer, the key attribute will be the customer's identity number or reference number.

- There are many similar entities in the system, each with the same set of attributes. A collection of similar entities is called an entity set. Examples of entity sets are therefore customers, suppliers, employees, orders, jobs and so on.

- Every entity in the system must have a relationship with at least one other different type of entity.

- Relationships are shown by means of a line, and are described in words in the ERM diagram.

Examples of relationships are as follows.

- Entities in a system might be employees and projects. An employee works on a project, and this is the relationship between the two entities. The relationship could also be expressed as 'a project requires employees'.

- Entities in a system might be factories and components. Components are made in a factory.

- Within a training system students go on courses and trainers teach on them. There is a relationship between students and courses, and a relationship between trainers and courses.

DEFINITION

An **entity** is something of significance to a system about which data must be held.

KEY POINT

An **entity** is an individual person or object.

An **attribute** is an individual piece of information about an entity.

A **relationship** is a logical link between two entities.

There are three types of relationship that might be shown in a system.

1   One-to-one relationship

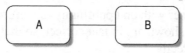

In this type of relationship between Entity A and Entity B, an occurrence of A is related to only one B; an occurrence of B is related to only one A.

2   One-to-many relationship

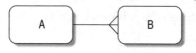

An occurrence of A is related to 1 or more occurrences of B; an occurrence of B is related to only one of A. The relationship is shown by a straight-line with a 'crow's foot' at the end where there could be many of the entities.

For example:

- in a sales ordering system, a single customer might place several orders

- in a job scheduling system, each job will use several different employees

- in a manufacturing system, each factory might make several different components.

3   Many-to-many relationships

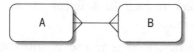

A many-to-many relationship is shown in an ERM diagram as a straight line between the entities with a 'crow's foot' at each end of the line.

An occurrence of A is related to one or more occurrences of B; an occurrence of B is related to one or more occurrences of A. For example, in a sales order system:

- for each customer order, several different products might be ordered

- each product might be ordered in several different customer orders.

The rules of data modelling state that a many-to-many relationship cannot exist; it usually implies that there is further analysis to be carried out to identify more data in the systems than has yet been discovered. When you find a many to many relationship, the solution is to draw a **link entity** between them, so that the link forms two one-to-many relationships instead. That principle is illustrated in the next section.

5.1   Constructing an entity relationship model (ERM)

The entities *Customer* and *Order* will have a relationship. This can be shown as follows:

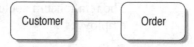

However, the model being developed needs to show that a customer may place many orders, but that a specific order can belong to only one customer:

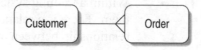

This model can be further extended to show that the order can be for many products. Each product, conversely, can be found on many orders:

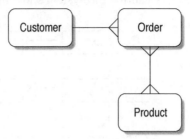

However, we have said above that many-to-many relationships are not allowed. We put another entity, a link entity, between the two many-to-many entities. In this case, the link entity would be an *Order line*. So, each order can have many order lines on it, while each order line belongs to only one order; similarly, each order line will be for only one product, while each product will appear on many order lines. This is always the case when using a link to resolve many-to-many relationships: the **crows' feet** always go at the link end of the relationship lines. This is shown below:

The model now shows that each order can have many order lines. Each order line is to a particular product. The entity *Product* however, will have many order lines on different orders.

We can continue building the model, with entities found for deliveries, invoices, suppliers, and whatever other features the business needs to store about its order processing.

Each entity will be made up of a number of attributes, i.e. data items that together describe the entity. Thus, *Customer* will have as its attributes ID, Name, Address, Telephone No., Credit rating, Discount code, Amount owing. *Order* may have Order No., Order date, Customer ID, Total value, Delivery instructions, and so on. The most important attribute is the key, a unique identifier that will be used to identify each occurrence of an entity.

The attributes will not be shown on the model, but will be recorded on a separate document, an 'Entity Description' form. This will comprise an entry for each entity on the model, and will give a brief description of the entity, and a list of all the attributes it has, including the key.

Activity 1

Describe the system shown in the following entity relationship model.

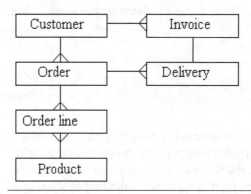

Feedback to this activity is at the end of the chapter.

5.2 Validation using ERM

The ERM can be used to help validate the data flow diagram: the data inside the entities must correspond with the data inside the data stores. Each piece of data should have a process at least to create it and one to delete it. There may also be processes to update it.

A more direct way, though, of validating the ERM itself is to test the model against the requirements. One method is to navigate the model with an access map. Here is an access map showing how we can answer an enquiry: 'Identify all orders for product X, and the customers who made them.' To answer that enquiry, our data model must let us find that particular product, and trace all the orders, with the customers who placed the order.

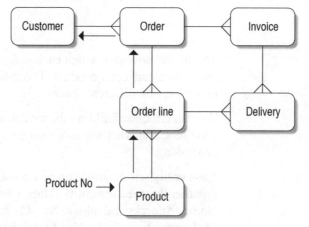

The arrows show how each product has many order lines, but we can track each one in turn, and for each order line, find that there is only one order, and only one customer who placed that order, so we can answer the query.

Activity 2

In a public library, borrowers are permitted to borrow up to six books at a time. Draw an ERM in which there are just one-to-many relationships, and no many-to-many relationships.

Feedback to this activity is at the end of the chapter.

6 Entity life histories (ELH)

While an entity relationship model reflects a static view of the relationship between different entities, an entity life history (ELH) – sometimes called a state transition diagram – shows details of the different events that cause an entity to be updated, from its creation right through to its deletion from the system. It is a diagram showing the processes and events through which an entity might go from its 'birth' to its 'death'.

An **event** is something that happens in the world that causes us to make a change to the data in our system (our entities). There are three types of event:

- External events, such as a customer placing an order (this will lead to creation of order and order line records, modification of product record, and possibly creation of customer record).

- Time-based events (e.g. at month-end, interest will be added to overdrawn credit accounts).

- Internal events, such as a management decision to discontinue a product line, which will result in modification, then deletion of the record.

As far as modelling the events goes, you do not need to distinguish one type from another – it's just that knowing the types helps you know where to look to find the events.

There are various conventions for recording entity life histories. The following diagram uses the conventions from SSADM and shows a selection of the events that can affect a bank account.

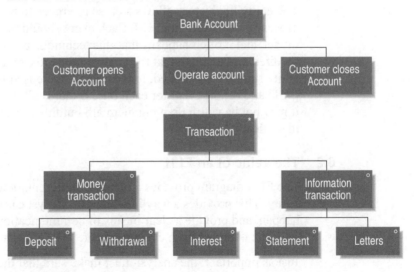

The structure is a **tree structure**, with the root at the top. The root is a single box with the name of the entity.

- The entity is the bank account, which is shown as a box at the top of the diagram.

- The events in the life of the entity are shown at different levels of detail, and the flow or sequence of events is from left to right (so in this example, the account cannot be operated until it is opened).

- At the next level of detail below the entity, the event on the left is something that 'gives birth' to the entity and the event on the right is something that brings the life of the entity to an end.

- Each event box contains one type of event. The diagram should avoid putting two different types of event in the same box, and to get round this problem, an entity life history diagram uses 'dummy boxes'. A dummy box is then taken down to another level of detail, where different types of event can be shown. In the diagram above, there are dummy boxes for 'Operate account' and 'Transaction'. (These might have been shown in a single dummy box, but 'Operate account' is a single dummy event and 'Transaction' can be repeated many times over during the life of the bank account. For this reason, they are shown as two separate dummy boxes, at different levels in the diagram.)

- An asterisk (*) in a box represents an **iteration**, or a repeated process. Everything on the branch below the iteration can be repeated. An iteration will mean that the event can affect this entity 0, 1 or many times

- A circle in a box (o) shows a **selection**, or a possible choice of events. If it is a 'money transaction', it will be a deposit, *or* a withdrawal *or* an interest calculation, only one of those. But if the first time the event happens, it is a deposit, the next iteration could happen because a withdrawal is being made, *or* because of another deposit, *or* it could be an information transaction, either a statement *or* a letter.

The asterisk in the Transaction box indicates that there may be repeated transactions during the life of the bank account. Each transaction may be a money transaction or an information transaction, indicated by the circles.

6.1 Validation of an ELH

The entity life history allows a cross reference to both the DFD (or other process model) and the ERM. Each event should be visible on the process model, and it often happens that this technique uncovers events – and hence required processing – that the analyst failed to capture earlier. Similarly, every entity should be modelled, to ensure that there is at least a creation and deletion (birth and death) event for each one. If that is all that happens in an entity's life, it may not be worth drawing them all, but those events should at least be identified.

6.2 The value of an ELH

The ELH diagram provides a pictorial representation of what happens to an entity. This provides a way in which the analyst can understand what is likely to happen, and provide a clear means of communication. The analyst must design methods to permit each event to occur.

Just as important, the analyst must make sure that the events can only take place in the correct sequence for that entity, according to the business rules. When the system is designed, each event will trigger a process to update the record; if the entity is not in the right state – i.e. the event happens at the wrong place in the life history – that transaction must be rejected with an error message. In an ELH for a customer, if the business declares that a customer cannot place an order if no payment for previous orders has been made, that rule must be shown on the diagram, so that the business rules are kept. The extract below shows this. *Either* the debt is still owing, *or* the order is met.

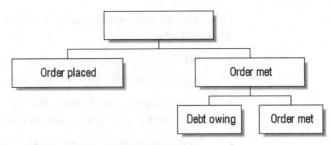

In this way, the ELH (or whatever state model is used) helps to preserve both the business rules and the integrity of the database.

7 Logical Data Structure (LDS)

The sole purpose of an information system is to support or automate business activities by storing and processing relevant business information or data.

It is therefore critical to the success of any IS development that the meaning, structure and business rules of the required data are fully analysed, understood and modelled.

What is a Logical Data Model?

In SSADM – the structured methodology we discussed earlier in this chapter – the Logical Data Model (LDM) is used for analysing the logical structure of an organisation's information. It is a way of *graphically* representing what that information is really all about, how it relates to other information and business concepts, and how business rules are applied to its use in the system.

The LDM comprises:

- Logical data structure (LDS), a diagram that defines the data entities and the relationships among them. Note that an LDS is simply the SSADM version of an Entity-Relationship Model (ERM) – there are a few differences in the notation.

- Entity Descriptions, which provide the background detail of the entities' attributes and keys.

- Data Catalogue defines the data dictionary of the data items used

7.1 Logical Data Structure – entities and relationships

What is a Logical Data Model?

Logical Data Structuring is based on the identification of the entities, their attributes, and the relationships between the entities within the system being modelled.

We have already discussed entities and relationships. The LDS is the same as the ER model in that:

- an **entity** is a thing about which data is kept e.g. Supplier.

- an **attribute** is a description of the data held about an entity. Examples of attributes for Supplier might be *supplier number, supplier name, supplier address,* and *supplier telephone no.*

- **relationships** are the connections between the entities. For example, an employee 'works on' a project; a student 'attends' a course or a part 'is made on' a machine.

However, all relationships in an LDS are based on the hierarchical concept of **Master/Detail.**

- Master entities are usually the 'one' end of a one-to-many relationship: e.g. one factory makes many parts.

- Detail entities are usually the 'many' end of a one-to-many relationship: e.g. each part is made only in one factory.

- All relationships must be named using verbs.

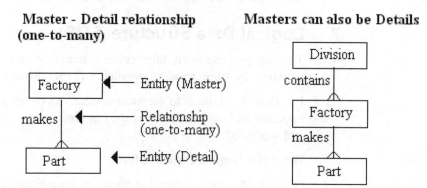

Attributes are data items that describe an entity. An *attribute instance* is a single value of an attribute for an instance of an entity. For example, Name and hire date are attributes of the entity EMPLOYEE. 'John Hathaway' and '3 March 1999' are instances of the attributes name and hire date.

The *primary key* (underlined in the diagram below) is an attribute or a set of attributes that uniquely identify a specific instance of an entity. Every entity in the data model must have a primary key whose values uniquely identify instances of the entity.

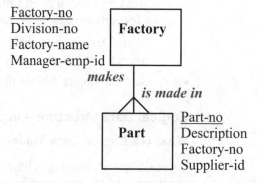

Given a factory we can tell which parts it makes and given a particular part we can tell which factory made it.

A formal description of the relationship shown in the diagram above is:

- One Factory may make zero or more Parts.

- One Part is made in one (and only one) Factory.

Note that, in a complete model, relationships are named from both directions. However, it is generally acceptable to only show the name from one direction in working models.

Constructing a database – what this means in a database system is that:

- one record in a table called *Factory* may be related to a number of records in a *Parts* table;

- but a record in the *Parts* table can only be related to one record in the *Factory* table.

(Note that the relationship is supported by the use of 'keys'. The factory identity is the key to the following relationships.)

Factory	
F1	UK
F2	Hong Kong
F3	Kuala Lumpur

Parts	
F1	Part P1
F1	Part P2
F1	Part P4
F2	Part P2
F2	Part P3
F3	Part P1
F3	Part P5
F3	Part P6

7.2 Optional and exclusive relationships

The LDS traditionally describes two different notations:

(i) **Optional relationships**

Some orders come via sales staff, others directly from customers. So the link may be to a sales person or to another entity (the customer).

(ii) **Exclusive relationships**

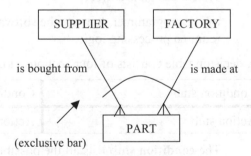

A Part *may* be bought from a Supplier OR be made at a Factory, but it must come from one or the other.

This can all be put together to construct an initial LDS:

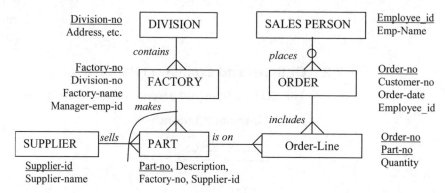

Adding the attributes will give us the following *entity-attribute-relationship* model, which looks like a useful starting point for creating a database system.

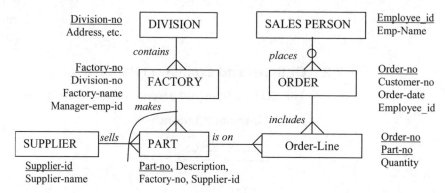

8   Decision tables

8.1   Purpose and structure

Decision tables are used to show the logic of a process. They can be used:

- by the computer user, to check that the logic of the process specified in a system design is correct

- by the programmer, to write the software so that it complies with the required processing logic.

A decision table consists of four sections or quadrants:

Condition stub	Condition entries
Action stub	Action entries

- The **condition stub** lists all the possible conditions that might occur, for which processing (a particular action) will be necessary.

- The **action stub** lists all the possible actions that might be taken, depending on the conditions that apply.

- The **condition entry** section shows each of the various combinations of conditions that could arise. There is a separate column for each set of conditions.

- The **action entry section** indicates what the particular action (or actions) should be for the given set of conditions. There is an action entry for each set of conditions, and this part of the decision table therefore has the same columns as the condition entry section.

There are three types of decision table:

- limited entry decision table
- extended entry decision table
- mixed entry decision table.

8.2 Limited entry decision table

In a limited entry decision table:

- the conditions described in the condition entry section are phrased as questions, for which the answer must be Yes, No or either Yes or No
- the only entries that are possible in the condition entry section of the table are Yes (Y), No (N) or a blank or hyphen (meaning Yes and No)
- the only entries that are possible in the action entry section of the tables are an X to indicate the appropriate action or actions for each given set of conditions.

Example

A company has a policy for allowing credit to customers and giving customer discounts. The rules are as follows:

- If an order is for less than £1,000 and the customer has been buying from the company for less than one year, the company asks for cash payment with the order.
- If an order is for £1,000 or more, the company will allow credit.
- If the customer has been buying for one year or more, the company will allow credit.
- If the customer has been buying for one year or more, a discount of 2% is given for all orders below £1,000.
- If the customer has been buying for one year or more, a discount of 5% is given for all orders of £1,000 or more.

A limited entry decision table to show the logic of this order processing is as follows:

Is the order for £1,000 or more?	Y	N	Y	N
Has the customer been buying for one year or more?	Y	Y	N	N
Ask for payment with order				X
Give credit	X	X	X	
Give 2% discount		X		
Give 5% discount	X			

8.3 Extended entry decision table

With an extended entry decision table:

- the entries in the condition entry section are not Yes and No, but contain other values or text narrative.
- the entries in the action entry section are not Xs, but specify an action in text or figures.

Example

A company has a policy for the length of credit it allows to its customers, and the discount it gives on its catalogue prices. This policy depends on the size of the order and the credit rating of the customer. The company uses three credit ratings in its rating system: A, B and C.

The policy is set out in the following extended entry decision table.

Credit rating	A	B	C	A	B	C
Order size (in £000)	< 10	< 10	< 10	10 +	10 +	10 +
Credit terms (days)	60	30	30	90	60	30
Discount allowed	3%	2%	0%	5%	3%	2%

8.4 Mixed entry decision table

In a mixed entry decision table:

- the entries in the condition entry section can be a mixture of Yes and No conditions and conditions described in figures or words

- the entries in the action entry section can be a mixture of Xs and other text.

An example is shown below.

Years of service	< 7	< 7	< 7	7 +	7 +	7 +	7 +
Management grade	A	A	B	A	A	B	B
Professionally qualified?	Y	N	-	Y	N	Y	N
Annual holiday (days)	25	25	20	30	30	25	25
Annual bonus	X			X	X		
Entitlement to stock options				X		X	

Activity 3

Delivery charges are calculated as follows:

(a) If the value of the order is £100 or more and the distance is less than 50 miles, no charge is made. If the distance is more than 50 miles, the charge is £5.

(b) If the value is less than £100 and the distance is less than 50 miles, the charge is £5. If the distance is 50 miles or more, the charge is £10.

(c) If the customer requests urgent delivery, a fixed charge of £20 is made.

Required:

Draw a decision table for delivery charges.

Feedback to this activity is at the end of the chapter.

8.5 Advantages of decision tables

Using decision tables can be helpful in systems development work for several reasons:

- **Analysis**. Using decision tables is a useful aid to analysing a decision-making process, to ensure that all possible conditions have been considered.

- **Understanding**. The computer user is often able to understand decision tables more easily than logic flowcharts or narrative, and decision tables can therefore be an aid to confirming that the logic of the decision-making process is correct.

- **Communication**. A decision table is a convenient way of explaining a decision-making process to someone else.

- **Programming**. A decision table can be a useful aid to a programmer whose task is to write the software that includes the decision-making logic.

9 Files and databases

In a conventional IS, the system is designed for a specific purpose. For example, a payroll system would be designed for calculating the wages and salaries of employees, and instructing the bank to make the payments. Similarly, a personnel system would be designed to hold and process the data required by the human resources department.

Each system has its own 'master file' containing standing data, for example, a payroll master file holds data about employees and their pay. Each file consists of records: in a payroll system there will be one record for each employee on the payroll master file. Each record consists of fields, such as employee name, employee number, department in which the employee works, bank identity and bank account number, and so on.

Within an organisation, a large number of different information systems might be developed, for payroll, personnel, accounts, sales, purchasing, inventory control and other applications. In many cases, the master files for each system will contain similar data. For example, a payroll file and a personnel file will both contain similar data about employees, such as their name, number and department, and their home address. Similarly, a purchasing system, inventory control system and accounts system will all hold some data relating to inventory quantities.

When there are several systems, each with their own separate files and each holding similar items of information, there are inefficiencies in data processing.

- Each file has to be updated separately. For example, if a new employee joins the organisation, the payroll file and the personnel file must both be updated.

- It is quite possible that information on one file will disagree with the information held on a file in another system. For example, the records for inventory levels might differ in the inventory control system and the cost accounting system.

- The different systems cannot 'talk to each other', and data on the master file in one system cannot be fed automatically into a different system for processing.

Databases are designed to overcome these problems of inefficiency.

9.1 Databases: a definition

A database is defined as a file of data, or files of inter-related data, that is structured and designed in such a way that many different processing applications can use the same data and update it. It is a common file of data for many different users and for a range of different applications. For example, a company can use the same database for its payroll system and its personnel records.

9.2 Database management system (DBMS)

All communications between the different software applications and the database files are controlled by special software called the database management system or DBMS. A DBMS can be defined as a set of programs that manages the database. It deals with all aspects of access, maintenance and security of data.

A distinguishing feature of a database system is that, since there is a common set of shared files for all applications, information to update the files is input just once (instead of several times, once for each application system).

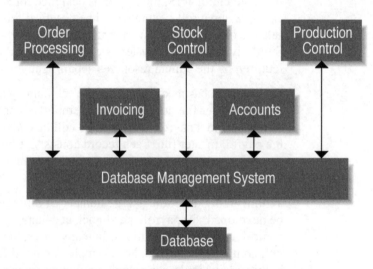

The DBMS has the effect of **decoupling the data from the applications that use it**. It will offer the following facilities:

- the ability to add, amend and delete records

- the ability to retrieve data for reference or processing

- the ability to present data in different forms and combinations

- the ability to control access to data on the files by means of passwords and other security procedures

- the ability to allow the database to evolve without requiring modifications to applications programs

- the ability to record transactions.

When a database system is large, the organisation might employ a **database administrator** to control and administer operations relating to the use of the database.

9.3 Advantages of a database

The advantages of a database are as follows:

- **Less duplication** – data is input once only to update the data on file. Data is held once, and is not duplicated in different files in different application systems. If data is held two or more times, there is data redundancy, because both sets of the same data should not be required. A database system therefore minimises data redundancy, and possibly eliminates it.

- Less processing – by minimising data redundancy, storage space in the system files is reduced, and **storage space is used more efficiently**.

- Updating is much easier, and data is equally up-to-date for all applications.

- There is **data consistency** (or **data integrity**). All users access the same data and therefore inconsistencies between data in different application systems do not exist.

- **Improving access to data**. Database systems are designed to allow many different users access to the shared files. They also allow access to a wide range of data for **management reports** that would not be obtainable if there were separate computer systems for each processing application, each with its own data files.

- **The data can be used by different users for different applications and in different ways**. The data on file is said to be **independent** of the application programs. This means that the physical layout of the database can be altered without having to alter the application programs that use it. The application programs access the DBMS and the DBMS looks after the physical layout of the database. Program independence. The programs using the database do not have to be changed if the database is changed; the database management system handles this.

The main disadvantage of a database can be the high cost of maintaining it, especially if it is large and complex.

9.4 Designing and managing a database

For the examination, you are not required to know about how databases are structured. However, you need to be aware of various aspects of database design, because these relate to aspects of IS design that have been described earlier in this chapter.

The main stages in designing and managing a database are:

- analysing the information needs of the user

- the logical design of the database

- the physical design and construction of the database

- data entry and upkeep

- data retrieval and reporting

- monitoring and maintenance.

Logical design

The data in a database is independent of the application programs that use it, and a database is designed by considering what needs to be held on file and how these items might be related to each other. Tools for designing the logic of a database therefore include **logical data structure (LDS) diagrams** and **entity relationship models (ERMs)**.

For example, a type of database called a relational database is structured logically as a number of entity sets with relationships between them. An entity set is structured as a table of the individual entities, each with attributes, including key attributes. By structuring the data in this way, it should be possible to ensure that:

- unnecessary duplication of data on the files is eliminated, and

- each table of data contains a logically distinct set of data.

This approach to structuring data logically in tables and eliminating data redundancy is called **normalisation**. However, when designing the logical structure of the data within the database, it must be possible to link different data items where necessary, by cross-referencing from one set of data to another. In the simplified example below, there are three sets of data (entity sets), with a link between the products table to the warehouse location table, using the warehouse ID field.

Product ID	Product	Warehouse location
1	Red	1
2	Blue	2
3	Green	1
4	Yellow	3
5	Orange	2

Warehouse location ID	Location	Address
1	UK	Birmingham
2	US	New Jersey
3	Japan	Osaka

Customer ID	Name	Address
1001	ABC Company	
1002	F and G Traders	
1003	Great Company	
1004	Big Business	
1005	Bulawayo company	

All the data held in a database should be clearly documented. The documentation containing the detailed descriptions of the data is called a **data dictionary**.

Data entry or upkeep

Data in the database that is independent of application programs can be updated separately. A specialised program language called a **data manipulation language** or **DML** may be used for this process of addition, amendment or deletion.

Data retrieval and reporting

Most database systems provide a variety of ways in which data on the file can be accessed and analysed.

- Data can be accessed by application programs that specify the data required.

- Items may be retrieved by specifying the parameters for the data required: for example, a university might wish to extract from its database of student records a list of all students who achieved a first class honours degree on any course between 20X5 and 20X7.

- Report generators are supplied with many database management packages, which allow users to summarise and report data.

- A specialised language called **structured query language** or **SQL** might be used to retrieve and report information from a database.

Summary

- When deciding whether to introduce a new computer system, there should be an evaluation of the costs and benefits.

- There might be some financial benefits from cost savings (improvements in efficiency) or higher sales. However, many benefits are qualitative (for example better and more timely information for decision-making) and difficult to quantify financially.

- The financial benefits and costs of a proposed computer system can be evaluated using techniques such as discounted cash flow analysis (DCF).

- When bespoke software is specially designed and written for an IS, the system development process may go through a 'life cycle' of feasibility study and report, system analysis, system design, system development, and testing and implementation, followed by review and maintenance.

- Prototyping is an approach to system development that speeds up the process of making a new bespoke system available for use. It also gives the user an opportunity to alter the system requirements through experimenting with prototypes, instead of having to specify the system requirements in full at the design stage.

- When computer users are involved closely in system development, a structured methodology for the system design might be used.

- With a structured methodology, a number of different techniques or tools might be used to specify the system and confirm the logic of the system. These include data flow diagrams, entity life histories, entity relationship models, logical data structures and decision tables.

- Many computer users use a database. A database is a common file or set of files containing data that is available for all computer applications. The data is held on file independent of the applications for which it is used.

- A database is controlled by software called a database management system or DBMS.

- The logical structure of a database can be designed with tools such as logical data structures and entity relationship models.

- Databases offer advantages for the computer user such as greater efficiency with data input and storage and file updating, better access to data on file and access to the same up-to-date data for all the users of the system.

Having completed your study of this chapter, you should have achieved the following learning outcome:

- evaluate, from a managerial perspective, new hardware and software and assess how new systems could benefit the organisation.

Self-test questions

1 What might be the costs of a new computer system? (1)

2 What might be the potential benefits of a new computer system? (1.1)

3 What might be the disadvantages of introducing a new computer system? (1.2)

4 What are the stages in a 'traditional' system development life cycle for a new system with bespoke software? (2.1)

5 What is prototyping and what are its main benefits? (2.3)

6 What are the features of a structured methodology approach to new system design? (3)

7 What are the seven stages of design work and documentation in the SSADM approach? (3.1)

8 What symbols are used in a data flow diagram? (4.1)

9 What are the limitations of data flow diagrams for system design? (4.3)

10 What is an entity life history and what is an entity? (5, 6)

11 What symbols are used to draw an entity relationship model? (5.1)

12 What is an attribute? (7.1)

13 What are the four sections or quadrants in a decision table? (8.1)

14 What is a limited entry decision table? (8.2)

15 What are the advantages to a computer user of having a database? (9.3)

16 What is normalisation in the process of designing the logical structure of a database? (9.4)

17 What is a DML and what is SQL? (9.4)

Practice questions

Question 1

Complete this sentence:

In an entity relationship model, relationships between entities are described in the model diagram using a _____ .

Question 2

Which of the following statements about an entity life history is incorrect?

A   It need not show an event that ends the life of the entity.

B   Each life history diagram must be for one entity only.

C   An entity life history diagram is drawn with several levels.

D   The flow in an entity life history is from left to right.

Question 3

Car agency

AB Agency is a vehicle hire and driver hire agency. It has a number of local offices throughout the country. Each local office owns and is responsible for its own vehicles. Customers tend to be regular customers and book vehicles through their local office. Each vehicle is separately booked out and, if required, a suitable driver is then found to take that booking. Customers are invoiced at the end of each quarter for all the bookings falling within the quarter.

Required:

Construct an entity relationship model to represent the above relationships.

Question 4

ELH

A customer's account is created when an order is received, and removed from the system if there has been no activity on the account for at least two years, or the company has ceased to trade. At present, each transaction that is processed through a customer's account can be to order products, to amend an existing order or to make a payment.

Required:

Construct an entity life history for the above procedure.

Question 5

Explain in English

The entity relationship model (or logical data structure) shown in the diagram below has been provided as a part of a functional specification document. The entities in this diagram are shown as rectangular boxes.

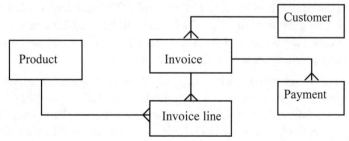

Required:

(a)   Explain the meaning of the model shown using a set of English statements.

(b)   The model shown contains a likely flaw in the relationship between invoice and payment. What should the relationship be?

(c)   Many methodologies decompose such relationships. Decompose (or break down), with a brief explanation, the relationship between invoice and payment.

(d)   What data items could be contained in the newly determined entity?

Question 6

Decision table

EC supplies a range of industrial cleaning materials and gives discounts on orders as follows:

Total order value	Discount
Less than £50	2%
£50 and over	5%

These discounts are only given if the customer's account is less than four weeks in arrears. If the account is four to eight weeks in arrears, the goods are despatched without discount. If the account is more than eight weeks in arrears a proforma invoice must be sent and settled before despatch.

The above discounts are increased by 1% if the customer has bought over £2,000 of materials in the past 12 months.

Required:

You are required to prepare a limited entry decision table to determine the correct discount for any order.

Question 7

WRF Inc

WRF Inc trades in a dynamic environment where it is essential that information is presented quickly and clearly to its staff. The information can come from the company's database or from other staff members. Significant processing of the information is also required on each individual's personal computer (PC) before effective decisions can be made.

WRF Inc intends to upgrade its computer system to improve speed and clarity of information. Each member of staff will have a PC linked to a local area network (LAN). Each PC will run Windows® XP Home and a word processor and spreadsheet on its local hard disk. The network will be used for centralised back up, access to a central database, and storage of data files. The LAN will also be used for communication within the office by e-mail.

The systems analyst in charge of the project thinks that users will require a Pentium processor running at 200 megahertz with 128 megabytes of RAM. The network will incorporate a central file server and run at a low baud rate. He is pleased that the system will cost only US$ 1,500 per user (about £1,000). The systems analyst is on a fixed-term contract that terminates when the system installation is complete.

Users have broadly welcomed the move, although they have not been formally told of the systems change. The requisitioning department of WRF Inc has now questioned the order for the computer hardware and software because of lack of authorisation from the Board.

Requirement:

Write a report to the Board briefly explaining the systems development life cycle (SDLC); and why it is preferred to the situation outlined above as a means of providing a systems changeover for WRF Inc.

(20 marks)

For the answers to these questions, see the 'Answers' section at the end of the book.

Feedback to activities

Activity 1

A customer might place several orders.

Each order might contain several lines.

There is one product specified on each line of an order, but products can be ordered on many order lines in different customer orders.

For each order there might be more than one delivery.

However, there will be one sales invoice for each delivery (rather than one invoice for each order).

A customer might receive many invoices.

Activity 2

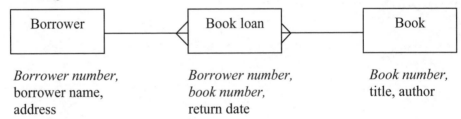

Borrower	Book loan	Book
Borrower number, borrower name, address	*Borrower number, book number,* return date	*Book number,* title, author

Activity 3
Your table should be as follows:

Delivery charges	1	2	3	4	5
Urgent delivery	Y	N	N	N	N
Value ≥ £100	-	Y	Y	N	N
Radius ≤ 50 miles	-	Y	N	Y	N
£20	X				
£10					X
£5				X	X
No charge		X			

Chapter 4

IS IMPLEMENTATION AND EVALUATION

Syllabus content

- The problems associated with the management of in-house and vendor solutions and how they can be avoided or solved.

- IT-enabled transformation (i.e. the use of information systems to assist in change management).

- System changeover methods (i.e. direct, parallel, pilot and phased).

- IS implementation (i.e. methods of implementation, avoiding problems of non-usage and resistance).

- IS evaluation, including the relationship of sub-systems to each other and testing.

- IS outsourcing.

- Maintenance of systems (i.e. corrective, adaptive, preventative).

Contents

1   IT-enabled transformation

2   Management of in-house and vendor solutions

3   Invitation to Tender

4   Evaluating supplier proposals

5   Outsourcing

6   Implementation – avoiding user resistance and implementation failure

7   Testing

8   File conversion

9   System changeover (implementation)

10 Documentation, support and training

11 System maintenance

12 System evaluation

1 IT-enabled transformation

1.1 Business transformation

DEFINITION

Business transformation
is the process of
translating a high level
vision for the business
into new services.

Business transformation is the process of translating a high level vision for
the business into new services. It involves developing a plan or design,
translating it into programmes of business change and implementation of
new services. The plan sets out:

- new ways of working

- how components fit together to deliver strategic objectives

- how customer needs will be met

- how IS and IT will be used to support the business.

It documents what needs to change: structure; processes; people/skills and the
supporting technology.

Process design is about coming up with a new, streamlined, possibly radical
way of doing things. The really difficult task is converting design into reality:
transforming innovative ideas into the new operational environment. Managers
prepare for the future with a model of what the business does – and could do –
together with a specification of how the business could work.

1.2 Managing the change

The key steps in managing change:

- gain an understanding of the environment, the organisation and its culture
  – knowing the organisation's capability to respond is a critical factor in
  deciding whether the changes can be coped with and how they might be
  handled

- set the strategic direction; communicate at all levels – both the
  organisation and its people need to have a clear idea of where it is going
  and why

- establish a change programme, led by a manager empowered as change
  champion to make things happen. Support the people through training
  and development

- expect the unexpected; keeping track of progress; continuing to improve
  and learn from experience.

Change should be managed through a formal process of **programme
management** to ensure that change is focused on meeting the objectives of the
organisation. There is a structured framework for defining and implementing
change within an organisation as summarised below.

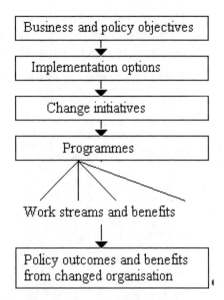

1.3   Different degrees of transformation

The diagram below shows different degrees of transformation and the range of potential benefits in relation to IT-enabled change.

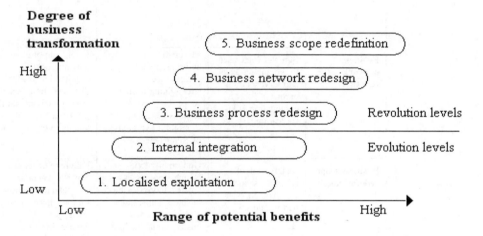

The table below provides an expanded summary of the levels of business transformation, with notes on strengths, potential weaknesses and the management actions required for transformation.

Table 1: A summary of five levels of IT-enabled business transformation

Level of transformation	Characteristics	Strengths	Potential weaknesses	Management transformation
Localised exploitation (automation)	Use existing IT functionality to reengineer individual, high-value areas of business operation.	Easy to identify potential capability, minimum resistance to change, addresses localised weaknesses in capability.	Duplication of effort: nothing new is learned; attractive relative to past practices, but fail 'best of breed' comparisons.	Identify high value areas. Benchmark results against best practice. Redesign performance assessment criteria to reflect exploitation.
Internal integration	Use the capabilities inherent in IT to integrate business operations: reflects a seamless process.	Addresses weaknesses in capability throughout the business: supports TQM: improves customer services.	Competitors may have moved on from this traditional concept to more radical concepts of reorganisation.	Focus on business inter-dependence and technical interconnectivity. Ensure that performance criteria are reassessed. Benchmark new capabilities.
Business process reengineering	Redesign key processes to provide business capabilities for the future: use IT as an enabler.	Move from outdated practices: opportunities to lead the market.	Benefits will be limited if too narrow a view is adopted (addressing current weaknesses, or historical issues): redesign of obsolescent processes.	Communicate the vision (are you eradicating weaknesses or designing for the future? Are you responding to competitors or leading the way?) Recognise that organisational issues are more important than selecting technology architectures to support the redesign.
Business network redesign	Strategic logic used to provide products and services from partners: exploitation of IT for learning.	Elimination of activities outside competence: streamlining business scope for responsiveness and flexibility: exploitation of competence of partners.	Lack of co-ordination may not identify required levels of differentiation: lack of streamlined internal IT infrastructure will hinder ability to learn.	Selected partners rather than extended array. Elevation of importance of partnerships in strategy. Radically new performance criteria. Definition of efficiency gains.
Business scope redefinition	Redefinition of corporate scope: what you do, what partners do, and what is enabled by IT.	Opportunity to use business processes to create a more flexible business: substitution of inter-company business relationships as an effective alternative to vertical integration.	Failure to develop a consistent area of competence for the future: enterprise may create gaps in competencies that are necessary for growth and survival.	Articulation of business vision through internal activities, external relations and business arrangements. Shift from assessing success on return on assets (internal) to measures such as return on value added or return per employee.

Although the example illustrated is for IT-enabled change, the same principles apply for any change programme to achieve new ways of working. Other examples might include a new school, a call centre or a radical change following the merger of two or more organisations. Radical change need not be carried out as a 'big bang'; it can be implemented in incremental steps or broken up into modules. Managers should identify the approach that best matches their organisation's capability and priorities.

2 Management of in-house and vendor solutions

Software can be developed in different ways:

- written bespoke in-house

- written bespoke externally

- purchased 'off-the-shelf' from an external supplier.

2.1   Writing in-house

In-house writing of software has a number of advantages over other options:

- **Cost** may be minimised because the organisation's own staff are writing the software. The staff are already on the payroll and therefore there is no additional cost of using those staff.
- The software can be clearly focused on the **needs of the organisation** as the internal staff know and understand those needs.
- The organisation may gain competitive advantage by writing the software to focus on its own unique selling methods or style.

However, there are problems with writing software in-house:

- The necessary resources may not be available meaning that these will have to be obtained externally. This will increase the cost and the risk that the software will not meet the specific requirements of the organisation.
- Staff may not necessarily have all the knowledge needed to write the software. This will increase the time of writing as staff are trained or learn 'on the job' how to write the software.
- There is an increased risk of errors being made due to rushed development or lack of skill again on the part of in-house staff.

2.2   Writing externally

Writing the software by a specialist third party supplier should help overcome the problems of in-house writing mentioned above. However, there will be additional issues such as maintaining confidentiality of the development and control of the third party supplier to consider.

Third party software development will therefore involve issuing an invitation to tender and then a contract to control the development, as noted below.

2.3   Purchase off-the-shelf

(a)   Issues in software selection

Requirements fit. It is important to assess the 'fit' of the package software to the requirements of the manufacturing company. It is unlikely that any of the packages will fulfil all the requirements defined in the Invitation to Tender and so the company has to decide either to make compromises and forgo certain requirements or to purchase a package and then commission bespoke changes to produce a system that exactly meets its needs. The flexibility of the package may be an important issue in evaluating each proposal. Some packages allow menus, dialogues and reports to be tailored to each organisation's specific requirements. Some vendors will also build in changes at low cost on the understanding that such functionality can be passed on to other users, so that their product becomes more functional and hence attractive to other customers in the marketplace.

System performance. The functionality of the system must be supported by acceptable performance. The company must be sure that the system can cope with the volumes of data that will be processed and stored. Many suppliers have tables of performance statistics showing the response time of their software under different loadings and configuration. It may be possible to achieve acceptable performance by relatively cheap hardware upgrades and so it might be unwise to reject a package on system performance alone.

Compatibility with existing software. The company currently has inventory control software that it wants to replace. This current system must store information about products, orders, despatch notes and so on, which the replacement system might need to access. Consequently the company should investigate issues of data conversion and compatibility, the willingness of the supplier to provide such facilities and the cost of these facilities.

Usability. Many software packages offer very similar facilities because they are supporting the same functional operation. Consequently, differences between packages may be limited to the user-friendliness of the software – general screen layout, meaningful error messages, context-sensitive HELP, report layouts and so on. A package may be judged against de facto industry standards (such as Microsoft Windows). Evidence suggests that users expect packages to be consistent across applications, so that they can take their skills from one area to another.

Security and audit. Many competing packages offer different security aspects. Some may offer only rudimentary password facilities (perhaps on initial entry into the package) whereas others provide several layers of passwords, supported by encryption and other measures designed to protect the data. The audit trail should also be inspected and its content discussed with internal auditors or external advisers.

Supplier factors. Package selection should include a general evaluation of the supplier. This might include an assessment of the financial strength of the supplier, the supplier's experience in the manufacturing industry and the number of solutions they have supplied to this sector (i.e. the number of packages they have sold). The supplier might also offer flexible supply options (for example, allowing the customer to rent the package for three months before deciding to purchase). Training, support and documentation should also be examined and assessed.

(b)   Weighted tables

The most common approach to assessing the strengths and weaknesses of each proposal is to compile a number of important factors and to give a weighting to their importance in the selection process. For example:

Factor	Weighting
Functionality	10
Cost	8
Compatibility with existing software	8
Performance	7
User-friendliness	7
Flexibility	5
Security	5
Supplier issues	4

The package of each supplier is given either a rank or a score for each of these factors and a weighted total is produced. The package with the highest weighted total figure is selected.

3 Invitation to Tender

An Invitation to Tender (ITT) is a document inviting suppliers to make a bid for the supply of some specific software (or hardware) to the purchasing company. The invitation may be sent out to specific suppliers, or made as a general invitation to any supplier, perhaps via an advert in a trade journal.

The ITT is likely to be for hardware, a substantial application package or for the development of a bespoke system by an outside contractor.

The ITT will define what needs to be done to achieve the system objectives and act as a basis for suppliers to put together and present their proposals.

3.1 Contents of an ITT

The invitation to tender will normally contain the following sections:

- letter of invitation
- instructions to tenderers
- conditions of contract
- form of letter and schedules
- requirements specification
- software engineering requirements.

The same format can be used for purchasing bespoke solutions or off-the-shelf packages although, in the latter case, details of software engineering may be very limited as the package is likely to require only minimal amendments.

Letter of invitation

This is the formal invitation to tender. It will specify:

- the date for submission of tenders
- contact names for technical queries
- contact names for contractual queries
- a warning that tenders received after the due date may not be considered.

Instructions to tenderers

These instructions advise the tenderer what to do and how to tender for the contract. Many of the points may seem obvious, but they have to be stated to avoid any misunderstanding. The instructions will include:

- alternatives and options where the tenderer may suggest different methods of achieving a requirement in the requirements specification, but with improved efficiency or reduced cost
- additional information that may be available from the supplier
- period of validity of the ITT
- a statement indicating whether or not prices can be varied for changes in labour rates or materials costs
- statement on the basis for prices
- statement on compliance – that is, areas of the tender that the tenderer cannot comply with, with reasons for this non-compliance.

Conditions of contract

The conditions of the contract apply to the terms of the supply of the software itself. The important areas to be included in this contract will include:

Visibility of the supplier's activities during development	The purchaser needs to be able to contact the supplier as the contract progresses to ensure that the software being designed actually meets the requirements specification and that the contract is running to schedule. As some of the work may be undertaken away from the supplier's premises, providing appropriate contact arrangements is important.
Purchaser response to queries	The contract will specify timescales for the purchaser to respond to queries raised by the supplier. The aim is to ensure that work is not unduly delayed by slow response times.
Ownership rights in software	The actual ownership of software is not always clear. The contract needs to state that ownership of bespoke software passes to the purchaser, normally after the supplier has been paid, to avoid subsequent dispute in this area.
Patents, design rights and copyright	The main issue here is intellectual property rights, and whether the software written infringes on copyright of any existing software. The supplier will normally indemnify the purchaser against any breach of copyright; in effect, the supplier is confirming that the software is original work and does not infringe any other copyrights.
Indemnity and insurance	The supplier will need to arrange for appropriate insurance covering areas such as professional indemnity, product liability and legal expenses. Third party consequential damages may also be considered, although consequential loss may also be excluded by the contract.
Acceptance	How the supplier will know whether or not the purchaser has accepted the software. Some formal sign-off agreement will be stated with an acceptance certificate being produced as evidence of this.
Warranty period	This is the amount of time during which the supplier will amend the software for errors found in it. The warranty will include any errors noted in the acceptance certificate, but will exclude defects caused by the purchaser amending the software.
Maintenance and enhancement	The purchaser may ask the supplier to continue to support the software by providing ongoing maintenance and upgrades to the software. Alternatively, responsibility for these can be taken in-house.
Insolvency or bankruptcy	In case of insolvency or bankruptcy of the supplier, the purchaser will normally need access to the source code of the software so that it can be amended and upgraded in the future. One method of achieving this aim is to place the source code with a third party, to be released only if the supplier is insolvent or bankrupt. This arrangement is commonly called an 'escrow' agreement.
Performance and completion time	The contract will provide a timetable showing important milestones and estimated completion time for the software.
Confidentiality	Both the supplier and the purchaser will agree to keep confidential information that is not in the public domain. Confidentiality constraints apply to any sub-contractors as well as the main contractor.
Insurance copies	An explanation of whether additional copies of the software are available in case of loss or damage.

Form of letter and schedules

The tenderer will need to commit, in relatively high-level terms, to some additional information regarding the supply of the software and subsequent support after successful installation.

The tenderer must indicate the price and timescales for completion of the work and also for amendments and maintenance in the future need to be specified.

The tenderer will be required to state whether they comply with the requirements in the ITT. If compliance to specific sections cannot be given then these will be stated within the response to the ITT.

The tenderer will also have to supply some basic technical and project information concerning the software to be written and the method of writing the software. This information may be supplied in a form which the supplier produces.

Requirements specification

The ITT will also include the detailed requirements specification. Details of a requirements specification are covered in Chapters 7, 8, 9 and 10.

Software engineering requirements

This section asks the tenderer to provide an overview of the life-cycle method that will be used to produce the software. It provides the supplier with confidence that recognised design principles will be used to write the software.

3.2   Identifying suitable suppliers

KEY POINT

To identify suppliers:
- check who supplies other organisations
- read trade magazines
- consult an expert.

Identifying potential suppliers of software can be difficult. Although there is no absolute rule for identifying all possible suppliers of software on the market, there are a number of avenues that can be explored:

1   **Suppliers to other organisations**. An examination of the hardware or software used by comparable organisations can reveal the existence of suitable products, and how popular they are with their current users.

2   **Trade magazines**. A trawl of trade magazines will find appropriate advertisements and trade reviews and articles. Each of these must be examined critically – it should not be assumed that the articles and reviews are necessarily independent or unbiased.

3   **Consult an expert.** The company may consult with an expert. This expert may be a computer consultant with experience in the application being computerised, or may be employed by a dealer or retail establishment. It is important to consider the independence and motivation of the advice given – a dealer, for example, may receive a higher profit margin on one product than another.

When a list of suppliers has been drawn up, then the ITT can be sent and responses to this awaited!

4   Evaluating supplier proposals

Once the proposals have been received from potential suppliers, they must be compared with what was requested in the tender document, and the best one selected. The criteria used to judge the proposals can be put into three categories:

KEY POINT

Main criteria:
- technical
- cost
- customer support.

Technical

How closely do the suppliers' proposals tally with the hardware and software requirements specified in the Invitation To Tender Document?

Cost

What is the overall cost of the package offered by each supplier?

Customer support

How good is the after-sales service and warranty offered by the supplier?

Attempt to obtain the hardware and software from the same source and with a guarantee that they will be compatible. If bought from different sources and the system does not work, one supplier can blame the other's product.

4.1 Evaluating software proposals

There are many points to consider when evaluating possible purchases of application software. It is often useful to make out a checklist of the points that are most salient to the user. Some of the points that may be included on the checklist are:

How well the software fits the needs of the organisation	This does not necessarily imply that every single requirement is satisfied – the users may be able to compromise, or to satisfy their information needs in some other way.
Can the software be tailored to fit the organisation's needs?	Sometimes packages can be modified by the supplier (at a cost) and, on other occasions, a package may have sufficient flexibility to allow the users to adapt it as required.
Other facilities	Has the software any extra facilities that can be exploited by the organisation?
How well does the organisational structure fit in with the demands placed on it by the software?	The users should only acquire the software if no changes in structure are needed, or if any such changes will increase efficiency. A centralised system to help the sales force plan its calls efficiently would not be suitable where the sales people do not regularly visit the head office.
Will existing hardware need to be upgraded or replaced?	Many modern PC applications are very hungry for internal memory or hard disk space, and may not be capable of running on older machinery.
Is the software compatible with existing software and file structures?	A change to a new word processing package, for example, may require all existing documents to be converted to the new format. A supplier that is eager for business may well agree to carry out the conversion process.
Is the software compatible with the organisation's future requirements?	The users may be planning to migrate to a new operating system, which would make it necessary to acquire software compatible with the new operating environment.
Under what conditions is the software being supplied?	Extra payments may be payable each year; use of the software may be restricted to single machines; a site licence may be needed for use on more than one machine; use may be restricted to machines at a single location.
What protective measures has the supplier taken against unauthorised duplication?	Although suppliers are justified in protecting their software, the measures they take can sometimes cause operational problems. The user may be unable to take a back-up copy of the original disk that the software was supplied on. If the system becomes corrupted the user may have to obtain a replacement from the supplier. There may be a delay of several days before the system can be used again.
How fast does the system run?	The user will need to be assured that the system can cope with the volumes of data that will need to be processed and stored – some software that looks satisfactory when demonstrated by a salesperson can be unusable when asked to deal with volumes of data that are greater than it was designed for.

KEY POINT

Points to check for when evaluating proposals:

- fit to organisation's needs
- can it be tailored?
- other facilities
- fit to organisation's structure
- hardware implications
- fit with current software
- fit with future needs
- conditions of supply
- duplication restrictions
- speed
- demonstration facilities
- ease of use
- documentation
- training
- size of customer base

- security features
- maintenance offered
- updates
- cost.

Can the software be adequately demonstrated?

The supplier is often able to show a special demonstration version of the software running. Sometimes a restricted version (or even a full version) of the software can be lent to the user for a period of time. Many suppliers make lists of existing customers. These can be visited to see the system running in a real situation. Seeing software running can give the user a 'feel' for how it works and can provide reassurance as to its suitability.

How user friendly is the software?

It must be both easy to use and tolerant to user error. Menus, graphical interfaces and clear prompts make the software easier to use, and attractive and uncluttered screen designs make the system enjoyable to use. One strategy used by software designers to make their products user-friendly is to mimic the look and feel of more familiar software. Lotus 1-2-3, for example, is often used as a pattern for other software – both spreadsheets and other types of software.

Documentation must be both comprehensive and comprehensible

Documentation can be at several levels, ranging from brief reference cards, through easily understood user guides to system manuals that can act as a technical reference to specialist and experienced users.

How will the user acquire the expertise to run the system?

Most suppliers offer training, and both internal and external courses may be appropriate ways for users to learn how to operate the system. Well-known packages often have many experienced users who may already be employed or who can be hired in. On-screen and written tutorials allow users to learn at their own speed.

How wide is the customer base of the software?

The existence of a large number of customers provides several benefits. Most of the bugs in the software will have been identified and corrected. There is likely to be a reservoir of expertise that can be exploited by the user, and books may have been written and training courses developed. The user can be assured that they will get what they expect from the software.

Does the software have any security features?

User numbers, passwords and encryption are useful for protecting confidential data on all types of software, and are absolutely vital in multi-user and networked systems.

What sort of maintenance and after-sales service is offered?

Maintenance and after-sales service is just as important for software as it is for hardware. A maintenance fee will usually be payable for bespoke software just as it is for hardware. The availability of a help desk is very helpful to an organisation. Many suppliers charge a subscription for access to a help desk, and some suppliers charge for each call asking for advice. The existence of this kind of charge may be a disincentive towards buying a particular software package.

Are future versions of the software likely to become available?

Many software suppliers allow users to obtain updated versions of packages at advantageous rates. If an updated version is *not* bought, the users must assure themselves that the supplier will continue to support the older versions. The user can suffer disastrous problems if support is not kept up. An example of what can happen is as follows:

A small business acquired one of the biggest selling PC accounts packages. The version of the software that they bought was one for a different type of microcomputer. This particular version of the package did not allow for a non-integer percentage Value Added Tax. By the time the software house had found someone capable of updating the package, the small business had been forced to go back to a manual invoicing system.

What is the cost of the software?

All aspects of cost must be included in the user's calculations – purchase price, site licences, maintenance, the cost of access to help, training costs, etc.

4.2 Selecting an application package

Organisations have a great deal in common with one another – the core information-processing activities are likely to be very similar from one company to the next. The basic accounting functions, for example, apply to a large majority of businesses. Many applications are served by packages that can be obtained off-the-shelf, although care must be taken in choosing the appropriate package for the specific organisation.

5 Outsourcing

5.1 Outsourcing and facilities management

IT outsourcing involves purchasing from outside the organisation the IS services required to perform business functions.

Outsourcing is often confused with facilities management but outsourcing is a broader definition to cover the contracting out of specified services to a third party within a controlled, flexible relationship. It covers facilities management types of services and a range of contracts with more intangible benefits. It includes such services as computer centre operations, network operations and application management, and also systems integration.

Facilities management – this literally means that an outside specialist manages the organisation's facilities. In the physical sense, all the IS elements may remain within the client's premises but their management and operation become the responsibility of the contracted body. FM deals are the legally binding equivalent of an internal service level agreement. Both specify what services will be received but with an FM contract legal redress is possible.

5.2 Different approaches to outsourcing

Recent research has shown that four distinct approaches to IT sourcing are in use. They are:

- Total outsourcing – where an organisation chooses to outsource more than 70% of its IT capability to a single supplier. These deals involve the transfer of IT assets and staff to a single vendor.

- Multiple/selective sourcing – when an organisation negotiates with a range of suppliers and may develop a framework agreement that outlines how the client and supplier will work together in the event of an outsourcing contract being signed.

- Joint venture/strategic alliance sourcing – this approach is when an organisation enters into a joint venture with a supplier on a shared risk/reward basis.

- Insourcing – is when an organisation decides to retain a large centralised IT department and 'insource' management and technical capabilities from the external market to accommodate the peaks of the work.

Cost reduction/containment continues to be a major factor in embarking on outsourcing, leaving the organisation free to concentrate on their core business.

5.3 Benefits of outsourcing

Overall the benefits of outsourcing have been seen as:

- Cost reduction – because of the economies of scale available in purchasing equipment and efficiencies in utilising specialist staff

- Business improvement – by management being able to concentrate on core competencies because of expertise and specialisation available to manage and staff the IT function.

- Avoid the growing shortage of IT and IS systems staff and keep up with technological change.

- Cost control – creating a 'customer/contractor' relationship tends to concentrate the focus on cost control which is sometimes lost when functions are performed internally.

- Other benefits include access to IT skills, improved quality, headcount reduction, flexible resourcing and the release of managers to concentrate on other activities.

5.4 The problems with outsourcing

Whilst the major reason for outsourcing is cost reduction, there are a number of disadvantages that include the following:

- dependency on supplier

- problems of security and loss of confidentiality – particularly where an outsourcing company is also working for competitors

- difficult contract terms

- length of contract (being locked in)

- lost expertise

- work that has been outsourced is difficult to switch to a new supplier if there are problems, or at the end of a contract period. This gives the external supplier significant bargaining power

- the contracting company will be seeking to minimise risk and maximise profit by maintaining stability and drive down its costs and is unlikely to suggest changes

- loss of competitive advantage (if information systems are a core competence then they must not be outsourced).

Activity 1

Suppose that a regional hospital authority agrees a contract with a software company. The software company agrees to develop a new system that the hospital will use for maintaining patient records, communicating with patients at home, scheduling operations and charging the patients for services that are not free. After the system has been implemented, the software company will operate the system itself for a contract period of five years, and the hospital staff will only be involved with the system to the extent of providing the software company with the data for input.

What would you consider to the risks, if any, in arranging the outsourcing agreement for the development and operation of this system?

Feedback to this activity is at the end of the chapter.

6   Implementation – avoiding user resistance and implementation failure

6.1   Introduction

This section discusses how user resistance to new systems can be minimised and the risk of implementation failure limited.

6.2   Overcoming user resistance

KEY POINT

The risk of project failure is reduced when users are involved in the system development as they feel more able to accept the project as 'theirs'.

The need to involve users during the initial design and development of the project has already been discussed in this chapter. The risk of project failure is reduced and users are more likely to accept a system and feel ownership towards that system when they have been involved in its development.

The implementation of a project can also fail if users are not involved in this stage of the project. In general terms, users will be more satisfied with an information system if they have been involved in its implementation, including receiving proper training.

However, users may still resist the implementation of a new system for a variety of reasons. Specifically, new systems will also bring organisational change, and users may reject the system because they do not like the changes, or feel that they have lost power within the organisation as a result of the implementation.

Resistance to information systems may include simply not using the system, where use is voluntary. However, where a system must be used, then resistance may involve increased error rates, disruption to the system or even sabotage. User resistance can be explained using the theories of Markus (1983) and Davis and Olson (1985). Resistance falls into one of three categories.

People-orientated theory

Change is resisted because individual users or a group of users do not wish to learn new programs or amend their working practices. This resistance is caused by factors internal to the individual or the group.

Strategies to overcome this resistance include:

- user training and education to show the benefits of the system

- interviewing users to identify reasons for not using the system and then finding methods of overcoming those reasons

- coercion by issuing memos or other communications requiring use of the system

- persuasion or threats.

The latter two 'strategies' are more likely, of course, to consolidate resistance and resentment. If management has to resort to threats to make users use a new system, serious damage has already been done to its chances of success, regardless of the merits of the system itself.

System-orientated theory

Resistance to a system is caused by poor usability and functionality, and users find it difficult to make the system work correctly. This resistance is system orientated because it relates to poor system design.

Strategies to overcome this resistance include:

- where possible, modifying the package to take account of user concerns. However, this may be difficult and expensive, especially where the package has already been implemented

- additional user training and education to explain in more detail how to use the package

- increased user participation in future releases of the package. Although this will not provide a short-term modification, users will see that action is being taken to rectify the problems in new releases.

Interaction theory

The system itself is well designed and accepted by some users. However, other users do not accept the system because they fear it will take away some of their power or influence in the organisation. Resistance to the system in this case is caused by poor interaction between people and the system. The source of this is cultural and political, rather than poor systems design.

Strategies to overcome this resistance include:

- restructure incentives for users so that they are not dependent on system usage

- try to address organisational problems prior to the introduction of any new system

- try to involve users in the implementation of the system to encourage acceptance and remove any interaction barriers by demonstrating the benefits of the system.

6.3 Level of management support

Providing an appropriate level of management support is important to the success of the whole project. This chapter has already outlined the problem that too much or too little support can result in overall project failure. To ensure project success, managers must be aware of the needs of the individual project team, and must then make decisions regarding the level of support that the specific team requires. An initial meeting with the project team to clarify the level of support expected will help managers make this decision.

6.4 Management of the implementation process

Management of the implementation process, and possible reasons for project failure arising from poor management, were discussed earlier in this chapter.

There are various methods of attempting to minimise risks:

Organisational impact analysis

An organisational impact analysis explains how a system will affect the organisational structure and the attitudes of staff within the organisation, and identifies changes to the decision-making process and operations, and the processing of data and information. This document will help to remove some of the risks such as poor communication by helping to identify areas of change and planning to communicate this information to staff prior to that change occurring.

Ergonomics

Ergonomics is the study of the interaction between people and computers in the workplace. It includes the design of the human/computer interface, and the physical environment such as desks and chairs to be used, as well as the overall job design. Ergonomics is important because providing an appropriate working environment for staff will help to increase the acceptance of any new system. Taking time to ensure that screen designs follow work methods, that tables and chairs meet legal requirements and are comfortable to work at, etc will significantly assist user acceptability of new systems.

Socio-technical design

An extension of ergonomics is socio-technical design. This design method attempts to blend technical efficiency of the IT systems with the need to meet organisational and human objectives for the system. The overall system design will hopefully result in more efficient working because both the users and the IT system will be working effectively. Socio-technical design is explored more fully in Chapter 14.

The human objectives for a system may include being placed in appropriate workgroups and being allocated appropriate tasks, as well as having jobs that are designed to meet human objectives, and not simply entering data into computer systems. Systems are designed by producing a technical and a social design, and then attempting to merge these to produce one overall system. When these systems are compatible, then it is expected that productivity will increase without any compromises being made regarding the human or social objectives. An expected outcome from this approach is that the users will accept and work with the system, rather than be inclined to resist its implementation.

6.5 Controlling the project timetable

There is a tendency for large projects to over-run their scheduled target date for completion, and are implemented behind schedule. This problem is particularly relevant for the development of bespoke software, since off-the-shelf software will usually be readily available.

The reasons for delay in project completion might be:

- poor project management

- changes to the system requirements by the computer user ('client'), resulting in revisions to the system design or to programs

- problems with the system design or the software, which are not revealed until testing.

Some of these problems can be avoided through good management.

Critical path analysis (CPA) charts

There are several techniques to help with the control of the project timetable. One of these is critical path analysis (CPA). With this technique, the project is divided into a large number of different tasks or activities. These activities are put into a logical time sequence, identifying which activities must be completed first and which activities cannot begin until certain others have been finished. For each activity, an estimate is made of the time that will be required to complete it. This analysis of activity sequencing and estimated times is then consolidated into a CPA chart. A CPA chart shows which activities are the most critical to the completion of the project on time, and so must be started at the earliest possible time in order to ensure that the project as a whole can be completed on schedule. For non-critical activities, the chart shows how much spare time or 'float' is available, so that starting or completing the activity can be delayed without affecting the overall completion time.

The CPA chart should be updated regularly throughout the course of the project, so that the project manager is fully informed about the current state of the project and its current expected completion time. Critical delays can be identified and action taken to deal with them.

Control over changes to specifications

The project manager should try to discourage the computer user ('client') from making changes to the system requirements that are not essential. Changing the requirements can result in the need to re-assess the system design and they take time – and cost money – to make.

7 Testing

When a new system is designed, and even when a new system is purchased as off-the-shelf software, it should be tested before the 'old' system is abandoned. The new system should be shown to work as planned and specified, and without serious problems or faults in the system.

There are four key stages of testing a bespoke system:

- testing the logic of the system and programs within the system

- program testing

- system testing

- acceptance testing.

7.1 Testing the system and program logic

Before programming work begins, the system and each individual program within the system should undergo a logic test. This is a test to make sure that the logic of the system and each program is valid, and that all possible conditions have been provided for by the system designers.

The tools for logic testing include logic flowcharts and decision tables. The systems analyst or programmer takes a number of transactions or other data items through the system structure diagrams or program flowcharts to make sure that the data will produce the expected results.

Errors in the logic can be identified and corrected. If the logic appears correct, programming work can begin.

7.2 Program testing

When each program has been written, it is tested thoroughly, usually by the programmer. Test data is created for input to the program. This data should be designed to ensure that all sections of the program will be tested, to make sure that they process the data correctly. The program testing process should be fully documented, with records made of:

- the data used for testing

- the expected results or output from the program

- the actual results and output from the program

- any corrective action taken because of the test results.

The documentation of the program tests is useful as a point of reference if there are problems with the program in the future.

When the program tests have been completed, the tests should confirm that each program taken independently can receive input and process it correctly to produce the expected output. Program tests do not, however, test whether the output from one program can actually be read and processed by another program. The system as a whole has not been tested, and there is a risk that the linkages between the different programs will contain faults.

7.3 System testing

Once it has been established that the individual programs are working correctly, the system as a whole must therefore be tested. Test data is used as original input to the system, and these tests are documented in the same way as the program tests.

System testing must be carried out before the system is installed on the computer hardware that will be used operationally (off-line testing) and also immediately after installation (on-line testing). The more off-line testing that can be carried out, the lower will be the risk of finding system faults and errors during implementation.

With a large computer system, system testing is unlikely to discover all the system faults, and some problems will only become apparent after the system has been handed over to the computer user.

7.4 Acceptance testing

KEY POINT

The computer user
should carry out some
acceptance testing of
the new system before
introducing it
operationally.

The computer user should carry out some acceptance testing of the new system before introducing it operationally. Acceptance testing should be carried out on off-the-shelf software (for large systems) as well as bespoke software.

The purpose of acceptance testing is to give the computer user an opportunity to check that the system works as intended, before accepting delivery of the finished software for operational use. The tests can check not only that the computer system works as planned, but that the interface works efficiently between the computer system and the user's other operational procedures and office systems.

The user should use acceptance testing:

- to confirm that the system meets the system specifications

- to give the staff an opportunity to familiarise themselves with the new system.

With a large system, the computer user will probably use much larger quantities of test data (based on 'live data') than were used in system testing.

The number of problems discovered by acceptance testing should be reduced through:

- involving the computer user throughout the development process, and

- prototyping.

7.5 Testing packages

When an organisation buys an established software package 'off-the-shelf', the program and system testing will already have been carried out by the company that produced the software. The computer user should, however, carry out acceptance testing in order to make sure that the package meets its requirements and to discover what the limitations of the package might be.

Testing should be thorough when a package is customised. Rigorous acceptance testing should be designed to satisfy the buyer that the customisation has been carried out properly. With customisation, the standard package is altered by the software provider, in order to meet certain specific requirements of the computer user. For example, the standard package might not have been written to process a particular type of transaction, and the buyer of the package might ask the software provider to alter the package so that it can do this additional processing. The risk with customisation is that the amended program will not have undergone any testing under operational conditions before the buyer acquires it.

When a software company develops a new off-the-self product, or a new version of an existing product, it will want to be satisfied that the package will be well-received by its purchasers (or that software users will be happy to upgrade to the new version). The company might therefore arrange for some pre-launch testing by sending pre-production copies to selected customers for their appraisal. This type of testing is called **beta testing** and it allows the software company both to carry out marketing tests on the software as well as identifying and eliminating faults.

8 File conversion

Most commercial systems are file-based, depending on the processing of one or more files. These files must be created before the system is operational. Creating the basic data files is an important but often time-consuming task. There are five different scenarios:

KEY POINT

File conversion scenarios:
- data exists in hard copy
- some data is missing or incomplete
- data is fully available on magnetic media
- data is partially available on magnetic media
- part or all of the data is contained in a central database.

1   **The data is available in hard copy.** This data must be collated onto input forms and then entered into the system. This process is likely to be time-consuming and labour intensive and may require the hiring of temporary staff to ensure that data entry is done in a timely manner. If the data entry is on-line, it is often better to use the temporary staff to carry out the ongoing work while the existing staff enter the data. This helps with training and helps test the system.

2   **The data is in hard copy form but some data is missing or incomplete.** If this data is crucial it must be researched or estimated.

3   **The data is fully available on magnetic media from existing applications.** This is the easiest situation to deal with, although it is still important to validate or verify the data after it has been converted.

4   **The data is partially available on magnetic media.** The additional fields should be researched or estimated as in 2 above.

5   **Part or all of the data is contained in a central database.** The data dictionary must be updated as appropriate.

8.1 The main stages in file conversion

The main stages in file conversion might be as follows:

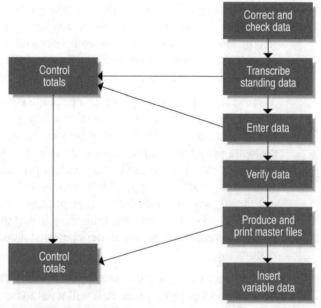

The diagram shows standing (or reference) data being set up first. This produces a skeleton file and can often be done well in advance of the changeover date, as the reference data is static. Only the variable data remains to be dealt with at the changeover date. Skeleton files therefore help to reduce the time pressure of file conversion.

Dead records will be identified and eliminated before conversion. The data must be as 'clean' and as accurate as possible before being printed into the new system. For example, records of former employees should be removed from an employee file if there is no requirement to hold the information. Similarly records from a customer file of customers who no longer buy or who have gone out of business can be removed. Missing items of data should be obtained and added where appropriate.

It is essential that adequate reconciliation details are maintained to agree the old system's control total with that produced by the new system. Control over conversion can be by:

1   **One-for-one checking.** This involves checking each record on the old system to a record on the new system.

2   **Sample checking.** Where numbers are too large for one-for-one checking, statistically monitored samples can be checked.

3   **Control total checking.** This involves checking the total number of records and transaction details from the old to the new system.

4   **Programmed validation.** This involves using a computer program to assist in the conversion, e.g. when converting from a bureau system to an in-house system, a computer program might be used to handle the conversion and reformatting of master files.

Input and verification

The transcribed data is input to the system, to create the standing data for the new files. If the data is keyed in from terminals, the error rate can be reduced by means of data verification and data validation.

- **Data verification** means re-keying the data, so that the data is keyed in twice. If there are keying errors by one of the operators, this is notified to the second operator via the terminal screen. The operator then checks what the correct data should be, and confirms the correct data to the program.

- **Data validation** describes logical checks within a program that are designed to look for errors in the input data that are logically incorrect or inconsistent. For example, if all inventory ID codes contain six digits, a validation check can be included in the program to count the number of digits in the inventory code for any record, and reject any record that does not have six. Errors found by validation checks are reported to the computer user for investigation and correction.

Dealing with large files

If the new system has large files, the file conversion might be in two stages. Standing data might be input first to create a 'skeleton file' and variable data is added later, closer to the time that the system is eventually implemented. For example, to create a customer file, the standing data might be input to create a new file well in advance of the system changeover date. This data would include the customer's name and ID number, address and other contact details, and possibly credit status details. Closer to the time that the new system is implemented, variable data containing details of the historical transactions with the customers might be added, so that the files become ready for operational use.

8.2 Middleware

Middleware is the name given to software that takes data from one system and converts it into data for another system. Middleware was first developed during the 1990s, when many large organisations wanted to convert the files in their old computer systems ('legacy systems') whose programs were mainly written in a language called COBOL, into a format suitable for a new system. Middleware removed the need to do this conversion manually, thus saving time and expense and reducing the error rate considerably.

8.3 XML

XML stands for 'extensible mark-up language'. This is now used extensively for holding data on file, and identifying elements of data with special 'tags'. A feature of XML is that it enables data held on file to be used for different applications. If files are stored in XML, it becomes easier for different computer programs to exchange data. In time, this means that when a new system is developed, file conversion will be much easier if the data files in the current system use XML.

9 System changeover (implementation)

System changeover is the change from operating the current system (if there is one) and introducing the new system operationally. This is a critical phase of system development and implementation because, until a system 'goes live', there will always be doubts about whether it will work properly.

- There is a risk that, if the new system does not work properly, the computer user will be unable to do any processing.

- With major new systems, there will inevitably be some initial difficulties and operational problems.

  - Staff might need some time to get used to the system.

  - Errors in the software might be discovered, requiring correction by writing a new version of the faulty program.

  - Management might also need to study the impact of the new system, on employees, customers or suppliers.

The initial period during which a new system becomes operational is therefore an important time, when the IT specialists and the user's management will spend considerable time monitoring, checking and correcting.

There are four approaches to system changeover, and the most appropriate approach will vary according to circumstances. The four approaches are:

- direct conversion

- parallel running

- pilot operation

- phased implementation/phased conversion.

9.1 Direct conversion

With direct conversion, the computer user ceases to operate the old system and switches completely to using the new system. The risk with this direct changeover is that, if the new system does not function properly, the computer user will not have any system at all.

Direct conversion might be appropriate, however, when:

- the new system has been used elsewhere (for example, an off-the-shelf package) and there is confidence that it will function properly

- the problems for the computer user will be tolerable, even if the system fails to function properly

- none of the other changeover methods are practicable.

9.2 Parallel running

With this method of changeover, the old system and the new system are both operated together for a while. They are operated 'in parallel'. The output from the new system and the efficiency of the system are compared with the output and efficiency of the old system. If the new system performs as well as expected, or at least as well as the old system, a decision can be taken to stop operating the old system, and change entirely to the new system.

The theoretical advantage of parallel running is that, if there is a major problem with the new system, the old system is still operational and up-to-date. In addition, the old and new systems can be compared in detail. However, parallel running is difficult to manage, and additional resources are required to operate two systems. This method of changeover is therefore now rarely used.

9.3 Pilot operation

With a pilot operation, the new system is tested operationally within a part of the organisation, such as one region or one department. For the region or department affected, there is direct changeover, but the rest of the organisation continues to operate the old system until the pilot operation has been successfully tested and is operating efficiently.

The new system is then extended gradually, department by department or region by region, to the entire organisation.

An advantage of a pilot operation is that IT specialists and the user's management can concentrate on a small part of the total organisation, to check that the new system functions properly and to identify and deal with problems.

A pilot operation is only practicable when the system is operated in different geographical areas, or in different departments.

9.4 Phased implementation/phased conversion

With phased implementation, a part of the new system is introduced to replace the corresponding operations in the old system. If this changeover is implemented successfully, another part of the new system is introduced. The new system is therefore introduced in parts or stages until everything has been changed over to the new system.

For example, if a company introduces a new accounting system by phased conversion, it might begin by introducing the new sales ledger system, followed by the new payables ledger system, followed by the new inventory system, and so on.

This method of changeover allows the computer user to become familiar with each part of the system before introducing the next part. It can, therefore, ease the problems for the staff in learning the new system, and gives them time to adjust to the new system.

When resistance to a new system is strong, phased implementation might also help to reduce the strength of the resistance, since staff will be asked to abandon the old system and deal with the new system in stages.

Where a new system will result in job losses, a phased changeover also allows more time to deal with staff retraining, to prepare them for working elsewhere.

9.5 Computer-based monitoring

Performance monitoring can be used as an aid in systems evaluation. The main computer-based monitoring methods are hardware monitors, software monitors and systems logs.

Hardware monitors

The purpose of a hardware monitor is to measure electrical signals in specific circuits of the computer hardware. Based on these electrical signals, idle time, the extent of CPU activity, or peripheral activity can be measured. The sensors send data to counters, which write to magnetic tape. A program is then used to analyse the data and produce the findings as output. Inefficiencies in performance could be identified in this way.

Software monitors

The software monitor is a computer program that records data about the application in use. During the monitoring process the application being monitored is interrupted; this results in a decrease in the operating speed of the program. Software monitors might be used to identify excessive delays during the execution of the program.

Systems logs

Computer systems often produce automatic system logs, the data from which can be useful for analysis of the system. The type of data recorded may be the times a job starts and finishes.

10 Documentation, support and training

10.1 Documentation

System documentation covers a number of different documents, each with a different purpose. All documentation should be updated whenever changes are made to the system or to any program.

Design documentation

The systems analysts and programmers for a tailored (bespoke) system prepare **system design specifications** and **program specifications**, setting out the logic of the system and the programs within the system. They also document the program tests and system tests. These documents will be used in future for checking errors that have been discovered in the system, and for writing amendments and updates to the software.

User manuals

Documentation should also be prepared for the user, to:

- training employees how to use the system

- provide a reference document for dealing with queries; for example, explaining the meaning of various error codes, or the significance of warnings displayed on a VDU screen.

A user manual should be written in non-technical and easy-to-understand language. Some software companies now provide user manuals for their packages in electronic form, within the package itself (with help menus and help screens), or possibly on a separate CD.

Technical manual

A technical manual might be prepared to supplement the system specification, program specifications and testing documentation. It will typically include:

- the system objectives

- an overview of the system

- a performance specification for the system

- a technical specification

- appendices, such as:

    - the data dictionary for any database in the system

    - data flow diagrams

    - entity relationship models and entity life histories

    - the program specifications.

10.2 Support services: specialist help

In spite of testing, user training and user manuals, problems will inevitably occur with new systems, especially large systems, and there must be arrangements in place to provide the computer users with specialist help when they need it.

Specialist help can take several forms.

- Specialists might be available to assist with purchasing special stationery or supplies or additional terminals.

- Technical staff might be available to deal with hardware and communication problems.

- Software specialists may be available to provide help. When an organisation buys an off-the-shelf package, it might enter into a contract with the software provider for a **help desk** or **help line** facility. The software provider might undertake to deal with queries from the user by e-mail or telephone. For a larger annual fee, the software house might undertake to send specialists to the user's premises in the event of a major operational difficulty with the software.

Providing users with access to relevant expertise is an important aspect of system implementation that is sometimes forgotten. The implementation plan should include provision for whatever support is considered necessary as soon as the system becomes operational.

10.3 Training

The individuals who operate a computer system should be given suitable training. This might be provided:

- in the office, by individuals with more experience and knowledge of the system (desk training)

- in special courses organised from time to time by the computer user

- in courses run by the software provider or a specialist training company.

Training might be appropriate even for general-purpose packages, to improve the user's skills with the package, and knowledge of different options and facilities.

11 System maintenance

When a system has been implemented, it must be maintained. System
maintenance involves:

- correcting any errors that are discovered in the system after it has
  been implemented

- updating the system for any changes that become necessary

- amending the system to meet any new requirements of the user.

11.1 Corrective maintenance

Corrective maintenance involves eliminating faults and errors ('bugs')
from a system. Although most errors should be identified and corrected
during the testing stages of system development, errors might be
discovered after the new system has been implemented. When errors are
discovered after implementation, correcting them is often an urgent
requirement, particularly if the consequences of the error are severe and the
computer user does not want it to happen again.

Corrective maintenance is an expensive process. If the correction is made by an
in-house programmer, the programmer will need time to become familiar with
the program in order to identify the incorrect logic and re-write the program.
The program should then be tested before being introduced to live operations.
There is also a risk that, by writing new program instructions to correct one
error, the programmer will inadvertently introduce a new error into the system.

When program corrections are written by an external software company, the
company might charge a high fee for the corrections.

To minimise the cost of corrective maintenance, it is important to minimise
errors at the system design stage and to test the programs and system thoroughly
before the system goes live.

11.2 Preventive maintenance

Preventative maintenance is maintenance carried out in advance of a problem
occurring, to reduce the risk of that problem. It is the same as having a car
regularly serviced in order to reduce the risk of breakdowns. In theory, more
preventative maintenance means less corrective maintenance. This is good, because
preventative maintenance can be carried out at a time most convenient to the
organisation, whereas corrective maintenance always seems to be required during
the busiest periods.

11.3 Adaptive maintenance

Adaptive maintenance is amending the system to adjust to changes in its
environment. There are several reasons why adaptive maintenance might
be required.

- The user's needs and requirements might change. The user might
  want the system to perform additional processing routines, or to hold
  additional data on file requiring some changes to the file design and
  the software.

- There might be changes in the system environment that necessitate
  changes. For example, an expert system on taxation will require
  amendment each time there are changes to the tax rules.

- The system might have grown beyond the capacity limits for which it was originally designed. For example, a system might have been designed to handle a maximum number of transactions or enquiries each day, or a maximum file size, or code numbers with a maximum number of digits. As a system reaches the limits of its design capacity, it often 'slows down' and becomes much less efficient.

11.4 Perfective maintenance

DEFINITION

Perfective maintenance is carried out to improve the efficiency and effectiveness of the system.

Perfective maintenance is carried out to improve the efficiency and effectiveness of the system. It might be prompted by new technology that has become available, or by the development of new techniques. Alternatively, a new data validation check might be written into a program to identify a type of error that had not been anticipated or foreseen when the system was originally designed. Introducing a new validation check should reduce the number of incorrect entries getting in to the system files undetected.

Changes to improve a system should provide additional benefits that justify the cost.

11.5 The systems maintenance lifecycle

It is important to see maintenance not just as a series of disconnected ad hoc reactions to problems but as a planned, formalised activity that is integrated into the system design process. The actual processes involved in maintenance can be set down as a cycle of activities.

Planning for maintenance

Good maintenance practice starts within the system design process, and a major objective in planning a new system is to make maintenance as easy as possible.

Flexibility and adaptability are major considerations when building a system. A flexible system can cope with widely varying volumes of transactions and can be adapted to cope with changes in procedures and requirements.

Another major consideration is the recognition of problems when they occur. Validation routines are built into programs to identify when data errors occur and to deal with them where possible. Not only should data be validated as it goes into the system but existing files and data should be checked periodically.

Monitoring the effectiveness and efficiency of a system is an important part of the maintenance process. Each system will have a number of performance indicators that are calculated during each run of the programs and compared with target values. When performance starts to fall below target, investigations can be carried out and remedial action taken if it is needed.

Once an existing problem has been identified, or a possible future problem predicted, action must be taken. Likely problems can be anticipated and contingency plans made during the initial design. Extra storage capacity, for example, can be made available to cope with increasing volumes of data as and when existing capacity is exceeded.

The maintenance lifecycle

The procedures involved in maintaining software can be presented in the form of a diagram:

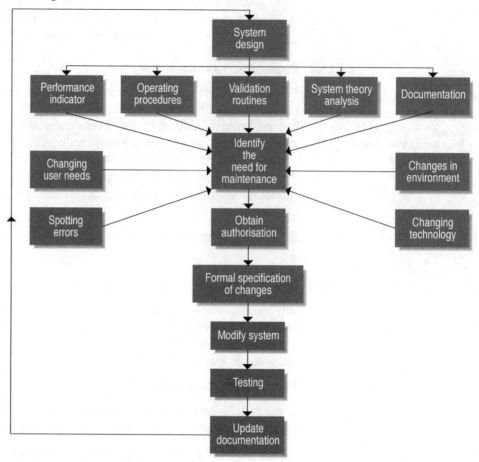

Performance indicators show that the software is not running as efficiently as expected. This may be caused by situations such as an increase in the number of transactions being processed or higher volume of network traffic. The reason for the poor performance will need to be identified and methods of improving performance agreed.

Finally, documentation may occasionally result in a change requirement, for example, new forms required by tax authorities may need additional output from the system.

Having identified the need for maintenance, then authorisation will have to be obtained for that change and a formal specification produced. The latter will be needed to help track exactly what changes are being made and so that appropriate testing can be carried out after the change has been made.

After the change has been made and tested, documentation must be updated to ensure that users have full information about any changes made. The whole process can then start again!

12   System evaluation

Measures of success remain less than clear. How do the designer and user know success when they see it?

Although no general set of standards exist, there are a number of ways of measuring success, each with its own criteria.

Several authors focus on the quality of the software in measuring success.

12.1 Characteristics of software quality

Portability – the amount of platform independence

Reliability – degree of completeness, accuracy, and consistency

Efficiency – degree of efficiency and accessibility

Human engineering – degree of communicativeness

Testability – degree of structure

Comprehensibility – degree of self-descriptiveness, conciseness, and legibility

Modifiability – degree of enhancement

12.2 Other measures of success

Attitudinal measures – one approach is to focus on the degree to which the system is actually used. Another is to measure user satisfaction.

Technical measures – often this involves a comparison of the features of the DSS to the original user requirements.

Organisational measures – focus is on the degree to which organisational needs have been met or exceeded.

12.3 Criteria for a successful IS

Improves the way decision makers think about problems.

Fits well with the organisation's planning methods.

Fits well with the political approach to decision making within the organisation.

Results in alternatives and choices that are implemented.

Is considered both cost-effective and valuable relative to its development costs.

Is expected to be used for a measurable period of time.

12.4 Measuring IS success

One framework contains four measurement categories:

1   System performance – response time, data entry, output format, usage, and user interface.

2   Task performance – decision quality, measured by time spent in the decision process. Also, trust, confidence and satisfaction.

3   Business opportunities – costs of development and operation. Increased income and changes in productivity.

4   Evolutionary aspects – degree of flexibility, overall functionality of the DSS.

Summary

- Business transformation is the process of translating a high level vision for the business into new services.

- Business change is complex because of the interdependencies between the business environment, the organisation, its people and supporting technologies; any change in one aspect will affect one or more of the others.

- In-house development of software does help to focus requirements on the organisation, although there are also benefits of external development such as the expertise.

- IT outsourcing involves purchasing, from outside the organisation, the IS services required to perform business functions.

- Four distinct approaches to IT sourcing are in use. They are total outsourcing, multiple/selective sourcing, joint ventures and insourcing.

- A new system must be tested before it is implemented. There are four stages of testing for a tailored or in-house system: logic testing, program testing, system testing and acceptance testing.

- For many new systems, it is necessary to create a new file. File conversion is the process of creating the file or files for the new system from the file data for the current system (plus any data that is required additionally for the new system).

- There are four possible approaches to changing over from the old system to the new system: direct changeover, parallel running, a pilot operation and phased implementation.

- There might be considerable resistance by the user's staff to a new computer system, and a reluctance to use the system.

- Systems should be fully documented. The user is likely to need specialist support when a new system is implemented, for example a help line facility. The user's staff should be given suitable training in how to operate a new system.

- There are different types of system maintenance: corrective maintenance, preventive maintenance, adaptive maintenance and perfective maintenance.

- When aspects of an IT project development, or IT operations, are outsourced, the relationship with the external supplier should be carefully managed. It needs to be a constructive relationship, and commercially beneficial to both sides.

- After its implementation, a system should be subject to regular evaluation. Issues to consider in an evaluation include costs, financial benefits, operating performance and efficiency (processing speeds, turn-round times, file sizes, processing volumes), the user's satisfaction with the system and the amount of use, the quality and value of reports from the system, error rates and security issues.

Having completed your study of this chapter, you should have achieved the following learning outcomes:

- recommend strategies to minimise the disruption caused by introducing IS technologies

- explain how to supervise major IS projects and ensure their smooth implementation.

Self-test questions

1   What are the five levels of IT-enabled business transformation? (1.3)

2   Outline the four approaches to IT sourcing. (5.2)

3   What is a CPA chart? (6.5)

4   What is acceptance testing? (7.4)

5   What is beta testing of an off-the-shelf package? (7.5)

6   What is file conversion and why is it needed? (8)

7   What is middleware and what is XML, and what is the relevance of each to file conversion? (8.2, 8.3)

8   What is a pilot operation for a new system? (9.3)

9   What is a phased changeover for a new system? (9.4)

10   What might be included in the technical manual for a new system? (10.1)

11   What is a help line facility? (10.2)

12   What is preventive maintenance? (11.2)

13   For what reasons might adaptive maintenance to a system be necessary? (11.3)

14   What issues might be considered in a system evaluation? (12)

Practice questions

Question 1

A system evaluation has found that within 18 months the system will no longer be able to handle the anticipated volume of processing unless file sizes are increased. Work carried out by IT staff to amend the system by increasing file size capacity is an example of:

A   corrective maintenance

B   adaptive maintenance

C   perfective maintenance

D   preventive maintenance.

Question 2

A computer user asks a software company to amend the software for its sales ordering system, so as to allow customers to place orders and pay by credit card through its website. This amendment to the system is an example of:

A   corrective maintenance

B   adaptive maintenance

C   perfective maintenance

D   preventive maintenance.

Question 3

Which of the following factors is the least likely to affect user satisfaction with a new system?

A GUI

B Response times

C File sizes

D Error rates

Question 4

State two benefits of using a pilot test or pilot operation as the method for changing over to a new computer system in a large organisation.

Question 5

Review of implementation

A small chain of four department stores is located in and around a major metropolitan area. It is about to implement, in all stores, a point of sale system with linkages to a central computer. The stores all currently use conventional cash registers. You have been asked to assist in the conversion to the new system.

You are required to produce:

(a) an evaluation of the various approaches to the system changeover **(8 marks)**

(b) a checklist, in sequence, of the activities likely to be carried out during implementation **(4 marks)**

(c) suggestions as to how the new system might be evaluated after three months of operational training. **(8 marks)**

(Total: 20 marks)

Question 6

Facilities management

The directors of DS are not satisfied with the GDC Ltd facilities management company, which was contracted two years ago to run the IT systems of the company. At that time, the existing in-house IT development and support department was disbanded and all control of IT systems handed over to GDC Ltd. The appointment of GDC Ltd was relatively rushed and, although an outline contract was agreed, no detailed service level agreement was produced.

Over the last few weeks, the number of complaints received from staff regarding the service has been increasing and the provision of essential management reports has not been particularly timely.

A recent exchange of correspondence with GDC Ltd failed to resolve the matter. Staff at GDC Ltd recognised the fall in standards of service, but insisted that it had met its contractual obligations. DS's lawyers have confirmed that GDC Ltd is correct.

Key features of DS's contract with GDC LTD facilities Management Company:

The contract can be terminated by either party with three months' notice.

GDC Ltd will provide IT services for DS, the service to include:

Purchase of all hardware and software

Repair and maintenance of all IT equipment

Help desk and other support services for users

Writing and maintenance of in-house software

Provision of management information

Price charged to be renegotiated each year but any increase must not exceed inflation, plus 10%

Required:

(a)   Explain, from the point of view of DS, why it might have received poor service from GDC Ltd, even though GDC Ltd has met the requirements of the contract.

(12 marks)

(b)   Explain the courses of action now available to DS relating to the provision of IT services. Comment on the problems involved in each course of action.

(8 marks)

(Total: 20 marks)

For the answers to these questions, see the 'Answers' section at the end of the book.

Feedback to activity

Activity 1

A suggested answer is as follows.

- The system might be imperfectly specified when system development work begins. If the hospital authority subsequently changes the specification, the software house might be able to increase its fee substantially.

- Since the software company will operate the system, it could be difficult for the staff of the hospital authority to test it.

- The software company will wish to make a profit from the contract, and will be reluctant to agree to changes, and might even argue against corrective maintenance, unless it is paid extra.

- Once the system becomes operational, the hospital authority might have very little control over the communications between the software company's staff and the general public (the patients or 'customers').

- If the system creates bad publicity, due to errors in the system relating to scheduling of operations or invoicing, the hospital authority will have no control over the damage to its reputation.

What happens at the end of five years? Will the hospital authority be forced to renew the contract with the software house because no one else understands the system? Alternatively, will the authority be obliged to abandon the system and buy a new system to replace it?

Chapter 5

CHANGE IN ORGANISATIONS

Syllabus content

- External and internal change triggers (e.g. environmental factors, mergers and acquisitions, re-organisation and rationalisation).

- The stages in the change process.

- The importance of managing critical periods of change through the life cycle of the firm.

Contents

1 Change in organisations

KEY POINT

Change is defined as the 'substitution or succession of one thing in place of another; substitution of other conditions; variety'.

Change is defined as the 'substitution or succession of one thing in place of another; substitution of other conditions; variety'.

Within any organisation there will be reasons why change is desirable or even inevitable and, simultaneously, resistance to that change.

Change happens constantly, at all levels within an organisation. Change management is concerned with the principles and practice of introducing change.

1.1 Planned or unplanned change

Change can be categorised as either planned or unplanned.

KEY POINT

Planned change is deliberate and conscious. There is an intention to move from the current situation to a new target position, and a plan is formulated for how to get there.

- **Planned change** is deliberate and conscious. There is an intention to move from the current situation to a new target position, and a plan is formulated for how to get there. When an organisation anticipates developments and find ways of dealing with them in advance, this is known as **proactive change**.

- **Unplanned change**. An organisation might simply change by responding to developments and adapting to new circumstances as they arise. This is **reactive change**. When an unplanned change is a necessary response to an unforeseen crisis, it is generally seen as a threat to be dealt with rather than an opportunity to exploit.

Change can also be categorised as either a 'one-off' major change (a change 'event') or as a continuing process of development. Until the 1980s, theories of change management focused on large-scale changes to deal with a major event, such as a merger or takeover, or a radical reorganisation in response to severe financial losses or loss of business. The emphasis is now perhaps more on continuous change within an organisation that learns and adapts, and the development of a change-oriented culture.

1.2 Four types of organisational change

According to the Nadler-Tushman model, there are four types of organisational change:

- **Anticipatory changes:** planned changes based on expected situations.

- **Reactive changes:** changes made in response to unexpected situations.

- **Incremental changes** – subsystem adjustments required to keep the organisation on course. This is a fairly small change. It is change that occurs within an organisation without the need for a change in its structure or culture. The organisation can adapt easily, and accommodate the change without any serious problem. When incremental changes occur regularly over an extended period of time, they are referred to as **evolutionary change**.

- **Transformational change** is a bigger and more radical change that cannot be accommodated without a change in the organisation structure and culture. Transformational change will therefore have an enormous effect and result in significant restructuring and reorganisation, and will call for a different way of thinking.

Employees and managers are often prepared to accept incremental change, but could resist transformational change.

1.3 Features of change in organisations

Buchanan and Huczyknski suggested that there are four basic features of organisational change:

- **Triggers.** A change is initiated by a trigger of some kind, arising either within or outside the organisation. In other words, change has one or more identifiable causes.

- **Interdependencies.** The various parts of an organisation are interdependent. Change in one aspect of an organisation creates pressure for adjustments in other aspects. It is important to look at the effects of change on the organisation as a whole, in both the long and the short term, and to understand all the implications of change. In this respect, it might be helpful to apply some of the ideas of general system theory.

- **Conflict and frustrations.** The technical and economic objectives of change that managers want to achieve will often conflict with the needs and aspirations of employees. This leads to conflict, with managers wanting to enforce changes and employees resisting it.

- **Time lags.** Change rarely takes place smoothly and all the change does not happen immediately. Instead it happens in an 'untidy' way. Some parts of the organisation change more rapidly than others. Some individuals and groups may need time to 'catch up' with everyone else.

2 Triggers for change

The circumstances or events that cause change within an organisation are referred to as 'triggers' for change. These can arise externally or within the organisation.

2.1 External triggers

External triggers are changes in the environment within which the organisation exists. Many different changes might occur within the general external environment of an organisation, but these can perhaps be classified by PEST analysis as:

- **P**olitical and legal change

   For example, the privatisation of a state-owned organisation, such as a government-owned transport service, will have major consequences for companies operating in the industry.

- Economic change

   For example, within Europe, many organisations have reacted to the opportunities (and regulations) provided by membership of their country in the European Union.

- Social and cultural change

   For example, changing public attitudes towards environmental issues could be significant for many companies, with customers choosing to buy from 'environmentally friendly' organisations.

- **T**echnological change

  Technological change is a major trigger for change in organisations, not least because it provides opportunities for new products, new services and new operating technologies.

The other main category of external triggers relates to change in the competitive environment, including:

- changes in competitive rivalry

- new entrants into the industry

- increased threats from substitutes

- increased customer power

- increased *s*upplier power.

Each of these will put more pressure on the organisation's profit margins. It will need to reduce costs and/or improve quality if it is to defend itself against such threats.

Activity 1

List an external change trigger that could lead to changes in organisational structure or operating methods in each of the following categories:

(a)   political change

(b)   economic change

(c)   social and cultural change

(d)   technological change.

Do not use any of the examples in the text above.

There is no feedback to this activity.

2.2   Internal triggers

Internal triggers for change originate within the organisation itself (although they can be affected by environmental change). Examples of internal triggers are as follows.

- **Innovation** – the company may develop a new product or a new manufacturing process that alters the economics of the market place.

- **Individual executive's ambition.**

- **Unforeseen internal events**, for example, incapacity of senior executives.

- **Pursuit of growth** – Starbuck has suggested several driving forces that stimulate company growth:

  (i)   companies may seek dominance of a particular market or area

  (ii)   a company may seek to grow in size in order to achieve 'critical mass', i.e. that state that enables a company to dictate the terms of its market and/or purchases, thereby generating stability for the future

  (iii)   growth may enable a company to reap economies of scale. This may be linked to the desire to maximise capacity utilisation

  (iv)   to seek maximisation of profit

> (v)   executives may seek the challenge and adventure of new projects. For example, a restless entrepreneur who is successful in one field may lose interest as that field becomes more stable and predictable
>
> (vi)   growth may increase the power, job security and earnings of executives. There is therefore an in-built desire amongst the management team to achieve growth.

- **Change of management**. A new boss might want to introduce new ideas about how things should be done.

- **Change of objectives and strategy**. Senior management might decide to change the objectives and business strategies of the organisation, for example by deciding to focus on a 'core business' and sell off 'non-core' operations, or by expanding into new geographical markets.

- **Acquisitions or mergers**. If a company grows through merger or takeover (acquisition), the enlarged organisation will have to be restructured, and a new combined corporate culture might have to be developed. Integrating an acquired company or merged companies is a notoriously difficult change to manage successfully.

- **Downsizing and reorganisation**. A company that is in serious financial difficulties might be forced to scale back the size of its operations, and make many employees redundant. Reorganising and restructuring inevitably result in big changes.

- **Rationalisation**. An organisation might be 'rationalised'. Rationalisation should mean that operations are reorganised in a way that makes them more logical, efficient and effective. Unfortunately, the term is commonly associated with large-scale redundancies and downsizing.

Changes resulting from internal triggers can result in either small adaptive change or sudden and major transformational change. Mergers and acquisitions, rationalisation and restructuring are all likely to trigger a transformational change. However, you should not lose sight of the fact that much change is adaptive and incremental.

3   Resistance to change

DEFINITION

Resistance to change is defined as 'any attitude or behaviour that reflects a person's unwillingness to make or support a desired change'.

Resistance to change is defined as 'any attitude or behaviour that reflects a person's unwillingness to make or support a desired change'.

However, resistance is not always something that has to be overcome, it can also be viewed as feedback to help the change agent to accomplish his or her change objectives.

It is a very human trait to resist change. At the deepest level we carry in our heads a picture of how the world works and test situations against this to understand them and to ensure they are acceptable. The picture is arrived at through years of working within a society and organisational culture. When what is happening does not match our picture, the so-called 'conservative impulse' kicks in and we are alerted to something that is about to infringe the norms, which we have adopted and which provide us with day-to-day guidance about how things should be.

This initial reaction to change leads to an automatic reflex to resist in most people, but there are lots of other issues at work as well. Rosabeth Moss Kanter in her article 'Managing the Human Side of Change' published in the *Management Review* identified a number of other reasons for resistance. These include:

- Loss of control – change done by us can be exciting and rewarding; change done to us can be threatening and unwelcome. The less in-control people feel, the less they will be inclined to co-operate in change.

- Low trust – when people are not certain where the next step will take them, comfort is impossible.

- Historical factors – a range of factors from an organisation's history can influence the success of a change project: change carries with it an implicit assumption that the 'old ways' were wrong and people do not like to feel embarrassed in front of their peers; people who have submerged a gripe against the organisation or particular managers within the organisation can find that the change gives them an opportunity to throw a spanner in the works.

- Concerns about future competence – people may have fear that 'old dogs can't be taught new tricks' and avoid change as a consequence.

- Sometimes the threat is real! – change often leads to people losing their jobs or having their career paths blocked. Often changes increase the pressures on people to perform, to reach targets, to work longer hours, to lose little privileges which they have accrued over time.

3.1 Job factors, personal factors and social factors

Individuals will often resist major change because they see it as a threat. The fears and worries of individuals facing change can be classified in terms of job factors, personal factors and social factors.

Job factors

Individuals might see change as a threat to their job.

- Fear of technological unemployment. There might be a concern that a new technological innovation will remove the need for the technological skills and knowledge of the employee. New systems could reduce the value that an employee thinks he or she offers, because the employee might have built up a deep knowledge of the existing system over many years: when the existing system is abolished, all the acquired knowledge will become useless.

- Fear of changes in working conditions. The employees might be concerned that a change will result in a change for the worse in their working conditions.

- Fear of demotion and reduced pay. Individuals might fear that a change will affect their status at work and the amount of their pay, for example because less overtime or weekend working will be needed.

- Fear of increased effort and less bonus. Employees might suspect that changes will result in them having to put in more effort at work, possibly for less reward. Changes by management to improve the efficiency of operations can often provoke this concern.

Personal factors

Individuals might resist change for personal reasons.

- They might resent the implied criticism that the present way of doing things is not good enough.

- They might also dislike the implied criticism that their performance has been inadequate.

- They might feel that the change will make them less valuable in the organisation.

- They might fear either that the change will make their work more monotonous and boring, or that the change will force them to work harder (which they do not want to do).

- They might resent having to learn new ways of doing things.

- They might simply dislike change and not knowing what the consequences of the change will be.

Social factors

Changes in the organisation structure and operating methods will affect:

- who the individual works with, and

- who he or she meets.

The work environment is a social environment in which individuals live together and react and respond to each other. Change will alter the nature of this society. Individuals might therefore:

- dislike the need to break up the present social environment at work

- dislike the new social environment that will be created

- fear that the new social situation will bring less satisfaction

- have a personal dislike of the individuals who are promoting and introducing the change

- resent the lack of consultation about the change and not being allowed to participate in the decisions leading to the change

- believe that the change will benefit the organisation at the expense of the individual, work group or society.

3.2 Sources of resistance

Another view of why individuals resist change and the possible response, was suggested by Schermerhorn.

Sources of resistance	*Possible response*
• Fear of the unknown	• Provide information and encouragement: invite involvement
• The need for security and the familiar	• Clarify the purpose of the change and how it will be made
• Having the opinion that no change is needed	• Demonstrate the problem or the opportunity that makes change desirable
• Trying to protect a vested interest in the existing system that the new system threatens	• Enlist key people in change planning
• Poor timing	• Wait for a better time
• A lack of resources to 'sell' and implement the change	• Provide the resources needed or reduce the performance expectations

Note: A **vested interest** exists when an individual benefits from the current system, and so will have a personal interest in opposing change. Individuals with vested interests might be individuals with expertise in the current system who are regarded as people with 'authority', trade union representatives who might benefit personally from leading resistance to change, individuals who earn bonuses or other benefits from the operation of the current system, and so on.

Activity 2

Changes in organisations can be seen as threatening. You will possibly know this from your own experience. Think about the possible effects of change and then list the reasons why people might fear or resist organisational change.

Feedback to this activity is at the end of the chapter.

4 Stages in the change process

4.1 Patterns of strategy development

Organisational strategy is a function of factors such as environmental opportunity, internal competence and resources, managerial interest and desires and social responsibility. Most planned organisational change is triggered by the need to respond to new challenges or opportunities presented by the external environment, or in anticipation of the need to cope with potential future problems. The strategy adopted should improve the ability of the organisation to cope with changes in its environment.

Mintzberg looked at the relationship between strategic decision-making and changes in the organisation, and whether changes in strategy could result in major changes to the organisation. His research discovered that:

- It is a mistake to think that strategy is developed through decisions to make a major strategic change: most strategies are developed within a consistent framework over a period of time.

- 'Revolutionary' change or 'transformational' change does happen occasionally, but typically strategic changes are small, incremental and piecemeal.

- There are periods when strategy remains unchanged, and periods of 'flux', when the organisation seems to have no clear sense of direction. The diagram below outlines the different patterns of strategic change.

- In some respects, organisations should seek to manage strategy in order to achieve incremental change. No organisation can function efficiently if it goes through frequent major strategic changes. Realistically, it is unlikely that the environment will change fast enough to make necessary frequent 'transformational' changes in the organisation and its strategy.

- Incremental change is adaptive change in a continually changing environment. It is beneficial for an organisation to adapt and change incrementally, because it builds on the skills, routines and cultures that it has built up over time.

- However, when the organisation changes very rapidly, incremental change is not possible if the organisation is to survive, and transformational change will then be necessary.

- Transformational change may come about either because the organisation is faced with major external events that demand large-scale changes or because the organisation anticipates such changes and therefore initiates action to make major shifts in its own strategy.

4.2 Strategic options

Whenever the organisation can identify differences between where it is and where it wants to be on any dimension, it can engage in a process of planned change or organisational improvement.

There are a number of strategic choices management can make in order that an organisation may achieve its stated objectives – firms pursuing virtually the same ends do not have to employ the same change strategies.

In 1980 Glueck classified the alternatives and identified the following usage frequencies:

- growth   54.4%

- stability   9.2%

- retrenchment (defensive)   7.5%

- combination of the other three   28.7%

Such strategies can be pursued internally using the company's existing resources and competencies or external means can be employed such as acquisition, merger or collaborating with other organisations.

4.3 Greiner's model of organisation growth

KEY POINT

Greiner suggested that, as organisations become more mature, and possibly get bigger, they go through a number of significant changes in order to sustain an acceptable level of performance.

There are several views about how organisations develop and change over time. In the 1970s, Greiner suggested that, as organisations become more mature, and possibly get bigger, they go through a number of significant changes in order to sustain an acceptable level of performance. There are five stages of organisation growth, and the change from one stage to the next is triggered by a crisis.

Phases of growth: evolution and revolution

Greiner identifies five phases of growth. Each evolutionary period is characterised by the dominant **management style** used to achieve growth, while each revolutionary period is characterised by the dominant **management problem** that must be solved before growth can continue.

Greiner's model can be shown as follows:

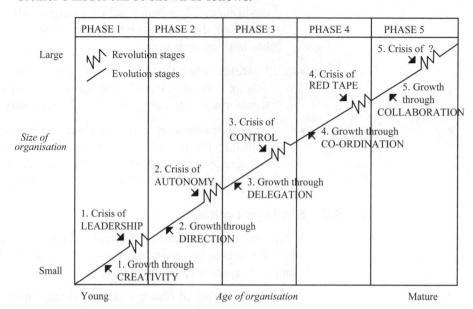

It is important to note that each phase is both an effect of the previous and a cause for the next phase. For example, the evolutionary management style in phase 3 (above) is 'delegation', which grows out of, and becomes the solution to demands for greater 'autonomy' in the preceding phase 2 - revolution. The style of delegation used in Phase 3, however, eventually provokes a major revolutionary crisis that is characterised by attempts to regain control over the diversity created through increased delegation.

The principal implication of each phase is that management actions are narrowly prescribed if growth is to occur. For example, a company experiencing an autonomy crisis in Phase 2 cannot return to directive management for a solution – it must adopt a new style of delegation in order to move ahead.

Five aspects of organisational growth

Greiner suggested that all organisations go through these phases and periods of crisis as they develop. However, several factors affect the nature and pace of change in organisations:

- Age of the organisation. The older an organisation is, the more difficult it is to change (due to the established culture and traditions).

- Size of the organisation. Larger and more complex organisations find it more difficult to change due to problems of communication and co-ordination when changes are attempted.

- Stages of evolution. Management are stable and focused on growth. Only incremental change is needed during periods of evolution.

- Stages of revolution – serious unrest in management due to major turbulence. Management are focused on solving the problems that are hindering growth. Transformational change is needed to get through crises (periods of 'revolution').

- Growth rate of industry – affects the pace of change, the organisation undertakes. Companies in high-growth industries are likely to go through the stages more quickly than companies in low-growth industries. As a result, they change more quickly.

If Greiner's model is valid, its implications for change management are that managers should be able to recognise the stage of development that their organisation has reached, and to prepare for the next crisis and the need for change to the next stage of development. The different approaches to management that might be required at each stage of the development process can be summarised as follows.

Phase	Phase 1	Phase 2	Phase 3	Phase 4	Phase 5
Growth through	Creativity	Direction	Delegation	Co-ordination	Collaboration
Management focus	Make and sell	Operational efficiency	Market expansion	Consolidation of organisation	Problem-solving, innovation
Organisation structure	Informal	Centralised and functional departments	Decentralised, geographical structure	Product groups. Advisory ('staff') management functions	Team structures
Top management style	Entrepreneurial	Directs	Delegates	Watchdog	Participates
Control system	Market results	Standards, cost centres	Reports, profit centres	Plans, investment centres	Mutual goal-setting
Management reward system	Reward owner	Salary. Merit increases	Individual bonus	Profit-sharing bonus, stock options	Team bonus

Note: Greiner's model focused on the stages of growth in organisations. It is worth remembering that organisations might grow to the point where they cease to be efficient or successful. In these circumstances, change might be triggered by divesting (selling off parts of the business) and demerging (splitting the business into two or more separate parts).

4.4 Development versus growth

Development involves policy decisions that will change objectives, while growth involves technical or administrative improvements, which will allow the organisation to achieve its objectives more effectively. Development is a broader concept, and can happen through innovation and/or acquisition, providing a framework for growth.

Growth occurs during a particular stage of the organisation's development; it is an evolutionary process. JR Hicks states:

'Growth asks: how does the organisation get more out of what it now has?

Development asks: how does the organisation achieve something different?'

Development usually changes the organisation fundamentally and can be 'revolutionary', which results in resistance to the changes.

Growth and development, while separate and distinct concepts, are also interrelated. Development creates the potential for new growth, and as growth reaches its limit, pressures often occur for development. New innovations or markets will lead to development, which if successful will create the opportunity for growth. This interaction is depicted below:

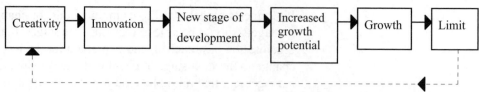

Relationship of creativity, development and growth (Hicks).

4.5 Growth by diversification

Johnson and Scholes stress that a company engaging in diversification considers: 'All directions of development away from its present products and its present market at the same time'.

They can be split into those related to the firm's core marketing system (**vertical integration***),* those related to the business of the firm (i.e. **concentric diversification)** and those unrelated to the firm and beyond the boundaries of its industry (i.e. **conglomerate diversification)**. Diversification strategies can be pursued internally or externally.

4.6 Mergers and acquisitions

Mergers and acquisitions are often made to achieve diversification but equally a company might seek to grow by taking over other companies or merging with other companies, to create a larger business. The failure rate for mergers and acquisitions shows that there are considerable risks and the operation should therefore be carefully planned.

There are various financial or economic reasons in favour of mergers and acquisitions, such as:

- achieving economies of scale within a larger organisation

- increased share of the market and influence over the market and its customers

- being in a better position to compete against rivals

- achieving a better bargaining power with suppliers

- putting up more effective barriers to the entry of new firms by acquisition in their own industry

- obtaining skills

- obtaining liquid resources (the acquiring company can defray the purchase price by the issue of additional equity capital, particularly where the price earnings ratio is high), etc.

A company might wish to be acquired because the owner wants to retire to obtain additional cash or to use the larger company's R&D facilities to assist its expansion or to provide more extensive career opportunities for the owner/directors, etc.

However, mergers and acquisitions are high-risk ventures, and often fail to achieve the benefits intended. The main reasons for the failure of mergers and acquisitions include:

- difficulties with integrating computer systems and other systems and procedures so as to achieve uniformity throughout the enlarged organisation

- difficulties in bringing together people from organisations with differing cultures and attitudes

- the problems of making some people redundant, and the problems this can create for morale and work relationships. Key individuals who are dissatisfied with the change might decide to leave the organisation. In service industries, in particular, the problems of 'asset walk' following a takeover – the loss of many key individuals – could be severe.

4.7 Reorganisation

Changes in the organisation's structure might involve creating new departments and divisions, greater delegation of authority or more centralisation, changes in the way plans are made, management information is provided and control is exercised.

Although reorganisation is intended to respond to changes in the organisational environment, there may be other compelling reasons. Those related to the enterprise environment include changes in operations caused by acquisition or sale of major properties, changes in product line or marketing methods, business cycles, competitive influences, new production techniques, changes in the number of people employed, government policy or the current state of knowledge or trends in organising.

The need for reorganisation may become apparent with the deficiencies in an existing structure. Some of these arise from organisational weaknesses, excessive spans of management, too many committees, slow decision-making, excessive costs or breakdown in financial control. Personality clashes between managers may be solved by reorganisation and staff-line conflicts may develop to such an extent that only reorganisation will resolve them. Other deficiencies may stem from management inadequacies or a lack of skill or knowledge on the part of a manager. These may have been avoided by moving the authority for decision-making to another position.

Some older companies provide ample evidence of inflexibility. Examples include an organisation pattern that is no longer suited to the times, a district or regional organisation that could be either abolished or enlarged because of improved communications, or a structure that is too highly centralised for an enlarged enterprise requiring decentralisation.

The need for reorganisation is outlined below:

Causes	Examples
Changes in the organisational environment	Greater competition may create pressure for cost cutting, leading to a reduction in employees
Diversification into new product/service market areas	As the organisation becomes more complex, there is a need for better lateral and vertical integration. There is also the problem of when or whether to switch from a functional to a divisional organisation structure
Growth	As more people are employed there are problems with extended hierarchies and poor communication
Technology	New developments can lead to fewer staff required in certain skills and shortages of staff in others
Changes in the capabilities of the staff	Changes in educational levels and the distribution of occupational skills, as well as the attitude towards work, can have an impact on the structure of the organisation

4.8 Downsizing and delayering

Downsizing is the scaling-back of the size of operations and closing uneconomic businesses in order to refocus the organisation to concentrate on core, profitable businesses.

- It should also involve rationalisation to reorganise operations in a way that makes them more logical, efficient and effective.

- It is likely to involve redundancy of significant numbers of employees.

Delayering is the removal of middle layers of the organisational hierarchy to develop a flatter structure.

- This will involve a reduction in the numbers of staff who are not directly involved in relating to customers.

- It should result in faster decision making and greater flexibility, making the organisation more responsive to customer needs.

5 Organisational development

5.1 Introduction

Organisational development (OD) is a response to change, a complex educational strategy intended to change the beliefs, attitudes, values and structure of organisations so that they can better adapt to new technologies, markets and challenges, and to the dizzying rate of change itself.

The essence of an OD programme is that it aims to improve enterprise effectiveness in all aspects of the company, i.e. it considers the company as an entity. It is seen as a continuous, all-embracing process that is focused on change.

5.2 Objectives of organisational development

OD is a contingency approach, designed to solve problems that decrease operating efficiency at all levels, using the diagnostic and problem-solving skills of an external consultant in collaboration with the organisation's management. Such problems may include lack of co-operation, excessive decentralisation and poor communication.

The objective of OD, and therefore of the consultant or change agent, are to:

- create an open, problem-solving environment in the organisation
- supplement the authority of role or status with that of the authority of knowledge and competence
- locate decision-making and problem-solving responsibilities as close to the sources of information as possible
- build trust among individuals and groups in the organisation
- maximise collaboration and make competition constructive
- develop reward systems that recognise the development of people as much as the achievement of organisational objectives
- increase acceptance of company objectives by active participation
- increase the degree of autonomy for individuals in the organisation.

5.3 OD process

Although various techniques are used, the process often includes the steps outlined below:

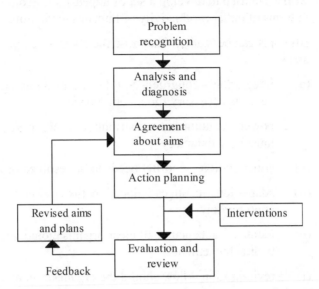

(a)   The preliminary stage is where the discussion of the aims and the implications of the programme takes place. The role of the third party is also sorted at this stage.

(b)   The analysis and diagnosis stage includes obtaining and analysing data to identify and clarify problems.

(c)   After analysing the data, management and the third party agree on aims and objectives of the programme.

(d)   The action planning involves planning the sequence of activities designed to improve the organisation, in the light of the problems diagnosed.

(e)   As with any planning activity, the progress needs evaluating and reviewing.

(f)   Resulting from the review, new plans may be required.

The interventions in the process may include a change in the organisation structure, a more effective procedure for handling customer complaints and/or the establishment of a team charged with the responsibility of implementing a cost reduction programme.

OD must be considered as a continuous process – planned, systematic and focused on change. The aim is to make the organisation more effective.

5.4 Diagnosis

The consultant will explore the possibility of embarking on a programme of OD and will investigate the people, products, processes and environment of the client, looking at the systems and sub-systems in use for answers to the following questions:

•   Are the learning goals of organisation development appropriate?

•   Are the client's set of values such as to be conducive to a system of OD?

•   Are the key people involved?

•   Are individuals in the client system ready for OD?

•   What are the main problems confronting the organisation?

With regard to the last question, OD practitioners claim that goals vary in clarity and kind and that they are always in the process of changing. W Bennis stated that, when he felt certain that he knew what the problem was, he began to worry. He tried to develop a set of hoped-for outcomes, which were measurable in terms of either productivity or human satisfaction.

Attempts can be made to diagnose the client's key problems under six basic areas:

(a)   integration – congruence of the organisation's goals and the individual's needs is necessary (goal congruence)

(b)   power and authority – distribution of the sources of power and authority must be satisfactory

(c)   collaboration – conflict needs to be resolved or managed

(d)   adaptation – changes induced by the environment must be responded to appropriately

(e)   identity – acceptance of clear organisational goals and commitment to their achievement

(f)   revitalisation – how should the organisation react to growth and decay?

There may be a need for one or more of the following:

- changing the organisation's culture (from a family concern to a professionally managed company for instance)

- changing managerial strategy

- changing the way work is done

- adapting to changes in the environment

- changing communications and developing trust between staff and line groups.

5.5   Education of managers

Management of change has become one of the most important parts of managers' jobs, and much more emphasis needs to be placed on the type of education needed to enable managers to cope with change. The qualities that are necessary, either within the company or externally, include:

- interpersonal competence – skill in communication, ability to manage conflict, and self-awareness can be improved by laboratory training activities, grid and sensitivity training

- training in problem-solving and decision-making

- goal-setting skills

- planning skills

- better understanding of the processes of change

- skills in systems diagnosis.

It is true that there is not much evidence that education or training will, in itself, influence attitudes; these might be improved in the process of the individual undergoing training, but their ability to apply a changed attitude to real-life situations may be limited. An awareness of problems is, however, a first step to accomplishing desirable changes in attitude.

5.6 Evaluation

The final phase of OD is the evaluation of the effects of a change programme on the organisation as a whole; this is a continuous process that does not stop once the consultant, or change agent, has left the client's premises. This evaluation may take the form of attitude surveys, survey-feedback projects, research projects by behavioural scientists, and internal employee-relations research groups.

A serious problem is the evaluation of an individual's contribution to the organisation. The evaluation of progress is often highly subjective; some, such as Blake and Mouton, use productivity figures, whilst others use a variety of other indicators, for example, satisfaction, communication patterns, morale, etc. Bennis endeavoured to determine whether the organisation was, after his assignment, able to maintain and continue its own organisation development programme. Initially, he saw his role as that of a catalyst, a necessary ingredient in the process of change in the early stages of OD. With guidance, the client should become less and less dependent upon the change agent, and more capable of self-support.

Summary

- Organisations are continually changing. Some changes are proactive, others are reactive in response to external events or developments.

- Changes within one part of an organisation can have a cascading effect, and lead to the need for change in other parts of the organisation. It can be helpful to take a general systems theory approach to understanding and analysing change in organisations.

- Change may be incremental (adaptive or evolutionary) or transformational (sudden and major changes). These different types of change need differing approaches to change management.

- Changes are initiated by external or internal triggers. External triggers might be categorised into political and regulatory change, economic change, social and cultural change and technological change. Internal triggers for change include changes in management, changes in strategy, mergers and acquisitions, rationalisation (downsizing) and reorganisation. These internal triggers usually result in transformational change, but other internal triggers can lead to incremental change.

- Mergers and acquisitions create difficulties for change management, due to problems with integrating the systems of the merged companies, the clash of cultures in the different organisations and problems caused by redundancies and reorganisation.

- Resistance to change by individuals can be due to a combination of job factors, personal factors and social factors.

- An organisation develops over time. Greiner suggested a five-stage model for organisation development, with change from one stage to the next caused by a crisis. There is evolutionary change during each stage, but revolutionary change at each crisis point.

- It is important to manage critical periods of change through the stages of development of the organisation.

Having completed your study of this chapter, you should have achieved the following learning outcomes:

- explain the process of organisational development

- discuss how and why resistance to change develops within organisations.

Self-test questions

1 What is the difference between incremental change and transformational change? (1.2)

2 List four job factors, four personal factors and four social factors that can create resistance to change. (3.1)

3 What is a vested interest opposing change? (3.2)

4 What are Mintzberg's views on incremental and transformational change resulting from a change in strategy? (4.1)

5 What are the five stages of organisation growth in Greiner's model? (4.3)

6 What problems for change management are characteristic of a takeover or merger? (4.6)

Practice questions

Question 1

Greiner identifies five phases of growth. Each evolutionary period is characterised by the dominant management style used to achieve growth, while each revolutionary period is characterised by the dominant management problem that must be solved before growth can continue. At which point on the graph is the crisis of control?

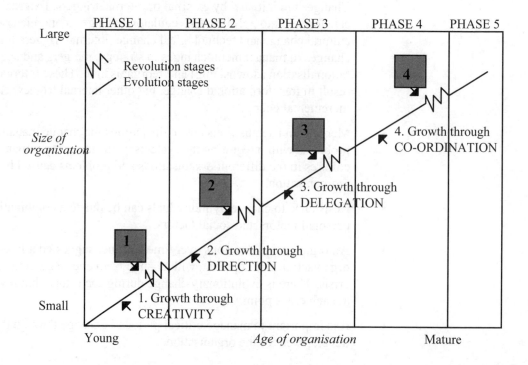

Question 2

According to Greiner's model, which type of crisis triggers change from the growth through delegation phase of evolution?

A   Crisis of red tape

B   Crisis of control

C   Crisis of leadership

D   Crisis of autonomy

Question 3

Explain, in no more than 20 words, the approach recommended by Lewin to getting change successfully introduced, when restraining forces are stronger than driving forces for change.

Question 4

Managing change

Required:

Explain **five** strategies for managing change, giving the advantages and disadvantages of **each.**

(20 marks)

Question 5

(a)   Describe the stages of an organisation's life cycle, according to Greiner's model. How useful do you think such models are?

(12 marks)

(b)   What changes do you think will occur in the role of the management accountant in each phase of the life cycle?   **(8 marks)**

(Total: 20 marks)

For the answers to these questions, see the 'Answers' section at the end of the book.

Feedback to activities

Activity 1

There is no feedback to this activity.

Activity 2

People tend to resist change because they fear one or more from the following list:

- A loss of job security.
- A loss of status.
- The loss of work they enjoy.
- Possibility of having to work for a different manager.
- A break up of working relationships.
- Having to work in a different location (moving home, etc).
- Having to work at a different time (shift work, etc).
- An inability to cope with new duties/responsibilities.
- Inconvenience of the change (training, etc).
- The closing of potential promotion (career implications).
- Economic aspects (loss of overtime, etc).

Chapter 6

MANAGING CHANGE

Syllabus content

- Approaches to change management (e.g. Beer and Nohria, Kanter, Lewin and Peters, Senge et al.).

Contents

1   Models of change

2   Approaches to managing change

3   Change-adept organisations

1   Models of change

1.1   Leavitt's model of change management

Leavitt argued that approaches to change that succeeded in one organisation were not necessarily successful in another. He suggests that the chosen approach to change in a particular organisation should reflect the underlying beliefs within that organisation.

Whilst change can never be fully planned due to unexpected problems and follow on effects, many organisations are adopting a positive attitude to the need for change. Leavitt recognised four variables, which can be affected by change and claimed that these 'entry points' can become specific targets for managerial efforts to instigate change. The variables are:

- task

- structure

- technology

- people.

Each of these can give rise to different approaches to change.

(a)   **Task approach** – Seeking improved solutions to tasks will be largely technical, that is, seeking to improve the quality of decisions. The task approach, even where it involves clear changes of methods, is clearly interrelated to the other three approaches.

(b)   **Structure approach** – This approach covers:

(i)   the traditional performance approaches of ensuring proper division of labour, levels of authority and responsibility, defining chain of command, span of control, etc

(ii)   decentralisation – the creation of project centres and localising of decision-making creating a high level of local autonomy

(iii)   communication patterns – the consideration of communication channels and flows; thus for repetitious, predictable work a highly centralised communication structure seems most efficient – whereas for novel, loosely structured tasks, a more open multi-channel communication network seems more appropriate.

(c)   **Technological approach** – Taylor's Scientific Management is an early example of this approach category, which includes method study approaches where an outsider views the work pattern and suggests changes in a technological approach. Updating and replacement of equipment is a natural example of an external approach. The essence is that the approach occurs outside of the work group itself.

(d)   **People approach** – Group working, attitude training, changes in styles of management are examples of the people approach.

Each change can therefore be approached by one of these main four methods but it must be remembered that there is strong interaction between these categories. For example, a change in **technology** (introduction of a computer) will influence **tasks** (output may be quicker or greater) and a change in structure could mean fewer staff needed. A change in any category is likely to have an effect upon the people approach.

The interdependence of these four variables can be illustrated as follows:

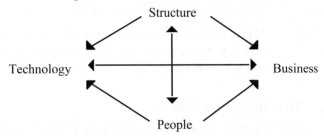

As a result of these interdependencies changes in one variable could lead to unanticipated, and possibly undesirable, changes to other variables. Moreover, it is possible to deliberately change one variable to bring about a desired change in another variable – the increasing adoption of mass production technologies has led to the spread of capitalist structures.

Leavitt points to the fact that, if there is too much rigidity in an organisation, it does not allow creative ideas to be introduced. Some methods used to overcome this are:

(a) **diversification** – enterprises with too narrow a product base may buy interests in other industries

(b) **decentralisation** – the parent company has overall control but units are given authority to make major decisions and the unit managers are held accountable to the parent company

(c) **venture groups** – a group is given the resources to develop a new idea, which may have come from a group member.

1.2 How organisations can create readiness for change

The senior management group has responsibility for establishing the organisation's vision and objectives and for making sure that the whole organisation pursues the same vision.

The managers are then responsible for creating the conditions that will promote change and innovation. To manage the change process successfully, the culture of the organisation will need to be permissive and flexible. Bureaucracies are very slow to change because they do not have this culture.

Managers need to encourage individuals to use their initiative and must put the emphasis on teamwork. An autocratic management style is not conducive to change because the manager should act as a facilitator of change rather than just telling people what to do.

Ronald Corwin, in his book *Strategies for Organisational Intervention*, argues that an organisation can be changed more easily:

- If it is invaded by creative and unconventional outsiders with fresh ideas.

- If those outsiders are exposed to creative, competent and flexible socialisation agents.

- If it is staffed by young, flexible, supportive and competent boundary personnel.

- If it is structurally complex and decentralised.

- If it has outside funds to lessen the cost of innovation.

- If its members have positions that are sufficiently secure and protected from status risks involved in change.

- If it is located in a changing, modern urbanised setting where it is in close co-operation with a coalition of other organisations that can supplement its skills and resources.

1.3 The role of the leader

There must be a leader of the change process who accepts the responsibility. Such a leader must have certain skills and attributes, such as:

- inspiration

- interpersonal skills

- the ability to resolve a multitude of interdependent problems

- the ability to plan

- opportunistic abilities

- the gift of good timing.

To maximise the advantages and minimise the disadvantage of the change process, the role of the leader should be to:

- Give all staff concerned the maximum possible warning of impeding change to give them time to get accustomed to the idea.

- Explain as far as possible the reasons for change as the provision of both adequate and accurate information scotches rumours before they can be circulated.

- Involve individuals and/or work groups in the planning and implementing of change as much as possible. Employees will be more likely to become committed to change if they feel they can have some influence on the change and its outcome. It is also a way of gaining valuable suggestions.

- Keep lines of communication going, monitor progress, give regular feedback and communicate results.

- Try to introduce changes gradually; phased change stands a better chance of success.

- Offer and provide appropriate training.

- Ensure the workforce are aware of the benefits to them of the change e.g. increased responsibility, job enrichment.

- Consider the effects of change on individuals, giving counselling where necessary.

- Follow up regularly and be supportive.

- Develop a favourable climate for any subsequent changes envisaged.

2 Approaches to managing change

2.1 The six change approaches (Kotter and Schlesinger)

The six change approaches is a model to prevent, decrease or minimise resistance to change in organisations. According to Kotter and Schlesinger (1979) there are four reasons that explain why certain people resist change:

(a) **Parochial self-interest** (some people are concerned with the implication of the change for themselves and how it may affect their own interests, rather than considering the effects for the success of the business).

(b) **Misunderstanding** (communication problems; inadequate information).

(c) **Low tolerance to change** (certain people are very keen on security and stability in their work).

(d) **Different assessments of the situation** (some employees may disagree on the reasons for the change and on the advantages and disadvantages of the change process.

Leaders can overcome resistance to change using different approaches like education, communication, participation, involvement, facilitation and support, negotiation, agreement, manipulation, co-optation and explicit and implicit coercion. Kotter and Schlesinger set out the following change approaches to deal with this resistance:

(a) **Participation** – this approach aims to involve employees, usually by allowing some input into decision-making. This could easily result in employees enjoying raised levels of autonomy, by allowing them to design their own jobs, pay structures, etc.

Employees are more likely to support changes made and give positive commitment as they 'own' the change. Another advantage of participation is the improved utilisation of employee expertise.

The possible disadvantages include:

- The time element – the process can be lengthy due to the number of people involved in the decision-making process.

- The loyalty element – there is a need for a strong trusting relationship to exist between management and workforce.

- The resistance element – management may suffer from restricted movement as the amount and direction of change acceptable to employees will have some influence.

(b) **Education and communication** – usually used as a background factor to reinforce another approach. This strategy relies upon the hopeful belief that communication about the benefits of change to employees will result in their acceptance of the need to exercise the changes necessary. The obvious advantage is that any changes could be initiated easily. However, employees may not agree about the benefits of proposed changes as being in their best interests. Also, the process of education and persuasion can be lengthy to initiate and exercise unless there is a firm mutual trust. Without this they are not likely to succeed.

(c)   **Power/coercion** – this strategy involves the compulsory approach by management to implement change. This method finds its roots from the formal authority that management possesses, together with legislative support. Management can fire, transfer or demote individuals. They can also stifle their promotion or career prospects. When there is a state of high unemployment, management enjoys greater power and is therefore able to use this strategy with more success. The advantages of this method are that changes can be made with speed and adhering to management's requirements is easy when opposition is weak from the work force. The disadvantages include the lack of commitment of the workforce and determination to reverse policy when times change and also poor support resulting in weak motivation, low morale and performance. Future implications also need to be considered. For example, when employees enjoy a stronger position, i.e. union representation, they are less likely to co-operate due to their experiences of past management treatment.

(d)   **Facilitation and support** – employees may need to be counselled to help them overcome their fears and anxieties about change. Management may find it necessary to develop individual awareness of the need for change.

(e)   **Manipulation and co-optation** – involves covert attempts to sidestep potential resistance. Management can put forward proposals that deliberately appeal to the specific interest, sensitivities and emotions of key groups involved in the change. The information that is disseminated is selective and distorted to only emphasise the benefits of the change. Co-optation involves giving key people access to the decision-making process.

(f)   **Negotiation** – this particular strategy is often practised in unionised companies. Simply, the process of negotiation is exercised, enabling several parties with opposing interests to bargain. This bargaining leads to a situation of compromise and agreement. Branching from this are two strategies:

        (i)   Each party involved seeks to negotiate for itself, at the cost of the other parties involved.

        (ii)   Each party aims to find an agreement with aspects advantageous to all concerned.

    The advantage of negotiation strategy is that it offers the company the opportunity to note possible conflict and allows it to be dealt with in an orderly fashion. This hopefully prevents such problems as industrial action. Also, when an agreement has been made, the outcome can be to encourage commitment, preserve morale and maintain output. The main disadvantage is that this approach may be time consuming and, should opposition be strong enough, the management might choose to adopt a power strategy instead.

    Where strategic change is sought, it is also suggested that different styles might be more effective in some circumstances, for example:

        (i)   Participation, education and communication are likely to be best suited to incremental modes of change or to situations of transformational change in which time horizons are long.

        (ii)   Coercion and power are likely to be effective only if there is a crisis or need for rapid transformational change, unless change is taking place in an established autocratic culture.

2.2 Force field analysis (Lewin)

Kurt Lewin, a social psychologist, developed force field theory to explain and analyse how interactions between human beings are driven by both the people involved and their environment. He used 'force field analysis' and 'force field diagrams' to visualise the 'tug-of-war' between opposing forces around a given issue. He was particularly interested in the forces that came into conflict around planned changes.

A force field diagram sets out, for a planned change:

- the driving forces that support the change and act towards making the change

- the restraining forces that are against the change and resist it.

The forces can include:

- habits (present and past practices)

- the persons involved, and their needs

- customs and traditions

- attitudes

- relationships

- vested interests

- organisational structures

- institutional policies

- vested interests in the existing system

- available resources to push through the change

- regulations

- events.

Each of these can be either a driving force or a restraining force. Each of the forces is given a measured strength, possibly shown as numerical values (say, from 1 to 5) or as arrowed lines with different lengths or thicknesses to indicate relative strength. Lewin argued that:

- change will not occur when the forces resisting the change are equal to or stronger than the driving forces, and

- changes are only possible when the driving forces are stronger than the restraining forces.

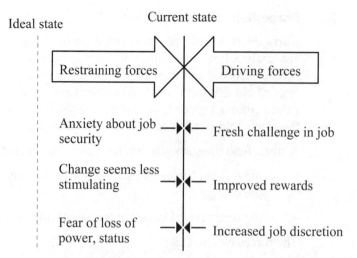

Restraining and driving forces in a change situation

Lewin advocates that managers should recognise that there exists a current state of equilibrium with forces pushing for change on the one hand and, equally, forces resisting change aiming to maintain the present situation.

Change can be brought about by either increasing the driving forces or by reducing the restraining forces. The tendency is to increase the pressure of the driving forces. Lewin contends that this is often counter-productive, because it causes increased pressure from the restraining forces. It is better practice to analyse the restraining forces with a view to reducing or eliminating their pressures. This can then move more smoothly to the new state of equilibrium.

Involvement in understanding the need for the change and also in the framing of the changes will achieve this reduction of restraining forces. The change process consists of:

(a)   identifying the restraining forces and overcoming/removing/getting round them

(b)   carrying out the change

(c)   stabilising the new situation by reinforcing the (now changed) behaviour of individuals and work groups with praise and encouragement.

Using a common individual and organisational problem, that of lack of time, the use of force field analysis can be illustrated. To work on the problem effectively the situation must be stated in terms of current and desired conditions, where we are and where we want to be. The current condition = no time spent on planned change and the desired condition = large blocks of time to critically appraise the organisation.

In order to understand the situation, the forces that are keeping us in equilibrium must be identified, i.e. no change from the current condition.

Driving forces

- Knowledge of theory that says it would be 'better'.

- Feeling that it would be 'better'.

- Success stories about increased productivity from current literature.

- Success stories from acquaintances in similar organisations.

- Consultants selling the virtues of a new approach.

Restraining forces

- Programmed activity increases to absorb available time.

- Current deadlines leave no time to analyse the problem of lack of time.

- We seem to be doing satisfactory work, there is no sense of urgency.

- Reluctance of participants to rock the boat by analysing group processes.

- Assumption that time is not currently wasted.

This list is not exhaustive but it leads to the next step, which is to pick one or more of the forces, starting with restraining forces and generating ideas for increasing them or decreasing them.

After alternatives have been evaluated, action plans can be designed and implemented.

Lewin went on to argue that force field analysis can be used to manage change by:

- investigating the balance of power around the planned change and the most important driving and restraining forces. Can the change get enough needed support, or are the restraining forces at least as strong as the driving forces?

- identifying the obstacles to introducing the change. Who are the most important opponents and allies? Considering actions to reduce the resistance. How can each of the major opposing forces be removed or reduced in strength?

Activity 1

A manager is in charge of a team that has been given the task of introducing a new management reporting system into regional offices. There is considerable resistance to the changes from the office managers, and comments that you have heard include the following:

- I have more important work priorities to take up my time.

- I'm used to the old system.

- The new system is too complicated.

- The new system will create more paperwork.

- The new system will make me more accountable.

- My job in the new system is not clear.

How would you try to deal with this resistance to change?

Feedback to this activity is at the end of the chapter.

Activity 2

All change is a threat since it involves moving into the unknown. How can managers introduce change and minimise staff's anxieties?

Feedback to this activity is at the end of the chapter.

2.3 Unfreezing and re-freezing (Lewin)

Kurt Lewin also put forward ideas about how planned change should be
introduced in an organisation. His views are sometimes called 'prescriptive
planned change theory'. A planned change process should begin with an
analysis and diagnosis of the current situation, in order to:

• identify the source of the problems, or

• identify the opportunities for improvement.

For large organisations, this often requires a major re-think of strategy, or a
re-definition of what the organisation does.

The change process should then go through three stages:

• unfreeze

• movement (change)

• re-freeze.

Planned change process

Lewin developed a programme of planned change and improved
performance, involving the management of a three-phase process of
behaviour modification. He demonstrated the effectiveness of using group
norms and consensus decision-making to change individual and
organisational behaviour. His views are sometimes called 'prescriptive
planned change theory'. A planned change process should begin with an
analysis and diagnosis of the current situation, in order to:

• identify the source of the problems, or

• identify the opportunities for improvement.

For large organisations, this often requires a major re-think of strategy, or a
re-definition of what the organisation does.

The process of change, shown in the diagram below, includes unfreezing
habits or standard operating procedures, changing to new patterns and
refreezing to ensure lasting effects.

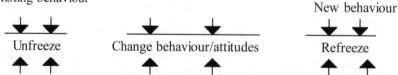

Existing behaviour

Unfreeze   Change behaviour/attitudes   Refreeze   New behaviour

Unfreezing implies that a change will mean abandoning existing practice
before new practices can be successfully adopted. If individuals are to
change, their current behaviour patterns must be unfrozen as a way of
reducing resistance to change. Unfreezing will lead to doubts and to fear of
the unknown. It will create the initial motivation to change by convincing
staff of the undesirability of the present situation. This is an opportunity for
managers to introduce education and training. However, in some cases an
ethical question may arise regarding the legitimacy of deliberately creating
discomfort that may initiate change.

Communication is an essential part of the unfreezing process. Managers must
communicate the plan for change, so that everyone affected by it understands it
and accepts it. Change might have to be explained to a variety of stakeholder
groups, in addition to employees; for example, shareholders, lenders, customers
or suppliers might be affected, and the process of unfreezing their attitudes
could be a necessary requirement for successful change.

KEY POINT

After unfreezing comes
the process of making
the change, and the
movement from the
current position to the
planned new position.

Movement (change) – after unfreezing comes the process of making the change, and the movement from the current position to the planned new position. The management of this process involves winning the support of the people affected in carrying through the changes.

- The change manager should try to create participation by others in the change process. Participation reduces resistance to a change, and helps the individuals affected to take ownership of the change and become motivated to make it work successfully. Participation also improves communication of the reasons for the change, what the planned changes are, and what the changes are intended to achieve.

- For a change to be successful, there has to be enough support to make the change happen. When certain groups resist the change, such as some employees and some customers, they will have to be persuaded to alter their opinion and start to see the change as a good thing. Some groups resistant to change, such as major suppliers, might be involved in the planning process for the change. Employees, represented by their trade union representatives, might be persuaded to agree to changes through an offer of improvements in pay or working conditions.

The managers responsible for making the changes should be given enough resources to do the job properly, in the form of money, personnel, training and (where required) support from management consultants.

Re-freeze – Lewin argued that even if the change is implemented successfully, the success could be short-lived because the employees might go back to their former behaviour and methods.

KEY POINT

The re-freeze process is
needed in order to
stabilise the change and
reinforce the new
pattern of working or
behaviour.

The re-freeze process is needed in order to stabilise the change and reinforce the new pattern of working or behaviour. An important way of making the change 'stick' is through the use of rewards. Motivation theory suggests that, if individuals have a strong need for reward, and if they see that they will probably achieve those rewards by acting in a certain way, a reward system can be important for making a change happen and remain in place. However, the organisation should ensure that the reward system (which could be tangible rewards such as more pay or intangible rewards such as greater job satisfaction) is effective, and that rewards are given for the desired behaviour and results.

Reporting systems are needed for monitoring performance and trying to ensure that the planned changes and targets are achieved. The control system might use benchmarks for comparing performance and standards of performance and specifying the responsibilities of key managers and work groups.

Performance should be monitored through feedback mechanisms. Both informal as well as formal feedback channels should be used.

Example: unfreeze, move, re-freeze

An example of the application of Lewin's model for change is the process that occurred at British Airways when it was privatised many years ago, and changed from being a bureaucratic public sector organisation to becoming a commercial organisation which had to be service-oriented, with a market-driven culture.

The planned change was to downsize the organisation from 59,000 to 37,000 employees, flatten the management hierarchy structure and introduce a variety of changes to operational systems and structures. The three stages that occurred were, briefly, as follows.

Unfreezing: getting acceptance of the need to change

- Introduce a new chief executive officer with a strong marketing background.

- Set up 'diagonal' task forces to work on different aspects of the changes. (A diagonal task force is a team consisting of members from different functional areas or departments, who are at different levels in the management hierarchy.)

- Large-scale training programmes for staff, with emphasis on training in customer services and direct contact with customers.

Movement

- Training programmes for senior and middle management.

- Chief executive's personal commitment to the change.

- Greater participation, through question-and-answer sessions.

Re-freezing: stabilising and maintaining the change

- Promotion of those who supported the change.

- New performance-related pay and appraisal systems.

- New logo and company uniforms.

Activity 3

UK listed companies were required to switch from using UK accounting standards to using international accounting standards from 1 January 2005. A survey by the Institute of Chartered Accountants in England and Wales, reported in July 2004, found that of 92 listed companies in the survey, only 17 had drawn up communication plans for informing investors and analysts about the change. The ICAEW view was that it was extremely important for listed companies to explain the likely changes to the financial markets.

Why do you think communication was necessary, and what form might it have taken?

Feedback to this activity is at the end of the chapter.

2.4 Theory E and Theory O (Beer and Nohria)

Beer and Nohria studied transformational changes in organisations, such as downsizing, restructuring and attempts to change the corporate culture, and suggested reasons why so many of these changes had a low rate of success. In their opinion, when management introduce major changes, they apply a range of different concepts and change management techniques, and get stuck in an 'alphabet soup of initiatives'. As a consequence, they lose focus on what they are trying to achieve.

According to Beer and Nohria, although business changes are unique in each organisation, all changes are based on one of two different approaches and unconscious assumptions of senior executives. They called these two approaches Theory E and Theory O.

- **Theory E** is an approach to change based on economic value. It is a 'hard' approach to change, in which shareholder value is the only legitimate concern. Change is therefore directed at improving shareholder value through measures such as economic incentives, large redundancy programmes downsizing and restructuring the organisation.

- **Theory O** is based on organisational capability and is a 'soft' approach to change. The assumption is that focussing on economic value can damage the organisation, and it is more appropriate to develop the corporate culture and the 'human' capability of its employees, through organisational and individual learning. Change is a process whereby feedback is obtained about each change that is made, the results are considered carefully and further changes are made. With the Theory O model, the company has a strong psychological contract with its employees.

The differences between Theory E and Theory O are summarised in the following table.

	Theory E	*Theory O*
Goals	Maximise shareholder value	Develop the organisation's capabilities
Leadership	Manage from the top down	Encourage participation from the bottom up
Focus	'Hard'. Structure and systems	'Soft'. Corporate culture. Employee behaviour and attitudes
Process	Plan and establish change programmes	Experiment and evolve. Learn from mistakes
Reward systems	Reward through financial incentives	Motivate through commitment. Use pay as a fair exchange, not a motivator
Use of consultants	Consultants analyse problems and develop solutions	Consultants support management and help managers to devise their own solutions

Beer and Nohria suggested the reasons why many organisations fail to introduce changes successfully.

- If a company adopts Theory E only, they lose the commitment and creativity of employees. However, this commitment and creativity are needed for achieving a sustained competitive advantage in the company's markets.

- If a company adopts Theory O only, it never has the impetus or drive to take hard economic decisions.

- A company might apply Theory E first and then switch to Theory O. For example, they might make redundant large numbers of employees (Theory E), but then reduce the management hierarchy and improve communications (Theory O). However, senior management often find it difficult to change from Theory E to Theory O, and the process also takes a long time. This approach is therefore likely to fail.

- A company might apply Theory O first and then switch to Theory E. This too is likely to fail. When management make the switch to Theory E, many employees will feel a sense of betrayal.

The solution, as recommended by Beer and Nohria, is to attempt a blend of Theory E and Theory O at the same time. The features of this blended approach are as follows.

	Theory E combined with Theory O
Goals	Embrace the paradox between economic value and organisational capability. Be open and explicit about the existence of this paradox and how it is being managed.
Leadership	Set directions from the top, and engage people from below.
Focus	Focus on both the hard and the soft.
Process	Plan for spontaneity.
Reward systems	Use incentives to reinforce change, not to drive change forward. Reward employees for meeting performance goals, not just financial goals.
Use of consultants	Consultants are expert resources who 'empower' employees.

2.5 The learning organisation (Senge)

Senge developed ideas about 'learning organisations', which he described as 'organisations where people continually expand their capacity to create the results they truly desire, where new and expansive patterns of thinking are nurtured, where collective aspiration is set free and where people are continually learning to see the whole together'.

In situations where change is happening rapidly, only those organisations that are flexible, adaptive and productive will excel. For this to happen, organisations need to 'discover how to tap people's commitment and capacity to learn at *all* levels'.

Senge argued that all individuals have the capacity to learn, but the situation in which they work does not always make learning possible. Individuals also lack the tools and the guiding ideas to make sense of the situations which they face.

In a learning organisation, there must be two types of learning.

- **Adaptive learning**. This is learning how to adapt to changes in order for the organisation to survive. However, adaptive learning on its own is insufficient.

- **Generative learning**. This is learning that enhances the capacity of individuals and the organisation to create (be innovative).

Mastery of five disciplines

Senge argued that learning organisations are different from other organisations because they have mastered five disciplines or 'component technologies':

1　Systems thinking

General Systems Theory, and its application to organisations, gives individuals the ability to look at the whole and examine the relationship between the different parts (sub-systems). A systems approach to organisation is generally oriented toward the long-term view. In many organisations, however, management thinking usually focuses on short-term 'solutions', in the mistaken belief that taking action to produce an improvement will have an effect within a fairly short time.

However, this is not the case. Short-term solutions can have long-term costs. The problem is made even greater because the feedback of information about the effects of a short-term solution can be reinforcing, encouraging management to do more of the same. 'Whatever movement occurs is amplified, producing more movement in the same direction. A small action snowballs, with more and more and still more of the same, resembling compound interest.'

An example of failure to take the systems view by concentrating on a short-term solution is a company that is faced with difficulties in its markets, which are very competitive, as a result of which forecast profits are expected to be lower than planned. A short-term solution would be to cut marketing spending. In the short-term, this might appear successful because the cutback in spending will have a direct impact on profit. This might encourage management to do more of the same, and cut back marketing spending still further. The short-term boost to profit, however, would be at the expense of the longer term. Reducing spending on marketing will eventually have an adverse effect on sales volume.

Senge would argue that learning organisations do not make this sort of mistake.

2　Personal mastery

Organisations learn only through the individuals they employ, who do the actual learning.

- Individual learning is not a guarantee that the organisation will be a learning organisation.

- However, without individual learning, an organisation cannot be a learning organisation.

Senge described personal mastery as a discipline of 'continually clarifying and deepening our personal vision, of focussing our energies, of developing patience and of seeing reality objectively'.

'People with a high level of personal mastery live in a continual learning mode. They never 'arrive'…. Personal mastery is not something you possess. It is a lifelong discipline. People with a high level of personal mastery are acutely aware of their ignorance, their incompetence, their growth areas. And they are deeply self-confident. Paradox? Only for those who do not see "the journey is the reward".'

3 Mental models

Mental models are deeply ingrained assumptions and generalisations, or even pictures and images, that influence the way in which we understand the world and take action. For Senge, the discipline of mental models involves looking at our own mental models and holding them up for scrutiny by others. The aim of a learning individual is to avoid having narrow and restricted views. People should expose their own thinking and should make it open to influence by others.

4 Building shared vision

Senge was critical of the 'vision statements' put out by many organisations, which he believed pay lip service to an idea but do not really mean it. He argued that when there is a genuine vision, people will excel and learn, not because they are told to but because they want to. However, he was critical of leaders who believe they can impose their personal vision on to others. No matter how heart-felt and strong a leader's convictions, these will not be accepted unquestioningly by others. The vision has to be shared by everyone, and this means building it collectively. For a leader, the practice of building a shared vision involves 'the skills of unearthing shared "pictures of the future" that foster genuine commitment … rather than compliance'.

5 Team learning

Teams should learn together. When teams learn together, the individuals in the team are able to learn more rapidly. 'The discipline of team learning starts with 'dialogue', the capacity of team members to suspend assumptions and enter into genuine 'thinking together'. To the Greeks, *dia-logos* meant a free-flowing of meaning through a group, allowing the group to discover insights not attainable individually.'

2.6 Thriving on chaos (Peters)

Tom Peters has written extensively on management theory. One of his ideas relates to 'excellent' companies that have succeeded by seeking to create a climate of continual and radical change. Peters called this 'thriving on chaos'. He suggested that:

- Incremental change is the enemy of true innovation, because it makes an organisation less willing to be truly innovative.

- Excellent firms don't believe in excellence, only in constant improvement and constant change.

- A constantly changing environment does not necessarily mean chaos: instead, it may mean that companies can handle the introduction of change successfully.

- Peters suggested that the advantages of having a climate of change are as follows:

- Innovation and the introduction of new products and new methods are actively sought and welcomed.

- People who are used to change tend to accept it without resistance.

- Employees develop an external viewpoint, and are less insular and defensive in their outlook.

However, there are possible disadvantages – with a climate of change morale might be damaged, and staff might become involved in office politics because of their concerns about the possible changes that might occur in the organisation.

Peters suggested that there are five areas of management that are important for success in a chaotic business world.

- An obsession with responsiveness to customers. This is expressed by developing customised products or services that create a new 'niche' in the market, and that add more value, through changes to features, quality and service. New products that add value achieve or maintain true competitive differentiation for the organisation in its markets, on which success is based.

- Constant innovations in all areas of the firm. Innovation should apply to all activities within the organisation, and to all products from their development to maturity phases of their life cycle.

- Involve everyone in everything. There should be wholesale participation by employees in the organisation in the change processes, and a sharing of the gains. There are no limits to what the average person can accomplish, if well-trained, well-supported and well-paid for performance.

- Leadership that loves change (instead of fighting it) and instils and shares an inspiring vision. The leaders develop a clear and exciting vision, through listening, assessing the external situation and obtaining all points of view. This vision nevertheless leaves plenty of scope for the pursuit of innovation and new opportunities.

- Control by means of simple support systems. The focus is on flexibility rather than rigidity. The process of developing objectives is truly 'bottom up'.

2.7 Key issues for success in takeovers (Drucker)

A takeover or acquisition can be a source of transformational change. **Peter Drucker** suggests five key issues for success in takeovers:

- The purchaser must be convinced that value can be added to the target.

- There must be a common core of unity between the two businesses.

- Management must understand the business being acquired.

- The purchaser must be able to put in a quality management team quickly.

- The purchaser must be able to hold on to the best management of both companies.

The first three of these are essentially strategic selection tools. The last two relate to how the change process is managed.

Activity 4

Many Japanese companies have long recognised the benefits of institutionalised learning based around quality improvement teams and associated issues.

Explain *five* competencies involved in building a learning organisation.

Feedback to this activity is at the end of the chapter.

3 Change-adept organisations

3.1 The views of Kanter

Rosabeth Moss Kanter looked at the characteristics of organisations that managed change successfully ('change-adept organisations'), and the qualities of their leaders and managers. She suggested that change-adept organisations share three key attributes:

- The **imagination to innovate**. Effective leaders help to develop new concepts, which are a requirement for successful change.

- The **professionalism to perform**. Leaders provide both personal competence and competence in the organisation as a whole, which is supported by workforce training and development. This enables the organisation to perform strongly and deliver value to ever-more-demanding customers.

- The **openness to collaborate**. Leaders in change-adept organisations make connections with 'partners' outside the organisation, who can extend the organisation's reach, enhance its products and services, and 'energise its practices'. 'Partners' will include suppliers working in close collaboration, joint venture partners, and so on.

Kanter argued that change should be accepted naturally by organisations, as a natural part of their existence. Change that is compelled by a crisis is usually seen as a threat, rather than as an opportunity for successful development. Mastering change means being the first with the best service or products, anticipating and then meeting customer requirements (which continually change) and applying new technology. This requires organisations to be 'fast, agile, intuitive and innovative'.

3.2 Skills for leaders in change-adept organisations

Kanter suggested the skills that leaders/managers should have in a change-adept organisation.

- **Tuning in to the environment**. A leader cannot possibly know enough personally, and be in enough places, to understand everything that is happening both inside and (more importantly) outside the organisation. However, a leader can actively gather information that might suggest new approaches, by tuning in to what is happening in the environment. Leaders can create a network of 'listening posts', such as satellite offices and joint ventures. Kanter suggested: 'Look not just at how the pieces of your business model fit together, but for what *doesn't* fit. For instance, pay special attention to customer complaints, which are often your best source of information about an operational weakness or unmet need. Also search out broader signs of change – a competitor doing something differently or a customer using your product or service in unexpected ways.'

- **Challenging the prevailing organisational wisdom**. Leaders should be able to look at matters from a different perspective, and should not necessarily accept the current view of what is right or appropriate.

- **Communicating a compelling aspiration**. Leaders should have a clear vision of what they want to achieve, and should communicate it with conviction to the people they deal with. A manager cannot 'sell' change to other people without genuine conviction, because there is usually too much resistance to overcome. Without the conviction, a manager will not have the strength of leadership to persuade others.

- **Building coalitions**. Change leaders need the support and involvement of other individuals who have the resources, knowledge or 'political clout' to make things happen. There are usually individuals within the organisation who have the ability to influence others – 'opinion shapers', 'values leaders' and experts in the field. Getting the support of these individuals calls for an understanding of the *politics* of change in organisations.

- **Transferring ownership to the work team**. Leaders cannot introduce change on their own. At some stage, the responsibility for introducing change will be handed to others. Kanter suggested that a successful leader, having created a coalition in favour of the change, should enlist a team of other people to introduce the change.

- **Learning to persevere**. Something will probably go wrong, and there will be setbacks. Change leaders should not give up too quickly, but should persevere with the change.

- **Making everyone a hero**. A successful leader recognises, rewards and celebrates the accomplishments of others who have helped to introduce a change successfully. Making others feel appreciated for their contribution helps to sustain their motivation, and their willingness to attempt further changes in the future.

3.3 'Power skills' of the change agent

Kanter also identified seven 'power skills' that change agents require to enable them to overcome apathy or resistance to change, and enable them to introduce new ideas:

(a) ability to work independently, without the power and sanction of the senior management hierarchy behind them, providing visible support

(b) ability to collaborate effectively

(c) ability to develop relationships based on trust, with high ethical standards

(d) self-confidence, tempered with humility

(e) being respectful of the process of change, as well as the substance of the change

(f) ability to work across different business functions and units

(g) a willingness to stake personal rewards on results, and gain satisfaction from success.

Kanter speaks of this management style in terms of 'business athletes' and a new entrepreneurial style. The new heroic model is an athlete that can manage the amazing feat of doing more with less, and who can also juggle the need to conserve resources and pursue growth opportunities. She outlines some techniques that change agents can use to block interference:

Wait them out	They might eventually go away
Wear them down	Keep pushing and arguing, be persistent
Appeal to higher authority	You better agree because they do
Invite them in	Have them join the party
Send emissaries	Get friends in whom they believe to talk to them
Display support	Have 'your' people present and active at key meetings
Reduce the stakes	Alter parts of the proposal that are particularly damaging
Warn them off	Let them know that senior management are on your side
And remember	Only afterwards does an innovation look like the right thing to have done all along.

3.4 Implementing change through power politics

If transformational change is required in an organisation, it is likely that there will be a need for the reconfiguration of power structures. Any manager of change needs to consider how it might be implemented from a political perspective. For example, a critical report by an outside change agency such as market research findings on customer perceptions of service may be 'rubbished' by the board because it threatens their authority and power.

Understanding these systems, there is a need to plan changes within this political context. The political mechanisms include:

(a) **The control and manipulation of organisational resources.** Acquiring, withdrawing or allocating additional resources, or being identified with important areas of resource or expertise, can be an important tool in overcoming resistance or persuading others to accept change. Being able to manipulate the information opposing the changes can also be important.

(b) **Association with a powerful group or elite** can help build a power base. This may be useful for the change agent who does not have a strong personal power base to work from. Association with a change agent who is seen as successful or who is respected can also help a manager overcome resistance to change.

(c) **Handling the subsystem effectively** can achieve acceptance of change throughout the organisation. Building up alliances and a network of contacts and sympathisers may help win over powerful groups.

(d) **Symbolic devices** that may take different forms. To build power the manager may become involved in committees, which reinforce and preserve the change model. Symbolic activity can be used for consolidating change by positive reinforcement towards those who most accept change. These rewards include new structures, titles and office allocation.

Summary

- A variety of approaches to change management have been suggested by various writers and theorists on management.

- Concepts in change management include 'change agents' (for example management consultants) who introduce change and 'change levers', which are tools for the successful introduction of change.

- Kanter described the characteristics of change-adept organisations and the qualities required from leaders in these organisations. Key factors are an imagination to innovate, the professionalism to perform and an openness to collaboration.

- Senge suggested that the most successful organisations are learning organisations, which have the ability to innovate as well as being able to adapt to environmental change. A learning organisation is based on the mastery of five disciplines: systems thinking, personal mastery, mental models, building a shared vision and team learning.

- Lewin was concerned about the resistance of individuals to change and acceptance of change by individuals. He suggested that change should be managed as a three-stage process: unfreezing, moving to the desired position, and re-freezing when this position has been reached. Different approaches should be adopted by management for each stage.

- Bennis set out views on organisational development (OD) in which he saw a key role for the management consultant as a change agent. An OD approach supports continuous change and development, through a repetitive cycle of identifying problems, analysing and diagnosing them, formulating and implementing plans to resolve them, review and further amendment.

- Beer and Nohria identified two conceptual approaches to managing change – a 'hard' Theory E approach and a 'soft' Theory O approach. Neither approach on its own is likely to be successful, nor is applying one approach followed by the other in succession. They suggested that the best approach is to use a combination of Theory E and Theory O at the same time.

- Peters suggested that excellent firms are able to 'thrive on chaos' and welcome rapid and continual change as a means of innovating and improving to gain competitive advantage.

Having completed your study of this chapter, you should have achieved the following learning outcomes:

- evaluate various means of introducing change

- evaluate change processes within the organisation.

Self-test questions

1   What are Leavitt's variables for change management? (1.1)

2   According to Lewin, what changes must occur during the unfreezing stage of organisational change? (2.3)

3   Itemise the main differences between Beer and Nohria's Theory E and Theory O models of managing change. (2.4)

4   According to Senge, what are the two types of learning that a learning organisation must have? (2.5)

5   What, according to Senge, are the five disciplines that a learning organisation has mastered? (2.5)

6   According to Peters, what five areas of management are important for success in a 'chaotic' business world? (2.6)

7   List four of the skills required by leaders in change-adept organisations, as suggested by Kanter. (3.2)

8   What, according to Kanter, are the 'power skills' required by a change agent? (3.3)

Practice questions

Question 1

According to Kanter, leaders in change-adept organisations should have certain skills. Which of the following is one of the skills she identified as necessary?

A   Expressing criticisms freely

B   Delegating responsibility for restructuring the organisation

C   Asking individuals to challenge the proposals of others

D   Building coalitions

Question 2

In a learning organisation, according to Senge, individuals should expose their own ways of thinking, and make them more open to the influence of other people. This is the mastery of which of the following disciplines?

A   Mental models

B   Building shared vision

C   Personal mastery

D   Team learning

Question 3

In less than 30 words, give a definition of organisational development.

Question 4

According to Lewin, what is the purpose of the 'unfreezing' stage in the three-stage model of organisational change?

Question 5

According to Lewin, which of the following methods would be inappropriate for management during the process of introducing change in an organisation (the movement stage)?

A   Participation

B   Communication

C   Enforcing the change

D   Negotiation

Question 6

Many Japanese companies have long recognised the benefits of institutionalised learning based around quality improvement teams and associated issues.

Required:

Explain **five** competencies involved in building a learning organisation.   **(20 marks)**

Question 7

Y is one of the five main high street banks in the country. Since banking deregulation in the late 1980s, Y, like other banks, has been facing increasing competition, first from other existing financial institutions but more recently from new entrants who have started to offer deposit accounts and a number of other financial services.

In seeking to respond to these competitive threats, the bank's senior management has started to implement a number of changes. These involve a significant restructuring of the organisation with the removal of a number of layers of management, and a consequent reduction in staffing levels in most divisions. The closure of a number of high-street branches is also planned. The telephone-banking arm is being substantially enlarged, and a major investment in IT is being undertaken. The effect on staff will be considerable. A programme of voluntary redundancy and redeployment is planned and, given the demand for new skills, a considerable amount of training will need to be carried out. Despite clear evidence of the threat to the future of the bank, the plans set forth by management are meeting resistance from the workforce. The banking unions in particular seem determined to obstruct the changes wherever possible.

Requirements:

With reference to the above scenario:

(a)   What do you understand by the term 'organisational change'?   **(5 marks)**

(b)   Explain why individuals tend to resist change.   **(5 marks)**

(c)   Why is change seen as a threat to groups within the organisation?   **(5 marks)**

(d)   Outline the main reasons for organisational resistance to change.   **(5 marks)**

(e)   Advise Y's management about the ways in which change can be facilitated.

    (5 marks)

(f)   Draw a force field diagram to explain the major driving force for change at 'Y'
    (5 marks)
    (Total: 30 marks)

For the answers to these questions, see the 'Answers' section at the end of the book.

Feedback to activities

Activity 1

Change introduced through the use of power or manipulation is likely to add to anxiety. Education and communication will rarely succeed on their own in introducing major change. However, they are useful as a support for a negotiation or participation approach. The negotiation approach requires the existence of organised representatives and a formal procedure which is suitable for some items such as change in employment terms but would be inadvisable for other items of changing procedures, organisational changes, decentralisation, etc. In these cases, participation offers the best opportunity of allaying staff anxieties by involving them early in the change process and continuing that involvement through to completion. Coch and French summarise the approach as 'involve those affected as early as possible, as deeply as possible'.

Activity 2

There is no single solution to this problem, but the key to implementing the new system successfully must be to win over the office managers and persuade them of the benefits of the new system. This is unlikely unless the managers are invited to contribute ideas and suggestions themselves. In other words, it is important to get them involved.

In addition, it seems clear that the benefits of the new system and the details of the new system have not been fully explained. There is a 'selling' job to be done. It might be appropriate to meet the office managers individually to discuss the new system. Alternatively, it might be more constructive to invite all the regional office managers to a conference on the subject.

Additional measures might be to:

- offer training in the new system to managers who need it

- try to convince the managers that the new system has the support of senior management, and is a major priority

- discuss the benefits of the new system for the individual managers personally, as well as for the organisation. A bonus arrangement for successful implementation of the new system might be considered.

Activity 3

The switch to international accounting standards was a planned change. Communicating information about the change would be a necessary part of the process of unfreezing the opinions of investors and stock market analysts. Although investors might not have any objection to the idea of the new accounting standards, it was probable that applying the new standards would have some effect on the reported profits. Listed companies were advised to inform investors about the change and the likely effect on their financial results, in order to avoid any unpleasant shocks and surprises when financial statements were eventually produced under the new rules. The chief executive of the ICAEW was reported as advising listed companies to explain the changes: 'otherwise, for analysts and investors, it will be like doing a jig-saw puzzle in a snowstorm at night'.

This aspect of change management is therefore concerned with maintaining investor support and avoiding adverse effects on the company share price as a consequence of the change. The method of communicating with shareholders could be through meetings or in a written document sent to shareholders. The content of the message should have been to explain the likely effect on reported profits and balance sheet valuations, the reasons for these changes, and reassurance that the businesses of the company are not changed in any way by changes in reporting rules.

Activity 4

A learning organisation can be defined as an organisation which facilitates the learning of all its members and continuously transforms itself.

According to Senge, there are five core competencies involved in building learning organisations:

- *Building a shared vision* – an organisation needs to ensure that its people or staff are working towards a common purpose. A sense of common purpose, and shared values, beliefs, norms and attitudes creates an environment conducive to continuous learning in contrast to only irregular, ad hoc learning when there is a crisis which brings all the people together.

- *Personal mastery of learning by individuals* – the need for members of the organisation to develop the ability to continually question taken-for-granted assumptions underlying their particular view of reality. This increases their perception beyond their accepted superficial view of 'reality' and enables them to create more of what matters to them.

- *Working with mental models to recognise unconscious assumptions and to see alternatives* – an extension of personal mastery by individuals to recognise their unconscious assumptions. This allows individuals to understand how an alternative reality can be created.

- *Team learning* – involves group interaction where individuals come together as teams. This goes hand in hand with personal mastery of learning by individuals so groups of people can deal with difficult issues and come up with specific decisions.

- *Systems thinking to understand inter-relationships and see the bigger picture* – instead of analysing and breaking down problems into discrete components, the emphasis here is on synthesis and the importance of understanding relationships.

Chapter 7

OPERATIONS STRATEGY

Syllabus content

- An overview of operations strategy and its importance to the firm.

- Design of products/services and processes and how this relates to operations and supply.

Contents

1 Operations strategy

2 Objectives

3 Porter's value chain

4 Design of products and services

1 Operations strategy

1.1 What is meant by 'operations'?

'Operations' involve the transformational process of changing inputs into outputs in order to add value.

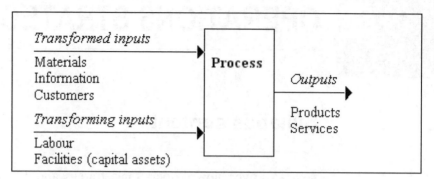

- **Inputs** may include capital, raw materials, people, information, managerial and technical skills and knowledge.

- **The transformation process** – in a manufacturing organisation, the transformation of inputs into outputs would be the production department; in an insurance company it would be the underwriting department. The maintenance process keeps the organisation functioning. It may repair and service the building. Alternatively, the human resource department can be seen as a maintenance sub-system, recruiting, retiring and counselling, etc employees.

- **Outputs** – the type of outputs will vary with the organisation. They generally include products, services, profits and rewards.

The nature of operations varies enormously between different types of organisation, but all operations can be described in terms of the transformation process model. Inputs to a process can be transformed in several ways:

- **Physical transformation, or change in nature/form** – a manufacturing operation transforms input materials, using labour and facilities, to produce manufactured products. A stockbroker takes instructions from clients to buy or sell shares (information) and carries out the instructions so that the customer has purchased or sold the shares (service delivered). An accountancy service transforms raw accounting data into financial reports and customers might undergo beauty treatment or medical treatment.

- **Change of location** – a courier service delivers parcels and packages from one location to another, and a mining operation extracts raw materials from under the ground. Data communications operations transfer data from one location to another and a service might transfer customers from one location to another (transport services).

- **Held in store** – a warehousing or storage company holds items for customers in a secure place for a period of time. A process might exist to store information for future use, such as information held in a data library. Customers might be given accommodation, for example by a hotel service or a prison service.

KEY POINT

All operations can be described in terms of the transformation process model.

- **Change of ownership** – the retailing process transfers ownership of products or a process might involve the transfer of ownership in rights to information, such as the transfer of information from a firm of management consultants to a client.

- **Psychological transformation** – a customer might be psychologically transformed by an item, such as an entertainment product or service (film, music or book).

Activity 1

Fill in the three missing sections in the table below:

	Inputs	Transformation	Outputs
1		Assembling bicycles	Completed bicycles
2	Students with limited knowledge and skills		Students with enhanced knowledge and skills
3	Client problem	Consulting: information analysis, evaluation and selection of alternatives, recommendation	

Feedback to this activity is at the end of the chapter.

KEY POINT

Operations management includes purchasing, warehousing and transportation – dealing with all the operations from the procurement of raw materials through various activities until the product is available to the buyer.

The term 'operations management' refers to the activities required to produce and deliver a service as well as a physical product. Production management used to be associated solely with the manufacture of goods but its expansion to operations management means that it now includes purchasing, warehousing and transportation – dealing with all the operations from the procurement of raw materials through various activities until the product is available to the buyer.

Operations management has a bearing on marketing, finance, research and development, administration and on job design, which has a knock-on effect on the tasks and the roles that human resources are involved in.

The design of an operations system requires decisions on the location of facilities, the process to be used, the quantity to be produced and the quality of the product.

1.2 Operations strategy and competitive advantage

As with other aspects of running a business, there is a strategic context to operations management.

KEY POINT

An organisation can achieve a significant competitive advantage over its rivals through superior operating capabilities of its resources.

An organisation can achieve a significant competitive advantage over its rivals through superior operating capabilities of its resources. The capabilities of the operating resources of an organisation will depend on:

- the quantity of resources available, and

- the capabilities of those resources.

Resources include not just physical resources (assets and workforce), but also intangible resources such as supplier relationships, the firm's reputation with customers and the skills and experience of the workforce.

The quantity and capabilities of the resources of an organisation act as a constraint on what the organisation is capable of achieving. An organisation cannot do more than its resources are capable of achieving. On the other hand, the capabilities of its resources also affect the strategic opportunities that can be exploited.

Strategic operational decisions are sometimes divided into two broad categories:

1   Decisions affecting the design and development activities of the organisation.

2   Decisions affecting the organisation of the workforce, the planning and control of operations and improvements in operations.

Strategic operational decisions affecting product design and development include:

- **Development strategy for new products or services.** How should the operation make decisions about which products or services to develop? Should the organisation take the lead in innovation, or should it wait for competitors to innovate and then copy what they have done?

- **Technology strategy.** In broad terms, what types of technology should the organisation be using? Should it be at the 'leading edge' of technological development, or not?

- **Vertical integration strategy.** How many stages in the supply chain should the organisation seek to operate itself? For example, an oil company has to make the strategic decision about how many stages it should operate itself in the supply chain from exploring for oil, extracting and refining the oil and distributing the refined oil products. Should it specialise in just one or two stages in the chain, or should it operate in all of them?

- **Facilities strategy.** How many separate geographical sites should the organisation operate from? Where should they be located? What should be the capacity at each location? What activities should be carried out at each location?

Strategic decisions affecting the organisation of the workforce, the planning and control of operations and improvements in operations include:

- **Structuring the workforce.** What skills should the workforce have, and how should it be organised? How should responsibilities for operations be divided or allocated?

- **Planning and control.** The operations function must have systems for making operational decisions, and for monitoring and controlling actual performance.

- **Improvements strategy.** There should be a strategy for improving operational performance standards. This strategy might be based on using benchmarks as targets, or based on a continuous improvement philosophy (kaizen), or based on a business process engineering approach. (These are all explained in later chapters.)

- **Supply/purchasing strategy.** An organisation might adopt different strategies for sourcing supplies of materials, components and services, such as single sourcing, multiple sourcing or delegated sourcing/network supply system.

- **Failure recovery strategy.** An organisation should have a strategy for what to do in the event of a major failure or breakdown in operations. For example, many large organisations have a disaster recovery strategy for handling disruptions caused by a terrorist attack.

- **Capacity and flexibility.** There should be a system for forecasting the expected volume of demand for the output of an operation, and adjusting capacity to meet the demand.

- **Inventory levels.** An organisation might set an operational strategic target for inventory levels. For example, a Just-in-Time strategy aims for zero inventories

1.3 Competitive factors

The objectives for operations should be consistent with the perceived requirements of customers. Various 'competitive factors' can be used to express customer requirements in terms of operational performance requirements. An organisation should establish its priorities for operational performance, and set target levels of achievement as a strategic objective.

- When customers want a low-priced product, the performance objectives in operational strategy should focus mainly on reducing costs and producing a low-cost output.

- When customers want a product or service with certain quality characteristics, and are willing to pay more for better quality, the performance objectives in operational strategy should focus on achieving the required quality standards, subject to a constraint that costs should be kept within certain limits.

- If customers want fast delivery of a product or service, the operational performance objective will concentrate on speed of operations or making the product or service more readily available.

- If customers want reliability, the operational objective should be to set targets for reliability and ensure that these are met. For example, a courier service meets customer requirements by ensuring that packages are delivered within a particular time to their destination, and without loss or damage. The operational target should be to meet these requirements on 100% of occasions.

- When customers want products or services to be designed to their own specification, the operational objective must be to achieve sufficient flexibility to handle the variations in customer requirements, and provide differing products or services accordingly.

- When customers want to alter the timing or delivery of services they receive, the main operational objective will also be flexibility. For example, a training company might have to be sufficiently flexible to deal with changes in the location, timing and duration of the training programmes required by their clients, and the number of delegates to be trained.

1.4 Operations strategy and operations management

In contrast to operations strategy, operations management is concerned with designing, implementing and controlling the transformational processes discussed above.

The table below shows how it differs from operations strategy:

Operations management	Operations strategy
Product/service design	Product/service innovation
Process design e.g. layout and technology	Process technology strategy
Job design	Human resource strategy
Capacity management	Capacity location, planning and dynamics
Planning and control e.g. JIT, MRP	Organisation and systems development
Inventory control	Supply network strategy
Quality control	Performance and improvement strategy

1.5 The four Vs of operations

Although all operations involve a transformation process, they can differ in four different ways, sometimes known as the 'four Vs' of operations:

Volume. Operations differ in the volume of inputs they process. For example, a large international airport such as London Heathrow and a small airfield both handle aircraft flights, but they differ enormously in character due to the volume of inputs they process. High-volume operations are likely to be more capital-intensive than low-volume operations, and there is likely to be a greater specialisation of labour skills.

Variety. Some operations handle a wide range of different inputs, or produce a wide range of output products or services. Others are much more restricted in the range of inputs they handle or outputs they produce. Where there is a large amount of variety, an operation might have to be very flexible and capable of adapting to different requirements and different customer needs. When variety is narrow, an operation might be much more standardised and inflexible.

Variation in demand. With some operations, demand might vary significantly from one season of the year to another, or from one time of the day to another, with some periods of peak demand and some periods of low demand. Other operations might handle a fairly constant volume of demand at all times. When variation in demand is high, there is a problem of capacity utilisation. If the operation is designed to handle peak capacity, there is idle capacity for much of the time.

Visibility. Visibility refers to the extent to which an organisation is visible to its customers. When an operation is highly visible, the employees will have to show good communication skills and interpersonal skills in dealing with customers. Visibility is usually greater in service operations than in manufacturing operations.

1.6 Operational planning: tactics

To be effective, strategies and policies must be put into practice by means of plans, increasing in detail until they get down to the nuts and bolts of operations. Tactics are the action plans through which strategies are exercised.

Tactical decisions are concerned with the efficient running and maintenance of operational activities within the defined strategic framework e.g.:

- achieving operational targets, covering volume and type of product

- product planning and scheduling

- defined levels of customer service

- acceptable levels of customer service

- personnel and industrial relations

- inventory levels and control procedures

- inspection arrangements

- purchasing of raw materials and bought out parts

- recruitment, training, deployment and dismissal of workforce

- achievement of financial and associated targets

- monitoring and control procedures relating to resource deployment.

2 Objectives

2.1 The five performance objectives

There are five basic types of performance objective that can be applied to any type of operation:

1   a quality objective

2   a speed objective

3   a dependability objective

4   a flexibility objective

5   a cost objective.

Quality objective. Quality can be defined in operational terms as 'doing things right' and meeting customer expectations. Customers often judge a product or service on their perception of its quality, and quality is therefore often an important performance objective. However, the definition of quality can vary widely from one organisation to another. For example, quality in a motor car is different from quality in a dental service or quality in a supermarket.

Quality also exists *within an operation* if it:

- reduces costs, or

- improves dependability.

Speed objective. Speed is concerned with how long a customer has to wait before receiving a product or service. For example, in a service operation, speed is related to the length of waiting times.

Speed *within an operation* can also be important. If an organisation is able to respond quickly to a customer order and make the product in a short time, it should be possible to minimise inventories. (Inventories are a costly resource and consist of items that customers might never actually want to buy, such as unsold goods in a retail shop.)

Dependability objective. Dependability means delivering a product or service to a customer exactly when promised, without delays or cancellations. Dependability is an important performance objective in operations such as public transport and the health service.

Within an overall operation, dependability relates to how reliable one stage in the operation is in delivering its products or services to the next stage in the operation.

Flexibility objective. Flexibility means being able to adapt and change the operation to meet variations in requirements or circumstances. Flexibility can relate to variability in the specifications for a product or service, or in the product mix or range delivered, or in the volumes delivered.

Within an operation, operational flexibility relates to the ability to respond to different requirements and changes in circumstances.

Cost objective. When companies compete on price, a cost objective is a critically important performance objective, because a company must produce its output at a cost below its selling prices in order to maintain profitability. However, costs are affected by other performance objectives, and it is usually necessary to spend more to achieve greater quality, speed, dependability or flexibility.

Activity 2

How might quality be defined for a company that operates a passenger train service?

Feedback to this activity is at the end of the chapter.

2.2 Order-winning factors and qualifying factors

KEY POINT

One method of establishing operational priorities is to make a distinction between:

- order-winning operational factors, and

- qualifying factors.

Performance objectives can therefore be expressed in terms of cost targets, quality targets, speed targets, reliability targets and flexibility targets. For any organisation, some of these targets will be more important than others, and strategic priorities must be decided. One method of establishing operational priorities is to make a distinction between:

- order-winning operational factors, and

- qualifying factors.

Order-winning factors are operational performance factors that assist the organisation to win orders from customers. If an organisation can improve its performance for an order-winning factor, it will obtain higher sales or larger customer demand, or will at least improve its prospects of increasing sales. The competitive advantage of the organisation will be improved.

Qualifying factors are aspects of operational performance that will not persuade customers to buy. However, a sufficient minimum level of performance must be achieved to prevent the customers from deciding not to buy. For example, customers for a private health clinic might not expect immediate treatment, and might be prepared to wait up to about four weeks before receiving treatment: however, if the waiting time is significantly longer, customers might decide not to use the clinic and to go elsewhere for service. In this example, speed of service would be a qualifying factor, whereas quality or flexibility of service might be the key order-winning factor.

2.3 Performance objectives and the product life cycle

The 'classic' life cycle for a product has four phases:

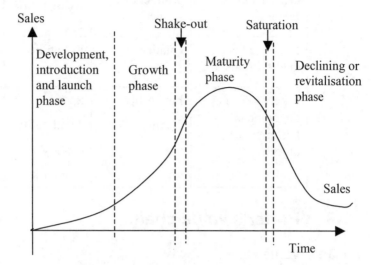

- An **introduction phase**, when the product or service is first developed and introduced to the market. Sales demand is low whilst potential customers learn about the item. There is a learning process for both customers and the producer, and the producer might have to vary the features of the product or service, in order to meet customer requirements more successfully.

- A **growth phase**, when the product or service becomes established, and there is a large growth in sales demand. The number of competitors in the market also increases, but customers are still willing to pay reasonably high prices. The product becomes profitable. Variety in the product or service increases, and customers are much more conscious of quality issues.

- A **maturity phase**, which might be the longest stage in the product life cycle. Demand stabilises, and producers compete on price.

- A **decline phase**, during which sales demand falls. Prices are reduced to sustain demand and to slow the decline in sales volume. Eventually the product becomes unprofitable, and eventually producers stop making it.

A large number of products have gone through this type of life cycle. For example, at the time of writing, it would appear that floppy disks for computers and video recorders are in the decline phase of their life cycle.

The key operational performance targets might vary over the different stages of the life cycle, as follows:

	Introduction	*Growth*	*Maturity*	*Decline*
Likely to be an order-winning factor	Features of the product or service	Quality Availability	Low price Reliable supply	Low price
Likely to be a qualifying factor	Quality	Reliability Price	Quality	Reliable supply
Likely to be key operational performance objectives	Flexibility Quality	Speed Availability Quality Reliability	Cost Reliability	Cost

3 Porter's value chain

3.1 Value

The aim of operations management should be to provide the output product or service in a way that adds value. Value can be defined in accounting terms as the difference between the sale value of the end product or service (the amount that customers are willing to pay) and the cost of providing the product or service. Value can therefore be added by:

- increasing the perceived value to the customers, in terms of what they are willing to pay, or

- reducing costs.

3.2 Value chain

According to Michael Porter, the business of an organisation is best described by way of a value chain in which total revenue minus total costs of all activities undertaken to develop and market a product or service yields value. Porter argued that competitive advantage arises out of the ways in which firms organise and perform activities. The value chain describes how an organisation uses its inputs and transforms them into outputs, which customers are prepared to pay for.

All organisations in a particular industry will have a similar value chain, which will include activities such as obtaining raw materials, designing products, and building manufacturing facilities, developing co-operative agreements, and providing customer service. An organisation will be profitable as long as total revenues exceed the total costs incurred in creating and delivering the product or service. It is therefore necessary that organisations should strive to understand their value chain and also that of their competitors, suppliers, distributors, etc.

The basic model of Porter's value chain, shown in the diagram below, displays total value and consists of value activities. Value activities are the physically and technologically distinct activities that an organisation performs.

Porter's value chain

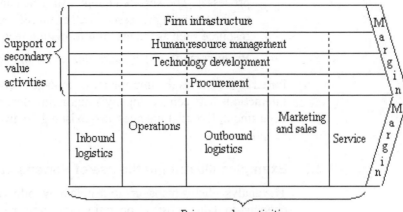

The term 'Margin' implies that organisations realise a profit margin that depends on their ability to manage the linkages between all activities in the value chain. In other words, the organisation is able to deliver a product / service for which the customer is willing to pay more than the sum of the costs of all activities in the value chain.

Porter groups organisational activities into five primary areas:

1   **Inbound logistics** – are the activities concerned with sources of funds (working capital, investment), relationship with suppliers, supply sources and costs, receiving, storing, and distributing the inputs to the organisation system (materials handling, stock control, transport, etc)

2   **Operations** – transforming inputs into final products/services includes production capacity and flexibility, plant location, labour numbers, skills required, machining, packing, assembly, testing and equipment maintenance

3   **Outbound logistics** – collecting, storing and distributing final products (for tangible products this includes order processing, warehousing, stock control, distribution, type of transport and vehicle scheduling. In the case of services it may be more concerned with arrangements for bringing customers to the service if it is in a fixed location e.g. theatre, sports event)

4   **Marketing and sales** – activities that attract customers to purchase (includes product planning, sales administration, advertising, selling, channel selection, pricing and promotion)

5   **Service** – activities that ensure that customers enjoy their purchases by providing information systems, installation, training, maintenance, repair and breakdown assistance, etc.

Each of these may be a source of advantage. All of these primary activities are linked to the secondary, or support activities:

•   **Firm infrastructure** – includes the systems of planning, finance, quality control and estate management. The infrastructure supports the entire value chain and can help or hinder the achievement of competitive advantage.

•   **Human resource management** – how people within the firm are managed.

- **Technology development** – covers know-how as well as machines and processes. The key technologies may be concerned directly with the product or with processes, such as oil refinery, or with a particular resource such as the use of information technology.

- **Procurement** – how the resources for the above are purchased

Porter also stresses the importance of linkages between activities e.g., the interactions between a company's marketing department and its production department. External linkages also exist e.g., between the company and its suppliers

3.3 Examples illustrating the use of Porter's value chain

The analysis helps managers to decide how individual activities might be changed to reduce costs of operation or to improve the value of the organisation's offerings. Such changes will increase 'margin' - the residual value created by what customers pay minus the organising costs. For example, a clothes manufacturer may spend large amounts on:

- buying good quality raw materials (inbound logistics)

- hand-finishing garments (operations)

- building a successful brand image (marketing)

- running its own fleet of delivery trucks in order to deliver finished clothes quickly to customers (outbound logistics).

All of these should add value to the product, allowing the company to charge a premium for its clothes. Another clothes manufacturer may:

- reduce the cost of its raw materials by buying in cheaper supplies from abroad (inbound logistics)

- making all its clothes by machinery running 24 hours a day (operations)

- delaying distribution until delivery trucks can be filled with garments for a particular request (outbound logistics).

All of these should allow the company to be able to gain economies of scale and be able to sell clothes at a cheaper price than its rivals.

3.4 The supply chain

A value chain is a sequence of activities within an organisation. However, there is also a supply chain within every industry. This is the series of organisations through which products or activities must go before they reach the end-consumer. Organisations rely on suppliers to provide them with raw materials, components, capital equipment and other items. Many organisations do not sell an end product to consumers, but instead produce goods or services that are consumed by other organisations. For example, a manufacturer of motorcars might purchase many components, such as tyres, brakes and engines, from suppliers, and assemble these components into a finished product. The finished product is then transferred to car distributors, who sell them to customers. The suppliers of the component parts to the car manufacturer will obtain parts and materials from other suppliers. The supply chain stretches from the producers of the basic raw materials (rubber, metal, plastic and so on) to the end-consumer. Each organisation has a position in the supply chain.

Operations management involves management of both the value chain within the organisation and also the supply chain, in order to deliver added value to its customers.

3.5 Processes within the overall process

The transformation process model shows the entire process as a single box. Every process consists of many different elements or sub-processes that are performed either sequentially or in parallel. Each separate element in the overall process has to be managed. For example:

- a manufacturing operation might consist of machining, assembly and finishing operations

- a magazine production process might consist of commissioning articles and features, gathering news, the writing, editing, artwork production and design, page layout, copy editing and then printing.

Every sub-operation or 'micro operation' within the overall operation can be described in terms of a transformation process model, with materials, information or a customer being transformed, to provide a product or service to the customer.

External suppliers perform some sub-operations. For example, in magazine production, some features and articles and some photographs might be provided from external sources. Other operations are performed internally. Sub-operations performed internally can be seen as the transformation of inputs for the benefit of an 'internal customer'.

The concept of the **internal customer** and **internal supplier** is important in operations management. Although an operation might be performed for another department or section within the same organisation, this department or section is an internal customer within the supply chain to the end-customer. The objective should be to add value for the next customer in the supply chain, no matter whether this is an internal or an external customer, in order to add value throughout the supply chain to the end-customer.

Porter's (1986) Value Chain Analysis can also provide valuable insights into make or buy decisions

A make or buy decision is concerned with whether an item should be made internally or purchased from an external supplier.

Advantages of making an item internally

- Producing a part internally reduces dependence on suppliers and may ensure a smoother flow of parts and material for production.

- Quality control may be easier when parts are produced internally.

- Profits can be realised on the parts and materials.

Advantages of buying an item from an external supplier

- By pooling the requirements of a number of users, a supplier can realise economies of scale and may be able to move more quickly up the learning curve.

- A specialised supplier may be able to respond more quickly and at less cost to changing future needs.

- Changing technology may make producing one's own parts riskier than purchasing from the outside.

4 Design of products and services

DEFINTION

Design is defined as 'all the activities relating to the development of a product or service, from inception, through all the developmental stages to the final model.

Design has been defined as 'all the activities relating to the development of a product or service, from inception, through all the developmental stages to the final model'. The design activity therefore is an integrating activity that lumps together all sectors of the organisation concerned with product development, manufacture, sales and finance

Product design indicates the formulation of articles to be made so as to specify shape and dimensions, materials and parts required and the type of finish. It has several aspects:

- Design for function – value in use implies quality and reliability: the product must satisfy the customer in its purpose and give long service.

- Design for aesthetics – although products should please the eye to attract customers, the appeal of the product may not be solely visual. Other senses are also often involved and sometimes characteristics such as smell, taste or texture may predominate.

- Design for production – to ensure component parts are made easily and economically, so that they can be assembled and transported easily and sold at an attractive price

- Design for distribution – to enable easy packing, reduction of storage space and packing costs.

KEY POINT

Commercial organisations need to continually look for new or improved products or services, to achieve or maintain a competitive advantage in their markets. Operations managers are not usually directly responsible for the design and development of new products and services.

Commercial organisations need to continually look for new or improved products or services, to achieve or maintain a competitive advantage in their markets. Operations managers are not usually directly responsible for the design and development of new products and services. However, the advice and assistance of both operations and marketing management is essential.

- Marketing management should help to identify the needs and requirements of customers, or potential customers, and suggest features for a new product or service that would meet those needs.

- Operations management should help in considering the ways in which a new product or service could be designed, within acceptable cost constraints, to meet the customers' perceived requirements for quality, speed, dependability, flexibility and price. There is an inter-relationship between the design of a product or service, and the **design of the processes** for making the product or delivering the service.

4.1 The effect of volume and variety on design

The design process and design activities differ between different types of organisation. For example, product design in a pharmaceuticals company is very different from product or service design in a hairdressing business. Factors that have a significant effect on design are:

- the volume or quantity of the product or service that will be planned, and

- the variety in the range of the products or services, or the variety in product or service features.

Typically, high volume is associated with low variety and large variety is associated with lower volumes.

- When the planned variety is large, the emphasis in design activities should be on the design of the product or service package itself. When the planned volume is high, the design of the production process is much more important.

- When variety is high, product or service standardisation is low. With high-volume output, there is much greater standardisation.

- When volume is low, production can be decentralised more easily than if volume is high. When output volume is high, manufacture must usually be centralised to achieve the required economies of scale.

- With low volume output, production is intermittent, and organised on a job production basis or a batch production basis. When volume is high, production is more likely to be organised as a continuous flow operation.

- When there is high variety and low volume, the technology used for producing the item or delivering the service will often be general-purpose technology, that is capable of making a range of different products or providing a range of services. With high volume and low variety, there will be much greater use of dedicated technology.

- With low volumes and high variety, labour skills need to be task-oriented and the workforce must be more flexible.

4.2 The product or service package

The aim of product or service design should be to satisfy the needs of customers. The first stage in a design process is therefore to identify the needs of customers, and produce a specification for a product or service 'package' that will meet those needs.

The initial ideas for a new or amended product or service, to satisfy customer needs, might come from a variety of sources, such as:

- customers themselves (market research, focus groups, from talking to customers, and so on)

- the activities of competitors

- the organisation's own staff, or

- new findings from research and development activities.

These ideas must then be turned into a product or service concept. It is perhaps convenient to think of a product as something that is tangible and manufactured, and a service as something intangible. In reality, this view is much too simplified, and products and services should be seen as a package of tangible and intangible features.

For example, providing a meal in a restaurant is a service operation, but the service consists of the food itself and the physical surroundings in the restaurant (table, chairs, cutlery, glasses and so on).

Similarly, a digital camera is a product that is used to take photographs, but the product design concept is much more. A digital camera:

- takes pictures of a very high resolution

- takes pictures of differing sizes

- is small and convenient to carry

- is easy to use and is reliable

- allows large numbers of photographs to be held on a single disk

- can be linked to a computer for editing

- allows the user to get rid of unwanted images or select parts of an image for printing

- allows users to print pictures easily.

These are just a few of the features of a digital camera that make up the product concept and product package. No doubt you can think of other features too, that digital cameras already have or should ideally have (for example, longer-life batteries).

When a product or service package contains many different features, another aspect of design is to decide how these different features should inter-relate with each other, and how all the different elements should come together in the unified package.

Activity 3

Take any product or service with which you are familiar, and list at least six features that make up the overall product or service package.

There is no feedback to this activity.

4.3 Concept screening

When a specification for a new product or service package has been devised, the concept should be 'screened'. Concept screening is the process of vetting a suggestion for a new product or service to decide whether the design and development process should continue.

A concept will pass the screening process only if it satisfies several evaluation criteria, relating to marketing, finance and operations.

- From a *marketing perspective*, the key issues are:

    - whether the total size of the market is likely to be big enough

    - whether the organisation will be able to win a sufficient share of this market with the product or service, and

    - what is the risk that it will fail to win a large enough share of the market?

- From a *finance perspective*, the key issues are:

    - does the organisation have enough finance to develop the product or service?

    - is the expected return on investment sufficient?

    - what is the risk that the return will be insufficient, or that the product or service will fail to achieve financial breakeven?

- From an *operations perspective*, the key issues are:

    - does the organisation have the operational capacity to make the product or provide the service?

    - how much reorganisation to the operations processes would be necessary?

    - what is the risk that the operations systems will fail to make the product or deliver the service to the design specifications?

New product or service concepts that pass the screening process go forward to further design and development.

4.4 The design process

There are different processes or procedures for designing and developing a new product or service in detail, and the design process differs from one organisation to another. Design techniques include the following:

- **Building a physical prototype or model of the product**. To build a physical prototype, the design engineers will need assistance from operations management.

- **Virtual prototyping**, which involves the construction of a three-dimensional prototype or model on a computer, using computer-aided design (CAD) techniques.

- **Value engineering** or cost engineering is a technique in which a firm's products, and maybe those of its competitors, are subjected to a critical and systematic examination by a small group of specialists.. The principle underlying value engineering is that a feature must add value to the product or service package; otherwise the feature serves no useful purpose and should be removed. In addition, the design engineers should consider whether the same feature could be provided within the package, but in a cheaper way. For example, is it really necessary to have a component made with a particular material, or would a cheaper material be just as effective? Will another dependable supplier provide it for less cost? The main purpose of value engineering is to simplify product design, eliminate unnecessary features and so improve the design or make the design cheaper.

4.5 Time-to-market

Time-to-market is the length of time between developing a new product concept and bringing the product (or service) to the market. Once a decision is taken to develop a new product or service, there is usually a competitive advantage to be gained in bringing the product or service to market as quickly as possible. With a short time-to-market:

- an organisation is more likely to bring its new product to market ahead of its competitors

- the costs of development are likely to be lower.

4.6 Product testing: supply issues in new product or service design

It is important that new products should be properly tested before they are introduced to the market to ensure that:

- the product or service meets the design specifications (an operations issue)

- the product or service meets customer needs as intended (a marketing issue).

Another aspect of new product design is that the product package might require new types of raw material or component, and in order to develop the product successfully, it is essential to find a supplier who is able to provide the required item or items to the required specifications.

When an organisation relies heavily on external suppliers for components, the supply relationship can be very significant, and the organisation has to rely on the co-operation and skills of its key suppliers.

Activity 4

Why might it be necessary to involve suppliers in a new product design and development project?

Feedback to this activity is at the end of the chapter.

Summary

- Operations strategy should be directed towards overall business objectives.

- Operational objectives might be expressed in terms of achieving target performance objectives, for quality, speed, dependability, flexibility and cost. Performance objectives can be set for the product or service, and for the process itself.

- Operational performance objectives might vary over the life cycle of a product.

- The operations function takes input resources and transforms them into outputs, in the form of products or services for customers. An operation can be described as a transformation process model, which transforms input materials, information or customers, using labour and facilities to create output products or services.

- Operations vary between different organisations. Differences in operations can be described in terms of the four Vs – differences in volume and variety, variations in customer demand patterns and the visibility of the product or service to customers.

- The sequence of activities within an organisation, from inbound logistics through operations to outbound logistics and marketing and sales, can be seen as a value chain. Each part of the chain should add value for the end customer.

- Operations within an organisation can also be seen as a part of the overall supply chain, from raw materials at the start of the chain to the final product or service for the end-consumer.

- Within an overall process or 'macro process', there will be a number of sub-processes or 'micro processes'. The output of one micro process is the input to another micro process. This gives rise to the concept of the internal supplier and internal customer.

- Operations management will be involved in new product or service design and development. A new product or service is conceived as a package of many different features, designed as a whole to meet the needs and requirements of the target customers.

- New product concepts should be screened, and only those that are considered potentially viable should be taken forward to detailed design and development.

- Time-to-market is often a key competitive factor in new product design. Companies that are able to achieve a short time-to-market for new products or services are likely to enjoy a competitive advantage over rivals.

Having completed your study of this chapter, you should have achieved the following outcomes:

- evaluate various aspects of the management of operations.

Self-test questions

1   Draw a transformation process model. (1.1)

2   What are the four Vs of operations? (1.5)

3   What are the five main categories of performance objectives for products, services and processes? (2.1)

4   What is added value and what is a value chain? (3.1, 3.2)

5   What is an internal customer? (3.5)

6   From what sources might ideas for new products or services originate? (4.2)

7   What is virtual prototyping? (4.4)

8   What is value engineering? (4.4)

9   What is time-to-market? (4.5)

Practice questions

Question 1

In a transformation process model, which of the following might be a transformed input?

A   A service

B   Labour

C   Facilities

D   A customer

Question 2

What is the sequence of operations that takes raw materials and converts them into an end-product or service for consumers known as?

Question 3

Continuous production is most likely to be the type of manufacturing process for:

A   production with a high volume of output

B   a high-cost operation

C   production with a high variety of output

D   products for which there are large fluctuations in demand.

Question 4

Why might operations management seek to reduce inventory levels?

Question 5

Woodsy is a garden furniture manufacturing company, which employs 30 people. It buys its timber in uncut form from a local timber merchant, and stores the timber in a covered area to dry out and season before use. Often this takes up to two years, and the wood yard takes up so much space that the production area is restricted.

The product range offered by the company is limited to the manufacture of garden seats and tables because the owner-manager, Bill Thompson, has expanded the business by concentrating on the sale of these items and has given little thought to alternative products. Bill is more of a craftsman than a manager, and the manufacturing area is anything but streamlined. Employees work on individual units at their own pace, using little more than a circular saw and a mallet and wooden pegs to assemble the finished product. The quality of the finished items is generally good but relatively expensive because of the production methods employed.

Marketing has, to date, been felt to be unnecessary because the premises stand on a busy road intersection and the company's products are on permanent display to passing traffic. Also, satisfied customers have passed on their recommendations to new customers. But things have changed. New competitors have entered the marketplace and Bill has found that orders are falling off. As the owner-manager, Bill is always very busy and, despite working long hours, finds that there is never enough time in the day to attend to everything. His foreman is a worthy individual but, like Bill, is a craftsman and not very good at man-management. The overall effect is that the workmen are left very much to their own devices. As they are paid by the hour rather than by the piece, they have little incentive to drive themselves very hard.

Required:

(a) What do you understand by the terms 'value chain' and 'value chain analysis'?

(5 marks)

(b) Use a diagram to give a brief explanation of the two different categories of activities that Porter describes. **(5 marks)**

(c) Analyse the activities in the value chain to identify the key problems facing Woodsy. **(5 marks)**

(d) Based on your analysis, prepare a set of recommendations for Bill Thompson to assist in a more efficient and effective operation of his business **(5 marks)**

(e) Explain the different aspects of design that Bill Thompson can consider for his garden furniture. **(5 marks)**

(f) Using Lewin's model, describe the process that might be adopted if Bill Thompson decides changes must take place at Woodsy. **(5 marks)**

(Total: 30 marks)

Question 6

The production process is one by which goods and services are brought into existence.

(a) Outline the strategic decisions that the operations manager is likely to encounter in a business that manufactures **toy** cars. **(12 marks)**

(b) Explain how these differ from operating and control decisions. **(8 marks)**

(Total: 20 marks)

For the answers to these questions, see the 'Answers' section at the end of the book.

Feedback to activities

Activity 1

Inputs	Transformation	Outputs
1 Plant, factory, machines, people and materials	Assembling bicycles	Completed bicycles
2 Students with limited knowledge and skills	Lectures, case studies and experiential exercises	Students with enhanced knowledge and skills
3 Client problem	Consulting: information analysis, evaluation and selection of alternatives, recommendation	Consulting report recommending course of action

Activity 2

Quality for a train company might be defined in terms of:

- trains being clean and tidy

- trains being comfortable

- trains being safe

- customer service, and staff being helpful to customers.

(Trains running to time is a dependability objective, not a quality objective; however, quality within the train company's operations might be the reason why trains run on time and the service is dependable. Scheduling trains to meet peaks in demand, such as rush hour commuter traffic, is a flexibility objective.)

Activity 4

- It is probably not necessary to involve suppliers of standard raw materials or components.

- It might be necessary to check that the supplier is able to produce a part or component to the planned design specification.

- It might be necessary to discuss with the supplier how a part or component might be produced within a target cost limit.

- The supplier might be able to contribute ideas for improving the specification for the product.

Supply relationships are described in a later chapter. However, it is appropriate to note at this stage that organisations might establish a long-term relationship with some key suppliers, and work together with those suppliers in new product design and development. The supply relationship is then a strategic relationship, with the organisation and the suppliers sharing common strategic business objectives.

Chapter 8

MANAGEMENT OF OPERATIONS

Syllabus content

- Methods for managing inventory, including continuous inventory systems (e.g. Economic Order Quantity, EOQ), periodic inventory systems and the ABC system (Note: ABC is not an acronym. A refers to high value, B to medium and C to low value inventory.)

- Strategies for balancing capacity and demand including level capacity, chase and demand management strategies.

- Systems used in operations management: Manufacturing Resource Planning (MRP), Optimised Production Technologies (OPT), Just-in-Time (JIT) and Enterprise Resource Planning (ERP).

Contents

1   Production planning and control

2   Inventory management

3   Capacity planning and control

4   Materials requirements planning (MRP I)

5   Manufacturing resource planning (MRP II)

6   Optimised production technology (OPT)

7   Enterprise resource planning (ERP)

8   Just-in-time (JIT)

1 Production planning and control

Production planning and control (or, in service industries, operations planning and control) is a process of reconciling the demand for resources and outputs with the supply of those resources and outputs.

- There are normally **uncertainties in the demand** for products, which means that the quantity produced should be increased or reduced accordingly. Production planning should provide for unforeseen variations in demand by providing ways of responding to them. For example, suppose that a production process has budgeted to make 1,000 units of an item during a month to meet anticipated demand. How would the planning and scheduling system respond to an unexpected increase in demand to, say, 1,500 units, or an unexpected fall in demand to 500 units?

- There might also be **uncertainties in supply**, caused either by:
  - insufficient supplies being available from external suppliers, due to shortages or delays in delivery, or
  - insufficient output of finished products, due to hold-ups or bottlenecks in production, inefficiencies in production or poor production planning.

1.1 Dependent demand

The demand for an item is either independent or dependent.

- **Independent demand** occurs when the demand for an item depends on factors that are difficult to predict. The demand for a finished product or the demand for a service is usually independent demand. An organisation has to make an estimate or forecast of what the demand is likely to be and schedule output and operations accordingly.

- **Dependent demand** is demand that is predictable, because it is dependent on a factor that is known and predictable. Typically, the demand for raw materials and components for making products is dependent demand, because the quantities required depend on the scheduled production quantities of the finished products.

MRP I, which is described later, is an example of a production planning system based on dependent demand for materials and components.

The methods used in production planning to schedule operations and purchases depend to some extent on whether demand is dependent or independent.

- When demand is dependent, an operation might only start to purchase the required raw materials and components when an order is received. This is known as *resource-to-order planning and control*. For example, a building company will only start to plan the acquisition of the materials and labour and other resources for constructing a building when a firm order is received from a customer. Planning and control activities can be carried out in the knowledge of the operational requirements. Similarly, a hotel will only plan the resources for a conference or reception when a firm order is received from a customer, with an estimate of the number of delegates or guests.

- With some operations, management might be confident that future demand for a finished product will arise. If so, it might retain a labour force in the expectation that future work will come for which the labour will be needed. It might also retain some inventories of items that it expects to be used in the future. This type of production planning and control is called *make-to-order*. Example of make-to-order production might be found in industries such as shipbuilding and aircraft manufacture, and also professional services such as audit work and legal services.

- Many companies make products or deliver services without any clear idea of what the future volume of demand will be. They consequently produce finished items and hold them as inventory, and acquire raw materials or components in anticipation of future demand. This type of production planning and control is known as *make-to-stock or make-to-inventory planning and control*. This type of system is very common. Where it is used, operations management must maintain suitable control over inventory levels and prevent inventories from becoming too large. (Inventories can be expensive. They tie up cash, because money is spent to acquire them, and there is a finance cost in the form of the interest cost of the cash or capital invested. Inventories also require accommodation and protection, and so incur warehousing or storage costs.)

1.2 P:D ratios

A P:D ratio is the ratio of production time or throughput time to demand time.

- Production time or throughput time is the time required for purchasing the resources for production, producing the item and delivering it to the customer.

- Demand time is the time a customer has to wait from placing an order to receiving delivery.

With a make-to-inventory production planning and control system, demand can be satisfied immediately out of existing inventories. The P:D ratio is therefore very high.

With a resource-to-order planning and control system, purchasing and production do not begin until after the order is received, and the P:D ratio will therefore be 1 or even less.

(With a make-to-order planning and control system, the P:D ratio will be somewhere between these two extremes.)

A significant difference between make-to-inventory and make-to-order systems is that:

- with make-to-inventory systems, measures by operations management to reduce the throughput time by improving production methods and efficiency will not have any effect on the demand time, whereas

- with make-to-order systems, measures by operations management to reduce the throughput time by improving production methods and efficiency will have a direct effect on the demand time, and so is likely to affect the customer's perception of the value of the product delivered.

1.3 The push and pull principles of inventory management

Two opposing forces are at work in business today:

- the need to reduce costs, and

- the need to improve service levels.

Bolstering one almost certainly causes the other to suffer. For example, when an organisation lowers its inventory to reduce costs it becomes difficult to meet varying customer demand. If it increases safety stock to meet peak demands it could wind up with a great deal of excess inventory on the books with nowhere to sell it.

Traditionally, two prevailing supply chain strategies have dominated the industry – push and pull.

In a push supply chain, production and distribution decisions are based on long-term forecasts. Push forecasts what demand will be like in the future and tunes manufacturing to that. It places the onus for inventory management decisions on the manufacturer. Typically, the manufacturer uses orders received from the retailers' warehouses to forecast demand. The problem with this strategy is that it depends on forecasts from outside the manufacturer's control. For retailers who have negotiated favourable terms, there is little risk: if the inventory doesn't move after a certain period of time, the manufacturer takes it back. For manufacturers, however, there is considerable risk: quality products may eventually wind up being sold at a reduced price.

With a pull supply chain, true customer demand, rather than forecasts, drives production and distribution. Pull places the purchaser at the centre of gravity for inventory management decisions. It prepares to fulfil demand as quickly and efficiently as it can, then actually waits for the future's demand to present itself, and replies to this demand when it comes. In other words, the manufacturer holds no inventory, but instead produces to order. On the surface, such a system is attractive because it allows the firm to eliminate inventory and the associated costs and increase service levels.

The pull strategy, however, breaks down when lead times are too long to react to demand in a way that satisfies the customer. A pure pull strategy also makes it more difficult to take advantage of economies of scale, because production and distribution are based on demand, and therefore only scheduled as needed.

There are ways to combine push and pull strategies. The place where push gives way to pull is known as the push-pull boundary. For example, a group of food manufacturers raise chickens in numbers that are based on projected demand, but only slaughter chickens based on actual demand. The push-pull boundary in this case is just before the slaughterhouse. The statistical methods used to determine an appropriate push-pull boundary are too complex to go into here, but it may be said that they essentially involve determining the point along the production chain where the savings that accrue from pull stop being worth the risk associated with pull. These calculations involve statistical facts and certainties and follow the model of all business planning.

2 Inventory management

All organisations hold inventories of some kind. Inventory exists because of differences in the rate of supply for a material or product and the rate of demand for using it. There are four different types of inventory:

- **Buffer inventory** or 'safety stock'. This is held as a precaution against the possibility that actual demand will exceed expectation. For example, suppose that a company uses an average of 10 units of an item each week, and buys a new supply of the item every four weeks. It might decide to hold a buffer inventory of, say 15 units, to guard against the possibility that demand during a four-week period might be as high as 55 units rather than the expected 40 units. Holding buffer inventory therefore reduces or eliminates the risk of running out of the item and having none of the item in inventory when it is needed.

- **Anticipation inventory**. This is inventory held in anticipation of future demand. For example, a manufacturer of skiing equipment might build up inventories of skiing equipment in anticipation of a large increase in demand at the beginning of the skiing season.

- **Cycle inventory**. This type of inventory is needed when a single process makes two or more items, but cannot make them simultaneously. The items are therefore made in batches. Each batch must be large enough to provide inventories for meeting demand in the period until the next batch of the item will be made. For example, suppose that Process X makes three products A, B and C. A batch of one of these products is made each day, so that a batch of Product A is made on day 1, a batch of Product B on day 2 and a batch of Product C on day 3, and so on. Each batch must be sufficient to meet the demand for each product for three days, which means that there will be some inventory of each product item.

- **Pipeline inventory**. This is inventory that has been allocated to a customer who has ordered it, but is still in the pipeline for delivery to the customer. The inventory has to be packed and loaded on to a transport vehicle and transported to the customer's premises. During this time, the inventory is still in the ownership of the supplier.

Inventory might also exist at different points in an operation or process. For example, in a manufacturing organisation there is inventory for raw materials and components, work-in-progress (part-finished items) and finished goods.

2.1 Inventory decisions

There are two main types of decision for inventory management:

- How much to order? When an order is placed with a supplier, what quantity should be ordered?

- When to order? How frequently should inventory be ordered? Should it be ordered at regular intervals, or when the inventory level has fallen to a reorder level?

The trade off is:

Ordering more frequently	Ordering less frequently
Higher ordering costs	Lower ordering costs
Smaller average inventory	Larger average inventory

The different departments within a firm (finance, production, marketing, etc.) often have differing views about what is an 'appropriate' level of inventory.

- *Financial managers* would like to keep inventory levels low to ensure that funds are wisely invested.

- *Marketing managers* would like to keep inventory levels high to ensure orders could be quickly filled.

- *Manufacturing managers* would like to keep raw materials levels high to avoid production delays and to make larger, more economical production runs.

2.2 Continuous inventory and periodic inventory systems

The method of making decisions about how much inventory to order, and when to order, differ according to the inventory management system that is used. There are basically two management systems, a continuous review system and a periodic review system.

- With **continuous review**, also called a **continuous inventory system**, the levels of inventory are kept under continual review. Each new addition of inventory and each withdrawal of an item from inventory is recorded when it occurs, so that there is a continuously up-to-date record of how much is currently held for each inventory item. Since the system records current inventory quantities, it can be used for re-ordering inventory items. A pre-determined quantity of an inventory item can be re-ordered from a supplier when the inventory level falls to a reorder level. For example, a system might automatically produce a purchase requisition for 1,000 units of item 12345 when the current inventory level for this item falls to, say, 500 units.

- With **periodic review**, also called a **periodic inventory system**, inventory levels are not kept under continual review. Instead, current inventory levels are counted at regular intervals (periodically), and a purchase order is placed with a supplier for each item so as to bring the total of inventory currently held plus the quantity on order up to a predetermined level. This predetermined level should be sufficient to meet the demand for the inventory item for the next period.

In a continuous review system, the inventory records might be kept on a computer file, but there is a risk that the actual inventory quantities might differ from the recorded quantities (for example, due to theft of inventory or errors in recording receipts or usage of inventory). There should therefore be a physical system to supplement the records system for inventory reordering. Two such systems are:

- a two-bin system, and

- a three-bin system.

In a **two-bin system**, the inventory for each item is held in two bins. One bin contains the reorder level quantity (including any safety stock or buffer stock). The other bin contains additional units of the item, and demand for the inventory item is met by taking items from this bin first, until it is empty. When this bin is emptied, a new order must be placed with a supplier immediately.

A **three-bin system** is similar.

- One bin holds a reorder level quantity, defined as:

  Average demand per day/week × Average supply lead time in days/weeks

- A second bin holds the safety stock or buffer stock units.

- The third bin holds all other units of the item. Demand for the inventory item is met by taking items from this bin first, until it is empty. When this third bin is empty, a new order must be placed immediately with a supplier. During the supply lead time, items issued from inventory should be taken from the bin containing the reorder level quantity.

With the three-bin system, the risk of a stock-out will be apparent if two bins are emptied and items issued from inventory have to be taken from the bin holding the safety stock.

2.3 Continuous review: how much to order? EOQ model

In a system of continuous review, there needs to be a method of establishing the reorder quantity for each item. One such method is the Economic Order Quantity model or EOQ model.

The EOQ model is used to calculate the order quantity for any item of inventory that minimises the total annual inventory costs. It is assumed that there are no price discounts available for larger-sized orders, and the total annual inventory costs therefore consist of:

- ordering costs for the inventory, and

- holding costs for the inventory.

Ordering costs might include:

- the costs of delivery, if these are payable by the buyer

- administration costs, if these are identifiable: administration costs might include the costs of asking several suppliers to submit a tender for the work and selecting the best tender, and costs of placing the order and monitoring its progress.

Holding costs might include:

- the finance cost of holding inventory, measured by applying the annual cost of finance to the cost of the average inventory level

- storage costs, but only if these are separately identifiable and traceable to individual units of inventory.

The EOQ model is based on several assumptions.

- There are no price discounts available for larger-sized orders.

- Demand for the item of inventory is a constant amount each day/week/month.

- Re-supply is immediate, so that the supply lead time is 0 days. (Alternatively, the supply lead time is constant, so that the reorder level can be fixed so as to ensure re-supply immediately the inventory level falls to 0 units.)

If none of these assumptions is valid (or largely accurate), the EOQ model is of doubtful accuracy and reliability.

Imagine that a firm sells A units a year and sales are constant. If it retails the product at a price p its turnover will be pA. The firm purchases stock at a wholesale price of w, sells it and, when stock has fallen to zero, obtains more stock. If the firm orders an amount Q, the stock level of the firm will follow the profile shown in the diagram below, where Q has been assumed to be 10 and stock usage is one unit a period. From the diagram it follows that the average stock level will be Q/2, in this case five units.

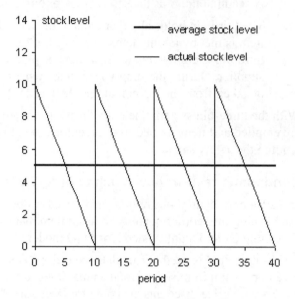

Total inventory costs are minimised when the combined cost of ordering inventory and holding inventory each period (each year) is minimised. To decide what to do, we must look at the demand and costs:

    C = ordering cost per order event (fixed cost to place an order, *not* per unit)

    H = holding cost per unit per unit of time eg, per year

    Q = is the reorder quantity

    A = total sales per annum

The equation below, which you will not need to derive, is the so-called *economic order quantity* or *EOQ*

$$Q = \sqrt{\frac{2AC}{H}} = EOQ$$

2.4 Reorder level: when to order in a continuous review system

When the demand for an item of inventory item is constant and predictable, and the supply lead time is also predictable, the reorder level for an item in a continuous review system should be:

Demand for the item each day/week × Supply lead time in days/weeks.

(The supply lead time is the length of time between initiating a new order for an inventory item and receiving the delivery of the item from the supplier.)

For example, if the daily demand for an inventory item is 10 units and the supply lead time is two weeks, the reorder level should be 20 units, so that there will be enough units of the item in inventory to meet the demand during the supply lead time. Similarly, if re-supply is 'instantaneous' and the supply lead time is 0, the reorder level can be 0 units. (This is the principle applied with just-in-time purchasing.)

2.5 The reorder level: uncertain demand and lead times

In practice, the demand for an inventory item is rarely predictable or constant, and the supply lead time might also be variable. When there is uncertain demand or an uncertain supply lead time, there could be some risk that demand during the lead time will exceed the reorder level quantity, and there will be a 'stock-out'. When a stock-out occurs, there will be some delay in operations until the new delivery of the item is made. There could possibly be a major disruption in operations, resulting in loss of output and sales or bottlenecks in production.

Imagine that the EOQ model is to be employed by a firm but the management is worried by the fact that the mathematics implies that stocks will be allowed to fall to zero. Given that, in reality, demand will not be constant as is implied by the regular fall in stocks as sales take place, it is quite likely that management would like to have a buffer stock (or safety stock) so that stock levels were never allowed to fall below a certain level. Assume that this safety level is given as S. If all of the other assumptions of the model hold, the path that stocks will follow will be that given by the diagram below where safety stocks of two units are assumed.

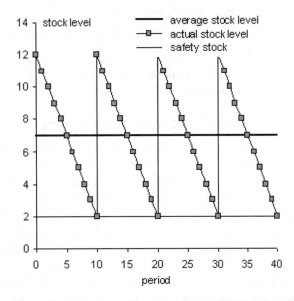

Thus, Q (10 units in the example) will be ordered but stocks will not fall to zero before the firm restocks. Rather stocks fall to S and then new stocks arrive at the warehouse. The question that is posed, therefore, is 'does this have any effect on the value of the economic order quantity? 'The answer is 'no'.

The use of buffer stocks leaves many features of the model unchanged. The cost of holding *one unit* of stock has not altered. Similarly, the cost of reordering stock has not changed. The only effect has been to increase the average stock level for any reorder quantity. In effect there is a permanent stock of 2 units in this example and a revolving stock that starts at *10* and falls to zero. The only difference now is that holding (storage) costs have increased because, at any time, more stock will be held. This does not affect the EOQ as it applies to all ordering frequencies.

2.6 Maximum and minimum warning levels

When a safety stock or buffer stock is held, there should be a control mechanism to warn management:

- if the size of the buffer stock might be too high, or

- if there is still some risk of a stock-out during the supply lead time.

A control mechanism can be provided by having, for each inventory item:

- a maximum inventory level, and

- a minimum inventory level.

If the actual inventory level exceeds the maximum warning level, this could be an indication that the buffer stock is too large, and the reorder level should perhaps be reduced. If the actual inventory level falls below the minimum warning level, this would give a notification of a possible stock-out during the supply lead time. If the actual inventory level falls below the minimum level during most supply lead times, this could indicate that the buffer stock is too small, and the reorder level should therefore be increased.

Formulae for establishing a maximum warning level and a minimum warning level for an item of inventory are as follows.

- Maximum inventory level =

  Reorder level + Reorder quantity – (Minimum demand per day/week × minimum supply lead time in days/weeks)

- Minimum inventory level =

  Reorder level – (Average demand per day/week × average supply lead time in days/weeks)

Other methods for deciding the reorder level and the maximum and minimum warning levels might be used.

2.7 ABC system of inventory management

The ABC system of inventory management is an inventory control method based upon a statistical principle discovered by a 19th century Italian economist, Vilfredo Pareto. He observed that a small number of situations in a population would often dominate the results achieved. Therefore, controlling the vital few would go a long way to controlling the overall situation. This observation is recognised today as Pareto's Law, which states that about 80% of total inventory usage can be accounted for by 20% of inventory items, and the remaining 20% of inventory usage is accounted for by the remaining 80% of items. When ABC analysis is applied to an inventory situation, it determines the importance of items and the level of controls placed on the items. By dividing a company's inventory into different classifications – A, B, or C, managers can focus on the items that account for the majority of the inventory. The adaptation of Pareto's Law of the vital few and trivial many follows a pattern:

- Category A items are those of particularly high value in terms of turnover or usage rate, so that if there were to be a stock-out, many customers might be disappointed. The turnover or usage rate can be measured as the value of the item consumed each week, month or year. Category A items might be the 20% or so items for which usage (by value) is highest, accounting for about 80% of total inventory usage by value.

- Category B items are those of medium value in terms of usage. Category B items might be the next 30% of inventory items, accounting for about 10% of total inventory usage by value.

- Category C items are the least-used inventory items, accounting for about 50% of inventory items and about 10% of total inventory usage by value.

The steps in doing the ABC analysis are:

- Determine annual quantity usage of each item.

- Multiply the annual quantity usage of each item by the cost of the item to obtain the total annual £ usage of each item.

- Add the total £ usage of all items to get the aggregate annual £ inventory expenditure.

- Divide the total annual £ usage of each item by the aggregate annual inventory expenditure to obtain the percentage of total usage for each item.

- List the items in rank order by percentage of aggregate usage.

- Review annual usage distribution and classify items as A, B, or C.

When doing an ABC classification, separate analysis should be performed for different types of inventory. For example, finished goods analysis is done separately from raw materials. An organisation applying an ABC system of inventory management might:

- apply a system of close inventory control for Category A items, for example by using a continuous review system for all the items in this category

- apply a less close system of control for Category B items, for example by using a periodic review system for all the items in this category

- apply a much less careful system of control for items in Category C, for example by holding large quantities of low value items (such as paper clips, staples, screws, nails and so on), or waiting until the inventory level falls to zero before ordering a new supply.

The presumption is that a stock-out of a Category A item could be costly, and should be avoided if possible, whereas a stock-out of a Category C item would be of little operational or financial significance.

ABC analysis puts emphasis on 'where the value is'. By focusing efforts on higher value inventory, a company can assign proper resources to attain the optimum inventory levels, reducing inventory costs and ensuring customers' needs are met.

2.8 Criticisms of traditional inventory management systems

Traditional inventory management systems assume that it is necessary to hold some inventory to avoid the risks and costs of stock-outs. An alternative view is that inventory is wasteful: it adds no value to operations. The aim should be to avoid inventory completely (at least for Category A inventory items, if an ABC approach is taken). To achieve this aim:

- items of raw materials or components should be provided by suppliers only when they are needed, and

- in a manufacturing system that has several consecutive stages of production, items of output from one stage of production should be manufactured only when they are needed by the next stage.

These are the aims of just-in-time purchasing and just-in-time production, discussed in detail in Section 8 below.

3 Capacity planning and control

Capacity planning and control is concerned with balancing the demand for output capacity with the supply or availability of capacity. The objectives of capacity planning should be to achieve a suitable balance between the demand for capacity and the provision of capacity, in order to achieve both high profits and satisfied customers.

- Costs are affected by the balance between capacity demand and supply. If an operation has capacity levels in excess of demand, there will be under-utilised capacity, and probably higher-than-necessary costs.

- Revenues are also affected by the balance between capacity demand and supply, but in the opposite way. If an operation has insufficient capacity to meet demand, there will be unsatisfied demand and some loss of revenue and profit.

- Quality might be affected by the management of capacity. An organisation might hire temporary labour when demand is high and in excess of normal capacity. If it does, there will be some risk of a fall in quality due to the comparative lack of skills and experience amongst the temporary staff.

- When capacity exceeds demand, the organisation might produce more output than it immediately requires for meeting the available demand. Inventories will therefore grow. This has a cash flow and a cost implication. Cash will be used up in the manufacture of items for inventory, and this investment of cash has an interest cost.

- The balance between demand and available capacity can affect dependability of supply. If demand is normally close to the available capacity level, the system will have difficulty in meeting demand on time if there is an unexpected increase in demand or an unexpected disruption to a part of the production process.

- The balance between demand and available capacity can also affect flexibility of operations, particularly volume flexibility. When there is excess capacity in the system, an organisation will be able to deal with an unexpected increase in demand by producing more output.

Capacity planning provides an operational framework and ensures the co-ordination of supplies and scheduling of resources. The starting points are:

- Market information – do we know what the demand is and by when? Can we forecast (predict) it?

- Shall we make goods to order only (MTO) or, being able to rely on a steady flow of orders with additional predictions of demand, make to stock (MTS)? Trends for both MTO and MTS must be predicted to ascertain capacity implications and generate plans.

3.1 Measuring capacity

Capacity can be measured in terms of either input resources available or output for a given period of time, such as a day, week or month.

- Input resources capacity might be expressed in terms of man-hours available in each department or each skills grade, or machine hours for each class of machinery.

- Output might be measured in terms of the number of units produced, the number of passenger-miles carried (transport systems) or the number of students graduating each year with a degree (university).

Design capacity is the theoretical capacity of an operation. For example, if a production department operates for six days each week and 14 hours each day, the design capacity of machines used in the department will be 84 hours (6 × 14).

However, in practice, the design capacity is unlikely to be achievable. For example, there might be some unavoidable loss in machine time due to the idle time between jobs, or due to routine machine maintenance and inspection checks.

Effective capacity is the design capacity minus loss of capacity that is outside management control. For example, the design capacity of a machine might be 84 hours each week but, owing to routine weekly maintenance and the down-time between batches, effective capacity might be, say, just 80 hours.

In practice, the **actual capacity** will be lower than effective capacity, for reasons within management control, such as machine breakdowns or bottlenecks in production. If capacity is measured in terms of available man-hours, actual capacity might be affected by employees being absent from work due to illness, or on a training course, or late for work.

When capacity is measured in terms of output rather than input resources, actual capacity is the actual volume of output produced. This might be less than capacity due to inefficiencies in production, or defective units of production.

For control purposes, useful measures of capacity might be:

- Utilisation $= \dfrac{\text{Actual capacity}}{\text{Design capacity}}$

- Efficiency $= \dfrac{\text{Actual output}}{\text{Effective capacity}}$

Overall equipment effectiveness (OEE)

Another measure for monitoring and controlling capacity of machinery or equipment is the overall equipment effectiveness (OEE) ratio. This is the product of three factors:

- output speed: the actual throughput or production rate as a percentage of the expected throughput rate

- output quality: the percentage of output that is 'good' and not rejected

- availability: the percentage of the time that the equipment was available for operations as a percentage of the time that it should have been available.

For example, suppose that a machine has the capacity to produce up to 200 units an hour but only produced 180 units an hour, of which 2% were faulty. If the machine should have been available for 50 hours in the week but was only available for 40 hours due to a major breakdown, the overall equipment effectiveness in the week was:

90% × 98% × 80% = 70.56%.

Activity 1

What is the overall equipment effectiveness in a period when the machines were available for 96% of the time, produced 2,900 units day and the defectives rate was 1%? Production capacity on the machines is 3,000 units per day.

Feedback to this activity is at the end of the chapter.

3.2 Balancing capacity and demand

There are several methods of planning capacity and trying to balance availability and demand. These include:

- a level capacity plan

- a chase demand plan

- a demand management plan

- a mix of these three types of plan.

Level capacity

With a level capacity plan, the aim is to maintain processing capacity at a uniform or level amount throughout the planning period, regardless of fluctuations in demand. Since planned output is constant throughout the period, labour and other resources (such as equipment) can also be kept constant.

- **Manufacturing operation**. If demand is less than output, the surplus output is added to inventory. When demand exceeds output, the excess demand is met from the inventory.

- **Service operation**. If demand is less than capacity, there will be idle resources. When demand exceeds capacity, the operation will have to turn away some of the customers.

Level capacity planning should result in a fairly high capacity utilisation ratio.

With level capacity planning in a manufacturing operation, inventories might build up to very high levels when capacity exceeds demand. When large inventories are held in anticipation of future demand, there is a risk that the demand will fail to materialise and the inventories will not be sold because they are no longer fashionable or because they are obsolete.

With level capacity planning in a service operation, management must accept that there will be idle resources for much of the time. This is often evident in operations such as retailing, and the hotels and restaurants business. Clearly such a strategy is unlikely to be compatible with a 'just in time' approach to inventory.

Chase demand

With a chase demand plan, the objective is to match capacity as closely as possible with demand. If demand increases, capacity is increased, and if demand falls, capacity is reduced. In order to achieve this objective, resources must be flexible.

- Staff numbers must be easily increased or reduced in numbers, possibly by hiring temporary and part-time staff, or staff must be prepared to work large amounts of overtime. Alternatively, it might be possible to sub-contract excess work to other organisations.

- Variations in equipment capacity must be achievable by methods such as equipment hire. In capital-intensive operations, a chase demand plan is unworkable, because equipment cannot be easily increased or decreased at short notice.

A chase demand plan might be appropriate in operations where it is impossible to hold inventories and meet customer demand by selling from inventory. This applies to various service industries such as hairdressing and training. For example, training companies are often able to match capacity with demand by using the services of independent self-employed trainers.

Demand management

An organisation might attempt to 'manage demand' with the aim of stabilising demand and making it more predictable. If demand is fairly stable and predictable, capacity levels can then be planned accordingly. An aim of demand management is often to encourage customers to use a service in an off-peak period rather than at peak times. Examples of demand management are:

- on the railways or buses, offering off-peak tickets at much lower prices

- lower prices for 'off-season' holidays

- lower prices for telephone calls at off-peak times.

A company might use *advertising* to boost demand during low demand seasons, such as encouraging consumers to eat more ice cream during the cold months of the year.

In some cases, an organisation might seek to boost demand in low-sales periods by offering a completely different product or service with the same resources. For example, mobile vans used for selling ice cream in the hot months might be converted to selling hot meals such as burgers and hot dogs during the colder months.

Mixed plans

Capacity planning might use a mix of level capacity, chase demand and demand management planning, in different parts of their operation.

Yield management

When an operation has a fairly fixed capacity level in the short to medium term, and it cannot raise or lower its capacity significantly in that time, it might pursue a yield management policy of maximising revenue with the available capacity.

A yield management approach can be particularly well-suited to an operation where:

- capacity is mainly fixed

- the market can be segmented into different sectors, to allow some price discrimination between sectors

- the output cannot be sold in advance

- the marginal cost of making additional output units within the available capacity is low.

Examples of yield management are often found in airline companies, where techniques to increase, decrease or switch demand are:

- Price discounting. To boost demand when capacity on certain routes is expected to be low, an airline might sell a block of tickets at a discount price to an agent, which then sells the tickets on to customers at a discount rate. Officially, the airline has not reduced its prices, although in practice it has reduced some (but not all) prices.

- Altering the seating capacity in airlines between first class, business class and economy class, to maximise revenue on each flight or route.

- Over-booking. An airline might sell more tickets than there are seats, expecting a proportion of customers to switch flights or cancel their booking. Occasionally, this will mean that more customers will turn up for a flight than the aeroplane can carry, and some passengers must be given inducements to take a later flight.

An organisation might be unsure which method of capacity planning would be most appropriate to its own circumstances. Techniques to assist in reaching a decision about how to plan capacity include modelling (such as simulation models or queuing models).

4 Materials requirements planning (MRP I)

DEFINITION

Materials requirements planning or MRP I is a computerised system for planning the requirements for raw materials and components, sub-assemblies and finished items.

Materials requirement planning, or MRP 1, is a computerised system for planning the requirements for raw materials and components, sub-assemblies and finished items.

It is a system that converts a production schedule into a listing of the materials and components required to meet that schedule, so that adequate stock levels are maintained and items are available when needed.

The aims of an MRP I system are to:

- make sure that:

  - all the raw materials and components are available in time to produce the finished products, and

  - the finished products are available on time in accordance with the production plan, to meet the expected sales demand

- minimise inventory levels, by trying to ensure that components are not manufactured until they are needed in production, and finished products are not manufactured until they are required by customers

- plan the purchasing of raw materials and other items from suppliers

- schedule the production of components in-house and the assembly of finished products, and the delivery of finished items to customers.

KEY POINT

MRP I takes a different approach to resources scheduling from the traditional 'fixed order quantity' and EOQ approach.

MRP I takes a different approach to resources scheduling from the traditional 'fixed order quantity' and EOQ approach.

- The traditional fixed order quantity approach is to purchase materials or manufacture parts and finished products in a predetermined fixed quantity, as soon as the inventory level falls to a given level.

- MRP I seeks to specify the exact number of items that must be purchased or manufactured, and when they are required, to meet a specific production schedule.

The principles of MRP I are quite straightforward.

- The starting point is a budget or forecast for sales demand.

- From this, it is possible to determine the quantities of finished output required in the planning period.

- These quantities are expressed as a master production schedule or MPS, which specifies both the quantities required and when they will be required.

- From the quantities of finished outputs required, it is possible to calculate the quantities of materials required to make the output. Materials quantities can be calculated at different levels of production.

For example:

- Product X might be made by assembling five components, and each of these components might be manufactured in-house.

- One of the components might consist of 12 different parts or sub-components, five of which are manufactured in-house and seven of which are purchased externally.

- One of these five sub-components might consist of ten parts, which are all purchased externally.

An MRP I system would calculate the quantities required for each component and sub-component, and the quantities of parts to be purchased externally for each component and sub-component. In addition, it would specify:

- when each purchase order for parts should be placed with the supplier

- when the production of each part for the sub-components should be scheduled, to be available for the manufacture of the sub-components

- when the production of each part for the components should be scheduled, to be available for the manufacture of the components

- when the manufacture of the finished products should be scheduled in order to meet the anticipated sales demand.

It might be apparent that an MRP I system works on the basis that the demand for all materials is a dependent demand, related to the master production schedule (MPS).

The elements of an MRP I system are as follows:

- The system has access to **inventory records**, for all items of stock (finished goods, sub-assemblies, components, raw materials) and so is aware of current stock levels. For each inventory item, there are also records for the production lead time or purchase lead time.

- The system has access to a **bill of materials** for each item of production. A bill of materials is simply a detailed list of the sub-assemblies, components and raw materials, including the quantities of each, needed to make the item.

- The system also has access to a **master production schedule**. This is a production schedule, detailing the quantities of each item that need to be produced, and the time by which completed output is required. The master production schedule is produced from firm sales orders and current estimates of future sales demand within the planning period.

- Taking the production schedule, the bills of materials and inventory records, the system computes what quantities of materials are required, and by when. In the case of items purchased externally, the system will report when the purchase orders must be placed. Where items are produced in-house, the system will provide a schedule for the commencement of production for each item.

- The system can produce works orders and materials plans and automatic purchase orders for use by the purchasing department.

- As information about sales orders changes, the production schedule can be altered quickly, and a new materials procurement programme prepared automatically.

A problem with MRP I systems is that the MPS is based to some extent on forecasts of future orders not yet received. In the short term, a company might have a full order book, and all production will be planned to meet existing orders. Over the longer-term however, sales demand will be based on uncertain estimates. Whenever it becomes apparent that actual sales will differ from the original plan, a new MPS should be produced, and also a new MRP schedule of purchasing and production requirements.

When there are only a few current orders, and most of the sales forecast is based on estimates of future demand, the operations management might choose to use a make-for-inventory system based on fixed production order quantities, rather than continually revise production schedules and MRP plans.

4.1 Comparing MRP I with a fixed order quantity system

With fixed order quantity systems, a company manufacturing parts and components for its own finished products will choose to manufacture each part or component, as well as each finished product item, in fixed quantities or batch sizes. Similarly, it will purchase items from suppliers in fixed order quantities (EOQ sizes).

A fixed order quantity system is therefore different from an MRP I system in a number of ways.

Fixed order quantity system	*MRP I system*
Order quantities determined individually for each end-product, component part and raw material separately	Materials requirements based on requirement for finished products
New supply of each item when inventory level is low	Production of parts and purchases scheduled to meet production requirements of end products.
Production or purchase orders triggered by inventory reaching reorder level	Production or purchase orders triggered by scheduled timing in MRP I plan
	Compatible with just-in-time manufacturing and JIT purchasing
Suitable when there is continuous random demand for the item	Suitable when demand is 'lumpy' and not continuous, or when demand is predictable.

4.2 Closed loop MRP

When MRP systems were first used for production scheduling, it was usual to produce a new materials requirements plan at the beginning of each week, based on a revised MPS. However, there was no feedback loop to inform operations managers whether:

- the plan was actually achievable, or

- whether it was actually achieved.

MRP systems were subsequently introduced that provided this feedback, and they were called 'closed loop MRP systems'. Closing the planning loop involves checking the production plans against available capacity and resources. If there are insufficient resources, the program changes the production schedule to something that is achievable.

Virtually all MRP systems now include a closed loop system.

4.3 Benefits of MRP I

An MRP I system can provide a number of benefits for production planning and operations management.

- An MRP I system produces a detailed production and purchasing schedule based on demand for the finished products, giving both quantities required and the timing of purchases and production.

- The MPS and MRP schedules can be amended quickly whenever estimates of demand change, because the system is computerised.

- The system can give an early warning of potential problems with production or purchasing due to bottlenecks or delays in the supply chain.

MRP I is consistent with a JIT system, which is described later.

4.4 Disadvantages of MRP I

MRP I is not suitable when it is impossible to predict sales in advance, or when sales demand for items is continuous and random. For example, an MRP I system would not be appropriate for a supermarket, or for systems that are used to manufacture non-standard items (such as contracting businesses or small jobbing businesses).

An MRP I system can also be fairly complex, and might therefore be difficult to use when the MPS has to be changed regularly or frequently.

5 Manufacturing resource planning (MRP II)

Manufacturing resource systems or MRP II systems are an extension of MRP I, and MRP I is a core feature of MRP II.

MRP II systems differ from MRP I systems by integrating into the same system other processes that are related to materials requirements planning, and in particular:

- financial requirements planning

- labour scheduling

- equipment utilisation scheduling.

KEY POINT

Manufacturing resource systems or MRP II systems are an extension of MRP I, and MRP I is a core feature of MRP II.

DEFINITION

Oliver Wight, another early advocate of MRP, defined MRP II as 'a game plan for planning and monitoring all the resources of a manufacturing company: manufacturing, marketing, finance and engineering'.

Oliver Wight, another early advocate of MRP, defined MRP II as 'a game plan for planning and monitoring all the resources of a manufacturing company: manufacturing, marketing, finance and engineering'.

- Without MRP II, the engineering function and the manufacturing function would have had separate files for bills of materials (BOM). Changes to the specification of a product might be entered on one BOM file but not on the other, resulting in differences and discrepancies between the activities of the two functions.

- Similarly, the finance function might use a different product database for producing estimates of costs and comparing actual costs against the budget. The product file used by the finance function might differ from the product specifications of the BOM file used by the manufacturing function.

Giving all functions access to the same product database removes the risks and problems of such differences and discrepancies.

6 Optimised production technology (OPT)

KEY POINT

Optimised production technology or OPT is another approach to production planning and capacity management. It was developed as a computerised scheduling system by Eli Goldratt in the 1980s and is based on his Theory of Constraints.

Optimised production technology or OPT is another approach to production planning and capacity management. It was developed as a computerised scheduling system by Eli Goldratt in the 1980s and is based on his Theory of Constraints.

The Theory of Constraints is based on the principle that the capacity of a system to produce output is limited or constrained by one or more bottlenecks in the system. In order to increase throughput, management should focus on the key constraint and seek to find ways of reducing it. Having removed one constraint, there will be another, different constraint that now restricts the capacity in the system and management should try to find ways of dealing with it. Operations management should therefore be a process of looking for the next constraint and dealing with it, and continually trying to improve capacity within the system.

An OPT system is a production scheduling system that focuses on bottlenecks. Production scheduling is based on the capacity of the bottlenecks, and the pace of throughput that these can handle.

Some of the principles or rules of OPT are as follows.

- A bottleneck or critical resource determines the production capacity for the entire system.

- The level of utilisation of non-critical resources should reflect the requirements of the critical resources.

  - An hour lost on a bottleneck is an hour lost to the entire production system.

  - An hour saved at a non-bottleneck has no real impact or value.

- Bottlenecks determine the amount of throughput and the size of inventories. Why produce a component faster than a bottleneck can use it? All that will happen is an unnecessary and costly increase in inventories of the component.

- The size of a batch transferred from one stage in production to another does not need to be the same as the batch size produced by the process.

- The process batch size should be variable, to optimise throughput, and should not be a fixed or standard quantity.

- Production schedules should be developed by looking at all the constraints in the system. Production lead times will be a consequence of what is feasible within the schedules, and are not a predetermined length of time.

7 Enterprise resource planning (ERP)

Enterprise resource planning (ERP) was developed from MRP, and some software companies such as SAP and Oracle have specialised in the provision of ERP systems to client companies. Some ERP systems are highly complex, as well as very expensive.

In an MRP system, the effects of any change in sales demand are calculated by the system, and new schedules for manufacturing and materials procurement are produced. An ERP system performs a similar function, but it integrates data from all operations within the organisation. As a consequence, decisions taken in one part of the organisation are reflected in the planning and control systems in other parts of the organisation.

Typically, an ERP system provides an integrated database for:

- operations (e.g. manufacturing)

- purchasing and supply

- financial applications

- human resource management applications

- sales and marketing applications

- delivery and logistics applications

- customer services applications

- strategic reporting to senior management.

Features of ERP systems include:

- allowing access to the system to any individual with a terminal linked to the system's central server

- decision support features, to assist management with decision-making

- in many cases, extranet links to the major suppliers and customers, with electronic data interchange facilities for the automated transmission of documentation' such as purchase orders and invoices.

8 Just-in-time (JIT)

'Traditional' responses to the problems of improving manufacturing capacity and reducing unit costs of production might be described as follows:

- longer production runs

- economic batch quantities

- fewer products in the product range

- more overtime

- reduced time on preventive maintenance, to keep production flowing.

In general terms, longer production runs and large batch sizes should mean less disruption, better capacity utilisation and lower unit costs.

Just-in-time systems challenge such 'traditional' views of manufacture.

A just-in-time (JIT) planning and control system is based on the idea that items should be purchased or produced only when they are required by the next stage in the production process, and products should only be manufactured when they are required to meet an existing customer order. Items should be available:

- not too early, before they are required, because this results in unnecessary inventory

- not too late, after they are required, because this results in a bottleneck in production and/or a delay in making a sale to a customer.

JIT has also been called 'stockless production' and 'fast throughput manufacturing'. It also has close connections with lean manufacturing, which is described in a later chapter.

8.1 Definitions of JIT

Just-in-time (JIT) is a system whose objective is to produce or to procure products or components as they are required by a customer or for use, rather than for stock. A JIT system is a 'pull' system, which responds to demand, in contrast to a 'push' system, in which stocks act as buffers between the different elements of the system, such as purchasing, production and sales.'

JIT applies to both production within an organisation and also to purchasing from external suppliers. An organisation using JIT must therefore seek to involve major suppliers in the JIT approach.

Just-in-time production is a production system that is driven by demand for finished products, whereby each component on a production line is produced only when needed for the next stage.

Just-in-time purchasing is a purchasing system in which material purchases are contracted so that the receipt and usage of the materials, to the maximum extent, coincide'. (CIMA *Official Terminology*)

8.2 Elements of JIT

The basic elements of JIT were developed by Toyota in the 1950s, and became known as the Toyota Production System (TPS). They include:

- **Product design**. In many cases, the design of a product has a big impact on operational costs. Production costs can be significantly reduced at the product design stage.

- **Just in time purchasing**. With JIT purchasing, an organisation establishes strategic and long-term relationships with major suppliers. The supplier undertakes to make its own production systems flexible, so that it is capable of delivering raw materials or parts only when they are required, but at the same time providing a reliable and dependable service, with no delays in delivery.

KEY POINT

A just-in-time (JIT) planning and control system is based on the idea that items should be purchased or produced only when they are required by the next stage in the production process, and products should only be manufactured when they are required to meet an existing customer order.

DEFINITION

Just-in-time (JIT) is a system whose objective is to produce or to procure products or components as they are required by a customer or for use, rather than for stock.

Just-in-time production is 'a system which is driven by demand for finished products whereby each component on a production line is produced only when needed for the next stage'

Just-in-time purchasing is 'a system in which material purchases are contracted so that the receipt and usage of material, to the maximum extent possible, coincide'

- **Work cells and employee involvement.** Machines or workers should be grouped by product or component instead of by the type of work performed. The non-value-added activity of materials movement between operations is therefore minimised by eliminating space between workstations. Products can flow from machine to machine without having to wait for the next stage of processing or returning to stores. Lead times and work in progress are thus reduced. Workers within each machine cell should be trained to operate each machine within that cell and to be able to perform routine preventative maintenance on the cell machines (ie to be multi-skilled and flexible).

- **Use several small, simple machines**, rather than a larger and more complex machine. Using smaller machines has the benefit of greater flexibility. They can be moved more easily than larger machines, and it is easier to organise work cells around simple machines.

- **Set-up time reductions.** 'Set-up' refers to the activities that have to be carried out between finishing one batch of output in a process and getting the process ready to start the next batch. For example, it might involve cleaning the equipment that has been used, making adjustments to the equipment and getting the parts and materials for the next batch. Set-up does not add value and time spent on setting up a process is wasted time. The aim should therefore be to reduce and minimise set-up times, for example by doing some of the set-up work for the next batch whilst the previous batch is still being processed.

- **Total productive maintenance.** (TPM). The objective of TPM is to eliminate breakdowns in equipment and unplanned halts in production by improving maintenance systems. Employees operating a particular process are encouraged to 'take ownership' of their machines and carry out simple running repairs and maintenance work on them. This gives maintenance specialists more time to spend on devising methods of improving maintenance systems rather than 'fire fighting' and carrying out routine repairs and maintenance operations.

- **Visibility in the work place.** With JIT production, the workplace is made much more visible, so that it is easy to see what is going on in each area of the factory floor, and to monitor the progress of work. Techniques for creating greater visibility include visual control systems (such as 'kanbans') see below), signal lights to indicate where a stoppage has occurred and display boards showing performance achievements.

Elimination of all non-value-added costs and waste. Value is only added while a product is actually being processed. Whilst it is being inspected for quality, moving from one part of the factory to another, waiting for further processing and held in store, value is not being added. Waste can be described as the use of resources that fail to add value to the product. All staff should be involved and encouraged to contribute to the processes of eliminating waste in the operation.

High quality and reliability. Disruptions in production due to poor quality production must be avoided, because disruptions caused by breakdowns and defective output create hold-ups in the entire system. Machinery must be kept fully maintained, and so preventative maintenance is an important aspect of production

Speed of throughput. All parts of the productive process should be operated at a speed that matches the rate at which the customer demands the final product. Production runs will therefore be shorter and there will be smaller stocks of finished goods because output is being matched more closely to demand (and so storage costs will be reduced).

Flexibility. In order to respond immediately to customer orders, the production system must be flexible, and capable of switching from making one product to making another. Batch sizes should be small. A flexible production system calls for a dedicated work force with appropriate skills, and a willingness by management to allow the work teams to use their initiative to deal with problems that arise.

Lower costs. Another objective of JIT is to reduce costs by raising quality and achieving a faster throughput. Production management should seek to eliminate scrap and defective units during production, and to avoid the need for reworking of units since this stops the flow of production and leads to late deliveries to customers. Cash flows should also improve if inventories are reduced towards zero

8.3 Close relationship with suppliers

A company is a long way towards JIT if its suppliers will guarantee the quality of the material they deliver and will give it shorter lead-times, deliver smaller quantities more often, guarantee a low reject rate and perform quality-assurance inspection at source. Frequent deliveries of small quantities of material to the company can ensure that each delivery is just enough to meet its immediate production schedule. This will keep its inventory as low as possible. Materials handling time will be saved because as there is no need to move the stock into a store, the goods can be delivered directly to a workstation on the shop floor. Inspection time and costs can be eliminated and the labour required for reworking defective material or returning goods to the supplier can be saved.

The successful JIT manufacturer deliberately sets out to cultivate good relationships with a small number of suppliers and these suppliers will often be situated close to the manufacturing plant. It is usual for a large manufacturer that does not use the JIT approach to have multiple suppliers. When a new part is to be produced, various suppliers will bid for the contract and the business will be given to the two or three most attractive bids. A JIT manufacturer is looking for a single supplier that can provide high quality and reliable deliveries, rather than the lowest price. This supplier will often be located in close proximity to the manufacturing plant.

There is much to be gained by both the company and its suppliers from this mutual dependence. The supplier is guaranteed a demand for the products as the sole supplier and is able to plan to meet the customer's production schedules. If an organisation has confidence that suppliers will deliver material of 100% quality, on time, so that there will be no rejects, returns and hence no consequent production delays, usage of materials can be matched with delivery of materials and stocks can be kept at near zero levels.

8.4 Elimination of waste

Waste is defined as any activity that does not add value. Toyota identified seven areas in which waste occurs.

1   **Over-production**. It is wasteful to produce more output at any stage of the production process than is needed for the next stage.

2   **Waiting time**. Time spent waiting for work is wasteful. Waiting time can be measured by labour efficiency and machine efficiency.

3   **Transport** (movement of materials). Moving items from one place to another does not add value, although it does incur costs and wastes time. The production system should seek to minimise the movement of materials, by re-arranging the layout of the factory floor.

4   **Waste in the process**. There might be waste in the process itself, which should be eliminated. Waste might be caused by poor maintenance or by poor design of products or processes.

5   **Inventory**. Inventory does not add value but it creates a cost and ties up cash. It is therefore wasteful. The aim should be to reduce inventory to zero by dealing with the problems that cause inventories to build up.

6   **Motion**. An employee does not necessarily create value by working, because many of the things that he or she does might be wasteful. For example, moving around from one place to another does not add value, but it takes up time and can be described as 'working'. The aim should therefore be to simplify work and get rid of unnecessary actions ('the waste of motion').

7   **Defective goods** are 'quality waste'. Producing defective items that have to be scrapped or re-worked is a major cause of waste in many organisations.

Activity 2

What is the difference between waste from transport and waste from motion? Explain how these different types of waste might be reduced.

Feedback to this activity is at the end of the chapter.

8.5 Involvement of all staff

JIT is an organisational culture, and the concept has to be adopted by everyone in the organisation if it is going to work. It is therefore associated with other concepts such as the 'empowerment' of the employee.

Authority should be delegated to the individuals who are directly responsible for a particular operation. The role of management should be to support individuals working on the factory floor, rather than spending their time giving instructions and telling them what to do. For example, if a quality problem arises in the production process, an employee working on the process should have the authority to bring the process to a halt (should have 'line stop authority') until the problem is resolved, and should not have to seek management permission to do so. Information about the performance of a production process should be given to the employees who carry out the process, and they should be given the opportunity to discuss any weaknesses in their performance and consider solutions to any problems they identify.

Employees should also be encouraged by their managers to be creative in devising improvements to the ways in which they do their work.

Equality should also extend to removing symbols of status within the workplace. For example, if employees in a factory are required to wear overalls or a uniform, managers in the factory should wear the same clothing. Everyone should use the same staff canteen and there should not be a separate management canteen or dining area.

Critics of JIT have argued that, in practice, management efforts to involve all staff are often patronising and unconvincing.

8.6 Kanban

'Kanban' is a Japanese word meaning both 'card' and 'signal'. Within a production system where output moves from one process to another, a system of coloured cards or kanbans can be used to give signals between one stage in the process and the next stage. For example, a card can be used by one stage in the process to give a signal to the previous stage that more output is now required from the previous stage. Details of the parts or materials required can be written on the card. Kanbans are therefore used to authorise a movement of materials within the production system, and without this authorisation there should be no movement.

Variations in the signalling system might be used.

- Colour-coded cards might be used for giving different signals. For example, different colours of card might represent different parts or material items, or differing degrees of urgency.

- When output is transferred from one stage of production to the next in standard batch sizes or container sizes, one card might represent a requirement for one container and two cards might represent a demand for two containers.

- A system might use 'kanban squares'. A kanban square is a physical space marked out on the factory floor. When the space is empty, this acts as a signal to the previous process to produce more output for the next process. When the square contains any items, this acts as a signal that no output from the previous process is required at the moment.

Activity 3

Refer to the earlier notes in this chapter on push and pull systems. Explain why JIT s is a pull system.

Feedback to this activity is at the end of the chapter.

8.7 JIT and service operations

Although it originated with manufacturing systems, the JIT philosophy can also be applied to some service operations. Whereas JIT in manufacturing seeks to eliminate inventories, JIT in service operations will seek to eliminate queues of customers (internal or external customers).

Queues are wasteful because:

- they waste the time of the customers in the queue

- a physical queue needs space for accommodating the individuals who must wait in it. This uses up resources and money, but adds no value

- having to wait in a queue gives customers an adverse impression of the quality of the service.

Other concepts of JIT, such as eliminating wasteful motion and seeking ways of achieving continuous improvement are also applicable to services as much as to manufacturing activities.

8.8 Problems with JIT

- Although it might be difficult to argue against the philosophy of JIT, there can be problems with applying the theory in practice.It is not always easy to predict patterns of demand.

- The concept of zero inventories and make-to-order is inapplicable in some industries. For example, retailing businesses such as supermarkets have got to obtain inventory in anticipation of future customer demand.

- JIT makes the organisation far more vulnerable to disruptions in the supply chain.

- JIT was designed at a time when all of Toyota's manufacturing was done within a 50 km radius of its headquarters. Wide geographical spread, however, makes this difficult.

- It might be difficult for management to apply the principles of JIT because they find the concept of empowering the employee difficult to accept.

Crucially, the success of JIT depends on employees and suppliers embracing the concept and the culture. Without their full support and commitment, a system that operates with zero inventories (or close-to-zero inventories) will be vulnerable to disruptions. This point was well-expressed by Oliver and Wilkinson (*The Japanization of British Industries*), as follows:

'Japanese systems of production, particularly JIT and total quality control, heighten the dependency of the organisation on its agencies or "constituents", especially employees and supplying companies. This means ... that the abilities of the organisation's constituents to exert leverage in their own interests is increased. The obvious implication is that it is imperative that such organisations take steps to counterbalance this by averting the possibility of such power being used .... We suggest that such a system will only work successfully where organisations have actively taken the appropriate measures to guard against disruption, or where social, economic and political conditions automatically provide safeguards.'

Summary

- Production planning and control involves trying to balance the demand for resources and outputs with their supply, given uncertainties in the volume and pattern of both demand and supply.

- Demand for end products is independent demand. The demand for resources (materials) to produce output is dependent demand and can be calculated from the production schedule for the period.

- The production planning system might plan for production on a resource-to-order basis, a make-to-order basis or a make-to-inventory basis. The basis used will depend to some extent on the ratio of production capacity to production demand for each product (the P:D ratio).

- In a push supply chain production and distribution decisions are based on long-term forecasts. With a pull supply chain, true customer demand, rather than forecasts, drives production and distribution.

- Inventory might be held as buffer stock, in anticipation of future demand, as cycle inventory or as inventory in the pipeline for delivery to the customer.

- When inventory is held, decisions about ordering fresh quantities of each inventory item might be based on continuous review or periodic review of inventory levels.

- With a continuous review system, the order quantity for new purchases might be calculated using the EOQ model. This model identifies the quantity that will minimise annual inventory holding costs plus ordering costs.

- With a continuous review system, there will also be a reorder level for each inventory item. There might also be maximum and minimum inventory levels, to act as warning signals for control purposes.

- The ABC system of inventory management is an inventory control method based upon the 80:20 principle discovered by a 19th century Italian economist, Vilfredo Pareto. In this system, the most valuable inventory items (in terms of the value of the inventory used) are controlled the most closely.

- For the purpose of capacity planning and control, a distinction might be made between design capacity and effective capacity. Actual capacity is compared with these.

- Methods of balancing production capacity and demand include a level capacity plan, a chase demand plan and a demand management plan.

- Materials requirements planning or MRP I is a computerised system for planning the requirements for raw materials and components, sub-assemblies and finished items.

- MRP I is incompatible with a system of continuous review of inventory and production in economic order/batch quantities.

- With a closed loop MRP system, there is a feedback loop to provide information about whether the production plan is actually achievable, and also whether it was actually achieved.

- Manufacturing resource planning (MRP II) is a development of MRP I and is based largely on MRP I. In addition it integrates related processes into the same system, using a common database. For example, it might integrate financial requirements planning, engineering planning, labour scheduling and equipment scheduling.

- Enterprise resource planning (ERP) is a further development of MRP, and requires an expensive and sophisticated software system.

- With optimised production technology (OPT), the focus is on identifying constraints in the production process and scheduling production to the pace or capacity of this constraint. Management also look for ways of removing constraints, in order to increase the capacity of the production system.

- Just-in-time is an approach to purchasing and production based on meeting demand immediately ('just in time'), with perfect quality and no waste.

- Operational requirements for JIT are high quality and reliability/dependability, fast throughput in production and flexibility in the purchasing and production systems. (The 'ideal' batch size is 1.) Other aims are to reduce costs through improvements in quality and zero inventory.

- Key elements in the JIT approach are the elimination of waste, the involvement of everyone, and continuous improvement. Seven areas of waste, identified in the Toyota Production System, are over-production, waiting time, transport, waste in the process, inventory, motion and defective goods.

- JIT techniques include simplifying the work flow (perhaps organising work around small work cells), reducing set-up times and visibility throughout the workplace (for example, using a Kanban signalling/card system).

- In service industries, a JIT approach might focus on eliminating queues, which are wasteful of customers' time.

Having completed your study of this chapter, you should have achieved the following learning outcome:

- evaluate various aspects of the management of operations.

Self-test questions

1 Define production planning and control. (1)

2 What is a P:D ratio and what might be the significance of the P:D ratio to the system of production planning and control used by an organisation? (1.2)

3 What is the difference between a push and pull system of inventory management? (1.3)

4 What is cycle inventory? (2)

5 What is pipeline inventory? (2)

6 What is the EOQ model formula? (2.3)

7 What is an ABC system of inventory control? (2.7)

8 What is a level capacity plan for scheduling production? How does it differ from a chase demand plan? (3.2)

9 How is a master production schedule prepared in a MRP I system? (4)

10 How are materials requirements calculated in a MRP I system? (4)

11 What is a closed loop MRP system? (4.2)

12 What are the rules or principles in an OPT system? (6)

13 What are the seven types of waste identified in the Toyota Production System? (8.4)

14 What is Kanban? (8.6)

15 What is a key problem with the successful implementation of a JIT system? (8.8)

Practice questions

Question 1

OPT stands for which of the following?

A   Output Production Technology

B   Optimised Planning Techniques

C   Optimised Production Technologies

D   Organisation Planning Technology

Question 2

Which of the following is a value-added activity?

A   Painting a car, if the organisation manufactures cars

B   Setting up a machine so that it drills holes of a certain size

C   Storing materials

D   Repairing faulty production work

Question 3

Overdrive Transmissions and Bearings (Overdrive) is a European manufacturer of gearbox and transmission systems for the car industry. Overdrive was formed in 1949 and is now one of the largest producers of such products in Europe. It has a turnover in excess of €300 million and employs 2,000 staff in three large factories in its home country.

Gearbox and transmission systems are complex products, with each typically containing over 200 parts. Each part must be manufactured to stringent quality standards, as the operating temperatures and stress levels involved are very high. There are also potential safety implications of quality failure in any component supplied to the car industry. Overdrive's customers (the major car manufacturers) demand high standards of quality, reliability and service level. Under the terms of the contracts between Overdrive and their customers, the car manufacturers can charge severe financial penalties for any failure in delivery or quality. Such penalties can amount to many millions of Euro for each incident. Because of this, overdrive has stringent quality control procedures.

While most of the parts and components used in Overdrive's products are manufactured by Overdrive itself, some components are bought in from other specialist manufacturers. One of these is component G4 – the gearshift selector assembly. Component G4 is used in most of Overdrive's products, and is currently bought from three small suppliers who each make the component to a design supplied by Overdrive. The suppliers are prohibited from supplying component G4 to any other organisation.

In a recent meeting, the purchasing manager of overdrive said, '… the modern trend in managing inbound logistics is to enter into sole supplier agreements. We should consider this for component G4.'

Required:

(a)   Explain what is meant by the 'inbound logistics' in Porter's value chain model.

(5 marks)

(a)   What types of decision for inventory management will the management of Overdrive need to take?

(5 marks)

(b)   What is the difference between continuous inventory and periodic inventory systems?

(5 marks)

(c)   Explain **three** advantages to Overdrive of having a formal agreement with a single preferred supplier for component G4.

(5 marks)

(d)   Explain **three** disadvantages to Overdrive of having a formal agreement with a single preferred supplier for component G4.

(5 marks)

(e)   Outline the problems of applying the theory of JIT to all industries in practice

(5 marks)

(Total: 30 marks)

Question 4

Operations managers have always been faced with dealing with the two conflicting objectives of inventory management, namely, to provide maximum components availability while keeping inventory investment low. The overall goal of inventory management is to provide the right item, at the right location, at the right time, at the best cost. To meet this goal, managers must work with two major objectives in mind:

(i)   maximising customer service, i.e. providing material when the customer needs it, and

(ii)   minimising inventory investment, i.e. controlling the money invested in parts and material.

Required:

(a)   Outline the main purpose of holding inventory and explain the differing views on inventory levels   **(8 marks)**

(b)   Describe the common techniques of inventory management   **(12 marks)**

(Total: 20 marks)

For the answers to these questions, see the 'Answers' section at the end of the book.

Feedback to activities

Activity 1

Overall equipment effectiveness = $2{,}900/3{,}000 \times 99\% \times 96\% = 91.87\%$.

Activity 2

Waste of transportation refers to the movement of materials and waste of motion refers to the movement of people in their work. Neither adds value to the process. Waste from transport might be reduced by reducing the distance that materials have to move during the production process, for example by organising work around small work cells on the factory floor. Waste of motion can be reduced by re-organising the work procedures or the layout of the work space, so that individuals do not have to walk as far in carrying out their tasks.

Activity 3

In JIT, production is only carried out in response to a customer order.

There is no production for inventory.

Production is therefore pulled through the system, only when needed by the next stage in the process.

Chapter 9

THE SUPPLY CHAIN AND SUPPLY NETWORKS

Syllabus content

- The role of the supply chain and supply networks in gaining competitive advantage, including the use of sourcing strategies (e.g. single, multiple, delegated and parallel).

- Supply chain management as a strategic process (e.g. Reck and Long's strategic positioning tool, Cousins' strategic supply wheel).

- Developing and maintaining relationships with suppliers.

Contents

1   Negotiating and managing supply relationships

2   The supply network: sourcing strategies

3   Supplier associations

4   E-procurement

5   Lean supply

1   Negotiating and managing supply relationships

For most organisations, relationships with major suppliers are an important aspect of business strategy. There are several reasons why supplies and suppliers are important.

- Purchases of materials, parts and services from external suppliers accounts for a large percentage of total operating costs for many organisations. The cost of purchases is therefore important.

- An organisation is only a part of the supply chain from raw materials to end product. Suppliers are a part of the same chain. The quality of supply from external suppliers affects the quality of supply by an organisation to its customers. An organisation relies on the ability of its suppliers to provide:

  - quality

  - speed of supply

  - dependability of supply, and

  - flexibility of supply.

There are a number of different ways that an organisation might use to deal with its suppliers. The relationship between an organisation and its suppliers might be anywhere between two extremes – these extremes could be described as a competitive relationship and a long-term strategic relationship.

Competitive relationship	Long-term strategic relationship
Seek the lowest prices possible.	The organisation collaborates with its key suppliers.
Negotiating on price with a supplier is a competitive activity. An organisation 'wins' if it gets a lower price and 'loses' if it has to concede a higher price.	It enters into a long-term supply relationship with key suppliers. This is seen by both the supplier and the organisation as a strategic partnership.
There is an 'us' and 'them' relationship.	Both the organisation and the supplier work together to add value, for their mutual benefit and the benefit of their end-customers.

Clearly, depending on the nature of the relationship between an organisation and its suppliers, the approach to negotiating a supply agreement will differ.

1.1   The supply chain and competitive advantage

A supply chain is a network that includes vendors of raw materials, plants that transform those materials into useful products, and distribution centres to get those products to customers.

Competitive advantage can be described as the ability to offer products or services to customers that give the customer better value than the products or services of competitors. Competitive advantage might be achieved by:

- offering a product or service to customers at a lower price than the price of rival products

- offering a product with more attractive features: in this sense product features include not just physical features and characteristics, but also features such as convenience of purchase, availability and image or prestige.

Some companies seek competitive advantage in a particular 'niche' of a market, by offering products with features that are intended to appeal to a particular type of customer.

Companies should have the strategic objective of achieving and maintaining competitive advantage in their markets. Some competitive advantage can be obtained through management of the supply chain.

It might help to think of a simple (or simplified) supply chain. For example, the supply chain for wooden furniture begins with the timber grower, moves on to the sawmill and timber yard, then to the furniture manufacturer and then to the furniture distributor or retailer. The furniture manufacturer is in the middle of the supply chain to the end consumer. It can seek some competitive advantage by looking for improvements in the supply chain, such as:

- reducing the supply lead time from its suppliers, the sawmills

- improving the administrative procedures for purchasing wood from suppliers

- persuading suppliers to improve their quality, so that the resources and costs of quality inspection can be reduced

- persuading suppliers to provide timber in a form that is better-suited to the production processes of the furniture manufacturer, so that wastage of wood in production can be reduced.

It has been suggested that the largest improvements in value added are often to be found by improving the interface between an organisation and its suppliers. The cost and quality of the end-product depends on what happens throughout the supply chain, and organisations cannot ignore the implications of this for their own competitiveness.

1.2 The strategic positioning tool (Reck and Long)

A number of writers on operations management, such as **Reck and Long**, have argued since the 1980s that purchasing and the supply chain are a strategic issue for organisations.

- It is inappropriate to look at the relationship with a supplier as an opportunistic relationship, where the buyer should try to obtain the lowest price possible and argue for a price reduction of relatively small amounts.

- The relationship with suppliers should be seen as a collaborative relationship, in which buyer and supplier seek together to find ways of enhancing value along the supply chain to the end customer, through:

  - lower costs, or

  - improving cycle times and reducing the time-to-market.

Collaborative relationships can bring medium- to long-term cost reductions, whereas opportunistic relationships can do no more than achieve short-term price reductions, in which the every price gain for the buyer is a loss for the supplier.

Reck and Long describe four stages of development that the purchasing function passes through to become 'a competitive weapon in the battle for markets': passive, independent, supportive and integrative, respectively, as detailed below:

Stage I	The Passive Stage
	• Purchasing normally begins as a reactor to requests from other departments.
	• The role of purchasing is essentially administrative.
	• The main emphasis is on processing transactions efficiently.
Stage II	The Independent Stage
	• Purchasing departments spend considerable time attempting to professionalise the purchasing function by introducing such things as computerised information systems, formalised supplier programs, and communication links with the technical functions.
	• There is a greater awareness of the financial implications of purchasing.
	• The main emphasis is often on price negotiations.
Stage III	The Supportive Stage
	• Purchasing departments are viewed by top management as essential business functions.
	• There is a greater awareness that purchasing can affect the firm's strategic goals.
	• Purchasing is expected to support and strengthen the firm's competitive advantage by providing timely information to all departments in the firm about potential changes in the price and availability of materials.
	• The main emphasis is on better coordination between departments.
Stage IV	The Integrative Stage
	• The firm's competitive success rests significantly on the capabilities of the purchasing department's personnel.
	• Purchasing's role within the firm changes from facilitator to functional peer.
	• This development process must be implemented and guided by management over a period of time.
	• Suppliers are seen as vital strategic partners.

1.3 Cousins: the strategic supply wheel

Another view of the relationship with suppliers was suggested by Paul Cousins, who defined a 'strategic supply wheel'. The basic idea is that several different aspects are important for an organisation to consider in its relationships with suppliers, and all these aspects should be given due attention.

Cousins' strategic supply wheel

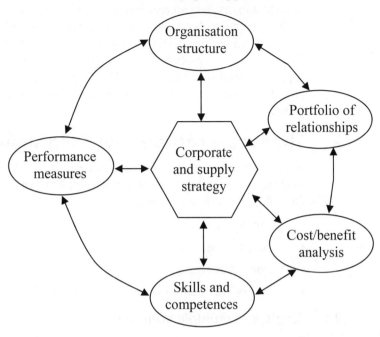

1.4 Supply agreements

An organisation might enter into a supply agreement with an external supplier if it expects a number of supply transactions to be made in the future. A supply agreement (or 'master agreement') establishes the terms on which all individual supply transactions will be undertaken, so that it will be easier and quicker to arrange individual purchase transactions whenever they occur. Every purchase transaction will be subject to the same terms of the service agreement.

The matters covered in a service agreement might include:

- an undertaking by the supplier about:

  - the range of products or services it will provide

  - response times or supply lead times

- an undertaking by the purchaser to purchase a minimum quantity or value of items within the period covered by the agreement.

The agreement might also contain details about price.

1.5 Maintaining the relationship

Having entered into a service agreement with a supplier, an organisation should try to manage the relationship, for as long as it lasts. This is likely to be the responsibility of the purchasing management.

Maintaining the relationship should involve communicating with the supplier regularly, to make sure that there are no problems and that everything is operating as it should. It is quite probable that the supplier will take much of the initiative in maintaining this relationship, through its sales representatives.

However, when an organisation and a supplier have a long-term strategic relationship, there is a greater responsibility on the organisation to communicate with the supplier. It should discuss its longer-term plans with the supplier, such as new product developments. Within a just-in-time purchasing arrangement, it should discuss its probable purchase requirements and ways in which the supplier can ensure the required JIT service. Ideas for new products or new processes, and ideas for the elimination of waste, might also originate with the supplier.

2   The supply network: sourcing strategies

A supply network is the term used to describe the nature of the arrangements made by an organisation to obtain its supplies. An organisation might use any of the following sourcing strategies:

- single sourcing
- multiple sourcing
- parallel sourcing
- a network chain or delegated sourcing.

2.1   Single and multiple sourcing

The 'traditional' model of supply relationships was that an organisation should have a large number of suppliers for each of its major raw materials or other purchased items, and should use the supplier offering the best prices or other terms (for example, the earliest delivery date). With multiple sourcing for each purchased item, an organisation should in theory:

- encourage suppliers to compete on price, and so obtain the lowest prices available

- avoid over-reliance on a single supplier, which might at some time be unable to meet the organisation's purchase requirements (for example, because it does not have sufficient production capacity, or suffers a loss of production capacity due to a strike by the workforce or fire damage in a factory).

However, there are circumstances in which an organisation might prefer to obtain all its supplies of a major item from a single supplier. Single sourcing can have several benefits.

- Procedures and processes for ordering and delivery can be streamlined when only one supplier is used. Supply lead times can be shortened.

- When time-to-market is critical for the development of a new product, research and development and design work can be shared between the organisation and its supplier, in order to shorten the development period. This calls for close co-operation between the organisation and the supplier, which is not achievable with a multiple sourcing arrangement.

- When the supplied item is in short supply, the buyer is likely to be treated more favourably if it has a single sourcing arrangement with the supplier.

- A strategic relationship can be developed with the supplier. The basic idea is that by taking away the competitive pressures that exist with multiple sourcing, an organisation should be able to develop a more open exchange of ideas with its supplier. The organisation and the supplier can work together to improve value in the supply chain, for example by reducing costs and improving efficiency. Close co-operation of this kind is not possible without a good long-term relationship.

Activity 1

What are the advantages and disadvantages of:

(a) short-term single sourcing for the supply of a major purchased item

(b) long-term single sourcing

(c) multiple sourcing?

Feedback to this activity is at the end of the chapter.

2.2 Parallel sourcing

KEY POINT

With parallel sourcing, a company uses a single supply at one of its plants or factories and a single but different source of supply at another plant or factory.

With parallel sourcing, a company uses a single supply at one of its plants or factories and a single but different source of supply at another plant or factory. For example, Factory 1 might buy all of its supplies of an item from Supplier X and Factory 2 might buy all of its supplies of the same item from Supplier Y.

It has been suggested that parallel sourcing combines the benefits of single sourcing and multiple sourcing.

2.3 Network sourcing

KEY POINT

The term 'network sourcing' is a system of sourcing raw materials and other supplies, based on a tiered network of suppliers, many of them small businesses.

The term 'network sourcing' is a system of sourcing raw materials and other supplies, based on a tiered network of suppliers, many of them small businesses. The concept originated in Japan, and the network sourcing model was first put forward by Professor Itsutomo Mitsui.

The network sourcing model has the following characteristics.

• A tiered supply structure, with a heavy reliance on small firms	In a tiered supply arrangement, an organisation deals with a small number of 'top-tier' suppliers. Each of these suppliers in turn obtains supplies from a small number of second-tier suppliers. These second-tier suppliers obtain their supplies for the first-tier suppliers from a small number of third-tier suppliers. A network might have any number of tiers or levels, in excess of one. By means of a tiered arrangement, an organisation obtains supplies from a large number of supplier firms, but only deals itself directly with a small number of them (the first tier suppliers).
• Single sourcing, but within a competitive dual sourcing arrangement	For any item of raw material or any part, there is often a single supplier under a long-term supply relationship. However, there is also an element of competition within the system.
• Risk sharing between suppliers and customer	Suppliers are prepared to invest in assets that are aimed at satisfying one specific customer only. This exposes the supplier to some risk, but the network sourcing system should provide the encouragement to take the risk.

•	Maximum outsourcing within the network, but minimum purchasing from outside the network	Suppliers seek to buy as much of their requirements from other firms in the network (lower down the hierarchy) and to make as little as possible themselves. However, the system also seeks to minimise purchases from firms outside the network. In this system, most supplies are therefore provided by firms at the bottom of the hierarchy, with firms higher up simply buying and selling on, usually for only a small profit mark-up.
•	A high degree of bilateral design	The organisation and all its suppliers within the network collaborate to develop products of higher quality and lower cost.
•	A high degree of supplier innovation in products and processes	In a network system, suppliers are willing to come up with new designs for products or processes that benefit the customer. The customer might specify just the basic size, shape and performance specifications for a product, giving its suppliers freedom to devise the detailed designs.
•	Close, long-term relationships between network members	There are close, long-term relationships between the organisation and its suppliers, and between suppliers at each level in the hierarchy and their suppliers. Clearly, for these relationships to exist and survive, there has to be strong mutual trust.
•	A high level of supplier co-ordination at each level or tier in the supply network	A key element of co-ordination of suppliers is a constant two-way flow of strategic information.
•	A significant effort by the organisation and by suppliers at each level of the network to develop and improve their suppliers	In Japan, this effort has been promoted through *kyoryoku kai* (described later).

The characteristics of a first-tier supplier in a network chain can therefore be summarised as follows.

- It is a direct supplier to the organisation (the 'top level purchaser').

- It is often the supplier of a high-cost or complex sub-assembly, that the top-level purchaser will incorporate into its end-product. For example, a first-tier supplier might supply engines to a manufacturer of motor cars.

- It is heavily dependent on the top-level purchaser, which in turn is heavily dependent on the first-tier supplier.

- Consequently, there is a close and long-term relationship between the supplier and the top-level purchaser. They share common strategic aims, and do not seek to obtain short-term profits at the expense of the other (by negotiating hard on price).

- The first-tier supplier will be involved in discussing new product ideas with the top-level purchaser.

- It is responsible for dealing with a number of second-tier suppliers, and so is put in charge of a section of the vendor base of the top-level purchaser.

- It must be a competitive producer to justify selection by the top-level purchaser as a first-tier supplier. It must also have good management capabilities in order to manage the second-tier suppliers successfully.

2.4   Tiering of suppliers: delegated sourcing

Network sourcing is not extensively applied in all its aspects by Western companies. However, the structuring of supply chains is an important strategic issue, and some aspects of network sourcing might be adopted.

Suppose that a manufacturing company wishes to maximise its own contribution to the 'value adding' process by producing as much of the finished product 'in-house' as possible and buying in relatively small quantities from outside suppliers. Within this strategy, the manufacturer is likely to deal directly with each of its raw materials or components suppliers. This type of supply chain can be illustrated as follows.

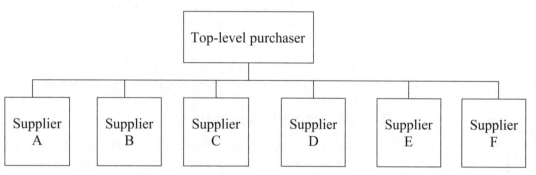

In contrast, if a manufacturer sees a strategic advantage in outsourcing, and using external suppliers for most stages of the production process, it is quite possible that the external suppliers in turn will outsource some of their own production requirements. When this happens, a tier of suppliers might be established, similar in structure to a network chain.

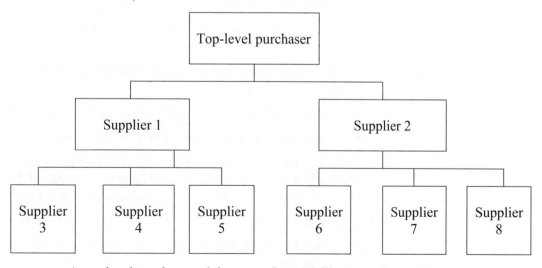

A top-level purchaser might even adopt a deliberate policy of tiering its suppliers, in order to reduce the number of 'first-tier' suppliers with which it has to deal and so 'reduce its vendor base'. In the diagram above, the top-level purchaser has direct dealing relationships with Supplier 1 and Supplier 2, but does not have to deal directly with Suppliers 3–8. It relies on the first-tier

Suppliers 1 and 2 to establish a good relationship with those suppliers in the second tier.

When the top-level purchaser has a tiered network of suppliers, it can concentrate on developing its strategic relationships with the small number of first-tier suppliers. The first-tier suppliers would be expected to work with the top-level purchaser in making improvements and adding value throughout the supply chain.

Benefits of tiering

The potential benefits of tiering suppliers are as follows.

- The top-level purchaser has fewer commercial relationships to manage and can focus its attention on improving these key relationships.

- The top-level purchaser can give more attention to strategic issues relating to the supply chain and adding value, without having to worry as much about the transactional and operational aspects of procurement/purchasing.

- The top-level purchaser can share a strategic objective with its first-tier suppliers of improving the supply chain. Co-operation on this issue is likely to bring more improvements than pursuing the objective alone.

- The first-tier suppliers might be able to co-ordinate activities throughout the supply chain more efficiently than the top-level purchaser.

3 Supplier associations

There are many industry associations, trade associations and supplier associations, organised on a regional, national or world-wide basis. The purposes of a trade association are to:

- promote the interests of their members, for example by lobbying or advising the government

- promoting industry-wide standards, for the benefit of both suppliers and customers

- providing information, news, statistics and education and training for members.

Formal collaboration between suppliers in an industry, through a suppliers' association, can help to:

- improve the level of skill and competence throughout the industry, and

- produce a uniform supply system for the industry.

Just one example of a suppliers' association is the European Association of Automotive Suppliers, which was set up in 1997 to co-ordinate the activities of various national associations of automotive suppliers. Its functions are to:

- represent the industry in talks with the European Commission

- develop European-wide technical regulations and standards for the industry

- promote co-operation within the industry.

3.1 Kyoryoku kai

In most countries, suppliers' associations are organised and run by the suppliers themselves. In Japan, there are supplier associations known as *kyoryoku kai*, which are organised by a major buyer/customer in the industry. For example, an association of suppliers in the automotive industry might be set up and organised by a major car manufacturer.

The first such association was set up by Toyota in 1943. Its original purpose was to provide an assurance of business to suppliers who were suffering from the consequences of the war effort in Japan. Over time, the main focus of interest in these supplier associations has been:

- improving quality

- reducing costs by means of efficiency improvements throughout the industry

- health and safety standards.

The benefit of having a supplier association organised by a major buyer is that the buyer is able to exert strong influence over its suppliers, and encourage the open exchange of ideas and information between suppliers.

4 E-procurement

E-procurement is the purchase of items over the Internet. There have been several developments in this area, and there will probably be more to come in the future. E-procurement can take a variety of forms.

- A company can send out requests to suppliers to submit a tender for a job, or can send out purchase orders directly from its own computer system to the computer system of the suppliers (for example, using Electronic Data Interchange or EDI).

- A company can make available to its suppliers real-time information about its own sales, in order to help its suppliers plan future production and supply schedules. For example, Wal-Mart, the US store chain, makes its sales data immediately available to its suppliers, through the Internet. This sales data allows the suppliers to make their own forecasts of expected future demand for their products through Wal-Mart and plan their production schedules on the basis of these forecasts, rather than waiting for an actual purchase order from Wal-Mart before making any scheduling decisions.

- An increasingly popular approach is to use extranets. An extranet is an intranet that has been extended to include business partners. The advantages are:

  - quicker information flow to/from partners

  - makes e-procurement easier as a supplier can check whether or not you need more stock

  - quicker transactions if partners are customers or suppliers

  - strengthens relationship with partners due to implied trust.

Activity 2

State one way in which e-procurement might:

(a)   strengthen strategic relationships with major suppliers

(b)   weaken strategic relationships with suppliers.

Feedback to this activity is at the end of the chapter.

5   Lean supply

The concept of lean supply originated in Japan in the 1940s and 1950s. It is based on the objective of eliminating waste in the supply chain. Waste is any activity that uses resources but adds no value. Examples of waste are therefore excessive inventories, unnecessary time-wasting procedures and the costs of rectifying or scrapping defective parts. Lean supply is associated with the just in time (JIT) approach to operations management, and JIT is sometimes called 'lean operations'.

A feature of lean supply is very close co-operation between buyer and supplier, in a 'partnership of equals'. Lean supply has been defined as a 'state of business in which there is dynamic competition and collaboration of equals in the supply chain, aimed at adding value at a minimum cost, whilst maximising end customer service and product quality' (Professor Richard Lamming).

Summary

- An organisation is only a part of the supply chain from raw materials to end-product. The quality of its own operations depends heavily on the quality of the service provided by its major suppliers. (Quality can be measured in terms of product quality, speed of supply, dependability, flexibility and cost.)

- The relationship with suppliers can be anywhere between the extremes of a competitive relationship based on negotiations about price and a long-term strategic partnership.

- Improvements in the supply chain achieved in collaboration with suppliers can give an organisation a competitive advantage over its rivals.

- Writers such as Reck and Long and Cousins have argued that purchasing and the supply chain are a major strategic issue for organisations.

- The broad terms of a relationship with a regular supplier might be set out in a supply agreement or service agreement, covering matters such as the range of products or services to be supplied and supply lead times.

- An organisation might use any of the following sourcing strategies – single sourcing, multiple sourcing, parallel sourcing or delegated sourcing (a network chain).

- With delegated sourcing, an organisation restricts the number of suppliers with which it deals directly. This should give its purchasing managers more time to devote directly to managing the supply relationships of the organisation.

- Suppliers might form associations with the aim of improving the quality of the service to customers provided by firms in the industry, and also to represent the interests of the industry, for example in lobbying government. In Japan, supplier associations have been established by a major buyer/customer in the industry.

- Lean supply is a concept based on eliminating waste from supply relationships. It might be applied where there is a long-term strategic relationship with a supplier.

Having completed your study of this chapter, you should have achieved the following learning outcomes:

- recommend ways to negotiate and manage relationships with suppliers

- evaluate a supply network.

Self-test questions

1 What are the main features of a long-term strategic relationship with a supplier? (1)

2 How might competitive advantage be obtained by improving the relationship with major suppliers? (1.1)

3 Draw a strategic supply wheel. (1.3)

4 Define parallel sourcing. (2.2)

5 Define delegated sourcing. (2.4)

6 What is the name given to supplier associations in Japan that are set up and managed by a major customer in the industry? (3.1)

7 What is the objective of lean supply? (5)

Practice questions

Question 1

Which of the following is not a feature of a long-term strategic relationship with a supplier?

A   Ensuring dependability of supply

B   Seeking the lowest purchase price possible

C   Collaborating for new product or new process design

D   Achieving greater flexibility in supply

Question 2

Which of the following is not a characteristic of a network supply chain?

A   Maximum purchasing from outside the network

B   Risk sharing between suppliers and customers

C   A small number of direct supply relationships

D   High level of supplier co-ordination throughout the network

For the answers to these questions, see the 'Answers' section at the end of the book.

Feedback to activities

Activity 1

	Advantages	Disadvantages
Short-term single sourcing	Lower costs and prices arising from economies of scale and bulk purchase orders. Better communications. Greater certainty for the supplier.	Risk to the security of supply: reliance on just one source for the product supply. Fewer competitive pressures for the supplier – removing the incentive for the supplier to perform well?
Long-term single sourcing	Better product quality, lower product variability. Better planning and control of supply. Greater probability of product and process innovations and improvements. Lower administrative costs.	Same potential disadvantages as with short-term single sourcing.
Multiple sourcing	Greater security of supply. Pressure on suppliers to be competitive. Buyer remains in touch with the supply market.	Economies of scale are lost. Uncertainty for suppliers, leading to difficulties with planning and scheduling. Possibly longer supply lead times. Suppliers will be less communicative, not wanting their knowledge to be passed on by the buyer to competing suppliers.

Activity 2

(a)   E-procurement can strengthen relationships with a supplier if an organisation and its supplier arrange to exchange data between their computer systems, in order to simplify and speed up the purchasing and supply process.

(b)   E-procurement can weaken supply relationships because a company can use the internet to identify new suppliers that it was not aware of, possibly in other countries.

Chapter 10

QUALITY MANAGEMENT

Syllabus content

- Methods of performance measurement and improvement, particularly the contrast between benchmarking and Business Process Re-engineering (BPR).

- Practices of continuous improvement (e.g. quality circles, Kaizen, 5S, Six Sigma).

- The use of benchmarking in quality measurement and improvement.

- Different methods of quality measurement (i.e. operational, financial and customer measures).

- The characteristics of lean production: flexible workforce practices, high commitment human resource policies and commitment to continuous improvement. Criticisms and limitations of lean production.

- Approaches to quality management, including Total Quality Management (TQM), various British Standard (BS) and European Union (EU) systems as well as statistical methods of quality control.

- External quality standards (e.g. the various ISO standards appropriate to products and organisations).

- Use of the Intranet in information management (e.g. meeting customer support needs).

- Contemporary developments in quality management.

Contents

1 The definition and importance of quality

1.1 Definitions

In order to control and improve quality it must first be defined. Most dictionaries define quality as 'the degree of excellence' but this leaves one having to define what is meant by 'excellence'. Who defines what is excellent and by what standards is it measured? In response to this problem, a number of different definitions of quality have been developed.

In an industrial context, quality is defined in a functional way. Here, quality means that a product is made free from errors and according to its design specifications, within an acceptable production tolerance level.

Such an approach also emphasises that every unit produced should meet the design specifications, so the idea of consistency becomes important. Note that consistency is a key aspect of quality standards such as BS5750.

This still leaves a problem, however. How should standards and specifications be set? Who decides what an 'acceptable' tolerance level should be?

An alternative approach to defining quality is thus to focus on the user.

- Japanese companies found the definition of quality as 'the degree of conformance to a standard' too narrow and consequently started to use a new definition of quality as 'user satisfaction'.

- Juran defines quality as 'fitness for use' (1988).

In these definitions, customer requirements and customer satisfaction are the main factors. If an organisation can meet the requirements of its customers, customers will presumably be satisfied. The ability to define accurately the needs related to design, performance, price, safety, delivery, and other business activities and processes will place an organisation ahead of its competitors in the market.

Taking these definitions together, Ken Holmes *(Total Quality Management)* has defined quality as 'the totality of features and characteristics of a product or service which bears on its ability to meet stated or implied needs'.

Quality is also normally seen in relation to price, and customers judge the quality of a product in relation to the price they have to pay. Customers will accept a product of lower design quality provided that the price is lower than the price of a better-quality alternative.

1.2 Importance of quality

The importance of quality for an organisation is that higher quality can help to increase revenues and reduce costs.

- Better quality improves the perceived image of a product or service and makes customers more likely to want to buy it.

- Higher demand should result in higher sales volume and higher profits.

- Higher volume might also result in lower unit costs, with economies of scale in production and selling.

- Higher quality in manufacturing should result in lower waste and defective rates, which will reduce production costs.

KEY POINT

In an industrial context, quality means that a product is made free from errors and exactly according to its design specifications.

KEY POINT

Japanese companies found the old definition of quality 'the degree of conformance to a standard' too narrow and consequently started to use a new definition of quality as 'user satisfaction'.

KEY POINT

Customers judge the quality of a product in relation to the price they have to pay.

KEY POINT

The importance of quality for an organisation is that higher quality can help to increase revenues and reduce costs.

- The need for inspection and testing should be reduced, also reducing costs.

- The volume of customer complaints should fall, and warranty claims should be lower. This will reduce costs.

- Better quality in production should result in shorter processing times and less capital equipment requirements.

1.3 Quality management

Quality management suggests a concern that the organisation's products or services meet their planned level of quality and perform to specifications. Managing quality is concerned with the prevention and detection of defects.

- Prevention is concerned with having the right tools for the job, skilled people and defined standards. This means appropriate methodology, project management, computer-based tools and education and training.

- Detection is concerned with inspection and testing of the products to ensure that any defects that are not prevented are found.

Management has a duty to ensure that all tasks are completed consistently to a standard, which meets the needs of the business. To achieve this they need to:

- set clear standards, after taking account of the quality expected by the customers and the costs and benefits of delivering different degrees of quality

- plan how to meet those standards – agree and document procedures, methods and controls to meet the standards, document responsibilities via job descriptions and terms of reference; and prepare and implement training plans for employees to ensure they are familiar with the standards, procedures, controls and their responsibilities

- track the quality achieved – gain employees' commitment and support by publishing and discussing the quality being achieved. Encourage ideas from the staff about improvements and consider introducing short-term suggestion schemes

- take action to improve quality where necessary.

2 Problems associated with quality

2.1 Association with inspection

Traditionally quality management was associated with inspection of finished output or goods inward. Quality was assured at the end of the process, often by specialised quality control staff.

The main problem with this approach is that the inspection process itself does not 'add value'. The production of defects is not compatible with newer production techniques such as just-in-time: there is no time for inspection.

Other problems include:

- the production of substandard products wastes raw materials, machine time, and human effort

- the inspection department takes up space, and has to be paid

- working capital is tied up in stocks which cannot be sold.

In other words, the 'inspection approach' allows for built-in waste. Where resources are scarce, this is not acceptable. Waste reduces profitability: the resources it consumes can perhaps be put to better use.

2.2 Quality failure

When customers are disappointed with the quality of a product or service, the reason for the 'quality failure' could be any of the following.

- The product design concept or service design concept is not matched by the actual design specification for the product or service. In other words, there is a gap between the concept and the specification.

- The design specification for the product or service fails to achieve the specification that customers would want it to have. In other words, there is a gap between the product design and customer expectations.

- The product that is manufactured or service that is provided fails to meet its design specifications. In other words, there is a gap between the actual product and its specification.

- The features of the product or service that are advertised or marketed to customers do not actually exist. In other words, there is a gap between what the organisation promises the product will do and what it actually does. (How many people, for example, have been disappointed by travel company promises of a 'holiday of a lifetime'?)

2.3 Quality-related costs

CIMA's *Official Terminology* defines quality-related costs as: 'the expenditure incurred in defect prevention and appraisal activities and the losses due to internal and external failure of a product or service, through failure to meet agreed specification'. Quality costs are classified in British Standard 6143 in terms of prevention, appraisal, internal failure costs and external failure costs.

Prevention costs are the costs of any action taken to prevent or reduce defects and failures before they occur. They include:

- designing products and services with in-built quality, to reduce defects and sub-standard quality

- designing processes with in-built quality

- training employees in the best way to do their jobs.

Appraisal costs are the costs of assessing the quality that has been achieved. These costs include:

- inspection and testing (including goods inwards)

- in-process inspection

- product quality audits.

Internal failure costs are costs arising within the organisation due to a failure to achieve the quality standards specified. In a manufacturing company these may include:

- re-inspection costs

- losses from failure of bought-in items

- losses due to lower selling prices for sub-quality goods

- costs of reviewing product specifications after failures

- the cost of scrapped parts

- the cost of re-working parts

- the cost of time lost due to failures and defects.

External failure costs are costs associated with the error or defect going outside the organisation to the customer. These costs include the costs of:

- dealing with complaints from customers

- the costs of carrying out work under guarantee or warranty

- costs of litigation, or payments to avoid litigation

- costs of recalling and correcting products

- the cost of lost goodwill, which is very difficult to measure but could be the factor causing the highest cost of poor quality due to loss of future sales.

Out of the four categories of costs, prevention costs and appraisal costs are subject to management influence or control. Internal and external failure costs are the consequences of weaknesses in prevention or appraisal. Of the two categories of cost that are subject to management influence, it is more appropriate to focus on prevention rather than appraisal ('inspection').

3 Contemporary thinking

3.1 Tom Peters

Tom Peters in his book *Thriving on Chaos*, concentrates on the 12 attributes of a quality revolution:

(i) Management obsessed with quality.

(ii) A guiding system or ideology.

(iii) Quality is measured.

(iv) Reward for quality.

(v) Training in technologies for assessing qualities.

(vi) Teams involving multiple functions or systems are used.

(vii) Concentration on small improvements.

(viii) Constant stimulation.

(ix) Creation of a shadow or parallel organisation structure devoted to quality improvement.

(x) Everyone is involved. Suppliers especially, but distributors and customers too, must be a part of the organisation's quality process.

(xi) Quality improvement is the primary source of cost reduction.

(xii) Quality improvement is a never-ending journey.

These are traits which companies like IBM, Ford and Federal Express share in their quality improvement programmes.

Peters argues that most quality programs fail for one of two reasons: they have a system without passion, or passion without a system. The type of system to follow, and the results obtained, causes some controversy. There are many ideologies used in quality processes. Should one follow Deming via statistical process control or Phil Crosby, author of *Quality is Free,* or Armand Feigenbaum's *Total Quality Control* or Joseph Juran's 'fitness for purpose'?

3.2 Deming

In the 1920s and 1930s in America, statistical quality control methods were used to monitor and control the quality of output in flow line production processes. These methods, the origins of modern quality management, were introduced into Japan by American consultants like Deming, who were involved in the aid program to rejuvenate the industry in Japan after the war.

Some companies (and governments) blame unions for having a negative impact on worker productivity. Deming insists that management is 90% of the problem. Organisations need to address the problems of the quality of direction being given to the workforce, the resources available to get the job done efficiently and the opportunities for workers to contribute ideas about how to do the job better.

Deming suggests that improving quality leads to improved productivity, reduced costs, more satisfied customers and increased profitability. His system for management to improve quality and competitiveness covers the following main areas.

- The organisation should have a constant purpose of improving their product or service.

- Quality objectives should be agreed and action taken to accomplish them.

- Systems for production and service delivery should be improved, eliminating all waste.

- Consideration of quality and reliability should be just as important as price when choosing a supplier.

- Attention must be paid to training people so they are better at their jobs and understand how to optimise production.

- Mass inspection of goods ties up resources and does not improve quality.

- Education and self-improvement should be encouraged in all members of the organisation. Management should enable staff to take a pride in their work.

- Barriers between staff areas should be broken down.

3.3 Crosby: zero defects and right first time

KEY POINT

According to Crosby management should aim for zero defects, and getting everything right the first time.

Crosby's thinking is based on zero defects. This defects concept and his assertion that a product should not have to be corrected once it is built (right first time) are embodied in his Four Absolutes of Quality Management.

- Quality is conformance to standards.
- Prevention is the system for advancing quality, not appraisal.
- The goal should be zero defects.
- The importance of quality is measured by the cost of not having quality.

3.4 Juran – fitness for purpose

Juran believes quality does not happen by accident: it has to be planned. Quality planning is one of the three key issues in quality management:

- quality planning
- quality control
- quality improvement.

As stated above, Juran defines quality as 'fitness for purpose'. This can be described loosely as 'that which relates to the evaluation of a product or service for its ability to satisfy a given need'. The elements of this theory are:

- quality of design, which can include customer satisfaction which is built into the product

- quality of conformance, or a lack of defects

- abilities, and

- field service.

Because customers incorporate such things as 'value for money' in their 'fitness for purpose' equation, Juran's theory is looking at quality from the point of view of the customer and is a more practical concept.

3.5 Feigenbaum

Feigenbaum emphasises the relevance of quality issues in all areas of the operation of a business. He believes that 'prevention is better than cure', stressing the importance of identifying the costs of quality in economic and accounting terms.

Organisations adopting his ideas are encouraged to change the role of the quality control function from inspecting and rejecting output to one in which quality is given a planning role, involving the design of systems and procedures to reduce the likelihood of sub-optimal production.

3.6 Taguchi

Taguchi developed a model to show that quality deteriorates with increasing significance as the design parameters for a product (or service) deviate further from their target values. The aim should therefore be to minimise the variation of the product (or service) design from these target values.

Taguchi recommended methods for testing the robustness of a design. His view was that a product or service should be capable of performing properly in extreme conditions. For example, a mobile telephone should still operate if it is dropped from a height on to a concrete floor. It is not normal for this to happen to a mobile phone, but it is a conceivable event. Similarly, a hotel service should be capable of handling an unexpected rush of customers, all arriving at the same time and expecting their room to be ready and available for use.

Taguchi identifies two aspects of quality control- off-line and on-line.

- Off-line quality control incorporates systems design, parameter design and tolerance design. Systems design should reflect appropriate technology.

- On-line quality control aims to minimise the loss due to variations between goods produced, weighing the cost of the variation against the cost of correcting the variation. Examples of these variations could include slight differences in weight between identical parts or slight differences in time to produce something.

Taguchi argued (1990) that:

- quality can be defined in terms of the (minimum) loss imparted to society from the time a product is shipped, or a service is delivered

- quality is therefore improved by reducing this loss

- reducing loss requires that quality should be built into the design of the product or service.

According to Taguchi, quality deteriorates with increasing significance as the design parameters for a product (or service) deviate further from their target values. The aim should therefore be to minimise the variation of the product (or service) design from these target values.

Taguchi recommended methods for testing the robustness of a design. His view was that a product or service should be capable of performing properly in extreme conditions. For example, a mobile telephone should still operate if it is dropped from a height on to a concrete floor. It is not normal for this to happen to a mobile phone, but it is a conceivable event. Similarly, a hotel service should be capable of handling an unexpected rush of customers, all arriving at the same time and expecting their room to be ready and available for use.

However, Taguchi recognised that there are many different designs that might be considered for meeting all the extreme circumstances under which the product or service might be required to operate. Taguchi devised a statistical procedure for carrying out relatively few experiments or tests whilst at the same time being able to decide on the best combination of design factors. 'Best' in this sense means the lowest costs of loss and the greatest uniformity.

3.7 Kauro Ishikauro

Kauro Ishikawa is noted for his proposals on quality circles and quality control. He argued that the development of quality in an organisation was an evolutionary process, from inspection in the 1920s to process control and now, to design improvements. In other words, once conformance quality is achieved, it is possible to carry on to design quality.

3.8 Quality circles

The idea of quality circles was first introduced by Ishikawa in Japan in the 1960s. He claimed that there had been too much emphasis on statistical quality control in Japan, with the result that employees felt that they were tightly regulated and disliked quality control. His solution was to encourage worker participation in TQM, and he believed that quality circles were a useful way of doing this.

A quality circle is a small group of employees, usually five to eight people, who come from the same area of work, but with a range of skills from those of the factory floor up to management. They meet voluntarily on a regular basis, to discuss work-related problems, identifying and analysing the problems and trying to find a practicable solution. Although they discuss mostly issues relating to quality, they might also talk about health and safety issues and productivity.

With quality circles, the process of decision-making about quality starts at the lowest level in the organisation, with ordinary workers encouraged to comment and contribute ideas and suggestions for improvement, as well as putting them into practice.

Quality circles are intended to supplement the more conventional procedures for quality control and quality assurance.

The possible benefits of quality circles are as follows:

- improvements in quality, leading to greater customer satisfaction

- better productivity

- employees at the factory floor level are able to understand better the problems of their supervisors and managers

- a culture of continuous improvement is encouraged

- the potential benefits exceed the costs of setting up and operating quality circles.

Some Western theorists, such as Crosby, encouraged the introduction of quality circles into Western manufacturing companies. However, putting the idea of quality circles into practice can be very difficult, particularly in organisations where the management hierarchy is firmly established and 'bottom-up' decision making is alien to its culture.

There are a number of ways in which firms can encourage the development of the use of quality circles:

- ensuring that there is high profile executive commitment to support the initiative

- ensuring that staff members have the training in problem solving and analysis which they need to identify problems and develop workable solutions

- ensuring that staff members who are involved in quality circles are free to spend the time necessary away from their day-to-day responsibilities to take part in meetings and activities; this may have budgetary implications

- reviewing the information system in the organisation to identify the information needs of quality circles and to ensure that any data required to assess performance and identify problems is available to them

- demonstrating that the senior management of the organisation takes the process seriously and takes any action to resolve problems which is identified as necessary by quality circles; this will encourage more staff to get involved

- developing a culture in the organisation that allows possible changes to be tested out, allowing for the possibility of mistakes

- providing training for all staff to increase awareness of the importance and value of quality circles.

3.9 Total quality management (TQM)

Total quality management (TQM) is a philosophy of quality management that originated in Japan in the 1950s. Some definitions of TQM are as follows.

CIMA defines TQM as 'the continuous improvement in quality, productivity and effectiveness obtained by establishing management responsibility for processes as well as outputs. In this, every process has an identified process owner and every person in an entity operates within a process and contributes to its improvement'.

The first definition of TQM in the US was given by Armand Feigenbaum in the 1950s in *Total Quality Control*. TQM is 'an effective system for integrating the quality development, quality maintenance and quality improvement efforts of various groups in an organisation so as to enable production and service at the most economical levels which allow for full customer satisfaction'.

KEY POINT

TQM is 'an effective system for integrating the quality development, quality maintenance and quality improvement efforts of various groups in an organisation so as to enable production and service at the most economical levels which allow for full customer satisfaction'.

- Total – means that everyone in the value chain is involved in the process, including employees, customers and suppliers

- Quality – products and services must meet the customers' requirements

- Management – management must be fully committed and encourage everyone else to become quality conscious.

Total quality management (TQM) is the name given to programmes, which seek to ensure that goods are produced and services are supplied of the highest quality. Its origin lies primarily in Japanese organisations and it is argued that TQM has been a significant factor in Japanese global business success.

KEY POINT

The TQM approach to quality costs is to get things right the first time.

The basic principle of TQM is that the cost of preventing mistakes is less than the cost of correcting them once they occur and the cost of lost potential future sales. The aim should therefore be to get things right first time consistently. This contrasts with the 'traditional' UK approach that less than 100% quality is acceptable as the costs of improvement from say 90% to 100% outweigh the benefits. Thus in the analysis of quality related costs there may be a trade-off between a lowering of failure (internal and external) at the expense of increased prevention and appraisal costs.

Which view is correct is a matter of debate but the advocates of TQM would argue that in addition to the cost analysis above the impact of less than 100% quality in terms of lost potential for future sales also has to be taken into account.

The philosophy of TQM is based on the idea of a series of quality chains, which may be broken at any point by one person or service not meeting the requirements of the customer.

The key to TQM is for everyone in the organisation to have well-defined customers – an extension of the word, beyond the customers of the company, to anyone to whom an individual provides a service. Thus the 'Paint shop' staff would be customers of the 'Assembly shop' staff who would themselves be the customers of the 'Machine shop' staff. The idea is that the supplier-customer relationships would form a chain extending from the company's original suppliers through to its ultimate consumers. Areas of responsibility would need to be identified and a manager allocated to each, and then the customer/supplier chain established. True to the principle outlined above the quality requirements of each 'customer' within the chain would be assessed, and meeting these would then become the responsibility of the 'suppliers' who form the preceding link in the chain.

Quality has to be managed – it will not just happen. To meet the requirements of TQM a company will probably need to recruit more staff and may also need to change the level of services on offer to its customers, which includes 'internal' customers. This would probably entail costs in terms of the redesign of systems, recruitment and training of staff, and the purchase of appropriate equipment.

John Thackray indicated the following features of companies that follow TQM:

- There is absolute commitment by the chief executive and all senior managers to doing what is needed to change the culture.

- People are not afraid to try new things.

- Communication is excellent and multi-way.

- There is a real commitment to continuous improvement in all processes.

- Attention is focused first on the process and second on the results.

- There is an absence of strict control systems.

4 Quality control, quality assurance and standards

4.1 Quality control

DEFINITION

Quality control is concerned with the management of quality and ensuring that actual quality standards, as measured, meet the target or benchmark standards that have been set.

Quality control is concerned with the management of quality and ensuring that actual quality standards, as measured, meet the target or benchmark standards that have been set. It is an approach to quality which involves:

- establishing quality standards for a product or service

- establishing procedures and processes which ought to ensure that these quality standards are met in a suitably high number of cases (in other words, quality acceptance standards are established)

- monitoring actual quality

- taking control action in cases where actual quality falls below the standard.

Quality control is concerned with maintaining quality standards, rather than improving them. It usually involves:

- procedures for inspecting and checking the quality of bought-in materials, and production output

- statistical quality control through sampling.

4.2 Statistical quality control

Statistical process control (SPC) is an aspect of quality management relating to the control of the production process. It is the continuous monitoring and charting of a process while it is operating, to warn when the process is moving away from predetermined limits. It means we can reliably assess the performance of any process, monitor it statistically and take steps to control it better. Typically the upper and lower control limits will be three standard deviations away from the mean. All points outside the control limits should be investigated and corrected.

Statistical quality control charts might be used to record and monitor important aspects of product conformance such as dimensional accuracy. A typical control chart is shown below.

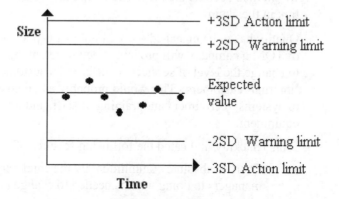

The horizontal axis is either time or a cumulative output volume. The vertical axis is a measure of a critical characteristic of the component such as its length or diameter.

Above and below the level of the expected dimension of the product are the control limits. The graph shows inner warning limits and outer action limits although in many cases only one limit is used. Normally, the values plotted on the chart would be the mean of a small sample taken at regular points in time. The outer limit is set at such a distance from the standard that a value outside it is very unlikely to have occurred by chance; the size of the deviation thus indicates that something may have gone wrong with the manufacturing process. The inner limit is used to monitor trends; if a sequence of samples displays increasing inaccuracy, action is taken when the inner limit is reached.

No matter how good the equipment or how skilful the operative, a number of articles produced by the same process will never be exactly alike, although with imperfect measuring instruments they may appear so. There will always be a slight variation from one to another. The causes of variation may be divided into *assignable causes*, such as mechanical faults or abnormalities in the raw material, which can be identified and eliminated, and *chance causes*, which are either unknown or impossible to eliminate. When only chance causes are operating, the process is said to be 'under control'. The data recorded will then vary about the process average, with a standard deviation measuring the residual variation i.e. the inherent variability of the process.

An empirical rule is used to assess whether a process is performing normally or is out of control:

If 8 successive values are on the same side of the mean, or 4 out of 5 are beyond 1 standard deviation, or 2 out of 3 are beyond 2 standard deviations or just 1 value is beyond 3 standard deviations then it must be assumed that there is an assignable cause for this and that this could not occur if the process were in control. Such outputs therefore indicate a process out of control.

Statistical quality control covers a wider range of topics:

- It can be used to process data to optimise plant performance. In its simplest form it is looking at the standard deviation of controlled variables and how close they are to the plant tolerance limits, and seeing if they can be pushed closer, making the plant more productive.

- It is an aspect of Total Quality Management (TQM), which is a way of managing a business to ensure complete customer satisfaction internally and externally. It is accepted that it is not possible to achieve perfection in products because of the variations in raw material quality, operating skills, different types of machines used, wear and tear, etc. but quality control attempts to ascertain the amount of variation from perfect that can be expected in any operation. If the expected variation is acceptable according to engineering requirements, then production must be established within controlled limits and if the actual variation is too great then corrective action must be taken to bring it within acceptable limits.

- It can be used to control buffer stocks or inventories. These are an accumulation of stock, usually raw materials, for use in case of supply problems, or cash-flow difficulties that prevent purchase of new stock. A buffer stock, or safety stock, is an insurance against unexpected problems, but excessive hoarding ties up assets and limits supplies of the resource to other companies. The use of just-in-time techniques has reduced the requirement for buffer stock.

- It can be used to record and monitor the accuracy of the physical dimensions of products. Representational samples of an output manufacturing process may be taken daily or even hourly, and faults in the process which are revealed may be fairly simple to correct by adjusting the appropriate machinery. If output exceeds the control limits consistently then more urgent management action would be required because this could indicate some inadequacy in production methods or quality of raw materials and components. It could even be due to inefficiency in production or excessively tight tolerances in the first place.

- Control charts can also be applied to the inspection of raw materials received from suppliers in order to confirm that the supplier is supplying materials, which conform to the size and standard specified in the purchase contract.

4.3 Quality assurance

Quality assurance is the term used where a supplier guarantees the quality of goods supplied and allows the customer access while the goods are being manufactured. This is usually done through supplier quality assurance (SQA) officers, who control the specification of the goods supplied.

One great advantage of SQA is that it may render possible reduction of the in-house quality control headcount, since there will be no need to check incoming materials or sub-assemblies or components. Items can be directed straight to production. This can give large savings in cost and time in flow production, and can facilitate JIT production.

In the past, failure to screen quality successfully has resulted in rejections, re-work and scrap, all of which add to manufacturing costs. Modern trends in industry of competition, mass production and increasing standards of quality requirements have resulted in a thorough reappraisal of the problem and two important points have emerged:

- It is necessary to single out and remove the causes for poor quality goods before production instead of waiting for the end result. Many companies have instigated 'zero defects' programmes following the Japanese practice of eradicating poor quality as early in the chain as possible and insisting on strict quality adherence at every stage – as Crosby points out in his book *Quality is Free*, this is cost effective since customer complaints etc. reduce dramatically.

- The co-ordination of all activities from the preparation of the specification, through to the purchasing and inspection functions and right up to the function of delivery of the finished product, is essential.

Suppliers' quality assurance schemes are being used increasingly, particularly where extensive sub-contracting work is carried out, such as in the motor industry.

4.4 Quality standards

TQM is considered to be a philosophy of management rather than a set of management practices. However, advocates of TQM support the concept of setting quality standards and monitoring actual performance against those standards.

Many quality standards are set internally by operations management, for their own particular operation. Quality standards can be set in terms of performance measurements: alternatively, a manufacturing system might use a system of statistical quality control for measuring compliance with operating specifications.

monitoring actual
performance against
those standards.

In addition to using internal quality standards, organisations might also use external quality standards. External standards might be set for a particular industry, or for all industries and organisations in general, depending on the nature of the quality item.

External quality standards are voluntary, but the underlying principle is that if producers in an industry give their support to achieving the established standards, the level of quality within the industry will rise.

- In the UK, the organisation still most closely associated with promoting both national and international standards is the British Standards Institute, now the BSI Group.

- At a European level, three standard-setting bodies operate with the support of the EU and EFTA:
    - CEN, the European Committee for Standardisation
    - CENELEC, the European Committee for Electrotechnical Standardisation
    - ETSI, the European Telecommunications Standards Institute.

In the UK, the British Standards Institute (now the BSI Group) introduced a British quality standard BS5750, which had three parts:

- specification for design

- specification for manufacture and installation

- specification for final inspection and test.

This standard influenced the development of quality standards by the International Organisation for Standardisation (ISO) in Switzerland, which issued the ISO 9000 series of standards. These were revised in 2000, and the ISO 9000 range now includes:

- ISO 9000:2000 'Quality management systems – fundamentals and vocabulary'. This defines the fundamental terms used in the ISO 9000 series of standards.

- ISO 9001:2000 'Quality management systems – requirements'. This specifies the requirements that must be met by the quality management system within an organisation if it is to meet the standard. Organisations can apply to obtain a certificate for meeting the ISO 9001:2000 quality standards.

- ISO 9004:2000 'Quality management systems – guidelines for performance improvements'. This provides guidelines for the continual improvement of the quality management system in an organisation.

Other standards in the ISO 9000 range cover specific topics. For example, ISO 9006:2000 deals with quality management in project management.

The ISO 9000 standards set out eight principles of quality management that organisations should apply.

1   **Customer focus**. There must be a customer focus. This means obtaining measurements of customer requirements, not just measurements of customer satisfaction. Measurements of customer requirements can be obtained by proactive methods (such as market research) or reactive methods (such as finding data from customer returns or complaints).

2   **Leadership**. Management must take an active role in implementing and sustaining quality improvement.

3   **Involvement of people**. Management must ensure that all employees are aware of how their activities contribute towards the achievement of quality objectives.

4   **Process approach**. There should be a process-based approach to quality management. In a process-based approach, the business is seen as a series of individual processes, with outputs from one process sometimes being the input to another process. Management should seek to define and improve the interaction and linkages between the different processes.

5   There should be a **system approach to management**. Management should not think departmentally.

6   **Continuous improvement**.

7   A **factual approach to decision-making**. Decisions affecting quality should be based on data about work processes that has been gathered and analysed.

8   **Mutually beneficial supplier relationships**. Relationships with suppliers should be based on openness and mutual trust, with a sharing of information about quality.

5   Methods of performance measurement and improvement

Performance measurement is a vital part of controlling operations and, in particular, quality because, as Tom Peters put it 'what gets measured gets done'.

There are three important questions:

(i)   What are the key aspects of the organisation, or of each separate part of the organisation, that should be measured?

(ii)   What is the appropriate measure of performance for each key aspect?

(iii) What is the appropriate benchmark, in each case, against which to evaluate performance?

5.1   What to measure

Traditionally, the focus of performance measurement has been on financial outcomes (effects) because:

- the profit motive is a driving force for commercial organisations

- financial outcomes (in terms of sales, costs and profit) are very measurable.

Gradually, but increasingly, there has been a recognition, in both the literature and in practice, that focus needs to be placed on the wide variety of underlying factors **(causes)** that influence financial (and other) outcomes (i.e. on the key drivers of sales, costs and thus profit). This should encompass the external as well as the internal environment in its scope, and in such a way that recognises the importance of an organisation's strategies and objectives.

Thus, for example, if the quality of customer service is a key element of an organisation's strategy then it should be measured in some way and will be a key indicator of sales performance. Factors such as customer satisfaction, competitiveness, product quality, order lead time, flexibility, resource use, speed and degree of innovation, quality of working life and employee satisfaction, and technological support may, for example, be seen as important in an organisation as indicators of financial performance.

As a result of this broader approach a wide variety of performance measures have developed which need to be tailored in each separate case according to:

- the nature of the organisation

- the competitive environment within which it operates

- the organisation's strategies.

The concept of the 'balanced scorecard' is now commonly used to help direct attention to, and collect together, a range of performance measures that consider customers, suppliers and competitors as well as the internal environment of the organisation itself. At each level of management in the organisation, and for each separate part of an organisation (e.g. market, division, function, department) critical success factors need to be identified.

5.2 How to measure

Measures used to assess performance in relation to the key aspects identified may be:

- quantitative or qualitative

- financial or non-financial

- absolute or relative.

Quantitative (rather than qualitative) measures are most common and should be used wherever possible because they are more objective. However, not everything can be easily quantified, for example standards of customer service or quality of working environment. Qualitative measures are more subjective and thus more open to interpretation/bias on the part of both, for example, customer and supplier or employee and employer.

Qualitative measures will be non-financial. Quantitative measures may be financial or non-financial. Both financial and non-financial measures have an important part to play in performance measurement. Direct measures of sales, costs and profit are obviously financial measures. Many supporting quantitative measures of key aspects of organisation performance will be non-financial, for example measures to assess:

- customer service (e.g. complaint response time)

- customer satisfaction (e.g. no. of customer complaints; complaints per customer; complaints per £ of sales)

- competitiveness (e.g. market share; customer base; % sales growth)

- product quality (e.g. no. of customer complaints; no. of product rejects; % rejects; customer returns % of total sales)

- delivery/lead time (e.g. no. of deliveries on time; % of deliveries on time) – applied to purchases as well as to sales

- resource utilisation (e.g. m/c hours worked % of capacity; m/c downtime % of m/c hours worked)

- employee satisfaction (e.g. labour turnover)

- innovation (e.g. length of product development cycle; % of total sales from new products).

Relative measures are frequently more useful than measures in absolute terms (contrast the examples above) because, by relating one aspect of business to another, they add meaning to absolute numbers and thus help to put performance into context/perspective. Thus, for example, complaints per customer may be more useful than simply the number of complaints; gross profit per unit (or as a % of sales) may be more useful than total gross profit; departmental costs in relation to an appropriate measure of activity/output may be more useful than simply total costs on their own; and cost control ratios may be more useful than standard cost variances in absolute terms.

The key question always is whether the measure used is the most appropriate, fair and useful way of assessing performance in relation to the critical success factors identified. If measurement leads to improvement in performance in relation to a particular aspect then it is important that this is positive for the organisation as a whole i.e. that actions taken enhance organisation performance overall in relation to strategy and objectives. For example, it may be counterproductive if an improvement in delivery times is achieved at the expense of holding excessive stocks.

Activity 1

A training company provides training courses for students preparing for their professional accountancy examinations. List two operational measures, two financial measures and two customer measures of quality that the company might use.

Feedback to this activity is at the end of the chapter.

5.3 Benchmarking performance

Benchmarking is a method of comparing the operational performance of a company with other companies, often competitors that are considered to be the 'best in class'.

The measurement of performance requires, in addition to each measure itself, a basis for assessing whether performance is below, above or in line with that reasonably expected. A benchmark is required which may be based upon:

- the trend of performance over time

- the performance in a similar organisation (internal or external) or similar part of an organisation

- a budget, target or standard (e.g. standard cost) set by management

- where performance is monitored over time, indices are a useful way of measuring the degree of change and of helping to assess what might be achievable.

Inter-business/inter-departmental comparisons can also be useful where similar measurements are available and reasonably comparative.

Budgets, and/or targets arising from the strategic planning process, are also used extensively as a performance yardstick.

In the context of budgets, cost standards are commonly used especially in manufacturing organisations that have repetitive operations. However, standards can be set at different levels of achievement (basic, ideal, attainable, current).

A **basic** standard is a standard established for use over a long period, rather than simply in a single budget period, where gradual but sustained improvement in performance against the basic standard may be expected and achieved. Thus favourable variances against standard (and control ratios >100%) would be expected and allowed for in targets set.

An **ideal** standard is a standard that can only be achieved under the most favourable operating conditions, with no allowance for normal losses, waste or machine down-time. Ideal standards are also established for use, without change, over a long period of time to measure progress towards the ideal. Adverse variances against standard (and control ratios <100%) would be expected and allowed for in targets set.

An **attainable** standard is a standard that can be achieved under reasonable expectations of operating conditions whilst a **current** standard is a standard that relates to current conditions. Both attainable and current standards are short-term standards that would be used solely to measure current performance. With current standards a target control ratio of over 100% may be set (i.e. expectation of a positive variance).

There are motivational aspects to consider. Also, the level at which standards are set influences the performance expected in relation to standard (as illustrated above), and thus the interpretation of the measure that results. The principles of setting standards on different bases can be more generally applied in target setting, for example should targets be set at a level that is very difficult to achieve or at a level that is more easily achieved?

There are different types of benchmarking.

KEY POINT

There are different types of benchmarking.

- internal benchmarking
- competitive benchmarking
- process benchmarking or activity benchmarking.

- **Internal benchmarking** is comparing the performance in key areas in one part of an organisation with the performance in one or more other parts of the same organisation. This might be useful, for example, when:

  - an organisation consists of several different regional or area operations, and some regions appear to perform better than others

  - one company takes over another and the practices in each organisation are compared to establish which are better.

- **Competitive benchmarking** is comparing your performance in key areas with the performance of your most successful competitors. A problem with competitive benchmarking is that it can be difficult to obtain much information about competitor performance and standards. However, there have been examples in the past of competitors agreeing to share information for benchmarking purposes. For example, at one time the US semiconductor manufacturers Intel, Motorola, Digital Equipment Corporation and Hewlett-Packard agreed to share information in the area of quality management standards so that they could compete more effectively against Japanese rivals.

- **Process benchmarking** or **activity benchmarking** involves identifying and making comparisons of processes, activities, products or services of other organisations in a different industry. The aim of this type of benchmarking is to identify best practice anywhere and to look at organisations that have acquired a reputation for excellence in particular areas of operation, such as fleet management, marketing or engineering.

An example of process benchmarking was the experience of Xerox with Bean, a catalogue retailer specialising in outdoor clothing. After looking at order fulfilment and processing activities in different organisations and industries, Xerox identified Bean as an outstanding leader in its industry. Xerox managers visited Bean to learn about its warehousing and order fulfilment processes. As a result, Xerox was able to improve order picking in its own warehouse.

Feedback to this activity is at the end of the chapter.

Activity 2

What are the potential benefits to be obtained from a benchmarking exercise?

5.4 Business Process Re-engineering (BPR)

Hammer has defined Business Process Re-engineering (BPR) as the fundamental rethinking and radical redesign of business processes to achieve dramatic improvements in critical contemporary measures of performance such as cost, quality, speed and service'. It involves a deep and comprehensive analysis of the way an organisation works and a complete revision of its processes.

BPR must ensure that activities are consistent with the enterprise's currently stated strategic and operational objectives. Different enterprises emphasise different objectives. For example, an enterprise that is competing on the basis of customer service will redesign its business processes with customer service as the primary goals, while an enterprise attempting to be a least-cost producer will redesign its business processes with cost as the primary goal.

It might be carried out as part of an overall strategic review of the organisation. Senior management might want to use a BPR programme as a way of:

- introducing a quality programme

- creating a focus on processes within the organisation that create value

- identifying internal barriers to meeting customer needs within the organisation

- creating a set of benchmarks against which the processes in the organisation can be measured against those of competitors.

In order to meet these enterprise-wide objectives, BPR focuses on achieving dramatic, breakthrough improvements in the effectiveness and efficiency of business operations. The overall aim is to satisfy multiple business objectives simultaneously.

The main principles of BPR have been described (by Hammer, 1990) as follows.

- There must be a complete re-think of business processes in a cross-functional manner. The work should be organised around the natural flow of information, or materials or customers (in other words, around the natural flow of the transformed inputs). The work should be organised around the outcomes from the process, not around the tasks that go into it.

- The objective is to achieve dramatic improvements in performance through a radical re-design of the process.

- Where possible, internal customers within an internal process should be required to act as their own suppliers, rather than depending on another stage in the process to do the work for them. If an internal customer can be its own supplier, this will simplify and speed up the process.

- The decision points for controlling the process should be located where the work is done. There should not be a division or separation between the people who do the work and the people who manage and control it.

Dong the work and controlling it are yet another example of an internal supply-internal customer relationship that can be merged.

In a BPR process, there will be a review of critical success factors for the organisation and a re-engineering of the critical processes in order to improve customer satisfaction.

5.5   Balanced scorecard (Kaplan and Norton)

The balanced scorecard is an attempt to align behaviour in the business to actions that create shareholder value. It considers four main areas of concern to organisations – two external and two internal:

- financial perspectives

- customer perspectives

- internal processes

- learning / growth.

The two external perspectives focus on how well the organisation is doing when looked at from the financial – mainly shareholder – perspective and the customer point of view. The internal perspectives are concerned with current business processes and with how the organisation is developing itself for the future.

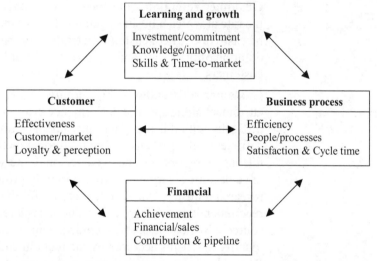

The model supplies a framework to translate a strategy into operational terms dealing with issues like:

- how do customers see us?

- what must we excel at?

- can we continue to improve and create value?

- how do we look to shareholders?

The customer perspective

In the customer perspective of the balanced scorecard, companies identify the customer and market segments in which they have chosen to compete.

These segments represent the sources of income that will deliver the revenue component of the company's financial objectives. As such, the customer perspective enables the business to align their core customer outcome measures – satisfaction, loyalty, retention, acquisition and profitability to customers and market segments. Essential to business success is value to the customer i.e., the ability to deliver the product/service that is valued by the customer. This could mean looking very carefully at the product and the market and identifying what the customer wants and values.

The five elements of the customer perspective are:

1   **Market share** – this reflects the proportion of the business in a given market expressed in terms of customer, pounds spent or volume sold. The size of the market can easily be obtained from trade associations, government statistics or even something like Yellow Pages.

2   **Customer acquisition** – this measures, in either absolute or relative terms, the rate at which a business unit attracts or wins new customers or business. Ratios can be monitored, the ratio of conversion to initial solicitation. How many cold calls? How many interested responses? How many follow ups needed? Literature requests? Existing customers can also be targets for developing related business.

3   **Customer retention** – this measures in either absolute or relative terms the rate at which a business retains its customers. Where customers can be easily identified, customer retention can be measured both by the duration of their stay, and the growth of that business with individual customers.

4   **Customer satisfaction** – this purports to measure the satisfaction level of customers along specific performance criteria. Large businesses have difficulty with this particular measure. The difficulty lies in obtaining sufficient valid responses. The traditional methods of mail surveys, telephone interviews, and even personal interviews are expensive and have become a very lucrative and rapidly growing part of the market research industry. One simple measure for the small business might be recommendation. Where the business has a record of the client, the source of the client can be included. Thus a measure is achieved by identifying clients acquired by the recommendation of other clients. Repeat business is another simple measure of satisfaction. If the customer was satisfied once, he/she will frequently return.

5   **Customer profitability** – this measures the net contribution from a customer or a segment.

The Business Process perspective

This perspective is about the internal value chain. The whole internal process must be driven, not by cost savings within the existing business but by a desire to identify and satisfy the external expectations. It involves three aspects of working:

- innovation
- operations
- post-sale services.

Innovation – to survive in the competitive world economy, companies must be effective, efficient and timely in the innovation process. The importance of the innovation cycle is most keenly felt where there are long design and development cycles such as in the pharmaceutical, agricultural chemicals, computer software and high-tech electronics industries. Most of the costs of such products are no longer in the production area, but in the development. What must drive efficient innovation is:

- knowing what range of benefits the customer is looking for

- performing the basic research to develop the new products/services

- exploiting existing technology to produce new products (this is important since it avoids 'reinventing the wheel')

- focusing the development efforts on new products/services for the market.

To achieve this, there must be better control and monitoring of the research and development function. Historically, control was always lax in this area because the emphasis was on high volume low-tech products and the investment was tied up in production. Now, advantage in the market place is derived from a stream of new products. To that end, effective control can be achieved by measuring:

- percentage of sales from new products

- percentage of sales from proprietary (patent protected) products (especially in the pharmaceutical industry)

- new product introduction versus competitors

- manufacturing process capabilities (how easy is it to make? how well does it use raw materials?)

- time to develop the next generation of products

- development break even time.

Operations – starts with the customer order and finishes with the delivery of the product/service to the customer. Kaplan and Norton are particularly critical of the use of traditional financial measures in controlling operational processes because they have emphasised efficiency variances in manufacturing and this excessive focus has frequently led to dysfunctional actions – stock-piling inventory to keep up production efficiencies, and penny pinching by switching suppliers with total regard for volume discounts, quality and delivery times.

It is suggested that measurements of quality, cycle time and minimal wastage arising from rectification might be more appropriate measures.

Post sale (or delivery) service – this covers the amount of time devoted to warranty and repair activities, treatment of defects and returns and the processing of payments, such as credit card administration.

Automobile manufacturers, especially where the traditional culture is less powerful, have dramatically improved the image for customer service in the realms of warranty work, periodic maintenance (longer periods between services) and repairs.

Many small businesses in the retail and service sector have only one opportunity to get it right, and the scope for warranty, repair and defects is minimal. A floral delivery has to be right first time, wreaths and wedding flowers cannot be wrong, and as such, a culture develops in keeping with that requirement. Bad news always travels faster than good; it might only be one defect that gets broadcast that results in immeasurable damage to the business. Monitoring becomes less and less pure financial. Speed of response is important, as is how quickly problems or calls are dealt with. When work has to be signed off as complete, and no money released until the work is signed off, then every effort must be made to minimise the delay in getting payment released.

The learning and growth perspective

The objectives in learning and growth create the infrastructure whereby the financial, customer and internal process objectives might be achieved. It is agreed that to continue to be successful, organisations must invest in their people, their systems and procedures.

Employee capabilities can be measured by:

- employee satisfaction
- employee retention
- employee productivity.

In a knowledge-worker organisation, *people* – the only repository of knowledge – are the main resource. In the current climate of rapid technological change, it is becoming necessary for knowledge workers to be in a continuous learning mode. Some organisations find themselves unable to hire new technical workers, and at the same time there is a decline in training of existing employees. This is a leading indicator of 'brain drain' that must be reversed. Measures can be put into place to guide managers in focusing training funds where they can help the most. In any case, learning and growth constitute the essential foundation for success of any knowledge-worker organisation.

Information systems – to be effective, employees need information about customers, internal processes and feedback on the consequences, particularly the financial consequences of their decisions. The obvious examples are where they eliminate waste, eliminate defects and drive out excess costs and time wastage out of the production system.

Motivation – measures that will make employees feel good are:

- number of suggestions submitted
- number of successful suggestions
- details of benefits from suggestions
- reward structure for benefits
- reduction in late deliveries, defects, scrap and absenteeism.

Such ideas among others, will both motivate people to do more and give them a sense that they are part of the team, rather than just pawns in a chess game.

The financial perspective

This perspective takes a view on how the organisation must, and should appear to shareholders. It will include the setting of measurable performance indicators that influence shareholder views – returns on equity, asset utilisation, growth and so on.

Top of the list of financial measures is return on capital employed (ROCE) – also known as return on investment (ROI) or accounting rate of return (ARR)

$$\frac{\text{Average annual profit after depreciation}}{\text{Initial investment}} \times 100\%$$

This has been a frequently criticised measure. Obvious difficulties are defining the capital employed, dealing with fluctuations, and the implications of low cost and low asset businesses. As a result of this latter drawback, ROCE/ROI can actually provide misleading information and lead to incorrect decision-making.

Another key financial measure is cash flow. A business must generate cash. In a strategic context, the organisation must understand the importance of the cash cow – the product that has recovered all its development costs, requires minimal advertising and marketing costs and as such generates the vital cash to enable the business to continue and fund new products. Cash flow must be regularly monitored, and the simple quick and current liquidity ratios will easily provide that. Such ratios can be usefully compared with previous year, previous month and readily projected. More to the point, projections can be made as to when cash will be generated and when it will be used.

Kaplan and Norton do not disregard the traditional need for financial data. But they argue that the current emphasis on financials leads to the 'unbalanced' situation with regard to other perspectives.

There is perhaps a need to include additional financial-related data, such as risk assessment and cost-benefit data, in this category.

Performance improvement

A major consideration in performance improvement involves the creation and use of performance measures or indicators. Performance measures or indicators are measurable characteristics of products, services, processes, and operations the company uses to track and improve performance. The measures or indicators should be selected to best represent the factors that lead to improved customer, operational, and financial performance. A comprehensive set of measures or indicators tied to customer and/or company performance requirements represents a clear basis for aligning all activities with the company's goals. Through the analysis of data from the tracking processes, the measures or indicators themselves may be evaluated and changed to better support such goals."

The balanced scorecard methodology builds on some key concepts of previous management ideas such as Total Quality Management (TQM), including customer-defined quality, continuous improvement, employee empowerment, and – primarily – measurement-based management and feedback.

Double loop feedback

In traditional industrial activity, 'quality control' and 'zero defects' were the watchwords. In order to shield the customer from receiving poor quality products, aggressive efforts were focused on inspection and testing at the end of the production line. The problem with this approach -- as pointed out by Deming - is that the true causes of defects could never be identified, and there would always be inefficiencies due to the rejection of defects. What Deming saw was that variation is created at every step in a production process, and the causes of variation need to be identified and fixed. If this can be done, then there is a way to reduce the defects and improve product quality indefinitely. To establish such a process, Deming emphasised that all business processes should be part of a system with feedback loops. The feedback data should be examined by managers to determine the causes of variation and the processes with significant problems and then they can focus attention on fixing that subset of processes.

The balanced scorecard incorporates feedback around internal business process *outputs*, as in TQM, but also adds a feedback loop around the *outcomes* of business strategies. This creates a 'double-loop feedback' process in the balanced scorecard.

Linkages between functions

All the measures are linked and must be viewed as a whole. For example, excess capacity can be a by-product of quality improvements. Increasing productivity may mean that fewer employees are required for a given level of output. Increasing sales may result in these improvements being exploited. The financial measurements remind management that improved quality, productivity and response time only benefits the organisation when it create a sustainable competitive advantage or is translated into improved financial results.

The goal of taking measurements is to permit managers to see their company more clearly – from many perspectives – and hence to make wiser long-term decisions. Measurements must derive from the company's strategy and provide critical data and information about key processes, outputs and results. Data and information needed for performance measurement and improvement are of many types, including: customer, product and service performance, operations, market, competitive comparisons, supplier, employee-related, and cost and financial. Analysis entails using data to determine trends, projections, and cause and effect - that might not be evident without analysis. Data and analysis support a variety of company purposes, such as planning, reviewing company performance, improving operations, and comparing company performance with competitors' or with 'best practices' benchmarks.

Activity 3

Many supporting quantitative measures of key aspects of organisation performance will be non-financial. Identify measures to assess the following:

- customer service
- customer satisfaction
- competitiveness
- product quality
- delivery/lead time
- resource utilisation
- employee satisfaction
- innovation.

Feedback to this activity is at the end of the chapter.

5.6 Three tier improvement plan

For a company wishing to introduce a balanced scorecard system to achieve business process improvements, the diagram below shows the procedure:

Three tier improvement plan

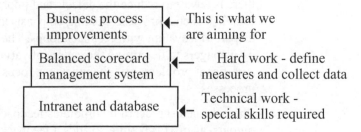

The foundation of the entire plan is an intranet connected to a relational database. This infrastructure is used to support the collection and distribution of data to all participants.

The balanced scorecard provides a management system based on measurements of the cycle time and cost of processes, employee growth and satisfaction, customer satisfaction, and financial data. The measures for the balanced scorecard are defined with reference to the strategic plan, so they can be used to assess alignment with this strategic plan.

The measurement system provided by the balanced scorecard allows us to measure processes and subprocesses, to identify candidates for improvement, and to make the improvements – this is the Business Process Improvements (BPI) Project. The organisation should expect to find significant overall cost reductions by the application of BPI analysis to some of these processes that may not been examined for a long time.

Conventional project management can manage the development of the three projects, but the balanced scorecard itself is *not a project:* it is a perpetual system that will be built into the information infrastructure of the organisation. Also, the BPI efforts may be managed continuously, rather than as focused projects.

5.7 Use of the Intranet in information management

Intranet technologies represent the next major step in the evolution of computing and hold the promise of increasing return on Information Technology (IT) investments. Almost every department in an organisation can benefit from an Intranet or Extranet site.

Intranet technologies, including Web browsers, Web-enabled databases, groupware, e-mail, ActiveX, Java, streaming audio and video, and countless new Web-based business applications represent a major advancement in the evolution of computing. Intranet technologies provide a common application development platform and an intuitive user environment that allows organisations to deploy applications much faster and at dramatically lower operating costs.

Here are some examples of business applications that can be supported by an Intranet (in conjunction with other server-side software such as a database):

Sales and marketing groups can take advantage of Intranets to enhance communication and collaboration with each other as well as with other functional groups, including external resources. The corporate Intranet enables centralised publishing of product, service and marketing information. It also provides quick but controlled access to relevant company databases that contain product or inventory availability data, sales forecasts, performance figures and the customer information knowledge base. An Intranet is a powerful tool for proposal development as well. Past projects and budgets can be referenced by size, scope of project and resources required to provide critical background information to insure future projects are successful and profitable. As a result, marketing and sales personnel can collaborate more effectively and ensure that the field sales staff, outside contractors, channel partners and distributors and dealers have immediate access to the information they need. The result is higher productivity and reduced costs.

Customer service representatives need instant access to up-to-date product, company and customer information. Field service and help desk personnel need access to customer problem and service history information for problem solving. This information must be accurate and content-rich, and it must be accessible and at their fingertips while they are interacting with customers. Customer service and support personnel also need to enter data into a variety of databases and knowledge bases, such as order information, problem tracking and technical support. In many cases, customers ask routine questions that do not require personal interaction. These include questions on pricing, product specifications and routine operational questions. Some companies have attempted to provide answers through fax-back and voice-response systems. However, these systems are often lacking in detail, and information is difficult to locate. As a result, these systems are not suitable for delivering timely information, and do not reduce call volume appreciably.

Intranets can enable organisations to create information systems that consolidate data from multiple databases or information systems within a single customer transaction. A Web-based application can be developed that enables representatives to use a single query to access multiple databases simultaneously. The application consolidates information in a single, easy-to-navigate window. For example, the application could enable fast access to both a customer database and a knowledgebase of known problems and solutions.

A knowledgebase is well suited for the hyperlinked search and retrieval capabilities associated with Web-based technology. Customer service personnel can easily navigate a large archive of data, which is constantly updated, to find the desired information. Faster access to this data dramatically reduces the time required to complete a customer transaction, so each representative can handle a higher volume of service calls. As a result, many companies find that they can handle a growing customer base without expanding the size of the service and support staff.

The company can also allow direct, yet controlled and secure, access to corporate information by customers, dealers and distributors. These external users enjoy ready access to the information they need without the intervention of service or support staff. This helps reduce the number of incoming calls that require human intervention, so service and support staff can spend more time solving complex problems.

Examples of ways to get more out of the customer services and support intranet are:

- **Online information** – post answers to routine questions for access by customer service. A knowledge base can also be made available on the intranet and guest access can be enabled to provide direct access for customers, distributors and dealers. One of the advantages is that customers can get answers to many questions on their own – 24 hours per day, 7 days per week

- **Customer information** – use the database to provide online forms for entering data about customer problems.

- **Problem escalation** – provide a discussion forum or database of information detailing problem escalation from field personnel to customer service to engineering

- **Bug fixes** – post all bug fixes on web site with capability to search quickly. Easy download of software upgrades.

- **Warranty claims and processing** – companies that sell warranted products can provide a self-serve mechanism for customers and/or distributors to make warranty or repair claims

- **Training** – post on-line training about products and customer service tools and techniques to the service and support staff.

- **Customer forum** – create a discussion group to allow customers to communicate with each other about key product and support issues

- **Customer feedback and ideas** – use the database to create a category of product requests, feedback and new ideas.

Finance and accounting – an Intranet provides a secure, central point for collecting and publishing financial information. It also provides a vehicle for online transaction processing, ensuring rapid updating of information and availability of accurate and timely information. As a result, an Intranet enables managers across the company to track financial performance and maintain effective control. Intranets also permit external business partners, shareholders and analysts to have limited access to financial data to build tighter relationships with these constituencies and provide them with timely, accurate information.

6 Lean production

The concept of lean production (sometimes called lean manufacturing) developed out of the Toyota Production System, the Japanese approach to operations management that emerged during the 1950s. (The Toyota Production System is also associated with the Just-in-Time operations management philosophy, and JIT and lean manufacturing are consistent with each other.)

It can be described as an operational strategy oriented towards achieving the shortest possible cycle time by eliminating waste in every area of production, including customer relations, product design, supplier networks and factory management. Its goal is to incorporate less human effort, less inventory, less time to develop products and less space to become highly responsive to customer demand while producing top-quality products in the most efficient and economical manner possible'

The seven wastes to be eliminated

1. Overproduction and early production - producing over customer requirements, producing unnecessary materials / products

2. Waiting – time delays, idle time (time during which value is not added to the product)

3. Transportation – multiple handling, delay in materials handling, unnecessary handling

4. Inventory – holding or purchasing unnecessary raw materials, work in process, and finished goods

5. Motion – actions of people or equipment that do not add value to the product

6. Over-processing – unnecessary steps or work elements / procedures (non added value work)

7. Defective units – production of a part that is scrapped or requires rework.

6.1 Principles and characteristics of lean manufacturing

Just as mass production is recognised as the production system of the 20th century, lean production is viewed as the production system of the 21st century.

The basic elements of lean manufacturing are waste elimination, continuous one-piece workflow, and customer pull. When these elements are focused in the areas of cost, quality and delivery, this forms the basis for a lean production system.

Four principles

- Minimise waste
- Perfect first time quality
- Flexible production lines
- Continuous improvement

The characteristics of lean manufacturing and a 'lean enterprise' are therefore:

- zero waiting time
- zero inventory
- scheduling production – production is initiated by external or internal customer demand rather than the ability and capacity to produce. In other words, production is initiated by 'demand-pull' rather than 'supply-push'
- moving from batch production to continuous flow production, or cutting batch sizes to one
- continually finding ways of reducing process times.

Compared to traditional manufacturing, lean production concentrates on the following:

- Reduced set up cost and times (for semi-versatile machinery such as big stamping presses) from months to hours thus making small lot production economically viable; achieved by organising procedures, using carts, and training workers to do their own set ups.

- Production is based on orders rather than forecasts; production planning is driven by customer demand or 'pull' and not to suit machine loading or inflexible workflows on the shop floor.

- Small lot production allowing higher flexibility and pull production (or just-in-time manufacturing).

- Employee involvement and empowerment – organising workers by forming teams and giving them training and responsibility to do many specialised tasks, for housekeeping, quality inspection, minor equipment repair and rework; allowing also them time to meet to discuss problems and find ways to improve the process.

- Quality at the source – total quality management (TQM) and control; assigning workers, not inspectors, the responsibility to discover a defect and to immediately fix it; if the defect cannot be readily fixed, any worker can halt the entire line by pulling a cord (called jidoka)

- Just-in-time purchasing.

- Pull production or Just-In-Time (JIT) – the method wherein the quantity of work performed at each stage of the process is dictated solely by the demand for materials from the immediate next stage; thus reducing waste and lead times, and eliminating inventory holding costs.

- Short order-to-ship cycles times; small batch production capability that is synchronised to shipping schedules. Fast (low) cycle times allow customer orders to be shipped quickly. Less money needs to be invested in inventory on the shop floor and in the warehouse. If inventories are low, there is less opportunity for the product becoming obsolete before it is shipped. Low Work-in-Progress inventory (WIP) means there is less potential scrap if defective parts are discovered after additional operations are complete.

- In small batch operations and administrative processes, it is frequently easier to quantify cycle time accurately than it is to measure defects. Focusing process improvement activities on reducing cycle time (eliminating the defects that cause unnecessarily long cycle times) will usually achieve better results faster than focusing on defects alone.

- Close integration of the whole value chain from raw material to finished product through partnership oriented relations with suppliers and distributors.

- Highly flexible and responsive processes.

- Quick changeovers from one operation to another.

- Integrated single piece continuous workflow.

- Machines, equipment, tools and people to make an item located together in the same work floor space.

- Compressed space.

- Continuous equipment maintenance – as pull production reduces inventories, equipment breakdowns must also be reduced; thus empowered operators are assigned primary responsibility for basic maintenance since they are in the best position do detect signs of malfunction.

- Multi-skilled workforce – as employees are empowered to do many jobs, they must be provided with adequate training.

- Supplier involvement – the manufacturer treats its suppliers as long-term partners; they often must be trained in ways to reduce setup times, inventories, defects, machine breakdowns, etc. in order to enable them to take responsibility for delivering the best possible parts/services to the manufacturer in a timely manner.

- Major reductions in defects.

Lean techniques are applicable not only in manufacturing, but also in service-oriented industry and service environment. Every system contains waste, i.e. something that does not provide value to your customer. Whether you are producing a product, processing a material, or providing a service, there are elements that are considered 'waste'. The techniques for analysing systems, identifying and reducing waste, and focusing on the customer are applicable in any system, and in any industry.

Example

IBM regularly compares part counts, bills of materials, standard versus custom part usage, and estimated processing costs by tearing down competitor products as soon as they are available. 'Through such tear-downs during the heyday of the dot matrix printer, IBM learned that the printer made by the Epson, its initial supplier, was exceedingly complicated with more than 150 parts. IBM launched a team with a simplification goal and knocked the part count down to 62, cutting assembly from thirty minutes to only three'.

Activity 4

Which of these characteristics of lean manufacturing is consistent with a JIT approach to production and purchasing?

Feedback to this activity is at the end of the chapter.

6.2 The six core methods of lean production

Lean manufacturing refers to the systematic identification and elimination of waste from a process while increasing responsiveness to change. While there are a number of specific tools that organisations use to implement lean production systems, the six core methods listed below are most typically used. Most of these lean methods are interrelated and some can occur concurrently. Implementation is often sequenced in the order presented below. Most organisations begin by implementing lean techniques in a particular production area or at a pilot facility and then expand use of the methods over time.

- Just in time/Kanban

- Kaizen

- 5S

- Total Productive Maintenance (TPM)

- Cellular manufacturing /One-piece flow production systems

- Six Sigma

6.3 Just-in-time/Kanban

Just-in-time (JIT) Production Systems, Kanban and cellular manufacturing are closely related, as a cellular production layout is typically a prerequisite for achieving just-in-time production. JIT uses the cellular manufacturing layout to significantly reduce inventory and work-in-process (WIP).

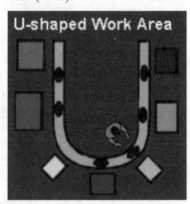

Orders must flow through production as efficiently as possible. They should flow continuously with queues between workstations as small as possible. Cells, like the U-shaped work area at the right, allow a single worker to operate several machines or do several operations. Maintaining a rhythm in operations (cell and otherwise) leads to better over-all efficiency. The workforce is cross-trained to allow flexibility in cell operation and scheduling.

JIT enables a company to produce the products its customers want, when they want them, in the amount they want. JIT techniques work to level production, spreading production evenly over time to foster a smooth flow between processes. Varying the mix of products produced on a single line, often referred to as shish-kebab production, provides an effective means for producing the desired production mix in a smooth manner.

Work is 'pulled' through production rather than 'pushed.' Final assembly (or final operations) is scheduled to meet customer delivery requirements. The operations just before final assembly (operations) are scheduled to meet the final assembly schedule, and so on back to the start of production. This is in contrast to starting jobs into production when orders are received or materials are received, and then trying to adjust schedules through production to maintain manpower and equipment productivity while meeting shipping requirements.

When designs and production volumes permit, Kanban systems are used. Storage space for standard components is limited to a number of standard containers. When a container is withdrawn for use in the next operation, an order is automatically generated to make another container of components. This 'pulls' production orders through the system and eliminates a lot of expediting.

The benefits of JIT systems are:

• Reduced inventory levels	• Increased equipment utilisation
• High quality	• Reduced scrap and rework
• Flexibility	• Reduced space requirements
• Reduced lead times	• Pressure for good vendor relationships
• Increased productivity	• Reduced need for indirect labour

6.4 Kaizen – continuous improvement

Kaizen is a Japanese term for the philosophy of continuous improvement in performance in all areas of an organisation's operations.

Kaizen, or rapid improvement processes, are often considered to be the building block of all lean production methods. Kaizen focuses on eliminating waste in the targeted systems and processes of an organisation, improving productivity, and achieving sustained continual improvement. This philosophy implies that small, incremental changes routinely applied and sustained over a long period result in significant improvements. The kaizen strategy aims to involve workers from multiple functions and levels in the organisation in working together to address a problem or improve a particular process. The team uses analytical techniques, such as Value Stream Mapping, to quickly identify opportunities to eliminate waste in a targeted process. The team works to rapidly implement chosen improvements (often within 72 hours of initiating the kaizen event), typically focusing on ways that do not involve large capital outlays. Periodic follow-up events aim to ensure that the improvements from the kaizen blitz are sustained over time. Kaizen can be used as an implementation tool for most of the other lean methods.

The concepts underlying continuous improvement are:

- The organisation should always seek perfection. Since perfection is never achieved, there must always be scope for improving on the current methods.

- The search for perfection should be ingrained into the culture and mindset of all employees. Improvements should be sought all the time.

- Individual improvements identified by the work force will be small rather than far-reaching.

The philosophy of continual small-scale improvements is in stark contrast to business process re-engineering, which seeks to make radical one-off changes to improve an organisation's operations and processes.

Quality management is not a one-off process, but is the continual examination and improvement of existing processes.

The idea of continuous improvement might appear to go against the principle of diminishing returns, in that it might be arguable that there is a limit beyond which there is no point in pursuing any further improvements.

Advocates of continuous improvement, however, believe that this principle does not always apply. Remember that continuous improvement does not only apply to the finished product, but also to the processes which give rise to it.

(a)   It is not easy to determine where diminishing returns set in.

(b)   A philosophy of continuous improvement ensures that management are not *complacent*, which can be a cultural disaster.

(c)   Customer needs change, so a philosophy of continual improvement enables these changes to be taken into account in the normal course of events.

(d)   New technologies or materials might be developed, enabling cost savings or design improvements.

(e)   Rarely do businesses know every possible fact about the production process. Continuous improvement encourages experimentation and a scientific approach to production.

(f)   It is a way of tapping employees' knowledge.

(g)   Reducing *variability* is a key issue for quality, if this is assessed on Taguchi's quality-cost model.

(h)   Improvement on a continual, step by step basis is more prudent in some cases than changing everything at once.

KEY POINT

Whereas BPR calls for a radical re-thinking of working methods and processes, continuous improvement takes a more gradual approach to improvement.

Whereas BPR calls for a radical re-thinking of working methods and processes, continuous improvement takes a more gradual approach to improvement. With a continual improvement programme, there is a permanent objective of aiming for further improvements in the efficiency and effectiveness of processes. Continuous improvement can be described as a never-ending cycle. Deming called this a Plan-Do-Check-Act cycle:

- **Plan.** Plan activities.

- **Do.** Implement the plan.

- **Check.** Check the results.

- **Act.** Improve the process.

The ISO 9004 standard for quality improvement describes continuous improvement as an eight-step method:

- involve the entire organisation

- initiate quality improvement projects or activities

- investigate possible causes of quality problems

- establish cause-and-effect relationships

- take preventative or corrective action to improve quality

- confirm the improvement

- sustain the gains

- continue the improvement.

The involvement of everyone was also emphasised by Masaaki Imai (1986) who defined kaizen as follows: 'When applied to the workplace, kaizen means continuing improvement involving everyone – managers and workers alike'.

It is not important whether each successive improvement is small. The key to success with continuous improvement is that it should be going on all the time. There should always be a momentum for change.

There are two parts that make up kaizen:

- improvement/change for the better, and

- ongoing continuity.

Both of these elements is essential for the kaizen approach to exist.

6.5 5S

The '5S' practice is an approach to achieving and maintaining a high-quality work environment. The 5Ss (Japanese words) are used to outline improvement actions workers/teams can apply in their work area. Translated these are:

Seiri – straighten up/sort – eliminate unnecessary things in the workplace. Decide what you need to do the work and what is not needed. Keep what is needed and remove what is not needed. Mark unwanted items with a red tag, so that they can be taken away to a central storage location.

Seiton – put things in order – arrange things properly. Place things where they will be easily found and reached whenever they are needed. 'A place for everything and everything in its place.'

Seiso – clean up – when you have got rid of all the unwanted items and stored everything else in a tidy way, the next step is to clean the work place thoroughly every day. When the workplace is clean, it becomes easier to spot problems such as oil leaks or water leaks.

Seiketsu – standardise – concentrate on standardising work practices to achieve 'best practice'

Shitsuke – sustain or self-discipline – having established a clean and efficient working environment, and established best practice, make sure that this is sustained. Do not slip back into old habits. Maintain the new work culture

In the daily work of a company, routines that maintain organisation and orderliness are essential to a smooth and efficient flow of activities. This lean method encourages workers to improve their working conditions and facilitates their efforts to reduce waste, unplanned downtime, and in-process inventory. 5S provides the foundation on which other lean methods, such as total productive maintenance, cellular manufacturing, just-in-time production, and Six Sigma, can be introduced.

6.6 Total Productive Maintenance (TPM)

Total Productive Maintenance (TPM) seeks to engage all levels and functions in an organisation in maximising the overall effectiveness of production equipment. Whereas traditional preventive maintenance programs are centered in the maintenance departments, TPM seeks to involve workers in all departments and levels, from the plant-floor to senior executives, in ensuring the effective operation of equipment. Autonomous maintenance, a key aspect of TPM, trains and focuses workers to take care of the equipment and machines with which they work. TPM addresses the entire production system lifecycle and builds a solid, plant-floor based system to prevent accidents, defects, and breakdowns. TPM focuses on preventing breakdowns (preventive maintenance), 'mistake-proofing' equipment (or poka-yoke) to prevent breakdowns or to make maintenance easier (corrective maintenance), designing and installing equipment that needs little or no maintenance (maintenance prevention), and quickly repairing equipment after breakdowns occur (breakdown maintenance). TPM's goal is the total elimination of all losses, including breakdowns, equipment setup and adjustment losses, idling and minor stoppages, reduced speed, defects and rework, spills and process upset conditions, and startup and yield losses.

6.7 Cellular Manufacturing/One-Piece Flow Systems

Cellular Manufacturing/One-Piece Flow Systems are work units arranged in a sequence that supports a smooth flow of materials and components through the production process with minimal transport or delay. Rather than processing multiple parts before sending them on to the next machine or process step (as is the case in batch-and-queue, or large-lot production), cellular manufacturing aims to move products through the manufacturing process one-piece at a time, at a rate determined by customers' needs. Cellular manufacturing can also provide companies with the flexibility to vary product type or features on the production line in response to specific customer demands. To make the cellular design work, an organisation must often replace large, high volume production machines with small, flexible, 'right-sized' machines to fit well in the process 'cell'. Equipment often must be modified to stop and signal when a cycle is complete or when problems occur, using a technique called autonomation (or jidoka). This transformation often shifts worker responsibilities from watching a single machine, to managing multiple machines in production cell. While plant-floor workers may need to feed or unload pieces at the beginning or end of the process sequence, they are generally freed to focus on implementing TPM and process improvements.

6.8 Six Sigma

DEFINITION

Six Sigma is a quality management program to achieve 'six sigma' levels of quality, derived from TQM. The aim of Six Sigma is that the total number of failures in a process (the number that exceed the established tolerance limits) should occur beyond the sixth sigma of likelihood or probability.

Six Sigma is a quality management program to achieve 'six sigma' levels of quality, derived from TQM. It is a data-driven approach, pioneered by Motorola in the 1980s, which is based on statistical measurements of variation from a standard or a norm. The aim of the approach is to achieve a reduction in variations and the number of 'faults' that go beyond an accepted tolerance limit.

The aim of Six Sigma is that the total number of failures in a process (the number that exceed the established tolerance limits) should occur beyond the sixth sigma of likelihood or probability. The 'sigma' refers to the Greek lower case letter representing a standard deviation (σ), and the acceptance rate for errors is measured statistically. For reasons that need not be explained here, it can be demonstrated that, if the error rate lies beyond the sixth sigma of probability, there will be fewer than 3.4 defects in every one million. This is almost total perfection. If this level of errors can be achieved, customers will have a reason to complain in fewer than four in one million cases.

In broad terms, there is a Six Sigma methodology for:

- existing processes (DMAIC), and

- new processes (DMADV).

The Six Sigma methodology for existing processes is DMAIC, as follows:

- D – Define what is meant by the out-of-tolerance range

- M – Measure the key internal processes that are critical to quality

- A – Analyse why defects occur

- I – Improve the process to stay within the tolerance limit
- C – Control the process to stay within this limit.

The Six Sigma methodology for new processes is DMADV, as follows:

- D – Define the process and where it would fail to meet customer needs
- M – Measure to determine whether the process meets these customer needs
- A – Analyse the options available that will meet customer needs
- D – Design in changes to the process to meet customer needs
- V – Verify that the changes have met customer needs.

The Six Sigma approach also uses experts who are trained in the Six Sigma methodology ('Six Sigma black belts') to provide advice and assistance to operations managers.

6.9 Criticisms and limitations of lean production

The concept of lean production has many supporters, but it also has critics. The alleged limitations of lean production include the following.

- It might involve a large initial expenditure to switch from 'traditional' production systems to a system based on work cells. All the tools and equipment needed to manufacture a product need to be re-located to the same area of the factory floor. Employees need to be trained in multiple skills.

- Lean manufacturing, like TQM, is a philosophy or culture of working, and it might be difficult for management and employees to acquire this culture. Employees might not be prepared to give the necessary commitment.

- It might be tempting for companies to select some elements of lean manufacturing (such as production based on work cells), but not to adopt others (such as empowering employees to make on-the-spot decisions).

- In practice, the expected benefits of lean manufacturing (lower costs and shorter cycle times) have not always materialised, or might not have been as large as expected.

7 Implementing a quality programme

7.1 A total quality programme

Quality seems such a desirable objective that you might wonder why it has not been implemented before now. As ever, quality inevitably encounters a variety of organisational problems. In practice all the techniques and approaches to TQM involve a significant shake up.

- TQM is associated with giving employees a say in the process (e.g. in the *quality survey*) and in getting them to suggest improvements.

- TQM implies a greater discipline to the process of production and the establishment of better linkages between the business functions.

- TQM involves new relationships with suppliers, which requires them to improve their output quality so that less effort is spent rectifying poor input. Long-term relationships with a small number of suppliers might be preferable to choosing material and sub-components on price.

- It requires both work standardisation and employee commitment.
- It requires long-term commitment.
- It involves the whole organisation.

Participation is important in TQM, especially in the process of continual improvement, where workforce views are valued. The management task is to encourage everybody to contribute. **Barriers** to participation include:

- an autocratic chief executive, who believes he or she is the sole key to the process;
- individualism, in which people 'possess' ideas in order to take credit for them rather than share them for mutual benefit;
- ideas of managers as leaders and directors rather than facilitators and supporters;
- middle managers who feel their authority is threatened.

7.2 Commitment to the plan

To gain commitment to the implementation of a quality programme, we need to begin at the top of the organisation.

- **Ensure management buy-in** – quality is led from the top down and implemented from the bottom up. The organisation and leadership team will not receive maximum benefits unless everyone is empowered and given the knowledge and skills necessary to take action and improve their responsible work areas. Leadership from the top of the organisation is necessary to define, prioritise and construct the quality culture. If the Chief Executive Officer or General Manager is not already committed to quality, the first step is to educate, develop the understanding, and generate active support. This is no easy task. It entails having a comprehensive understanding of the concepts of quality and using persuasion skills.

  One way to get attention and build momentum for a quality programme is to highlight the many problems and daily 'fires' of the organisation. Look for repeated customer visible defects and complaints, calculate financial savings from reducing defects, and try to quantify employee frustration with the current process.

- **Examine the organisation and culture** – each organisation has a specific culture and way of doing things. The culture of an organisation is the result of the beliefs and values of its employees. If the company is long established, the culture may be difficult to modify if employees are not used to change. Management must focus on the fit between the culture and quality and determine how best to implement quality within the organisation. The end result should focus on recommendations, specific next steps and the long-range plan for implementation.

- **Establish a mission** – having gained support from the management team and come to agreement on the best way to implement quality within the organisation and culture, the final step before actual implementation is to develop the quality mission. The mission statement sets the direction and priority for developing and implementing the quality plan. It clearly states the nature of the organisation's commitment to quality and should then be tied to the organisational operations through programmes, projects, actions and rewards/recognition. Only through clear, strong and persistent actions by top and middle leadership can the employees who doubt be convinced and the employees who fear reassured. Implementation actions must directly involve the CEO or GM to show what the culture now expects.

Once the management is on board, the main characteristics of a total quality programme should be addressed:

- Everyone in the organisation is involved in continually improving the processes and systems under their control and each person is responsible for his or her own quality assurance.

- A commitment to the satisfaction of every customer.

- Employee involvement is practised and the active participation of everyone in the organisation is encouraged.

- There is an investment in training and education to realise individual potential.

- Teamwork is used in a number of forms e.g. quality circles.

- Suppliers and customers form an integrated part of the process of improvement.

- Process re-design is used to simplify processes, systems, procedures and the organisation itself.

7.3 An outline plan

1 Identify the goals you want to achieve

Typical goals may be:

- Be more efficient and profitable

- Produce products and services that consistently meet customer requirements

- Achieve customer satisfaction

- Increase market share

- Maintain market share

- Improve communications and morale in the organisation

- Reduce costs and liabilities

- Increase confidence in the production system.

2 Identify what others expect of you

These are the expectations of interested parties (stakeholders) such as:

- Customers and end users

- Employees

- Suppliers

- Shareholders

- Society.

3 Apply the ISO 9000 family of standards in your management system.

Decide if you are seeking certification that your quality management system is in conformance with ISO 9001:2000 or if you are preparing to apply for a national quality award.

Use ISO 9001:2000 as the basis for certification.

Use ISO 9004:2000 in conjunction with your national quality award criteria to prepare for a national quality award.

4   Obtain guidance on specific topics within the quality management system

There are topic-specific standards for project management, measurement systems, documentation, training and auditing.

5   Establish your current status, determine the gaps between your quality management system and the requirements of ISO 9001:2000

You may use one self-assessment or assessment by an external organisation.

6   Determine the processes that are needed to supply products to your customers

Review the requirements of the ISO 9001:2000 section on Product Realisation to determine how they apply or do not apply to your quality management system including:

- customer-related processes

- design and/or development

- purchasing

- production and service operations

- control of measuring and monitoring devices.

7   Develop a plan to close the gaps

Identify actions needed to close the gaps identified in step 6, allocate resources to perform these actions, assign responsibilities and establish a schedule to complete the needed actions. ISO 9001:2000 Paragraphs 4.1 and 7.1 provide the information you will need to consider when developing the plan.

8   Carry out your plan

Proceed to implement the identified actions and track progress to your schedule. Undergo periodic internal assessment.

You may need or wish to show conformance (certification/registration) for various purposes, for example:

- contractual requirements

- market reasons or customer preference

- regulatory requirements

- risk management

- to set a clear goal for your internal quality development (motivation).

7.4   The TQM Excellence Model TQMEX

Samuel HO's TQMEX model is an integrated approach to the process of continuous improvement and the management of quality which shows the relationship between quality management and other aspects of operations management.

The TQMEX model gives a step-by-step approach to developing TQM and incorporates a range of other recognized models, as shown in the diagram below.

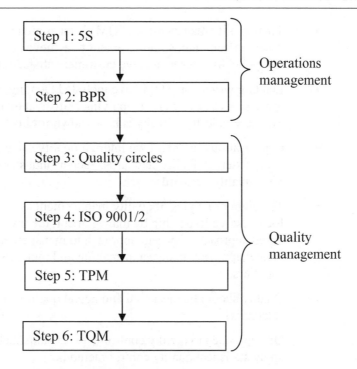

The rationale for this sequence is as follows:

- 5S is key to a total quality environment so needs to be the first step

- BPR involves redefining your business process to meet customer needs more effectively

- Quality circles then encourage employee participation in continuous improvement

- ISO 9000 builds on the previous three steps to develop a quality management system

- TPM results from applying 5S within this quality management system and flows naturally from ISO9000 procedures

- If the above five steps have been successfully implemented then the organization should be much closer to TQM

Summary

- Quality is an important aspect of operations, although it can be defined in different ways. Better quality can result in lower costs and higher sales. Quality is often judged in relation to the price of the product or service.

- Problems with quality can occur when there are gaps between actual achievement and expectations – a gap between a product design concept and the actual product design specifications, a gap between the product design specifications and customer expectations, a gap between the product design specifications and actual production, and a gap between the marketed features of the product package and its actual features.

- Costs related to quality are prevention costs, appraisal/inspection costs, internal failure costs and external failure costs. One approach to managing these costs is to minimise total quality costs up to the point where further improvements in quality would cost more than the value that would be added by the improvements. Another view is that the aim should be to improve quality continuously and there is no optimal level of quality costs.

- Total quality management (TQM) is an approach to the management of quality based on continuous improvement to achieve quality at a low cost by involving everyone, in order to achieve customer satisfaction.

- Leading writers on TQM have included Deming, Juran and Crosby. Deming's greatest successes were in applying statistical quality control methods in Japanese industry. Crosby is best known for his 'zero defects' philosophy.

- Organisations set their own internal quality standards. They might also seek to apply external quality standards, such as industry quality standards and the ISO 9000 quality standards.

- The eight principles of quality management as set out in ISO 9004 are customer focus, active leadership by management, the involvement of people, a process-based approach, a system approach to management, continuous improvement, a factual approach to decision-making and mutually beneficial relationships with suppliers.

- Quality should be measured and actual quality compared with target quality standards.

- One approach to quality control is to set statistical targets for performance and apply statistical quality control methods.

- Benchmarks might be used to compare quality standards and to set targets for quality. Benchmarks used for comparison might be internal benchmarks, competitive benchmarks or process or activity benchmarks.

- Business Process Re-engineering (BPR) is an approach to improving quality based on a study of the entire process and a radical re-design of the process based around the outputs from the system, rather than based on functional inputs. It calls for a complete re-think of the process in a cross-functional way.

- Continuous improvement (kaizen) is an alternative approach to quality improvement, based on the continual search for improvements in the process, no matter how small. Kaizen is based on the philosophy of involving everyone in the search for quality improvements, possibly using quality circles.

- Lean manufacturing is an approach to manufacturing based on JIT and TQM.

Having completed your study of this chapter, you should have achieved the following learning outcomes:

- analyse problems associated with quality in organisations

- evaluate contemporary thinking in quality management

- explain the linkages between functional areas as an important aspect of quality management

- apply tools and concepts of quality management appropriately in an organisation

- construct a plan for the implementation of a quality programme

- explain the concept of quality and how the quality of products and services can be assessed, measured and improved.

Self-test questions

1   Define quality. (1.1)

2   What problems might arise with the actual quality of products or services? (2.1, 2.2)

3   What are the four categories of quality-related costs? (2.3)

4   According to Juran, what are the three key elements of quality management? (3.4)

5   What is a quality circle? (3.8)

6   Define TQM. (3.9)

7   What are the main elements of TQM? (3.9)

8   What are the quality standards in the ISO 9000 range? (4.4)

9   What are the eight principles of quality management set out in ISO 9000? (4.4)

10   What types of benchmarking might be used? (5.3)

11   What are the potential benefits of benchmarking? (5.3)

12   What are the main principles of Business Process Re-engineering? (5.4)

13   What are the five elements of the 5S approach to achieving high quality? (6.5)

14   What is the aim of the Six Sigma approach? (6.8)

Practice questions

Question 1

A company providing an internet-based service for the home-delivery of supermarket items has recently compared its order processing and delivery system with a company that sells clothing to consumers using catalogues and web-based selling. This type of benchmarking is:

A   internal

B   competitive

C   process

D   BPR.

Question 2

What has been described as 'the fundamental re-thinking and rational re-design of the business processes to achieve dramatic improvements in … measures of performance such as cost, quality, speed and service'?

A   BPR

B   Kaizen

C   Lean manufacturing

D   TQM

Question 3

Which 'S' in the 5S approach advocates arranging things properly and putting them where they will be found easily when needed?

A   Sort

B   Straighten

C   Shine

D   Sustain

Question 4

What is the likely error rate if it lies beyond the sixth sigma of probability?

A   1 defect in 100,000

B   3.2 defects in 600,000

C   3.4 defects in 1,000,000

D   4 defects in 6,000,000

Question 5

Which writer on TQM advocated a zero defects philosophy?

A   Deming

B   Peters

C   Crosby

D   Juran

Question 6

Pump manufacturer

The Dose Company was established over a century ago and manufactures water pumps of various kinds. Until recently it has been successful, but imports of higher quality pumps at lower prices are now rapidly eroding Dose's market share. The managing director feels helpless in the face of this onslaught from international competitors and is frantically searching for a solution to the problem. In his desperation, he consults a range of management journals and comes across what seems to be a wonder cure by the name of Business Process Re-engineering (BPR).

According to the article, the use of BPR has already transformed the performance of a significant number of companies in the USA which were mentioned in the article, and is now being widely adopted by European companies. Unfortunately, the remainder of the article, which purports to explain BPR is full of management jargon and he is left with only a vague idea of how it works.

Required:

(a)   Explain the nature of BPR and describe how it might be applied to a manufacturing company like Dose. **(10 marks)**

(b)   Describe the major pitfalls for managers attempting to re-engineer their organisations. **(10 marks)**

(Total: 20 marks)

Question 7

Quality circles

The production director in a large manufacturing company wants to introduce quality circles into the company's factories, because he has heard of their success in several Japanese companies. He asks for your advice about introducing a system of quality circles, and he tells you: 'My objectives in wanting to introduce these circles are to arrive at decisions for change in product designs and production methods and to get a maximum degree of acceptance. Quality circles can improve quality, productivity, interdepartmental communication, teamwork, team spirit. They can reduce costs and absenteeism and create more job satisfaction. I want them.'

He asks you for your views about whether you can foresee any problems with introducing quality circles, and how you would set about implementing a programme for setting them up and using them. How would you respond? **(10 marks)**

Question 8

Sun and Sand Travel

Michael Medici has just been appointed as the Managing Director of Sun and Sand Travel Ltd. This is a small package holiday company (travel, accommodation and on-site services all being pre-booked and included in the package price) focusing on the mass and cheaper end of the market. Company sales have grown at an annual rate of 10% over the past five years but profits have not risen at the same rate. The company has used price as its main competitive tool and the company has been more concerned with 'bottom-line' financial results than with customer service.

Medici has spent the first two months of his work at Sun and Sand Travel Ltd, acting as a 'trouble shooter'. Customer complaints have risen to a record high – almost 20% of recent customers have registered complaints including poor accommodation, flight delays and time of travel changes. The company is also facing hostile media criticism – both the press and television media are publicising the difficulties of the company. The outlook is not good – advance bookings are 30% lower than a year ago. Medici realises that the obsession with profit at the expense of other criteria has been both foolish and short termist. He recognises that if you do not get the service right then the profits will inevitably suffer.

Medici has set up a working party to advise him on what to do to improve the situation. One of the recommendations of the working party is to use performance indicators other than profit to assess how well the company is performing.

Required:

(a)   Assess which performance indicators are particularly relevant for Sun and Sand Travel Ltd. **(10 marks)**

(b)   Identify and discuss the critical success factors required of a company operating in this market segment. **(10 marks)**

(Total: 20 marks)

For the answers to these questions, see the 'Answers' section at the end of the book.

Feedback to activities

Activity 1

Operational measures

- Pass rates (percentage of students attending the course who pass the examination).

- A measurement of the number of questions or proportion of the total marks in each examination paper that were directly covered by tuition during the course.

Financial measures

- The cost of carrying out regular appraisals of tutor performance.

- The cost of updating and improving course materials.

Customer measures

- Measuring customer satisfaction by asking students to complete a course assessment (feedback) form at the end of the course. Assessments can be graded or scored.

- Percentage of students returning for a course for the next stage of their examinations.

Activity 2

The potential benefits to be obtained from a benchmarking exercise are:

- learning and applying best practices

- learning from the success of others

- minimising complacency and self-satisfaction with your own performance

- encouraging continuous improvement.

Activity 3

Measures for assessment include the following:

- customer service (e.g. complaint response time)

- customer satisfaction (e.g. no. of customer complaints; complaints per customer; complaints per £ of sales)

- competitiveness (e.g. market share; customer base; % sales growth)

- product quality (e.g. no. of customer complaints; no. of product rejects; % rejects; customer returns % of total sales)

- delivery/lead time (e.g. no. of deliveries on time; % of deliveries on time) – applied to purchases as well as to sales

- resource utilisation (e.g. m/c hours worked % of capacity; m/c downtime % of m/c hours worked)

- employee satisfaction (e.g. labour turnover)

- innovation (e.g. length of product development cycle; % of total sales from new products).

Activity 4

All the listed characteristics of lean manufacturing are consistent with a JIT approach.

Chapter 11

THE STRATEGIC MARKETING PLAN

Syllabus content

- Introduction to the marketing concept as a business philosophy.

- An overview of the marketing environment, including societal economic, technological, physical and legal factors affecting marketing.

- Market research, including data-gathering techniques and methods of analysis.

- Segmentation and targeting of markets, and positioning of products within markets.

- The role of marketing in the strategic plan of the organisation.

- Market forecasting methods for estimating current and future demand for products and services.

Contents

1   The marketing concept

2   Segmentation, targeting and positioning

3   Environmental analysis – SLEPT or PEST analysis

4   Marketing research

5   Market forecasting methods

6   Social responsibility in a marketing context

1 The marketing concept

1.1 What is marketing?

The Chartered Institute of Marketing define marketing as 'The management process responsible for identifying, anticipating and satisfying customer requirements profitability'

Philip Kotler defines marketing as 'satisfying needs and wants through an exchange process'.

The key aspect of both of these definitions is a focus on customer needs. Customers' needs are anticipated and identified by **marketing research** and **segmentation** and then a **marketing mix** is employed to satisfy customers.

1.2 The marketing concept and its alternatives

An organisation that adopts the marketing concept is accepting the needs of potential customers as the basis for its operations. This type of organisation will develop a structure designed to identify and interpret customer needs, to create goods and services appropriate to those needs, and to persuade potential customers to purchase those goods and services. This involves integrated marketing, i.e. using all the marketing variables in a balanced and co-ordinated manner. In addition all departments of the organisation will need to appreciate that they have an impact on the customer, and are therefore part of a marketing system.

A marketing oriented business is one that has adopted the marketing concept although a number of alternative 'orientations' – sales, production and product – may be adopted:

Sales orientation – some companies concentrate on generating additional sales of the product or services which they already have available. Organisations that adopt this approach will be expected to make full use of selling, pricing, promotion and distribution skills. However, unlike a marketing orientation, there is no systematic attempt to identify customer needs, or to create products or services that will satisfy them.

Production orientation – the business is mainly preoccupied with making as many units as possible. Improved profitability will be achieved through economies of scale and production rationalisation. Customer needs are subordinated to the desire to increase output. This approach works when a market is growing more rapidly than output, but it offers no security against a reduction in growth rate and takes no account of changes in customer preference.

Product orientation – the business concentrates on its product, potentially without sufficient reference to the customer requirements.

1.3 What is a market?

The word 'market' can be misleading to a student learning marketing for the first time. We are not talking about a market-stall or a shop. One of many definitions simply states that a market is a number of potential customers. This group may be defined in several ways, for example:

(a)   geographically e.g. the Middle East market

(b)   by industry type e.g. the electronic engineering market

(c)   demographically e.g. the teenage market.

Often, however, markets may be defined in terms of the products or services for sale:

- the used-car market
- the property market
- the machine tool market.

Marketing managers often find the term 'market' too imprecise for their purposes. When they plan to sell to an identified customer type, the term target market is used so as to eliminate people or organisations for whom the product is not primarily intended.

Frequently, marketing effort is more effective if different groups of customers within the target market are treated differently. This process is called market segmentation, and it will later be described more fully.

Activity 1

As the new Marketing Manager for LM Ltd, a newly formed PC Manufacturer, you plan to give a talk to the rest of the management team about meeting customer needs, and discuss with them what marketing is about.

If you were delivering the speech what would you cover? List some points.

Feedback to this activity is at the end of the chapter.

1.4 Strategic marketing

Strategic planning is covered in detail in Paper P6. However, you are expected to understand marketing from a strategic perspective so it is useful here to look at strategic planning in more detail. The key steps are as follows:

1 **Strategic analysis**

- Detailed analysis of the organisation itself to identify strengths and weaknesses, core competences and resources.

- Detailed analysis of the external environment to identify opportunities and threats.

- Detailed analysis of stakeholder expectations and power.

2 **Strategic choice**

- Which markets to compete in?

- How to compete (nature of competitive advantage)?

- Which expansion vehicle to use (organic growth, acquisition, joint venture, etc)?

3 **Strategy implementation**

- Detailed functional strategies.

- Target setting.

- Monitoring and control.

The marketing process impacts all of these steps. For example:

1   **Strategic analysis**

- Analysis of brand strength, product quality, reputation, etc.

- Analysis of competition.

- Market research to determine market attractiveness (see Sections 3 and 4 below)

- Detailed analysis of customer expectations and power.

2   **Strategic choice**

- Market segmentation, targeting and positioning (see Section 2 below).

- The marketing mix strategies (see Chapter 12).

3   **Strategy implementation**

- Budgets set for advertising, etc.

- Target setting – sales revenue, market share, brand awareness, etc.

- Monitoring and control.

2   Segmentation, targeting and positioning

2.1   Introduction

Segmentation, targeting and positioning are marketing tools used by a company to gain competitive advantage in the market. They help the company to differentiate its product offering from that of its competitors and ensure that it reaches the exact market profile for which it is intended.

Market segmentation is the process of dividing the market into similar groups according to the characteristics intended for the product at hand.

Targeting is the process of selecting the most lucrative market segments for marketing the product.

Positioning involves the formulation of a definitive marketing strategy around which the product at hand would be finally marketed amongst the target audience.

2.2   Levels of market segmentation

DEFINITION

The **market** is the set of all actual and potential buyers of a product.

Market segmentation is the subdividing of a market into distinct subsets of customers.

The **market** is the set of all actual and potential buyers of a product.

A **market segment** is a group of consumers with distinct, shared needs.

Market segmentation is the subdividing of a market into distinct subsets of customers, where any subset may conceivably be selected as a market target to be reached with a distinct marketing mix.

It allows companies to treat similar customers in similar ways, whilst distinguishing between dissimilar customer groups. Each customer group has slightly different needs, which can be satisfied by offering each group, or segment, a slightly different marketing strategy. This is discussed in more detail under 'targeting' below.

2.3   Methods of market segmentation

Many different bases are used to segment a market. The traditional
method was segmentation on demographic grounds. This is still the
starting point for many segmentation exercises, though further
investigation often finds that demographic influences are not the prime
determining factors of purchase.

Demographic segmentation – market research studies are frequently
broken down by age, income, social class, sex, geographical area,
occupation, family unit, etc. This can be highly relevant with some
products. For example, certain brands of breakfast cereals have regular
sales only in families where there are children aged under eight, whereas
other brands (e.g. Bran Flakes and Shredded Wheat) sell almost entirely
to adults. In other areas, demographic influences appear to have no
effect, for instance, own-label products are believed to sell equally to high
and low incomes, to families and single people, and across age groups.

The most widely used form of demographic segmentation in the UK is the
socio-economic classification shown in the table below:

Class	Social status	Job descriptions
A	Upper middle class	Higher managerial, administrative and professional
B	Middle class	Middle management, administrative and professional
C_1	Lower middle class	Supervisory, clerical, junior management, administrative staff
C_2	Working class	Semi and unskilled manual jobs
D	Subsistence	Pensioners, widows, lowest grade workers

While such a class-based system may seem out of date, the model is still widely
used, particularly in advertising. Socio-economic class is closely correlated with
press readership and viewing habits, and media planners use this fact to
advertise in the most effective way to communicate with their target audience.

Geographic segmentation – markets are frequently split into regions for sales
and distribution purposes. Many consumer goods manufacturers break down
sales by television advertising regions.

Value segmentation – is present in most markets. Value can be defined as the
customer's view of the balance between satisfaction from the product and its
price. Thus, many products have a premium-priced, high quality segment, a
mid-priced segment and a low-price segment, e.g. shoes. In such a market,
fashion and quality differences can outweigh price variations. In other markets,
e.g. petrol and cigarettes, small differences in price can outweigh the small
differences in satisfaction perceived by the purchaser.

Psychological – consumers can be divided into groups sharing common
psychological characteristics. One group may be described as security-oriented,
another as ego-centred, and so on. These categories are useful in the creation of
advertising messages.

Life style segmentation – a recent trend is to combine psychological and socio-demographic characteristics to give a more complete profile of customer groups. This kind of segmentation uses individuals to represent groups, which form a significant proportion of the consumer market. It defines these individuals in terms of sex, age, income, job, product preferences, social attitudes and political views.

Purchasing characteristics – customers may be segmented by the volume they buy (heavy user, medium user, light user, non user), by the outlet type they use, or by the pack size bought. These variables, and many others, are useful in planning production and distribution and in developing promotion policy. A food manufacturer will approach supermarket chains very differently to the small independent retailer probably offering better prices, delivery terms, use different sales techniques and deliver direct to the supermarket chain. They might also supply own label product to the large chain but they are unlikely to be able to offer the same terms to the corner shop.

Benefit – customers have different expectations of a product. Some people buy detergents for whiteness, and are catered for by a particular brand. Others want economy, for which another brand may fit the bill. Some customers may demand stain removal: one of the biological products is appropriate. An understanding of what benefits a customer is seeking enables the manufacturer to create a range of products, each aimed precisely at a particular benefit.

Family life cycle segmentation – a form of demographic segmentation dividing customers by their position in the family life cycle.

Life cycle stage	Characteristics	Examples of products purchased
Bachelor	Financially well off. Fashion opinion leaders. Recreation oriented.	Cars, holidays, basic furniture, kitchen equipment.
Newly married couple	Still financially well off. Very high purchase rate, especially of durables.	Cars, furniture, houses, holidays, refrigerators.
Full nest (i)	Liquid assets low. Home purchasing at peak. Little money saving.	Washers, TVs, baby foods, toys, medicines.
Full nest (ii)	Better off. Some partners work. Some children work part time. Less influenced by advertising.	Larger size grocery packs, foods, cleaning materials, bicycles.
Full nest (iii)	Better off still. Purchasing durables.	New furniture, luxury appliances. Recreational goods.
Empty nest (i)	Satisfied with financial position. Home-ownership at peak.	Travel, luxuries, home improvements.
Empty nest (ii)	Drastic cut in income. Stay at home.	Medicines, health aids.

The benefits of segmentation to the company adopting this policy are that it enables them to get close to their intended customer and really find out what that customer wants (and is willing to pay for). This should make the customer happier with the product offered and hence lead to repeat sales and endorsements.

Activity 2

Give reasons why demographic segmentation, by itself, is not a successful basis for car manufacturers targeting their customers.

Feedback to this activity is at the end of the chapter.

2.4 Industrial segmentation

Industrial segmentation is different from that used in consumer marketing. The following factors influence the way industrial customers can be segmented:

Geographic is used as the basis for sales-force organisations.

Purchasing characteristics – is the classification of customer companies by their average order size, the frequency with which they order, etc.

Benefit – industrial purchasers have different benefit expectations to consumers. They may be orientated towards reliability, durability, versatility, safety, serviceability or ease of operation. They are always concerned with value for money.

Company type – industrial customers can be segmented according to the type of business they are, i.e. what they offer for sale. The range of products and services used in an industry will not vary too much from one company to another.

Company size – it is frequently useful to analyse marketing opportunities in terms of company size. A company supplying canteen foods would investigate size in terms of numbers of employees. Processed parts suppliers are interested in production rate, and lubricants suppliers would segment by numbers of machine tools.

2.5 Targeting

Having segmented the market, the organisation can now decide how to respond to the differences in customer needs identified. Two questions need answering:

1 Which segments are worth investing in?

When evaluating potential target markets, the following issues should be considered:

- size

- growth potential

- profit potential

- degree of competition

- accessibility (whether suitable distribution channels exist)

- barriers to entry

- critical success factors and whether the organisation has the resources to achieve them.

2 *Whether / how to vary the marketing strategy between segments*

For example, the market for package holidays can be split up into a variety of different sub-markets – the family market, the elderly market, the young singles market, the activity holiday market, the budget holiday market, etc. It would be virtually impossible to provide one single holiday package that would satisfy all people in the above markets. Because the people in the different sectors will have different needs and wants, a holiday company has a choice in terms of its marketing approach. It can go for:

Niche or target marketing (sometimes referred to as concentrated marketing) specialises in one or two of the identified markets only, where a company knows it can compete successfully. It acquires a great deal of expertise in its market segment, which must be large enough to sustain profitability. For example, Saga holidays offers a variety of holidays for the older market niche only. Ramblers concentrate on walking holidays. Ferrari is something special for a very small group.

Differentiated or segmented *marketing* offers a variety of products to suit all of the needs. Companies like Thompson Holidays offer a variety of holiday types to appeal to most markets. These holidays may be at different prices, in different resorts, at different times of the year and advertised in different brochures. However, not all businesses have to use market segmentation.

Mass or undifferentiated marketing is the opposite of differentiated marketing, in that it treats all customers and potential customers as identical; the whole market is the target for the firm, served with a single variety of products marketed in a single way. When Henry Ford began manufacturing cars he offered any colour 'as long as it is black'. Most firms in the holiday industry follow either a niche or a differentiated approach.

2.6 Product positioning

After the target market has been chosen, marketers want to position their products or fix them in the minds of the target customers.

Perceptual mapping is used to chart consumers' perceptions of brands currently on offer and to identify opportunities for launching new brands or to reposition an existing brand. Marketers decide upon a competitive position that enables them to distinguish their own products from the offerings of their competition (hence the term 'positioning strategy').

The marketer would draw out the map and decide upon a label for each axis. They could be price (variable one) and quality (variable two), or comfort (variable one) and price (variable two). The individual products are then mapped out next to each other. Any gaps (strategic spaces) could be regarded as possible areas for new products. The analysis below illustrates a local grocery market.

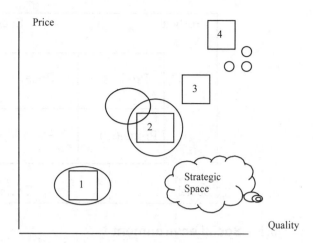

The two critical success factors here are price and quality. Of course, others, such as location, opening hours, marketing expenditure, and so on might be important too under some circumstances.

Group 1 are the price discounters. The business cuts cost wherever it can. Product ranges are restricted and there are few attempts to make the store decorative or service friendly.

Group 2 are the main market retailers. They compete on price, but offer more and better ranges, better customer service, and so on.

Group 3 offer a higher quality range, and do not attempt to compete on price at all.

Group 4 are delicatessens. They offer a great deal of service and specialist items. Prices are very high.

It is a great strategic mistake to try to position oneself where there are no customer groups. For example, several companies have tried to cross between groups 1 and 2, usually without success.

Activity 3

Wakefields had struggled to maintain its position in strategic group 1 because it could not keep its costs down. A new MD decided to go upmarket by renaming the chain, updating the shop dress and a national advertising campaign showing higher quality products than the store had previously stocked. It was a spectacular failure, as most attempts to move up market tend to be. What might have gone wrong?

Feedback to this activity is at the end of the chapter.

3   Environmental analysis – SLEPT or PEST analysis

Organisational performance will be dependent on the successful management of the opportunities, challenges and risks presented by changes in the external environment. One popular technique for analysing the general environment is a SLEPT analysis.

This analysis divides the business environment into five related but separate systems – Social, Legal, Economic, Political and Technical. Other versions of essentially the same model refer to PESTLE (the second E can mean ethics, or the Ecological factors) and PEST or STEP (where legal is subsumed into political). Looking at the SLEPT model we can apply each of these factors in turn to the marketing function.

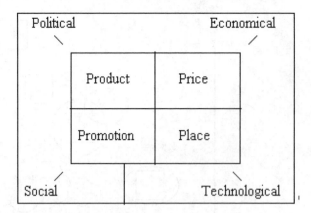

3.1 Social environment

Within society forces such as family, friends and media affect our attitude, interest and opinions. These forces shape who we are as people and the way we behave and what we ultimately purchase. For example, within the UK people's attitudes are changing towards their diet and health. As a result the UK is seeing an increase in the number of people joining fitness clubs and a massive growth for the demand of organic food. On the other end of the spectrum the UK is worried about the lack of exercise its youngster are obtaining. These 'fast food games console' children are more likely to experience health problems in their future because of the lifestyle they are living now.

Population changes also have a direct impact on all organisations. Changes in the structure of a population will affect the supply and demand of goods and services within an economy.

In Japan the fall in the birth rate has had a major impact on the sales of toys, as demand falls competition for the remaining market becomes very intense. If this trend continues it will have an impact on other sectors within the future affecting teen products, 20s products and so on.

As society changes, as behaviours change organisations must be able to offer products and services that aim to complement and benefit peoples lifestyle and behaviour.

According to Johnson and Scholes the social influences should be monitored include the following:

- **Population demographics** – a term used to describe the composition of the population in any given area, whether a region, a country or an area within a country

- **Income distribution** – will provide the marketer with some indication of the size of the target markets. Most developed countries, like the UK, have a relatively even distribution spread. However, this is not the case in other nations.

- **Social mobility** – the marketer should be aware of social classes and the population distribution among them. The marketer can use this knowledge to promote products to distinct social classes within the market.

- **Lifestyle changes** – refer to our attitudes and opinions towards things like social values, credit, health and women. Our attitudes have changed in recent years and this information is vital to the marketer.

KEY POINT

According to Johnson and Scholes the social influences should be monitored include the following:

- population demographics
- income distribution
- social mobility
- lifestyle changes
- consumerism
- levels of education.

- **Consumerism** – one of the social trends in recent years has been the rise of consumerism. This trend has increased to such an extent that governments have been pressured to design laws that protect the rights of the consumer.

- **Levels of education** – the level of education has increased dramatically over the last few years. There is now a larger proportion of the population in higher education than ever before.

3.2 Legal environment

Regulations governing business are widespread; they include those on health and safety, information disclosure, the dismissal of employees, vehicle emissions, use of pesticide and many more.

Changes in the law can affect organisations in many ways. A tightening of health and safety legislation may increase costs. Premises failing to meet the higher standards could be closed down. Particularly damaging might be the imposition of a complete ban on the organisation's product, clearly made worse should they have failed to develop a product portfolio sufficiently broad to absorb such a loss.

3.3 Economic environment

All businesses are affected by economical factors nationally and globally. Interest rate policy and fiscal policy will have to be set accordingly. Within the UK the climate of the economy dictates how consumers may behave within society. Whether an economy is in a boom, recession or recovery will also affect consumer confidence and behaviour.

The business cycle

An economy that is booming is characterised by certain variables. Unemployment is low, job confidence is high, and because of this confidence spending by consumers is also high. This has an impact on most businesses. Organisations have to be able to keep up with the increased demand if they are to increase turnover. An economy that is in a recession is characterised by high unemployment, and low confidence. Because of high unemployment spending is low, confidence about job security is also low. Businesses face a tough time, consumers will not spend because of low disposable income. Many businesses start cutting back on costs i.e. labour, introduce shorter weeks and cut back on advertising to save money.

Economies globally also have an impact on UK businesses, cheaper labour abroad affects the competitiveness of UK products nationally and globally. An increase in interest rates in the USA will affect the share price of UK stocks or adverse weather conditions in India may affect the price of tea.

A truly global player has to be aware of economic conditions across all borders and ensure they employ strategies and tactics that their protects their business.

3.4 Political environment

Political factors can have a direct impact on the way business operates. Decisions made by government affect our every day lives and can come in the form of policy or legislation. The government's introduction of a statutory minimum wage affects all businesses, as do consumer and health and safety laws and so on. The current increase in global petrol prices is having a profound impact on major economies, it is estimated that £200bn has been added to the global fuel bill since the price increases started.

The political decision as to whether the UK signs up to the Single European Currency is again having an impact on UK businesses. Firms like Nissan who have invested in the UK have signalled that they will withdraw their business from the UK if the government fails to sign up.

3.5 Technological environment

This is an area in which change takes place very rapidly and the organisations need to be constantly aware of what is going on. Technological change can influence the following:

- changes in production techniques
- the type of products that are made and sold
- how services are provided
- how we identify markets.

Much has been made of the application of new technologies to communications and business, particularly the Internet and, although IT is perhaps the main technological driver for change in business practice, other major changes appear to be widespread.

Within any industry, failure to exploit information technology and new production technology can lead to an organisation falling behind its rivals and losing its competitive edge.

Traditional methods of delivering services have been turned upside down by rapid developments in information technology. This erosion of entry barriers to industries such as banking and insurance through easier access to distribution channels (the Internet rather than a High Street presence) and much lower start-up costs has created threats to the established players which, if they do not respond to them, could lead to decline in their sales.

New technology can lead to the emergence of substitutes. The cinema industry went into decline in the early 1980s as a result of the emergence of the video. Examples of recently developed new products can be found in biotechnology, and pharmaceuticals and data storage devices. The rate of change in these industries, and the high costs of research and development have profound effects on the structure of the industry and the way that the industry competes.

Activity 4

Environmental analysis might relate to PEST factors. What does this mean?

Feedback to this activity is at the end of the chapter.

4 Marketing research

4.1 Overview

Marketing research is the systematic and objective search for, and analysis of, information relevant to the identification and solution of any problem in the field of marketing. It is not just obtaining information, but involves:

- framing questions whose answers will provide data to help solve problems

- asking questions to those best qualified to answer them

- recording answers correctly

- interpreting answers, and

- translating interpretations and making recommendations for marketing action.

Marketing research consists of:

- *market research* (analysis of the market size, trends, market shares, etc)

- *distribution research* (analysis of present channels of distribution, warehouse and other storage locations, discount policy, transport needs, etc)

- *economic research* (analysis of trends including social and forecasting)

- *evaluation of product(s)* (customer requirements analysis, product life cycles, quality measurements, reliability), and

- *communication analysis* (of the media usage, suggested media combinations e.g. T.V. and newspaper advertising, etc).

'Market research is the means used by those who provide goods and services to keep themselves in touch with the needs and wants of those who buy and use those goods and services.'

The main object of attention, as far as marketing is concerned, is the customer (or market place). This is the area that gives rise to most of the problems which marketing research is applied to. A typical problem could be that of a falling market share for one or more of the organisation's products or services. To be able to clarify the problem and put it in perspective, a number of questions could be posed, for example:

Regarding the marketplace:

- Is the market stable, expanding or declining?

- Is the threat from domestic competitors, or from overseas?

- What is the situation for competitors?

- What advantages, if any, do the competitive products have?

Regarding customers:

- What is the organisation's reputation with its existing customers?

- How often do customers purchase?

- How likely are they to purchase from you?

- What is the expected market price?

- How do they select a vendor?

- Are there enough customers to build a viable business?

- What are the main factors considered by customers in a purchase decision?

The detailed tools required to analyse market competition are covered in Paper P6. Here we focus on researching customer needs. Some of these questions can be answered by analysing secondary data (desk research) and others by analysing primary data (field research).

4.2 Desk research

Desk research – sometimes called secondary research – is concerned with the collection of information from secondary sources. It does not derive information first-hand but obtains existing data by studying published and other available sources of information. Thorough desk research at the beginning of a survey can often eliminate the need for extensive field work, or limit it to checking the main features of the study.

Somebody else may have collected this information, perhaps for a different purpose. Although the research data is unlikely to be exactly what the current researcher wants and may not be totally up to date, it has the advantage that it is available and at relatively low cost.

Thorough desk research at the beginning of a survey can often eliminate the need for extensive fieldwork, or limit it to checking the main features of the study. Thus collection of primary information by fieldwork should not be carried out until existing information has been carefully investigated and appraised.

There are three main types of information that can be collected by desk research:

- **Economic intelligence** can be defined as information relating to the economic environment within which a company operates. Economic intelligence is concerned with such factors as gross national product (GNP), investment, expenditure, population, employment, productivity and trade. It provides an organisation with a picture of past and future trends in the environment and with an indication of the company's position in the economy as a whole. A great deal of information is freely available in this area from sources such as government ministries, the nationalised industries, universities and organisations such as the OECD.

- **Market intelligence** is information about a company's present or possible future markets. Such information will be both commercial and technical, for example, the level of sales of competitors' products recorded by the Business Monitor or Census of Production; the product range offered by existing or potential competitors; the number of outlets forming the distribution network for a company's products; the structure of that network by size, location and relation to the end user; and the best overseas markets for a company.

- **Internal company data** is perhaps the most neglected source of marketing information. Companies tend to record their sales information for accountancy purposes or for the management of the sales force. Rarely is the information collected in a form in which it can readily be used by marketing management.

Desk research has the advantages of being cheaper and quicker than field research. The disadvantages of this method of research lie in the fact that you do not know if the findings are accurate, or how relevant they will be to your product or service.

4.3 Field research

Field (or primary) research is research by direct contact with an identified (or targeted) group of potential customers.

Field research falls into two chief types: motivational research and measurement research.

Motivational research – the objective is to unearth factors that influence why consumers do or do not buy particular products. Some of the more common techniques in motivational research are:

- *Depth interviewing* – undertaken at length by a trained person who is able to appreciate conscious and unconscious associations and motivations and their significance.

- *Group interviewing* – where between six and ten people are asked to consider the relevant subject (object) under trained supervision.

- *Word association testing* – on being given a word by the interviewer, the first word that comes into the mind of the person being tested is noted.

- *Triad testing* – where people are asked which out of a given three items is least like the remaining two, and why. If the three are brands of a given type of product (or three similar types), replies may show a great deal about attitudes.

Measurement research – the objective here is to build on the motivation research by trying to quantify the issues involved. Sample surveys are used to find out how many people buy the product(s), what quantity each type of buyer purchases, and where and when the product is bought.

It is also possible (less accurately) to assess roughly the importance of some reasons in buying or not buying a product. The main types of measurement are:

- *Random sampling* – where each person in the target population has an equal chance of being selected. Such samples are more likely to be representative, making predictions more reliable. However, the technique may be unfeasible in practice.

- *Quota sampling* – where samples are designed to be representative with respect to pre-selected criteria.

  For example, if the target population is 55% women and 455 men, then a sample of 200 people could be structured so 110 women and 90 men are asked, rather than simply asking 200 people and leaving it up to chance whether or not the gender mix is typical.

  The main disadvantage of quota sampling is that samples may still be biased for non-selected criteria.

- *Panelling* – where the sample is kept for subsequent investigations, so trends are easier to spot.

- *Surveying by post* – the mail shot method. Unfortunately the sample becomes self-selecting and so may be biased.

- *Observation* – e.g. through the use of cameras within supermarkets to examine how long customers spend on reading the nutritional information on food packaging.

Activity 5

A company is thinking of adding a new baby milk substitute to its existing range of baby foods.

Suggest secondary sources of information for its market research (also referred to as desk research).

Feedback to this activity is at the end of the chapter.

5 Market forecasting methods

5.1 Overview

When discussing market-forecasting methods, it is important to distinguish between sales forecasts and estimates of sales potential.

- *Sales potential*: the maximum sales level that can be reached *under ideal conditions.*

- *Sales forecast*: a prediction of the actual sales volume that is expected in a future time period *for a given level of marketing support*

Top-down approaches

A typical 'top-down' approach to forecasting would have the following steps:

1   Analyse industry trends and economic forecasts, incorporating the 'PEST' analysis factors described above.

2   Use this to determine the overall market potential i.e. the total potential demand for the product.

3   Use this to determine the local area market potential.

4   Determine the organisation's sales potential by considering its past performance, resources and future predicted market share.

5   Determine the sales forecast by incorporating a specified level of marketing effort.

The sales forecast

A sales forecast is an estimate of probable sales for one company's brand of the product during a stated time period in a specific market segment and assuming the use of a predetermined marketing plan. Other features include:

- It is based on a specific marketing plan.

- It can be expressed in £ or product units.

- It is best prepared after market potential and sales potential have been estimated.

- It typically covers a one-year period.

- Marketing goals and broad strategies must be established before a sales forecast is made.

Once the sales forecast is made, it becomes a key controlling factor in all operational planning throughout the company.

Bottom up approaches

An alternative to the above 'top-down' approach is a 'bottom-up' approach:

- Generate estimates of future demand from customers or the company's salespeople.

- Combine the estimates to get a total forecast.

- Adjust the forecast based on managerial insights into the industry, competition, and general economic trends.

5.2 Techniques

The choice of forecasting method depends on costs, type of product, characteristics of market, time span of the forecast, purpose of the forecast, stability of historical data, availability of required information and forecasters expertise and experience.

Quantitative forecasting methods include:

- **Fitting a trend line** – assumes sales influences fall into four categories

  1   Trends (long-term changes)

  2   Cyclical changes

  3   Seasonal changes

  4   Irregular changes

  Uses least squares to determine slope and intercept of a straight line

- **Moving average**: computes the average volume achieved in several periods and then uses it as a prediction for sales in the next period. With a strong trend in the series, the moving average lags behind. With more periods, the moving average forecast changes slowly.

- **'Simple' regression**: try to estimate the relationship between a single dependent variable (Y or sales) and a single independent variable (X) via a straight-line equation. $Y = a + b(X) + e$.

- **Multiple regression**: estimate the relationship between a single dependent variable (Y or sales) and *several* independent variables.

The most important criterion in the choice of a forecasting method is *accuracy*, as measured by error and tracking turning points.

Non-quantitative techniques for forecasting sales include:

Sales force composite – a bottom-up method consisting of collecting estimates of sales for the future period from all salespeople.

- Salespeople each estimate their territory

- May consult supervisor

- Individual forecasts are combined and adjusted for each office

- Used by 60–70% of all companies.

The main advantages and disadvantages of this technique are shown in the following table:

Advantages	Disadvantages
• Salespeople know the actual sales potential in their territories. • Salespeople are closest to the source. • Salespeople accept the forecast because they did it. • Put responsibility for forecasting in the hands of those that can make it happen. • Statistical and technical errors are minimised. • Detailed final forecast is done by product, customer, market. • Can be done with little or no data or history.	• Sales personnel can overestimate or underestimate the number of sales for various reasons. • Detailed plans sometimes needed to prevent bias. • If estimates are biased, correcting the data can be expensive.

Jury of Executive Opinion

Application – a small group should be used. They should be very well informed and they need access to data

Characteristics:

- opinions of a group of executives are pooled

- data may be compiled by each executive or by marketing research

- individual forecasts may be combined by a specialist, or

- individual forecasts may be combined by negotiation as a group.

This method is valued as most important to marketing managers.

Advantages	Disadvantages
• Easy, quick, not much mathematics • Opinions from all over the firm are integrated • Usually inexpensive	• Opinion based not data (fact) based • Takes executives away from their jobs • People with no marketing knowledge, like accountants, are making market forecasts • Hard to break down to territories • Hard to break down for tasks

Delphi Technique – a variation of the Jury of Executive Opinion

Characteristics:

- Jury members never meet face to face.

- Comprehensive and representative jury of experts.

- Jury members make anonymous forecast.

- Leader averages and sends it back to jury members.

- Jury members then resubmit.

- Keep repeating until a consensus is reached.

Market-test method

This method involves making a product available to buyers in one or more test areas and measuring consumer responses to distribution, promotion and price, for example, Cadbury's Wispa bar first appeared in the Tyne Tees television region.

5.3 The limitations of forecasting

- A good sales forecast costs money.

- Sales forecasters seldom have all the time they deem necessary.

- Sales forecasts are estimates.

- Changes in fundamental conditions can cause the forecast to vary from actual results.

There is no best technique for forecasting. Two forecasts done with different approaches are better than one.

6 Social responsibility in a marketing context

6.1 Social responsibility

Corporate social responsibility is generally considered to be the 'duty' of an organisation. An organisation should conduct its activities with due regard to the interests of society as a whole. A social responsibility audit can be defined as follows:

'An evaluation or assessment of the policies and practices of an organisation to establish how and to what extent it is behaving in a socially responsible manner, e.g. in terms of employment practices, relationships with its local community, environmental protection, etc.'

From this it can be seen that corporate social responsibility covers issues of interest to marketing as well as other functions. Consumers now expect more than just products and services, which satisfy their needs and wants. They look for the added bonus of the Societal Marketing Concept, where the well being of society is also catered for.

The situation has now arisen where it has become impossible in some industries to produce what customers want, without an accompanying high cost in environmental terms. Marketing issues concerning social responsibility, for example, cover areas such as the ozone layer, global warming and animal welfare.

6.2 Social criticisms of marketing

Social criticisms of marketing include:

- high prices

- poor service

- planned obsolescence

- shoddy or unsafe products

- high pressure selling

- deceptive practices.

The marketing function is accused by society of creating:

- false wants and too much materialism

- too few social goods

- too much political power

- cultural pollution.

Critics charge that a company's marketing practices can harm other companies and reduce competition through:

- acquisition of competitors

- marketing practices that create barriers to entry

- unfair competitive marketing practices.

6.3 Ethical responsibilities

Social responsibility refers to the responsibility a firm has for the impact of their product and activities on society. Ethical responsibilities refer to the moral basis for business activity and whether what the business does is 'right' and is underpinned by some moral purpose i.e. doing what is 'right'.

The problem arises when asking the question: 'Doing what is right for whom?' A private sector firm is primarily responsible to its shareholders – the owners of the business – who in turn will wish to see the firm grow, expanding sales and profits. In so doing there may be a conflict with the responsibility a firm has for the health and welfare of its customers. In the case of food products, companies have a responsibility to develop new products, market them and generate profits for their shareholders. But should they be doing so if this were at the expense of the health of those who consume their products?

Many businesses will claim to have a socially responsible code of practice that they adhere to as well as an ethical stance to their activities but such claims are sometimes refuted and criticised by opponents: for example, a company might claim to put no artificial colouring and preservative in their food products, while adding sugars instead.

If companies cannot be trusted to be responsible themselves, then it will be up to the government to do it for them, either by legislation or regulation. Part of the policy response by the government could be passing legislation that forces businesses to give clearer information on packaging to help consumers make more informed choices about what they buy. Such legislation would impose additional costs on businesses and ultimately would put up the price of the product to the consumer. Are we willing to pay such a price for the extra information? The issues therefore are complex and open, as with so many in business and economics, to subjective interpretation.

Summary

- The marketing concept holds that achieving organisation goals depends on determining the needs and wants of the target market and delivering the desired satisfactions more effectively and efficiently than competitors do.

- No organisation operates in a vacuum. Every decision an organisation takes affects several parties. Because of this an organisation must carefully consider the likely impact of its decisions.

- Analytical tools used in environmental analysis include SLEPT analysis. This analysis divides the business environment into five related by separate systems. Social, Legal, Economic, Political and Technical.

- Marketing research is the systematic and objective search for, and analysis of, information relevant to the identification and solution of any problem in the field of marketing.

- Corporate social responsibility is generally considered to be the 'duty' of an organisation.

Having completed your study of this chapter, you should have achieved the following learning outcomes:

- explain the marketing concept

- evaluate the marketing processes of an organisation.

Self-test questions

1   Explain the term 'marketing concept'. (1.2)

2   What is the difference between a 'selling concept' and a 'marketing concept'? (1.2)

3   Outline three strategic marketing decisions. (1.4)

4   Why is desk research sometimes called secondary research? (4.2)

5   Give two techniques in motivational research. (4.3)

6   Give three social criticisms of marketing. (6.2)

Practice questions

Question 1

Which of the following does not represent the marketing concept?

A   Has the market as a starting point

B   Focuses on customer needs

C   Uses methods of selling and promoting

D   Gains profits through customer satisfaction

Question 2

Which of the following statements is true?

A   Niche marketing offers a variety of products to suit all of the needs in a market

B   Niche marketing specialises in one or two of the identified markets only

C   Niche marketing deals with the older market only

D   Niche marketing is another term for mass marketing

For the answers to these questions, see the 'Answers' section at the end of the book.

Feedback to activities

Activity 1

1   Marketing is about providing benefits not products/services.

2   The benefit LM Ltd products offer to their target market.

3   The importance of continuous research to meet consumer needs.

4   The importance of understanding competitors and competitor products.

5   The importance of understanding the industry and industry trends.

6   The importance of managing differentiation and positioning.

7   The importance of after sales services in the computer industry.

Activity 2

With demographic segmentation customers are defined in terms of age, sex, income, socio-economic class, country of origin or family status. Reasons for it not being a successful basis include the following:

A car manufacturer may use the customer's age as a way of developing its target market and then discover that the target should be the psychologically young and not the chronologically young. The Ford Motor Company in America used the customer's age in targeting its Mustang car, designing it to appeal to young people who wanted an inexpensive sporty car. They found to their surprise that all age groups were purchasing the car.

Income is another segment that can be deceptive. You might imagine families on lower incomes would buy Ford Escorts and those on higher incomes would buy BMWs. However, Escorts are bought by middle-income people, often as the family's second car. The upgrading urge for people trying to relate to a higher social order often leads them to buy expensive cars.

Personal priorities also upset the demographic balance. Middle-income people often feel the need to spend more on clothes, furniture and housing which they could not afford if they purchased a more expensive car. Some parents, although 'well off', pay large fees for the private education of their children and must either make do with a small car, or perhaps no car at all.

Activity 3

Possible reasons for the failure of the attempt to reposition include:

- The target position (group 2?) was already saturated by the major market retailers. Competitive rivalry thus got more intense rather than less.

- The firm struggled to match the cost base of its larger competitors and so could not compete on price.

- Customers were not convinced by the renaming and still viewed the stores as the 'old' Wakefields.

- Product quality failed to match the advertising claims.

- The costs of improving quality were too high.

- Problems sourcing higher quality products – presumably this involved switching suppliers in some cases.

Activity 4

PEST factors are:

- Political – legislation may affect a company's prospects through the threats/opportunities of pollution control or a ban on certain products, for example.

- Economic – a recession might imply poor sales.

- Social attitudes.

- Technology – new products or means of distribution may be developed.

Activity 5

In this case possible sources of secondary information include:

(a) Past market research. It is quite probable that the company will have undertaken relevant research in connection with similar products.

(b) Existing sales. Indicate current consumer preferences which together with past sales may show trends.

The NHS may have significant information regarding baby foods together with its current advice to parents.

The Milk Marketing Board may have undertaken relevant research or have useful information regarding trends.

Supermarket/baby food retailers may have analyses regarding consumer choices and apparent preferences.

Other sources of information include trade organisations, universities and colleges, welfare organisations and specialist consumer groups.

Give reasons why demographic segmentation, by itself, is not a successful basis for car manufacturers targeting their customers.

Chapter 12

THE MARKETING MIX

Syllabus content

- Devising and implementing a pricing strategy.

- Marketing communications (i.e. mass, direct, interactive).

- Distribution channels and methods for marketing campaigns.

- Social responsibility in a marketing context.

Contents

1 The marketing mix

1.1 Marketing mix

DEFINITION

The marketing mix is the set of controllable tactical marketing tools that the firm can use to influence the buyers' responses (Kotler) – the four Ps.

According to Kotler et al. (1999) the marketing mix is a set of controllable tactical marketing tools ... that the firm blends to produce the response it wants in the target market'. Hence, in an effective marketing programme all of those elements are 'mixed' to successfully achieve the company's marketing objectives.

The marketing mix is concerned with how to influence consumer demand and is primarily the responsibility of the marketing department.

1.2 The four Ps

The variables are commonly grouped into four classes that Jerome McCarthy refers to as 'the four Ps' – product, price, promotion and place (or distribution):

- Price – an organisation may attack competitors by reducing price or increasing the size for the same money. The question of price policy in terms of competitors may be stated as Jet petrol's statement, 'We will always sell at 1– 2p below the market leaders'.

- Promotion – advertising, money-back coupons, special prizes are all means of boosting sales without cutting price. Whereas a price cut may lead to a retaliatory war from competitors, a money-off coupon is seen as a temporary initiative and competitors may ignore it.

- Place – refers to the outlets, geographic areas and distribution channels. Some manufacturers have specified that only their goods can be sold in an outlet, e.g. most car manufacturers stipulate this requirement. Others choose a competition strategy involving vertical integration by which they takeover distribution outlets and block a competitor's products. An example of this is the retail shoe industry.

- Product – refers to anything offered for attention, acquisition, use or consumption that might satisfy a want or need. Products can be **physical objects, services, persons, places, organisations** and **ideas.** An organisation may choose to lead the competition by being the best performer in those areas that it believes customers count as important and competitors can be outscored.

The marketing mix is essentially the working out of the tactical details of the positioning strategy. An organisation should ensure that all of the above elements are consistent with each other. This is the primary way to project a consistent and believable image. Thus a firm that seizes upon the 'high quality position' knows that it must produce high quality products, charge a relatively high price, distribute through high-class dealers and advertise in high quality magazines. A high-cost product with a wide range of features and advertised in up-market magazines would not sell if sold in newsagents.

Activity 1

Describe how McCarthy's marketing mix model could assist in the process of strategy formulation for an ice cream manufacturer.

Feedback to this activity is at the end of the chapter.

1.3 Variations in marketing mix settings

Different companies put different emphasis on each of the four components of the marketing mix.

For example, some companies place all the focus on making a good quality product; other companies place the emphasis on making it at a cheap price or emphasise the promotion and advertising to sell it. A manufacturer of desks might wish to sell to both the consumer market and the industrial market for office furniture. The marketing mix selected for the consumer market might be low prices with attractive dealer discounts, sales largely through discount warehouses, modern design but fairly low quality and sales promotion relying on advertising by the retail outlets, together with personal selling by the manufacturing firm to the reseller. For the industrial market, the firm might develop a durable, robust product that sells at a higher price; selling may be by means of direct mail-shots, backed by personal visits from salespeople.

An interesting comparison can be made between different firms in the same industry; for example, Avon and Elizabeth Arden both sell cosmetics but, whereas Avon relies on personal selling in the consumer's own home, Elizabeth Arden relies on an extensive dealer network and heavy advertising expenditure.

2 Product

2.1 Product definition

'Product' means everything that is used by the organisation to provide consumer satisfaction. A product can be a physical commodity, a service, a group of either of these, or a product-service combination.

The product has two roles in the marketing mix. First, it plays a key role in satisfying the customer's needs. Second, product differentiation is also an important part of the firm's competitive strategy.

The product can be viewed or defined in a number of different ways:

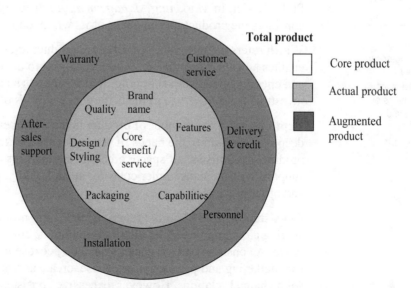

The core product – what is the buyer really buying? The core product refers to the use, benefit or problem solving service that the consumer is really buying when purchasing the product, i.e. the need that is being fulfilled.

The actual product is the tangible product or intangible service that serves as the medium for receiving core product benefits.

The augmented product consists of the measures taken to help the consumer put the actual product to sustained use, including installation, delivery and credit, warranties, and after-sales service.

An automobile offers personal transportation (core product), has many different features and attributes (actual product), and may include a manufacturer's warranty or dealer's discounted service contract (augmented product).

A product, therefore, is more than a simple set of tangible features. Consumers tend to see products as complex bundles of benefits that satisfy their needs. Most important is how the customer perceives the product. They are looking at factors such as aesthetics and styling, durability, brand image, packaging, service and warranty, any of which might be enough to set the product apart from its competitors.

2.2 Product portfolio issues

After determining the type of products it will offer, the organisation needs to outline the variety and assortment of those products.

A product line is a group of products that are closely related. This may be because they satisfy a class of need, are used together, are sold to the same customer groups, are marketed through the same type of outlets or fall within given price ranges. For example, Campbell sells many types of soup, Macmillan publishes a number of textbooks on marketing and the airlines provide different services e.g. economy, business and first class.

A product mix (or product range) includes all the products (or product lines) that a particular strategic business unit (SBU) offers for sale to buyers. For example, Gillette has a product mix which includes razors, shaving cream, deodorants, shampoos and appliances. In rapidly changing product markets, companies are constantly planning product improvements in order to encourage customer migration to higher-value, higher priced items. This definition could be amended to allow for services, since such organisations as banks and insurance companies face similar mix decisions to those of manufacturers.

KEY POINT

Philip Kotler, in *Marketing Management, Analysis, Planning & Control*, considers the product mix in terms of its width, depth and consistency.

Philip Kotler, in *Marketing Management, Analysis, Planning & Control*, considers the product mix in terms of its width, depth and consistency.

Width refers to the number of different product lines it has. A wide mix enables a firm to diversify its products, appeal to different consumer needs and encourage one-stop shopping. It also requires substantial resource investment and expertise in the different categories of product or service.

Depth refers to the number of product items within each product line. A deep mix can satisfy the needs of several consumer segments for the same product, maximise shelf space, preclude competitors and sustain dealer support. It also means higher costs for stock holding, product alterations and order processing.

Consistency is based on the relationship among product lines in terms of their sharing a common end-use, distribution outlets, consumer group and price range. A consistent mix is easier to handle because it allows the organisation to use marketing and production expertise, create a strong image and generate solid channel relations. However, excessive consistency can leave the organisation vulnerable to environmental threats e.g. resource shortages.

The elements of the product mix that the marketer can control include quality, styling, design, packaging, reliability, durability and available sizes. Trade-offs are involved between the various elements of product mix. The build quality of the car may be at a high production cost. The durability of a vehicle may be a trade-off with increased weight, reduced economy and performance.

The product mix needs to take into account changes in cultural values and society. Fashions change. Legal requirements change. Environmental pressures may require the repackaging and reformulation of the product. The changing age structure of many countries – with increasing proportions of older people – may shift the emphasis from fashion to durability and utility as the cultural norm.

2.3 Key aspects of the 'actual' product

Key aspects of the actual product include:

- Quality.

- Features and capabilities include combinations of product attributes.

- Styling refers to the design, aesthetic, or ergonomic aspects.

- The brand name.

- Packaging protects and promotes.

Quality

Product quality is the overall ability of a product to satisfy customer expectations. The level of quality is determined by comparison with other brands in same product category. Key aspects of quality are:

- Consistency – customers experience the same level of quality in product time after time.

- Reliability – likelihood of breakdown.

- Conformance – conformance to specification.

- Technical durability – length of time before the product becomes obsolete.

- Serviceability – ease of service.

- Aesthetics – look, smell, feel, taste.

- Perceived quality – reputation.

- Value for money.

The quality of a product (involving its design, production standards, quality control and after-sales service) must be properly established and maintained before a sales campaign can use it as a selling feature.

Design

Design involves the creation of an attractive product that works. The success of Apple Computer's iMac can be attributed to its distinctive design features. Successful design depends on the following factors:

- Aesthetics: how the product looks. A car manufacturer may introduce a new model by changing the bodywork and the fittings as these appeal to people's senses. The engine may not change at all.

- Function: the product must do the job intended. Some car manufacturers are so confident in their design that they give their cars a five-year warranty.

- Economics: the design must be economically viable.

- Environmental impact: many companies try to minimise the impact of their product on the natural environment. Careful design can reduce waste in the production and distribution of the product.

Brand

A brand is a name, symbol, term, mark or design that enables customers to identify and distinguish the products of one supplier from those offered by competitors. The supplier has to decide which products to brand, the quality level aspired to and the targeted position in the market place.

Successful brands have established recognisable images that allow consumers to readily identify and distinguish the product from all others, often from a considerable distance. Consider, for example, how far away you can be and still recognise the Coca-Cola 'disk'. A powerful brand has high brand equity; this is described as 'the value of a brand, based on the extent to which it has high loyalty, name awareness, perceived quality, strong personality associations and other assets, such as patents, trademarks, and customer relationships.

In the creation of a brand strategy, an organisation needs to be aware of the effect the brand name can have on the product or service. Some fortunate companies have had their name adopted for the product, regardless of the manufacturer, e.g. Hoover instead of vacuum cleaner and Sellotape instead of sticky tape. Market research in the UK has shown that most people believe that an organisation with a good reputation would not sell poor quality products. This is a competitive advantage for those companies when it comes to promoting new products.

Developing and maintaining a brand is a rather expensive affair. However there are other possibilities such as 'distributor's brands' or 'licensed brand names'.

Nike is a powerful brand, but the company that owns the brand does not own a single shoe production facility. They contract other shoe producers to make the shoes to their specifications. In this situation it is better to have a market than to own a factory.

Packaging

Most products require some form of packaging and labeling. In fact, many marketers believe that packaging is so important that it can be considered as a separate element of the marketing mix. Other marketers believe that packaging should be considered as a promotional element. The packaging of any product has five main purposes or functions:

- The product must arrive at the point of consumption (the customer) in perfect condition and it is the packaging which will achieve this.

- In the design of packaging the marketer must consider the impact of the weather during distribution to ensure that neither the packaging nor its contents are damaged.

- Damage can also be caused by human tampering which may not always be obvious.

- Packaging is an added cost and so the marketer should ensure that cost is considered against the benefits if provides.

- The quality, shape and colour of the packet should be consistent with the brand image that is being pursued.

- The packaging impact on channel intermediaries must also be considered. A manufacturer will want distributors, wholesales and retailers to stock the product.

What is also important is the requirements of the reseller (retailer). A 'good' consumer package is one that has display impact. This is what moves goods from the stores shelves. Packages, to the retailer, should be appropriately sized, convenient for stacking, easily price-marked and tough enough to handle normally (not only by shop staff, but by potential buyers) and protect the product, keeping it fresh and in good condition.

Thus, a great many decisions have to be made on package design. The aspects include size, shape, materials, colour, the text that appears on the package, the text for any enclosed leaflet and the brand mark.

2.4 The 'augmented' product

As we have already noted, the augmented product consists of the measures taken to help the consumer put the actual product to sustained use, including installation, delivery and credit, warranties, and after-sales service.

Service factors

Instructions – the type and complexity of instructions will vary enormously from product to product and from market to market. Complete and effective instructions are an important method of reducing post purchase dissatisfaction. Instructions can also serve to promote other products in the range by emphasising synergistic relationships.

Warranties and guarantees – associated with the packaging will be the requirement in many markets to provide warranties or guarantees. For many sectors, particularly in the industrial market, such warranties will be a vital part of the product benefit.

Control requirements

Copyright is the ability to establish ownership of a particular form of printed matter or artistic invention and is controlled by international convention. Rights are however limited to those developments that can be described as unique, with the result that extending copyright to design has generally been unsatisfactory.

Patent protection extends to original product developments, and is limited to an initial period followed by a possible extension. Organisations need to register patents and to establish that the patent concept is different from pre-existing patents. Though patent registration is expensive, it provides the ability to effectively control products by civil court actions against infringements.

Trademark – specific aspects of the name or design of the product can achieve trademark protection. Trademark protection is more complex than either patent or copyright, as different countries have different procedures for establishing them.

Product/service complaints – the effective management of complaints is a crucial part of reducing post purchase dissatisfaction and increasing the level of repeat sales. Companies that offer no-argument refund policies always rank more highly in surveys of customer satisfaction than those that do not.

2.5 Product adoption

The adoption process focuses on the stages that individual consumers or organisational buying units pass through in making a decision to accept or reject an innovation. The process can be modelled in the form of a bell-shaped diffusion curve similar to the following:

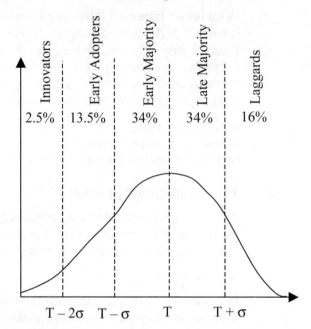

Innovators are the first to adopt an innovation and are characterised as venturesome, less risk averse, younger, with higher incomes and better education than later adopters. Innovators represent the first 2.5% to adopt the product.

Early Adopters – based on the positive response of innovators, early adopters then begin to purchase the product. They tend to be educated, self-confident opinion leaders and represent about 13.5% of consumers.

Early Majority are middle-class, cautious, deliberative decision makers. They adopt the product once the Early Adopters have tried it.

Late Majority are older, careful, conservative, skeptical consumers, who tend to avoid risk, and are doubtful of the benefits of adoption.

Laggards are those who avoid change and may not adopt a new product until traditional alternatives no longer are available. Laggards represent about 16% of consumers.

2.6 Product life cycle

A new product progresses through a sequence of stages from introduction to growth, maturity, and decline. This sequence is known as the **product life cycle** and is associated with changes in the marketing situation, thus impacting the marketing strategy and the marketing mix.

The product revenue and profits can be plotted as a function of the life cycle stages as shown in the graph below:

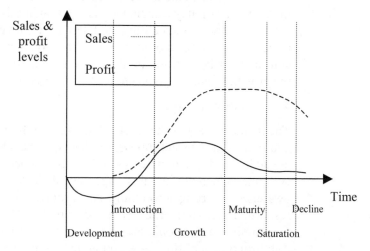

The life cycle concept may apply to a brand or to a category of product. Its duration may be as short as a few months for a fad item or a century or more for product categories such as the petrol-powered car.

It must be appreciated that the curve of the life cycle is a general one and only the experience of the marketing manager can possibly identify the stages of a given product's life cycle. The six stages are outlined below:

1 Product development.

Product development is the incubation stage of the product life cycle. There are no sales and the firm prepares to introduce the product. As the product progresses through its life cycle, changes in the marketing mix usually are required in order to adjust to the evolving challenges and opportunities. This is when there are only outgoings since money is invested in design costs and the production of prototypes. After this comes the product launch.

2 Introduction stage

When the product is introduced, sales will be low until customers become aware of the product and its benefits. **Product branding** and **quality** level is established, and intellectual property protection such as patents and trademarks are obtained. Some firms may announce their product before it is introduced, but such announcements also alert competitors and remove the element of surprise. **Advertising** costs typically are high during this stage in order to rapidly increase customer awareness of the product and to target the early adopters. **Pricing** may be low penetration pricing to build market share rapidly, or high skim pricing to recover development costs. **Distribution** is selective until consumers show acceptance of the product. During the introductory stage the firm is likely to incur additional costs associated with the initial distribution of the product. These higher costs coupled with a low sales volume usually make the introduction stage a period of negative profits.

3   Growth stage

The growth stage is a period of rapid revenue growth. Sales increase as more customers become aware of the product and its benefits and additional market segments are targeted. New product features and packaging options are introduced as well as improvement of product quality. Once the product has been proven a success and customers begin asking for it, sales will increase further as more retailers become interested in carrying it. **Price** is maintained at a high level if demand is high, or reduced to capture additional customers. The marketing team may expand the distribution at this point. When competitors enter the market, often during the later part of the growth stage, there may be price competition and/or increased promotional costs in order to convince consumers that the firm's product is better than that of the competition. During the growth stage, the goal is to gain consumer preference and increase sales.

4   Maturity stage

The maturity stage is the most profitable. **Product** quality is maintained and additional features and support services may be added. **Distribution** channels are added as demand increases and customers accept the product. While sales continue to increase into this stage, they do so at a slower pace. Because brand awareness is strong, advertising expenditures will be reduced. Competition may result in decreased market share and/or prices. The competing products may be very similar at this point, increasing the difficulty of differentiating the product. The firm places effort into encouraging competitors' customers to switch, increasing usage per customer, and converting non-users into customers. Sales promotions may be offered to encourage retailers to give the product more shelf space over competing products.

5   Saturation

The saturation stage is sometimes overlooked in many PLC models but is seen as the first sign of product/service decline. At this point, the product/service has no future for profits because there are too many competitors or the product/service is no longer popular. More products are available than the market can absorb. Competition is intensified and prices fall. Producers begin to leave the market due to poor margins. Promotion becomes more widespread and uses a greater variety of media.

6   Decline stage

Eventually sales begin to decline as the market becomes saturated, the product becomes technologically obsolete, or customer tastes change. If the product has developed brand loyalty, the profitability may be maintained longer. Unit costs may increase with the declining production volumes and eventually no more profit can be made. During the decline phase, the firm generally has three options:

(i)   Maintain the product in hopes that competitors will exit. Reduce costs and find new uses for the product.

(ii)   Harvest it, reducing marketing support and coasting along until no more profit can be made.

(iii) Discontinue the product when no more profit can be made or there is a successor product.

Activity 2

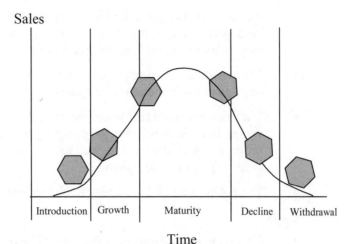

Put the following products on the product life cycle diagram:

1   MS-DOS

2   Internet Telephones (WAP or 3G)

3   Palmtop computers

4   Play Station 2

5   Sega Megadrive

6   Fax machines.

Feedback to this activity is at the end of the chapter.

3   Price

3.1   Pricing considerations

When pricing its products a firm needs to consider the following issues:

Corporate objectives

*   Is it trying to make short-term profits (perhaps before competitors enter the market)?

*   Is it trying to build up its market share through low prices?

*   Is it trying to complement a high quality and brand image through higher prices?

*   Is it trying to exclude competitors by setting low prices?

Customers

As a general point, products will not sell unless they are priced in such a way that customers are prepared to buy them. This has the following implications.

*   Pricing should be consistent with making the required profits at the expected level of demand.

*   A suitable balance should be found between price and quality.

*   Prices should be reviewed in the context of a product's stage in its life cycle.

*   Pricing should be consistent for the organisation's product range.

*   The value of the product as it relates to the value of the price. People may pay more for a similar product if they think they will get more out of it.

Competition

When pricing a product strategically, management needs to look at:

- The competition (or lack of it) the product faces. If the product is one of a kind, particularly if it is in the technology field, then higher initial prices may be more palatable to consumers (and even expected).

- The sensitivity (or insensitivity) of the customers to pricing for this type of product (as in the case of airlines).

- The price elasticity (the lower the price the more that is sold and vice versa). Keep in mind what the company has to sell in order to make a profit, and then chart out the variations in prices and quantities to sell in order to pinpoint the right one.

- The positioning that has been established for the product.

Costs

- Cost issues are discussed in Section 3.3 below.

3.2 Pricing strategies

There are many ways to **price** a product, as you can see from the matrix below.

Quality

	Low	High
Low	Economy	Penetration
High	Skimming	Premium

Price

Pricing strategies matrix

Premium Pricing – we use a high price where there is uniqueness about the product or service. This approach is used where a substantial competitive advantage exists. Such high prices are charged for luxuries eg, Cunard Cruises, and Savoy Hotel rooms.

Penetration Pricing – the price charged for products and services is set artificially low in order to gain market share. Once this is achieved, the price is increased. This type of pricing is used for products identified as being in the 'introductory' stage of the product life cycle to enable the product to get a foothold in the market. Prices are artificially reduced to attract the largest possible audience. It is often used to prevent or discourage competitors from capturing the market and used for products that are mass-produced.

Economy Pricing – this is a no frills low price. The cost of marketing and manufacture are kept at a minimum. Supermarkets often have economy brands for soups, spaghetti, etc.

Price Skimming – you can charge a high price because you have a substantial competitive advantage. However, the advantage is not sustainable. The high price tends to attract new competitors into the market, and the price inevitably falls due to increased supply. Manufacturers of digital watches used a skimming approach in the 1970s. Once other manufacturers were tempted into the market and the watches were produced at a lower unit cost, other marketing strategies and pricing approaches are implemented. This type of pricing structure works very well for products that are in demand or where there are few competitors, electronic equipment for example. Caution has to be used when employing this strategy as competitors may well take advantage of these high prices and enter the market quickly with a realistic price thus stealing the market. Again this type of pricing strategy might be used when the product is in its growth stage in the product life cycle as demand is high and sales are high.

Psychological Pricing – is used when the marketer wants the consumer to respond on an emotional, rather than rational basis. For example, 'price point perspective' 99 pence not one pound.

Product Line Pricing – where there is a range of product or services the pricing reflects the benefits of parts of the range, for example car washes. Basic wash could be £2, wash and wax £4, and the whole package £6.

Optional Product Pricing – companies will attempt to increase the amount customers spend once they start to buy. Optional 'extras' increase the overall price of the product or service. For example airlines will charge for optional extras such as guaranteeing a window seat or reserving a row of seats next to each other.

Captive Product Pricing – where products have complements, companies will charge a premium price once the consumer is captured. For example a razor manufacturer will charge a low price and recoup its margin (and more) from the sale of the only design of blades that fit the razor.

Product Bundle Pricing – here sellers combine several products in the same package. This also serves to move old stock. Videos and CDs are often sold using the bundle approach.

Promotional Pricing – to promote a product is a very common application. There are many examples of promotional pricing including approaches such as BOGOF (Buy One Get One Free).

Geographical or Differential Pricing – allows the same product to be priced differently when the product is sold in areas with differing economic climates, when sold through differing distribution channels, to appeal to a different market segment. For example, you could choose to charge a wholesaler less for buying in bulk than for an individual who only bought a single item. You could also decide to charge more in London than you would in the North of England, simply because the economy is more stable in London than in the North of England. This is evident where there are variations in price in different parts of the world, for example rarity value or where shipping costs increase price.

Value Pricing – is used where external factors such as recession or increased competition force companies to provide 'value' products and services to retain sales e.g. value meals at McDonalds.

Loss Leader Pricing – this involves lowering prices on a number of key products in order to attract a customer to purchase the products. Customers obviously like a bargain and may be attracted to buy this item even if they had never considered purchasing it before. Price reductions could be used to entice customers to look at your other products, and any profit lost might well be made up should the customer be persuaded to shop around and purchase other produces that are not reduced in price. Loss leader pricing might be used to sell off or stimulate interest in products considered to be in the maturity or decline stage of their life cycle.

3.3 Cost plus strategy

Sometimes a cost-plus strategy is recommended for the product's introduction stage. However, this raises a number of issues. These include:

(a)   Are standard costs used to provide a basis for measuring costs? How are adverse variances recovered through the pricing mechanism?

(b)   What is the basis for identifying fixed and variable elements of the cost structure? Are marginal costing and contribution accounting techniques used to assist pricing decisions?

(c)   If full cost absorption costs are used, how are the subjective matters dealt with that concern:

- the basis for apportioning overhead costs between cost centres?

- the basis for reapportioning service cost centres overhead costs between production cost centres?

- the basis of absorbing production cost centres overhead costs into jobs?

- the basis of absorbing other costs such as administration, research and development, selling and distribution into jobs?

(d)   What is the basis for ongoing verification of the validity of cost elements that affect pricing decisions? Are amendments made where necessary?

(e)   Are differences between historical costs, current costs and replacement costs acknowledged when appropriate?

(f)   What is the basis for fixing the mark-up percentage rate? The following aspects should be considered:

- published list prices

- negotiated discounts

- rebates

- allowances

- credit terms

- supplementary services, samples, etc

- promotional support.

3.4 Discount strategy

Discounts on the listed prices are also frequently used as a deliberate pricing strategy. The following discount strategies can be distinguished:

- **cash discounts** – for prompt payment

- **quantity discounts** – price reductions given to customers buying large quantities

- **functional discounts** – offered to traders if they perform certain specific functions, such as promoting the product

- **promotional pricing** – these are temporary discounts with a special promotional objective e.g. to attract first-time buyers during introduction.

Activity 3

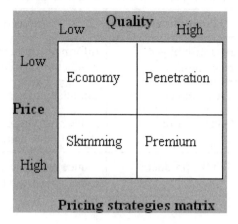

Listed below are a series of pricing strategies/polices. Place them onto the correct section of the matrix

1 Asda launch a new range of own-label soups.

2 Cunard launch two new cruise ships.

3 A cable TV provider moves into a new area and needs to achieve a market share.

4 Holiday Inns try to fill hotels during winter weekends.

5 Burger King introduces a new range of value meals.

6 Nokia launch a new videophone.

Feedback to this activity is at the end of the chapter.

4 Promotion

4.1 Introduction

Promotion is the communications strategy of the marketing plan. It will be where the message the organisation wants to use is devised and also the tools to spread it to the world.

There are a number of methods management may choose to use to make customers aware of their products. They include:

• media advertising (television, magazines, Internet, radio)

• personal selling (involving a sales person)

• non-personal communication (persuasion advertising - competitions, free samples

• other promotional types include public relation exercises and free publicity.

Each company has a different promotion-mix setting; even companies in the same product area can successfully adopt widely differing promotion policies.

4.2 Stages in the buying process

It is the function of promotion to bring people to the point at which they actually purchase a product. Some potential customers might be completely unaware of a product; others could be vaguely interested in it; whilst the remainder may want to own it. There are several complex models which illustrate the stages through which people pass on their way to a decision, but one of the simplest and easiest to remember is the AIDA model:

A awareness

I interest

D desire

A action

The customer must be made aware of the product or service, should become interested in it, then desire it and finally act by purchasing.

The following table, taken from *Marketing Theory & Application* (Wentz & Eyrich, Harcourt Brace) relates that model to the task and effect of marketing:

Buyer stage	Promotional task	Advertising effect
Awareness	Establish buyer awareness	Inform potential customers about the product or service.
Interest	Create buyer interest	Stimulate interest in the product.
Desire	Create desire	Induce favourable attitude, especially in relation to competing products.
Action	Sell the product	Induce purchase by stressing the immediate desirability of the product.

4.3 Advertising

Advertising is a 'paid for' communication. It is used to develop attitudes, create awareness and transmit information in order to gain a response from the target market. There are many advertising 'media' such as newspapers (local, national, free, trade), magazines and journals, television (local, national, terrestrial, satellite) cinema, Internet and outdoor advertising (such as posters, bus sides). Advertising is sometimes called above-the-line promotion.

It is not enough to say that advertising is expected to increase sales. The objective of a campaign must be more precisely stated, e.g:

Introduce new products. Advertising is the most effective way to acquaint a market with a new or revised product. Some authorities distinguish between informative and competitive advertising. The former type is definitely informative, and is useful in accelerating sales on launch so that profitability is achieved as soon after launch as possible.

Improve the competitive position. The company may decide to increase sales by inducing potential customers to switch brands. It may do this by claiming a product feature or benefit which is unique. Alternatively, it can claim its product is more efficient than the competition, e.g. *'this toothpaste leads to 30% fewer fillings'* or *'this soap powder washes whitest of all'*.

Sell in to dealers. If a product is being heavily advertised, dealers and retailers will be more likely to buy it. The effect can be enhanced both by advertising to the trade and by salespeople briefed to refer to the main promotion.

Develop the company's image. Many large companies use institutional advertising to reassure the public about the company's intentions, and to create an image of progressiveness, reliability, or good service. Whilst not directly aimed at selling a product, this type of advertising could have a pronounced long-term effect on sales.

Build or maintain brand loyalty. For a company with a strong brand and a high market share, a major objective is to keep brand loyalty high, ie, to prevent brand switching. One of the best examples of this type of advertising was the Coca-Cola campaign with its catch phrase *'it's the real thing'*. Companies in this position sometimes emphasise the tradition and quality of their product.

Bring salespeople and customers together. One of the effects of most advertising is an increase in the morale of sales personnel. Some advertising, however, is specifically designed to put potential customers in touch with salespeople. A good example is the use of return-coupons in industrial advertisements.

4.4 Personal selling

Personal selling is an effective way to manage personal customer relationships. The sales person acts on behalf of the organisation and tends to be well trained in the approaches and techniques of personal selling. However, sales people are very expensive and should only be used where there is a genuine return on investment. For example they are often used to sell cars or home improvements where the margin is high. The advantages of personal selling are that questions can be answered straight away and problems can be sorted out at a personal level.

4.5 Sales promotion

Sales promotion (sometimes called below-the-line promotion) is non-media promotional activity aimed at increasing sales, which includes a variety of techniques such as give-aways, competitions, coupons and exhibitions. It is intended to stimulate the actual purchase, rather than to be informative or interesting. Sales promotion can be aimed at the ultimate customer, to encourage pull or, at the trade, to push goods into dealerships or the retail system. Some of the more important objectives and techniques are:

'Sell in' to the trade. Appropriate techniques would be dealer discounts (or '11 for the price of 10' offers), trade competitions, or incentive offers to company salespeople.

Gain new users. A company could distribute free samples of the product, offer a trial use or use a banded pack in which a sample of a new product is attached to the pack of one of the existing lines.

Counteract competition. Price discounting is common. Other possibilities are to offer twin packs at an advantageous price or to run a consumer competition.

Gain repeat purchase. Can be encouraged by coupons on the pack that can be traded in at the next purchase. Other possibilities are to have a series of give-aways in the packs, send-away offers which require several labels or coupons, or a competition that requires proof of purchase of several items.

Improve display/shelf position. Shelf display may be improved by the use of free gifts attached to the pack, by container premiums (in which the container is attractive in its own right), by consumer competitions or by competitions in which retailers are given prizes for the best window display.

Clear old stock prior to the launch of a new product.

Add excitement to a well-established product that may be suffering from consumer familiarity.

There are some types of below-the-line activity not listed above. For example, discount cards are issued to encourage loyalty to retail outlets. One of the most important below-the-line activities in industrial marketing is attendance at exhibitions. This is intended to gain new users, but afterwards it is difficult to determine whether a sale resulted from an exhibition or another source.

Activity 4

Can you think of some more examples of types of customer promotion incentives?

Feedback to this activity is at the end of the chapter.

4.6 Public relations

Public relations is the creation of positive attitudes regarding products, services or companies by various means, including unpaid media coverage and involvement with community activities. The 'public' can include company employees, customers, suppliers, investment managers, financial institutions, shareholders, a particular geographical area and the general public.

At the core of almost all PR exercises is the company's desire to develop and express its corporate identity. Its aim is to spread knowledge and educate people, in order to achieve understanding, according to the prescribed objectives. For example, BP had a campaign showing beauty spots that have oil pipelines laid underground. Lever Brothers can claim the first recorded public relations exercise in the UK; in 1890, they issued the first in-house journal.

4.7 Marketing communications (mass, direct, interactive)

Mass media was for mass markets and the incredible explosion of technology of the last two decades has, for all practical purposes, shattered the mass market and made many of the traditional techniques of mass marketing obsolete. Mass media primarily serves the purpose of large advertisers who want to reach the greatest number of viewers. They generally use the broadcast model (i.e. shows on TV) to reach out to a large audience. However, to maintain consistency in fragmented markets and multiple media, marketers need to adopt new and better ways of understanding, reaching and connecting with consumers and therefore they are resorting to using newer forms of media in addition to mass media.

Direct marketing is where organisations communicate directly with target customers to generate a response and/or a transaction. Direct marketing is much more than direct mail and mail-order catalogues. It involves a variety of activities, including database management, direct selling, tele-marketing, and direct-response ads through direct mail, the Internet and various broadcast and print media.

Interactive media allow for a back-and-forth flow of information whereby users can participate in and modify the form and content of the information they receive in real time. Unlike traditional forms of marketing communications such as advertising, which are one-way in nature, these new media allow users to perform a variety of functions such as receive and alter information and images, make inquiries, respond to questions and, of course, make purchases. In addition to the Internet, interactive media also include CD-ROMs, kiosks and interactive television. However, the interactive medium that is having the greatest impact on marketing is the Internet, especially through the World Wide Web.

Direct and interactive marketing are discussed in more detail in Sections 6.4 and 6.5 below.

4.8 Marketing campaigns and communication channel planning

Through the segmentation process the marketer should already have some knowledge of his or her customers. There should be some idea of who potential customers are, their buying behaviour, the influences on their buying decision and their role in the decision making unit.

The target audience is usually formed of current and potential customers but could also be any stakeholder or other member of the proximate environment. It is only through knowledge of the target audience that effective campaigns can be planned.

Kotler's framework for campaign planning suggests the following phases:

- Identify the target audience.
- Determine the communication objectives.
- Design the message.
- Select the communication channels.
- Develop the total promotional budget.
- Decide on the promotion mix.
- Measure the promotion results.
- Manage and coordinate the total communication process.

5 Place

5.1 Channel intermediaries

While the word 'place' is chosen rather than 'distribution', partly to suit the mnemonic of four Ps (product, price, promotion and place), it does have the benefit of emphasising that decisions have to be taken about how to get the goods from producer to purchaser, about the design of the channels of distribution, and about the logistics of the physical distribution management. The process of distribution may involve one or more intermediaries, though in some cases manufacturers may not need intermediaries or may perform this function themselves. The customer will want the goods to be available locally in the right quantity and form. There may also be a need for sales support staff and customers may require a local after-sales service. The design of a channel of distribution will be influenced by the type of product, the abilities of the intermediaries and the expectations of the consumer.

There are six basic 'channel' decisions:

1   How do we decide upon a distributor? Do we use direct or indirect channels (e.g. 'direct' to a consumer, 'indirect' via a wholesaler)?

2   Single or multiple channels?

3   Length of the multiple channels?

4   Types of intermediary? The distributor must be familiar with your target consumer and segment. Changes during the product life cycle mean that different channels can be exploited at different points in the PLC e.g. Foldaway scooters are now available everywhere. Once they were sold via a few specific stores. How much training and support will your distributor require?

5   Number of intermediaries at each level? A qualification assessment will establish the experience and track record of your chosen intermediary.

6   Which companies to choose as intermediaries to avoid 'intrachannel conflict' (i.e. infighting between local distributors). Is there a match between their polices, strategies, image, and yours? Look for 'synergy'.

There are many types of intermediaries such as wholesalers, agents, retailers, the Internet, overseas distributors, direct marketing (from manufacturer to user without an intermediary), and many others.

1   Channel Intermediaries – Wholesalers

- They break down 'bulk' into smaller packages for resale by a retailer.

- They buy from producers and resell to retailers. They take ownership or 'title' to goods whereas agents do not (see below).

- They provide storage facilities. For example, cheese manufacturers seldom wait for their product to mature. They sell on to a wholesaler that will store it and eventually resell to a retailer.

- Wholesalers offer reduce the physical contact cost between the producer and consumer e.g. customer service costs, or sales force costs.

- A wholesaler will often take on the some of the marketing responsibilities. Many produce their own brochures and use their own telesales operations.

2   Channel Intermediaries – Agents

Agents are mainly used in international markets. An agent will typically secure an order for a producer and will take a commission. They do not tend to take title to the goods. This means that capital is not tied up in goods. However, a 'stockist agent' will hold consignment stock (i.e. will store the stock, but the title will remain with the producer). This approach is used where goods need to get into a market soon after the order is placed e.g. foodstuffs.

Agents can be very expensive to train. They are difficult to keep control of due to the physical distances involved and they are difficult to motivate.

3   Channel Intermediaries – Retailers

In the consumer market there is a range of distribution channels. Examples are the traditional high street shops and, more recently, out-of-town shopping precincts or malls.

- Retailers will have a much stronger personal relationship with the consumer.

- The retailer will hold several other brands and products. A consumer will expect to be exposed to many products.

- Retailers will often offer credit to the customer e.g. electrical wholesalers or travel agents.

- Products and services are promoted and merchandised by the retailer.

- The retailer will give the final selling price to the product.

- Retailers often have a strong 'brand' themselves e.g. Debenhams and John Lewis.

4   Channel Intermediaries – Internet

The Internet has a geographically disperse market. The main benefit of the Internet is that niche products reach a wider audience e.g. Scottish Salmon direct from an Inverness fishery. Other benefits include:

- low barriers to entry as set up costs are low

- use of e-commerce technology (for payment, shopping software, etc.)

- a paradigm shift in commerce and consumption which benefits distribution via the Internet.

5.2 Distribution strategies

Some firms deliver to wholesalers, who then deliver to retailers. Direct marketing avoids intermediaries. This includes mail order, telephone ordering and the use of the Internet for e-business. The distribution strategy being developed could be aimed at a wide distribution or it could be focused on the target market depending on whether a cost leadership or differentiation strategy is used.

Traditional distribution methods such as franchising, licensing and distributors are good choices, but businesses must also explore newer options such as strategic partnering and the Internet. The Internet has provided a distribution channel for information-based products and consumer goods. Strategic partnering can increase revenues and provide fast access to new customers and new markets.

The two best-known distribution strategies are called 'pull' and 'push'.

A 'pull' strategy means massive advertising to create consumer demand and this demand more or less forces the retailers to include this product in their assortment (not having this product in stock means disgruntled consumers that may go elsewhere to shop).

A 'push' strategy means that the producer does not try to create consumer demand through heavy advertising, but instead offers high margins to the trade channel members (retailers and wholesalers) and expects that in return they will actively promote and market the product.

Also companies may adopt strategies such as:

- exclusive distribution – using just one retailer in each geographical market

- selective distribution – using more than just one, but less than all distributors that are willing to retail your product. Good working relations (loyal resellers) may develop if indeed the company succeeds in making the product attractive in the eyes of the final consumer (pull strategy)

- intensive distribution – placing the product with as many outlets as possible.

When assessing/evaluating the distribution structure of a company economists use concepts such as the level of penetration (the numerical distribution, the number of shops in which your product is actually being sold as a percentage of the total number of shops selling this kind of produce in a given geographical area) and 'weighted' or real distribution (the proportion of the total market covered by those shops that are also selling your product).

As with pricing, the places where the product is available say a lot about its quality and 'status'. The channels of distribution must match the image goals of the product and the customers' perception of the product. Marketers must stay on top of changes in the market that might make them change the distribution strategy. They must also make sure the product can get the attention it needs in the chosen channel, both from the sales staff (are they knowledgeable?) and from a shelf-space standpoint (how many competing products does the distributor also carry?).

6 Three extra Ps – service marketing mix

The traditional marketing mix was primarily directed at tangible products; Booms and Bitner have extended the number of controllable variables from the four in the original marketing mix model to seven. The three extra Ps to be considered in service marketing are described below.

People

If the organisation is providing a service, rather than selling a product, the people involved become even more important. The quality of personal relationships between company and clients becomes vital. New staff joining in the business will need thorough training and constant monitoring. People leaving a business may take customers with them. Staffing costs are likely to form a higher percentage of your cost base and recruiting specialist staff may be time-consuming and expensive. The marketing plan should have strategies and tactics for recruiting, training and safeguarding relationships.

Physical evidence

If the organisation does not have a product to sell, it will need to show people the quality of its service. Recommendations, case studies and printed materials can give prospective customers good reasons to buy from the organisation. Physical evidence includes the elements of 'marketing mix' which customers can actually see or experience when they use a service, and which contribute to the perceived quality of the service, e.g. the physical evidence of a retail bank could include the state of the branch premises, as well as the delivery of the banking service itself

Process

If the organisation sells a service, its processes can give it the edge. The way in which a good or service is delivered has an impact on the way in which customers perceive the organisation.

Processes must help customers get what they want. What processes, systems or services would make life easier for customers? And could new systems – or new technology – help one particular organisation stand out from the competition?

The process is sometimes referred to as the 'whole customer experience'. A customer of a top class restaurant, for example, experiences the food, the atmosphere, the surroundings, the service and so on. Process can also refer to the efficiency of the service. For example, the ease with which a well-designed loan application form can be completed could be an important element in a bank's loan service.

7 Developing your marketing plan

One of the learning outcomes for this part of the course is for you to produce a strategic marketing plan for the business.

Your marketing plan should include everything you do to get your customers to buy your product or service. It will include both your strategies for growing sales as well as the tactics you will employ to achieve it, along with an overview of the competition in your market.

The marketing plan section of a business plan is made up of five subsections:

1 Target market

2 Services or products

3 Pricing strategy

4 Sales and distribution plan

5 Advertising and promotions plan

Target market

You need to have an understanding of the size of the target market for your product/service and the niche you are trying to carve out for your business. Explain the type of person or business that is likely to buy your product or service and how large this market is. Describe your direct competition and your indirect competition. Your indirect competitors are the businesses that sell a product that is not the same as yours but could be used as an alternative by your customer.

Give a summary of the major trends in the marketplace. You will have to do a lot of research to complete this section and it is important that you credit your sources since this will add credibility to your facts and figures.

The Target Market section of your marketing plan should cover the following:

- An outline of your target market. Include demographics statistics such as age, gender, where they live, income, etc. Also explain the psychographics of your target market. What do they have in common? What motivates them?

- Estimate the total size of the target market for your product or service in terms of gross sales and units of product or service sold.

- Describe the trends are affecting the target market for your product or service. Consider industry trends, socioeconomic trends, government policy and demographic shifts.

- Summarise your competition. Includes estimates of their market share, and your sense of their financial health. Compare their product or service to yours in terms of quality, price, service, warranties, image, etc. Include both your direct competition and your indirect competition.

Services or products

Your marketing strategy should communicate what makes your product or service unique. It is important to describe both the features and the benefits of your product or service. Features are descriptive attributes of your product such as the colour, weight, etc. The benefits describe what good things the customer will enjoy by using your product or service (e.g. save time, save money, feel better, etc.).

This section should cover the following:

- The one thing above all else that makes your product or service unique (USP).

- Other features of your product or service. Consider packaging, quality, price, service, etc.

- The benefits your customers will enjoy by buying your product or service? Will they save money, feel better, be smarter, etc.?

Pricing strategy

An important part of your strategy is determining how you will price your product or service. The secret here is to establish a reasonable base price that will enable you to make a fair profit. You may believe the easiest route is simply to set your prices in accordance with those of your competitors. Before you set a base price, you have to look at your own objectives and special considerations.

The pricing strategy section should cover the following:

- Your base price and how you arrived at this figure. Provide a brief summary of your fixed and variable costs.

- The prices of similar products and services. Explain how the price of your product or service will compete with market prices. If your price is higher, why would a customer choose your product? Do you offer superior service or a higher quality product? If your price is lower, how are you able to charge less? Is the quality different, is your production process more efficient, do you sell in large volumes?

- What your costs include. Are you offering discounts to students or seniors or for those who pay in cash rather than by credit? Are you allowing trade-in?

- What kind of a return are you looking for in your investment and how soon are you anticipating recouping your investment?

Sales and distribution plan

Your sales and distribution plan should detail how the transaction between you and your customer will take place. It should include a discussion about how you plan on selling your product or service and it should outline all of the different people and companies involved in getting your product into the hands of your customer. You should explain in detail what type of distribution channels are available to you (account representatives, salespeople, Internet, delivery services, other companies that will carry your product), what benefits you will have by choosing them and the length of time it will take to get your product to your customer. You should also summarise your returns policy and describe any warranties or after-sales support you will offer customers.

This part of the plan should cover the following:

- How you will distribute your product or service. Will it be by mail, through a wholesaler, through retail, through a Website and/or an independent sales representative, etc.? Outline all of the players or technology involved in getting your product/service to the end customer.

- How you expect your customers to pay for your product. What credit terms will you extend to your customer? Include any discounts you will offer for early payment or penalties for late payment.

- Describe your return policy, service guarantees and/or any warranties you intend to offer customers. What after-sales support will you offer? Will you charge for this service?

Advertising and promotions plan

Your advertising and promotions plan must detail how you are going to communicate to your customers. There are many ways your business may communicate including advertising, public relations, brochures, a Website, trade shows, etc. If possible, include an example or mock-up of your communications pieces.

Your advertising and promotions plan should cover the following:

- A description of how you will advertise your product. Include what medium you will use (i.e. direct mail, Internet, radio, television, etc). How much will this cost? How much business do you anticipate this will bring in?

- An outline of the plans you have to generate publicity for your business. What type of media will you target?

- An outline of the kind of marketing material you will produce. Include brochures, fliers, business cards, etc.

- Details of your Website if you plan to have one and a description of how you will use it to market your business.

- Details of any other forms of marketing you will use. Consider trade shows, telemarketing, etc.

Summary

- The marketing mix is the set of controllable variables that the firm can use to influence the buyers' responses – the four Ps.

- The marketing mix describes the specific combination of marketing elements used to achieve objectives and satisfy the target market. The mix consists of four major factors: product or service; distribution; promotion; and price.

- 'Product' means everything that is used by the organisation to provide consumer satisfaction.

- The elements of the product mix that the marketer can control include quality, styling, design, packaging, reliability, durability and available sizes.

- A **brand** is a name, symbol, term, mark or design that enables customers to identify and distinguish the products of one supplier from those offered by competitors.

- Many marketers believe that packaging is so important that it can be considered as the fifth 'P' (i.e. the fifth element of the marketing mix).

- A new product progresses through a sequence of stages from introduction to growth, maturity and decline. This sequence is known as the **product life cycle.**

- **Advertising** is a 'paid for' communication. It is used to develop attitudes, create awareness, and transmit information in order to gain a response from the target market.

- The design of a channel of distribution will be influenced by the type of product, the abilities of the intermediaries and the expectations of the consumer.

Having completed your study of this chapter, you should have achieved the following learning outcomes:

- evaluate the marketing processes of an organisation

- apply tools within each area of the marketing mix

- produce a strategic marketing plan for the organisation.

Self-test questions

1   What are the four Ps? (1.2)

2   What is the difference between a 'core' product and an 'actual' product? (2.1)

3   Describe two of the stages in the product life cycle. (2.6)

4   What are the advantages of personal selling? (4.4)

5   How does an agent differ from a wholesaler? (5.1)

Practice questions

Question 1

A skimming price is:

A   a no frills low price

B   the price charged for products and services is set artificially low in order to gain market share

C   a high price where there is uniqueness about the product or service

D   a high price because you have a substantial competitive advantage.

Question 2

Marketing mix decisions

You are required to:

(a)   Explain the role of advertising in the promotional mix, using a model to depict the way in which promotion works.   **(5 marks)**

(b)   Describe the role of advertising as an element in the marketing communications mix for companies manufacturing and marketing chocolate confectionery.

(5 marks)

(c)   Describe the role of advertising as an element in the marketing communications mix for companies manufacturing and marketing fork-lift trucks.

(5 marks)

(d)   Describe how 'below-the-line' promotional activity differs from advertising.

(5 marks)

(e)   Explain why manufacturers use brand names.   **(5 marks)**

(Total: 25 marks)

Question 3

The marketing mix

Describe the key elements of the marketing mix. What criteria should you consider to develop an optimum balance between them?

(20 marks)

For the answers to these questions, see the 'Answers' section at the end of the book.

Feedback to activities

Activity 1

Using McCarthy's Marketing Mix model will ensure that the management of the ice cream manufacturer considers the different aspects of each of the four Ps, both individually and in combination. This should result in a co-ordinated and, therefore, more effective strategic plan for each firm.

Activity 2

You would plot the products in the PLC as follows. You may disagree with some of the positioning. However, the exercise demonstrates the way in which marketers would use such a tool.

- Introduction – Internet Telephones (WAP or 3G)

- Growth – Palmtop computers

- Early maturity – Play Station 2

- Late maturity – Fax machines

- Decline – MS-DOS

- Withdrawal – Sega Megadrive

Activity 3

Here is the 'Pricing Strategies Matrix' with the answers overlaid.

	Quality	
	Low	High
Low	Asda	Cable TV
	Holiday Inn	
	Economy Burger King	**Penetration**
High	Nokia videophone	Cunard
	Skimming	**Premium**

(Price — on the left axis: Low at top, High at bottom)

- Asda launches a new range of own-label soups. This is an economy brand.

- Cunard launches two new cruise ships. The service is high price and high quality with a premium price.

- A cable TV provider moves into a new area and needs to achieve a market share. The company uses a penetration approach to gain market share. Prices could be increased at a later date.

- Holiday Inns tries to fill hotels during winter weekends. This is an example of 'off peak' pricing.

- Burger King introduces a new range of value meals. There is a lot of price competition in the fast food market, hence the value approach.

- Nokia launch a new videophone. This is a new innovative product that can claim a higher price. Skimming is only an option in the short-term since competition will be inevitable.

Activity 4

More examples of types of customer promotion incentives include:

Home, magazine or newspaper couponing where a coupon with monetary value, redeemable against a specified brand, is either distributed to homes or cut from a magazine or newspaper.

Reduced price packs with a price reduction marked on package by producer. Value of typical price reduction varies between 3% and 12% of retail price.

Bonus (or free) packs where the customer is given an extra product at no additional cost (e.g. four for the price of three).

Buy 'X' number and get one free where the consumer sends in packets or labels and will receive a coupon inviting him/her to a free pack or product. (There are a number of variants of this scheme.)

Free merchandise packs where the customer gets a gift that is attached to brand package.

Re-usable container packs where the product has a special container with an intrinsic value. The container may be free or involve the consumer paying extra for it.

Home sampling where a free sample is distributed by hand or mail to individual homes.

Contests e.g. card and stamp game, rub-off cards, skill competition, sweepstake or draw contest.

Chapter 13

MARKETING PROCESSES

Syllabus content

- Understanding consumer behaviour, such as factors affecting buying decisions, types of buying behaviour and stages in the buying process.

- Marketing Decision Support Systems (MDSS) and their relationship to market research.

- How business-to-business (B2B) marketing differs from business-to-consumer (B2C) marketing.

- The differences and similarities in the marketing of products and services.

- Use of the Internet (e.g. in terms of data collection, marketing activity and providing enhanced value to customers and suppliers) and potential drawbacks (e.g. security issues).

- Internal marketing as the process of training and motivating employees so as to support the firm's external marketing activities.

Contents

1 Analysing buyer and customer behaviour

2 Business contexts of marketing

3 The role of technology in marketing

1 Analysing buyer and customer behaviour

A crucial element in the marketing process is understanding why a buyer purchases or does not purchase an organisation's goods or services. If the organisation does not understand the process, it will not be able to respond to the customer's needs and wishes.

1.1 Maslow's hierarchy of needs

Maslow proposed a hierarchy of needs that he used to explain human motivation. Conventionally used to explain the motivation to work, his hierarchy can also be applied to customer motivation.

Maslow's hierarchy of needs (discussed in more detail in Chapter14):

(a) Physiological needs – heat, air, light, etc.

(b) Safety needs – the need for the familiar, the secure.

(c) Love needs – the need to be loved by family, friends.

(d) Esteem needs – the need to be regarded as important, having prestige.

(e) Self-actualisation needs – the need to initiate, to achieve for oneself.

The five-part hierarchy is arranged in the order in which human needs must be satisfied. Thus, a 'safety' need is a motivating factor only when 'physiological' needs have been satisfied. When the 'safety' need is satisfied, 'love' needs become important, and so on:

Products and services could be considered against this hierarchy. For example, insurance and banking are involved with safety needs; cigarettes and alcohol are frequently dependent upon love needs in their promotions; a fast car exploits customers' esteem needs.

It is the job of the marketing team to persuade the potential customer that the product will satisfy his or her needs.

1.2 Influence of other people

So far we have considered customers as individuals. This is unrealistic, however, because each customer is a part of larger social groupings. When people make purchase decisions, they reflect the values of their social and cultural environment. Among the more obvious influences are those of family and of reference groups.

The family is often important in engendering brand purchasing habits in grocery lines, although it also has a far broader influence in forming tastes in its younger members.

Reference groups, which may be school-friends, working colleagues, fellow club members etc., exert a strong normative influence. That is, they cause members of the group to buy similar things and tend to disapprove of those who behave in too individualistic a manner. It is a bold person who reads the Sun in an office of *Financial Times* readers, and groups of teenagers can be seen to dress with almost identical styles.

1.3 Stages in the buying process

Research suggests that customers go through a five-stage decision-making process in any purchase. This is summarised in the diagram below:

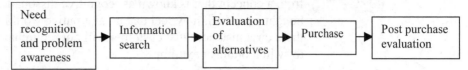

This model is important for anyone making marketing decisions. It forces the marketer to consider the whole buying process rather than just the purchase decision (when it may be too late for a business to influence the choice!)

The model implies that customers pass through all stages in every purchase. However, in more routine purchases, customers often skip or reverse some of the stages.

For example, a student buying a favourite hamburger would recognise the need (hunger) and go right to the purchase decision, skipping information search and evaluation. However, the model is very useful when it comes to understanding any purchase that requires some thought and deliberation.

The buying process starts with need recognition. At this stage, the buyer recognises a problem or need (e.g. I am hungry, we need a new sofa, I have a headache) or responds to a marketing stimulus (e.g. you pass Starbucks and are attracted by the aroma of coffee and chocolate muffins).

An 'aroused' customer then needs to decide how much information (if any) is required. If the need is strong and there is a product or service that meets the need close to hand, then a purchase decision is likely to be made there and then. If not, then the process of information search begins.

A customer can obtain information from several sources:

- personal sources: family, friends, neighbours etc
- commercial sources: advertising; salespeople; retailers; dealers; packaging; point-of-sale displays
- public sources: newspapers, radio, television, consumer organisations; specialist magazines
- experiential sources: handling, examining, using the product.

The usefulness and influence of these sources of information will vary by product and by customer. Research suggests that customers value and respect personal sources more than commercial sources (the influence of 'word of mouth'). In the evaluation stage, the customer must choose between the alternative brands, products and services.

Why should a marketer need to understand the customer evaluation process?

The answer lies in the kind of information that the marketing team needs to provide customers in different buying situations.

In high-involvement decisions, the marketer needs to provide a good deal of information about the positive consequences of buying. The sales force may need to stress the important attributes of the product, the advantages compared with the competition; and maybe even encourage 'trial' or 'sampling' of the product in the hope of securing the sale.

Post-purchase evaluation – cognitive dissonance

The final stage is the post-purchase evaluation of the decision. It is common for customers to experience concerns after making a purchase decision. This arises from a concept that is known as 'cognitive dissonance'. The customer, having bought a product, may feel that an alternative would have been preferable. In these circumstances that customer will not repurchase immediately, but is likely to switch brands next time.

To manage the post-purchase stage, it is the job of the marketing team to persuade the potential customer that the product will satisfy his or her needs. Then after having made a purchase, the customer should be encouraged that he or she has made the right decision.

1.4 Different roles in the buying process

The following roles have been identified in the buying process:

- An *initiator* starts the buying process, usually by identifying a need.

- The *influencer* will affect which product is bought, perhaps based on their expertise.

- The *buyer* buys it.

- The *user* uses it.

As such, this terminology could be applied to B2C or B2B marketing:

Example: Purchasing a child's bike (B2C)

Member	*Role*
Initiator	Child pesters parents for new bike
Influencers	Older siblings have an opinion on the choice of bike, once parent recognises child has grown out of present one
Buyer	Parent pays the bill
User	The child

Example: Purchasing new machinery (B2B)

Member	*Role*
Initiator	Machine breaks down, the operator reports it, thus initiating the process
Influencers	User may influence purchase. May also involve supervisor, R&D staff, accountant, sales reps, etc
Buyer	Buyer handles search for and negotiations with supplies
User	Operator

However, the terminology is more often used within the context of B2B marketing.

2 Business contexts of marketing

2.1 Consumer and industrial markets

One of the most commonly used divisions between types of market is that between consumer and industrial markets.

The **business-to-consumer market** (B2C) is the market for products and services bought by individuals for their own use or for that of their family. Goods bought in consumer markets can be categorised in several ways:

Consumer durables – these have low volume but high unit value. Consumer durables are often further divided into:

- *white goods* (e.g. fridge-freezers; cookers; dishwashers; microwaves)

- *brown goods* (e.g. DVD players; games consoles; personal computers).

Soft goods – these are similar to consumer durables, except that they wear out more quickly and have a shorter replacement cycle. Examples include clothes, shoes.

Services (e.g. hairdressing, dentists, childcare).

KEY POINT

The **business-to-business (B2B)** or **industrial market** consists of organisations (and individuals) that buy goods or services so as to use them in creating the goods or services they offer for sale.

The **business-to-business (B2B)** or **industrial market** consists of organisations (and individuals) that buy goods or services so as to use them in creating the goods or services they offer for sale. These are goods that are not directly aimed at consumers. Industrial markets involve the sale of goods between businesses.

Industrial goods may be categorised as follows:

Raw materials, which have been extracted from the natural state, but subject to very little processing e.g. steel, coal, gas and timber.

Processed materials and components, which have been transformed into a condition in which they can be incorporated into either finished goods or more complex processed parts. Americans often refer to the former as semi-manufactured goods.

Capital goods, which consist of equipment used in the creation of goods and services and in their marketing, but are not consumable e.g. office furniture, computer systems.

Supplies, which is the industrial equivalent of fast-moving consumer goods, and covers all industrial consumables.

Industrial markets often require a slightly different marketing strategy and mix. In particular, a business may have to focus on a relatively small number of potential buyers (e.g. the IT responsible for ordering computer equipment in a multinational group). Whereas consumer marketing tends to be aimed at the mass market (in some cases, many millions of potential customers'), industrial marketing tends to be focused.

Salient features of B2B marketing:

- **Derived demand**: the more distant the manufacturer is from the production of a specific consumption good, the less direct will be the impact of a change in demand for that good.

- **Rational buying motives**: there is a difference in the degree of rationality in B2B marketing; that is, the buyer will emphasise objective criteria to a greater degree than the average consumer.

- **Concentration of buyers:** the number of potential buyers for an industrial good is generally far smaller than in the case with consumer goods.

- **The scale of purchasing:** in absolute money terms this is generally, but not always, true.

- **Technical complexity:** a greater degree of technical complexity, generally true, but not absolutely true.

- **A group process:** more often a group process.

- **Role of service:** this depends on the nature of the product and type of service, although after-sales service if often required.

Activity 1

Kotler suggests that 'the industrial market consists of all the individuals and organisations that acquire goods and services that enter into the production of other products or services that are sold, rented or supplied to others'. The industries making up the industrial market are the public sector, banking, insurance, transportation, manufacturing, agriculture, and so on. Consider the industrial market in which a brick manufacturer operates and describe its characteristics.

Feedback to this activity is at the end of the chapter.

2.2 Services markets/industries

Service industries are extremely varied: the not-for-profit sector with its many charitable organisations contrasts with the business sector with its finance, transportation, hotels and numerous professional services such as legal and accounting. There is also the public sector, which contains health, education and emergency services, which have their own distinguishing features. In this context one should also acknowledge the existence of the manufacturing sector with its business services.

Philip Kotler has provided a definition that helps to focus upon service elements in the economy: 'A service is any act or performance that one party can offer to another that is essentially intangible and does not result in the ownership of anything....'

What exactly are the characteristics of a service? How are services different from a product? In fact many organisations do have service elements to the product they sell, for example McDonald's sell physical products i.e. burgers but consumers are also concerned about the quality and speed of service; are staff cheerful and welcoming and do they serve with a smile on their face?

Kotler suggests that there are four major characteristics that impact upon the design of a marketing plan when considering the service sector.

Intangibility – you cannot hold or touch a service unlike a product. In general there can be no results prior to purchase, you cannot use your perceptual senses and therefore one will seek 'assurance' of quality to predict outcomes and reduce uncertainty.

Inseparability – whilst physical goods are frequently sold through sophisticated outlets and often after storage, this is not the case with regard to services, which are often produced and consumed simultaneously. The existence of such chains of marketing outlets adds to the feeling of comfort or 'quality' for the consumer of products. However, the chain is absent for the service client.

Variability – it is very difficult to make each service experience identical. If travelling by plane the service quality may differ from the first time you travelled by that airline to the second, because the steward is more or less experienced. Services vary greatly and such variations can precipitate confusion

---

KEY POINT

Kotler suggests that there are four major characteristics that impact upon the design of a marketing plan when considering the service sector:

- intangibility
- inseparability
- variability
- perishability.

---

and, in the worst-case scenario, distrust in the purchaser of services. Since the purchaser may often engage in large searches prior to reaching a purchase decision, the standardisation of staff and services seeks to ensure 'quality' and therefore satisfaction.

Perishability – services last a specific time and cannot be stored like a product for later use. If travelling by train, coach or air the service will only last the duration of the journey. The service is developed and used almost simultaneously. This removes the buffer frequently employed by manufacturing businesses to cope with fluctuations in demand. Controlling quality and matching supply to demand are therefore significant management problems within service-oriented organisations.

Activity 2

How would a public library regard marketing success?

Feedback to this activity is at the end of the chapter.

DEFINITION

Internal marketing is 'the means of applying the philosophy and practices of marketing to people who serve the external customers so that (i) the best possible people can be employed and retained and (ii) they will do the best possible work'.

2.3 Internal markets

Internal marketing is 'the means of applying the philosophy and practices of marketing to people who serve the external customers so that (i) the best possible people can be employed and retained and (ii) they will do the best possible work'. Internal marketing is about building morale, motivating employees and maintaining post-sale customer relationships. It means that the service firm must invest heavily in employee quality and performance. It must effectively train and motivate its customer-contact employees and all the supporting service people to work as a team to provide customer satisfaction. The company may have a strong marketing strategy and active advertising campaign, but without their employee's support it will not be as effective. If advertising promises are not kept through the services and products provided, eventually the company's reputation will suffer and the customers will stop coming. For the firm to deliver consistently high service quality, everyone must practise a customer orientation.

Employees have a particularly great bearing on services marketing where:

- employees account for a high proportion of total costs

- customer-employee encounters are an important part of the service offer.

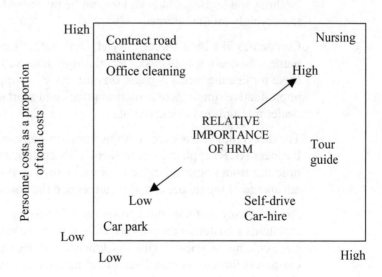

An internal marketing programme will communicate the customer focus concept and objectives to all employees. This process needs to be continuous and integrated into every process, training session and internal communication to ensure it becomes part of the company culture. This also needs to be incorporated into the induction process so that new employees have an understanding of the company vision and culture.

Employees should be given both on- and off-the-job training. On-the-job training should encompass empowerment and role training. Off-the-job training could include professional certification, language skills and any other personal development that will motivate and fulfil employees.

Counselling should also be used and staff should feel able to discuss their problems and work stresses.

Other strategies to keep employees informed and motivated are company clothing, awards, annual reports, events, newsletters, handbooks and manuals.

Activity 3

Describe why internal marketing is important to an organisation.

Feedback to this activity is at the end of the chapter.

2.4 Direct marketing

Direct marketing is a method of distribution in which transactions are completed between buyer and seller without the intervention of a sales person or retail outlet. It can be defined as the process in which individual customers' responses and transactions are recorded and the data used to inform the targeting, execution and control of actions that are designed to start, develop and prolong profitable customer relationships.

It involves the use of mail, telephone, fax, email and other non-personal tools to communicate directly with specific consumers or to solicit a direct response. Because of its rising importance, modern marketers have frequently referred to it as the fifth element of the communications mix. However, direct marketing techniques are not just communication devices; they are also sales channels in their own right. For example, many companies use direct channels to sell their products. A wide range of products and services, including computers, software, financial services, clothing and household appliances can be purchased by phone, mail and increasingly on the Internet.

Companies like First Direct, easyjet, Dell and La Redoute are pure direct marketers, dealing with customers through their websites and call centres. The logic for dealing direct is based on efficiency – stripping out overheads or unproductive running costs such as bricks and mortar outlets, sales forces, dealer margins and stockholding.

The direct model works for both business-to-consumer (B2C) and business-to-business (B2B) applications. In fact Dell's customers range from individuals ordering from home to large corporations such as Barclays Bank. Another advantage of the model is that it can reduce the cost of international expansion.

Any company that uses direct response advertising, on-line or off-line, and maintains a customer database is using direct marketing. Tesco maintains a huge customer database with its Clubcard and uses it to tailor offers to its customers through personalised direct mail using past purchasing behaviour to predict future behaviour.

Successful direct marketing practice depends on four elements: targeting, interaction, control and continuity (TICC).

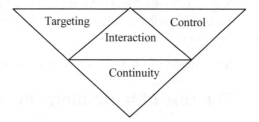

Targeting refers to the decisions on who will receive the message and includes the media selection: TV, banner ads, print advertising, direct mail, telemarketing, e-mail and so on. By examining the results of previous attempts to target correctly, companies can keep on refining their future targeting.

Interaction is at the heart of direct marketing. It includes the stimuli that marketers create in the hope of producing a response from the people in their target market. The completeness and accuracy of the data within the interaction triangle will be crucial to the exercise of control. Interaction quantifies the *effects* of the marketing. Customer interactions may not just be orders. They may be returns (of unwanted goods), queries, complaints, requests, suggestions, questionnaire responses and so on.

Control is the management of the marketing. It includes setting objectives, planning at the strategic and operational levels, budgeting and assessment of results. The process is cyclical, future planning being informed by past results.

Continuity is about retaining customers and cross-selling other products to them. In the vast majority of business enterprises, the bulk of profit arises from dealings with established customers.

Recording **interactions** enables communications with customers, recognising their interest and showing appreciation of their custom. The special challenge of e-commerce and of contact centre management is to respond to customers in real time.

All four of the TICC elements are critical. Direct marketing is not direct marketing unless they are all in place.

Multi-channel marketing also uses direct marketing. Tesco is a multi-channel retailer, although its website sales are dwarfed by its store-based sales. Car manufacturers such as GM and Ford sell a few cars directly to private motorists on the web. IBM sells direct and through dealers. Some magazine publishers (*Reader's Digest* and the *Economist*) sell through newsagents as well as through direct subscription. Charities raise funds through direct mail, street collections, charity shops and special events.

2.5 Interactive marketing

Interactive marketing is direct marketing through new media. It can be described as the exploitation of the new interactive electronic mediums to deliver unique and customised products and services to customers at a mass-produced price. It is a powerful combination of the concepts of one-to-one marketing with mass customisation.

Interactive marketing can exploit any and many of the new technologies, especially the interactive ones, as well as established methods:

Interactive technologies include the Internet, interactive TV, web-TV, kiosks, fax, e-mail, voice mail, personal data assistants, mobile phones, fixed phones, pagers and postal mail. All these allow personal messages and encourage customer feedback. Many allow interaction at a time and a place that suit the customer.

Key aspects of the role of newer technologies are discussed below.

3 The role of technology in marketing

3.1 Marketing Decision Support System (MDSS)

Marketing Decision Support Systems consists of information, systems, tools and techniques such as models, with supporting software and hardware. With these information systems an organisation can gather and interpret relevant information, in order to improve the decision making process and proceed with marketing actions.

A marketing information system can be defined as 'a structured, interacting complex of persons, machines and procedures designed to generate an orderly flow of pertinent information for use as the basis for decision-making in specified responsibility areas of marketing management'.

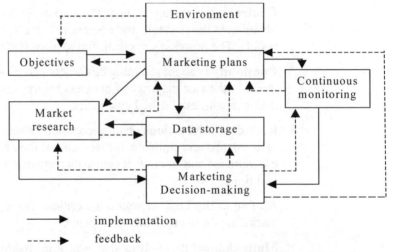

In the system outlined above the organisation begins with a statement of their objectives, which are influenced by environmental factors such as competition, government and the economy. The objectives provide broad guidelines that direct market planning.

After marketing plans are outlined the data needs of the marketing department can be specified and satisfied.

3.2 Marketing databases

Some companies have designed marketing databases (computerised) to gain faster access to the required data, whether from internal sources, such as customers' sales details or from external sources through networks such as Compuserve or the Internet, which allow access to a wide variety of databases.

A marketing information system offers many advantages:

- organised data collection

- broad perspective

- retention of important data

- co-ordination of marketing plan

- speed of access to information

- quantifiable results

- cost-benefit analysis.

Specialist databases, which are established externally to a company, are often available from government departments, industry associations, regional development bodies, research establishments, etc. Such databases often contain information that is relevant to a company in making decisions regarding marketing initiatives, control of the marketing mix variables, R&D budget, etc.

Data is normally purchased from the database provider who is offering a range of data, defined and analysed, for many users. Since the data collection, definition and analysis are not designed for one customer company, it is often necessary to check the validity and relevance of the data.

Aspects that a company would check include the accuracy of the data provided. The relevant specialists within the company could check a sample of the data and could compare results with information available elsewhere. Where errors are located the company can correct the data or apply a tolerance margin in its decision-making.

The company would need to check the definitions upon which the data is collected and analysed. For example, a major retailer could obtain details of the store's catchment area, in order to plan a local customer transport service. The database could readily provide number of households and number of car owners but not the number of households who would require a public transport service to visit the store. Similarly, a database might provide number of dogs in a locality but not the number of dog owners. Where a variation in the basis of the data is identified, then it is necessary for the relevant specialist section in the company to make an assumption and provide a correcting factor to the data (e.g. assume that each dog owner has 1.2 dogs).

A specialist database can provide information that affects the variables involved in major marketing and stocking decisions. For example, a motor factor chain of companies considering whether to have 'own label' goods supplied, would be influenced by the sales volumes of different car models and manufacturers. Also, the motor factor would seek to learn the replacement period for each model in order to gauge order and stock quantities. If there is uncertainty regarding the validity or accuracy of the information then decisions would be qualified.

Market research is concerned with understanding consumer attitudes towards the company's products and its competitors. A market researcher seeks to understand and measure the size and characteristics of the market. Although most market research information is collected external to the company (e.g. Nielsen data, consumer panels, etc.), an important source can be the control data in the company's central database.

A central database would typically hold historical information such as:

1   sales levels analysed by month, region, type of outlets, grade of goods, etc

2   prices and discounts

3   growth of demand in various segments of the market

4   cost profile of products

5   marketing spend

6   production levels and stock levels.

Although this information is historical, it provides the market researcher with a base from which to check sales forecasts. Knowledge of a company's production performance (e.g. high wastage with a particular size or blend) can assist a market researcher in providing more meaningful sales performance indicators.

Cost information can often be important; a comparison of budgeted and actual costs may indicate the need for a price rise. The central data held on database would enable the market researcher to check back on the effect on sales of a previous price increase.

In summary, central data from a company's database is an important secondary source of information for market research.

3.3   Economic models

Economic models are frequently used by marketeers to test responses of company sales figures to variations in underlying factors. Most economic models that are familiar to the general businessman are macro-economic models that reflect economy changes as a whole. An economic model is usually formulated from analysis of historical data and is constantly updated. It is a complex and major exercise to create a macro-economic model, e.g. the London Business School model of the UK economy.

Once a model is functioning the parameters are self-adjusting so that each initiative envisaged by the company can be tested under different parameter conditions. For example, the effect upon furniture sales of a falling £ may lead some households to refurnish rather than take continental holidays. This effect could be evaluated in the model against different rates of interest (1989 shows the strong depressing effect of high interest rates on furniture sales).

The special value of a model to a marketer is, therefore, that each separate marketing initiative can be gauged in many different scenarios, each of which could involve several factors.

Other economic models can be developed within a company: for example, to maximise production of a family of products from limited production capacity. The marketer is keenly interested in the interrelationships within such a production model and would provide some of the parameters upon which the model is based. The marketeer would also need to be aware of the output of the model in making his marketing decisions.

Some economic models are predictive and can extrapolate current information into future forecasts. Such predictions are relevant as a basis for marketing plans.

A major danger with all economic models (especially predictive versions) is the incompleteness of the parameters. It is difficult to incorporate all possible parameters and to state the interaction between them. The use of models for budgeting purposes is therefore limited. A marketer will use a model to test ideas and as a basis for a marketing strategy but not for detailed planning and control.

3.4 Use of the Internet

The World Wide Web is an extremely powerful medium for all marketing activity – planning, research, market segmentation and targeting, positioning, building customer satisfaction, designing, pricing, promoting, and placing product. Apart from these, there are as well as some particular benefits to be enjoyed by connecting to the Internet and using WWW. Those are: improve corporate image, improve customer service, find new prospects, increase visibility, perform transactions, expand company market, meet customer expectations, reduce cost, get up to speed before it was too late.

The WWW is a pull medium, not push medium. By definition promotional mix is affected by whether the company chooses 'push' or 'pull' strategy. The Web provides information to people who might be willing to reach in and pull it out.

Online marketing differs from traditional marketing in many important respects.

- **It is an interactive process.** Instead of creating a message for the lowest common denominator, as does broadcast advertising, online marketers can create interactive catalogues that allow the consumer to choose the information he wants to see, when she wants to see. Companies can create interactive sales materials that meet the needs of every type of consumer.

- **Consumers are actively engaged in many dynamic activities.** They can control their navigation through interactive video, they can leave feedback, send e-mail, leave comments, orders, etc. Communication is two-way, not one way.

- **Electronic marketing is part of virtual reality.** As Virtual Reality Transfer Protocols (VRTP) becomes available virtual showrooms and product demonstrations can become part of the Web. The consumer can walk through a mall and talk to his personal digital assistant.

- **Web marketing is direct marketing.** Market aggregation is somewhat different than in conventional marketing. The Internet is not generally understood as a mass market; rather it involves one-to-one promotion.

- **Marketing research is facilitated by Web technology.** Customer surveys, product interest and reaction surveys can be carried out automatically. Web marketing provides fast feedback from potential and actual customers. This can assist with product development and niche information for product placement. Logging of a mall or storefront may include automatic data collection and statistic manipulation.

- **Electronic marketing offers new forms of public relations**. It is increasingly common to do short informational releases of new products and services online, giving your page's URL to refer inquiries for more information. These releases are typically posted to appropriate newsgroups and to mailing lists such as net-happenings. Another promotional activity is that of page sponsorship for conferences, public information, government or non-profits. By sponsoring a homepage for a large event sponsors gain considerable visibility for their company, products or services

- **Web advertising is different from the conventional one.** In traditional media advertising is everywhere. On the Internet intrusive or aggressive advertising is not permitted by AUPs and is strongly disliked by the citizens of the network – potential customers. On the Internet, advertising is accomplished by gaining visibility. Making your page a good place to visit is the best Internet advertisement.

Interactive marketing via a website has the following advantages over traditional direct marketing:

- A trading website is always open. There is no downtime to re-stock, correct programming errors or repair broken links to other business systems.

- A website deals with customers in real time, raising expectations of instant query resolution, immediate response to requests and, even faster delivery. Furthermore customer interaction data is being gathered continuously.

- A website can be personalised to a greater degree than personalised print. It can be based on a variety of data sources (e.g. cookies, clickstream, personal data and previous purchases) and used within a single site visit if appropriate.

- A website can collect much higher volumes of data of different types than can be collected from other reception points. This poses a systems integration problem and a potentially crippling data volume problem.

- Customers do not phone call centres just for a chat. But the Internet is different. It is open, democratic and even revolutionary. The plus side may be viral marketing. The downside could be flaming (abusive replies).

- Comparison shopping is so easy. The pricing policy may need to be changed for interactive marketing.

- The reach of the website may be wide but logistical or legal constraints may apply. It may be necessary to restrict orders geographically.

- The cost of handling on-line orders and information requests is much lower. This may permit lower ticket or lower margin transactions. However, credit card payment queries will be high and delivery costs will remain the same.

While the Internet has great power for marketing, it also has the power to damage your business's reputation. Sending unsolicited message to newsgroups or mailing lists can result in angry responses from those on the Net. Negative posting about your company to key discussion lists and groups can reach millions within hours.

3.5 Other forms of electronic marketing

As well as the obvious use of websites to advertise products and process sales, there are other ways a website can be used for marketing purposes:

Discussion Lists. The Internet discussion lists are a method for individuals to network with others on a focused topic. Having your own discussion list will provide opportunities for professional networking, and large-scale distribution of information (newsletters).

Usenet Newsgroups. The best approach is to locate groups by getting their FAQ and reading their charters. This will tell you more about the groups, including whether advertisements or product announcements are permitted.

Companies can learn a lot about the norms and culture of the network by monitoring a number of groups. You can also create your own group under the existing usenet hierarchies.

Mail Servers and E-mail. The mail server is an automated mail reply feature that can automatically return message to someone requested information. Because the e-mail message is being requested the reply can be made context-sensitive to the specific needs of the customer.

Announcements. Many companies make regular announcements to various newsgroups regarding the availability of product information. These announcements include only general information and are usually used to drive the customers' attention to more specific topics.

FAQ. These are documents that present a compilation of frequently asked questions and answers to these questions. These documents are developed so that regular readers of the postings to a usenet group or discussion list would not have to see the same questions and same answers month after month. FAQ usually play an important role in customer support services where the same questions are asked by several groups of customers.

Greeting Cards. They can be viewed as a variation of an e-mail message. Some companies are using them as mailings to current customers. They should not be sent to individuals who do not already have a relationship with your business

Newsletters and 'Zines. Electronic newsletters are used to provide information of all kinds to current and potential customers. Most newsletters are distributed upon request through e-mail, listservs, or Gophers. Many are attached at FTP sites. Some newsletters are redistributed on Usenet. Electronic 'zines are small magazines created to grab attention.

3.6   Security and other issues

While Internet connectivity offers enormous benefits in terms of increased access to information, Internet connectivity is dangerous for sites with low levels of security. The Internet suffers from glaring security problems that, if ignored, could have disastrous results for unprepared sites. Inherent problems with TCP/IP services, the complexity of host configuration, vulnerabilities introduced in the software development process, and a variety of other factors have all contributed to making unprepared sites open to intruder activity and related problems.

Organisations are, rightly concerned about the security implications of using the Internet: Problems include:

- Ease of eavesdropping and spoofing – the majority of Internet traffic is not encrypted. E-mail, passwords and file transfers can be monitored and captured using readily available software.

- Hackers disturbing internal systems.

- Valuable organisational data being compromised (changed or read) in transit.

- Systems being attacked by viruses and similar programes (worms, trojans, etc).

- Sites being copied by crooks who then get information on passwords from customers. The crooks then log on to the 'real' website and misappropriate funds.

3.7 Viral marketing

Viral marketing refers to ways in which businesses can get messages about their business to target audiences through 'word of mouth'. The use of the term 'viral' is based on the hope that the way the message spreads will be exponential in nature. For example, one person triggers the message to two others who in turn spread the word to another two friends who in turn do the same thing. Very quickly you are creating a massive growth in the number of people who are aware of your product.

Hotmail is a well-known example of the viral marketing technique. At the foot of the mail message received is the offer to get a free account. The expectation is that others will then open accounts as the network of messages begins to widen. You e-mail your friends; each of them opens up a Hotmail account and in turn e-mail their friends who do the same. It is not difficult to imagine the speed by which the 'viral' message spreads.

Other examples include short video advertisements that are amusing or outrageous enough for people to want to send them to their friends.

Activity 4

Outline how a car manufacturer could benefit from computerised assistance in selling cars.

Feedback to this activity is at the end of the chapter.

Summary

- An understanding of consumer needs and the mechanics of the buying process can assist firms in marketing their products more effectively.

- There are many differences between B2C and B2B marketing.

- The business contexts within which marketing principles can be applied include internal marketing, services marketing, direct marketing and interactive marketing.

- A service is any act or performance that one party can offer to another that is essentially intangible and does not result in the ownership of anything.

- New technology, in particular the Internet, has opened up many new marketing opportunities.

Having completed your study of this chapter, you should have achieved the following learning outcomes:

- evaluate the marketing processes of an organisation

- describe the business contexts within which marketing principles can be applied (consumer marketing, business-to-business marketing, services marketing, direct marketing, interactive marketing)

- evaluate the role of technology in modern marketing.

Self-test questions

1   When is a safety need a motivator? (1.1)

2   Outline the stages in the buying process. (1.3)

3   What is the difference between consumer marketing and business-to-business marketing? (2.1)

4   Identify three characteristics of services marketing. (2.2)

Practice questions

Question 1

ABC Group plc

The ABC Group plc manufacture specialist hinges but one of its problems is its inability to market its products successfully so as to gain a significant market share. It fails to use a corporate approach to marketing yet its more flexible company-specific approach does not provide it with the market penetration required. The group needs to be more knowledgeable about its markets and to be more focused in its approach to them.

Required:

(a)   Discuss the key differences between the industrial buying environment and the consumer goods buying environment, and show how knowledge of these differences can help ABC Group plc.   **(10 marks)**

(b)   Describe how ABC might effectively segment its industrial market, and discuss the criteria, which the company should consider in deciding upon the appropriate segments.   **(10 marks)**

(Total: 20 marks)

Question 2

Pains Fireworks

Pains Fireworks is one of the UK oldest companies. These days, most of its revenue comes from Firework displays, rather than the manufacturing of fireworks themselves. When asked about the marketing issues he faces, MD Bill Deeker said:

"You know how to buy a pair of shoes because you know what leather looks like, you know what good stitching looks like and you can pull the sole and the top and the upper apart to see if it's glued or stitched. You can't do that with firework displays because you're not buying the products when you're buying the display. You don't see it."

What are the additional factors to be taken into account when marketing services, rather than products?   **(20 marks)**

For the answers to these questions, see the 'Answers' section at the end of the book

Feedback to activities

Activity 1

A brick manufacturer's industrial market has characteristics that contrast sharply with consumer markets. These are described below:

(a) **Fewer buyers**

There are fewer buyers in the industrial market than in the consumer market. Although the ultimate users of houses and structures built from using bricks number in the millions, the company's fate critically depends on getting orders from perhaps only a few thousand property developers.

(b) **Large buyers**

Even in popular markets, a few large buyers normally account for most of purchasing. The buyers can thus exert some power over suppliers in terms of price fixing, distribution and product design. These buyers are often geographically concentrated.

(c) **Fluctuating demand**

The demand for industrial goods, such as bricks, tends to be more volatile than the demand for consumer goods and services. A certain change in consumer demand can lead to a much bigger percentage change in demand for the industrial good. Sometimes change in industrial demand can be over twenty times that of the consumer demand change. Economists refer to this as the **acceleration principle.**

(d) **Derived demand**

The demand for bricks is ultimately derived from the demand for houses and structures built using bricks. If the demand for these declines, so will the demand for bricks decline.

(e) **Inelastic demand**

The total demand for many industrial goods and services is not much affected by price changes. Property developers are not going to buy many less bricks if the price for bricks rises, unless they can find suitable substitutes such as glass, metal and wood. However, construction companies will use price to decide which suppliers to purchase from, although price levels will have less impact on the quantity purchased.

(f) **Rational buying**

Industrial goods are usually purchased by professional buyers, who are continually learning new methods of how to make better purchasing decisions. Consumers on the other hand are not so well trained in the art of careful buying.

(g) **Direct purchasing**

Industrial buyers often buy direct from producers rather than through middlemen

Activity 2

A public library might regard marketing success as an increase in demand, and a switch to book borrowing by the public from book buying or watching television, etc as a pastime.

Activity 3

Effective internal communications and internal marketing has the potential to really improve employee contributions by aligning what they do, how they do it and their values, with the direction of the organisation.

Activity 4

The following computerised assistance could help boost demand:

- Website-based selling that could reduce the overheads associated with a traditional showroom and allow the firm to offer lower priced vehicles. A website has the additional advantages of always being open and being able to show more detailed information, involving product reviews and comparisons.

- Viral marketing – the Citroën TV advert with a car performing a Justin Timberlake-style dance routine was originally a small video file that the firm hoped people would email to their friends as it was very original when it first came out.

- Maintaining a database of previous customers so they can be contacted directly to encourage them to replace their old cars with a new one.

- Use of emails to advertise ('spam').

- If 'computerised assistance' extends to enabling greater flexibility in the production process, then the sales staff can offer customers a greater range of choices without significantly delaying delivery times.

- The company can ensure that its stock is listed on various car search websites to enable customer and dealer to find each other. This is particularly useful for second hand and rare cars.

Chapter 14

MANAGING WORK ARRANGEMENTS

Syllabus content

- Theories of Human Resource Management (e.g. Taylor, Schein, McGregor, Maslow, Herzberg, Handy, Lawrence and Lorsch).

- High performance work arrangements.

- Issues in the design of reward systems (e.g. the role of incentives, the utility of performance-related pay, arrangements for knowledge workers, flexible work arrangements).

- Personal business ethics and the CIMA Ethical Guidelines.

- HR in different organisational forms.

Contents

1 Theories of human resource management

2 Contingency approaches

3 High performance work arrangements

4 Reward schemes

5 Ethics

1   Theories of human resource management (HRM)

Since strategies can only be implemented by and through people, the manner in which human resources are managed and co-ordinated is a central management challenge.

In general terms, there are two approaches to HRM theories:

The **industrial organisation approach:**

- is based on economic theory deals with issues like competitive rivalry, resource allocation, economies of scale

- assumptions – rationality, self interested behaviour, profit maximisation.

The **sociological approach:**

- deals primarily with human interactions

- assumptions – bounded rationality, satisfying behaviour, profit sub-optimality.

HRM theories can also be divided into those that concentrate mainly on efficiency and those that concentrate mainly on effectiveness. **Efficiency** is about doing things the right way. It involves eliminating waste and optimising processes. **Effectiveness** is about doing the right things. There is no point in acting efficiently if what you are doing will not have the desired effect. A good strategy will blend both efficiency and effectiveness. This distinction is linked to the formulation/implementation distinction made above. We will Taylor, Schein, McGregor, Maslow, Herzberg, Handy, Lawrence and Lorsch.

1.1   Taylor

Frederick Taylor was an American engineer who invented scientific management, which consisted of rationalising organisational behaviour through extensive and detailed task analysis, systems and routines. He took the view that there is a right (meaning best) way to perform any task. It is management's job to determine the right way. Workers gain from this approach because the 'right way' is easier and pay is enhanced as a result of increased productivity. Taylor considered welfare to be of secondary importance; he firmly believed in high-priced man. His four underlying principles of scientific management are:

- A science of work to replace old methods – the best way of doing a job. Fulfilling optimum goals would earn higher wages; failure to do so would result in a loss of earnings.

- Scientific selection and development of the worker – training each to be first class at some job.

- Bringing together the science of work and the scientifically selected and trained workers for best results. Then co-operating with the man so as to ensure all of the work being done is in accordance with the principles of scientific management.

- Equal division of work and responsibility between workers and management, co-operating in close interdependence. The management should take over all the work for which they are better fitted than the workmen.

While Taylor's principles have a certain logic, most applications of it fail to account for two inherent difficulties:

- it ignores individual differences: the most efficient way of working for one person may be inefficient for another;

- it ignores the fact that the economic interests of workers and management are rarely identical, so that both the measurement processes and the retraining required by Taylor's methods would frequently be resented and sometimes sabotaged by the workforce.

1.2 Schein's view of employee behaviour

Edgar Schein believed that if a manager wants to motivate employees successfully, the way the employees actually behave must match the way the manager thinks that they behave. He suggested that management ideas about how people behave could be grouped into four sets.

- **Rational-economic man** – This view states that the pursuit of self-interest and the maximisation of gain are the prime motivators of people. It lays stress on man's rational calculation of self-interest, especially in relation to economic needs. The implications for motivating seem to be a reward system based on methods of recognition for individual performance.

- **Social man** – This view sees people as predominantly motivated by social needs and finding their identity through relationships with others. Acceptance of this view by managers concentrates on 'people needs' rather than 'task needs'. Studies have shown that productivity and morale can be improved by fostering social relationships in order to improve co-operation and teamwork. Attention should be given to the dynamics of formal and informal group formation in the enterprise. Further, the role of the manager changes from controller, commander and organiser to guide, supporter and facilitator of better individual and group performance.

- **Self-actualising man** – relates to the highest level of Maslow's pyramid of needs and derives from the idea that the driving force is to satisfy basic needs. The managerial strategy that follows from this approach is to provide the right demanding, challenging and rewarding work. It aims for greater responsibility and autonomy at work. This strategy can be seen today in many companies' reduction of the number of levels in the management structure, establishing two-way communication channels to ensure high levels of involvement and participation in decision-making, increasing flexibility and responsibility, and increasing the amount of choice and accountability given to the employee.

- **Complex man** – this view sees people as being more complex and variable than the previous ones. The requirement for management is an ability to diagnose the various motives that may be at work with their staff.

1.3 McGregor's Theories

Douglas McGregor presented **two opposite sets of assumptions** implicit in most approaches to management, which he called **Theory X** and **Theory Y**. These theories are opposite ends of a continuum.

- **Theory X:** assumes that people dislike work and responsibility. Therefore they must be coerced, controlled, directed and/or threatened with punishment to get them to make an effort towards achievement of organisational objectives. Managers assume that subordinates prefer to be directed, wish to avoid responsibility, have relatively little ambition, and want security above all.

- **Theory Y:** assumes that physical and mental effort in work is as natural as play or rest. The average human being does not inherently dislike work, because it can be a source of satisfaction. Managers assume control and the threat of punishment are not the only means of bringing about effort towards organisational objectives. People can exercise self-direction and self-control to achieve objectives to which they are committed.

Theory X is the traditional approach greatly influenced by the results of specialisation, standardisation and mass production techniques. Jobs have been sub-divided to such an extent that initiative and discretion have been reduced; conformity, obedience and dependence have been demanded from the members of the organisation. This appears to be the approach of the scientific managers and classical theorists and the supporters of Weber's type of bureaucracy.

1.4 Maslow's theory

Abraham Maslow proposed that humans possess unique qualities that enable them to make independent choices, thus giving them control of their destiny.

He advanced the following propositions about human behaviour:

- The behaviour of an individual at a particular time is influenced by his or her needs.

- The strongest need is likely to have the greatest influence on his or her behaviour.

Maslow identified a **hierarchy of human needs** that individuals pursue in a predicted sequence. He showed how an individual's emphasis on needs moved from basic to the higher needs as satisfaction at that lower level occurred.

Maslow's hierarchy of needs

The peak of each level must be passed before the next level can begin to assume a dominant role. Needs do not have to be completely satisfied before higher needs emerge, a sufficient level of satisfaction is acceptable as opposed to the maximum or optimum level. Maslow's theory may be summarised and simplified by saying that everyone wants certain things throughout life, and these can be placed in five ascending categories, namely:

- **Basic or physiological needs** – The things needed to stay alive: food, shelter and clothing. Such needs can be satisfied by money.

- **Safety or security needs** – People want protection against unemployment, the consequences of sickness and retirement as well as being safeguarded against unfair treatment. These needs can be satisfied by the rules of employment, i.e. pension scheme, sick fund, employment legislation etc

---

KEY POINT

Maslow identified the following human needs: **physiological, safety, relationships, esteem** and **self-actualisation.** He arranged these as a hierarchy: **Maslow's hierarchy of needs.**

- **Social needs** – The vast majority of people want to be part of a group and it is only through group activity that this need can be satisfied. Thus the way that work is organised, enabling people to feel part of a group, is fundamental to satisfaction of this need.

- **Ego needs** – These needs may be expressed as wanting the esteem of other people and thinking well of oneself. While status and promotion can offer short-term satisfaction, building up the job itself and giving people a greater say in how their work is organised gives satisfaction of a more permanent nature. An example might be being asked to lead groups on a course.

- **Self-fulfilment needs** – This is quite simply the need to achieve something worthwhile in life. It is a need that is satisfied only by continuing success, for example opening and running a new office.

The significance of Maslow's hierarchy of needs is that it underlines the relative importance of money. Status gives little satisfaction to a person desperate for food and shelter. Equally it demonstrates that money alone is not enough, and indeed as basic and safety needs become satisfied people are likely to concentrate their attentions on social and ego needs.

1.5 Herzberg's theory of motivation

Herzberg's theory of motivation is known as a two-factor theory. It is based on the idea that motivation is based on two needs, namely, hygiene factors and motivational factors. The 'hygiene' factors are those to do with non-job related features such as the working environment, whilst the motivational factors are those concerned with a need for personal development.

The most important part of this theory of motivation is that the main motivation factors are not in the environment but in the intrinsic value and satisfaction gained from the job itself.

Herzberg considers the following factors to be determinants of job satisfaction and therefore 'motivators':

- a sense of achievement and the intrinsic value obtained from the job itself
- the attraction of the job itself
- the level of recognition by both colleagues and management
- the level of responsibility
- opportunities for advancement and the status provided.

Motivators lead to satisfaction because of the need for growth and a sense of self-achievement.

Hygiene factors are also often referred to as 'dissatisfiers'. They are concerned with extrinsic factors associated with the job itself but are not directly a part of it. The important fact to remember is that attention to these hygiene factors prevents dissatisfaction but does not necessarily provide positive motivation. Typically, salary is given as an example of a 'dissatisfier', however, others might include:

- perceived differences with others
- job security and working conditions
- the quality of management
- organisational policy
- administration and interpersonal relationships.

Such extrinsic factors attract people to the job and persuade them to remain – the 'golden handcuffs' of many organisations.

As distinctly separate factors are associated with job satisfaction and job dissatisfaction, Herzberg concluded that the two feelings are not the opposite of one another, but that they are concerned with two different ranges of an individual's needs.

Hygiene factors are purely preventive: if the organisation provides them it will prevent the workers from being dissatisfied with their job, but they will not motivate positively. To help them to do creative, satisfying, responsible work the organisation must provide motivators.

Herzberg defines three avenues that management can follow in attempting to improve staff satisfaction and motivation.

KEY POINT

Herzberg proposed **job enrichment**, **job enlargement** and **job rotation** to improve satisfaction and motivation.

- **Job enrichment** (sometimes called 'vertical job enlargement') – a deliberate, planned process to improve the responsibility, challenge and creativity of a job. Typical examples include delegation or problem solving. For instance, where an accountant's responsibilities for producing quarterly management reports end at the stage of producing the figures, they could be extended so that they included the preparation of them and the accountant could submit them to senior management. This alteration in responsibilities could not only enrich the job but also increase the workload, leading to delegation of certain responsibilities to clerks within the department, the cascading effect enriching other jobs as well.

- **Job enlargement** – widening the range of jobs, and so developing a job away from narrow specialisation. There is no element of enrichment. Argyris calls this 'horizontal job enlargement'. Herzberg contends that there is little motivation value in this approach.

- **Job rotation** – the planned rotating of staff between jobs to alleviate monotony and provide a fresh job challenge. The documented example quotes a warehouse gang of four workers, where the worst job was tying the necks of the sacks at the base of the hopper after filling; the best job was seen as being the forklift truck driver. Job rotation would ensure that equal time was spent by each individual on all jobs. Herzberg suggests that this will help to relieve monotony and improve job satisfaction but is unlikely to create positive motivation.

Activity 1

List the hierarchy of needs and hygiene/motivation factors. What parallels can you draw between the two approaches?

Feedback to this activity is at the end of the chapter.

KEY POINT

Handy argues that **psychological contracts** exist between individuals and organisations. Needs will be met in return for their energy and talent. Contracts can be classified as **coercive**, **calculative** and **co-operative**.

1.6 Handy's psychological contracts

Psychological contracts exist between individuals and the organisations to which they belong, be they work or social, and normally take the form of implied and unstated expectations. According to **Handy**, individuals have sets of results that they expect from organisations, results that will satisfy certain of their needs and in return for which they will expend some of their energies and talents. Similarly, organisations have sets of expectations of individuals and its list of payments and outcomes that it will give to them.

An individual belonging to more than one organisation will have more than one psychological contract. Only if each contract is perceived identically by all parties will conflict be avoided.

Psychological contracts can be classified as follows:

- **Coercive contracts** – which are not freely entered into and where a small group exercise control by rule and punishment. Although the usual form is found in prisons and other custodial institutions, coercive contracts exist also in schools and factories.

- **Calculative contracts** – where control is retained by management and is expressed in terms of their ability to give to the individual 'desired things' such as money, promotion and social opportunities. Most employees of industrial organisations 'enter into' such a contract.

KEY POINT

All behaviour is motivated. Our performance of a task is the product of ability and motivation.

- **Co-operative contracts** – where the individual tends to identify with the goals of the organisation and strive for their attainment. In return the individual receives just rewards, a voice in the selection of goals and a choice of the means to achieve such goals. Most enlightened organisations are moving towards such contracts but it must be emphasised that if they are to be effective, then the workers must also want them – if such a contract is imposed on the workforce, it becomes a coercive contract.

In all cases the employees must know the results of their increased efforts and the management must understand the individual's needs.

1.7 Lawrence and Lorsch

Lawrence and Lorsch claim that managing an organisation consists of two basic processes, which they term differentiation and integration:

Differentiation can be defined as 'the state of segmentation of the organisation into sub-systems, each of which tends to develop particular attributes in relation to the requirements posed by its relevant external environment.'

Differentiation occurs through a division of labour and technical specialisation. However, too much differentiation causes miscommunication, conflict and politics.

Integration is 'the process of achieving unity of effort among the various subsystems in the accomplishment of the organisational tasks'. Integration occurs when specialists co-operate to achieve a common goal. Integration is essential for utility of direction – towards the common goal.

Lawrence and Lorsch's view of integration was not the minimising of differences between departments and the provision of a common outlook. It was the recognition that different departments could have their own distinctive form of structure according to the nature of their task, and the use of mediating devices to co-ordinate the different outlooks of departments.

In their study of the firms in the plastics industry, Lawrence and Lorsch found a clear differentiation between the major departments of R&D, production and sales.

- **R&D** – was more concerned with the long-run view and was confronted with pressures for new ideas and product innovation. The department operated in a dynamic, scientific environment and had the least bureaucratic structure.

- **Production** – was more concerned with the short-term problems such as quality control and meeting delivery dates. The department operated in a fairly stable, technical environment and had the most bureaucratic structure.

- **Sales** – was in the middle between research and production. The department was concerned with chasing production and had a moderately stable market environment.

The aim of the study was to discover what forms of organisation structure were required for different environments. It was concluded that the extent of differentiation and integration in effective organisations would vary according to the demands of the particular environment.

- The more diverse and dynamic the environment, the more the effective organisation will be differentiated and highly integrated.

- In more stable environments, less differentiation will be required but a high degree of integration is still required. Differences in the environment will require different methods of achieving integration.

2 Contingency approaches

2.1 The contingency way of thinking

Lawrence and Lorsch (1967) coined the label *contingency theory* to capture the notion that different environmental contexts place different requirements on organisations. Contingency 'theorists' do not ignore the lessons learnt from earlier theories, but adapt them to suit particular circumstances. Their approach is to identify the conditions of tasks (scientific management school), managerial jobs (administrative management school) and persons (human relations school) as parts of a complete management situation and attempt to integrate them all into the solution that is most appropriate for a specific circumstance.

2.2 Contingent factors

There are three types of contingent factor:

Environment will affect the control system according to the degree of predictability (control systems are more helpful to management where the organisation operates in a relatively stable environment), the degree of competition in the market place and the number of different products/markets. A competitive market will require more sophisticated systems of control.

Organisational structure includes size and the degree of decentralisation. As the organisation gets bigger it will tend to require more formal controls

Technology factors include the degree of mechanisation of the production process and the length of the production run. Organisations with large batch and mass production may require a very formal control system.

2.3 Concept of contingency

The concept of contingency implies that there is no one, absolute 'best' design - rather, there are many possibilities and the best or preferred choice will be contingent on the situation being analysed. Universal models designed to suit all situations are therefore rejected. This is consistent with the fact that most organisations are networks of a variety of bits of design rather than conforming, as one entity, to a particular model. So we might find units of bureaucracy, units of matrix structures, units with project teams, units with extremely loose, almost *ad hoc* structures – and all these within, say, the same company. In this sense, the contingency theorists merely reflected the findings of hundreds of researchers. There are common elements in the hierarchies of different organisations but there are also very many differences peculiar to the local situation.

The most appropriate structure is dependent, therefore, upon the contingencies of the situation for each individual organisation. These situational factors account for variations in the structure of different organisations.

2.4 Flexibility in work organisation

Whatever the criticisms or limitations of contingency models, the application of modern contingency theory can help contribute to more effective performance. The effects of increased economic pressures and demands for greater competitiveness have drawn attention to the importance of structural variables. The nature of work is being redefined and this has created strong pressures for greater flexibility in patterns of work organisation and the workforce.

According to Atkinson, organisations are looking for three kinds of flexibility:

- **functional flexibility** to permit the rapid redeployment of employees among different activities and tasks (perhaps involving the practice of multi-skilling)

- **numerical flexibility** to restructure and adjust the number of employees to match the level of demand for labour

- **financial flexibility** so that pay and other employment costs reflect the supply and demand of labour and in order to shift to new pay and remuneration systems.

As a result, Atkinson suggests that flexible firms have attempted to develop an organisation structure based on a central, stable 'core' group of full-time permanent career employees who undertake the organisation's key, firm-specific activities and with emphasis on functional flexibility; supported by peripheral and numerically flexible groups of workers including agency temporaries, subcontracting, self-employed and part-time staff, whose numbers, in theory, can expand or contract according to market conditions.

2.5 Handy's shamrock organisation

An example of Handy's changing perception of organisations is provided by his use of the shamrock. Handy uses this symbol to demonstrate three bases on which people are often employed and organisations often linked today. People linked to an organisation are beginning to fall into three groups. Each has different expectations of the organisation and each are managed and rewarded differently.

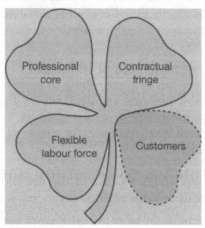

Representation of Handy's shamrock organisation

KEY POINT

The professional core are essential to the continuity of the organisation, and have detailed knowledge of it, and of its aims, objectives and practices.

Professional core – the first group is a core of qualified professional technicians and managers. They are essential to the continuity of the organisation, and have detailed knowledge of it, and of its aims, objectives and practices. They are rewarded with high salaries and associated benefits, in return for which they must be prepared to give commitment, to work hard and to work, if necessary, long hours. They must be mobile. They work within a task culture, one within which there is a constant effort to reduce their numbers.

Contractual fringe – the second group consists of contracted specialists who may be used, for example, for advertising, R&D, computing, catering and mailing services. They operate in an existential culture; and are rewarded with fees rather than with salaries or wages. Their contribution to the organisation is measured in output rather than in hours, in results rather than in time.

Flexible labour force – represents all those part-time and temporary workers who make up the fastest growing group in the pattern of employment. It provides for flexibility in human resourcing. People are brought in as occasional extra part-time labour or temporary staff as changing work situations demand. Their commitment will be to a job and work group rather than to a career or organisation. Part-time or temporary work may be a matter of choice, not just a necessity.

The increase in the flexible labour force is particularly noticeable with the growth of flexible service industries. Services are created and consumed simultaneously. Unlike manufacturing, services are time-perishable and cannot be stored. The flexible labour force has increasingly been used as a cheaper and more convenient means of dealing with the peaks and troughs of demands, and as a means of adjusting the level of service to match changing customer requirements.

Customers – Handy considered adding customers as a possible fourth leaf in his shamrock organisational model because in many service businesses the customer is asked to do some of the work (e.g. filling in forms; monitoring service quality; or even serving themselves). However, he decided to exclude them because they are not paid by the organisation so this fourth leaf cannot exist as part of the formal structure of the shamrock.

The concept of the shamrock organisation can encourage managers to question the operations of their organisations. It gives rise to important decisions concerning what activities, and which people, should belong to the core; and concerning the management and control of sub-contracting, and of the flexible workforce.

Activity 2

Could you put forward an argument to suggest that the organisation does pay customers?

Feedback to this activity is at the end of the chapter.

3 High performance work arrangements

High performance can be described as producing results much better than expected both in individuals and in organisations. The essence of high performance work arrangements is reliance on all organisational members for their ideas, intelligence, and commitment to making the organisation successful.

High performance work organisations seek to elicit the discretionary effort of workers by giving them:

- the opportunity to participate in decisions

- autonomy, self-directed teams, offline teams, communication structures

- training and skills

- formal and informal training, education, employment tenure

- incentives and motivation

- pay for performance, employment security, promotion opportunities.

3.1 High performance job designs

Job design is the process by which managers plan and specify job tasks and the work arrangements through which they are accomplished. The best job design is the one that:

- meets organisational requirements for high performance

- offers a good fit with individual skills and needs

- provides opportunities for job satisfaction.

Job simplification standardises work procedures and employs people in clearly defined and highly specialised tasks. The intent is to increase efficiency, but it may in fact be decreased due to the motivational impact of unappealing jobs.

When designing high performance jobs we should look at the following:

- The **alternative job design approaches** include job enlargement, job rotation and job enrichment. Job enlargement increases task variety by combining into one job two or more tasks that were previously assigned to separate workers. Job rotation increases task variety by periodically shifting workers among jobs involving different tasks. Enlargement and rotation use horizontal loading to increase job breadth.

- The **keys to designing motivating jobs** means identifying the core job characteristics that are particularly important to job design eg, skill variety, task identity and significance and autonomy. Combined together, the core job characteristics create a motivating potential score (MPS). MPS indicates the degree to which the job is capable of motivating people.

- **Technology and how it influences job design** – sociotechnical systems reflect the importance of integrating people and technology to create high performance work systems. These are essential for new developments in job design, given the impact of computers and information technology in the modern workplace. Automation and robotics can be used instead of people to do highly simplified jobs that lack intrinsic motivation. Flexible manufacturing systems are adaptive computer-based technologies and integrated job designs that are used to shift work easily and quickly among alternative products. Workers develop expertise across a wide range of functions and the jobs offer a wealth of potential for enriched core job characteristics. Electronic offices offer job enrichment possibilities for workers equipped to handle the technology.

- **Goal setting** can improve performance. Goals are important aspects of any job design. They are needed to give proper direction to workers. Goal setting is the process of developing, negotiating, and formalising the targets or objectives that a person is responsible for accomplishing.

3.2 Alternative work arrangements

The movement towards tighter and leaner organisations has drawn attention to the importance of alternative forms of structure and placed increased emphasis on the demand for flexibility. Alternative work arrangements are designed to influence employee satisfaction and help employees balance the demands of their work and non-work lives. They include:

- **Compressed work weeks** involve any scheduling of work that allows a full-time job to be completed in fewer than the standard five days. Four days amounting to 40 hours (4/40) is the most common form. The advantages for workers is added time off and lower commuting costs. For organisations it means lower absenteeism and improved recruiting of new employees. The disadvantages for workers is increased fatigue and family adjustment problems. For organisations it is work scheduling problems, customer complaints, and possible union opposition.

- **Flexible working hours** – also known as flexitime – give individuals a daily choice in the timing of their work commitments. It is becoming an increasingly popular valuable alternative for structuring work to accommodate individual interests and needs. The advantages for workers include shorter commuting time, more leisure time, more job satisfaction, and greater sense of responsibility. For organisations it means less absenteeism, tardiness, and turnover; more commitment; and higher performance.

- **Job sharing** – one full-time job is assigned to two or more persons who divide the work according to agreed-upon hours. This can be done on a daily, weekly, or monthly basis. It is practiced by a relatively small percentage of employers. The advantages for workers are less burnout and higher energy level. For organisations it can mean attracting talented people who would otherwise be unable to work.

- **Work sharing** is different from job sharing. It occurs when workers agree to cut back on the number of hours they work in order to protect against layoffs.

- **Telecommuting** is work done at home or in a remote location via use of computers and advanced communication linkages with a central office or other employment locations. Variants of telecommuting include Flexiplace, Hotelling and the virtual office. The individual works 'from the road' and while traveling from place-to-place or customer-to-customer by car or airplane or the worker remains linked electronically to the home office. The advantages for workers include flexibility, the comforts of home, and choice of work locations consistent with one's lifestyle. For organisations it means costs savings, efficiency, and improved employee satisfaction. The disadvantages for workers include isolation from co-workers, decreased identification with work team, and technical difficulties with computer linkages.

- **Part-time** arrangement enables an employee to work less than a standard full-time schedule per week. This appeals to people who want to supplement other jobs or do not want full-time work. For organisations it means lower labour costs, ability to better accommodate peaks and troughs of business cycle, and better management of retention quality. The disadvantages for workers is added stress and potentially diminished performance if holding two jobs, failure to qualify for benefits, and lower pay rates than full-time counterparts.

KEY POINT

Alternative forms of structure include **compressed work weeks, flexible working hours, job and work sharing, telecommuting and part time, V time, gradual retirement, leave and sabbaticals.**

- **Voluntary reduced work time (V time)** is a time/income trade-off that gives employees a range of choices for reducing their hours (and income) by a fixed percentage over a set period of time. V-time programmes incorporate a variety of work reduction percentages, typically 2.5, 5, 10, 20, 25, or 40 percent of full-time. Employees may be given a choice of time off in the form of a shorter work day, shorter work week, or extended vacation time. Employees are usually given periodic opportunities (every three, six, or twelve months) to enroll/renew and must commit for a fixed amount of time (six or twelve months for example) to facilitate staff planning. V-time can be a creative alternative to lay-offs by spreading the available work around.

- **Gradual retirement** allows employees to reduce their working hours or reduce their workload over a period of time rather than switching from full time employment to retirement abruptly. This phased period can be used to train the replacement employee, help others adjust to restructuring within the company, or to adjust for the redistribution of tasks among the remaining employees.

- **Leave and sabbaticals** are authorised periods of time away from work without loss of employment rights. Paid or unpaid leave is usually granted for family, health care, education or leisure reasons. Sabbaticals are usually paid (or partially funded) and occur on a regular basis in addition to vacation time. In some cases, self-funded leave is also possible where a portion of the employee's salary is withheld and returned to the employee 'as pay' during the time away from work.

Activity 3

Under what category of job design would you place flexi-time?

Feedback to this activity is at the end of the chapter.

4 Reward schemes

4.1 Reward systems

KEY POINT

Achievement of high performance may be through **positive rewards** or the fear of job insecurity.

Management action is usually designed to keep staff highly motivated to meet their performance standards. Achievement of high performance may be through offering **positive rewards**. Equally, achievement may be through the employees having the perception that if they do not perform up to standard, then something unpleasant may result. It may be reduced pay, less chance of promotion, or in the current world employment climate, reduced job security or no job at all. Either way, it is important to identify opportunities for development and advancement and conduct regular performance reviews so that performance can be monitored.

4.2 Money as a motivator

KEY POINT

Pay can be related to motivation in the theories of **Maslow,** and **Herzberg**.

Money in the form of pay is a powerful motivator and can be viewed as all embracing, as a basis for comparison or as a reinforcement. The multiple meanings of **pay** can be related to the motivational theories examined as follows:

- **Maslow** – Pay is unique in that it can satisfy all types of need: directly, in the case of lower-level needs, and otherwise indirectly; for example, the prestige of being on a high salary level can be a source of ego-fulfilment.

- **Herzberg** – Pay is normally viewed as a hygiene factor but it can be a motivator when it occurs as a merit increase that gives special recognition for a job well done.

The most direct use of money as a motivator is payment by results schemes in which an employee's pay is directly linked to their results. All such schemes are dependent upon the belief that people will work harder to obtain more money.

4.3 Purchasing power and status

KEY POINT

Money is important not only for its **purchasing power** but also as a **status indicator**.

In discussing **money** as a motivator it is necessary to recognise its effects at two levels.

- Money, in absolute terms, is important because of its **purchasing power**. It is what money can buy that gives it value. Because money can be exchanged for satisfaction of needs, money can symbolise almost any need an individual wants it to represent. The next increase in salary could mean affording a better car, or an extra holiday.

- Money is also important as an **indication** of **status**. Increasing differentials between jobs creates feelings of a senior status in the person enjoying the higher salary. Money is a means of keeping score.

4.4 Non-financial motivators

KEY POINT

Non-financial motivators might be **participation**, **quality of work life** and **job design**.

We have already noted the content theories of Herzberg etc., which point to the job itself as a source of motivation. The job content can be interesting and challenging. It can meet needs for advancement, social standing, professional recognition, self-esteem, etc. This can sometimes compensate for lower earnings and cause people to hold back from pursuing a higher-paid position because the job content is seen to be less interesting. Examples of **non-financial motivators** are:

- **Participation** – This is frequently quoted as a means of stimulating motivation. There is no doubt that being involved in the actions and decisions that affect them motivates people. Participation is also a recognition of the value of staff, since it provides a sense of accomplishment and 'being needed'. A manager seeking to raise performance by increasing motivation could involve staff in the planning and inspection aspects of the work encouraging staff to participate in the design of the work planning schedules. Staff would be motivated to achieve the targets that they had helped establish.

- **Quality of work life** – The approach is a very wide-ranging application of the principles of job enrichment. The intention is to improve all aspects of work life, especially job design, work environment, leadership attitudes, work planning and industrial relations. It is an all-embracing systems approach, which usually starts with a joint management and staff group looking at the dignity, interest and productivity of jobs.

- **Job design** – As we have already noted, Herzberg defines three avenues that management can follow in attempting to improve staff satisfaction and motivation: job enrichment, job enlargement and job rotation.

4.5 Performance-related pay incentives

KEY POINT

Examples of incentives built into payment schemes are:

- piecework or payment by results
- measured day work
- commission
- productivity plans
- profit sharing.

Performance pay schemes cover the various methods of linking pay to a measure of individual, group or organisational performance. They all share the idea that where a worker can vary output according to effort the prospect of increased pay will lead to greater performance. There are many such schemes in existence, some of the most popular being:

(a) **Piecework or payment by results** – where employees are paid according to their output. There are a number of variations possible but the schemes all pay employees for either the number of items produced (or quantity of output) or for the completion of work in less than the allowed time. The bonus may be paid either to the individual or to the group.

(b) **Measured day work** where the pay of the employee is fixed, on the understanding that a specified level of output will be maintained. This level of performance, known as the 'incentive level', is calculated in advance and the employee is put under an obligation to achieve the level specified so that pay does not vary from week to week.

(c) **Commission** is a form of payment by results scheme paid on sales achieved or on profits gained from sales.

(d) **Productivity plans** involve some extra payment based on the success of employees in reducing costs, increasing production or expanding sales, usually measured by some overall index (e.g. company or divisional performance). There are a number of such plans e.g. Scanlon or Added Value.

(e) **Individual performance related pay** (IPRP): bonus earnings or pay levels based on the assessment or appraisal of an employee's (or team's) performance against previously set objectives, usually part of a performance management system.

(f) **Profit sharing** is a company-wide scheme where payments are made in the light of the overall profitability of the company or some other measure of results. Differentials can be built into the schemes to take account of factors such as level of responsibility or length of service.

(g) **Organisation-wide incentives**: bonus earnings or pay levels based on measured quantities or values for the whole establishment; this is frequently the basis of contract price or tender-led schemes.

A development in profit sharing has been the introduction of Profit Related Pay (PRP) whereby a proportion of salary can be paid tax-free on a part of company profits allocated on a predetermined basis. The take-up of the scheme has been disappointingly low, mainly due to the costs and time involved in maintaining the necessary records.

Performance related pay cannot be determined unless there is a measuring system in place to assess output. It also provides a limiting factor to the use and extension of incentive pay in instances where work is difficult to measure.

Payment by results schemes

A variety of incentive schemes (e.g. piecework, time bonuses, sales commission) tie some part of the employee's earnings to the results/outputs achieved by the employee. The proportion of the income determined by the payment by results scheme varies considerably; in some cases a textile worker or a salesman might receive all of his or her income on the basis of output, whilst at the other extreme 'bonus' earnings can represent only a very small proportion of total earnings.

However, in all cases, the assumptions underlying the scheme remain the same i.e. if it is possible to demonstrate to the worker that there is a direct link between the level of sales/production reached and the level of earnings, then the worker will be motivated to increase his or her level of sales or production. This principle forms the basis of both individual and group payment by results schemes. Such schemes are widespread in contemporary business.

Performance-related pay

Paying for performance simply means measuring the performance of individuals and rewarding them accordingly. In general, it is only true that money will motivate if the prospective payment is significantly large in relation to the normal income of that person. Small increases can prevent feelings of dissatisfaction but to create motivation in a person who will be motivated by money it is necessary for the amounts to be large.

4.6 The role of incentives

Apart from, or as well as performance related pay incentives, there are other financial and non-financial incentives that can be offered to employees as motivators.

Direct financial benefits	Indirect financial benefits	Non-financial benefits
• Pensions • Illness/health/ accident / life insurance • Clothing / accommodation allowance • Travel allowance • Child care allowance	• Subsidised meals / clothing / accommodation • Subsidised transport • Child care subsidy / crèche provision	• Holiday/vacation • Flexible working hours • Access to / support for training and education • Sabbatical, study leave • Planned career breaks • Occupational health / counselling • Recreational facilities

4.7 Pay and flexible work arrangements

- Typical flexitime arrangements define core hours during which all employees must be present on the job. Employees will be paid under the assumption that they are working a standard number of hours; some adjustment may be necessary if the paid hours differ from the actual hours worked. These adjustments are made at the end of a 'settlement period' which may be anywhere from a day to several weeks.

- Job sharing is a voluntary work arrangement in which two or more people share the responsibilities and duties of a full time job. The benefits and salary are prorated based on the hours of work of each individual.

- A part-time working arrangement means working less than the full-time hours (40 hours per week in many instances). Salary should be prorated for the actual number of hours worked and hourly wages should be equal to those of the full-time employee. Benefits are generally prorated in proportion to the number of hours worked compared with a full-time employee. The employee is recognised as permanent.

- Telecommuting can be an exclusive arrangement, whereby the employee carries out all or almost all of their job assignment from home and is paid a normal salary with the same benefits as employees working from an office.

- V-time employee income and benefits will be proportionally reduced by the work reduction percentages.

4.8 Arrangements for knowledge workers

It is generally accepted that knowledge is now a critical asset for organisations. As we move from a traditional manufacturing to a service/knowledge economy, it is recognised that knowledge is a primary source of competitive advantage, particularly because it is so difficult to emulate.

Knowledge management requires a wide range of traditional people management and development policies and practices to be reshaped to take account of the new priority given to the creation, transfer, application and retention of knowledge. Issues that the human resources function will need to consider include:

- the selection criteria for knowledge workers may need to be changed, to take account, in particular, of the greater importance of teamwork

- approaches to career development will need to reflect the importance of knowledge retention by creating career paths that motivate key workers

- performance appraisals must prioritise the development of knowledge skills if employees are to believe that the organisation takes these seriously. This highlights the need to develop metrics in this area

- work/life balance appears to be more important for younger workers, and reward systems will need to take this into account.

There are also new developments inspired by a focus on knowledge that human resources professionals should consider. These include:

- communities of practice, which aim to help develop knowledge. These are not shaped by organisational structures, but by the common interests of the participants

- the role of intermediaries between those engaged in creating and developing knowledge and the users of that knowledge

- the use of space to encourage knowledge transfer.

Key contributing factors to employee commitment are:

- The degree of flexibility and autonomy within the workforce.

- An emphasis on performance-related pay. Performance could be measured by, for example, the amount of quality information about a product published professionally on a web site that will help sell more of that product. The more motivated the knowledge worker is, the more quality information he or she will create.

- Appraisal systems that monitor and reward knowledge contributions and application e.g. knowledge turned into information, into documents, into content.

- Profit-sharing or equity-based forms of reward. Quality information about a product published professionally on a web site will help sell more of that product. The more motivated the knowledge worker is, the more quality information he or she will create.

- Career progression – make it clear that those who contribute quality information on a consistent basis will move up through the organisation.

5 Ethics

5.1 Introduction

Ethics is concerned with distinguishing 'right' from 'wrong' courses of action. There are three approaches to solving this problem:

(a) 'Deontological' approaches focus on describing moral actions or duties and see some actions as absolutely right or wrong, regardless of the consequences. An example of such an approach would be the Ten Commandments and its place within religious thinking.

(b) 'Teleological' or 'consequentialist' approaches judge whether an action is right or wrong by looking at the consequences – the end justifies the means. Such an approach might view lying as acceptable to protect people in certain situations.

(c) Ethical or moral 'relativism' applies to people who believe that an act is right if it is approved by the social group to which a person belongs and wrong if it is not. Otherwise, moral beliefs should be regarded as the private concern of each individual.

On a practical level, these get formulated into the political, social and professional environments that the management accountant operates in:

- the political environment consists of laws, regulations and government agencies

- the social environment consists of the customs, attitudes, beliefs and education of different groups in society

- the professional environment consists of, amongst others, the CIMA Ethical Guidelines – a set of well-established rules of personal and organisational behaviour.

5.2 Ethics at three levels

Ethical issues regarding business and public-sector organisations exist at three levels:

(a) At the **macro level,** there are issues about the role of business in the national and international organisation of society. These are largely concerned with the relative virtues of different political/social systems, such as free enterprise, centrally planned economies, etc. There are also important issues of international relationships and the role of business on an international scale.

(b)   At the **corporate level,** the issue is often referred to as corporate social responsibility and is focused on the ethical issues facing individual corporate entities (private and public sector) when formulating and implementing strategies. These could include whether it is ethical to use cheap labour in countries with less robust employee rights legislation or whether it is unethical for the firm to insist on employees having very short employment contracts to avoid them gaining additional rights relating to sickness leave, for example.

(c)   At the **individual level,** the issue concerns the behaviour and actions of individuals within organisations. These could include whether a particular manager is acting fairly towards his /her staff. In many countries this would be covered by legislation relating to anti-discrimination or unfair dismissal, say, but what if no such legislation exists?

Most ethical dilemmas involve a clash between two or more stakeholder groups. For example profits for shareholders could be boosted by forcing them to work longer hours. Legislation regarding working time directives would counter such behaviour but even if the practise is legal it may still be considered unethical.

5.3   Varying standards of ethics

The problem is compounded by the fact that in a world of multinationals, where competition is now international, the standards of ethics vary from nation to nation. Some countries have higher standards than those of the West, whilst others have standards that are very much lower.

The payment of contributions to political parties is an interesting example. In England, it is allowed and it must be declared in the published accounts, but other than in the rare cases such as where the future of the organisation is threatened, it is not tax deductible. This practice is not permitted in the US. However, in several countries of the world, payments to government officials and other persons of influence to ensure the expedition or favourable handling of a business transaction are not regarded as unethical bribes, but rather as payment for services rendered. Indeed, in many cases such payments to ensure the landing of a particular contract are considered a desirable and acceptable way of doing business. There have been instances where foreign nationals have even threatened to close operations down if payments are not met.

5.4   Ethics and the individual

Handy cites the problem where an organisation's standards of ethics may differ from the individual's own standards. For example, what is the responsibility of an individual who believes that the strategy of their organisation is unethical? Should the individual report the organisation; or should they leave the employment of the company on the grounds of a mismatch of values? This has often been called 'whistle blowing'.

5.5   The CIMA Ethical Guidelines

KEY POINT

The CIMA Ethical Guidelines state that members have a duty to observe the highest standard of conduct and integrity.

The CIMA Ethical Guidelines state that members have a duty to observe the highest standard of conduct and integrity. They set standards of conduct for professional accountants and state the fundamental principles that should be observed by professional accountants in order to achieve common objectives. These guidelines also assume that, unless a limitation is specifically stated, the objectives and fundamental principles are equally valid for all members, whether they be in industry, commerce, the public sector, public practice or education.

They set standards of conduct for professional accountants and state the fundamental principles that should be observed by professional accountants.

The guidelines recognise that the objectives of the accountancy profession are to work to the highest standards of professionalism, to attain the highest level of performance and generally to meet the public interest requirement. The objectives require four basic needs to be met:

(a)   In the whole of society there is a need for credibility in information and information systems.

(b)   There is a need for individuals who can be clearly identified by employers, clients and other interested parties as professional persons in the accountancy field.

(c)   There is a need for assurance that all services obtained from a professional accountant are carried out to the highest standards of performance.

(d)   Users of the services of professional accountants should be able to feel confident that there exists a framework of professional ethics which governs the provision of these services.

In order to achieve the objectives of the accountancy profession, professional accountants have to observe a number of prerequisites or fundamental principles.

The fundamental principles

(a)   **Integrity** – a professional accountant should be straightforward and honest in performing professional services.

(b)   **Objectivity** – a professional accountant should be fair and should not allow prejudice or bias or the influence of others to override objectivity.

(c)   **Professional competence and due care.**

(d)   **Confidentiality** – a professional accountant should respect the confidentiality of information acquired during the course of performing professional services. He or she should not use or disclose any such information without proper and specific authority or unless there is a legal or professional right or duty to disclose.

(e)   **Professional behaviour** – a professional accountant should act in a manner consistent with the good reputation of the profession and refrain from any conduct which might bring discredit to the Institute.

(f)   **Technical standards** – a professional accountant should carry out professional services in accordance with relevant technical and professional standards.

KEY POINT

In order to achieve the objectives of the accountancy profession, professional accountants have to observe a number of prerequisites or fundamental principles:

- integrity
- objectivity
- professional competence and due care
- confidentiality
- professional behaviour
- technical standards.

Activity 4

Suggest where ethical codes clash with business needs.

Feedback to this activity is at the end of the chapter.

Activity 5

How would you apply ethical considerations to the following dilemmas?

(a)   A rival company creates the legally permitted maximum of toxic waste. Your company has a range of expensive systems that keep waste to much lower levels. Not using these would reduce costs, and there is increasing pressure from industry analysts to increase the return on investment.

(b)   A young, talented and ambitious team leader wants you to dismiss a member of his team, who is much older than the rest and does not really fit in. However, the worker in question has worked at the company a long time with a good record of service.

(c)   You are forced to make redundancies in a department. The Human Resources manager has said, off the record, that it must not seem that gender or ethnicity is an issue, so you must make it look fair. However, this would require you to keep some weaker individuals, and lose some good ones.

Feedback to this activity is at the end of the chapter.

Summary

- There are a number of variables and other factors that affect the choice of the most appropriate organisation structure and systems of management, the manner in which the work of the organisation is carried out, and how people actually behave within the formal structure and system of the organisation.

- **McGregor** proposed two theories to describe value judgements inherent in management: **Theory X** and **Theory Y**.

- The types of motivation theory include:
  - content theories
  - process theories.

- Herzberg proposed job enrichment, job enlargement and job rotation to improve satisfaction and motivation.

- **Contingency theory** captures the notion that different environmental contexts place different requirements on organisations

- There is a clear link between theories of motivation and the reward system. Money is not always a strong motivator, and non-monetary rewards such as a sense of achievement can lead to higher levels of performance.

- Performance management is practised in many organisations and can help to provide a 'collaborative' approach towards employee development.

- Ethical behaviour depends on the personal ethics or values of its members, which shape its culture.

- A person's own values have a considerable influence on their ethical standards, and these are often reinforced and supported by the actions of superiors and peers.

- Professionals are also considerably influenced by the ethical standards maintained within the various institutions of which they are members.

Having completed your study of this chapter, you should have achieved the following learning outcome:

- evaluate the role of incentives in staff development as well as individual and organisational performance

- explain the importance of ethical behaviour in business generally and for the Chartered Management Accountant in particular.

Self-test questions

1   How does the industrial organisation approach differ from the sociological approach? (1)

2   Explain what Theory X and Y are. (1.3)

3   Give two examples of integrating mechanisms. (1.7)

4   Sketch Handy's shamrock organisation. (2.5)

5   Does money motivate? (4.2)

6   Explain the expectations placed on a manager by the CIMA Ethical Guidelines. (5.5)

Practice questions

Question 1

Which of the following **theories** of employee motivation distinguishes between 'satisfiers' and 'dissatisfiers'?

A   Herzberg's Maintenance Theory

B   Maslow's Need Hierarchy

C   Schein's view of employee behaviour

D   McGregor's Theory X and Theory Y

Question 2

Schein's models

With reference to motivation theory, explain three of the following concepts:

- rational-economic man
- social man
- self-actualising man
- complex man.

Your explanation should include the significance of each concept to a manager.

(20 marks)

Question 3

You are required to contrast and compare the Classical and Contingency/Systems approaches to organisations.   **(20 marks)**

For the answers to these questions, see the 'Answers' section at the end of the book.

Feedback to activities

Activity 1

Hierarchy of needs	Motivating factor	Hygiene factors
Self-fulfilment needs	Opportunity for advancement	Sports/social facilities
Esteem needs	Acknowledgement	Working conditions
Social needs	Increased responsibility	Pension
Safety needs	Work challenges	Pay
Basic needs		

There is a clear relationship between Herzberg's 'Hygiene Factor' and the lower levels of Maslow's 'Hierarchy of Needs'. Likewise there is a close correlation between the motivating factors and Maslow's higher needs.

Activity 2

It can be argued that customers often are 'paid' for the work that they do for an enterprise. For example, customers who pay their bills early may be given a discount; airline passengers who book and pay for their flights well in advance may be given cheaper fares; taxpayers who maintain adequate records of their expenditures may avoid extra tax liabilities or other penalties; customers who transact their business outside peak periods may be given discounts; fast food patrons who report deficiencies in service quality may be given their meal free; etc. Consequently, for many organisations, customers can arguably be included as an important contributor to the organisation's objectives. They will be particularly important in the case of enterprises providing a personal service of some kind.

Activity 3

Flexi-time is a familiar example of job enrichment, where employees are given the responsibility of fulfilling their contractual hours at times, which can be more suited to them individually.

Activity 4

In spite of the investment in human capital, the employees cannot be obliged to remain in their company. In some cases, the cost of the development can be recovered, but the intellectual capital can only be protected by legal means. The expertise walks with the employees. This is not an ethical issue, but a business risk, common in many sectors.

From time to time, employees find themselves in ethical dramas concerning the wrong-doings of an organisation. The employee then has to consider the possibility of a public declaration – commonly known as 'whistle-blowing'.

Activity 5

In all these examples, the dilemma cannot be resolved, but much can be done to defend the values that are creating the problem in the first place. For example, there may be some competitive advantage in asserting the cleanliness of the product, or supporting an older worker's experience that might be interpreted as dissent by a younger worker. Making redundancies based on the image of fairness, rather than rewarding ability and application, is poor business.

The answers are often legitimately found in steering between the two extremes of the dilemma.

Chapter 15

HUMAN RESOURCE MANAGEMENT

Syllabus content

- The relationship of the employee to other elements of the business plan.

- Determinants and content of a human resource (HR) plan (e.g. organisational growth rate, skills, training, development, strategy, technologies and natural wastage).

- Problems in implementing an HR plan and ways to manage this.

Contents

1   The role of human resource management (HRM)

2   The role of HRM in strategic planning

3   The relationship of HRM to other parts of the organisation

4   Human Resource Planning (HRP)

5   Changes affecting HRP

1 The role of human resource management (HRM)

1.1 Overview

Human resource management (HRM) can be viewed as a strategic approach to acquiring, developing, managing and motivating an organisation's key resource.

The people in most organisations are of central importance, and human resource management should be in a position to complement and advance the organisation's objectives.

Michael Armstrong's definition sees the role of HRM as:

'A strategic and coherent approach to the management of an organisation's most valued assets: the people working there who individually and collectively contribute to the achievement of its objectives for sustainable competitive advantage.'

The role of HRM, as defined by Armstrong, can be viewed as:

- suggesting a strategic approach to the personnel function

- serving the interests of management

- dealing with gaining employees' commitment to the values and goals laid down by the strategic management

- aiding the development of the human resources that help the organisation add value to their products or services.

1.2 The role of personnel versus the role of HRM

The traditional view of 'personnel management' includes activities that are described by Michael Porter as 'maintenance' functions in the value chain. They include:

- record maintenance, human resource planning, recruitment and selection

- placement and termination

- training and career development

- grievance and discipline procedures

- terms of employment

- negotiation on wages and salaries, and

- other matters and procedures for avoiding disputes.

These are necessary tasks, but have left the personnel function without a genuine insight into how its actions affect the organisation's achievement of its objectives.

The traditional role offered scope for specialisation, leading to the personnel function being staffed by people who have spent their entire careers in the personnel field. They may have started by specialising in job analysis and have ended up as company personnel manager or personnel director, but only in rare instances with a seat on the board.

KEY POINT

Michael Armstrong describes human resources management as: 'A strategic and coherent approach to the management of an organisation's most valued assets: the people working there who individually and collectively contribute to the achievement of its objectives for sustainable competitive advantage'.

KEY POINT

Human resources management (HRM) can be viewed as a strategic approach to acquiring, developing, management and motivating an organisation's key resource.

The HRM approach believes firmly in what is known as 'empowerment'. This means passing authority as far down the line as practicable and sensible for the enterprise.

HRM can be defined as the process of achieving outstanding organisational performance through empowering people to achieve and give of their best. As such, it is directed at building a sustainable competitive advantage and is a strategic activity. Because of this approach, HRM is not the exclusive province of the specialist in the human resource area. It is an activity that should actively involve not only line managers, but also all those responsible for the strategic direction of the organisation.

2 The role of HRM in strategic planning

2.1 Overview

New themes in planning are concerned with the improvement of competitive performance. Organisations are in the middle of an industrial revolution based on a wave of new technologies: electronics, computers, robotics and automation, biotechnology, and various new materials. The success of Japanese industry has encompassed all of the above, but another competitive edge is their human resource strategies and their ability to engage, involve and motivate people, thus tapping their energy and ideas. This success has encouraged many western firms to re-examine their approaches to personnel. Multinational companies are now investing as much in human resource programmes on leadership, competitive benchmarks, quality improvement and employee involvement as they are spending on new equipment. The emergence of flexible organisational arrangements such as short-term contracts, teleworking, part-time working and the use of consultants and bought-in services are being seen.

2.2 Objectives of Human Resource Strategy

Human resource plans and corporate plans cannot exist in isolation, since each will automatically influence the other. Heads of all company functions are involved in the process of considering the changing staffing needs over the period of the corporate plan, starting from the present position. HRM's responsibility is that of drawing the functional requirements together within the framework of company human resource policy, including funding. The basic aim is to assess the quantity and quality of people required at each level within each department of the business and to ensure that these positions are filled on a continuous basis.

Effective human resource planning will, therefore, help to remove the need for redundancies and avoid shortages of labour. Age planning can deal with some of the people problems arising from time to time. An effective human resources strategy (HRS) must include realistic plans and procedures. The objectives will include the following:

(a) Identifying, in precise terms, the kinds of talent the organisation needs to achieve its strategic goals in the short, medium and long term.

(b) Recruiting an adequate supply of people with the potential to become outstanding performers, allowing for wastage and for the actions of competing organisations.

(c) Developing people's potential by training, development and education.

(d)   Retaining as high a proportion as possible of those recruited in this way whose potential is demonstrated in the early years of employment.

(e)   Ensuring that everything possible is done to prevent poaching of talent by competitors.

(f)   Recruiting an adequate number of talented people of proven experience and accomplishment, and easing their adjustment to a new corporate culture.

(g)   Downsizing to reduce staff numbers when necessary.

(h)   Motivating the employees to achieve high levels of performance and to build ties of loyalty to the organisation.

(i)   Searching for ways of improving performance and productivity.

(j)   Creating an organisational culture in which talent is nurtured.

2.3 Environmental analysis

To make a valid contribution to the enterprise, human resource planners must look both within and outside the internal environment. The organisation does not exist in a vacuum but is influenced by political, economic, social and technological (PEST) factors. By analysing these areas, the planner can consider changes that have taken place or are likely to occur in society at large and build them into scenarios to clarify plans for the future.

Political factors – A change of government could affect the way people are employed. Legislation can be introduced that changes industrial relations' procedures. This could result in fewer days lost through industrial action. Governments may introduce incentives to encourage young people to remain in full-time education, or they may fund businesses to encourage training and development for them. Specific areas of the economy may be given special attention, in the form of funding, to encourage growth.

Economic factors – National economies may experience growth or decline and governments may have a special commitment to change cultures through economic interventions. Companies in the South of England looking to relocate and/or recruit new staff might develop scenarios based on the environmental forecasting associated with buying or renting houses in the area. Experts could be asked to assess probabilities directly. Factors considered could be buoyancy of housing market in general, availability and price of existing and planned housing stock in designated area, the local infrastructure, interest rates and availability of mortgage funds.

Social factors – in recent years, customers' tastes have changed towards certain products, e.g. environmentally friendly and genetically modified products. There may be significant changes in the composition of the labour force, e.g. the average age of workforces may increase because of a fall in the birth rate or more women may be represented in traditionally male sectors because of changes in social attitudes.

Technological factors – New production methods may be developed that reduce the need for operational or supervisory staff. The advent of new technologies may spark a requirement for the acquisition of new skills to maintain the new machines. Old skills and knowledge, which were previously valued, may become superfluous.

Activity 1

Describe your own situation as a CIMA student in terms of the PEST factors.

Feedback to this activity is at the end of the chapter.

3 The relationship of HRM to other parts of the organisation

3.1 Strategic integration

Strategic integration is the process of linking HRM policies and activities to explicit business strategies.

This integrating process will aim to match available human resources to the ever-changing requirements of the organisation. It will also establish the competencies required at all levels in the organisation to ensure that business strategies are implemented and will then take the human resource development initiatives required to provide those competencies. Finally, it will provide the levers required to manage strategic change.

A coherent approach to strategic integration is, however, only possible where the whole top team works together in developing and managing the process.

3.2 HRM and the corporate plan

Competitive pressures have stressed the need for managements to concentrate on innovation, quality enhancement, customer service and cost reduction. This has influenced the way in which organisations have been structured and managed. The need to be more responsive to external events has resulted in a greater emphasis on operational flexibility, and the need to make managers more accountable for results has resulted in more decentralisation and devolution of authority. The 'flexible firm' is one in which teamwork is more important but it also means the setting up of core groups of employees consisting of managers, technicians, knowledge workers and multi-skilled craft workers. These groups are supported as and when required by contract staff and part-timers. The creation, development and control of teams and core workers operating in a state of constant change places even greater demands on all managers in the organisation and it is these demands which have accentuated the need to adopt a human resource management approach based on a belief that:

- people are the most important assets an organisation has

- HRM makes a major contribution to the achievement of corporate objectives and strategic plans

- the achievement of excellence will require HRM to manage the corporate culture, values, organisational climate and managerial behaviour emanating from that culture

- HRM will need to make a continuous effort to encourage all the members of the organisation to work together with a sense of common purpose. It is also particularly necessary to secure commitment to change.

3.3 The nature and importance of Human Resource services

The 'operational' aspects of HRM are referred to as 'personnel services'. The personnel department play an important role in supporting and servicing other parts of the organisation. For example, other organisational divisions or departments will require services, such as:

(a) **Organisational structure and manning levels** – most organisations, and almost every large one, are structured on bureaucratic lines. Emphasis is on chains of responsibility and authority up and down the organisation. There is a strong commitment to the principle that the tasks the business needs to perform are structured into the work of defined jobs or offices.

For each office a formal job description is documented defining the job category, the tasks to be done and other features. Similarly, for each jo,b a person specification is drawn up defining the attributes of the ideal person for the job. The jobs as defined make up the organisation's establishment. This establishment gives the details of the 'offices' of the whole company. It includes the numbers of jobs in the organisation, and at each grade, with a defined pay category attached. A major task of the department is to regularly review jobs, numbers of people and the establishment in general so that the numbers and types of employees best match production needs.

(b) **Redundancy, redeployment, recruitment and selection** – a major asset of organisations not shown in the conventional balance sheet is the carefully recruited labour force. To make the best use of the human resource, there should be regular reviews of staff levels. Human resource plans are updated and decisions taken about recruitment, selection and redundancy. Many organisations feel they have a social responsibility to employees and they are reluctant to make any employees compulsorily redundant. Recruitment is important in that it brings fresh people into the company, and even at times of recession the organisation will want to have an appropriate age profile for its staff.

(c) **Reward issues and procedures** – depending on the nature of the business, labour costs may be the major cost of providing output. Wage costs account for around 60 per cent of the expenses of banks in the UK. The control of such costs is an important element of profit making. Most management nowadays do believe that wages are the primary element of employee motivation and therefore performance-related pay is becoming increasingly widespread.

(d) **Staff appraisal procedures** – an important tool for motivating and controlling the employee is the formal managerial appraisal of employee performance. As the HRM philosophy becomes increasingly accepted, it is becoming part of the 'common sense' of society that all employees should be subject to performance appraisal and that it is 'irrational' to think otherwise. Staff appraisal requires the careful administration of suitable appraisal techniques and feedback to employees.

(e) **Employment records** – there is clearly a need for basic information about employees. This data is needed for day-to-day operations and can also be used for the effective planning of staff numbers and the development and training of individuals.

KEY POINT

Employee
communications and
relations are an
increasingly important
aspect – not just as part
of a motivation strategy
but as part of
developing a company
culture.

(f) **Employee communications and relations** – communica
the workforce are an increasingly important aspect – not j
of a motivation strategy but as part of developing a compa
This culture is designed to elicit a high degree of commitm
the employee. The employee will identify personal individual
interests closely with the interests of the organisation. This involves
two-way communication and efficient formal networks through
meetings and the circulation of written material. This is of central
importance to the HRM approach.

KEY POINT

The company needs to
have control
procedures, which
attempt the
improvement of
unsatisfactory
performance and,
where necessary, make
sure unsatisfactory
performance is
eliminated.

(g) **Disciplinary and dismissal procedures** – there are several aspects
to disciplinary and dismissal procedures. At the legal level the
company must ensure that it conforms to the required procedures for
the dismissal of employees. There is a requirement in most
companies that these are seen to be fair and implemented with
justice and uniformity. The company needs to have control
procedures, which attempt the improvement of unsatisfactory
performance and, where necessary, make sure unsatisfactory
performance is eliminated.

KEY POINT

Staff training and
management
development always
have to respond to
change.

(h) **Staff training and management development** – the organisation's
operations are dynamic – they always have to respond to change.
The relationship with every employee can be seen as part of a cycle.
Employees are hired and trained, they may progress in the
organisation and, sooner or later, they leave voluntarily or not. In
addition to that cycle there are many other changes in a business,
some arising from internal pressures, some a response to the external
environment.

KEY POINT

The working
environment should be
a safe and healthy
place in which to work.

(i) **Health and safety procedures and training** – virtually every
organisation recognises that not only is it required by UK law that
the working environment should be a safe and healthy place to work
in, but that it is also part of their social responsibility to employees
and all who come into contact with the organisation. This requires
that the organisational culture as well as its procedures, practices and
training should have a commitment to health and safety.

4 Human Resource Planning (HRP)

4.1 Introduction

KEY POINT

Capital investment
brings economies,
which lead to lower
prices, leading to
growth, leading to
greater human resource
requirement. The mix of
grades will tend to
change from unskilled
to skilled, from
production to
maintenance, from
technical operating to
planning, researching,
marketing, purchasing
and accounting.

Human Resource Planning (HRP) cannot, of course, be considered in
isolation. It is related to all other resources strategies and particularly to
capital investment. Capital investment often means less human resource. It
can, however, lead ultimately to an increased human resource requirement,
but with a change in the mix of grades required.

Capital investment brings economies, which lead to lower prices, leading
to growth, leading to greater human resource requirement. The mix of
grades will tend to change from unskilled to skilled, from production to
maintenance, from technical operating to planning, researching, marketing,
purchasing and accounting. Such changes must be planned for as far in
advance as possible. Re-training schemes must be organised.

If an overall drop is going to be necessary, an attempt should be made not
to build up too much only to be cut back later. (The 'hire and fire' attitude
is definitely 'out' these days.) If any cuts are necessary, planned use should
be made of early retirement schemes, voluntary redundancy, etc.

DEFINITION

The main aim of HRP is to acquire and retain the number and kinds of people needed by the organisation to achieve organisational goals.

The main aim of HRP is to acquire and retain the number and kinds of people needed by the organisation, looking inside the company to develop suitable people, as well as buying in from outside.

It should also consider organisational design and job analysis to see if there are better ways of organising the way that people perform at work. This consideration has powerful implications for staff development and for theflexibility of workers, and the content of a human resource plan.

A typical human resources plan should look forward from three to five years in an organisation's lifetime. It is a cyclical process having four main stages.

(a) Analysing corporate and departmental objectives – to determine the overall shape and size of the organisation required, and the strategies and tactics to be employed in the implementation of operational plans.

(b) Demand forecasting – projecting future staffing requirements required achieving the corporate objectives by the target date.

(c) Assessing present human resources and producing a supply forecast, which is an estimation of likely changes in the existing staff resources by the end of the forecasting period, i.e. target date.

(d) Devising policies and plans, in detail, whereby shortages or excesses in labour numbers and skills deficiencies can be overcome.

The HRP process should also consider the broader environmental factors. These include:

- changes in population trends (e.g. ageing populations)

- patterns of employment – more flexible structures of work organisation

- competition for labour from other organisations

- changes in the educational system

- developments in information technology and automation

- government intervention, e.g. initiatives on employment, training and enterprise programmes and information technology, and employment legislation.

4.2 Stages in a human resource plan

DEFINITION

HRP can be described as a strategy for the acquisition, utilisation, improvement and retention of an organisation's human resources.

HRP can be described as a strategy for the acquisition, utilisation, improvement and retention of an organisation's human resources. After the strategic review, the four main stages are auditing, forecasting, planning and controlling resources.

(a) The auditing stage involves the analysis of the strategic environment (trends in population growth, education, pensions, employment rights of women and ethnic minorities) in the light of the organisation's strategic objectives. The strategy chosen will have implications on the numbers of employees and the mix of skills required.

(b) The forecasting stage analyses the demand for and supply of labour in terms of number, type and quality of people the organisation should employ to meet planned requirements and cover expected turnover.

(c)   The planning stage involves policies to recruit, train and develop the labour force indicated in the forecast.

(d)   The controlling stage involves measuring the effective use of the human resources and their contribution towards the achievement of the organisation's objectives.

The stages of HRP are outlined in the diagram below:

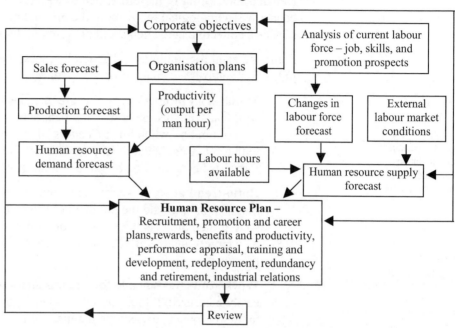

4.3   Analysing corporate and departmental HR objectives

DEFINITION

Human resource strategy is a reconciliation process between what an organisation might do (opportunities) and what it can do (resources).

Human resource strategy is a reconciliation process between what an organisation might do (opportunities) and what it can do (resources). This is an impossible process without consideration of human resource requirements. Similarly, HRP needs, as its base data, predictions of future output and some indication of available finance. Within this framework, HRP serves two functions:

*   It fulfils a problem-solving role by identifying human resource requirements, controlling the flow of labour, developing skills and increasing adaptability.

*   It also has a strategic role in contributing towards the shape of the organisation as required by external and internal changes.

In both cases, HRP represents an important flow of information to aid decision-making and the formulation of policies.

The management accountant can assist the HR manager in the control stage of the plan. Any control system needs to set objectives, measure performance, note deviations and act to eliminate them. The management accountant will be able to advise the HR manager if any of the environmental factors – economic, technological or market trends – changes in an unpredicted way. This will allow the recruitment, training or redeployment plans to be updated accordingly.

4.4 HR demand and supply forecasting

Demand forecasting is closely linked with an organisation's corporate strategy. Any strategic decisions will have a human resource implication, e.g. decisions to invest in new equipment, to reorganise, acquire, increase or decrease productivity, to change the method of production, to diversify into new product markets and to market products more effectively. Demand forecasting is, therefore, tied in with changes in the state of the economy, technological innovation, the product market, demand for services, collective agreements and government legislation.

Future demand for employees is generally measured by managerial judgement, ratio-trend analysis or work-study.

- **Managerial judgement** – is where managers consider future workloads and decide how many people they need. The process may be 'bottom up', when line managers submit proposals for agreement with top management, or 'top down', with senior management forecasts being verified by the line managers.

- **Ratio-trend analysis** – looks back over several years at trends in the numbers of staff and the numbers of products or services made or sold. It then projects these ratios forward, taking into account the new targets and the effects of new technology and new working practices.

- **Work-study** – is suitable for circumstances where work can be easily measured. It looks at output plans and at how long each unit takes to produce, to give the planner required annual hours – taking into account absenteeism, turnover and new technology.

People are a crucial resource, and therefore long-term plans are needed to ensure availability of the right type of skills. The main problem with HRP is that, with the speed of change in technology, it is difficult to predict not only how many workers will be needed in n years' time, but also what type of skills they will need. Some jobs, which now form a major part of the work content, may be completely automated within a few years. In addition, the rate of growth of the firm's business cannot be accurately predicted. There is thus considerable uncertainty on the demand side.

Supply forecasting begins by assessing present human resources and analysing:

- staff numbers by age, abilities, grade, type, skills and experience, etc

- turnover of staff and rates of absenteeism

- overtime rates and periods of inactivity

- staff competencies and potential.

Analysis by age would enable the department to draw a graph to show when the vacancies due to retirement would occur, and would enable the personnel department to draw up better detailed pension plans. In addition, analysis by age would remove 'bottle-necks' or 'age gaps' within the company. It would show where the bulk of people were and if any likely problems could occur in the future because of a particular age spread (e.g. if the bulk of employees are aged 55 to 58 and retirement is proposed to be brought forward to age 60).

Analysis by ability would involve appraisals of the staff in the department. This would require written reports, at six-monthly intervals, from the manager for whom each member of staff worked. These reports are read through by both the manager and the person being appraised, and discussed together. They should cover his or her ability in detail. All the skills of each employee must be detailed, not merely the ones they use at present.

One of the problems with supply forecasts is that people cannot be treated like other resources. They are unpredictable and might leave the company. Although there is uncertainty on the supply side, an attempt must be made to assess the numbers, which will be required in each type of work for some years ahead, even though the estimates will be subject to wide error. Demand and supply must then be reconciled, with decisions being taken as to the level of recruitment required, the extent of internal promotion, the amount of internal training needed, etc. This in turn will lead to decisions about the size of the personnel department needed to handle interviews, training, etc.

The management accountant can assist the HR manager in both of the forecasting stages. Because labour must be recruited and trained or shed and made redundant as required at the most appropriate time, the forecast must be based on the predictions gathered from the analysis of all the organisation's forecasts. The management accountant can quantify the objectives for a given period in the future (generally five years) and draw up a list of current and future requirements.

5 Changes affecting HRP

5.1 Changes in organisational requirements

In organisations that are large enough to draw up business plans from the overall corporate objectives, it is important that there is a relationship between the various business plans drawn up in different functional areas. This link can be highlighted when the areas of change affecting an organisation's human resource requirements are looked at.

(a) **Expansion or contraction of the enterprise** – expansion will almost certainly involve the planning of recruitment while contraction may involve decisions concerning redundancy.

(b) **Changes in the demand for output** – certain products or services may be showing increasing demand while others may be declining. This may well involve changes, if not in the numbers employed, then certainly in the skills' composition of the workforce, necessitating retraining. These changes may be of a seasonal nature, as in the hotel industry, and organisations must plan for such fluctuations in demand.

(c) **Product changes** may affect the composition of the labour force. For example, an organisation that has traditionally supplied fitted kitchen furniture to the highest specification may decide to change to factory-produced home assembly kits. Different skills may well be required to manufacture these.

(d) **Changes in the method of output** brought about by changes in technology will undoubtedly affect human resource requirements. Automation in a production department or the introduction of a computer in an accounts or records department will undoubtedly call for different skills, if not a reduction in the number of people employed.

(e) Finally, **changes in productivity** may occur through techniques to improve efficiency or productivity bargaining. This, too, will affect the quantity and perhaps the skills required of the labour force.

It can be seen that some of these changes will affect most organisations at some time or another. Recently, strong arguments have emerged for the application of HRP techniques to cope with such changes. These are:

(a) In many firms, **wage costs** are a significant proportion of total costs. Firms, therefore, need a clear indication of likely future wage costs for effective budgeting exercises.

(b) The increased importance is given to **training and career planning**, because of technical change and the expectations of the workforce, necessitates some form of HRP.

Firms are now under much greater pressure to appear socially responsible. Both social expectations and successive legislation have affected traditional policies of 'hire and fire' according to market demands. Human resource planning is a key technique in avoiding over-recruitment or lay-offs and redundancy.

Activity 2

Explain the term 'demand' and 'supply' forecasting.

Feedback to this activity is at the end of the chapter.

5.2 Policies and plans to plug the gap between supply and demand

A human resource plan provides the trigger for a HRM action programme aimed at reconciling differences between supply and demand. It provides a framework in which action can be taken to help overcome staffing difficulties facing the organisation. HR planning is a continuous process, which seeks to ensure flexible resourcing related to internal and external environmental influences.

Acquiring adequate numbers of staff of the right grades is not the end of HRP. HRP involves promotion, recruitment, training and promoting good industrial relations. It also involves a continuous review of working conditions by comparison with other organisations: pay, wage comparisons between different grades, pensions, holiday and sickness pay, physical working conditions, safety aspects, sports and social facilities, other fringe benefits.

Tactical plans to implement these policies include pay and productivity bargaining, conditions of employment, career development, organisation and job specifications, redundancy, recruitment, training and retraining.

Shortages or surpluses of labour that emerge in the process of planning may be dealt with in various ways. A deficiency may be met through internal transfers, promotion, training, external recruitment and reducing labour turnover (by reviewing possible causes). A surplus may be dealt with by running down staff levels by natural wastage, restricting recruitment or, as a last resort, redundancies.

• **Recruitment** – to recruit the appropriate numbers of employees the supply of labour must be such that workers are available of the right skills, age and health in the area. Labour generally is regarded as relatively immobile. Many organisations will decide where to locate new operations on the basis of knowledge about available labour. The labour that is required could be attracted away from existing employers if higher salaries are offered.

- **Redundancy** – selection of labour for redundancy is a very difficult task. The bond of loyalty between organisation and employee may be considerable and threats of redundancies will usually result in a demotivated workforce who fear for the future. The impact on the level of motivation and on company performance has to be taken seriously by management.

- **Training** – changes in products and methods of production often require a new skill or understanding on the part of the workforce. The personnel function will often establish a training programme to cope with changes in the work environment and to increase the motivation of employees. In situations where an expansion requires more skilled workers, the training programme may be used to upgrade the skills of existing workers, or to provide the skills for new employees. This is particularly likely to be the case when the local labour supply cannot provide sufficient numbers of the appropriately skilled workers.

- **Management development** – the level of education and training available in the existing labour supply is unlikely to provide potential employees with the exact skills, experience, and enterprise required for management within a particular organisation. Managers must therefore be trained to fulfil the role expected of them. The management team must also keep abreast of developments in all areas of business, which may often require training programmes and attendance at various courses. Frequently the emphasis is on self-development.

- **Estimates of labour costs** – a forecast of the labour requirements will enable organisations to estimate the associated costs. The factors influencing these will not simply be the numbers and grades required, but also the state of the labour market. A labour surplus in an area may lead to the lowering of wage rates, although trade union pressure may not allow this.

5.3 Dismissal, retirement and redundancy

The organisation should have a responsible attitude towards employment legislation requirements and codes of practice, union activities and communications with staff.

When general principles are converted into practice, they should take the form of good pay and working conditions and high quality training and development schemes. They should also extend to dismissal, retirement and redundancy policies.

Dismissals will be inevitable in any large organisation, but careful recruitment methods should manage to keep such demoralising events to a minimum. Recruitment of staff is very important. If an organisation recruits individuals who turn out to be unsuitable, they will have to sack them.

Organisations have different ways of providing for staff nearing retirement, apart from pension schemes. One of the problems for retired people is learning what to do with their leisure time. Some companies provide training courses and discussion groups to help them plan their future time constructively.

Dealing with redundancies is a more difficult problem. Even for organisations that show an ethical sense of responsibility towards their employees, there may be occasions when parts of the business have to be closed down, and jobs lost. In such a situation, the organisation should have a meaningful and cost-effective programme to deal with staff identified as surplus to future requirements. This might include redeployment and redundancies, although more creative schemes will also involve early retirement provisions, flexible pension planning and secondments. For employees who are made redundant, there are measures the organisation can take to help them to get a job elsewhere, for example:

- providing funds for training in other skills that employees could use in other industries and organisations

- counselling individuals to give them suggestions about what they might try to do

- providing generous redundancy payments that employees could use to either set up in business themselves, or tide them over until they find suitable employment again.

5.4 Problems in implementing the HRP

People resources are costly and like all other resources of the company have to be carefully planned. Apart from problems of providing the funds to meet 'labour cost', other current problems underline the need for HRP. Knowledge, expertise and skill are constantly changing. Rapid social and technical changes represent more problems in the environment within which planning takes place.

All types of forecasting are subject to several potential drawbacks. These are:

(a) Problems may arise due to the uncertainty of the environment. Significant changes can occur which can render earlier predictions virtually useless. For example, cheap imports can seriously affect developments in the British industry. The strength of the pound against foreign currencies adversely affects the tourist industry and hence employment in the hotel, catering and entertainment industries. Unforeseen changes in legislation may have an impact on manning levels in affected sectors and rapid technological developments may seriously affect earlier human resource forecasts.

(b) Such forecasts cannot take complete account of factors related to the unpredictability of human behaviour.

(c) The data being used by the planners may be incorrect or wrong estimations may be made of unknown data.

The value of HRP is that it can assist organisations to foresee changes and identify trends in staffing resources, and to adopt personnel policies that help to avoid major problems.

Effective HRP can anticipate future difficulties while there is still a choice of action. Coupled with good communications, consultation and participation with staff involved, planning should help alleviate harmful effects to individual members of staff or to the performance of the organisation.

Summary

- The concept and role of HRM and the part the function plays in supporting other parts of the organisation.

- HRP is a part of the process and deals with human activity directed towards a specific economic aim, and so provides the organisation with the right number of employees who have the skills to achieve the organisation's objectives.

- Human resource strategy is a reconciliation process between what an organisation might do (opportunities) and what it can do (resources). This is an impossible process without consideration of human resource requirements and we examine the methods available for forecasting.

- HRP needs, as its base data, predictions of future output and some indication of available finance.

- A human resource plan aims to reconcile the differences between supply and demand. It provides a framework in which action can be taken to help overcome staffing difficulties facing the organisation. This can mean recruitment, training, career development, dismissal, retirement and redundancy.

Having completed your study of this chapter, you should have achieved the following learning outcomes:

- explain the role of the human resource management function and its relationship to other parts of the organisation

- produce and explain a human resource plan and supporting practices

- identify features of a human resource plan that vary depending on organisation type and employment model.

Self-test questions

1 Define the modern view of HRM. (1.1, 1.2)

2 Briefly describe three objectives of the human resource strategy. (2.2)

3 What are the factors in a PEST analysis? (2.3)

4 Identify three environmental factors that affect HRP. (4.1)

5 What are the main problems of implementing HRP? (5.4)

Practice questions

Question 1

A PEST analysis is made up of which of the following factors?

A Political, Economic, Social and Technological

B Political, Environmental, Social and Technological

C Political, Environmental, Social and Transport

D Political, Environmental, Service sector and Technological

Question 2

Human resource planning

(a) Describe the human resource planning process. **(10 marks)**

(b) Why is human resource planning an important feature of the strategic management of organisations that employ significant numbers of accountants and other professionally qualified staff? **(10 marks)**

(Total: 20 marks)

For the answers to these questions, see the 'Answers' section at the end of the book.

Feedback to activities

Activity 1

Political – increased regulation due to failures such as Enron with increased demand for a CIMA qualification.

Economic – this will lead to a shortage of supply and increased price of the commodity, reflected in salaries.

Social – decreasing respect for professions, coupled with scandals in other areas, pressures for increased regulation. Provision of CIMA courses not well spread over the UK leading to local shortages.

Technological – increasing use of JIT and other measures requires better, faster management information.

All these point to a bright future for a CIMA student once qualified!

Activity 2

Demand forecasting is closely linked to an organisation's corporate strategy. Any strategic decisions will have a human resource implications. For example, decisions about:

- investing in new machinery or equipment
- reorganisation
- acquisitions
- increase or decrease productivity
- change of method of production
- to diversify into new product markets
- to market products more effectively.

Demand forecasting is therefore tied in with the changes in the state of the economy, technological innovation, the product market, demand for services, collective agreements and government legislation.

Supply forecasting begins by assessing present human resources and analysing:

- staff numbers by age, abilities, grade, type, skills and experience
- turnover of staff and rates of absenteeism
- overtime rates and period of inactivity
- staff competencies and potential.

Chapter 16

THE PROCESS OF INDUCTION, RECRUITMENT AND SELECTION

Syllabus content

- The process of recruitment and selection of staff using different recruitment channels (i.e. interviews, assessment centres, intelligence tests, aptitude tests, psychometric tests).

- Issues relating to fair and legal employment practices (e.g. recruitment, dismissal, redundancy, and ways of managing these).

- The importance of negotiation during the offer and acceptance of a job.

- The process of induction and its importance.

Contents

1 The importance of recruitment and selection

1.1 Introduction

Recruitment and selection play an important part in the organisation's strategy. It is inextricably linked with the organisational goals and objectives and much of the training and development, which follows it. Its position is shown in the diagram below:

The aim of most organisations is to produce goods or services at a profit, so the people working in these organisations will need to be good at their jobs. There is always the possibility of training someone to do the job efficiently but it is obviously better if people are placed in jobs where their natural abilities and interests are reasonably suited.

Choosing the right candidate for the job, or selecting the right person for promotion, is a critical organisational decision for a number of reasons. Incorrect decisions can lead to frustrated employees and poor performance levels for the organisation. Selection and appraisal procedures can be costly and time-consuming and it is annoying to have to repeat them to recover from previous errors.

1.2 Outline of the recruitment and selection process

Recruitment and selection are parts of the same process and some people often refer to both as 'recruitment'. This is not accurate; the process of recruitment, as distinct from selection, involves the attraction of a field of suitable candidates for the job.

There is no 'ideal plan' for recruitment and selection – no super model to be followed. All organisations have their own way of doing it, with varying degrees of success. What is important is for an organisation to be aware of what has been useful and successful in the past and to try to develop a system that is well designed and properly applied.

The process of recruitment involves several stages:

- The clarification of the exact nature of the position to be filled – is the job really necessary or can it be covered adequately by reorganising or re-allocating to other jobs? If the job is necessary, what does it entail? What are the duties and responsibilities attached to the job?

- Determining the skills, aptitudes and abilities required for the job – what qualities and attributes are required for a person to perform the job effectively?

- Establishing a profile of the ideal candidate.

- Attracting candidates by advertising or other means – is it necessary to recruit outside the organisation? If so, where are suitable applicants most likely to be found? Which are the best sources of labour and methods of recruitment?

Once this has been achieved, the selection processes begin; these are aimed at selecting the best person for the job from that field of candidates. The processes include collecting information about the candidates and planning the selection process to decide on the most appropriate methods of selection.

The last part of the recruitment and selection process is the induction and follow-up – how to undertake the socialisation process and introduce the new member of staff to the policies, procedures and working practices of the organisation.

A general outline of the recruitment and selection process is shown below:

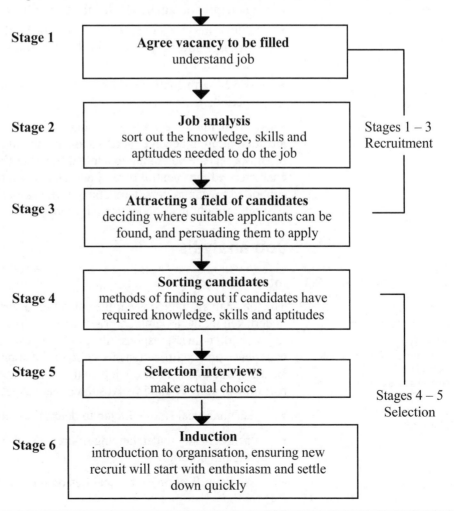

Stage 1	**Agree vacancy to be filled** understand job	
Stage 2	**Job analysis** sort out the knowledge, skills and aptitudes needed to do the job	Stages 1 – 3 Recruitment
Stage 3	**Attracting a field of candidates** deciding where suitable applicants can be found, and persuading them to apply	
Stage 4	**Sorting candidates** methods of finding out if candidates have required knowledge, skills and aptitudes	
Stage 5	**Selection interviews** make actual choice	Stages 4 – 5 Selection
Stage 6	**Induction** introduction to organisation, ensuring new recruit will start with enthusiasm and settle down quickly	

1.3 Assessing the need to recruit

When considering recruitment, there are two questions that managers must address. The first is whether there is really a job, and the second is whether there is someone suitable who is already employed by the organisation. There are many alternatives to recruitment, e.g.

- promotion of existing staff (upwards or laterally)

- secondment (temporary transfers to another department, office, plant or country) of existing staff, which may or may not become permanent

- closing the job down, by sharing out duties and responsibilities among existing staff

- rotating jobs among staff, so that the vacant job is covered by different staff, on a systematic basis over several months

- putting the job out to tender, using external contractors.

1.4 Alternative employment arrangements

The majority of new recruits are still appointed on a full-time, permanent basis. However, because the profile of working people is changing organisations are beginning to turn towards other methods of employing staff. Alternative working arrangements include:

- Home working (or teleworking) – technical advances mean that a great deal of work can now be done from home.

- Job-sharing – where two or more employees split a job between them, normally doing the whole job for half the time.

- Flexitime – where core hours must be worked but employees can arrange how they make up sufficient hours over a period of a week or a month.

- Fixed term contracts – where employees are contracted to work for set periods.

There are many more ways of solving staffing problems and organisations are attempting to become more responsive to employee needs. Many organisations are beginning to adopt a 'flexible firm' model, which is characterised by a central core of permanent workers, surrounded and supported by contractors, temporary staff, seasonal workers and part-timers, who are brought in as and when required.

2 Job analysis

2.1 Introduction

DEFINITION

Job analysis is 'the determination of the **essential** characteristics of a job'. British Standards Institution (BSI 1979).

The job analysis will consider the collection of tasks, i.e. the job, to be undertaken by the job holder, procedures involved, relationships with other jobs and job holders, responsibilities of the post, the personal qualities, experience and qualifications required of the applicant. According to the British Standards Institution, job analysis is a vital preliminary to any recruitment activity and involves three main aspects; these are:

- an analytical study of a job to determine accurately the work done

- achieving an understanding of the work in relation to other tasks in the organisation

- an identification of the qualities required of the jobholder.

Such an exercise is frequently necessary since all too few organisations have a precise picture of the work that people do to achieve organisational objectives. It has often been said that discrepancies occur between what superiors believe is taking place, what job-holders believe is taking place, and what subordinates believe is taking place and all these can differ from what is actually taking place.

2.2 Job analysis: its importance

Effective recruitment depends upon accurate job analyses. Precision in identifying the type of person required by an organisation can save time and money and avoid unwanted personnel. For instance, if the exact nature of the job is known, then it facilitates precisely worded advertisements, which assist in attracting a suitable field of candidates. If the advertisement is loosely worded, based upon an insufficient analysis, then totally unsuitable candidates may be attracted to apply, thereby causing an increase in the costs of recruitment. Job analysis is helpful to the recruitment process in another way, since it may establish that the job is no longer necessary or that it can be done elsewhere in the organisation or that it can be shared amongst other employees. Thus, job analysis may eliminate the need for recruitment. However, apart from its value in the recruitment process, job analysis as a technique is useful in many areas of personnel work. The list below gives an indication of its many uses.

(a) To assist in determining the most appropriate method of selection.

(b) To help identify the need for training and the most appropriate training method.

(c) As part of a job evaluation exercise. Job analysis is the first step in establishing differences between jobs so that wage and salary differentials may be determined.

(d) As an important preliminary to any job redesign exercise, as in work improvement through job enrichment.

(e) It may be useful in the field of industrial relations by providing information vital to negotiating exercises.

2.3 Job descriptions

A job description specifies the tasks, details responsibilities, sets authority limits, distinguishes accountability and outlines the organisational relationships that the job entails. It can be used in job evaluation, which is a process of analysing and assessing jobs to ascertain their relative worth and using the assessments as a basis for a balanced wage structure.

After a full job analysis has been carried out, a job description can be drawn up identifying the precise nature of the job in question. There are various methods of classification but most include all of the following points.

(a) The title of the job and the name of the department in which it is situated.

(b) The purpose of the job, identifying its objectives in relationship to overall objectives.

(c) The position of the job in the organisation, indicating the relationships with other jobs and the chains of responsibility. For this purpose, many firms refer to existing organisation charts.

(d)   Wage/salary range.

(e)   Principal duties to be performed, with emphasis on key tasks, and limits to the jobholder's authority. Usually under this heading is included an indication of how the job differs from others in the organisation.

(f)   A further breakdown of principal duties is made identifying specific tasks in terms of what precisely is done and in what manner, and with some explanation, both in terms of quantity and quality.

(g)   Aspects of the 'job environment' should be considered. Descriptions should be made of how the organisation supports the job, in terms of management and the provision of key services. The working conditions should be considered in terms of both the physical environment and the social environment (is the job part of a group task?). The opportunities offered by the job should be identified; these are especially important in a recruitment exercise.

(h)   No job description is complete without a full identification of the key difficulties likely to be encountered by the jobholder.

2.4   Job evaluation

Job evaluation is used to determine wage and salary differentials. It is essentially concerned with relationships not absolutes. It provides data for developing basic pay structures but cannot determine what the pay levels should be. It is the job that is evaluated, not the person doing the job. However, job evaluation methods depend, to some extent, on a series of subjective judgements made in the light of concepts such as logic, justice and equity and the progressive refinement of job evaluation techniques is an attempt to minimise the subjective personal element.

Methods of job evaluation are both non-analytical and analytical. Non-analytical methods include job ranking and job classifications.

Job ranking – the simplest method of evaluation is an attempt to determine the relative position of each job in the undertaking in comparison with all other jobs though without indicating the extent of the difference between jobs at different levels. A committee usually undertakes the ranking.

Job classification – is similar to job ranking, except that instead of ranking jobs and then devising grades, the grades are pre-determined and the jobs are then evaluated and allocated to a grade identified by a number or letter. This system is used in the Civil Service with eight grades A–H in ascending order of work complexity.

Analytical methods include points rating and factor comparison

Points rating – involves several steps:

- the definition of job factors, e.g. skill, responsibility, education, working conditions
- determination of the number of points to be awarded to each factor, e.g. skill 100–300 points, responsibility 100–500 points, education 100–400 points
- breaking down of factors into a number of degrees on which jobs will be compared; thus education may be 4 GCSE levels or equivalent = 50 points, A levels =150 points, HNC = 200 points, second class honours degree = 300 points, higher degree = 400 points

- ranking of each job on each factor and determining the total number of points

- multiplying the total number of points by the value allocated to a point or group of points.

Factor comparison – like the points system, this is based on the assumption that jobs can be broken down into factors. Points, however, are not awarded to each factor; instead jobs are compared with each other on the basis of common factors. The steps involved are:

(a)   a number of representative 'key' jobs (15–20) are selected for comparison

(b)   the representative jobs are ranked according to the factors selected, e.g. skill, education

(c)   the portion of the current wage attributable to each factor for each representative job is chosen and the apportionment ranked.

Analytical methods allow a finer distinction to be drawn between jobs and so provide a more acceptable basis for showing whether jobs that have changed in content should also change in pay. Control over the wage structure is thus made easier. The main cause of wage inflation is that workplace bargaining often takes place in a piecemeal fragmented way, giving rise to anomalies and compensatory counterclaims from individual work groups. Job evaluation means the comparison of jobs, not employees, in a systematic analysis to determine their place in a hierarchy. It offers a basis for a structure of pay, which can at least be presented as rational. Job evaluation forces on management the same disciplined approach to personnel problems as is required in other spheres. For the employee, job evaluation means that increased skills and responsibility can be rewarded and recognised.

2.5   Person specifications

This is variously referred to as the personnel specification, the job specification and even the man specification. Its aim is to construct a blueprint of the qualities required of the jobholder. It is based firstly on the job description and secondly upon an analysis of successful as well as unsuccessful jobholders. Such a specification is of obvious value in framing recruitment advertisements and as a guide to the selection process. Several classifications have been produced, the most famous of which is undoubtedly the **Seven Point Plan** devised by Alec Rodger in the 1950s. Rodger's classification involves the following factors:

KEY POINT

Rodger's seven point plan: 'SCIPDAG'.

S   **Special aptitudes** – some jobs carry specialised requirements such as the ability to drive a car or bus, the ability to type, or the ability to speak a foreign language.

C   **Circumstances** – may include such factors as availability for working irregular hours or the home address of the candidate. For example, if a firm requires its employees to be on regular call, it may be difficult for someone living in an isolated rural community.

I   **Interests** – certain interests may be appropriate to certain jobs. Any interest in helping people may be considered a necessary requirement for social work. Candidates for certain teaching posts may be favoured if they express an interest in extra-mural activities such as drama or running a soccer team.

P   **Physical make-up** – this can be extremely precise, as in the case of listing minimum height requirements for recruits to the police force, or it can refer to more general attributes such as a pleasant appearance, a clear speaking voice and good health.

D   **Disposition** – all firms require their employees to be honest and reliable. A friendly disposition is usually essential in jobs that involve a great amount of contact with the general public as in the case of a receptionist. Jobs without close supervision invariably call for employees who are self-reliant and can make decisions.

A   **Attainments** – relate to both job attainments and educational attainments. It is quite common for organisations to stipulate minimum entry requirements in terms of the number of GCSEs, A-levels or a degree, and in some cases, as with jobs in the Civil Service, the class of degree. People aspiring to the professions, as in the case of accountancy, must have minimum educational qualifications to enable them to tackle the required professional examinations. Many jobs require applicants to possess specific work experiences such as typing speed, experience of working with certain types of computer language or proven ability at operating a certain machine.

G   **General intelligence** – many attempts have been made by psychologists to link measured intelligence levels with the ability to do certain jobs. Many jobs require such abilities as a good memory, verbal and numerical skills and problem solving.

KEY POINT

Munro-Fraser's 5-point plan: 'FIRMI'.

A similar blueprint was devised by Munro-Fraser. He referred to it as the **Five Point Plan**, to include the following considerations:

F   Flexibility and adjustment – emotional stability, ability to get on with others and capacity for stress.

I   Impact on other people – appearance, speech and manner.

R   Required qualifications – education, training, and experience.

M   Motivation – determination and achievement.

I   Innate abilities – 'brains', comprehension and aptitude for learning.

Whichever classification system is used it must be adapted to the job in question. It may be useful to distinguish between essential and desirable attributes. Plumbley suggests that it is also important to identify contra-indications, i.e. attributes that would disqualify a candidate. It can clearly be seen that a person specification can be helpful in not only the recruitment process but also as a template by which candidates may be selected. It is important to reiterate an earlier point about the need to be flexible and to draw up the specification in terms that can be recognised and measured – not a list of abstract human qualities. Finally, care must be taken not to transgress one of the laws relating to discrimination, as in the case of a job advertisement seeking 'a female Scottish cook and housekeeper', which was barred both on the grounds of race and sex discrimination.

3 Channels of recruitment

3.1 Internal or external recruitment

Once the content and value of each job and the ideal requirements of the jobholder have been determined, recruitment can begin. Management must make a decision as to whether the organisation is seeking to recruit from within or from outside. Each has its own advantages and disadvantages.

Internal recruitment occurs when a vacant position is filled by one of the existing employees. It generally applies to those jobs where there is some kind of career structure, as in the case of management or administrative staff. Most firms invariably recruit supervisors from their own shop floor staff. If a policy of internal recruitment is to be pursued the following points should be noted:

(a) Recruiting from within by promoting existing employees can act as a source of motivation and may be good for the general morale of the workforce.

(b) In dealing with existing staff, selection can be made on the basis of known data. The old adage of 'better the devil you know' applies here.

(c) The internal recruit may be fully conversant with the work involved and will certainly know the people with whom they will be dealing; they may even have been carrying out the duties either as part of their own job or as the understudy to the incumbent.

(d) It can save considerable time and expense in recruitment and selection.

(e) If training is required this can be costly, but generally no induction is needed, and the firm may be able to train employees to its own specifications.

External recruitment occurs when an organisation seeks to bring in someone from outside the organisation to fill a vacancy. In general its advantages and disadvantages are opposite to those of internal recruitment, but the following specific points should be noted:

(a) External recruitment may be essential if an organisation is seeking specific skills and expertise that is not available internally. At some stage external recruitment is necessary to restore manning levels, depleted by employee wastage and internal promotion policies.

(b) It may be necessary to inject new blood into an enterprise. People from outside the firm often bring with them new ideas and different approaches to the job, gleaned from their experience working in other organisations. With internal promotion policies there is a real danger of producing a succession of employees all with the same ideas; indeed, this may be a barrier to progress in the organisation. On the other hand, it should be remembered that newcomers can be equally set in their ways and have difficulties of adjustment to new techniques and approaches.

(c) Although training costs may be reduced since there is the opportunity to recruit personnel with the required expertise, external recruitment does add to replacement and selection costs, and induction is still necessary.

(d) Bringing in someone from outside may create dissatisfaction among existing employees.

(e)   In order to attract people to change their jobs a firm may have to pay initially higher wages.

3.2   Types of advertising

The national press is probably most suitable for the recruitment of managerial, some professional and senior technical staff. More popular daily papers such as the *Daily Mirror* may be used where large numbers of skilled or semi-skilled workers are required, and incentives are offered for moving area. The main advantages include the following:

*   There is regular publication, so space is usually available for an immediate insertion.

*   The layout is usually attractive.

*   There is a wide circulation and readership, thereby increasing the field of potential candidates.

*   Many British newspapers are sold in other countries, so that overseas coverage is achieved at no extra cost. This may be important in recruiting for jobs requiring the experience of working in another country, as in some marketing posts.

*   Certain newspapers such as *The Times* have a certain status, which may enhance the reputation of the firm.

*   Some newspapers have regular job features. The *Guardian*, for instance, devotes particular days to certain types of job advertisements; Monday is devoted to media appointments, Tuesday to teaching appointments and so on.

The main disadvantages include the following:

*   The fact that approximately 95% of the circulation is wasted.

*   The advertisement has a relatively short life; many people do not keep daily newspapers beyond the day of issue.

*   Since national papers are popular sources of recruitment, competition is fierce. A firm may find that its advertising is surrounded by others of a similar nature, perhaps offering more attractive jobs.

*   The national press is very expensive. A column centimetre can cost anything from £10 – £20 and a large block display can be £1,000 or more; and these rates apply for only one issue.

Local newspapers are probably most suited for the recruitment of skilled manual, clerical, local authority and lower management positions. The main advantages include the following:

*   It is usually much cheaper than the national press (but it still may constitute a considerable expense for some firms).

*   It can reduce recruitment and selection costs by eliminating the costs of resettlement in that readers are usually from the local area.

*   The firm may already be well known so that the length of advertisements may be reduced.

*   The use of local papers has the added advantage of contributing to good public relations and vacancies may attract editorial coverage.

*   Most local papers have a longer life than their national counterparts.

The main disadvantages include the following:

- A sufficient number of people with the necessary requirements may not be available in the local area.

- Circulation is usually limited and issues are often only on a weekly basis.

- The quality of layout is very variable.

Specialist journals include the publications of the professional bodies and various trade journals. As such they are most suited for recruitment in the professions and specialist trades. The main advantages include the following:

- The readership is particularly homogeneous; there is already a degree of pre-selection, which may reduce eventual recruitment and selection costs.

- Many, because of their small circulation, have relatively cheap advertising rates, although this may not be the case for the more popular accounting journals.

- It may be assumed that likely readers are those who wish to keep up-to-date with developments in their field.

- The main disadvantages include the following:

- Closing dates for advertisements usually occur well before publication; this can inhibit speedy recruitment.

- Because they are so specialised there is considerable competition from other advertisements.

- Many give little space to job advertisements.

- Circulation can be slow and haphazard, particularly where it involves subscription readership.

Radio and television – using radio and television is increasing in popularity particularly since the advent of commercial radio. Whilst there is wide exposure, the desired audience may not be listening or watching. In some cases firms using television have been overwhelmed by the response, which creates significant problems of selection. Although television advertising can be more expensive than the national press, the use of television, along with the cinema, may be appropriate for mass recruiting in situations of severe labour shortage.

Activity 1

What might happen if the organisation failed to keep internal applications for vacancies a secret from the applicant's line manager?

Feedback to this activity is at the end of the chapter.

4 The application form and references

4.1 The application form

A common procedure is to invite inquirers to complete a standard application form accompanied by a short hand-written letter of application. The application form usually seeks information about the applicant on several fronts, namely:

- personal details of address, age, family background, nationality

- education and experience history

- present employment terms and experience

- social and leisure interests.

The application form should be regarded by the applicant as an opportunity to qualify for the interview. It usually includes a general section enabling the applicant to express career ambitions, personal preferences, and perhaps even aspects of motivation, ambition and character, in their own words.

The application form has advantages over the personal CV in that it allows for standard comparisons between applicants and it includes all areas of interest to the company. As well as obtaining all the essential information about the applicant, the purposes of the application form are:

- To eliminate totally unsuitable candidates; a standardised form speeds the sorting and short-listing of applicants and can be most useful where the ratio of applicants to vacancies is high. At a basic level it is a test of literacy and the ability to understand simple instructions.

- To act as a useful preliminary to selection interviews. Basic information can be gained which would otherwise take up valuable interview time. Some interviewers use the form as the framework for the interview itself; it can be a particularly useful guide for inexperienced interviewers. Some organisations have extended the role played by the application form compared to the interview by asking for much more detailed information, sometimes asking candidates to answer questions relating to their motivation towards applying.

- It forms the nucleus of the personal record of individual employees. A well-designed application form contains all the relevant data relating to address, age, qualifications, previous experience and so on. This should be updated at regular intervals.

4.2 References

Generally the personnel department issue a standard letter requesting a reference because this is relatively easy, but it places a considerable workload on the referee. Using the telephone as a means of gaining a reference, although more time-consuming, often leads to better and more accurate information on the applicant.

The type and number of references taken up varies with different organisations. Many companies suggest going back five years or two previous jobs. Applicants' present employers are contacted only after a decision has been made to make an offer of employment.

4.3 The purpose of references

References are used by most employees as a key part of their selection process, but mainly to verify facts about the candidate rather than as an aid to decision making. The reference check is usually the last stage in the selection process and referees should be contacted only after the applicant has given permission. Good referees are almost certain to know more about the applicant than the selector and it would be foolish not to seek their advice or to treat the reference check as a mere formality.

As well as the applicant's suitability for employment, the reference may provide information on strengths and weaknesses, training needs and potential for future development.

4.4 The problems with references

Unfortunately, references are notoriously poor predictors of future performance. Some referees take the task seriously but many do not, and because most of them are well known to the applicant, they hesitate to say anything critical.

Where people are dissatisfied or frustrated in their present jobs, they could come out badly in a reference. Star students can turn out to be less than star employees, and sacked employees could turn out to be real winners in a different organisation. Employers wishing to rid themselves of an unsatisfactory employee could write a glowing reference, or one that leaves a lot unsaid. Some references are too ambiguous to be useful, e.g. 'Any manager would be lucky to get Miss Jones to do the accounts'. The skilful reference reader learns to look for what is conspicuous by omission, although there is a risk that the writer merely forgot.

The poor predictive validity of the reference may be due to the blandness of the request. To overcome this, employers should ask direct and meaningful questions. One question that might be included is whether the employer would re-employ the candidate and, if not, why not.

Activity 2

Why might an employer give a poor reference to a member of staff?

Feedback to this activity is at the end of the chapter.

5 The selection process

5.1 The process

Selection is the process, at the end of which a decision is made as to whether an individual is offered and takes up employment with an organisation. Not only is the firm selecting the individual but also, invariably the individual is making decisions as to the suitability of the job offered, the terms of employment and the firm.

Methods of selection include the short-listing of applicants, collecting information about the applicants and the design and preparation of the selection process.

The diagram below outlines the process:

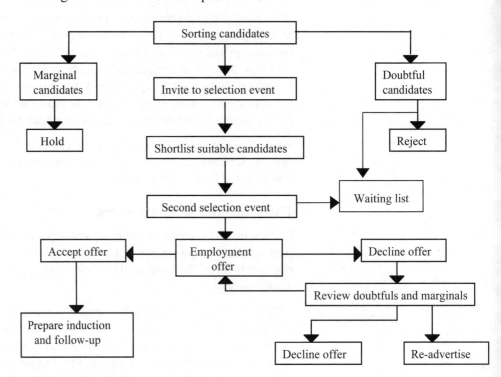

5.2 Screening and short listing

Before selection can take place the number of applicants must be reduced to manageable proportions. The employer must decide the criteria that are essential and desirable to do the job effectively. Candidates should be screened according to these conditions and placed in one of three categories, e.g. potential, doubtful and marginal. The doubtfuls should be sent a standard letter briefly, but tactfully, dismissing them. The marginals will be kept on hold and informed of the situation and the potentials, assuming there are enough, will be invited for a selection event.

In general, selection events should be tailor-made for a particular organisation and job. The thoroughness of the procedure will depend on a number of factors

- The consequences of faulty selection; obviously an organisation will take more care in selecting its Financial Director than it will in selecting its car-park attendant.

- The time and finance available; these are both constraints on the process. A firm may have neither the time nor the money to invest in lengthy, complicated selection methods.

- The company policy, which may lay down certain rules for the composition of selection panels or the use of certain tests. Some companies have policies of over-hiring certain types of trainees, to ensure that the most able graduate is available for all positions. This will often offset losses through labour turnover.

- The selection process becomes more important the longer the length of the training period, since this represents a considerable investment on the part of the organisation.

The selection event can include the application form, interviews, tests, references, medical examinations, group selection methods, situational tests and/or assessment centres.

5.3 The selection interview

The interview is a third stage in the selection process.

The purpose of the interview must be clear. It has three main aims:

- finding the best person for the job
- making sure that the candidate understands what the job is and what the career prospects are
- making the candidate feel that they have been given fair treatment in the interview.

Other objectives to be achieved at the interview include:

- To confirm and expand on the information about candidates given in the application form, in other documents or on the telephone.
- To assess candidates' personality and motivation.
- To obtain further details on certain matters.
- To ensure applicants have a reasonable knowledge of the job and the organisation and to provide them with more information if required.
- To evaluate the suitability of the candidates for the job.
- To encourage the most suitable candidate to take the job.
- To agree terms of employment.

5.4 The selection interview process

An interview process can be:

A face-to-face interview – carried out once by a single representative, usually of the employing organisation. It is considered the best situation for establishing rapport and is certainly cost effective in terms of people employed. While it does have the advantage of placing candidates at ease, enabling the interviewer to gain a true picture of the applicant, the selection decision relies heavily on the judgement of one individual.

A problem-solving interview – this is a face-to-face interview where the candidate is set a hypothetical problem. For example, a problem may be posed to a prospective industrial relations trainee concerning the action they would take following a fight between a foreman and a shop steward where both participants told a different version of the incident and a work stoppage had ensued. The drawback with such interviews is that the quality of the answers is very difficult to assess and compare to those given by other candidates.

A stress interview – this is another face-to-face interview, where the candidate is put under deliberate stress usually by an aggressive interviewer, who attempts to disparage the candidate's answers at every opportunity. This method of interviewing proved successful during the war for selecting undercover agents and was in vogue a few years ago for selecting managers, based on the theory that their ability to handle stressful situations was the best test of their ability. Research evidence concerning stress interviews suggests they are of dubious value and can actually cause harm by alienating favourable candidates.

Succession of interviews – by different interviewers (e.g. operating manager and personnel officer). Common practice in leading companies is to conduct several face-to-face interviews, rather than a single panel interview. Obviously this type of exercise is more costly and can be more wearing on the candidate, but it may enable a more balanced judgement to be made.

Group interview – where candidates are brought together and observed by assessors, who give the group a problem to discuss or a situation to sort out. It is a sort of committee exercise. This method can identify personal reactions such as tact, dominance and persuasiveness.

Panel interview – candidates are interviewed before a panel of two or more people, in some cases as many as six or seven. For some senior posts in some local authorities in Britain, panels of 20 or more can be found. The usual panel size is between two and six interviewers, depending upon the nature of the job and the customs of the employing organisation. Panel interviews have the advantage of sharing judgements and most panels have the authority to reach immediate decisions. Their main drawback is the question of control: with so many people, irrelevancies can be introduced and a particular line of questioning can soon be destroyed. The success of a panel interview often depends upon careful planning and effective chairmanship. While they can be impressive in terms of ritual, panel interviews can be particularly unnerving for some candidates.

5.5 Assessment centres

These are centres where groups of around six to ten candidates are brought together for one to three days of intensive assessment. They are presented, individually and as a group, with a variety of exercises, tests of ability, personality assessments interviews work samples team problem solving and written tasks. As well as being multi-method, other characteristics of assessment centres are that they use several assessors and they assess several dimensions of performance required in the higher-level positions.

Traditionally, the main purpose of assessment centres has been to contribute to management decisions about people, usually the assessment of management skills and potential as a basis for promotion decisions. Assessment centres are better at predicting future performance than judgements made by unskilled managers, and it is the combination of techniques that contributes to their apparent superiority over other approaches.

5.6 Selection testing

Selection testing includes medical examinations, attainment testing, psychological tests and observation of the candidate in group situations. The tests used usually take the form of pencil and paper tests, and it is argued that such testing helps:

DEFINITION

A test is a standardised type of examination given to an individual.

- to assess the ability and quality of existing employees

- to assess the potential of shortlisted future employees

- to reduce the cost of recruitment by cutting down the time spent on subjective interviewing

- to eliminate or at least reduce the risk of making costly mistakes

- to minimise staff turnover, which is also costly.

The main problem with any form of selection test is ensuring that it is relevant to the type of appointment. The main types of testing are.

(a) **Intelligence tests** – such as general IQ tests. These involve the setting of some kind of task or problem, which is designed to gauge levels of reasoning, understanding, memory and speed of thought. The need for such tests is not considered necessary where existence of a formal education path can be shown.

(b) **Aptitude tests** – aim to measure some inborn potentiality of a certain kind, rather than acquired skill or knowledge. They are basically used to obtain information about such skills as mechanical ability, clerical and numerical ability and manual dexterity.

(c) **Competence tests** – sometimes called attainment tests, measure the depth of knowledge or grasp of skills that have been learned in the past. For example, a car mechanic could be asked to tune a car engine using a machine that they claim to be experienced in using.

(d) **Personality tests** – usually take the form of personality inventories. These are lists of multiple choice questions where the aim is to reveal 'what a person really is' or how a person would react in certain situations. The importance of personality in employment is that what people are determines what they do. A typical personality test asks people to report on their likes, dislikes, attitudes and what they would do in certain situations.

(e) **Medical examinations** – eliminate candidates with health problems that might affect their attendance at work or endanger the health or safety of colleagues, and protect prospective staff from being employed in work for which they are physically unsuitable. These are mandatory for some jobs, notably for airline pilots, bus drivers and hospital workers. Apart from a general check on fitness they can assist in the placement of employees, especially when dealing with disabled candidates. In some firms a medical examination is required as part of that firm's agreement with an insurance company.

(f) **Group selection methods** – the classic format for such methods is where a group of leaderless candidates are presented with a simulated work problem. Such tests are much used by the British Army as part of their officer selection programme and are also used by several large organisations in the selection of graduate trainees.

(g) **Situational tests** – are developed to meet the criticism of most other types of test, where answers are either right or wrong. Those in favour of situational tests argue that most work situations are probabilistic and the most useful tests are those of problem-solving and creative thinking in a work simulated setting. The classic format for such tests is in group selection.

5.7 The criteria for effective selection

The selection decision is a very important one. It should be as objective as possible by using the job analysis, a clear interview plan containing meaningful comments, a fair grading scheme and by acknowledging the following criteria.

Discrimination – whichever method of selection is used, the manager must be able to discriminate between candidates to make a selection decision. For example, if ten candidates are given a written test as part of the selection procedure and all score 100%, then the test has failed to discriminate between candidates. This criterion is particularly important in the design of tests; in some cases questions must be eliminated which prove to be too difficult or too easy for all candidates.

Reliability – this is a question of the dependability of the method of selection.

Regardless of the method and approach chosen, good selection will ultimately rest on the firm understanding of the requirements of the job and job holder and a sensible use of techniques, which will objectively measure the extent to which the candidates possess those qualities and skills.

5.8 Making the offer of employment

Once an eligible candidate has been found, an offer can be made, in writing or by telephone, subject to satisfactory references.

The organisation should be prepared for its offer to be rejected at this stage. An applicant may have received and accepted another offer, may have disliked their first view of the organisation, may have changed their mind or may have just been testing the water in applying in the first place. A small number of applicants will be kept in reserve to cover this eventuality.

An effective offer of employment must not contain anything that cannot be delivered and should contain the following elements:

- Must be a written document – a written statement is a legally binding document, which should help to seal the offer. A telephone call to break the good news to the successful candidate is fine, but should not go into too much detail about the offer in conversation.

- Must contain sufficient detail – must contain the job title and location with details of pay, benefits, hours of work, holiday as well as the terms and conditions of employment, including notice period, sickness payment schemes, pension scheme details, disciplinary and grievance procedures and an outline of the probationary period where one is in force.

- Should offer an opportunity to make further contact before a final commitment is made – a clear but informal opportunity for further discussion, which may lead to negotiation on terms and conditions of employment.

5.9 Negotiation of the employment offer

After the offer of employment is made, it may be necessary to reach a mutually agreeable compromise over some aspects of the employment contract. This could mean negotiating over pay, hours of work, holiday arrangements or the type of car on offer.

Negotiating is an activity that seeks to reach agreement between two or more starting positions, enabling parties with opposing interests to bargain. This bargaining leads to a situation of compromise and agreement. Regardless of the nature of the dispute, the same principles will apply and the aim will be to reach a solution that is acceptable to both parties – a 'win-win' situation. A 'win-lose' situation culminates where one group has achieved its objectives at the clear expense of the other. This solution tends to cause dissatisfaction and the situation could deteriorate into a 'lose-lose' position where the benefits originally gained by the winner are continuously eroded by resistance and a lack of commitment.

Activity 3

You are a manager of quite a large accounts department. You have three deputies and the rule is that only one of them can be away on holiday or attend a course at a time. All three approach you in March asking for the same two weeks off in June. Tom, who is the most senior of the three, wants to do a sponsored bike ride in Cuba. Dick wants to take his family to Las Vegas for his brother's wedding. Harry has been accepted on a special course that will enhance his promotional prospects.

Each of them hears about the other's applications and they have a furious row and now only talk to each other about work-related matters.

Outline five different ways of dealing with this situation.

Feedback to this activity is at the end of the chapter.

6 The induction process and fair and legal employment practices

6.1 Induction

A new entrant's first impressions can be very important in shaping their attitude to the company and colleagues. A warm welcome, introductions to other members of the organisation and a well-planned induction programme will reassure the new member. Reassurance will aid motivation and attitude to work performance. Induction courses are arranged for new recruits to an organisation to enable them to familiarise themselves with the firm and to adjust to the requirements of the organisation.

Induction is an opportunity to affirm corporate values and objectives while the employee is still likely to be comparatively receptive and before they have been subjected to dissenting views. It is also an opportunity to provide the employee with an organisational context for their own duties and responsibilities. Induction covers the rules and regulations, methods of operation and personal training and development needs. Effective induction is an extension of the recruitment and selection procedure, starting with the selection process and covering the first few months at work.

6.2 Process

The first stage might involve a tour of the offices and factory, talks or films on the history and products or services of the organisation, and an explanation of the policy relating to holidays, sickness, trade union membership, flexitime, etc. On the first day, the paperwork will need to be sorted, e.g. P45, banking details, confirmation of educational qualifications etc. Induction is a matter of telling and showing, to build familiarisation swiftly, enabling new entrants to maximise their contribution to the company in the minimum time.

Someone joining an accounts department would then require an introduction to the structure of the departmental organisation and their role in it. Here, the idea is to familiarise the new recruit with colleagues. Arrangements should be made at this stage for someone to go to lunch and/or tea with the new person, mainly because it can be very lonely on your first day sitting on your own in the canteen. If at all possible the new employee's manager and head of department should be available over the first few days to give a clear indication of their commitment to ensuring that things work out well. Details of the methods of working would also be given (much of this may be embodied in an office manual) and instruction given by a supervisor on the requirements of the post for which the recruit was engaged.

For staff who are seeking membership of one of the accountancy bodies the selection of the most appropriate qualification and methods of study will have to be determined in discussions between the student, the accountant and the training officer (this may have been agreed at the selection interview). In addition a training programme must be initiated so that the correct practical experience is obtained to satisfy the requirements of the accountancy body.

Within the accountancy profession there is much emphasis on post-qualifying education (PQE) and details of courses provided by all the accountancy bodies, and other organisations, should be readily available. Staff should be encouraged to attend to keep their knowledge up to date and, in some instances, staff may be directed to attend, e.g. to update skills and knowledge.

Staff at all levels should be encouraged to develop their knowledge and abilities to as far as they are capable (and wish). In accounts departments, there are many opportunities to specialise and this should be encouraged, provided it is compatible with the policies and requirements within the organisation, and there are understudies for all areas of knowledge.

After about two months on the job, it is good practice to arrange a meeting where the new employee can discuss areas of concern and find out how they are getting on. The meeting may be timed to coincide with the end of the probationary period or with the presentation of the formal statement of terms and conditions of employment.

This follow-up should be designed to explore issues of satisfaction, expectation and motivation. Attention should be given to the quality of training received and the nature of interpersonal relationships within the workgroup. The outcome should be a positive one but, when it is negative, action must be taken to investigate areas of dissent to help that employee and to make sure it does not happen in the future.

6.3 Fair and legal employment practices

The culture of an organisation is 'the general pattern of behaviour, shared beliefs and values the members have in common'. It is the culture of the organisation that helps to determine whether the procedures and practices used in the organisation are just and fair.

'Equal Opportunities' is a generic term describing the belief that there should be an equal chance for all workers to apply and be selected for jobs, to be trained and promoted in employment and to have that employment terminated fairly. Employers should only discriminate according to ability, experience and potential. All employment decisions should be based solely on a person's ability to do the job in question; no consideration should be taken of a person's gender, age, racial origin, disability or marital status. In the recruitment process the following legislation can protect an individual in employment:

- **The Equal Pay Act (1975)** that allows employers to gradually eliminate gender differentials relating to pay.

- **The Sex Discrimination Act (1975)** that renders it unlawful to make any form of discrimination in employment affairs because of gender or marital status. Discrimination, either direct or indirect, and victimisation are outlawed under this Act.

- **The Disabled Person Act (1958)** that encourages employers to provide for disabled persons in the workplace and outlaws discriminatory practices in employment.

- **The Race Relations Act (1976)** uses a broadly similar approach to that of the Sex Discrimination Act and uses the same categorisations of direct and indirect discrimination and victimisation.

- **The Rehabilitation of Offenders Act (1974)** provides that a conviction, other than one involving imprisonment for more than 30 months, may be erased if no other serious offences are committed during the rehabilitation period.

6.4 Managing employee relations

A certain amount of conflict in an organisation is not only inevitable, it is often beneficial, for conflict is both a cause and an effect of change. Managing conflict is a key part of a manager's role and within an organisation there are policies and procedures that help a manager carry out this particular role. Procedural agreements are agreements made between employers and employee representatives. Procedural agreements may relate to:

- grievances
- discipline
- disputes
- promotion, and
- redundancy.

7 Redundancy

This is covered by the Employment Protection (Consolidation) Act 1978. In the statutes, redundancy is defined as occurring when ...The employer has stopped or is about to stop carrying on business in the place or for the purpose for which the employee in question was employed, or where the requirements of the business for work of a particular kind, or in a particular place, have ceased or diminished or are likely to do so.

7.1 Reasons for redundancy

Redundancy arises when the employer:

(a)   has ceased to carry on business at the place at which the employee was employed

(b)   no longer has a requirement for the work that the employee was employed to carry out.

The most frequent causes of redundancy at the present time are:

(a) Organisations taking advantage of technological advances to reduce staffing levels. This is a significant factor in both blue and white collar employment. However, new technology does not necessarily always lead to conspicuous manpower savings.

(b) Organisations taking initiatives to reduce overmanning in industries where trade unions had maintained unrealistic staffing levels or industries which required streamlining to meet new economic conditions.

(c) Changes in the structure of employment with the increased use of 'peripheral' workers at the expense of 'core' workers.

(d) 'Cut backs' in public expenditure with resultant enforced redundancies.

(e) Shedding of employees unable to deal with the necessary changes taking place in the organisation.

(f) Changes in the structure of organisations with fewer lower level workers and consequently, fewer middle managers.

The pace of changes in our society is increasing. Economic, social and technological change will influence dramatically all organisations and as such stable employment patterns, where 45 years of employment in a single organisation was possible, will be unknown. The future pattern of work is uncertain and is likely to remain so, but it would be true to say that organisations are being forced to make more intensive use of manpower. They have also resorted to unusual employment practices as an alternative to redundancies – job sharing, networking, consultancy contracts, part-time and temporary assignments, use of manpower agencies. However, it is fair to say that redundancy will continue to play a large part in the work of personnel specialists.

7.2 Redundancy pay

Compensation for redundancy is available to all employees with over two years' service (with certain exceptions) and is paid according to a sliding scale related to age, length of service and the weekly amount of pay, as follows:

(a) One and a half weeks' pay for each year of service wherein the employee is 41 years of age or over.

(b) One week's pay for each year of service wherein the employee is between 22 and 41 years of age.

(c) Half week's pay for each year of service wherein the employee is between 18 and 22 years of age.

In all cases the pay referred to is the most recent weekly rate subject to a statutory minimum. In addition firms making more than ten employees redundant must notify the Secretary of State for Employment and consult the trades unions involved at **the earliest opportunity**. Employees who are being made redundant are expected to be given a reasonable amount of time off with pay to seek alternative employment.

Many firms go beyond the statutory requirements and offer redundancy payments in excess of the minimum required. Some personnel departments have instigated a redundancy counselling service whereby employees who are to be made redundant are given advice on how to cope with their changed status and also offered facilities including contacts with other employers in the area.

7.3 Selection for redundancy

When companies devise redundancy policies or agreements they often spend much time and effort on drawing up a detailed list of selection criteria and order of discharge.

(a)   The practice of last-in-first-out is not necessarily the starting point for declaring redundancies. Indeed in many cases it is the final stage when all else has failed. If a company has insufficient volunteers, whether for redundancy or early retirement, part-time staff and so on, then the last criterion usually used is last-in-first-out. Two points have to be taken into consideration:

  (i)   the need to retain a balanced staff, and

  (ii)   the length of company and departmental service.

(b)   Any hint of discrimination either negative or positive should be avoided. Perceived 'favourites' will have an adverse effect on the workforce preserved. There is always the danger in 'value to the organisation' of subjective judgement entering into the equation. However, justification can be made even in breach of an agreement where the special skills of the employee can be shown to be necessary for the continued functioning of the department, process, etc.

(c)   Most agreements provide for the acceptance of voluntary redundancy before any attempt is made to terminate employment compulsorily. Companies prefer to use voluntary severance as it avoids problems over selection, also hardship and resentment. The most common combination of voluntary terms are indeed large lump sums for those with little service (and therefore little entitlement under the statutory scheme) and early retirement for those aged over 55 or 60.

Companies can face two problems when asking for volunteers – maintaining a balanced workforce and selecting from volunteers when they get a massive oversubscription. The bulk of organisations get round the problem of a balanced workforce by reserving the right to refuse a volunteer.

(d)   Early retirement is probably the first method to be used by most companies in a situation which requires the workforce to be reduced. The plea of a company for individuals over a certain age to take early retirement is nowadays construed as the 'thin end of the wedge.' However, there are those to whom this form of 'redundancy' might appeal. If the compensation and pension rights are generous and available to those within five years of retirement, there is every possibility that there may be acceptors. For those aged 55, however, the scheme would involve further employment which could be difficult in the present climate.

In making any redundancy decisions, many factors have to be taken into account. Early retirement, under reasonable terms, does seem to be the least harsh way to deal with such a situation, but the organisation has to be careful to preserve a balance of age and experience. Failing a satisfactory result on early retirement, voluntary redundancy opens the way to individual choice. It is only when both methods have proved ineffective that organisations resort to compulsory redundancies under whatever guise.

8 Dealing with grievance and disciplinary matters

8.1 Grievance

A grievance occurs when an employee feels that there is something in the work situation that is wrong, unjust, unfair or unreasonable. Some grievances are individual – such as a dislike of something that is said or a manager's approach. Others are group grievances, where one person volunteers to represent others. Many grievances are about pay but in times of economic uncertainty, grievances may be about job security and employees will express this in 'territory defending' behaviour.

A grievance may become a complaint to express the employee dissatisfaction or it may become a dispute, which is a formal expression of dissatisfaction at organisational level.

When an individual or group has a grievance, there should be a procedure to enable the problem to be resolved. Some grievances are resolved informally by the appropriate manager but, if an informal solution is not possible, there should be a formal grievance procedure.

Some grievances are genuine and well founded, others may be imaginary. But they must all be treated seriously because if they are left unresolved they can grow until they become a grievance of the whole workforce and a subject of dispute.

8.2 Discipline

The word discipline tends to be associated with authority, force, warnings, threats and/or punishment. However, discipline can also be used to maintain sensible conduct and orderliness. Most mature people accept the idea that following instructions and fair rules of conduct are normal responsibilities that are part of any job. They believe in performing their work properly, in following instructions, in coming to work on time and in refraining from fighting, drinking, stealing or taking drugs at work.

The types of disciplinary situations that require attention by the manager include:

- excessive absenteeism

- defective or inadequate work performance

- breaking safety rules and other violations of rules, regulations and procedures

- improper personal appearance.

The purpose of discipline is not punishment or retribution. The goal of disciplinary action is to improve the future behaviour of the employee and other members of the organisation. The purpose is avoidance of similar occurrences in the future.

Many organisations adopt a progressive discipline approach following a list of suggested steps:

(i)   The informal talk – where the infraction is of a relatively minor nature and the employee's record has no previous marks of disciplinary action. The manager discusses with the employee his or her behaviour in relation to standards that prevail in the organisation.

(ii)   Oral warning or reprimand – emphasises the dissatisfaction with the subordinate's repeated violation, which could lead to serious disciplinary action.

(iii)   Written or official warning – becomes a permanent part of the employee's record and may be used as evidence in the case of grievance procedures.

(iv)   Disciplinary layoff or suspension without pay is used when previous steps were of no avail.

(v)   Demotion is a form of constant punishment due to losing pay and status over an extended period of time.

(vi)   Discharge/dismissal is a drastic form of disciplinary action reserved for the most serious offences.

8.3 Role of procedures in handling conflict

An important part of any employee relations' policy is to set out the broad standards of conduct that the organisation intends to follow in respect of unacceptable behaviour on the part of the employee (disciplinary matters) and grievances raised by the employee.

The role of procedures in handling conflict is to:

- create a means of solving problems and grievances while allowing work to go on

- provide a means by which justice can be seen to be done

- allow time for issues to be judged more calmly

- remove problems from immediate source of dispute for examination at objective levels

- give protection to the individual against personal animosity

- redress the balance of power towards the individual

- specify time scales and appeals procedures.

8.4 Grievance procedures

Grievance procedures should provide a speedy means by which employees can seek redress for any grievances they may have at work. A good procedure aims to achieve a solution to a grievance as near as possible to the point of origin or to process the grievance without delay to a higher level in the management chain. In a grievance situation, the manager concerned should aim to establish the facts relating to the grievance and eventually reach a mutually acceptable solution.

Formal grievance procedures should be set out in writing and do the following:

- clarify the categories of employees to which they apply and ensure they are aware of their rights

- specify who employees can take their grievance to in first instance (usually their immediate boss) and subsequent steps

- allow friend or representative involvement

- define time limits between processes

- define distinctions between collective and individual grievances.

A typical grievance procedure usually follows the stages set out below:

(i) The employee should first raise the matter with the immediate supervisor or manager and may be accompanied by a fellow employee. The supervisor or manager will endeavour to resolve the problem without delay.

(ii) If the employee is not satisfied with the response of the superior, he or she may refer the grievance to the department manager or other senior manager, who will hear the grievance within five working days. A fellow employee may accompany the employee and the company HR manager will be present.

(iii) If the employee is still dissatisfied after the second stage, he or she may appeal to a director who will arrange to hear the appeal within five working days. The results of the appeal will be recorded and distributed to all the parties concerned.

8.5 Disciplinary procedures

The aim of this type of procedure is to correct unsatisfactory behaviour, rather than punish it. A good disciplinary procedure should be clearly stated, in writing and should enable employees to feel assured of fairness and consistency of treatment if ever they should become subject to the procedure. It should specify as fully as possible what constitutes 'misconduct' and 'gross misconduct' and state what the most likely penalty is for each of these categories and how long an offence is kept on the records. In cases of proven gross misconduct, this is most likely to be immediate dismissal, or suspension followed by dismissal. There should be a definition of who has the authority for dismissal. In cases of less serious misconduct, the most likely consequence is that a formal warning will be given. For repeated acts of misconduct, it is likely that the employee concerned will be dismissed.

Employees should have right to reply to complaints against them and be given an opportunity to have a friend or representative with them at each stage in procedures. There should be an appeals procedure, with times clearly specified between each stage.

8.6 External means of dealing with grievance and disciplinary matters

The Employment Protection (Consolidation) Act 1978 defines the terms of a contract of employment. The express terms are specifically stated in the contract, which must provide the names of the parties concerned, the date of the commencement of the job, its title, terms of payment, working hours, holiday, sick pay and pension entitlements, notice of termination of employment, discipline and grievance procedures.

Wherever possible, the employee should be given a statement of the conditions and the regulations of service in writing. This should be completely understood by the employee and he or she should be able to ask for any clarification – which should be offered willingly. Only in this way can there be a clear understanding and the avoidance of conflict in these issues.

As far as the discipline and grievance procedures are concerned, the contract must state the person appointed to deal with grievances and the person to whom employees may express dissatisfaction concerning any disciplinary matters relating to themselves.

The contract must also indicate a document that sets out the disciplinary rules (and this must be available to all employees) or it must specify the rules itself. Alterations must be notified to all employees.

The Advisory, Conciliation and Arbitration Service (ACAS) was established under the Employment Protection Act 1975, and operates services of conciliation, both on an individual and group basis, arbitration, mediation and enquiry. In addition ACAS offers advice to organisations, particularly in its preparation of Codes of Practice, e.g. in the area of disciplinary procedures. The code proposes that disciplinary procedures should follow certain guidelines as follows:

- should be in written form

- must identify to whom they apply (all, or some of the employees)

- should be able to deal speedily with disciplinary matters

- should indicate the forms of disciplinary action which may be taken (e.g. dismissal, suspension or warning)

- should specify the appropriate levels of authority for the exercise of disciplinary actions

- should provide for employees to be informed of the nature of their alleged misconduct

- should allow employees to state their case, and to be accompanied by a fellow employee and/or union representative

- make sure that every case is properly investigated before any disciplinary action is taken

- must inform employees of the reasons for any penalty they receive

- should state that no employee will be dismissed for a first offence, except in cases of gross misconduct

- should provide for a right of appeal against any disciplinary action

- should specify the appeals procedure.

Where employees feel that they have been unfairly dismissed they have the right to take their case to the Industrial Tribunal. The tribunal will normally refer the case to ACAS in the hope of gaining an amicable settlement. Most cases are settled by some form of conciliation and arbitration.

It should be noted that industrial tribunals always compare the company procedures with ACAS recommendations when making judgements. If an organisation follows the ACAS procedures, an employee will be less successful in suing for unfair dismissal.

8.7 The role of management

Because of the serious implications of disciplinary action, only senior managers are normally permitted to carry out suspensions, demotions or dismissals. Other managers and supervisors are restricted to giving the various types of warnings.

When it comes to handling grievances, all supervisors and managers will have a role to play because one of the key features of an effective grievance procedure is that it should aim to settle the dispute as near as possible to the point of origin. Another important role of the manager when conducting the grievance interview is to aim for a mutually beneficial outcome. The employee concerned should be able to go away feeling reassured that, either there is no problem or, if there is, it has been tackled constructively by the immediate superior. The manager should feel that the grievance has been handled correctly and that both parties had 'won'.

8.8 Disciplinary interview

These are very formal affairs where managers control the proceedings and can plan in advance how they will deal with the guilty party and future consequences. This type of interview seeks to establish the facts and, assuming the complaint is valid, confirms that a company rule has been broken to the offending employee. The employee is warned that a penalty is, or will be, enforced either now or in the event of further misconduct. The seriousness of the offence, such as gross misconduct, is identified, and at this stage the consequences of further offences must be discussed. It is hoped by this means to prevent further misconduct and so ensure the future efficiency and appropriate conduct of the employee. An employee has the right to bring a friend or colleague as a witness to the details of the interview.

Activity 4

Can the manager plan a grievance interview in advance?

Feedback to this activity is given at the end of the chapter.

8.9 Dismissal

Dismissal is usually seen as the last step, the ultimate sanction in any disciplinary procedure. However, dismissals occur most frequently in the form of redundancy. Statistics published by the Department of Employment list the major reasons for dismissal as redundancy, sickness, unsuitability and misconduct in that order. Legislation in Britain during the 1970s, notably the Industrial Relations Act 1971, the Trades Unions and Labour Relations Act 1974 and the Employment Protection Acts 1975 and now the Employment Protection (Consolidation) Act 1978 makes it a difficult and costly business to dismiss employees. There are now provisions for employees to challenge the employer's decision. However, in recent statistics published by the Department of Employment it was revealed that only a proportion of cases of unfair dismissal actually reach Industrial Tribunals. The majority are dealt with by some form of conciliation and arbitration.

Fair dismissal

There is a statutory obligation for an employer to show that a dismissal is fair. In this case a dismissal is fair if it is related to:

(i)   A lack of capability or qualifications

This involves cases where the employee lacks the qualifications, skill, aptitude or health to do the job properly. However, in all cases the employee must be given the opportunity to improve the position or in the case of health be considered for alternative employment.

(ii) Misconduct

This includes the refusal to obey lawful and reasonable instructions, absenteeism, insubordination over a period of time and some criminal actions. In the last case, the criminal action should relate directly to the job; it can only be grounds for dismissal if the result of the criminal action will affect the work in some way.

(iii) A statutory bar

This occurs when employees cannot pursue their normal duties without breaking the law. The most common occurrence of this is the case of drivers who have been banned.

(iv) Some other substantial reason

This is a separate reason and will include good work-related reasons for dismissal (e.g. a need for the business to change and the employees refusing to adapt to the change required).

Unfair dismissal

In all cases of unfair dismissal there are two stages of proof. Firstly, the circumstances which represent fair grounds for dismissal must be established, and secondly, the tribunal must decide whether dismissal is fair in the circumstances of the case in question.

For dismissal to be automatically unfair, it must be for one of the following reasons:

(a)   trade union membership or non-membership

(b)   pregnancy

(c)   sex or race discrimination

(d)   revelation of a non-relevant spent conviction.

Provisions for unfair dismissal

Where employees feel that they have been unfairly dismissed they have the right to take their case to the Industrial Tribunal. The tribunal will normally refer the case to ACAS (Advisory Conciliation and Arbitration Service) in the hope of gaining an amicable settlement. Most cases are settled by some form of conciliation and arbitration. The possible solutions or remedies for unfair dismissal are set out below.

(a)   **Withdrawal of notice** – by the employer. This is the preferred remedy as stated in the Employment Protection Act.

(b)   **Reinstatement (order of Industrial Tribunal)** treats the employee as though he had never been dismissed. The employee is taken back to his old job with no loss of earnings and privileges.

(c) **Re-engagement (order of Industrial Tribunal)** in this case, the employee is offered a different job in the organisation and loses continuity of service. Both reinstatement and re-engagement were provisions introduced by the Employment Protection Act.

Compensation (order of Industrial Tribunal) – if an employer refuses to re-employ then the employee receives compensation made up of a penalty award of 13–26 weeks' pay (more in the case of discrimination), a payment equivalent to the redundancy entitlement and an award to compensate for loss of earnings, pension rights and so on. Some form of compensation may also be appropriate in cases of reinstatement and re-engagement.

Summary

- Recruitment and selection plays an important part in the organisation's strategy. It is inextricably linked with the organisational goals and objectives. In this chapter we give a general outline of the recruitment and selection process.

- For the person specification we outlined two useful classifications – Rodger's seven-point plan 'SCIPDAG' and Munro Fraser's five-point plan 'FIRMI'.

- Recruitment, as distinct from selection, involves the attraction of a field of suitable candidates for the job. There are various methods to do this, which we have examined. Only when this is done does the selection process begin, the aim being to select the best person for the job from that field of candidates.

- The main aim of the selection interview process is to find the best person for the job and encourage him or her to accept the position with terms that are agreeable to both parties.

- Induction involves the introduction of a new member of staff to other members and to the environment of the organisation, its culture, policies and practices.

- Employment legislation provides the basis for 'fair employment practices' in organisations. However, the legislation itself does not protect employees. It is essential that the organisation, and the management within it, believe just and fair practice is an employee right and not a matter of choice.

- Disciplinary procedures and their operation, including the form and process of formal disciplinary action and dismissal (e.g. industrial tribunals, arbitration and conciliation).

Having completed your study of this chapter, you should have achieved the following learning outcomes:

- evaluate the recruitment, selection, induction, appraisal, training and career planning activities of an organisation

- evaluate the role of incentives in staff development as well as individual and organisational performance.

Self-test questions

1   Define selection. (1.1, 1.2)

2   List the elements of job analysis. (2.1)

3   What is the purpose of job analysis? (2.2)

4   Outline four factors that feature in Alec Rodger's seven point plan. (2.5)

5   Describe the types of recruitment advertising an organisation might run. (3.2)

6   What advantages does the application form have over the personal CV? (4.1)

7   What types of interview processes are there? (5.4)

8   At what stage of the induction programme would management organise the follow-up? (6.2)

Practice questions

Question 1

You have a big test tomorrow and you are in the living room studying for this test when you are interrupted by your little sister, Amy, who has had a tough day and needs to have some fun and relax. She turns on the music and starts dancing. You need quiet. You argue. Discuss the possible outcomes using the following chart.

	Your sister gets what she needs	Your sister does not get what she needs
You get what you need	WIN-WIN	WIN-LOSE
You do not get what you need	LOSE-WIN	LOSE-LOSE

Question 2

Engineering company

You work for a large engineering company, which is under severe pressure to significantly reduce costs and improve performance. Your Chief Accountant is retiring after a lifetime's service with the firm. In recent years they have lost interest and their department has performed badly – producing poor quality information behind schedule. Although there are some able people in the department everyone has become demoralised and demotivated. Sickness and absenteeism is high. There is confusion over areas of responsibility within the section, systems are out-dated and you sense that there is a lot of duplication.

(a)   Describe the recruitment and selection process the company would go through to fill this vacancy.   **(12 marks)**

(b)   Identify the options available to you and explain the reasons for your choice.

        You are required to describe the recruitment and selection process the company would go through to fill this vacancy, explaining the options that are available to you and the reasons for your choices.   **(8 marks)**

        (Total: 20 marks)

For the answers to these questions, see the 'Answers' section at the end of the book.

Feedback to activities

Activity 1

It could result in the line manager blocking attempts by their staff to move into another job, especially if it is a post outside their department. Alternatively, and worse, such employees may be 'blacklisted' by their line manager, who may see their request to move jobs as a personal slight against them.

Activity 2

A poor reference may be submitted on a worker an employer does not wish to lose.

Activity 3

As the manager you could deal with the situation in the following ways.

- Call them all together and explain they must sort the matter out themselves, but if they fail to do so, you will sort the matter out for them by exercising your right to determine the holiday rota, and that no one will be allowed to go that fortnight anyway. If you go for this option, you are choosing the power route. This is fine if jobs are scarce, but highly risky. If you win, they all lose!

- Call them all together and tell them they must sort the matter out themselves. By choosing this option and letting them sort it out themselves you are avoiding the situation.

- Talk the matter over with each of them separately to discuss the facts with them. Make a decision as to whose need is the most pressing, get them all together and announce your decision. This option is an attempt at a compromise, although not allowing very much input from them.

- Tell them individually not to be silly, and suggest they take an afternoon off and talk the matter over with their families/friends/training officer. This solution of patting them on the head and telling them to talk to others is trying to defuse the situation.

- Discuss all the problems the situation raises with each fully, and if the matter still cannot be sorted out, go to the training officer and see if there is an alternative course; and the Chief Officer to see if on this occasion two deputies can be allowed on holiday at the same time. Bring them all back to hear the outcome. Only this option begins to address the problems. Even though there is no knowing there will be a successful outcome you are trying to resolve all the conflicting needs.

Activity 4

It is very difficult to plan in advance, because the subordinate will want to determine the content of the interview. Prior to the interview the manager should have some idea of the grievance and its possible source, and should have done some investigations in preparation.

Chapter 17

TRAINING AND DEVELOPMENT

Syllabus content

- The distinction between development and training and the tools available to develop and train staff.

Contents

1 The importance of training and development

2 The benefits of effective training and development

3 Training needs analysis

4 Meeting training needs

5 Staff evaluation

6 Development programmes

7 Career and succession planning

8 The learning process

1 The importance of training and development

1.1 Introduction

Effective training and development requires a systematic approach, which will start with the needs defined by the human resource plan. This will outline the job requirements for the future and the performance criteria necessary. Past appraisals or a skills analysis exercise could determine the existing position of the current and proposed jobholder. From this base of future need and present capability, a systematic, step-by-step training and development scheme can be defined.

1.2 Development and training

Human resource development may be seen as a process of building and enhancing the skills, knowledge and attitudes of employees. Apart from the benefits accruing to the individual worker – greater versatility, extra skills, etc. – many advantages accrue to the organisation. Employees become more flexible, the productivity and quality of work should improve, job satisfaction might increase – with consequent reduction in absenteeism and staff turnover rates – and the organisation need not fear the consequences of new technology. A common confusion that exists is the distinction between training, development and education. In practice the distinction is often blurred but for the sake of clarifying the following discussion, the definitions quoted here will be used.

Training is a planned process to modify attitude, knowledge, skill or behaviour through learning experiences to achieve effective performance in an activity or range of activities.

Development is concerned more with changes in attitudes, behaviour and potential than with immediate skill. It relates more to career development than job development.

The definition of training stresses the relationship between training and human resource planning.

The definition of development, on the other hand, suggests a fulfilment of innate potential and ability through continuous involvement rather than just timely interventions to satisfy gaps in knowledge and ability.

1.3 Training and development policies

As with recruitment and selection, training and development is inextricably linked with the organisational goals and objectives. Organisations formulate training and development policies in order to:

(a)   define the relationship between the organisation's objectives and the current and future human resource needs

(b)   provide a framework for facilitating development, and training

(c)   provide information for employees. For example, to stress the performance standards expected and to inform employees of opportunities for training and development

(d)   enhance public relations. For example, to help attract high calibre recruits, reassure clients and the public about the quality of products or services.

2 The benefits of effective training and development

2.1 Introduction

A systematic approach to training should be adopted. It will involve

- defining training needs

- deciding what training is required to satisfy these needs

- using experienced trainers to plan and implement training

- following up and evaluating training to ensure that it is effective.

This approach can be illustrated diagrammatically:

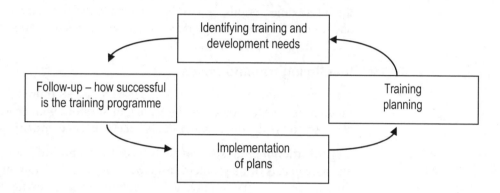

2.2 Benefits to the organisation

The benefits to the organisation of effective training and development are:

- provision of trained manpower

- improvement of existing skills

- increased employee knowledge

- improved job performance

- improved customer service

- greater staff commitment

- increased value of the organisation's human assets

- the personal development of employees.

2.3 Benefits to the individual

The benefits to the individual of effective training and development are:

- increased motivation

- individual goals equating with those of the organisation

- needs and aims to develop abilities and talents satisfied

- newly acquired skills for future use.

3 Training needs analysis

3.1 Job training analysis

The training needs will be indicated by a job training analysis.

A job analysis will reveal the 'training gap' which is the difference between the knowledge and skill required for the effective performance of a specific job and the knowledge and skill already possessed by the employee.

Some of this training requirement will relate to the longer term, for example where a company has a strategy to enter a particular overseas market or move into a new industry. The knowledge and skill gap will be defined for the future needs of the organisation and expressed for each of the future time periods. It will then be detailed in the human resources plan and used to define training and development needs as well as the recruitment and promotion of staff.

3.2 Identifying training needs

There are a number of means that are used to assess training needs. These range from a very broad analysis of **organisational goals** and **corporate strategy** to the details of individuals' **performance appraisal**.

Organisational analysis – an analysis of the features of an organisation and a diagnosis of its problems may well indicate that training is necessary. Such an analysis may involve consideration of the following factors.

(i) The overall performance of the organisation or any part of it in terms of output, sales, profit, costs and so on. For example, if materials wastage is high for a batch of new recruits, it might show a need for improvement in the training programme they have been through.

(ii) The policies of an organisation may involve training as a means of achieving future goals. Forecasts of technical change and plans for expansion have implications for training with the requirements to train for new skills or increase the supply of traditional skills. Similarly changes in personnel policies, e.g. a new promotion policy or a career development plan, will create new training needs.

(iii) There are various indicators of organisational health, which may well suggest that training is necessary. Such indicators might include labour turnover, absenteeism or the level of grievances. For example, several studies have shown that inadequate training often leads to workers failing to achieve production targets, which affects their chances of gaining financial incentives. Many such employees experience frustration, which manifests itself in grievances and labour turnover.

(iv) Governmental influences, and legislation in particular, have caused and still do cause organisations to reconsider their position concerning the provision of training.

Performance appraisal – individual training needs can be established by feedback on individual assessments. A major objective of appraisal schemes is to make both superior and subordinate aware of the need to train and/or re-train employees.

(c) **Job analysis** –there are a variety of approaches to job analysis which involve greater or lesser degrees of detail but the basic procedure is similar for all and covers the following stages:

(i) A broad analysis of the requirements of the job and any special problems surrounding it as seen by the job-holder, the superior and, possibly, colleagues.

(ii) An analysis of the particular skills needed to do the job.

(iii) A detailed study of the responsibilities, duties and tasks carried out. This forms the basis of the job description.

(iv) An analysis of the knowledge and skills required by the job-holder. This forms the basis of the job specification.

(v) A description of the training requirements for the job, i.e. the training specification.

(d) **Other approaches** – include information gained from records of employee performance, feedback from customers or simply from observation of employees. Other methods available include surveys of staff with questionnaires or interviews of superiors and subordinates and customer surveys covering their **satisfaction** and **dissatisfaction.**

4 Meeting training needs

4.1 Training interventions

The organisation has to determine exactly what it hopes to achieve by the training and development intervention. There are five stages for the organisation to consider:

- **Determination of the development and training objective** – This will specify the task, procedures, techniques, skills and ability that employees should be able to perform/exhibit and the standards required.

- **Determination of the appropriate strategy** – The criteria used to determine the appropriate strategies are:

  – compatibility with objectives

  – estimated likelihood of transfer of learning/development to the work situation

  – available resources

  – employee considerations.

- **Planning and implementation** – Careful briefing of employees and their managers should take place, in order that they know what is happening, when and why.

- **Evaluation of the programme** – This is perhaps the most difficult stage of the process. The aim is to evaluate the effectiveness of the investment, in terms of resources, and find out whether it has achieved the stated objectives. The following questions need to be asked:

  Was the training effective? Did the employees acquire the knowledge and skills that the activity was intended to provide? Can the employees do the job, which requires the knowledge and skills that they have acquired?

Was it worthwhile in terms of return on expenditure incurred in giving the training? Is there some other way that the organisation can secure a suitably skilled employee that is less expensive, e.g. effecting different training arrangements, buying-in the skills.

- **Reviewing the system** on a regular basis to ensure that it is still satisfying the organisation's training and development needs.

4.2 Training solutions

Once the training needs are collated, the training funds available, and the priorities established in relation to the urgency of the training, the training decisions must be made. These include decisions on the scale and type of training system needed, and whether it can best be provided by the organisation's own staff or by **external consultants**. Training methods (covered in the previous chapter), timing and duration, location and the people actually doing the training also needs to be decided.

Training may be carried out '**in-house**' or **externally**. If any of the training is done in-house, decisions will need to be made on such things as:

- training workshops

- location and equipping of classrooms

- selection of **training officers**.

Colleges, **universities**, **training organisations** and **management consultants** may provide external courses. There are also open and distance learning facilities via the Open University and other providers. To make sure that the training needs are being met, separate training and development co-ordinators may be allocated the responsibilities for training within the firm and for any external training. They may also be responsible for reviewing the system on a regular basis to ensure that it is still satisfying those needs.

Activity 1

What does your own personal development programme look like?

Feedback to this activity is at the end of the chapter.

5 Staff evaluation

5.1 The evaluation of training

Every organisation should ask itself at the end of any substantial training activity:

- Was the training **effective**? Did the employees acquire the knowledge and skills that the activity was intended to provide? Can the employees do the job, which requires the knowledge and skills that they have acquired?

- Was it **worthwhile** in terms of return on expenditure incurred in giving the training? Is there some other way that the organisation can secure a suitably skilled employee that is less expensive, e.g. effecting different training arrangements, buying-in the skills.

It is important to evaluate the effectiveness of the training programmes. To do this an organisation needs information about the training arrangements such as the content, objectives and assessments. The organisation must also be clear about the criteria by which it will evaluate the training programme.

KEY POINT

Implementation of training can be either in-house or external.

External sources of training include: **colleges**, **universities**, **training organisations** and **consultants**.

For in-house provision, **infrastructure** and **staffing** must be carefully considered.

DEFINITION

Evaluation of training is 'any attempt to obtain information (**feedback**) on the effects of a training programme and to assess the **value** of the training in the light of that information' (Hamblin).

KEY POINT

To evaluate the effectiveness of training, an organisation needs information about training arrangements, such as

---

content, **objectives** and
assessments, and
criteria by which to
evaluate the training.
Evaluation criteria could be
the subsequent behaviour
of the trainees, and the
organisational benefits.

If the evaluation is to be used to improve training, then the organisation will also need machinery for feeding the evaluation into the training design activity so that courses and programmes can be adjusted as necessary.

It has been suggested that evaluation can take place in relation to the trainees' subsequent behaviour.

- **Trainees' behaviour**

    - What was the trainees' reaction and response to the training? Did they enjoy it or feel that they had benefited from it?

    - Has there been a transfer of learning to the job, i.e. has the trainees' job behaviour been modified in the desired way?

- **Organisation behaviour**

    - Has the training had a beneficial effect on quality, costs, output and employee morale?

    - Has the training improved the quality of the welfare and its commitment to the organisation?

    - Evaluation leads to control, which means deciding whether the training was worthwhile and what improvements are necessary to make it better. Evaluation is not always easy because it is hard both to set measurable objectives and to obtain the information or results to see if objectives have been met.

KEY POINT

Hamblin's five levels of
evaluation:

- reactions

- learning

- job behaviour

- organisation

- ultimate value.

5.2 The five levels of evaluation

Hamblin suggests that there are five levels at which evaluation can take place:

- **Reactions** – of the trainees to the training, their feelings about how enjoyable and useful it has been, etc.

- **Learning** – what new skills and knowledge have been acquired or what changes in attitude have taken place as a result of the training.

- **Job behaviour** – at this level evaluation tries to measure the extent to which trainees have applied their training on the job.

- **Organisation** – training may be assessed in terms of the ways in which changes in job behaviour affect the functioning of the organisation in which the trainees are employed in terms of measures such as output, productivity, quality, etc.

- **Ultimate value** – this is a measure of the training in terms of how the organisation as a whole has benefited from the training in terms of greater profitability, survival or growth.

Hamblin's general approach to the assessment of training can be seen in the diagram below.

Hamblin's general approach to the assessment of training

Results of training	Evaluation strategy
Training ↓	Training-centred – assesses inputs and methods
Reactions ↓	Reactions-centred – trainee reaction
Learning ↓	Learning-centred – measures learning achieved, eg, tests, exams
Changes in job behaviour ↓	Job-related – measure of learning applied in workplace
Changes in organisation ↓	Organisation development – measures organisational changes resulting from training
Impact on organisational goals	Cost benefit – what has training done for profitability?

5.3 Role of management

The role of management in a learning organisation is to encourage continuous learning and acquisition of new knowledge and skills and to transform these into actual behaviour, products and processes within the organisation. To enable learning to take place within the organisation, management should adopt the following approach:

- The process of strategy formulation should be designed with learning in mind, and should incorporate experimentation and feedback.
- All members of the organisation should be encouraged, and given the opportunity, to contribute to policy making as part of the learning process.
- Information should be seen as a resource to be exploited by all members of the organisation, not as a 'power tool' reserved for a chosen few.
- Accounting systems should be designed in such a way that members of the organisation can learn how the cash resource is used.
- Employees should be encouraged to see internal users of their outputs as 'customers'.
- Employees should be encouraged to see the diversity of rewards they enjoy (not just cash), and there should be openness about why some people are paid more than others.
- The structures of the organisation – everything from office layout to managerial hierarchy – should be regarded as temporary arrangements that can be altered in response to changing conditions.
- Employees who have contacts outside the organisation – salesmen, customer service staff, purchasing staff etc. – should impart the knowledge they determine from such contacts to improve the organisation's knowledge base.
- Management must foster a climate in which workers understand that part of their task is to improve their own knowledge, and to share knowledge with other members of the organisation.
- A priority for management should be the provision of opportunities for structured learning – courses, seminars, etc.

Activity 2

What are the five levels of evaluation that Hamblin describes?

Feedback to this activity is at the end of the chapter.

6 Development programmes

6.1 Introduction

The manager must have the following basic skills as well as specific skills such as coaching and teaching to cope with the training and development of subordinates.

(a) *Planning* – Preparing schemes or schedules for achieving the targets that have been set by either themselves or the management.

(b) *Organising* – Allocating tasks, delegating and arranging the work and resources in such a way as to enable the realisations of the plan.

(c) *Controlling* – Ensuring that the workers' performance in terms of cost, quality and quantity of output matches the plan, if necessary by correcting deviations.

(d) *Communication* – Keeping all concerned adequately informed and himself or herself in touch.

(e) *Problem solving and decision taking* – Handling day-to-day difficulties and problems and deciding what needs to be done to ensure the effective performance of the supervised.

(f) *Motivating and maintaining discipline* – Encouraging people to give their best within the rules that govern their employment.

Coaching – where on the job training is the responsibility of the line manager or supervisor, he or she will need to be a good coach. To be effective the training must be done in a climate of confidence and trust between superior and subordinate. Wisdom and patience are required. Managers must be able to delegate authority and give recognition and praise for jobs well done. Effective coaches will develop the strengths and potential of their subordinates and help them overcome their weaknesses.

Teaching requires the manager to:

- know what the training objectives are

- analyse and break down the job into separate elements

- demonstrate the skill to the trainee

- allow the trainee to try the skill, making adjustments where errors are spotted.

6.2 Management development

Planning for succession is one part of ensuring the successful future of the organisation. Management development must be geared to planning for succession; the board must think in terms of planned recruitment of managers involving particular selection methods – headhunting or training entrants direct from university.

If development is to be effective it must make those managers into better managers from the point of view of the company employing them. It must also take into account the future managers and what their potential is likely to be. Thus, to establish a management development programme the following steps should be taken:

(a) Assess the strengths, weaknesses and training needs of existing managers and future managers.

(b) Chart the planned growth of the organisation over the next five or ten years.

> (c)   Match the potential strengths to future posts.
>
> (d)   Develop potential strengths to meet future posts.

6.3 Management development programmes

Management development programmes may take many forms. The main schemes are:

- **Student sponsorship** – the method by which the armed services recruit and train graduates and a method favoured by many large concerns. The undergraduate attends university sponsored by his or her future employer with an undertaking to join them on qualification. For the undergraduate the advantages include a salary whilst training and the prospect of a definite job, whilst the employer benefits by the early training and recruitment of staff of potentially high ability.

- **Professional and technical qualifications** – such as membership of ACCA. Schemes like this mean that the employee is given an opportunity to develop his or her skills and the employer is assured of well-trained, often externally examined and highly motivated staff.

- **General management development** – the UK is well behind the USA in its use of business degrees and the existence of business schools. The realisation that management is a skill to be learned and that there is much research to be done is gradually gaining ground in the UK. There are now courses of one and two years' duration at the various business schools intended to attract the already professionally qualified manager who now wishes to add business skills to his abilities in order to enhance his promotion prospects.

- **Internally organised management development** – good management training can be obtained in the sophisticated multinational companies simply by being seconded to a variety of departments to learn how to run them and their area of work.

The full and perfect management development programme will cater for the raw recruit from his school sixth form and the 48-year-old entrepreneur and managing director, and will involve a combination of all the above types of management development.

6.4 Career management

Many organisations have elaborate schemes for planning the career progression of all, or most, of their managerial staff. This is generally done with the objectives of providing each individual with a satisfactory career and ensuring that the organisation makes the best use of its managerial resources.

Charles Handy argues that career planning in many organisations is not a development process so much as a weeding-out process. Because career development is a series of hurdles such as appointments and levels of authority, only the strong survive to the end. The need to provide a large number of hurdles, or promotion possibilities also leads to clutter in the organisation, with many more levels of authority than often necessary.

7   Career and succession planning

7.1 Introduction

Career management was once the chosen way of ensuring that the organisation had the right people in the right places at the right times. It meant understanding the direction and objectives of the organisation, grooming and developing the appropriate staff, managing individual career expectations and matching them with the current and future needs outlined in the human resources plan. It also involved succession planning to ensure a stock of skilled and trained people to fill anticipated vacancies.

This type of planning still exists and succession planning and career management are still a part of many organisation's human resource plan. However, the current situation in some industries is a little different. They are seizing the opportunity, offered by delayering and restructuring, to influence the way individuals think about their career. Businesses like banks used to have a grading system that encouraged an expectation of promotion and life-long employment. This is now unrealistic and creates false career aspirations. Because of the removal of levels of management and changes to jobs through technological advances, these types of organisation have people who are at a plateau and are unlikely to move any further in the company.

From our understanding of motivation theory, we know that, among other things, people seem to place a high value on responsibility, opportunities for achievement, advancement and clear links between performance and reward. Many of us will want a greater say in how we organise our work and there are a number of ways in which jobs can be redesigned to improve the satisfaction and productivity of those who do them.

7.2 Development and career planning

KEY POINT

If the organisation does not address the problem of career development it will have to rely on filling vacancies by ad hoc methods either from internal or external sources.

If the organisation does not address the problem of career development it will have to rely on filling vacancies by ad hoc methods either from internal or external sources. The risks are great that the correct human resources will not be available or that current managerial resources will be wasted, with consequent effects on commitment and morale. The questions raised by this area are:

(a)   What basic job and professional training needs to be provided to prepare new and existing staff to fulfil their roles satisfactorily?

(b)   Should we concentrate on in-service training or external courses?

(c)   How can induction procedures be improved?

(d)   What special programmes need to be developed to deal with re-training and updating?

(e)   How can internal procedures be improved to aid the movement of staff to jobs where they can exercise greater responsibilities?

(f)   What new succession plans need to be drawn up for key management and supervisory roles?

(g)   How well is training linked to career development?

Human resource planning also requires a method of plotting career progression so that the organisation can ascertain the rate of the employees' progress, and whether factors such as age-spread will lead to promotion blockages or the over-promotion of inexperienced employees. Managing careers is a difficult part of human resource planning. Expectations of employees seem to change and higher levels of education may add to the difficulty. A key decision is whether careers are expected to fall within specialist areas, such as the professions, or in departments, or whether a broader base is required.

7.3 Career development: objectives

Many organisations have elaborate schemes for planning the career progression of all, or most, of their managerial staff. This is generally done with the objectives of:

- providing each individual with as far as possible a satisfactory career

- ensuring that the organisation makes the best use of its managerial resources.

Charles Handy argues that career planning in many organisations is not a development process, so much as a weeding-out process. Because career development is a series of hurdles – appointments and levels of authority – only the strong survive to the end. The need to provide a large number of hurdles, or promotion possibilities also leads to clutter in the organisation, with many more levels of authority than often necessary.

Most managers are not only interested in their current job but are concerned about where this job is going to lead to in the future. The objective of many managers is to ensure that they 'grow' during their career. This objective can obviously benefit the organisation as well as the individual. It is the personnel department's responsibility that the career-growth cycle is achieved.

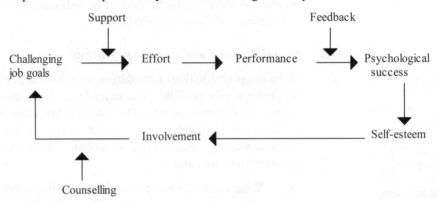

The growth is triggered by a job that provides challenging, stretching goals. The clearer and more challenging the goals, the more effort the person will exert, and the more likely it is that good performance will result. If the person does a good job and receives positive feedback, they will feel successful (psychological success). These feelings will increase a person's feelings of confidence and self-esteem. This should lead to the person becoming more involved in work, which in turn leads to the setting of future stretching goals.

7.4 Succession planning

Succession planning should be an ongoing process so that the personnel department is continuously working with heads of departments to ensure that the staff requirements are anticipated and met within the dynamic framework of the corporate plan.

Consideration of the process might be assisted by starting from the present position. An assessment of current staff resources should be available, analysed by departments, the types of jobs at each level (job description) and the number and quality of staff in those jobs (staff appraisal).

A forecast of the staffing requirements, by grades and skills, should then be assessed and agreed within the corporate plan (both the short and long-term needs) to highlight any surplus staff as well as shortages.

In the case of a mismatch between job specification and existing employees, every opportunity should be made to provide retraining or to undertake staff development. Again, the personnel appraisal records should indicate staff who have been willing or who are keen to widen or change their skills.

Where there are shortages, recruitment programmes should be agreed. Vacancies should be identified and using the job description and job specification, recruitment and selection of appropriate staff should be carried out. The plan may require that training should then be provided for new recruits, as they will be unlikely to have the specific job knowledge required. In such cases, recruitment would be geared to the selection of people with the necessary ability and aptitude.

Succession planning is a difficult task. Whilst the process must seek to achieve the organisation's goals and objectives, it must also take into account the aspiration of individuals in trying to achieve a realistic fit between the person and the job.

7.5 Management succession

One of the most important aspects of human resource planning is ensuring the management succession. It is, of course, both possible and desirable to bring in top managers from outside the company, thereby adding a breadth of experience to the top management team, but it is still necessary to have people at the top who have come from within the business. They bring specialist knowledge of different aspects of the firm itself and provide an inspiration for more junior managers who can aspire to the same position. It is thus essential that people with management potential are identified early in their careers.

Good training schemes must be provided for such people, to integrate with planned career patterns, including a number of development moves, to widen experience. However, care must be taken that grooming the chosen few does not take precedence over everyone else's career: if certain people are known to have been singled out, resentment will be caused and the company may miss out on spotting late developers. This points to the need for a thorough appraisal system throughout the organisation. Everyone should be made to feel that his actual and potential contribution is of value.

Management succession planning will probably entail compiling:

- for each post, a list of perhaps three potential successors
- for each person (at least from a certain level upwards) a list of possible development moves.

These lists then form the basis for long-term plans and development moves, and in addition supply a contingency plan to provide a successor for any post that becomes suddenly and unexpectedly vacant (e.g. through death).

8 The learning process

We have already noted that for a training and development intervention to be considered effective, learning must take place. This might be the acquisition of knowledge, a new skill or modified behaviour. Learning theory highlights the importance of feedback in sustaining and improving human performance at work and the implications of this view for managerial practice are also investigated.

8.1 Learning in the workplace

DEFINITION

Learning is the process of acquiring knowledge through **experience** which leads to a change in **behaviour**.

Learning might be the acquisition of a new **skill**, new **knowledge**, a modified **attitude** or a combination of all three. Learning is the result of **experience**. People use their knowledge of the results of past behaviour to change, modify and improve their behaviour in future. Learning cannot take place without appropriate **feedback**. The experience may be planned, as in studying this book, or it may be accidental, such as learning from one's mistakes. However, learning cannot be seen; it can only be inferred by observing changes in behaviour.

KEY POINT

Learning occurs in new situations and may be triggered by questions – these may be about **facts**, **processes** or **purposes**.

Learning frequently occurs when an individual has to deal with a situation new to them. It is about developing new skills, competencies and attitudes to meet new situations. It begins when we ask ourselves a question. This may be a simple **factual** question, such as: 'How much of product X did we sell last year? – or a question about **process**, such as: 'How can I arrange for my results to be available three days earlier each month?', or it could be a question about **purpose**, such as: 'What is the main aim of this organisation?'

EXAM HINT

Be careful when answering questions in an exam to stress the aspect of **experience,** because behaviour can also change in ways, which are not classed as learning, e.g. behaviour changes due to alcohol, drugs, ageing and fatigue.

These questions may come about because we considered a particular situation and doing so has raised questions. Alternatively it may have come about because a situation has forced the question upon us. Whatever the source of the question, the situation will demand an answer. Then the answer needs to be tested out in practice. If it works, then something has been learnt. If it does not, then the process starts again with the question.

8.2 Learning curve

The ability of employees to learn is more important to organisations that are preoccupied with controlled performance; needing to know what the staff must do, how they are to do it and how well they are expected to perform. In these organisations learning theories influence all the induction of new recruits, job training, reward systems and performance evaluation.

Changes in workplace behaviour and comparison of individuals can be quantified using a '**learning curve**'. A fictitious curve for learning from a study guide such as this one is shown below:

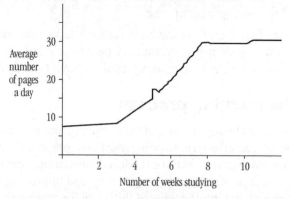

Number of weeks studying

KEY POINT

The pace of learning or progress changes with familiarity – this is the **learning curve**. The shape of the learning curve depends on the

The shape of the curve depends on the type of work, the task and the individual learner. Experience has shown that learning does not take place at a steady rate. Initially progress may be slow with sudden improvement followed by further progress for some time. There will be a final levelling off when, without enormous effort, little further progress will be achieved.

When you have finished reading this study guide you will expect to have

type of work or task and the individual.

learnt something. The test is whether or not you will be able to do things that you could not do before you read the book.

8.3 Learning theories

There are four theories of learning; the first two are '**behavioural theories**' concentrating on observable behaviour, and the other two are '**cognitive theories**', focusing on what goes on internally to create learning. **Behaviourists** and **cognitive psychologists** agree that experience influences behaviour, but disagree on how this happens.

• **Reinforcement theory** – **Burrhus Skinner** states that we learn by continually looking for ways to achieve more positive reinforcement, in terms of **rewards**, and avoid negative reinforcement or **punishment**.

• **Information theory** looks at the way that learners seek out feedback and use it to control performance and modify behaviour in an automatic way like a thermostat in a central-heating system.

• **Cognitive** or **problem-solving** approaches to learning argue that knowledge is information which can be used to modify or maintain previous behaviour. The information has to be perceived, interpreted, given meaning and used in decision making about the future behaviour.

• **Experiential learning theory** – **Kolb**, **Rubin** and **McIntyre** see learning as a continuous cyclical process with four stages (see following diagram):

  – **experience**, which may be either planned or accidental

  – **reflective observation**, which is looking back at the experience and introspectively reviewing the general issues raised and their significance

  – **abstract conceptualisation**, which can be viewed as generalising from reflection and analysing to develop a body of ideas, theories or principles, which can then be applied to other similar problems or situations; hypotheses are developed, based on experience and knowledge

  – **active experimentation**, which is consciously trying out the learning in similar situations; it involves creativity, decision-making and problem-solving.

Experiential learning theory: learning as a cyclical process

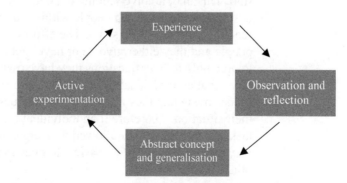

The experiential learning method proposes putting learners in active problem-solving roles and using a form of self-learning which encourages them to be committed to the chosen learning objectives.

Activity 3

What types of punishment or negative reinforcement are commonly used in the workplace?

Feedback to this activity is given at the end of the chapter.

8.4 The effect on learning of individual differences

Honey and **Mumford** believe that there are different learning styles which suit different individuals and have drawn up a classification of four learning styles:

- **theorist** – where the person seeks to understand underlying concepts and to take an intellectual 'hands off' approach based on logical argument

- **reflector** – the person who observes phenomena, thinks about them and then chooses how to act

- **activist** – a person who likes to deal with practical, active problems and who does not have much patience with theory

- **pragmatist** – a person who only likes to study if they can see a direct link to practical problems; they are not interested in theory for its own sake.

The implications for effective learning are that people react to problem situations in different ways and so there should be harmonisation between the learning methods and the preferred learning style for the learner.

8.5 The barriers to learning

In order to facilitate learning we need to be aware of the potential blocks and avoid them. There are three types of **barrier**:

- **The questions are not raised** – Some individuals appear to have no natural curiosity or, because of their mental set, rarely question why something has happened to them. Organisations can miss questions because it is no one's responsibility to raise them. The questioning habit and natural curiosity becomes dulled if existence is predictable. **Predictability** raises no questions. However, when the routine is disrupted, panic occurs because we have come depend on routine. Therefore in order to cope with learning and change, it is important to maintain curiosity and to experiment with ideas and skills.

- **Finding the answers is difficult** – Answers can require major effort to find. This may involve seeking out data, talking to suppliers and customers, meeting with people within the organisation with who we feel uncomfortable and so on. The effort can frequently be too much for people and they either give up or never get beyond asking the question. People only answer questions they have **ownership** in. This does not mean that an individual must raise the question in order to answer it, but it does mean that they must feel that the question is relevant to them or their situation. Therefore if an individual is employed to do a specific task and never asked or allowed to operate outside a clear boundary, they are unlikely to offer answers to questions that they see and perhaps others don't.

- **Testing the answers** – It is not until the testing stage is reached that the commitment of substantial resources is required. The answer must be tested to find out if it is the right one – unless we are dealing with factual situations. Because of the commitment of resources, testing can be quite difficult in organisations. In any test there is the risk of failure, and organisations generally hate failure. Testing consists of nothing more than a **tolerance to mistakes**. You have to be capable of living with your own failure and being able to try again. People often find it difficult to view a failed test as part of the learning process. Few organisations regard 'mistakes' as part of a learning process that will eventually lead to success.

8.6 Learning organisations

Learning organisations encourage testing and experimentation, because they want to find new answers, and they recognise that failed answers are as important as successful ones. Therefore actions that are carried out have two purposes – to resolve the immediate problem and to learn from the process.

Pedler, Burgoyne and Boydell are the main proponents in the UK of the 'learning company'. It can be defined as 'an organisation that facilitates the learning of all its members and continuously transforms itself'.

The aim is to design an organisation that is capable of adapting, changing, developing and transforming itself in response to the needs, wishes and aspirations of people, inside and outside. These organisations will be able to achieve their objectives without predatory takeovers, mergers or divestments. They will be able to avoid the large-scale restructurings that are now commonplace in industry. The authors believe that the current state of an organisation is due to three forces:

- the idea behind it
- the phase of its development
- the era it is in.

Although these three perspectives are in principle independent, in practice they may be linked.

When an organisation is going through a **development phase** that **integrates** its activities, employees and ideas, this is when the organisation starts to take a '**learning approach**' to change.

Self-development and **action-learning** are also foundations of the learning organisation: as the organisation learns from the actions that it carries out, so does the individual.

8.7 Role of management

The **role of management** in a learning organisation, is to encourage continuous **learning** and acquisition of new **knowledge** and **skills** and to transform these into actual behaviour, products and processes within the organisation.

To enable learning to take place within the organisation, the following approach should be adopted by management:

- The process of strategy formulation should be designed with learning in mind, and should incorporate experimentation and feedback.
- All members of the organisation should be encouraged, and given the opportunity, to contribute to policy-making as part of the learning process.

- **processes**.

- Information should be seen as a resource to be exploited by all members of the organisation, not as a 'power tool' reserved for a chosen few.

- Accounting systems should be designed in such a way that members of the organisation can learn how the cash resource is used.

- Employees should be encouraged to see internal users of their outputs as 'customers'.

- Employees should be encouraged to see the diversity of rewards they enjoy (not just cash), and there should be openness about why some people are paid more than others.

- The structures of the organisation – everything from office layout to managerial hierarchy – should be regarded as temporary arrangements, which can be altered in response to changing conditions.

- Employees who have contacts outside the organisation – salesmen, customer service staff, purchasing staff etc. – should impart the knowledge they determine from such contacts to improve the organisation's knowledge base.

- Management must foster a climate in which workers understand that part of their task is to improve their own knowledge, and to share knowledge with other members of the organisation.

- A priority for management should be the provision of opportunities for structured learning – courses, seminars, etc.

Summary

- The purpose of training in the work situation is to develop the abilities of the individual and to satisfy the current and future manpower needs of the organisation.

- Training begins with a clear definition of the organisation's training needs.

- Different types of training can be identified to meet the differing needs and staff involved.

- A systematic approach to training will involve, defining training needs, deciding what training needs to take place, using experienced trainers to plan and implement the training, and following up and evaluating the training.

- Training and development methods vary tremendously depending on the person, the job, the resources, the organisation and the economic environment.

- Organisational learning is the process by which an organisation, like an individual, adapts its behaviour based on experience.

- The key features of this type of learning are where the organisation can transform knowledge into actual behaviour, encourage questions and explicitly recognise mistakes as part of the learning process.

Having completed your study of this chapter, you should have achieved the following learning outcomes:

- evaluate the recruitment, selection, induction, appraisal, training and career planning activities of an organisation

- evaluate the role of incentives in staff development as well as individual and organisational performance.

Self-test questions

1   Outline the benefits to the individual of effective training and development. (2.3)

2   What is the role of management in a learning organisation? (5.3)

3   What are the objectives of career progression? (7.3)

4   Define the learning process. (8.1)

5   Outline three types of barrier to learning. (8.5)

Practice questions

Question 1

Learning propositions

Comment on each of the following learning propositions:

(a)   an individual should be motivated to learn   **(3 marks)**

(b)   active participation is better than passive reception   **(3 marks)**

(c)   clear objectives and standards should be set   **(3 marks)**

(d)   timely and relevant feedback on performance and progress should be given

(3 marks)

(e)   positive and negative reinforcement should be used judiciously.   **(3 marks)**

In a business and accounting environment that is constantly changing, it is vital that you as an accountant to adopt a learning style that ensures individual and organisational success. There are different learning styles and approaches to suit different individuals.

Required:

(f)   Identify and describe two different schools of thought on approaches to learning.   **(5 marks)**

(g)   What are the four stages in the experiential learning theory of Kolb?   **(5 marks)**

(h)   Briefly describe the experiential learning cycle.   **(5 marks)**

(Total: 30 marks)

Question 2

Installing a training system

You are required to:

(a)   describe the steps that should be taken to set up a training system in an organisation   **(10 marks)**

(b)   identify **five** ways in which such a system would benefit the accounting function.   **(10 marks)**

(Total: 20 marks)

For the answers to these questions, see the 'Answers' section at the end of the book.

Feedback to activities

Activity 1

Your immediate ambition is to achieve your accounting qualification. You may be undertaking this entirely on a distance learning basis or you may be attending college on a day release or full time basis. You may be receiving support from your organisation for this in terms of money and time. Or you may be entirely self-financing. This qualification may just be one element in a complex and highly structured development programme that might also include secondments, rotation, in-house training or mentoring or it may stand alone as the only example of career development your organisation has planned for you.

Activity 2

Evaluation is not always easy because it is hard both to set measurable objectives and to obtain the information or results to see if the objectives have been met. Hamblin suggests that there are five levels at which evaluation can take place:

- **Reactions of the trainees** – their feelings about how enjoyable and useful it has been, etc.

- **Learning** – what new skills and knowledge have been acquired or what changes in attitude have taken place as a result of the training.

- **Job behaviour** – at this level evaluation tries to measure the extent to which trainees have applied their training on the job.

- **Organisation** – training may be assessed in terms of the ways in which changes in job behaviour affect the functioning of the organisation in which the trainees are employed in terms of measures such as output, productivity, quality, etc.

- **Ultimate value** – this is a measure of the training in terms of how the organisation as a whole has benefited from the training in terms of profitability, survival or growth.

Activity 3

The types of sanction that are commonly used include:

- informal spoken warnings
- formal written warnings
- loss of pay
- suspension from work
- dismissal.

Chapter 18

THE PROCESS OF APPRAISAL

Syllabus content

- The importance of appraisals, their conduct and their relationship to the reward system.

Contents

1   The importance of appraisal

2   Appraisal process methods

3   Effective staff appraisal

4   Relationship between appraisal and the reward system

1 The importance of appraisal

1.1 Introduction

An early HRM model, developed by Fombrun *et al,* shows four key constituent components – selection, appraisal, development and rewards, as outlined below:

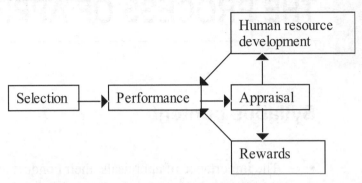

As the diagram shows, the information relative to the behaviour and performance of an individual can lead to activities in the human resources department. Performance appraisal data can be used as predictors in the planning, recruitment and selection processes and can determine employee rewards.

1.2 The appraisal scheme and the organisational structure

The organisation's appraisal scheme is inextricably linked to its control structure. It clarifies specific jobs, it assesses competencies, it uses feedback and reward to improve performance, it links performance to organisational goals and it aims to make the behaviour of employees predictable and, hence, controllable.

The overall purpose of appraisal must be to create a more effective organisation where employees know, not only what is expected of them, but also the reason for doing the job the way they do it, and how good/bad they are at their work. The other side of this is that management is fully aware of what the staff are supposed to be doing and how they are actually doing it. This can be achieved if performance criteria are established jointly, appropriate on-the job behaviour is mutually understood and the review is a continual process focussed on growth and development.

Assessment is the process used for obtaining information about an individual employee's past and current work behaviour and performance. This allows appraisal.

Performance appraisal is a procedure where the managers or supervisors in an organisation discuss the work of their subordinates. They see each person individually and consider the progress they have been making in their job, their strengths and weaknesses and their future needs as regards training and development and the employee's potential for promotion.

1.3 Appraisal as a management tool

In a sense all individuals are constantly appraised but a systematic appraisal involves more than a casual assessment of individual performance. Systematic performance appraisal is a vital management tool for the following reasons:

(a)   It enables a picture to be drawn up of the human 'stock' of an organisation – its strengths and weaknesses, enabling more effective human resource planning.

(b)   By identifying weaknesses in an individual's performance it may identify training needs and once training has taken place, performance appraisal enables some evaluation of training effectiveness.

(c)   It allows managers and subordinates to plan personnel and job objectives in the light of performance.

(d)   In some circumstances it may be used to assess the level of reward payable for an individual's efforts, e.g. in merit payment systems.

(e)   By encouraging two-way communication it permits an evaluation of a subordinate's strengths and weaknesses and the reasons for them. Thus, for example, if a subordinate's failure to perform is due to some failure in the work system corrective action can be taken quickly.

(f)   It is the ideal situation for assessing potential. At the organisational level this permits career and succession planning. At the individual level it permits superior and subordinate to assess the most effective development plans for the subordinate.

It is, however, important if the appraisal is to fulfil the last point that it is regular and systematic, based on objective criteria and permits a two-way flow of communication in a reasonably trusting atmosphere. No subordinate is likely to admit to weaknesses or training needs in a climate of distrust.

1.4 Categorising training needs

DEFINITION

Training needs analysis (TNA) identifies, shortcomings or 'gaps' in performance which are then used as indicators of the training required to achieve improvements.

Training needs may be identified from the appraisal process, in which actual performance is compared with pre-defined objectives. At the same time, training based upon the appraisal process can be used to develop and build individual personal capacity and competence and to develop and build group/departmental capacity and competence.

The process of appraisal may also be used to review and develop departmental role objectives and job descriptions, from which further training needs' analysis can be undertaken. Actual training needs may be categorised on the basis of:

(a)   competencies associated with work quality, e.g. accuracy and consistency, exercise of judgement and discretion, communication skills and cost consciousness

(b)   competencies associated with work quantity, e.g. personal planning and time management, capacity to meet deadlines or work under pressure and capacity to cope with upward variations in work volume

(c)   supervisory and managerial skills and competencies, e.g. planning and organising, communication and interpersonal skills, directing, guiding and motivating, leadership and delegation, co-ordination and control, developing teamwork and developing and retaining staff.

1.5 The benefits of appraisal

(a) Effective appraisal is grounded in the belief that feedback on past performance influences future performance, and that the process of isolating and rewarding good performance is likely to repeat it.

(b) Agreement on challenging but achievable targets for performance motivates employees by clarifying goals and setting the value of incentives offered.

(c) Effective appraisal can allow employees to solve any workplace problems and apply creative thinking to their jobs.

1.6 The conduct of appraisals

The process of performance appraisal usually entails:

- clarifying a person's job

- identifying criteria for assessment

- assessing competence

- interviewing the job holder

- identifying and agreeing future goals and targets

- agreeing action points, e.g. training needs

- giving regular feedback.

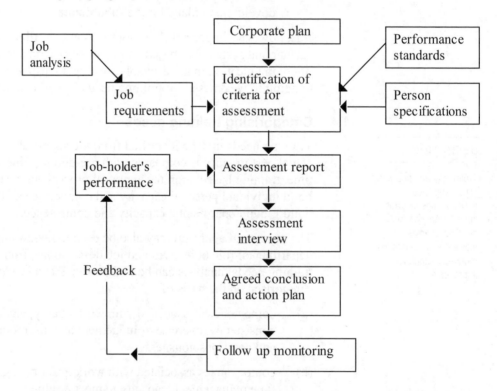

Appraisal can be highly motivating if it builds on expectations of appropriate effort leading to desired performance, and includes positive reinforcement with rewards that are equitable in the eyes of all parties concerned.

1.7 Who appraises?

In any organisation there are a number of alternative individuals or groups who might be involved in the appraisal of others. This section briefly examines the alternatives.

(a) **Appraisal by the immediate superior** – this is the most common arrangement. The advantage of this is that the immediate superior usually has the most detailed knowledge of the tasks and duties carried out by the subordinate and the most intimate awareness of how well they have been carried out. The formal appraisal session should also be seen as part of the continuous appraisal and feedback process that goes on all the time between a superior and subordinate.

(b) **Appraisal by superior's superior** – they may be involved in the appraisal process in two ways. First, they may be required to countersign the appraisal of the immediate superior in order to legitimise it and show that it has been carried out fairly. Secondly, the superior's superior may directly carry out the appraisal. This is felt to offer a fairer appraisal in many situations, reducing the chances of 'victimisation' and ensuring that common standards are applied.

(c) **Appraisal by the personnel department** – frequently it may be responsible for the administration and organisation of the appraisal system but this does not normally mean that it actually carries out appraisals. However, it can happen in situations where there is no logical immediate supervisor to do the job, as, for example, in a matrix organisation.

(d) **Self-appraisal** – how people rate themselves is of crucial importance to the realisation of many of the objectives of an appraisal system. If a person feels the present system is unfair and that criticisms of performance are ungrounded then the individual is not going to be concerned about self-improvement and development. Self-appraisal as the sole form of appraisal is very rare but an element of self-appraisal is quite common. This may consist of getting individuals to prepare for the appraisal meeting by filling out a self-appraisal form or perhaps to complete one section of the superior's assessment form. This differs from full self-appraisal in that it is always the superior who has the final say.

(e) **Appraisal by peers** – it can be argued that a person's peers will have the most comprehensive view of their performance, and hence will be able to make the most acceptable and valid appraisal. However, managers do not often accept this method.

(f) **Appraisal by subordinates** – though not widely used certain benefits may be claimed for this approach. In particular, subordinates are likely to be very closely aware of the performance of their boss. As part of a more comprehensive appraisal method an appraisal by subordinates can play a useful role.

(g) **Development centres** – are used to appraise the potential of employees as supervisors or managers. They use tests, group exercises and interviews to assess this potential.

The openness of the appraisal process is one of the most crucial issues in performance appraisal and it concerns the extent of participation by the jobholder in the assessment of their own performance. However, what is meant by participation in appraisal? In many cases it is used only to denote that the employee has been allowed to see the appraisal. In only a minority of cases does the employee actually participate in assessing their performance as an integral part of the appraisal system.

1.8 General principles of appraisal

The following list represents the generally agreed set of criteria, which should be fulfilled for an appraisal scheme to be effective:

- It should be systematic in that all relevant personnel should be appraised using the same criteria.

- It should be objective. Critical remarks that are factual may be acceptable but citing personality defects or subjective judgements is not.

- It should be based on factors that are relevant to the performance on the job and not consider those factors, which may relate more to the personal prejudices of a particular assessor.

- It should be carried out on a regular basis so that the assessment of any individual is based on current information.

- Wherever possible it should be mutual and there should be a large amount of agreement between superior and subordinate about the subordinate's performance. This is seen as essential for motivation purposes if the subordinate is to improve performance.

- It should be constructive, helping the improvement of performance. Destructive appraisals will lead to resentment and a worsening of superior/subordinate relations.

- Before an appraisal scheme is established there should be an agreement between management and the trade unions involved concerning the need for appraisal, the uses that will be made of it and the method of operation.

- There should be adequate training given to those responsible for carrying out the appraisal.

- The standards should be consistently applied in all functions at all levels.

Appraisals should be fair, consistent and disciplined in approach, relying more on objective than subjective input and aiming to help the person being appraised consider future planning.

KEY POINT

Appraisals should be fair, consistent and disciplined in approach, relying more on objective than subjective input and aiming to help the person being appraised consider future planning.

2 Appraisal process methods

2.1 Types of staff appraisal

KEY POINT

There are a few types of staff appraisal processes:

- review and comparison

- management by objectives

- task-centred appraisal method.

There are a few types of staff appraisal processes in use, these include the **review and comparison** method, **management by objectives** and the **task-centred** method.

(a) **Review and comparison** – consists of the individual being assessed and analysed in terms of objectives, tasks, workflows and results achieved. These are then compared with previously agreed statements of required results and performance levels.

(b) **Management by objectives** – a system whereby managers agree certain objectives with their subordinates and then review the results achieved. It is a common-sense approach to staff appraisal based on the idea that if subordinates know their objectives they are more likely to reach them. Motivation will also be higher as they have more control over the setting of objectives and targets and also the methods by which those objectives and targets can be met.

(c) The **task-centred appraisal method** – relates to what the subordinate is doing and how they do it. It avoids the more formal approach to staff appraisal and adopts a continual assessment approach. After the completion of each task an assessment is carried out and performance monitored.

Activity 1

Explain the general principles of appraisal.

Feedback to this activity is at the end of the chapter.

Whichever type of appraisal method is used the criteria must be clearly stated, understood and agreed by the subordinate. Subordinates must also be clear about the objectives and results required.

The objectives set, and statement of results required, must also relate to the job description, personnel specification and salary grading. The appraisal criteria may include the following.

(a) Volume of work produced, e.g. within time period, evidence of work planning, personal time management and effectiveness of work under pressure.

(b) Knowledge of work, e.g. gained through experience, gained through training courses and gained prior to employment.

(c) Quality of work, e.g. level of analytical ability, level of technical knowledge, accuracy, judgement exercised and cost effectiveness.

(d) Supervisory or management skills, e.g. communication skills, motivation skills, training and development skills and delegation skills.

(e) Personal qualities, e.g. decision-making capabilities, flexibility, adaptability, assertiveness, team involvement, personal motivation and commitment to the organisational goals.

2.2 Techniques of assessment

KEY POINT

Techniques of assessment:

- employee ranking
- rating scales
- checklists
- critical incident method
- free reporting
- results oriented methods.

(a) **Employee ranking** – employees are ranked on the basis of their overall performance. This method is particularly prone to bias and its feedback value is practically nil. It does, however, have the advantage that it is simple to use.

(b) **Rating scales** – under this method the individual's performance is usually broken down into several characteristics or areas of performance, such as

(i) quantity of acceptable work

(ii) quality of the work

(iii) understanding of the work

(iv) initiative, and

(v) application.

The individual's performance in each of these areas is then rated. The rating scales used for this exercise vary. The simplest methods used are those where a score (e.g. out of 10) or a grade (e.g. A, B, C, D and E) is awarded. A commonly used method is the *Graphic Rating Scale*. In this method each characteristic is represented by a scale, which indicates the degree to which the individual possesses the characteristics. It is called 'graphic' because the scale visually graphs performance from one extreme to the other. The advantage of this method is that the person rating often finds it easier to relate to descriptions of performance rather than allocating a score or a grade.

The main problem associated with rating scales is the 'clustering' of results around the 'average' or 'satisfactory' level with little use made of the extreme levels. This negates the whole purpose of an appraisal scheme. To overcome this, some specialists replace terms like 'poor', 'satisfactory' or a numbering system with a series of statements. Each statement is tested for best match with the jobholder's performance.

Despite their popularity there are problems with the use of rating scales. They provide little information to the individual as to how to improve their performance. There is no identification of training needs so it is difficult to design training programmes on the results of rating scales. Frequently rating scales will induce resistance on the part of superiors doing the rating because they are required to assess on factors where they do not feel they have adequate information. For the person being assessed, rating scales can readily provoke resistance, defensiveness and hostility. Telling someone that they lack initiative or that their personality is unsatisfactory can strike at the heart of their self-identity and self-esteem.

(c) **Checklists** – with this method the rater is provided with a list of statements relating to job performance. The rater must choose the most (and sometimes the least) appropriate statements for each individual.

(d) **Critical incident method** – this is based on the assumption that performance is best assessed by focussing on critical incidents. An incident is considered critical when an employee has done, or failed to do, something that results in unusual success or unusual failure in some part of the job. Such a method involves spotting critical incidents and then recording them on a record sheet for each employee. While the method is useful in highlighting strengths and weaknesses in important areas, it relies upon critical incidents being identified by a superior. It can also be extremely time-consuming.

(e)   **Free reporting** – this method usually involves the completion of a report on each employee. It has the advantage of giving complete freedom in the assessment process. However, it does make comparisons difficult to draw between employees, and to a certain degree depends upon the standard of literacy of the assessor.

(f)   **Results oriented methods** – advocates of methods such as Management by Objectives claim their superiority in assessing performance. The method involves setting individual targets and identifying the actions necessary to achieve them. At the end of a period of time (usually six months), results are reviewed. However, some writers feel that such methods lead to an over-reliance on results at the neglect of individual counselling. Another major criticism is that results may not reflect performance but may be the product of external factors outside the control of any individual.

2.3   Rating scales: bias

Bias can occur when using rating scales for a number of reasons:

(a)   **Halo effect** – this refers to the tendency of people to be rated similarly on all of the dimensions or characteristics being assessed. Thus if quality of work is rated as fair, then there will be a likelihood that all other factors in the assessment will be rated as fair. The term halo is used because all of the ratings fall within a narrow range or within a halo.

(b)   **Recency effect** – though appraisal should normally relate to a person's performance over the whole period since the last appraisal it is found that, in fact, assessors tend to be most strongly influenced by their most recent observations. Thus what is supposed to be an annual review is actually based on performance only in recent weeks.

(c)   **Contrast effect** – this can happen when appraising a number of subordinates within a short space of time. A manager's appraisal of an individual can be affected by the evaluation of the preceding subordinate. For example, a poor performance by one individual can make the next person to be appraised look excellent in comparison even though the performance is really only average.

(d)   **Attribution errors** – since we are appraising a person, good and bad performance will be explained in personal terms. Success or failure will be attributed to factors in the individual rather than any situational factors that have had major effects on performance.

2.4   Reducing rating errors

Though it is difficult to eliminate all sources of error it is possible to minimise them by applying the following general guidelines:

(a)   Superiors should be encouraged to observe performance regularly and keep records of their observations.

(b)   Rating scales should be constructed so that each dimension on the scale is designed to measure a **single, important** work activity or skill.

(c) Appraisers should not be required to appraise a large number of subordinates at any one time.

(d) Those rating should be made aware of the common sources of error and helped to avoid them.

(e) There should be training in the effective use of performance appraisal techniques and in the conduct of an appraisal interview.

2.5 Behaviourally anchored rating scales (BARS)

These differ from the common rating scale in two major respects. First, rather than rate personality, BARS evaluate employees in terms of the extent to which they exhibit **effective behaviour** relevant to the specific demands of their jobs. Secondly, each item to be assessed is 'anchored' with specific examples of behaviour that correspond to good performance, average performance, poor performance and so on.

A simplified example is given below which relates to performance in communicating and co-operating with others in a production control environment.

Rating	Behaviour
Excellent	Reports, oral and written, are clear and well organised; speaks and writes clearly and precisely; all departments are continually informed; foresees conflict and handles with initiative.
Good	Conveys necessary information to other departments; does not check for misunderstandings, but willingly tries to correct errors.
Unacceptable	Does not co-operate with or inform other departments; refuses to improve on reports or to handle misunderstandings.

To arrive at the behavioural examples for all jobs in an organisation is a complex task, which involves the collection of much data and the discussion and participation both of management and of those who are to be appraised.

Advantages of BARS

- Rating errors can be reduced because the choices are clear and relevant.

- Performance appraisal can become more reliable, meaningful and valid for both the appraiser and the appraisee because of their participation in establishing the scheme.

- The degree of conflict and defensiveness is reduced because people are being assessed in terms of specific job behaviour and not their personalities.

- The feedback that is generated can clearly identify deficiencies and identify needs for training and development activities.

Disadvantages of BARS

- Decision-making, inventiveness and resolution of problems are difficult to incorporate.

- The time, effort and expense involved is considerable and the investment may only be worthwhile if there are a large number of people doing the same or similar jobs.

- Since BARS are concerned with **observable** behaviours then jobs with a high mental content such as a research scientist or a creative writer do not lend themselves to evaluation using BARS.

- There is an inevitable level of generalisation involved, so that BARS cannot hope to cover all examples of employee performance at all levels.

- Overall it is felt that BARS are superior to graphic rating scales and they are increasingly popular.

2.6 The appraisal interview

The interview is a common feature of many appraisal schemes and is normally used in conjunction with one of the rating methods discussed above. It is the vehicle for giving feedback to the employee where they can find out about their strengths and weaknesses and discuss what steps to take to improve future performance. As such it is a crucial part of the appraisal process. However, the fact that an interview takes place does not inevitably lead to desirable outcomes. It requires skill and insight on behalf of the appraiser to ensure that feedback is positive and the motivational effects are beneficial to the individual and the organisation.

KEY POINT

The effectiveness of the interview will depend very much on the skill of the superior conducting the interview.

The effectiveness of the interview will depend very much on the skill of the superior conducting the interview. It is important to listen to the subordinate and be prepared to change an evaluation in the light of new evidence. The emphasis should be on the future rather than the past, stressing opportunities rather than trying to apportion blame. There is a better chance of progress in an appraisal interview if the discussion centres on specific job behaviour or results rather than on general issues of personality or attitude. The focus should be on an employee's strengths so that they know those behaviours that they should maintain and develop as well as where there are weaknesses to be remedied.

KEY POINT

A properly conducted appraisal interview can have a major effect on an individual's self-appraisal.

A properly conducted appraisal interview can have a major effect on an individual's self-appraisal and it is this self-appraisal that will be the main determinant in the continuation of excellent performance and the willingness to improve and develop in those areas where necessary.

However, problems can readily arise. The person being assessed will experience a conflict between presenting themselves in the best possible light to get the best evaluation and being frank and open about weaknesses to gain help and coaching to deal with difficulties. Appraisal interviews can readily lead to defensive reactions to critical statements. People feel threatened and self-esteem is seen as being under attack. This is common where pay discussions and appraisal are merged.

---

3 Effective staff appraisal

3.1 Introduction

Performance appraisal has to determine what constitutes valid criteria or measures of effective performance. The problem is made more difficult because almost all jobs have many dimensions so that performance appraisal must employ multiple criteria or measures of effectiveness in order to accurately reflect the actual job performance of the employee.

Although it is impossible to identify any universal measures of performance that are applicable to all jobs, it is possible to specify a number of characteristics that a criterion of job performance should possess if it is to be useful for performance appraisal:

(a) A good criterion should be capable of being measured reliably. The concept of reliability of measurement has two components. Firstly, stability, which means that measures taken at different times should yield the same results. The second is consistency, which means that if different people use the criterion, or a different form of measurement is used, the results should still be more or less the same.

(b) A good criterion should be capable of differentiating among individuals according to their performance. If everyone is rated the same the exercise rapidly becomes pointless.

(c) A good criterion should be capable of being influenced by the jobholder. If a person is to improve performance after appraisal then it must be about matters over which the individual has discretionary control.

(d) A good criterion should be acceptable to those individuals whose performance is being assessed. It is important that people feel that their performance is being measured against criteria that are fair and accurate.

3.2 The criteria of effectiveness

A key issue that has to do with the criteria of effectiveness is the question of whether they should focus on the activities (tasks) of the jobholder or the results (objectives) achieved. For example, a salesman might be assessed in terms of activities, e.g. number of cold calls or speed of dealing with complaints or in terms of results, e.g. total sales volume or number of new customers. Measures of results pay no attention to how results were achieved.

There are advantages and disadvantages of using either results or activities as criteria. Appraisal based on results has the advantage of encouraging and rewarding the results desired by the organisation. However, it has the disadvantage that it might encourage people to break rules or go against company policy to get the desired results. It may lead to frustration if the failure to achieve results is due to factors beyond the control of the individual. Assessment in terms of results also has the shortcoming that it does not generate information about how the person is doing the job and hence has limited value in suggesting ways of improving performance.

A major advantage of appraising in terms of activities is that it helps in generating information that can help in the training and development of poor performers. However, it may only encourage people to concentrate on their activities at the expense of results achieved. This can result in excessive bureaucratic emphasis on the means and procedures employed rather than on the accomplishments and results. There are then problems in incorporating the successful non-conformist into the appraisal system.

An effective appraisal system needs to have a balance of both measures of results and measures of activities.

3.3 Appraisal: negative effects

There have been studies on the effects of appraisal, which show some negative effects, e.g.:

- criticism had a negative effect on goal achievement

- subordinates generally reacted defensively to criticism during appraisal interviews

- inferior performance resulted from defensive reactions to criticism

- repeated criticism had the worst effect on subsequent performance of individuals who had little self-confidence.

3.4 Appraisal: barriers

Too often appraisal is seen as a personal criticism session, and therefore staff become very suspicious and uncooperative as it may announce financial disadvantage or lost promotion opportunity. The superior might show bias towards certain employees or may be reluctant to 'play God' with the subordinate's future.

Any appraisal scheme is doomed to failure and will cause frustration among the staff if:

- the top management does not give the appraisal system continuous support

- the appraisal procedures are not made clear to everybody

- the scheme does not get full support at all management levels. As wide a range of staff as possible should be involved in the formulation of the scheme

- potential appraisers are not given experience of interviewing before they are involved in appraisals. Too often a manager has not been trained in this field and their valuations simply reflect their own temperament

- interviews designed to improve performance are often trying to weigh up at the same time salary and promotion issues

- fear, ignorance, lack of involvement and the suspicion of unfairness can create open hostility. A scheme should be seen to be fair, with an appeals procedure for those who consider themselves unfairly treated

- the facts are not recorded

- uncontrollable factors are introduced, and

- it is not felt to be taken seriously.

3.5 Other problems

Despite the growing popularity of performance appraisal schemes in many organisations, several problems have been revealed and various criticisms have been made of appraisal as a technique. The main problems and criticisms are as follows:

(a) Many organisations seek too many objectives with their appraisal schemes. To try to use them to assess potential, to motivate employees, to review salaries, to control training etc. is asking too much of such schemes.

(b) Many appraisal schemes generate a mass of paperwork, which is wasteful of management time and costly to administer.

(c) Some studies have revealed a lack of commitment to such schemes by top management that means that the schemes are not properly implemented. This often means a lack of follow up to appraisal so that adequate provision for increased training or new levels of pay has not been made.

(d) Assessments made in appraisals are very prone to errors of judgement because of subjectivity, prejudice, inappropriate criteria, pressures of time etc.

(e) Frequently there is little attention given to the training of people to carry out appraisals.

(f) In some organisations appraisal becomes little more than an annual ritual with little concern for its consequences and even less concern for critically reviewing the process itself.

(g) The criticism of 'recency' is often made. Superiors may appraise subordinates only in terms of recollections of events immediately preceding the appraisal.

(h) Employee resistance to appraisal is not uncommon. This is particularly noticeable when a scheme has been introduced without full consultation with all the interested parties.

Despite criticisms, appraisal is becoming more widespread and is seen as an important part of staff relationships.

KEY POINT

Despite criticisms, appraisal is becoming more widespread and is seen as an important part of staff relationships.

4 Relationship between appraisal and the reward system

4.1 Introduction

In many organisations there is a link between performance and pay. The extent to which performance is linked to pay can cause many problems some of which can be overcome with training for those who carry out the process. Many employees think that the appraisal system should be definitely linked with the reward system, on the ground that extra effort should be rewarded. Although this appears to be common-sense and fair view there are some drawbacks to rewarding performance with a monetary reward. For example:

- Funds available for pay rises rarely depend on one individual's performance alone: the whole company has to be successful.

- Continuous improvement is always necessary and perhaps should be expected of employees as part of their work and not rewarded as an extra.

- In times of economic recession or low-inflation pay rises can be fairly small.

- Performance management is partly about future performance levels rather than rewards for past performance.

4.2 Types of reward

The three main objectives of reward management are:

- to attract and retain suitable employees

- to maintain or improve levels of employee performance

- to comply with employment legislation and regulations.

The types of reward used in an organisation will result from decisions made concerning the nature of the effort in relation to the reward.

4.3 Pay and performance

Relating pay to performance comes from the theories of motivation. The 'need' theories emphasise what motivates people, rather than how people are motivated. Maslow argued that higher order needs become progressively more important as lower order needs are satisfied. Herzberg found that pay becomes significant as a source of satisfaction when it is seen as a form of recognition or reward.

An incentive scheme ties pay directly to performance. It can be tied to the performance of an individual or a team of employees. The scheme includes the following performance-related pay:

- **piecework – or payment by results** – is a system where rewards are related to the pace of work or effort. The faster the employee works, the higher the output and the greater the reward

- **bonus schemes**

- **commission** – this a reward paid on the performance of an individual, typically to salaried staff in sales functions, where the commission earned is a proportion of total sales

- **measured day work** – where the pay of the employee is fixed, on the understanding that a specified level of output will be maintained. This level of performance, known as the 'incentive level', is calculated in advance and the employee is put under an obligation to achieve the level specified so that the pay does not vary from week to week

- **productivity plans** – involve some extra payment based on the success of employees in reducing costs, increasing production or expanding sales, usually measured by some overall index (e.g. company or divisional performance)

- **profit-sharing** – a company-wide scheme where payments are made in the light of the overall profitability of the company of some other measure of results. Differentials can be built into the schemes to take account of factors such as level of responsibility or length of service.

KEY POINT

Reward is very hard to define, especially as between individuals. In an organisation, a Reward System refers to all forms of financial returns and tangible services and benefits employees receive as part of an employment relationship.

4.4 Performance-related pay linked with appraisal

In order to be able to match pay to individual performance and to take into consideration individual competencies, skills and team outputs, there is a clear need for the design and implementation of a sophisticated appraisal scheme. Because of this link, appraisal schemes are sometimes viewed by many employees with distrust, suspicion and fear. Broadly speaking, the appraisal system can be seen to have two main purposes:

- to assess performance with the intention of linking it to a pay award

- to assess performance to highlight training and development needs.

The linkage between individual appraisals and performance related pay schemes rely on:

- jointly agreed performance objectives and criteria

- an objective and reliable means of assessment

- developing the link between performance and pay.

4.5 Difficulties in linking pay to performance

There are many problems in linking pay to performance and the notion of there being a direct relationship between performance and pay include:

- employees concentrating on goals that have a definite link to the reward system

- inducing conflict when rewarding some employees more than others

- financial constraints due to recessionary factors, or poor company results.

To overcome some of the difficulties of linking pay to performance it is necessary for appraisors to be well trained and skilled at carrying out the process. Schemes need to be uncomplicated, free from bias and subjectivity, and perceived to be fair by those who are to be appraised.

Activity 2

If an appraisal session does not include a discussion on salary, then what is its relevance?

Feedback to this activity is at the end of the chapter.

Summary

- Appraisal acts as an information processing system providing vital data for rational, objective and efficient decision-making regarding improving performance, identifying training needs, managing careers and setting levels of reward.

- In any organisation there are a number of individuals or groups who might be involved in the appraisal of others. This chapter briefly examined the alternatives.

- Appraisals should be fair, consistent and disciplined in approach, relying more on objective than subjective input and aiming to help the person being appraised consider future planning.

- Staff appraisal processes include the review and comparison method, management by objectives and the task-centred method. There are also quite a few techniques of assessment and we focus on the rating scales method, as this seems to be the most widely used technique.

- Determining what constitutes valid criteria or measures of effective performance.

- Establishing the relationship between appraisals and the reward system.

Having completed your study of this chapter, you should have achieved the following learning outcomes:

- evaluate the recruitment, selection, induction, appraisal, training and career planning activities of an organisation

- evaluate the role of incentives in staff development as well as individual and organisational performance.

Self-test questions

1   What can performance appraisal data be used for? (1.1)

2   Give three examples where performance appraisal is a vital management tool. (1.3)

3   Identify the stages in the performance appraisal process. (1.6)

4   What is the main problem associated with rating scales? (2.3)

5   What does the acronym BARS stand for? (2.5)

6   Outline some of the problems associated with appraisal interviews. (2.6)

7   What are the three main objectives of reward management? (4.2)

Practice questions

Question 1

What does TNA stand for?

A   Task-centred needs analysis

B   Training new appraisal

C   Training needs analysis

D   Task-centred new appraisal

Question 2

What type of bias happens when when appraising a number of subordinates within a short space of time and the appraisal of one individual can be affected by the evaluation of the preceding one?

A   Halo effect

B   Recency effect

C   Contrast effect

D   Attribution error

Question 3

Appraisal systems

You have been asked to write a report on performance appraisal systems and in it you have been asked to describe the following:

(a)   the purpose of an appraisal system   **(8 marks)**

(b)   the objectives of appraisals from the viewpoint of the individual and the organisation. Include in your answer the barriers to effective appraisal.

(12 marks)

(Total: 20 marks)

For the answers to these questions, see the 'Answers' section at the end of the book.

Feedback to activities

Activity 1

The general principles of appraisal include the following:

- It should be systematic, objective and based on factors tha are relevant to the performance of the job.

- It should be carried out on a regular basis and the information on which it is based should be current.

- wherever possible it should be mutual and there should be a large amount of agreement between appraisor and appraisee.

- It should be constructive and help improve performance.

- there should be adequate training given to those responsible for carrying out the appraisal.

- standards should be consistently applied in all functions at all levels.

Activity 2

Current practice suggests that involving pay matters in appraisal sessions inhibits discussion on other aspects. The appraisee is reluctant to be open in case it affects the salary award and will react defensively to criticism.

Without pay discussions, the appraisal session can fulfil its key purpose of staff counselling and development. This would involve such matters as:

- feedback on performance and problems encountered

- career development

- identifying job interests and likely development areas

- define performance targets

- review promotability

- enable individuals to appreciate where their jobs fit in the overall company scheme.

Chapter 19

ANSWERS TO PRACTICE QUESTIONS

Chapter 1

Components and structure of a computer system

Question 1

The answer is **A**.

A firewall is software that acts as a barrier between a computer system and the telecommunications network (Internet), preventing unauthorised access from the Internet by hackers.

Question 2

The answer is **B**.

Check the text of the chapter for typical storage capacities of electronic storage devices.

Question 3

Real time.

Question 4

With data compression, the data held on the file is reduced in size, so that it does not require one byte to represent one character.

Question 5

The answer is **D**.

A compiler is an item of software that translates programs written in a high level language into programs in machine-readable form (machine language).

Question 6

National Counties Hotel plc

Memorandum

To: Head Office official

From: Advisor

Date: Today

(a)   The major components in the National organisation appear to be:

- Each hotel – running the local operation.

- Head office – co-ordinating and managing hotels; some central bookings.

Within each hotel the sub-systems are:

- The bar – sale of drinks and, perhaps, bar snacks.

- The restaurant – sale of food and drink.

- Room letting – individuals

- Room letting – group bookings from tour companies

- The housekeeping department – looks after laundry, cleaning and furnishings in rooms.

- Conference arrangements – liaising with conference organisers and marketing the hotel's facilities.

All of these areas are closely linked. For example:

- Activities in the restaurant will affect bar takings.

- Lettings and conference arrangements will affect the restaurant and the bar and, for residential conferences, room lettings

- The rooms that can be let to individuals will be sometimes dependent on the rooms which have been let to groups.

- Housekeeping workload will depend on room lettings.

Each hotel will be linked to head office (many bookings are referred from a central booking department) and will also be linked to other hotels in the chain so that onward accommodation can be arranged.

Typically, head office will carry out the functions of accounting, marketing, senior appointments, finance, strategic planning, investment decisions, pricing.

(b)   Operating systems are specialist pieces of software which are normally supplied with the computer. In microcomputers, commonly found operating systems are MS-DOS (often simply called DOS) and Windows.

Operating systems do not ensure that an organisation's operating procedures are foolproof; nor do they guarantee that only correct data and accurate data is processed. The main functions of an operating system are to:

- Communicate with the user.

- Enable the user to carry out certain routine tasks.

- Monitor the computer for error conditions.

- Oversee the running of programs, including disk access.

Errors can be detected by the operating system. For example, if the user or a program attempted to copy data onto a file where there was no room, the operating system would intervene, prevent any transfer and warn the user. Occasionally, programs begin to operate incorrectly, perhaps trying to interfere with other programs that are running simultaneously, and the operating system may intervene to limit the damage.

Operating systems such as Windows present users with a graphical user interface (GUI). GUI systems are usually regarded as being more user-friendly than text based systems.

(c)   It is common for guests in hotels to be given a card showing their room number, name and period of residence. Many hotels ask to see this before items can be charged to room accounts.

The card is usually printed as the guest registers and it would be possible to include a bar code on it. This would encode the same information as was printed normally, but could be scanned by a reader each time the guest asked for an item to be charged.

The advantages of this system would be:

- accurate recording of information
- fast recording of information
- valid bar codes can be made difficult to forge
- the card would still be very cheap to produce and could be discarded by the guest after use
- guests should find the system no more awkward to use than conventional cards
- bar code scanners are cheap and can be connected to lightweight, portable recording devices.

If you have any questions regarding the above, please do not hesitate to contact me.

Chapter 2

Information systems

Question 1

The correct answer is **B.**

Both negative and positive feedback provide information about actual results. Negative feedback results in control action to bring actual results back into line with the target. Positive feedback results in action to maintain or increase the divergence between actual and target results. Feedforward control information compares current forecasts (not historical results) with a target or plan.

Question 2

The correct answer is **A.**

This is a simple definition of an open system.

Question 3

An open system reacts to stimuli or inputs from its environment. Unless it receives continual inputs, it will become more disordered and chaotic. Entropy is a measure of the resulting disorder in a system.

Question 4

HZ Hospital

(a)   The MIS provides routine information to doctors and other staff, and contains historical factual information. The information is used by the MIS in fairly predictable ways, for example to inform the doctors about their patients' case histories and circumstances (for example, their age).

An expert system provides information to assist with unstructured decisions about recommended treatments for patients. The output is provided in response to non-standard input requests.

(b)   The hardware for the expert system will probably consist of a number of terminals (with keyboard, mouse and screen) linked in a local area network to a central computer. The system will have some other peripheral equipment, such as printers.

There must also be a link to the database of the MIS. However, these might be housed in the same physical computer.

The software consists of a powerful off-the-shelf package (with a knowledge base, an inference engine and an explanation program). This package should be updated regularly by the software company supplying it.

Question 5

Competitive edge

In recent years, the strategic and competitive value of information technology has advanced to the forefront of overall systems planning issues. The high capital expenditure that new systems require, together with the greatly enhanced information processing capacity provided by technological developments, has meant that organisations are reviewing in detail the positive commercial advantages that can accrue from an imaginative application of information technology to their activities as a whole.

An organisation's perception of the *future* strategic and competitive value of its information systems will depend partly on the role information systems *currently* play in the organisation. If management simply view the function of information systems as the provision of support for other production or managerial structures, then the strategic and competitive value of future systems will not be regarded as particularly significant.

Alternatively, information systems might by viewed as a type of information production 'factory', enabling the organisation to produce its goods or services efficiently. The systems might be felt to be vital in providing competitive edge in existing products or markets, making new kinds of products possible.

Michael Porter emphasises that tomorrow's successful organisation will be a collection of skills and capabilities, which are ready to pounce on any market opportunity. Possessing competitive edge means having those factors, which lead customers to consistently prefer your products. He has suggested three overall competitive strategies that an organisation can implement.

1   The use of information technology to provide *overall cost leadership*. This objective may be held by companies in very competitive price-sensitive markets, where any means of reducing costs can lead to price reductions in goods and services offered to clients or customers (or where margins can be maintained on lower prices).

2   Information systems can reduce staff time spent on clerical work and more on business development. Cost containment can include detailed control of stock levels: enhanced information systems might allow a company to tie up its purchasing services directly with its suppliers, reducing stock-holding costs, or delays in processing orders.

3   *Product differentiation.* Information systems can enhance an organisation's ability to compete by providing it with up-to-the-minute information as to customer needs, and comparing customer purchases of the organisation's goods with those of other suppliers. This allows an organisation to differentiate its products on factors other than price.

4   *Focus.* Information technology may permit the identification or exploitation of a market niche not yet serviced. An example of the competitive value of information technology is the introduction of automated teller machines.

Additional to the provision of competitive advantage in the market place, internal changes in an organisation's structure can enhance its competitive edge, by encouraging more effective use of its human and material resources. Sometimes changes can be radical: a distribution organisation may get rid of one of its warehouses and employ a more efficient computerised distribution system to manage the inventory.

Information systems might be used to foster innovation, by encouraging a free flow of ideas in a large organisation. A computer conferencing system, where individuals communicate their ideas with relative informality is an example of such a system.

Information technology does not guarantee an enhanced competitive ability for the simple reason that any advantage due to information technology alone is likely to be temporary as competitors can also use it. Moreover, improved information does not *necessarily* lead to better decision-making

Chapter 3

Design of information systems

Question 1

Verb

Question 2

The correct answer is **D**.

The ELH diagram must show the events that begin and end the 'life' of the entity.

Question 3

Car agency

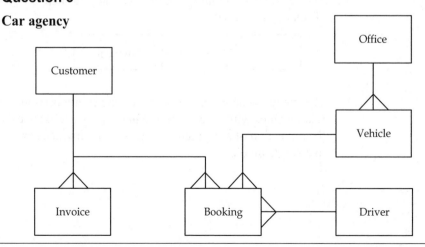

Question 4

ELH

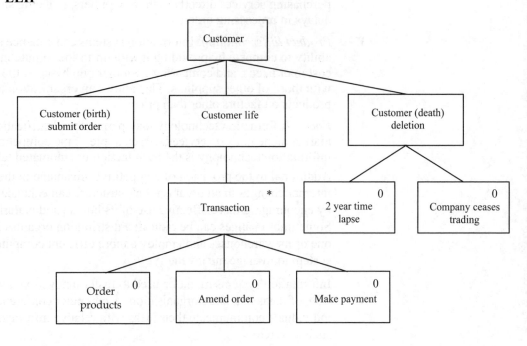

Question 5

Explain in English

(a)   The interpretation of the entity relationship model using a set of English statements is as follows.

- Each customer receives one or many invoices.

- Each invoice is sent to only one customer.

- Each invoice has one or many invoice lines.

- Each invoice line is for only one invoice.

- Each invoice is paid through one or many payments.

- Each payment refers to only one invoice.

- Each product is on one or many invoice lines.

- Each invoice line is for only one product.

(b)   The relationship should probably be many-to-many so as to maximise the efficiency of the data.

(c)   The many-to-many relationship can be decomposed into two one-to-many relationships with a new intermediate entity probably called allocation. This is the allocation of a payment to one or more invoices or more than one payment to a single invoice.

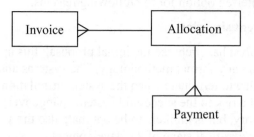

(d) The likely contents of the entity 'allocation' will be:

- payment number (the key of payment)

- invoice number (the key of invoice)

- amount.

Question 6

Decision table

Total order less than £50	Y	N	–	–	–
Account less than 4 weeks in arrears	Y	Y	N	N	Y
Account 4 – 8 weeks in arrears	N	N	Y	N	N
Account more than 8 weeks in arrears	N	N	N	Y	N
Bought over £2,000 in 12 months	–	–	–	–	Y
Give 2% discount	X				
Give 5% discount		X			
Do not give discount			X		
Pro forma invoice				X	
Add 1 to discount					X

Question 7

WRF Inc
Report

To: The Board of WRF Inc

From: Chartered Certified Accountant   Date: 23 May 200X

Subject: Systems development life cycle approach to providing a successful systems changeover

1   Introduction

The systems development life cycle (SDLC) is a disciplined approach to developing information systems. It is a model that is based upon a phased approach. There are many versions of the SDLC, and different terminology may be used, but the basic intent is similar. It covers the following stages:

- requirements and specification

- design

- implementation.

SDLC is the preferred option for the following reasons:

2 The current situation

The systems analyst has prepared the initial proposal; this appears to have been done without following any formal methodology. The systems analyst is on a fixed-term contract that is due to terminate when the system installation is complete. These two factors represent a risk to the successful system changeover: the solution provided may be satisfactory, but is unlikely to be optimal; also the systems analyst's contract may terminate at a critical stage of the development.

Before embarking on the phases of the SDLC, it is worth considering that prior to a new system being designed and built, the existing system needs to be fully understood; therefore, it is important that a study of the current system is undertaken.

3 Requirements and specification

Initially it is important to ascertain the purpose of the new system, what the new system is required to do, and what level of performance is expected etc.

At this stage, business requirements are clearly defined: the inputs, files, processing and outputs of the new system. Resulting from this initial analysis, performance criteria can be set and solutions developed, resulting in appropriate specifications; the specification of a 386 processor running at 20 MHz and 2 Mb RAM running Windows® 3.1 was arrived at because the systems analyst 'thinks the users will require' this.

4 Design

This stage considers both computerised and manual procedures, and how the information flows are used. Computer outputs are normally designed first; inputs, program design, file design, database design, and security are also areas to be addressed.

It will also be necessary to consider operability at this stage i.e., who should have access and capability to do what to which data.

At this stage a detailed specification of the new system is produced. A 386 processor running at 20 MHz may well be considered to be too slow: a 486 processor running at, say, 33 MHz may be necessary to produce the required results.

5 Implementation

This stage may include the building of prototypes and the finalisation of specification requirements e.g. 2 Mb will almost certainly be considered insufficient RAM; 4 or 8 Mb may be deemed more appropriate.

The implementation stage takes the development through from design to operation. This involves acquiring or writing software, program testing, file conversion, acquiring and installation of hardware and training.

When following a formal methodology, implementation and all it embraces should be considered from the initial analysis stage so the likelihood of problems should be substantially diminished.

6 Review and maintenance

This final stage ensures that the project meets with the objectives set, that it is accepted by users, that its performance is satisfactory, and allows for future enhancements and development.

7   **Recommendation**

It is recommended that the Board of WRF Inc approve the utilisation of SDLC for the systems changeover. Not only does this approach encourage discipline during the development process, communication between the developers and the users, and recognition of the importance of analysis and design, but it also ensures that business needs are met and provides a useful basis for future development.

Signed: Chartered Certified Accountant

Chapter 4

IS implementation and evaluation

Question 1

The correct answer is **D**.

The work is carried out to prevent the system from being unable to handle the anticipated growth in volume.

Question 2

The correct answer is **B**.

This is adaptive maintenance, because the system is being altered to meet new user requirements.

Question 3

The correct answer is **C**.

It might be argued that the question calls for subjective judgement. However, user satisfaction will clearly be affected by the interaction between the computer user and the computer system through the screen displays (GUI), response times (the length of time it takes for the system to respond to input from the user) and errors in the system. File sizes are not directly related to user satisfaction.

Question 4

(a)   With pilot testing, the IT specialists (systems analysts) and the user's management are able to focus their attention on and devote their time to the part of the organisation where the test is carried out. This should improve the monitoring of the tests.

(b)   Introducing a new system into parts of the organisation gradually allows management to compare operations with the old and new systems operating together, but without the complexity and cost of parallel running.

(c)   Introducing a new system gradually means that the departments or regions that implement the new system first can use their experience to assist the departments or regions that do not implement the system until later.

Question 5

Review of implementation

(a) **Essentially, there are four approaches from which to choose:**

Direct changeover

The existing system is abandoned for the new at a given point in time. *Prima facie* this seems an economical approach, but this is balanced by the risk that the new system will not work perfectly. Furthermore, there will be no safety net, in terms of existing procedures and staff, with which to recover the situation. It is not suitable for large systems crucial to the well-being of the organisation. If the new system bears little or no similarity to the old, this may be the only route. In the context of the department store, it should be obvious that this is not a viable option; if the new system collapses, then the store potentially loses all sales until it is remounted.

Parallel running

This involves the running at the same time of both old and new systems, with results being compared. Until the new system is proven, the old system will be relied upon. This is a relatively safe approach, which also allows staff to consolidate training in the new system before live running commences. It is expensive, however, because of the extra resources required to run two systems side by side. Parallel running is necessary where it is vital the new system is proven before operation. In the case of the POS system, this would be the most suitable method of changeover.

Phased changeover

Here the new system is introduced department by department, or location by location. This is less drastic than direct changeover, and less costly than parallel running, although each department may still be parallel run. For the department store group it might well be a sensible approach to introduce the new POS system into just one store, initially, and parallel run at that store first, before switching to phased changeover, and subsequently to implementation at all other stores.

Pilot changeover

This is another compromise approach, involving the running of the new system, or functions/subsystems thereof, on a sample of users, transactions, files, etc. in parallel with the new system. This might be followed by full parallel running, or a switch to phased changeover. Care must be taken with the choice of sample. The nature of the new system here makes it unlikely that this approach could be adopted.

Whichever approach, or combination of approaches, is adopted, good management control, including thorough monitoring, will be essential if the new system is to be successful.

(b) **Checklist of implementation activities should include:**

- development of a changeover timetable

- involvement of all affected personnel in planning

- advance notification to employees, followed by periodic progress bulletins

- development of training programme

- consider possible needs for external resources

- delivery of POS equipment

- testing of equipment

- installation and testing of software

- completion of documentation

- training for systems operators

- system trials

- changeover period

- acceptance of new system

- operational running.

(c)   **Systems evaluation**

This is a vital and important part of system implementation. Its objective is the systematic assessment of system performance to determine whether the established goals are being achieved.

Several criteria are commonly used to measure the performance of the systems:

Time, i.e. the time required for a particular action to be performed. Response time is the time that elapses before a system responds to a demand placed upon it; for the POS system, this must be measured in seconds. Turnaround time is the length of time required before results are returned; for a POS system, little processing is done, and this may not be significant.

Costs, sometimes the only measure applied, are used to determine whether the various parts of the system are performing to financial expectations, and include labour costs, overheads, variable costs, maintenance costs, training costs, data entry costs, data storage costs, etc. For the POS system, all of these should be considered.

Hardware performance should be measured in terms of speed, reliability, maintenance, operating costs and power requirements. The performance of the POS devices in the various store departments, the central computer servicing the POS system and any networking components must be evaluated.

Software performance should be measured in terms of processing speed, quality and quantity of output, accuracy, reliability, maintenance and update requirements. Again, this is necessary for all software involved in the POS system.

Accuracy is a measure of freedom from errors achieved by the system and can be measured in several ways; but it is important that the type of errors as well as volume is analysed to ensure that serious errors are quickly identified. In the POS system, it is essential, for example, that the prices charged to customers are accurate.

Security means that all records are secure, that equipment is protected and that unauthorised or illegal access is minimised. It is important that the central database containing product prices is not corrupted, for example.

Morale is reflected in the satisfaction and acceptance that employees feel towards their jobs. Absentee rate and employee turnover are two factors that can be used to assess morale of the POS operators in the stores.

Customer reactions are an important factor in the context of the POS system; large numbers of complaints from customers would indicate that the system is not performing satisfactorily.

All the data gathered from the various components of evaluation should be studied to assess the success or otherwise of the system and, if the latter, to help pinpoint the reasons why performance is not reaching expectations.

Question 6

Facilities management

(a)   It is not clear from the scenario whether GDC Ltd inherited a system that was already running or whether they were involved in any of the system design and development. From the point of view of DS, there are many reasons why it may have received poor service, even though the terms of the contract have been fulfilled.

The terms are as follows:

(i)   **Purchase of all hardware and software.** GDC may have a preference for hardware and software that they are familiar with and this may not be a suitable fit to the existing system. Unfortunately, hardware and software become obsolete very quickly and GDC Ltd may not have been replacing it fast enough to keep up with the demands of the company. It could be that they have bought software to upgrade the system e.g. moved from Windows 95 to NT, and they have no staff trained sufficiently to maintain it. A similar situation could have occurred with networking and routing equipment. Problems can occur that are very difficult to sort out without available expertise.

(ii)   **Repair and maintenance of all IT equipment.** This is a tall order for any company. When the equipment was purchased, DS should have arranged maintenance service through the manufacturers themselves. There could easily be a misunderstanding over the type of maintenance required from GDC Ltd. Are they supposed to fix faults when they occur or do regular maintenance checks to ensure the smooth running of the equipment?

(iii)   **Help desk and other support services for users**. Users often have an inadequate understanding of existing systems and develop unrealistic expectations. This means that they may generate unreasonable and unmanageable volumes of requests for change. GDC Ltd. might suffer from high programmer turnover rates. Their employees may not have the necessary skills or motivation. Many programmers prefer development work to maintenance work and may be reluctant to get involved in help desk support.

(iv)   **Writing and maintaining software.** There are two main areas of software maintenance:

- changes to the specification, requiring the software to be changed, and

- bug fixes or rectifying deficiencies so that the system performs as originally specified.

There are three types of maintenance activity:

- **Corrective**, where behaviour or performance fails to be as specified due to faulty implementation;

- **Adaptive**, where a change in the environment has not been anticipated, and causes a departure from the specification. Adaptive changes may arise from.

    –   changes in the law

    –   alterations in taxation regulations

    –   changes forced by technical advances by competitors

        –   improvements in hardware within the company

        –   the evolution of new standards and procedures.

- **Perfective**, where some feature is enhanced though it was within the tolerances of the specification, e.g. the program may be made more user-friendly, or the processing speed may be increased.

Since the contract is vague and the scope so large, there are bound to be areas of poor service from GDC Ltd.

(v)   **Provision of management information**

Unless the type, content and timing of the management report required is specified, then there is ample scope for poor service. A new person at GDC Ltd. may be responsible for producing the reports and he or she may not know the full routine. The report may have been left in the wrong place, or delivered to the wrong person first. However, the problem may not be due to a fault at GDC Ltd. To obtain essential management reports, the information must be kept up to date by the staff at DS. If the employee responsible for maintaining the database is sick or the files containing the data get damaged or corrupted, then the production of reports is likely to be delayed.

(b)   There are several options available to DS.

The first is to re-write the contract with the help of GDC Ltd so that there is some flexibility but no vague areas and each party knows what is expected from them. This could be done through negotiation while the existing contract is still running. The problems with this course of action is that DS are locked into the current arrangement and GDC Ltd will be aware of the problems it could cause by giving three months' notice and leaving DS. They would be in a very strong position to increase the price substantially or restrict their commitment to DS in any negotiations that might take place.

The second would be to obtain help in re-writing the contract and, when satisfied, give GDC Ltd three months' notice and ask them, and other facilities management companies, to tender for the new contract. The problems with this course of action is that DS might just be trading in one company that is giving poor service for another that they do not know. There is no guarantee that service standards will always be as expected.

The third option would be to revert to an in-house IT development and support department solution. This would require a lot of effort and expense and, if new staff have to be recruited, there will be a long period before they could understand the system and be in a position to do what GDC Ltd are already doing.

Chapter 5

Change in organisations

Question 1

The correct answer is in phase 3 when delegation leads to additional problems of co-ordination and control.

Question 2

The answer is **B**.

A crisis of control results in a transformational change from growth through delegation to growth through co-ordination.

Question 3

Use measures to remove significant restraining forces or reduce their strength.

Question 4

Managing change

(a) **Participation** – this approach seeks to involve employees in the decision making process. There are cases where this has been extended to the designing of own jobs, payment systems, etc. The advantage of this method is that it enhances commitment to change, since the employees have developed their own change. In addition, the wider range of input into the change process will bring in an equally wide range of knowledge and experience.

However, there are a number of significant disadvantages. First of all, there must be the culture and climate to permit participation in change. Townsend boasted how change worked in Avis but the type of person working for a car-rental firm is likely to be different, and probably more adaptable, than someone who is in a very highly programmed job with little scope for creativity.

Secondly, the greater number of people in the decision-making process can give rise to an extremely protracted decision-making process, because no-one is responsible and hence accountable for the decision.

Thirdly, there is a need for a high degree of trust between the management and their subordinates. Again, there may not be the culture and tradition of this, with the result that the invitation to participate will be treated with considerable suspicion.

Fourthly, participation must be honest. Pseudo-participation is always exposed for the sham that it is, and only serves to exacerbate the problem. This can easily happen, since with the wide variety of people being involved, there is a high risk that plans for change degenerate into a talking shop.

(b) **Education** – there is a mistaken view that if people are better educated and trained, then they will be receptive to change. While better education and training may make changes easier, and create an environment where people are prepared to participate in the change process, it will also raise the expectation of the individual. This could mean an increased turnover as people become more marketable, or an exacerbated hostility derived from frustration where enhanced expectations have not been met.

(c) **Communication** – this assumes that if the plans for change are effectively communicated, then people will understand the need for change and accept the changes. This would lay the foundations for change to be implemented fairly easily and painlessly.

Sadly, the communication of the plans for change is subject to misinterpretation and, if the wrong medium is selected, can be manipulated into disinformation by self-seeking interests. In addition, communication can be a two-edged sword. People may learn of the need for change and morale may drop, exacerbating the current situation. Similarly, the more marketable people may move, and this will also create a situation where change is needed, but the best people to implement it have left.

(d) **Power** – this is where management exerts what is perceived as its 'right to manage' and imposes change unilaterally. Management has the formal authority to do this within the parameters of appropriate legislation, and the de facto situation in relation to the labour market. In periods of high unemployment, management may elect to take this option, knowing that if employees do not like the situation, then they should look very carefully at the alternatives. It is argued that this draconian method is a viable option only in times of high unemployment, but it could be argued that in times of full employment those people who are not prepared to go along with the changes can be eased out less painfully.

Such a strategy has the obvious advantage of being easy and quick to implement, especially if the workforce is in a weak and demoralised position. However, there are two significant potential disadvantages. First, in the short term, there is the obvious problem identified by Etzioni that such a coercive strategy will fail to gain the wholehearted support of the workforce, with the result that the desired levels of motivation, morale and output will not be achieved. Secondly, in the long term the company may be building up further problems for itself. Unions have long memories, and a coerced, demoralised workforce provides a fertile area in which confrontation and antagonism will develop. As a result, when the time becomes ripe for a more co-operative approach, the management is unlikely to find the unions and the employees very helpful, or predisposed to comply with managerial wishes.

(e) **Manipulation** – this can be very similar to the power strategy. It is ostensibly less coercive. A management team may use the media of pseudo-participation and pseudo-effective communication to persuade the workforce about the need for change. Ideally it will be done through a mass meeting, similar to union meetings outside the factory gate. Agreement comes from position power and an unwillingness to step out of line. The benefits are the same as from the power strategy, as are the considerable disadvantages.

(f) **Negotiation** – this moves along the spectrum from autocratic styles to a more consultative approach, usually through the media of the unions. The objective is an acceptable compromise solution. Two possibilities exist. First, that one side wins and one loses. Compromises are often unsuccessful, so this approach may be the best way. Secondly, is the possibility to work towards a compromise. This option may not exist or it may be very unpalatable. The obvious example is where rationalisation is required. The unions may resist the closures, but the future of the whole company or even the industry may be at stake. This may mean that the path towards a compromise is really not available. It also means that one party to the negotiations is fighting with a considerable handicap.

The obvious advantage of negotiation is that it recognises potential conflict and seeks a solution without running the risk of creating damaging industrial disputes. It has the further advantage that the resultant agreement will produce a commitment to the changes and maintain the morale of the workforce and the output that management requires. However, it can be a protracted process and if it goes on too long, patience may be lost on both sides. It also depends upon the level of confidence that exists in the union and the negotiating team. If there is a feeling that the unions have sold the employees out, if they could have got a better deal, and if they feel they have been the victims of cynical manipulation, then the whole process will fail.

Note: Any five of the above strategies would be sufficient for a complete answer.

Question 5

(a) **Greiner's model**

The organisation life cycle model was suggested by Greiner. It assumes that, as an organisation ages, it grows in size, measured perhaps by the number of employees and diversity of activities. This growth is characterised by a number of discrete phases. Each phase is characterised by:

(i) a distinctive factor that directs the organisation's growth

(ii) a crisis, through which the organisation must pass before achieving the next phase.

Phase 1. The organisation is small, and is managed in personal and informal ways. The founders of the business are actively involved in operations. Apple Computers, for example, started up in a garage. However, sooner or later there comes a need for distinct management skills, relating less to products and marketing issues and more to co-ordination of the organisation's activities. This is a crisis of leadership.

Phase 2. Clear direction is provided by professionalising the management. At the same time, there are more employees. This initial enthusiasm might be tempered by loss of autonomy and the growth of hierarchy. The problem arises in that of delegation. The top finds it harder and harder to keep in detailed control as there are too many activities and it is easy lose a sense of the wider picture. Employees resent the lack of initiative and their performance falters. There is a crisis of autonomy.

Phase 3. The response to the problems **of Phase 2 is** delegation. This has the advantage of decentralising decision-making and giving confidence to junior managers. However, this in itself leads to additional problems of co-ordination and control. Over-delegation can result in different departments acting sub-optimally. There is a crisis of control.

Phase 4. The addition of internal systems, procedures and so forth to ensure co-ordination of activities, optimal use of resources etc. This increased complexity results in a crisis of red tape.

Phase 5. The crisis of red tape is resolved by increased informal collaboration. Control is cultural rather than formal. People participate in teams. Greiner thinks that this growth stage may lead to a crisis of psychological saturation, in which all become exhausted by teamwork. He postulates a sixth growth phase involving a dual organisation: a 'habit' structure for daily work routines and a 'reflective structure' for stimulating new perspectives and personal enrichment.

Greiner's model describes organisational growth as inevitably punctuated by crisis. Another criticism is based on the fact that not all organisations **are founded by a visionary** controlling entrepreneur, selling a product or service.

(i) A new organisation can be formed from the merger of two existing ones.

(ii) Two or more companies might collaborate jointly on a joint venture. The Airbus project, for example, did not start as a small business, but as a result of co-operation between governments and existing companies.

(iii) New organisations are created by existing ones and have a substantial complement of staff.

The model perhaps combines too many issues: organisation structure, organisation culture, product/market scope, leadership and management style.

(b)   **The management accountant's role in each phase**

Management accounting deals with management information and control.

In Phase 1, it is unlikely that there would be a distinct management accounting function at all. This is because the organisation is small, and will not be able to afford an elaborate finance department. It is possible that bookkeeping will be contracted out to a firm of accountants. Or perhaps a small team of technical staff, reporting to the accountant, who may have a seat on the Board as a finance director, will do all the accounting jobs, including tax returns, company accounts, monthly management accounts etc.

In Phase 2, the management as a whole becomes professionalised, and you would expect to see the finance function growing in importance. If no qualified accountant has been employed until now, one will be found. The accountant will have to exercise staff authority over other professional managers. Increased attention will be paid to supplying detailed management information to the senior management.

In Phase 3, extensive delegation would suggest a need for systems of performance evaluation, profit centre analysis, etc. Specific management accounting skills come into their own in this stage.

Phase 4, which is ended by a crisis of red tape, might be characterised by an efflorescence of accounting controls, exercised by functional authority.

Phase 5 should engender a more sober look at the nature and purpose of accounting controls. Informal collaboration can be supported by information systems, which contain modelling facilities, executive information systems should be able to drill down into basic data.

Chapter 6

Managing change

Question 1

The correct answer is **D**.

Options A, B and C in the question were identified by Kanter as actions that will *stifle* initiative and change.

Question 2

The correct answer is **A**.

Check the text if you are not sure about the five disciplines of a learning organisation, and what each of them means.

Question 3

Organisational development, according to Bennis, is a continual approach to solving problems that decrease efficiency within an organisation, supported by management consultants using their diagnostic and problem-solving skills.

Question 4

To create dissatisfaction with the current position, and so reduce resistance to change or apathy about change.

Question 5

The correct answer is **C**.

Lewin was interested in the forces that drive change and resist change, many of which are psychological. He argued that the appropriate way to reduce the resistance to change is to persuade individuals to accept it, rather than impose it on unwilling employees.

Question 6

A learning organisation can be defined as an organisation which facilitates the learning of all its members and continuously transforms itself.

According to Senge, there are five core competencies involved in building learning organisations:

- *Building a shared vision* – an organisation needs to ensure that its people or staff are working towards a common purpose. A sense of common purpose, and shared values, beliefs, norms and attitudes creates an environment conducive to continuous learning in contrast to only irregular, ad hoc learning when there is a crisis which brings all the people together.

- *Personal mastery of learning by individuals* – the need for members of the organisation to develop the ability to continually question taken-for-granted assumptions underlying their particular view of reality. This increases their perception beyond their accepted superficial view of 'reality' and enables them to create more of what matters to them.

- *Working with mental models to recognise unconscious assumptions and to see alternatives* – an extension of personal mastery by individuals to recognise their unconscious assumptions. This allows individuals to understand how an alternative reality can be created.

- *Team learning* – involves group interaction where individuals come together as teams. This goes hand in hand with personal mastery of learning by individuals so groups of people can deal with difficult issues and come up with specific decisions.

- *Systems thinking to understand inter-relationships and see the bigger picture* – instead of analysing and breaking down problems into discrete components, the emphasis here is on synthesis and the importance of understanding relationships.

Question 7

(a) Change is an inescapable part of both social and organisational life. Most planned organisational change is triggered by the need to respond to new challenges or opportunities presented by the external environment or in anticipation of the need to cope with potential future problems. Change has both positive and negative attributes. It can represent the creation of something new or the discontinuity and destruction of familiar social structures and relationships. Despite the potential positive outcomes, change is often resisted at both the individual and the organisational level because it involves both confrontations with the unknown and loss of the familiar. Change presents those caught up in it with new situations, new problems, ambiguity and uncertainty. People are naturally wary of change. Many individuals, groups and organisations find change, or the thought of change, painful and frustrating.

(b)   Individual resistance – there is a tendency for some people to find a sense of security in the past; they wish to retain old and comfortable ways and try to protect the status quo because they have a fear of the unknown. They worry about whether they will be able to cope with the new pressures that the change will place on them and develop a vested interest in the perpetuation of particular organisation structures and accompanying technologies. It is not unnatural that they should feel personally threatened because they are really being asked to question their existing beliefs Changes may mean the loss of jobs, power, prestige, respect, approval, status and security. If the change is seen as likely to prove inconvenient, make life more difficult, reduce freedom of action or result in increased control, there will be resistance. In the case of 'Y', people may find it personally inconvenient for a variety of reasons. It may disturb relationships and arrangements that have taken much time and effort to establish. It may force an unwanted location or geographical move or alter social opportunities. There could be problems with learning new skills. Some employees will fear that they will fail and be reluctant to take on retraining. Perceived, as well as actual threats to interests and values, will be likely to generate resistance to change.

(c)   Group resistance – change may be seen as a threat to the power or influence of certain groups within the organisation eg, managers may perceive change as leading to a loss of their control over decisions, resources or information. Middle management groups, fearing de-layering, will be looking to their trade union to protect their interests. Even a small change such as the introduction of quality circles or worker directors may seem like a threat to some managers because they see it as increasing the role and influence of non-managerial staff and a risk to the power in their own positions. There may well be calls for industrial action or action to obtain the highest possible severance pay or redeployment terms. Even without the help of a trade union, groups may collude informally to resist change. They may do this by withholding information or by not being wholly co-operative with those seeking to implement change.

(d)   Organisational resistance – although organisations have to adapt to their environment, they tend to feel comfortable operating within the structure, policies and procedures that have been formulated to deal with a range of present situations. They often set up defences against change and prefer to concentrate on the routine things they perform well. Some of the main reasons for resistance against change are:

- the organisational culture – may have developed over a long time and be difficult to change. The pervasive nature of culture in terms of 'how things are done around here' also has a significant effect on organisational processes and the behaviour of staff. Firms that change from a role culture, in a relatively stable and a large-sized organisation, to a different culture that requires a flatter, more organic, organisational structure to cope with competition in the open market, will have problems in surviving such a dramatic change

- structural stability – the need for formal organisational structure with the division of work, narrow definitions of assigned duties and responsibilities, established rules, procedures and methods of work can result in resistance to change. The more mechanistic or bureaucratic the structure, the less likely it is that the organisation will be responsive to change

- the existing investment in resources – change often requires large resources, which may already be committed to investments in other areas or strategies. Assets such as buildings, technology, equipment and people cannot be altered easily

- past contracts and agreements with various organisational stakeholders can limit the changes in behaviour. For example, it is especially difficult to renegotiate the terms of fixed price contracts or change agreements with trade unions on compulsory redundancies.

(e) There are a number of ways to facilitate change. Kurt Lewin developed a programme of planned change and improved performance. His force field model suggests that when any change is being considered, it is important to consider the forces involved – those that are driving change and those that are impeding or restraining it. People driving the changes will encounter resistance in the form of countervailing pressures or forces. Very often the drivers for change are economic, e.g. to increase market share, to increase profits, to expand into new markets. In contrast, the reasons for the resistance are more concerned with the social implications than with the economic logic. They tend to be emotional and based on personal losses and gains.

(f) A manager must expect resistance to some if not many of the changes that he or she is seeking to bring about and a force field analysis is a good start to see where resistance to change might lie and where to seek allies. A force field diagram (see below) shows the balance between the forces driving change and those impeding it.

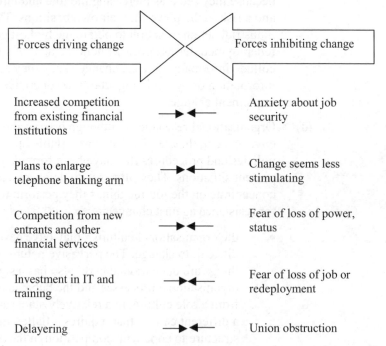

Using this diagram, we can show that the major driving force for change at 'Y' is the increasing competition brought about by changes in the environment. There are few options available except to become leaner and more effective. Delayering and its consequent reduction in staffing levels should help to cut costs. The strengthening of the telephone banking division and the investment in IT and training should help the bank's competitiveness.

Despite clear evidence of the threat to the future of the bank, the employees are not convinced by the plans that management have produced. This is perhaps because the message has not been communicated effectively to managers and other employees. It is not clear from the scenario what methods have been used to explain to the workforce the seriousness of the bank's situation and the rationale behind the plans to solve the problems. But clearly this must be an early priority for the senior management team.

Chapter 7

Operations strategy

Question 1

The correct answer is **D**.

Transformed inputs in a process might be materials, information or customers. Customers might be transformed physically (for example, by a hairdresser or a transport service) or intellectually (for example, by entertainment).

Question 2

The sequence of operations that takes raw materials and converts them into an end product or service for consumers is known as a transformation process.

Question 3

The correct answer is **A**.

When output volumes are high, it is usually economical to arrange production as a continuous process operation (rather than as a batch process operation). Output will usually be in small batches when there is low volume of demand for individual products and a large variety in the range of products manufactured.

Question 4

Inventories represent purchasing in advance of requirements for production or production in advance of customer demand. Inventory therefore represents incurring expenditure earlier than is really necessary.

Incurring expenditure earlier than necessary involves spending cash earlier than necessary. This has a cost in the form of an interest cost.

Inventory is also at risk of loss through damage, deterioration and theft.

Question 5

(a) '**Value chain**' describes the full range of activities which are required to bring a product or service from conception, through the intermediary of production, delivery to final consumers, and final disposal after use. It is a way of looking at a business as a chain of activities that transform inputs into outputs that customers value. Customer value derives from three basic sources:

- activities that differentiate the product
- activities that lower its cost
- activities that meet the customer's need quickly.

The value chain includes a *profit margin* since a markup above the cost of providing a firm's value-adding activities is normally part of the price paid by the buyer – creating value that exceeds cost so as to generate a return for the effort.

'**Value chain analysis**' views the organisation as a sequential process of value-creating activities, and attempts to understand how a business creates customer value by examining the contributions of different activities within the business to that value. Value activities are the physically and technologically distinct activities that an organisation performs. Value analysis recognises that an organisation is much more than a random collection of machinery, money and people. These resources are of no value unless they are organised into structures, routines and systems, which ensure that the products or services that are valued by the final consumer are the ones that are produced.

(b)   Porter describes two different categories of activities.

Porter's value chain

The primary activities, in the lower half of the value chain are grouped into five main areas.

- Inbound logistics are the activities concerned with receiving, storing and handling raw material inputs.

- Operations are concerned with the transformation of the raw material inputs into finished goods or services. The activities include assembly, testing, packing and equipment maintenance.

- Outbound logistics are concerned with the storing, distributing and delivering the finished goods to the customers.

- Marketing and sales are responsible for communication with the customers e.g. advertising, pricing and promotion.

- Service covers all of the activities that occur after the point of sale e.g. installation, repair and maintenance.

Alongside all of these primary activities are the secondary, or support, activities of procurement, technology, human resource management and corporate infrastructure. Each of these cuts across all of the primary activities, as in the case of procurement where at each stage items are acquired to aid the primary functions.

(c)   The key problem areas are as follows:

- Inbound logistics – Woodsy has problems with the procurement of the raw materials, labour and machinery. The company is buying its raw materials two years in advance of using it. This must be tying up capital that could be used to purchase new machinery and tools. Storing the timber entails large amounts of money being tied up in stocks, which are prone to damage, restrict the production area and is very slow moving.

The workmen are being paid by the hour rather than by the piece and this means that they have little incentive to work harder.

- Operations are concerned with the transformation of the raw material inputs into finished goods or services. At Woodsy, employees work at their own pace on the assembly of the garden seats and tables, using very basic tools. The production methods used make the finished product relatively expensive. The linkages between the support activities are also causing some problems. Both the owner and the foreman have no man-management skills. Technological development is non-existent and the company needs re-structuring.

- Outbound logistics are concerned with the storing, distributing and delivering the finished goods to the customers. Woodsy does not seem to have a system for distributing and delivering its goods.

- Marketing and sales are responsible for communication with the customers e.g. advertising, pricing and promotion. This seems to be non-existent at Woodsy as, in the past, satisfied customers have passed on their recommendations to new customers. The company relies on its position on a busy road intersection to displays its products, for customers to carry away themselves.

(d) For Bill Thompson, the main task is to decide how individual activities might be changed to reduce costs of operation or to improve the value of the organisation's offerings. The recommendations would include the following:

- The business needs managing full-time. A new manager, or assistant manager, could encourage Bill to streamline the manufacturing process, introduce new technologies and new production and administrative systems. He or she could also negotiate new payment methods to give the workforce an incentive to work harder.

- To increase the production area the alternative strategies that the company could explore include storing the timber elsewhere, or purchasing it after it has dried out and seasoned.

- Holding high levels of finished goods might give a faster customer response time but will probably add to the total cost of operations.

- The purchase of more expensive power tools and equipment may lead to cost savings and quality improvements in the manufacturing process.

- The company needs a marketing and sales department to research the market, inform the customers about the product, persuade them to buy it and enable them to do so. The product range may need to be extended and alternative outlets for the products sought.

(e) The purpose of design is more than to improve the appearance of a product. It must also satisfy the customer in its performance, durability, simplicity of operation and cheapness. Bill Thompson can consider the following different aspects of design for his garden furniture:

- Design for function – value in use implies quality and reliability: the product must satisfy the customer in its purpose and give long service

- Design for appearance – although products should please the eye to attract customers, the appeal of the product may not be solely visual. Other senses are also often involved and sometimes characteristics such texture may predominate.

- Design for production – to ensure component parts are made easily and economically, so that they can be assembled and transported easily and sold at an attractive price

- Design for distribution – to enable easy packing, reduction of storage space and packing costs

(f) Kurt Lewin suggested that change occurs in three phases: unfreeze, change and refreeze.

- Unfreeze – the current situation is unacceptable and will only result in job losses or even closure. Staff have to be convinced as to why the current practices are undesirable.

- Change – in this stage it is important to demonstrate to the employees what the new situation should be – the new ways of working, the streamlining of operations, the improvement in quality and in deliveries – and show how the changes can be accomplished. Attitudes and culture need to change.

- Re-freeze – the final stage involves the 're-freezing' of this newly 'accepted' position. This can be done be providing reassurance - the potential for job security and trying to incorporate the employees personal values into those of the organisation. Having accomplished the change then rewards such as praise and career development must be used to embed this new culture and so prevent a reversion to the old, bad practices.

Question 6

(a) The basic features of management decision-making are the same, no matter whether a manager specialises in production, selling, purchasing or any other operating function. Similarly, the decisions of a production manager in a toy car manufacturing business are the same as the decisions of a production manager in a different type of manufacturing business.

If we assume that the production manager is fairly senior in the management hierarchy, but that a business manufacturing toy cars will be a fairly small organisation, it could be presumed that the production manager would be involved in strategic decision-making, budgeting and weekly or daily production planning and control. Strategic planning decisions that the production manager might be involved with are as follows.

Planning new products. Product research and design might be a specific responsibility of an 'engineering' manager, but the production manager would need to be consulted about operational considerations involving new product development and manufacture. Similarly, he or she would be involved in decisions to develop existing products, promotion methods, and the timing and duration of advertising or promotion campaigns.

Deciding capital expenditure plans. The production manager will make recommendations about capital expenditure on production fixed assets. Such decisions would include re-siting the production plant, introducing new production technology (e.g. to make a new range of toy cars, such as cars with microtechnology in their remote control system) or replacing worn-out existing plant.

The quality of products is a key factor in the marketing mix. When a strategic decision is taken about the target market position for the organisation's toy cars, the choice of balance between quality and price will have to be made, and the production manager will be involved in this decision because he should be able to advise on what quality of output can be achieved with given production resources.

Decisions to shut down a plant, or to 'rationalise' production so as to achieve lower costs or greater efficiency, are either strategic or 'budgeting' decisions.

The production manager will be involved in production budgeting decisions. The production budget will be a plan of how many of each product should be made, what resources will be required to make them, and how much they will cost.

The resource utilisation budget will state the planned requirement for materials, labour and machine time. To determine these requirements, a decision must be made about standard rates of efficiency for material usage, labour productivity and machine operations. (Standard rates might be renegotiated annually with the work force as part of a pay and productivity arrangement.) A decision might be needed on second shift working, or overtime. The production manager might also be involved in deciding the appropriate levels of raw materials inventories, and the optimal size of batches, if the toy models are made by a batch production method.

Methods of working might be reviewed periodically, and improvements agreed by the production manager in consultation with trade union representatives.

Where limiting factors exist whereby some production resources place a constraint on what the business can make and sell, the production manager might need to decide whether to pay extra to overcome the production constraints (e.g. by suggesting that some work could be subcontracted, if this is technically feasible).

(b) Management control is the level below strategic planning. While strategic planning is concerned with setting objectives and strategic targets, management control is concerned with decisions about the efficient and effective use of an organisation's resources (personnel, materials, machines and money) to achieve them. Efficiency in the use of resources means that optimum output is achieved from the input resources used. Effectiveness in the use of resources means that the resources are used to reach the intended objectives or targets.

Within the framework of the budget, the production manager will be involved with weekly and day-to-day operating decisions. These will include production scheduling (deciding on output quotas, the allocation of different jobs to different groups, assigning priorities to jobs, etc).

Operating decisions consist of putting plans into effect and control decisions. Control decisions might involve some strategic control (monitoring the success or failure of the organisation in achieving its strategic plans) but most control decisions will be at a 'tactical' (budgetary) or operational (day-to-day) level.

Budgetary control involves a comparison of actual results against the budget plan, and the highlighting of excessive variances, which might indicate that control action is required. Control might then involve decisions about improving efficiency and labour productivity, controlling expenditure levels, postponing expenditure, reducing idle time improving capacity-utilisation of the plant, or quality control. Similar comparisons of actual results against production schedules might be carried out daily or weekly, involving control decisions by the production manager.

Chapter 8

Management of operations

Question 1

The correct answer is **C**.

OPT stands for Optimised Production Technologies.

Question 2

The correct answer is **A**.

The other activities are non-value-adding activities.

Question 3

(a) **Inbound logistics** in the value chain is the systems and procedures relating to the acquisition, movement and storage of inputs to the organisation. The buyer will study commodities, sources of supply, systems and procedures, inventory problems and market trends, methods of delivery, whether maximum discounts are being earned and the amount and use of waste materials. Inbound logistics also includes warehousing, stock control, transport etc. From the point of view of corporate financial strategy, storing inputs entails vast amounts of money being tied up in stocks, which are prone to damage and shrinkage and are perhaps slow moving. There is also the creation on the shop floor of a mentality that pushes components through to satisfy stocks (just in case) rather than pulling them through made to order (just in time). This means yet more stock is ordered and so on. While the choice of supplier is a 'procurement' function in the value chain, the management of the supplier relationship tends to be classified as inbound logistics, particularly when it comes to more closely integrating the organisation's purchasing systems with the sales systems of the supplier.

(b) There are two main types of decision for inventory management:

- How much to order? When an order is placed with a supplier, what quantity should be ordered?

- When to order? How frequently should inventory be ordered? Should it be ordered at regular intervals, or when the inventory level has fallen to a reorder level?

The trade off is:

Ordering more frequently	Ordering less frequently
Higher ordering costs	Lower ordering costs
Smaller average inventory	Larger average inventory

(c) There are two methods of inventory control: the periodic review system and the continuous (or perpetual) review system. In the **periodic review** system, the inventory position is reviewed at regular intervals (usually at the time of a scheduled reorder). The inventory is counted and the order quantity is calculated by subtracting the amount of stock on hand from the desired maximum inventory. A manager using this system determines the re-supply schedule by establishing a reorder interval (the number of months between orders), and places orders based on this schedule.

In the **continuous** or **perpetual review** system, the inventory level is reviewed on an ongoing basis for every transaction in which stock is dispensed. When the amount of stock reaches a predetermined reorder level, an order is initiated. Each time the stock is replenished, it is for a standard quantity (usually for that amount which will raise the stock level backup to the desired maximum level). This system is based on stock levels rather than on time intervals

(d) The main advantages of sole supplier agreements are as follows: *(Any three required)*

1   Overdrive should be able to negotiate lower initial prices due to the increased volume of business to be transacted with the supplier. The suppliers are all currently small organisations, so a trebling of the order quantities from any one of them should allow that supplier to exploit economies of scale.

2   Overdrive should be able to gain better control over their inbound logistics through direct involvement with the supplier. Giving the sole supplier more attention and management time should improve the reliability of deliveries and also reduce the risk of quality failure.

3   There is an opportunity to integrate the systems of Overdrive with those of the supplier, as mentioned above. For example, Overdrive could give the supplier access to production forecasts, which would allow the supplier to amend production plans for component G4 to meet forecast demand. This would allow a move towards just in time (JIT) logistics, and reduce (or eliminate) finished goods inventory at the supplier and component inventory at Overdrive.

4   Overdrive should be able to ensure better quality due to the extent of the supplier's reliance on Overdrive. The supplier would probably not wish to disappoint such a major customer.

(e) The main disadvantages of sole supplier agreements are as follows: *(Any three required)*

1   Once the agreement is signed, there is a risk over future price rises. It could be argued that the sole supplier agreement leads to increased supplier bargaining power over Overdrive, though this will depend on how well the relationship is managed.

2   There is a significant risk in relation to possible delivery failure by the supplier. Overdrive has contracts with car manufacturers that include 'liquidated damages' clauses for late delivery. These would have to be written into any contract with a supplier, and a small supplier may not be able to afford the cost of such a high exposure to possible penalties.

3   There is a risk of falling quality from the supplier if the relationship with Overdrive becomes too 'comfortable'. Overdrive must continually remind the supplier of its quality expectations. This is a big issue for Overdrive, as they are buying a high technology component that forms a key part of their product. There are also safety implications associated with product failure, and these could lead to legal action against Overdrive.

4   If Overdrive only uses one supplier, they might miss out on future innovations in the industry. Overdrive should change their planning process to ensure that they take advantage of any future developments by other suppliers.

(f)   Although it might be difficult to argue against the philosophy of JIT, there can be problems with applying the theory of JIT to all industries in practice.

- It is not always easy to predict patterns of demand.

- The concept of zero inventories and make-to-order is inapplicable in some industries. For example, retailing businesses such as supermarkets have got to obtain inventory in anticipation of future customer demand.

- JIT makes the organisation far more vulnerable to disruptions in the supply chain.

- JIT was designed at a time when all of Toyota's manufacturing was done within a 50 km radius of its headquarters. Wide geographical spread, however, makes this difficult.

- It might be difficult for management to apply the principles of JIT because they find the concept of empowering the employee difficult to accept.

Question 4

(a)   Holding inventory is cost effective and helps achieve sales at competitive prices. The other objectives of holding inventories are:

- To ensure prompt delivery.

- To obtain quantity discounts.

- To reduce the order cost.

- To avoid production shortage.

Managers will have different views on the levels of inventory to hold:

- The financial manager's view is to keep inventory levels low, to ensure the firm's money is not invested in excess resources.

- The marketing manager's view is to have large inventories of the firm's finished products to ensure all orders could be filled quickly, eliminating the need for back orders.

- The operations manager's view is to keep raw materials inventories high to avoid production delays.

- The purchasing manager's view is to have correct quantities at the desired time at a favourable price.

- An uncoordinated inventory system can allow these competing views to create conflicts and inefficiencies in the firm

(b)   The common techniques of inventory management include:

- **Economic order quantity (EOQ):** This refers to the optimal ordering quantity that will incur the minimum total cost (order cost and holding cost) for an item of inventory. Order costs include the costs of purchasing, receiving goods, and maintaining inventory records. These costs are fixed regardless of the size of the order. Holding costs include interest, insurance, taxes, handling, warehousing, and shrinkage. If money has been borrowed to purchase inventory, interest payments may consist of a large portion of these costs. With the increase in the order size, the ordering cost decreases but the holding cost increases and the optimal order quantity is determined where these two costs are equal. The company should also keep an eye on the level of safety stock and the lead-time associated with the orders made.

- **The ABC system:** This is also referred to as 'always better control'. It is founded on the 20/80 concept, where 20% of inventory accounts for 80% of sales. It divides inventory into three groups by sales value:

  - A group (the 20%) largest value and is actively managed

  - B group next largest and less actively managed

  - C group smallest and least managed.

  The items falling in category A are those that involve the maximum investment. Likewise, the items that require minimum investment are classified into group C.

  This approach helps in selective control of inventories. It helps in pinpointing the obsolete stocks, reducing the clerical costs and resulting in better inventory planning.

- **JIT system.** This is an inventory management technique that minimises inventory investment by requiring suppliers to deliver goods to manufacturers just in time to be used in production. It pushes the task of carrying inventory back onto the suppliers. The goal of JIT is manufacturing efficiency. For a JIT system to work, a great deal of faith and extensive coordination must exist between the firm, its suppliers, and shipping companies to ensure that material inputs arrive on time. In addition, the inputs must be of near perfect quality and consistency given the absence of safety stock.

- **Material Requirements Planning system (MRP).** MRP systems are used to determine what to order, when to order, and what priorities to assign to ordering materials. The goal of MRP is to lower inventory investment without impairing production. The technique uses EOQ concepts but uses a computer program to compare production needs to available inventory balances and determine when orders should be placed for various items on a product's bill of materials.

Chapter 9

The supply chain and supply networks

Question 1

The correct answer is **B**.

Seeking the lowest purchase price possible is a feature of a competitive relationship with a supplier. However, if an organisation and its supplier are able to find ways of adding value to the supply chain, by improving efficiency and reducing costs, there might be some reduction in costs and prices over the longer term.

Question 2

The correct answer is **A**.

Within a network structure, there might be maximum outsourcing by suppliers within the network to suppliers at a lower tier in the network. However, there is minimum outsourcing from suppliers outside the network.

Chapter 10

Quality management

Question 1

The correct answer is **C**.

Comparing similar activities or processes with a company in a different industry or business is called activity or process benchmarking.

Question 2

The correct answer is **A**.

This definition was provided by Hammer and Champny.

Question 3

The correct answer is **B**.

Question 4

The correct answer is **C**.

It might be useful to remember this six sigma statistic. It might be examined in a short question in your examination.

Question 5

The correct answer is **C**.

Crosby advocated a zero defects approach and Deming and Juran disagreed with it.

Question 6

Pump manufacturer

(a)   Business Process Re-engineering (BPR) is one of a number of techniques that have been advanced to overhaul existing business processes and practices with a view to improving organisational performance. It is an approach where management ask radical questions about why things are done in a particular way, and ask whether alternative methods could achieve better results. The aim is to reinvigorate a staid management structure and culture, and end up with a company better able to serve customers' wants at lower cost.

It seems as though the structural and cultural emphasis of the Dose Company has remained static over its whole existence. They probably exist in isolation from their suppliers and customers with each department handling different functions with no idea of their place in the value chain. Re-engineers are not constrained by existing methods, people or departments. They ask 'why' and 'what if' questions about everything that happens in the organisation and then begin to explore better ways of doing it. They start form the future and work backwards.

The first step for the management of Dose is to look at the customer interface and improve sensitivity to the customer needs. Unless Dose is providing the best quality at the best price, it will face extinction.

To achieve this it needs to address the primary processes and:

- re-develop the demand process of customer links, marketing and service

- re-develop the product – looking at innovation in design

- ensure that quality is built into the product from inception and not merely inspected in afterwards

- re-design the order fulfilment process – investigate the acquisition of resources, reduce development and production costs and reduce the lead time between product inception and commercial sale and delivery.

The secondary processes that may need re-engineering include the support services of administration, finance and personnel management.

After BPR the company should see itself as part of a longer value chain and organise along activity streams (or processes) running through the business

In this respect, there is a similarity to other management theories. Value Chain Analysis looks at the physically and technologically distinct activities that an organisation performs and looks for the sources of advantage that can be obtained form each stage. Activity Based Management also discards the old departmental approach of R&D, Finance, Marketing, Personnel, Purchasing, Production and Sales, and re-organises these activities along tightly-linked systems running through the business.

As a manufacturing company, the managing director of Dose will be able to find numerous examples of similar businesses that have tried BPR. Some have succeeded in adding profits by improving the processes and the efficiency of activity flows in the business. Others have failed at huge cost because it was either too late when they applied the re-engineering or the reforms were not suitable for the culture and structure of the company.

Dose, like other manufacturing companies, needs to examine radical change ideas as they come up, but healthy scepticism is also wise. Although outdated management techniques and manufacturing methods are a significant reason why new competitors are taking market share from established industrial groups, other reasons are also important. Manufacturers need to look at their fundamental cost structure (labour rates, automation, capital costs) and at their responsiveness and innovation in design, delivery, service etc.

Dose needs to appreciate the lessons learned by others over the last few years and, if the BPR path is chosen, it needs to be done with commitment and leadership from the top. The managing director should not rely too heavily on expensive and temporary external consultants. Top management need to understand the likely impact and thorough analysis of what the business is about with no preconceptions. Once plans for change are decided, management must ensure they implement the appropriate changes fully and carefully, guiding through any cultural change needed to match structural ones.

(b) In attempting BPR, managers might encounter the following major pitfalls:

- There are many consultants advertising their services as BPR experts. Companies could be tempted to pay exorbitant fees and have somebody else implement the re-engineering. However, successful BPR depends on a hands-on approach with management's personal commitment, communal ownership and shared learning.

- BPR is sometimes regarded as a means of making small improvements to existing practices. In reality, it is a radical approach that questions whether existing practices make any sense in their present form.

- As the managing director at Dose found out, BPR is seen as a fashionable cure-all where the advantages are widely written about, but the explanation of how to do it is surrounded by management jargon.

- Enthusiasm for BPR may encourage management to throw out much that is good within the organisation without achieving the potential gains of BPR.

- During the re-processing programme, managers may be distracted from changes in their markets, changes in technology, and the more routine, gradual advances their competitors might be making in the secondary processes areas eg, human resource management.

- Any new ideas or methods will challenge traditional power hierarchies and this will leave some employees – even managers – feeling threatened. Radical change makes staff feel like they have not been doing their job well previously. It also exposes management to resistance and high stress in a climate of uncertainty. The disruption costs can be very high.

- It is tempting for management to use BPR as a cover for something much more familiar such as cost-cutting. Re-engineering may have the intention of lowering costs, but the benefits come through a much bigger re-working than a mere trimming exercise. It is very difficult to do re-engineering properly. With so many other calls on organisational effort, and the high risk inherent in a BPR type of strategy, the company often makes a mess of re-engineering.

Question 7

Quality circles

Quality circles are a method of trying to encourage innovative ideas in production, and by involving employees they are likely to improve the prospects for acceptance of changes in products and working methods.

The production director should be advised that the nature of the changes recommended by the quality circle will depend on the range of skills and experience of the circle members. The wider their skills are, and the broader their experience, the more significant and far-reaching will be the changes they might suggest. Groups of workers with similar skills are more likely to make suggestions for limited changes, within the sphere of their own work experience. What range of skills should the circles have?

The 'terms of reference' of the circles should be made clear. Are they to recommend changes to senior management, or will they have the authority to decide changes, and make them?

Since the purpose of quality circles is to encourage innovation, the co-operation of employees will be crucial. The plans for setting up quality circles should therefore be discussed with the employees who will provide membership of the circles.

Possible problems with the introduction of quality circles might be:

(a)   not enough support from top management

(b)   no co-operation from middle management

(c)   discouragement because of unrealistic expectation of what the circles can do

(d)   lack of support from trade unions

(e)   poor choice of circle leaders

(f)   insufficient training of circle members

(g)   interference from non-circle members to deter the circle's operations

(h)   unwillingness to participate among employees

(i)   individual egos won't join in the circle 'team' spirit

(j)   individual talkers dominate the circle

(k)   poor communication

(l)   lack of enthusiasm due to inadequate publicity.

The keys to a successful programme are:

(a)   creating a proper atmosphere in which to launch them – a positive approach and good publicity

(b)   giving circle member adequate training in quality circle techniques

(c)   introducing circles slowly, one or two at a time, instead of setting up too many all at once. Learning from experience. Getting employees to accept the value of circles from their experience and observations over time

(d)   full support from top management

(e)   an enthusiastic 'facilitator' – a manager in charge of making the circles a success

(f)   setting up a good system for following up and evaluating proposals for change

(g)   giving recognition to circle members – for instance, rewards for successful changes.

Question 8

Sun and Sand Travel

(a)   Sun and Sand Travel has recently focused too much attention on its financial profitability. Whilst ultimately profit is important to survival and growth it is short-sighted to concentrate solely on financial outcomes. Without a good service record and a satisfied customer group, business (and ultimately profits) will decline. This has happened to this company. Reputation and customer satisfaction have been sacrificed for short-term profitability. Michael Medici needs to understand the company and its customer base more and concentrate on those issues that will win back customer support. Operational performance needs to be improved so as to rectify the recent financial performance. Kaplan's 'balanced scorecard' is a set of operational measures which complement the financial measures which so far Sun and Sand Travel appear to have concentrated on to the detriment of other areas. Apart from the traditional financial indicators of performance, Kaplan identifies three other key perspectives – customer perspectives, the internal business perspectives and the innovation and learning perspectives.

There are some obvious customer-centred issues that need to be addressed by Medici. The scenario highlights three areas that need improvement. Performance in these areas can all be examined and measured – are flight delays getting worse? Is the hotel accommodation deteriorating? And are clients being faced with unacceptable changes to holiday schedules at short notice? These parameters all need to be watched closely, with targets set for measurable and noticeable improvements.

Other factors can be used as indicators to measure the performance of the company with respect to its customers. The following are just a few of the potential indicators.

- How many customers are repeat purchasers of holidays?

- How many new customers have chosen Sun and Sand Travel as a result of recommendations?

- How many letters of complaint are received annually and how many letters of congratulation?

With respect to the internal business perspectives it is possible to assess how well the company responds to customer queries.

- How quickly are complaints dealt with? It is possible to measure the waiting time on telephone queries and indeed how swiftly the telephone is answered.

- How long does it take to process an order?

- How accurate are the brochures and how quickly can they be distributed?

These internal performance criteria will help the company to assess how efficiently the company operates in its dealings with the general public.

The final set of measurement criteria focuses on the ability of the company to be innovative and to transfer that innovative learning.

- How many new products are developed annually – new locations and new experiences. Customers are looking for adventure and change. To maintain and improve its position and reputation, Sun and Sand Travel must be in the vanguard with new ideas and new products.

It is possible to measure how much business is dependent upon old favourites and how much is from innovative products.

Also it is important to be able to calculate how long it takes to get a new 'product 'up and running.

If Sun and Sand Travel can utilise these and other non-financial performance indicators it will improve its reputation and should attract more clients, so enhancing its long-term profitability. This is more sensible than relying solely on short-term profits to measure performance and should ensure the company 's future survival.

(b) Sun and Sand Travel operates in a highly competitive environment and to survive and grow the company must demonstrate that it possesses a number of key competences in areas considered critical if success is to be assured.

As the company is operating in the consumer service field, it is important that Sun and Sand Travel has a strong brand name. Potential customers relate more easily to a well-known name. It often connotes reliability and quality, attributes useful in selling holidays.

The company also needs to have strong financial controls. The margins in this type of business are usually very small, resulting from intense competition, and any major variances will have a damaging effect on profitability.

It is also critical that the company has good negotiating and planning and control skills. The company has to deal with numerous suppliers – hotels, airlines, coach companies. Without these skills it will be difficult to integrate all the aspects which contribute to make a successful holiday.

It is also important that the company possesses good people relations skills. Holiday representatives can be so important in ensuring that clients enjoy their holidays whilst they are away. The company must employ and train staff in an appropriate and acceptable manner.

Administrative competence is also a prerequisite for any successful company. The company will be dealing with thousands of holiday-makers and hundreds of supplying companies. Managing these relationships is a fundamental skill.

Apart from the skills necessary in administering and organising the holidays, it is important that the marketing function is skillfully deployed. There must be a good and comprehensive product portfolio. The range of holidays must be sufficiently wide and varied to appeal to a large customer base. The holidays must be regularly re-vamped so as never to appear old-fashioned. Customers are always on the look-out for something or somewhere novel which provides interest and good value.

The company must possess the skills to put together a good holiday brochure. This is usually the prime vehicle for promoting and selling the holidays. Without a good brochure, the success of the company will be placed in jeopardy. It is also essential that the company has good coverage in retail travel agents. This is becoming more problematical as major travel companies now own many retail outlets. Without comprehensive exposure it is difficult to sell holidays. It will be too expensive for the company to run its own retail agencies, therefore the company will need to build up good relationships with the major retail chains. It might consider a direct mail approach or develop its business on the Internet.

The above are just some of the critical success factors which Sun and Sand Travel must be able to demonstrate if it is to improve its performance.

Chapter 11

The strategic marketing plan

Question 1

The technique that management will probably adopt is (B) Major strengths and profitable opportunities can be exploited

Question 2

The one that does not represent the marketing concept is C – uses methods of selling and promoting. A marketing concept uses methods of co-ordinated marketing

Chapter 12

The marketing mix

Question 1

The answer is **D**.

Skimming price is a high price because you have a substantial competitive advantage.

Question 2

Marketing mix decisions

(a)   To depict the way in which promotion works we can use the model AIDA:

A =   awareness

I   =   interest

D =   desire

A =   action

Advertising can be effective in making people aware of products, in generating interest in them, in encouraging desire for them, and in stimulating the actual purchase. Sales promotion is effective mainly at the action end. Sales forces are more successful if advertising has been used to promote awareness and interest, and PR is concerned with improving attitudes to the product and to customers.

For both types of product, chocolate and fork lift trucks, advertising is one of four main elements of the **promotion mix.** The other three are personal selling, sales promotion and public relations.

(b)   A manufacturer of chocolate confectionery may well spend as much as, say, 6 – 7% of the sales price of the product on the advertising budget. Much of this may be spent on TV and daily press advertising. The message would be designed to promote brand preference. The message would be simple and clear, and might exploit psychological characteristics such as the need for 'belongingness' or friendship. If the product were already well-known, the advertisement would be expected either to improve customer preference ('desire') for the brand or to stimulate interest in it in some other way.

(c)   A fork lift truck manufacturer would probably spend a lower proportion of the goods' price on advertising, with trade magazines and perhaps up-market newspapers selected as the media. In industrial advertising, it is common to find advertisements designed more explicitly as an aid to the sales force (for example, the use of a return coupon). The message would be more complex, to persuade economically conscious managers about claimed product advantages. The promotion mix in industrial marketing is more salesforce-oriented than in consumer marketing, and sales promotion also is less important.

(d)   Whereas 'advertising' refers to promotional messages transmitted through the media (TV, radio, press, posters, and cinema), 'below-the-line' promotion refers to the use of non-media methods, such as competitions, free gifts, retail displays, etc.

The major factors to be considered in planning an advertising campaign are the advertising budget, the message to be communicated, the media to be used, and the location and timing of the advertisement.

The budget size should be considered in relation to the resources available, the effect on company profitability, and the estimated advertising expenditures of competitors. Advertising expenditure is often fixed by companies as a proportion of the sales for each line, but this criterion, and the others mentioned, may be overridden in order to achieve a particular objective.

Message design involves the creation side of advertising – what is said, what images appear on the TV screen, the layout and pictorial features of press advertisement. Creative factors must be appropriate to the market segments at which they are aimed, catering for the tastes and needs of that segment.

Media selection depends upon the viewing, reading or listening habits of the potential customer. Cost-effectiveness is the major criterion, and the ratio used is cost per thousand of the target audience. The decision as to which media are actually used generally rests with the advertising agency; there is no 'either-or' choice, since many products use several media in integrated campaigns.

Location and timing (in TV and radio advertisement placing), and frequency of placement must be decided. The placement of the advertisement should be next to items or programmes of particular interest to the target audience, and the size or duration of the advertisement must be decided in relation to the budget, the required response, and the complexity of the message.

(e) Branding is a means of identifying a product or group of products. It provides a means of distinguishing the product clearly from competitive items and frequently, in the mind of the consumer, symbolises the particular qualities that apply to the branded manufacturer. It tells the customer roughly what to expect of the product, and is of great value in promotion of the company's goods.

The manufacturer making goods for a retailer's 'own branding' would clearly lose the benefit of those points mentioned above. There would be no control over the pricing and distribution of their product; in fact, the retailer gains by assuming direction of these variables.

For the manufacturer, selling to large retail outlets may be a relatively economical form of trading. An annual contract, for example, does not require frequent visits from the sales team. The predictability afforded by a guaranteed, large sale means that production can be more closely and efficiently planned. Distribution, in large planned batches rather than small highly varying quantities, will be cheaper and promotional expenditure will be greatly reduced. The manufacturer relies on the 'pull' generated by the retail outlet for their sales; indeed, the retailer may advertise extensively.

The manufacturer may well continue to make the product using their own, manufacturer's brand label. However, the retailer will often take a significant proportion of the manufacturer's turnover. The retailer may thus expect to exercise considerable influence on their supplier, especially in terms of quality and of regular supply. They will receive 'own-branded' goods relatively cheaply, and will sell them at a lower price than the manufacturer's brand, thereby attracting more people to their stores.

Some customers, of course, will still prefer the original manufacturer's branded product, but the stores can cater for this by stocking a quantity of the manufacturer's brand. This 'double stocking' is one of the disadvantages to a retailer, but is nevertheless widely practised.

One of the main disadvantages for both parties is the question of a heavy reliance on a single source or customer. In the event of extreme business problems (such as bankruptcy) or drastic policy changes by either partner, the other may experience a severe drop in the profitability of the product concerned.

Question 3

The marketing mix

The marketing function encompasses a wide variety of techniques and activities. It is concerned with identifying and analysing markets, understanding how consumers are motivated and how they behave in those markets as well as identifying groups of consumers which are of particular interest to the business. To build the link between the business and its consumers requires the development of an appropriate marketing mix, commonly referred to **as** the 'four Ps'. The components of this marketing mix are:

(a)   product

(b)   price

(c)   promotion

(d)   place

and these must be managed to ensure that the right type of product is available at the right price, in the right place and that the consumer is aware of this. It is often argued that the marketing mix for services such as banking includes a fifth 'P' – people, processes and physical evidence – to emphasise the importance that will be attached by the consumer on the attitudes and performance of the individuals supplying the service, the process by which the service is delivered, and the environment in which the service is supplied.

(a)   *Product.* The success of a new product will be improved if the product has certain distinguishing characteristics and features.

   (i)   If it is an innovative product, it must appeal to certain consumer needs in a way that no other product can do as well.

   (ii)   If there are rival products, it should have features that give it some edge, such as a better quality/price mix, new technology or 'environmentally sound' attributes.

(b)   *Place.* The producer must plan for the availability of the product, and the distribution channels to be used. The product must be readily available where the expected consumers are likely to be found.

(c)   *Price.* If the consumer's buying decisions are strongly influenced by price factors, a new product must be launched either at a competitive price or at a price which is promoted as giving excellent value for money given the quality of the product. More sophisticated pricing policies may also be used.

(d)   *Promotion.* Advertising and sales promotion are critical aspects of a successful product launch, to build up customer awareness. Depending on the nature of the product, factors to betaken into account should be:

   (i)   the scope of advertising and the advertising message

   (ii)   special sales promotions when the product is first launched

   (iii) brand image.

The 'design' of the marketing mix will be decided on the basis of management intuition and judgement, together with information provided by marketing research. It is particularly important that management should be able to understand the image of the product in the eyes of the customer, and the reasons which make customers buy a particular product. As an example, a newspaper publisher must try to understand the image of its paper; thus the *Financial Times* tries to sell on the basis of well informed opinions on world and particularly financial affairs, the *Guardian* tries to sell on the basis of socially concerned reporting, and the *Sun* has prospered on its 'page three' image.

It is nevertheless likely to be the case that elements in the marketing mix act as substitutes for each other. For example, a firm can raise the selling price of its products without adversely affecting sales volume if it also raises product quality or advertising expenditure; equally, a firm can perhaps reduce its sales promotion expenditure if it is successful in achieving a wider range and larger numbers of sales outlets for its product and so on. Kotler suggests that the rate of 'substitutability' to achieve a given volume of sales is variable.

If a firm has a fixed marketing budget which it can use to offer price discounts or to spend on advertising, there will obviously be many possible combinations of expenditure-sharing; however, for every £1 extra spent on advertising and taken away from the sales discounts budget, sales volumes will be subject to increasing and then diminishing returns.

Other aspects of the marketing mix design which should be noted are as follows.

(a) A manufacturer of consumer goods will need a marketing mix for the end consumer, and an additional marketing mix for the intermediaries (wholesalers and/or retailers) to whom the manufacturer sells directly.

(b) The optimum marketing mix will change over time as the marketing environment changes. The growth of discount stores and warehouses, for example, might persuade some manufacturers to switch to lower prices for selling through these outlets. The time of year might also be relevant to the mix; for example, in spring when demand for mortgages is traditionally highest there will be much higher promotional expenditure than in the rest of the year. In a recession, banks may cut back on distribution channels (mainly by reducing the size of the branch network).

(c) The marketing mix will also change over time as the product goes into different stages of its life cycle. When a product is in its 'growth' stages of life, the marketing mix might emphasise the development of sales outlets and advertising; in its 'mature' phase, there might need to be more concern for product quality; and to postpone the eventual decline, it may be necessary to reduce prices and spend more on advertising.

The ideal marketing mix is one which holds a proper balance between each of these elements.

(a) One marketing activity in the mix will not be fully effective unless proper attention is given to all the other activities. For example, if a company launches a costly sales promotion campaign which emphasises the superior quality of a product, the outlay on advertising, packaging and personal selling will be wasted if the quality does not live up to customer expectations. Expensive packaging and advertising will be wasted if distribution inefficiency reduces the availability of goods to the consumer, or the price is too high to attract buyers.

(b) A company might also place too much emphasis on one aspect of the marketing mix, and much of the effort and expenditure might not be justified for the additional returns it obtains. It might for example, place too much importance on price reductions to earn higher profits, when in fact a smaller price reduction and greater spending on sales promotion or product design might have a more profitable effect.

The marketing mix must be customer oriented and the main principle behind the marketing mix is that the arrangement and allocation of resources should be such as to maximise returns per unit of outlay.

Chapter 13

Marketing processes

Question 1

ABC Group plc

(a)   One of the key weaknesses of ABC Group plc has been its inability to develop a strong position within the markets in which it is involved. It is extremely important that managers understand the markets in which they operate and appreciate that any differences specific to industrial markets may influence the way in which they ultimately operate.

Closeness to the buyers – a major distinction between industrial and consumer buying is the fact that although the markets may be fragmented there are fewer buyers, some of which may dominate the market (the 80:20 rule). It is critical that the sales force not only knows who these buyers are, but understands what motivates their buying patterns. Promotion will need to be much more precise and targeted as mass advertising that is used in the consumer environment will not work. Within the industrial environment purchase decisions are often made by a group – the decision-making unit (DMU). It is important that ABC identifies and targets the influential parties within the DMU for each major buyer.

Product branding – the development of a strong brand awareness is of critical importance. However, as the company has currently no strong reputation in branding it may need to spend in order to develop market awareness.

Derived demand – the concept of derived demand demonstrates that the majority of products made by ABC are dependent upon the demand for consumer goods and services further down the production chain, ie demand for aircraft or demand for products manufactured with the machine tools produced by the group. Therefore it is important to monitor overall business trends to assess where future growth is to be obtained. With ABC operating throughout the world, and with business cycles being lagged (the Far East, say, might be in recession, whereas USA and Europe may be growing steadily), knowledge of potential growth points by examining international business activity will help the group.

Product pricing – a significant fact in many industrial markets is that demand is inelastic. Total demand is not often influenced by price. Unfortunately ABC appears to have used price as a major tool within its marketing mix. This may enable it to increase market share in the short term, but other companies with better product quality and performance are unlikely in the long run to allow ABC to obtain increased market share without retaliation. The group is not equipped to fight a price war. It would be well advised to concentrate on improving product design and development rather than relying on price-cutting. This coincides with another characteristic of industrial buying behaviour: rational buying. Professional customers usually base their decisions on economic reasons – price, quality or delivery. The impulse purchase or the decision based upon subconscious or barely understood motivations rarely occurs within the industrial environment. Consequently the need for careful research as distinct from a haphazard sales approach is required.

Direct purchasing – distribution chains are shorter in industrial markets. Whilst the use of agents may be appropriate in the smaller overseas markets, it would nevertheless be advantageous if the group could develop closer links with the bigger customers. In this way not only would commissions paid to distributors be saved but ABC could develop a closer working relationship with buyers, so providing ABC with more detailed knowledge of their needs and their intentions.

(b)   Segmentation of markets into specific sub-groups allows the development and implementation of marketing strategies to appeal specifically to those groups. This allows actions of the groups to be monitored more closely, and a marketing mix programme to be created to meet more precisely the needs of those groups.

Geographic segmentation – with a company operating on an international scale the most obvious mode of segmentation is geographic. Although customer needs are unlikely to vary as much as with consumer goods, there is still potential here for refining promotional and distribution strategies.

Benefit expectations – some companies are price-sensitive, whereas others may be more concerned with guarantee of supply, quality or innovative design. ABC should target those companies who are expecting the performance, service or price that the group can provide.

Customer size – smaller companies may need fewer deliveries, whilst bigger companies could be expecting just-in-time deliveries.

Product types – industrial customers can be segmented according to what products they manufacture. ABC could identify a number of customer groups, for example:

- aircraft furniture manufacturing

- vehicle manufacture

- users of electric motors.

Each group would be driven by different considerations.

Purchasing characteristics – companies can also be classified according to purchasing characteristics, i.e. frequency and size of orders. This type of segmentation is particularly useful when designing sales force visits.

When segmenting the market it is important to consider the following.

Measurability. Is there sufficient published data to enable the group to identify and select accurately companies to include within the segment?

Accessibility. How can the segments effectively be reached by either a sales force or promotional media?

Appropriateness. Is the segment compatible with the objectives and resources of the group?

Stability. Is the segment sufficiently constant so that it can be predicted in the future?

Substantiality. Is the segment of sufficient size to be financially viable and attractive?

If a segment fails on a number of these tests then it will be difficult to develop and maintain a successful segmentation strategy.

Question 2

Pains Fireworks

There are many differences. You may have observed the following:

- The producer / provider of the service is present at the point of consumption.

- The users of the service interact with the providers of the service rather more than they do with a manufacturer.

- There is greater variation in the delivery, quality and experience of the service than with product quality.

- The benefits of a service are frequently intangible.

- There is little that can be done to experience service quality in advance of a purchase – how could a customer try out an insurance policy or a film first?

- In order to incorporate these kinds of considerations, marketers have extended the elements of the marketing mix for services with three items, *people, physical evidence and process.*

People

Since the customer and the service provider often meet, it is important that those involved in the service are sensitive to customer needs. Perversely, in many countries and occupations, there is almost a pride in treating the customer poorly. For example, many medical receptionists in the UK public sector still see their job as protecting the doctor from bothersome patients, rather than helping them get the service they need. The attitude is less common in the private sector, although far from unknown. In the private sector, many services are traditionally handled very poorly, including almost all of those involved with conveying property. As Tom Peters famously remarked, 'any company that treats its customers with common decency is likely to get the lion's share of any market it wants, because it's alone'.

Much can be done to improve the customer interface, including training and appropriate recruitment. The service can often be outsourced – BA use external companies to deal with some important aspects of the customer interface although this is not obvious from the way the service is delivered.

Physical evidence

Since the user cannot trial the service directly, other clues will be used to infer service quality. This can be somewhat unreasonable. The head of an American airline once remarked that coffee stains on cabin trays imply that engine maintenance might be equally sloppy.

Service providers can do much to indicate the experience of the service in advance:

- *Users charters and performance indicators.* Indicators of what might be expected by users might be used in publicity material. In the UK, the authorities impose this on some sectors – particularly in education – by compiling performance indicators, and publishing them in the form of a league table. A parent can thereby see which of the local schools perform particularly well. Similarly, an insurance company might use information about the average time taken to process a claim

- *External validation* of quality by the national quality. Such awards as ISO 9000 can be used to imply service quality. Membership of appropriate trade bodies will usually imply some standards of performance.

- *Ambience* at first point of contact and the point of service delivery can convey much about how the service operates. In such businesses as catering and beauty treatment, a great deal turns on first impressions.

- *Corporate image.* Where the firm is big enough, it is possible to set standards that will be recognised. For example, the experience of eating in at McDonalds or Burger King can be predicted in advance anywhere in the world.

In cases where service quality cannot be regulated so effectively, it is possible to create a corporate image through other elements of the communications mix, described below.

Process

Quality can be instilled into the process whereby the service is produced. Much of this will result from the people in the organisation who provide the service to customers. In this context 'non-technical' (receptionists, telephonists, etc.) members of staff may be just as important as those actually producing the service. Training, supervision, quality controls and complaints procedures may all have a major part to play here.

Chapter 14

Managing work arrangements

Question 1

The answer is **A** Herzberg's Maintenance Theory.

Question 2:

Schein's models

Motivation is the urge and drive to achieve a certain goal or to do better. The chain of motivation states that people's needs dictate their behaviour and this specifies their actions. Many authors have sought to categorise people into types that can be seen as requiring different motivation approaches because of differing needs and behaviour. Edgar Schein developed a theory of four models, which defined different driving forces and different motivation needs.

- **Rational-economic man** is seen as a passive individual who will go through the motions of work unless there is a direct financial reward or penalty attached to performance. Schein sees such an individual as responding to direct offers of financial reward and fringe benefits. Taylor's scientific management approach is geared to motivate the rational-economic man since it related reward to specific performance. On the other hand, Herzberg's belief that pay is a 'hygiene' factor which can cause dissatisfaction but is not a motivator, seems to be at variance. Clearly, the rational-economic man is motivated by an external stimulus: there is little self-motivation.

- **Social man** seeks self-fulfilment through contact and relationships with others. Social man is deeply concerned about how others view him; acceptance into groups and being personally liked are important factors in his behaviour. The way in which the work is organised is a key factor in this model. If the manager organises the work so that social man feels isolated or is forced into an unwelcome group, then work performance will suffer. Further, this is the individual who may refuse a promotion or more interesting work since it would take him away from his established circle. Sensitive to the feelings of others, social man will perform badly in an atmosphere of friction or argument. Mayo's Hawthorne experiment first highlighted the significance of social pressure and peer group influence.

- **Self-actualising man is not seeking to meet outside pressures or inducements,** instead there is an internal self-fulfilment need. This can express itself in many ways. It can mean: being free to do one's own thing in one's own way; being able to settle for what one has got, and having continual, expanding ambitions as, for instance, Sir Richard Branson. This is the highest level of Maslow's pyramid of needs and indicates that each individual has his own set of potentialities and his own internally defined goals. Managers will find that self-actualising man responds to opportunity and challenge. He will perform well under delegation and will be goal-driven not task-led. Such an individual will work long hours and at a fast pace when challenged but will quickly become bored and restless with repetitive work. There is a regular need for the manager to ensure that the goals of the organisation and those of self-actualising man coincide – then peak performance will follow.

- **Complex man.** Schein says that the majority of people do not fall neatly into any one of these three categories, instead they are complex and have a balance of all three. This balance can change as circumstances alter. So motivating forces need to be variable since complex man's main motivating factor can vary over time and in different circumstances. Complex man is unlikely to respond to any one motivating force in isolation. Instead, there will be the need to develop a package of variable elements. This means that a manager must be able to ascertain the balance of models within complex man and then vary the approach accordingly.

Note: Only three of the models were required.

Question 3

The classical school

The classical school included writers such as Taylor, Fayol, Urwick, Weber, and Gantt. The main conclusions of their scientific approach were that a set of rules or conditions, if met, would satisfy the organisational needs of most companies. These rules, however, concentrated only on the company and work requirements, and omitted to study in detail the motivational needs, personal aspirations, and potential of the employee. Man was regarded as a tool to get work done to company standards, and was often referred to as 'economic man'. The principles expounded by these writers have given a framework for organisation design, and many of the rules still retain their value in today's business environment.

The main features of their approach were as follows:

- belief in one central controlling authority

- clear division between line and staff functions

- use of optimum spans of control

- responsibility and authority clearly specified

- use of delegation

- specialisation of tasks

- unity of direction and command

- fair pay and good working conditions, decided by management

- decentralisation to be implemented where needed

- authority is derived from the position held in the formal organisation.

The main criticisms of the classical school are as follows:

- It is based on the concept of 'economic' man, with little consideration for the human aspects of work.

- The proposal that it offered a universal solution to the organisational needs of all companies is obviously unacceptable in the present age of rapid change in task, technology and structure that are features of the systems concept.

- It was not geared to react quickly to the changing business environment.

- If a system worked it was not changed. Potential improvements could be overlooked.

The contingency approach

This was developed as a wholehearted belief that the 'human relations' or 'behavioural school' was on the wane.

Lawrence and Lorsch studied the effects of the business environment on organisation systems, and Joan Woodward, with her Essex Studies, developed the contingency school.

The systems / contingency school suggested that there was no one best method because of the large number of variables that influence operations. Thus flexibility and acceptance of change was a key component of the systems theory.

The main features of the systems/contingency approach are as follows:

- organisation structure reflects the need for co-ordination, often by the use of matrix systems

- communication and decision making involvement is encouraged

- regular updating of targets, which are discussed, defined and agreed

- an awareness that change is inevitable for success, and accepted as a challenge rather than a threat

- because of the basic interaction of key factors, staff are able to move away from being specialists, and thus have personal development goals

- high technology companies were seen to be dependent on the acceptance of change.

The implication of the systems/contingency approach is that the best organisational design will depend on:

- the technological environment

- the diversity of the tasks

- the size of the organisation

- type of personnel

- the culture of the organisation.

The main criticisms of this approach are as follows:

- Some staff may find the flexibility required by the systems organisation rather difficult to absorb.

- Reporting to more than one superior can cause problems.

- Constant reaction to change can be stressful, but hopefully it will be a stimulus, rather than a health hazard.

- Change is not always handled effectively.

Conclusions

From what has been written it can be seen that it is unlikely that any one design of organisation will satisfy the needs of companies operating in a period where change tends to be the order of the day. The most likely solution is the use of a combination of the above organisational systems.

Chapter 15

Human resource management

Question 1

The answer is **A** Political, Economic, Social and Technological.

Question 2

Human resource planning

(a)   Human resource planning is 'a strategy for the acquisition, utilisation, improvement and retention of an organisation's human resources'. It attempts to predict how many and what types of people will be needed in the future and the extent to which these needs are likely to be met. It should take into account how existing conditions might change, both inside and outside the organisation, and devise appropriate policies to ensure that the demand for staff is met. Its purpose in both the short and the long term is therefore:

- to estimate the (uncertain) demand for each grade and skill of employee

- to estimate the (uncertain) supply of labour of the appropriate grades and skills

- where there is a discrepancy between demand and supply to take measures, which will reduce the demand or improve the supply.

In other words, have the right people in the right jobs at the right time.

The process that the organisation might use for human resource planning is shown below:

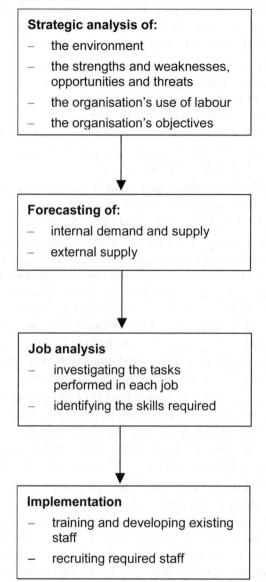

Strategic analysis of:

- the environment
- the strengths and weaknesses, opportunities and threats
- the organisation's use of labour
- the organisation's objectives

Forecasting of:

- internal demand and supply
- external supply

Job analysis

- investigating the tasks performed in each job
- identifying the skills required

Implementation

- training and developing existing staff
- recruiting required staff

The human resource plan is prepared on the basis of the analysis of labour requirements and the implications for productivity and costs. The plan may consist of various elements, according to the circumstances. For example:

- The recruitment plan – numbers and types of people and when they are required, culminating in the recruitment programme.

- The training plan – numbers of trainees required and/or existing staff needing training, culminating in the training programme.

- The redevelopment plan – programmes for transferring and retraining employees.

- The productivity plan – where and when redundancies are to occur; policies for selection and declaration of redundancies; redevelopment, retraining or relocation of redundant employees; policy on redundancy payments, etc.

- The retention plan – actions to reduce avoidable labour wastage.

  The plan should include budgets, targets and standards. It should allocate responsibilities for implementation and control – reporting and monitoring achievement against the plan, etc.

(b) One of the most valuable assets owned by an organisation is its staff. They sit at the centre of strategic planning. Whilst strategic planning seeks to minimise the uncertainty of the enterprise's environment (within a given set of constraints on its actions), it is the employees that actually implement the strategy ands take the opportunities offered. They must be motivated and developed and this is of the greatest importance when the people under consideration are professionally qualified. This is for a number of reasons:

   (i) If the organisation seeks excellence, it must realise that high quality of product and service is crucially dependent on a similarly high quality of staff. Excellence and human resource planning are closely related.

   (ii) Developing such staff is generally quite expensive, and there are therefore quite considerable investment implications for the medium to long term. This is emphasised by the relatively long lead-time required in such development. If this is combined further with the high level of uncertainty inherent in attempting to develop individuals to a very high level of expertise and performance, the potential investment in these employees is clear. The uncertainty arises because some will fail to reach the required standard if the standard is very high, and even those that do reach it may take their expertise elsewhere.

   (iii) Since professional skills tend to be at a premium, the development of 'home grown' experts may well be desirable. The influence of competitive employment markets is reduced and it may well be that professional employees, that are developed in-house, will show greater commitment and loyalty to the organisation as a result.

   Professional employees are highly important to an organisation because it is through them that vital skills are acquired for such processes as the management of innovation, change and development. If accountants are taken as an example, the management of cash flows from new product lines is crucial to the flow of funds for the continuing development and success of future products. They will also be necessary for the budgeting process and the analysis of variances from the budgeted figures.

Chapter 16

The process of induction, recruitment and selection

Question 1

	Your sister gets what she needs	Your sister does not get what she needs
You get what you want	Your sister uses a Walkman and you continue to work	You intimidate your sister into turning off the music
You do not get what you want	You go up to your bedroom for some piece while your sister continues to enjoy her music	Your parents come in and find you arguing and you are both in trouble

In this situation, you needed quiet while your sister wanted the same space for music. If you held on to these positions, no win-win solution was possible. The win-win solutions were based on satisfying underlying needs ie. your need to have some acknowledgment of the importance of your work, and your sister's important need for lighthearted fun. Underlying needs are often basic human needs for security, economic well-being, a sense of belonging, recognition and control over one's life. Once identified, these needs can often be met with win-win solutions.

Question 2

Engineering company

(a)   The first step will be to decide whether to keep the job in its current form or, particularly in view of the difficult financial climate, whether to combine the duties with another job or reallocate the duties. The Managing Director would need to be involved in this decision.

There is a clear requirement to analyse the post carefully because it is a senior vacancy, where there have been specific problems of performance where the job-holder has done the job for a long time and where there is confusion over areas of responsibility. Therefore, it will be essential to draw up a proper job description, clarifying the key responsibilities of the role. It will then be necessary to determine the person specification – the type of person sought to fill the job. Clearly a qualified, high-calibre accountant is required. But there are other requirements. The section has been poorly managed and uses out-dated systems. The person will need strong management skills and experience, perhaps with a qualification or experience. Part of the company's strategic plan may be to invest in a new system and, if so, the person appointed would need to demonstrate a knowledge of the latest systems. They will have a successful track record to date, will be dynamic with strong leadership, inter-personal and social skills.

Because of the problems of the firm as a whole and the section in particular, a strong candidate is clearly required. It is likely therefore that the job will need to be evaluated to ensure that candidates of sufficiently high-calibre are attracted. For example it will be necessary to determine a salary and benefits package which is competitive in the market place, will be attractive to the right candidate but which does not completely distort the pay differentials within the firm.

(b)   Once the decisions have been taken about the job description, the person specification and the value of the job, the recruitment and selection can take place. First there is a need to decide whether there are any suitable internal candidates. There are some bright young staff in the department with the potential for development but it is unlikely that any of them will have the experience or all-round breadth of skills required for the job. However it might be a good idea to give them a chance to apply – it is good for morale and there might be a surprise!

It is unlikely that there will be anyone on file who has written 'out of the blue' but it would be worth checking. There will be a need for the company to decide whether to advertise the post themselves or use recruitment consultants or head-hunters although head-hunters and agencies are expensive and times are hard!

It is therefore probably best to advertise. It will probably be more beneficial to advertise nationally to attract a sufficient breadth of applicant – because there is a requirement for a broad range of skills at a senior management level. A combination of the national press (*Sunday Times*) and trade magazine (*Accountancy Age*) would be advisable. The company should arrange for an attractive advert to be designed – making sure details of the broad-range and level of skills required as well as what the job can offer the candidate in terms of career growth and development are identified. Details of the job and salary and benefits range will also be included. Applicants who reply to job advertisements are usually asked to fill in a job application form, or to send a letter giving details about themselves and their previous job experience (their CV) and explaining why they think they are suitable for the job.

The application form or CV should be used to find out whether the applicant is obviously unsuitable for the job or whether they may be of the right calibre and worth inviting to an interview. It is likely that the Finance Director with the help of the personnel manager will select an initial list of people to interview. It may be decided, because the job is important and inter-personal and social skills are required, to subject the final short-list candidates to psychometric testing.

Interviewing is a crucial part of the selection process because it gives the company a chance to assess the applicant directly and it also gives the applicant a chance to learn more about the organisation. Because of the importance of the post a short-list of the two to three best candidates from the first interviews may be drawn up and then seen at a final interview with the Managing Director and the Finance Director.

With the personnel manager, the Finance Director should ensure that the interviews are properly organised and structured with key questions being prepared and detailed notes being taken and the action at the end of each interview agreed.

Finally, once the preferred choice is agreed upon and references are sought and acceptable, the job offer is made.

Chapter 17

Training and development

Question 1

Learning propositions

(a) The individual should be motivated to learn. The advantages of training should be clarified according to the individual's motives in terms of money, opportunity or valued skills.

(b) Active participation is better than passive reception - this is because of its effect on the motivation to learn, on concentration and on recollection. Participation has the effect of encouraging 'ownershop' of the process of learning and change and committing the individual to it as their own goal, not just an imposed process. If a high degree of participation cannot be achieved, practice and repetition can be used to reinforce reception of the learning.

(c) Clear objectives and standards should be set. This is to give each task some meaning. Each stage of learning should present a challenge, without overloading the learner or making them lose confidence. Specific objectives and performance standards for each task or activity will help the learner in the planning and control process that leads to learning. They will also provide targets against which performance will constantly be measured.

(d)   Timely and relevant feedback on performance and progress should be given. This will usually be provided by the trainer and should be concurrent (not delayed) with the progress or lack of it. For example, if progress reports or performance appraisals are given only at year-end, there will be no opportunity for behaviour adjustment or learning in the period in-between.

(e)   Positive and negative reinforcement should be used judiciously. Recognition and encouragement enhance an individual's confidence in their competence and progress: punishment for poor performance, especially if iot without explanation and correction, discourages the learner and creates feelings of guilt, failure and hostility

(f)   The **behaviourist approach** suggests that learning is the development of associations between stimuli and responses through experience. Skinner introduced the concept of shaping behaviour by selectively reinforcing desired pieces of behaviour - conditioning based on reinforcement. His reinforcement theory suggests that our responses are modified in accordance with feedback on whether previous experiences have been rewarding or punishing. We learn to adjust our behaviour according to which pattern produces the best results for us.

The **cognitive or problem solving approaches** to learning are based on the idea that the mind processes information. Reinforcement is always knowledge about the results of past behaviour; it is feedback on how successful our behaviour has been. That knowledge is information, which can be used to modify or maintain previous behaviour. The information has to be perceived, interpreted, given meaning and used in decision-making about the future behaviour. Cognitive psychology is therefore not concerned with the relationships between stimuli and responses, but with the plans and sub-plans that people choose, the means they adopt for pursuing them and the way that they are modified and improved with experience.

(g)   There are different ways of learning and people learn more effectively if they are aware of their own learning style preferences. Honey and Mumford identified four learning styles:

1   Activists are interested in novelty. They willingly become involved in new experiences and are attracted to different ideas and approaches. However, they tend to give insufficient attention to the application that attracts them.

2   Theorists are most concerned about linkages and relationships. When presented with new information, they need to fit it into their overall existing framework. They are keen to reject ambiguities.

3   Reflectors must have time to think about new experiences or ideas that confront them. They are cautious with new material and can be viewed as indecisive because of their reluctance to draw quick conclusions.

4   Pragmatists are driven by a need to ensure that any new material they encounter can be applied in practice. They need to know if new ideas can work. They want to act quickly on new ideas and material.

(h)   Kolb suggests that learning is a series of steps based on learning from experience. He believes that classroom learning is false and that actual learning comes from real life experiences. Experiential learning comes from 'doing', thus ensuring that learners actually solve problems. Kolb's experiential learning cycle (shown below) identifies the four steps:

•   the first step is where the person is learning something new

•   then the experience is reviewed

- then the experience is accepted or rejected, and
- the fourth step is when the person calculates how and when to apply what has been learned.

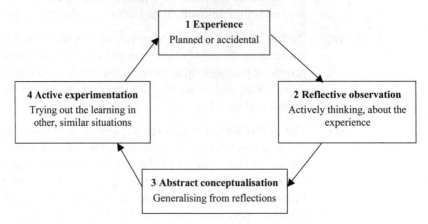

Question 2

Installing a training system

(a) All organisations, whatever their size and level of complexity, will need some form of training if staff resources are to be used properly. Even smaller firms who tend to recruit staff ready trained will need to train existing staff to cope with new systems and to teach new staff the finer details of their working practices. The main difference between the different types of organisation is likely to be the degree of formality involved in the training system.

The steps that should be taken to set up a training system will depend on its formality, but would normally include:

(i) an analysis of the organisation's training needs, based on a comparison of the skills possessed by its employees with those needed for its smooth operation

(ii) a decision on the scale and type of training system needed, and whether it can best be provided by the organisation's own staff or by external consultants

(iii) the allocation of responsibilities for training within the firm, including a co-ordinator for any external training

(iv) planning specific training courses and ensuring that they are properly timed to allow normal operations to continue

(v) reviewing the system on a regular basis to ensure that it is still satisfying the organisation's training needs.

(b) The most likely benefits of a training system for the accounting function of an organisation are:

(i) more efficient use of staff resources as staff understand their duties more clearly, so that, for example, difficult accounting entries will be dealt with more intelligently

(ii) greater flexibility of operation as more staff acquire more skills, allowing for replacement of those concerned with maintaining one set of records by those working on others if workload or absences demand it

(iii) greater ease in introducing new techniques as a training system will exist to help with the changeover, particularly useful if the accounting records are being computerised

(iv) greater capability for dealing with staff turnover as the training programme automatically provides for career succession

(v) general improvements in efficiency and staff morale.

Chapter 18

The process of appraisal

Question 1

The answer is **C** Training needs analysis.

Question 2

The answer is **C** Contrast effect.

Question 3

Appraisal systems

Report on Performance Appraisal Systems

For the attention of Accounts Manager

June 20X9

1   **Terms of reference**

This report was requested to provide the following information:

(a)   The purpose of an appraisal system.

(b)   The objectives of appraisals from the viewpoint of:

(i)   the individual

(ii)   the organisation.

(c)   The barriers to effective appraisal.

2   **The purpose of an appraisal system**

The general purpose of any assessment or appraisal is to improve the efficiency of the organisation by ensuring that the individual employees are performing to the best of their ability and developing their potential for improvement. It enables a picture to be drawn up of the human 'stock' of an organisation – its strengths and weaknesses, enabling more effective personnel planning.

Staff appraisal is a procedure where the managers or supervisors in an organisation discuss the work of their subordinates. They see each person individually and consider the progress they have been making in their job, their strengths and weaknesses and their future needs as regards training and development and the employee's potential for promotion.

The purpose therefore is:

- to assess the level of reward payable for an individual's efforts by measuring the extent to which the individual may be awarded a salary or pay increase compared with their peers

- to review the individual's performance, identify training needs and plan follow-up training and development. By encouraging two-way communication, it permits an evaluation of a subordinate's strengths and weaknesses and the reasons for them. Thus, for example, if a subordinate's failure to perform is due to some failure in the work system, corrective action can be taken quickly. This will help the individual to do their job better and assist the organisation to achieve its objectives

- to review the individual's potential by attempting to predict the type and level of work that the individual is likely to be capable of in the future. At the organisational level, this permits career and succession planning. At the individual level, it permits superior and subordinate to assess the most effective development plans for the subordinate.

The objectives of appraisals from the viewpoint of the individual

An appraisal is a process where the progress, performance, results and sometimes personality of an employee are reviewed and assessed by their immediate superior. The objectives of an appraisal from the individual's point of view include the following:

- it compares the individual's performance against a set and established standard

- it identifies work of particular merit done during the review period

- it provides a basis for remuneration

- it establishes what the individual has to do, regarding the objectives of the organisation

- it determines the future employment of the individual, e.g. to remain in the same job, be transferred, promoted or retired early

- it determines whether the individual is in a job where proper use is being made of their skills and talents

- it establishes key results which the individual needs to achieve in work within a set period of time

- it identifies training and development needs.

The objectives of appraisals from the viewpoint of the organisation

An appraisal system is used by the organisation to review and change, to inform and monitor and to examine and evaluate employees. The objectives from the organisation's point of view include the following:

- it monitors human resource selection processes against results

- it identifies candidates for promotion, early retirement, etc

- it helps to identify and provide a record of any special difficulties/hazards surrounding the job, perhaps not previously realised

- it identifies areas for improvement

- it provides a basis for human resource planning

- it helps formulate the training plan

- it improves communication between managers and the managed where the organisation adopts the joint problem solving approach in their appraisal system.

The barriers to effective appraisal

There have been studies on the effects of performance appraisal that show some negative effects, e.g.:

- criticism had a negative effect on goal achievement

- subordinates generally reacted defensively to criticism during appraisal interviews

- inferior performance resulted from defensive reactions to criticism

- repeated criticism had the worst effect on subsequent performance of individuals who had little self-confidence.

Index